Aesthetics of Religion

Religion and Reason

———

Founded by
Jacques Waardenburg

Edited by
Gustavo Benavides, Michael Stausberg, and Ann Taves

Band 58

Aesthetics of Religion

A Connective Concept

Edited by
Alexandra K. Grieser and Jay Johnston

DE GRUYTER

ISBN 978-3-11-068633-3
e-ISBN (PDF) 978-3-11-046101-5
e-ISBN (EPUB) 978-3-11-046045-2
ISSN 0080-0848

Library of Congress Cataloging-in-Publication Data
A CIP catalog record for this book has been applied for at the Library of Congress.

Bibliographic information published by the Deutsche Nationalbibliothek
The Deutsche Nationalbibliothek lists this publication in the Deutsche Nationalbibliografie;
detailed bibliographic data are available in the Internet at http://dnb.dnb.de.

www.degruyter.com

Foreword

This volume aims to present a newly emerging perspective in the Academic Study of Religion, its results and potentials. Developing innovative perspectives, such as the Aesthetics of Religion, requires a driving force that individuals will utilise to propose a topic and a debate. However, first and foremost, rethinking and re-configuring a status quo builds upon long-term developments, diverse influences and many more people than the single names that might be associated with the new approaches.

It was early sociologist of science Ludwik Fleck, in his *Genesis and Development of a Scientific Fact* ([1935] 1979), who made clear that the dynamics of gaining new insights, asking questions differently and designing a new *thought style* rarely develops in a linear way, or on argumentative grounds only. Endeavours leading to new approaches are also historical and social activities. They develop in waves and over long periods of time; they bundle ideas and practices, accidents and purposes; and they are dependent on people who read each other's work and meet at the right moment to exchange their thoughts and ideas in what we describe in this book as a *connective* way of thinking and researching.

This volume is the outcome of a creative encounter between scholars of religion from different backgrounds who share an interest in using aesthetics as a frame of reference for their work. Some of these scholars are members of a research network that was founded after a year-long collaboration in 2007 (the working group on the "Aesthetics of Religion", a sub-group of the German Association for the Study of Religion, DVRW; now developed into AESToR.net, a DFG-funded network programme); other scholars developed their approaches in different contexts, or on the basis of their discontent with concepts available for the realities they encountered in their research. It was exactly the conglomerate of purpose, accident and curious engagement that created the circumstances to bring together these scholars for the first international conference on the topic at the University of Groningen in 2013, titled "How Religion Becomes Effective: Aesthetics as a Connective Concept for the Study of Religion".

This pioneering event would not have been possible without many earlier encounters: in the stimulating research environment of the Department of the Comparative Study of Religion in Groningen, facilitated by Kocku von Stuckrad, where Jay Johnston and Alexandra Grieser spent time as researchers; in the creative atmosphere of Birgit Meyer's projects located at the University of Utrecht; and at the many panels at international conferences, deliberately organised as meeting points for scholars who were interested in studying religions as an embodied and sensory cultural practice. When scholars from Denmark, Ireland, and the UK, from Switzerland and Germany, the Netherlands, the US and Australia met in Groningen, many people contributed to the intellectual and personal curiosity and the truly experimental character of the conference: financial support was provided—for the biggest part—by the Royal Dutch Academy of the Sciences. The Faculty of Theology and Religious Studies, University of Groningen, made available the impressive environment of its location and enabled the organiser to invite scholars from abroad; Birgit Meyer generously opened up her international network and made possible the participation of another colleague from the USA. Her expertise, intellectual curiosity and integrative presence were constitutive for the intensity of the encounter. The support of the colleagues in Groningen reached far beyond practicalities; Kim Knibbe has especially been a catalyst and advisor in many ways and over the years. Annet van der Meer and Ella Sebamalai brilliantly covered all organisational aspects of the event, skilled, professional and full of humour and ideas.

Special thanks go to those speakers who gave additional lectures and master classes to make this event happen: Manual Vasquez, Christoph Uehlinger, and Niklaus Largier. Hans G. Kippenberg invigorated the *genius loci* of the venue by returning to the place where he co-founded the first journal of the field during the 1980s, *Visible Religion.* We are grateful to all contributors for their openness to bridge the gaps between different disciplinary backgrounds and to share also unfinished thoughts and projects, and especially to those colleagues who embarked the project at a later stage, adding their commentary essays.

It has been a pleasure to work with Alissa Jones Nelson and Sophie Wagenhofer from de Gruyter Academic Publishers, and with the series editors of "Religion and Reason", Michael Stausberg, Ann Taves and Gustavo Benavides. Their thorough feedback and the discussions it stimulated has undoubtedly improved this volume.

As a project on understanding the sensory aspects of religion and culture is at the same time an intellectual and a sensory endeavour itself, the graphic design that accompanied the conference was vital to its structure and to its reflective quality. Painter and graphic artist Volker Scheub's countless impulses given in discussions and experiential sessions kept on shifting perspectives and reminding us that there is much to learn for 'doing science' from people whose expertise it is to question any fixed relationship between 'form and content', and what it means to productively 'think through the senses'. How much Alexandra owes to these impulses can best be expressed by an insight and an experience: that critique can be beautiful.

On a personal note Jay wishes to thank the Aesthetics of Religion group for their generosity of spirit, encouragement and collegiality and Alexandra in particular for her commitment, patience and vision without which this volume would never have been created. Enormous thanks also to Iain Gardner and Lili Kamala Johnston for their ongoing support and for the many oft-needed escapades we share.

We hope that this volume will inspire more people to explore, discuss and apply the concepts on offer, and that it will stimulate connectivity—between diverse spheres of knowledge and expertise, and between people who like to think, and sense, across borders.

Jay Johnston & Alexandra Grieser
Sydney and Dublin, 2017

Bibliography

Fleck, Ludwik. [1935] 1979. *Genesis and Development of a Scientific Fact*, edited by Robert K. Merton and Thaddeus J. Trenn. Translated by Fred Bradley and Thaddeus J. Trenn. Chicago: University of Chicago Press.

Table of Contents

Alexandra Grieser and Jay Johnston

What is an *Aesthetics of Religion?* From the Senses to Meaning—and Back Again

1 Introduction

In recent years, investigating the role of the body and the senses in religion has constituted a most dynamic field in the Academic Study of Religion/s.[1] What is now a fast-growing area of research, publishing and teaching was in deficit for a long period of time. Its development not only added topics and themes to the research agenda, but it has also initiated reconsiderations of the theoretical foundations of Religious Studies in general. The present volume contributes to this broader development by introducing the Aesthetics of Religion as a framework for studying religion as a sensory and mediated practice. In close theoretical relation with approaches such as Sensory Studies,[2] Material Religion,[3] the Anthropology of the Senses[4] and the Cognitive Science of Religion (CRS)[5], an

---

1 When using "religion" and "religions", we are referring to terms theorised in the Study of Religion/s as operative tools rather than denoting unchallenged entities.

By *religions*, we mean the relatively stable communicative systems and practices which are fluent yet identifiable as traditions with specific institutions, organisational forms, practices, interpretive patterns and culturally differing relations to other societal subsystems such as juridical regulation, politics or education. Religions in their diversity are not separate units, but rather emerged and developed in exchange and mutual demarcation.

By *religion*, we refer to a more general term which has been derived from Western religious and scholarly discourse, a category which allows us to speak about a vast variety of practices, media and institutions across cultures. Moreover, it allows us to speak about influences not obviously related to religions; in a Weberian sense, societies are influenced by religious traditions in many, and often unexpected ways, for instance regarding concepts of personhood, being "on offer" in popular culture, or contributing to the emergence of economic structures. The terms are subject to ongoing theory work to which this volume aims to contribute. However, we decided not to use the /slash version throughout the text, but rather as a reminder that the more general term only exists on the basis of the concrete empirical practices we conceptualise as religious.

2 Sensory Studies have been established by Constance Classen and David Howes as a culture-historical project (Classen 1993, 1998; Howes 2005; Classen and Howes 2014; http://www.cen treforsensorystudies.org/). Also other areas in anthropology, for instance ethno-medicine and ritual studies added to the focus on the cultural diversity of sense perception.

3 The best insight into the breadth of this field is provided by the journal *Material Religion: The Journal of Objects, Art and Belief*. The journal covers not only material studies in the more specific sense, but also aesthetics, visual culture and theoretical debate about embodiment, etc.

4 For an assessment of the phases and strands of this approach: Michaels and Wulf (2014).

https://doi.org/10.1515/9783110461015-001

Aesthetics of Religion[6] focuses on understanding the *interplay* between sensory, cognitive and socio-cultural aspects of world-construction, and the role of religion within this dynamic.

The Aesthetics of Religion framework has been developing since the 1990s. It takes as its starting point the Greek term *aisthesis:* an epistemological concept that denoted *sensory perception,* but also referred to the larger process of how human beings make sense of their environment and of themselves through their senses. Building upon a critical revision of aesthetic history during the 1980s and '90s, the recent understanding of aesthetics has changed from a normative philosophy of art and beauty into an analytic concept for the study of culture. In this introduction, we will outline this revised understanding of aesthetics, and the reasons why scholars consider it as providing a pool of descriptive terms, analytical concepts and systematic questions that allow us to understand better how religions in their variety become "effective" on the levels of intellect, emotions, intuition and sensation. We then discuss what has been achieved by applying aesthetic concepts in the Study of Religion to date, differentiating between a repertoire of *religious aesthetics* to be investigated, and an *aesthetics of religion* as providing a platform for theorising religion in light of the perception of time, space and self. As we are introducing a perspective 'in the making', we also outline some of the potentials and opportunities which can be further developed. Before this, however, we begin by reflecting on some of the reasons why—throughout the history of the Academic Study of Religion—the aspect of matter and form, perception and sensation has long been neglected.

The aesthetic approach we are suggesting asks, How in the context of religious practice are the senses stimulated, governed and disciplined? How are religious experiences emotions and attitudes created, memorised and normalised? How do religious perceptual orders interact with those of a larger culture? Focusing on the process *aisthesis,* and how humans understand their world through the senses is not an overall critique directed against text and belief, or questions of meaning. On the contrary, sensing, perceiving and meaning making are viewed as a continuum that we distinguish for analytical purposes, and not in order to make ontological statements.

However, to be able to go beyond a symbolic understanding of aesthetic forms, theories specific to the sensory and bodily aspects of recognition are

---

5 CSR has been launched mainly by psychologists aiming to explain religion by applying knowledge about the human mind and how it has developed in universal evolutionary terms. Meanwhile, good overviews are available, for instance in Taves (2015).
6 We will elaborate on the development of the concept below; for an overview see Grieser (2015b).

needed, without transposing text hermeneutics and semiotics onto the realm of the sensual. Herein lies the opportunity and the challenge of an aesthetic approach. Just as the new 'science of images' (visual culture; *Bildwissenschaft*) has scrutinised different modes of seeing and the specific nature of visual media, the aesthetics of religion strives to unfold this for the whole spectrum of the senses, for instance of religion/s being heard and felt, as tactile or kinaesthetic phenomena, as architecture or as soundscapes within a society.

Stating that religion/s need to be acknowledged as rooted in both bio-somatic and cultural-historical grounds, it is necessary to undermine simplistic ideas about the senses providing the "raw material" for an intellect "refining" meaning. What André Leroi-Gourhan already pointed out in 1964, in his study about the relationship between thinking in images and in language, is also valid for the relationship between perception and meaning: it should be investigated as "one of coordination, not of subordination" (Leroi-Gourhan [1964] 1993, 195). We perceive this as a two-way dynamic: sensation and perception are as much "naturally" and "culturally" shaped, and they actively select information according to human needs as thinking and reasoning do. We will show further in section 3 why scholars think that aesthetics as a framework and intellectual tradition provides debates and concepts that help to better understand these modes of coordination implicit to religious ways of perceiving and interpreting the world. However, prior to that the next section articulates the dominant intellectual background that both 'silenced' such an approach and held the seeds for its emergence.

2 Background: Reasons for the Disembodied Study of Religion

When directing attention to the engagement of the body and the senses in all things religious, it is rather obvious that religion/s are as much felt, sensed and experienced as they are thought and believed. However, as our "letter-pic" image on the first page demonstrates, sensory practices are not merely *expressions* of beliefs and doctrines; rather, religion/s *consist* of sensory practice and, as it is shown in the picture, this includes reading and writing as much as dancing and singing, feeling pain as well as comfort or building and inhabiting architecture. Religious bodies—the walking pilgrim, the bowing worshipper, smelling the presence of the gods—are cultivated in ritual routines and extraordinary practices; practices are symbolised (e. g., St. Jacob's shell on the picture), communities identify with the symbols which support perceptions of the "own" and the "other" (the Cross and the Star and Crescent; senses provide metaphors, for instance, when the sense of seeing is turned into the all-seeing eye of Horus; time is structured religiously, even for non-believers: daily, weekly, yearly, cosmically); and space is divided into heavens and hells, holy and unholy places, virtual and real; religions are sanctifying media (e. g., holy scriptures and sacred dance), but they are also dependent on, and trapped in, how (secular) media depict them and influence how they are perceived. Religions are involved in how people sense their body, value their money and appreciate or repudiate theatre or music. Even the most spiritual practice requires a body to experience the disembodied, and what is called spirituality today has maybe never been so strongly related to the well-being of the physical body (e. g., meditation, mindfulness, Yoga). It is a far-reaching question that emerges from these observations—among scholars as well as in western popular perception—namely why the idea has been so successful that being religious is mainly a matter of belief and doctrines, or of an inwardly felt personal and individual emotion? We contend that the answer to this question is inevitably related to the reasons why *aisthetic* knowledge and theories of perception are only now being applied to understand how religion/s contribute to the ways humans relate to, and create, their worlds.

Most scholars responding to these questions are critically engaging with the legacy of the Academic Study of Religion, putting into a broader perspective its disciplinary history and viewing it as entangled with religious history and with the normalised western epistemological practice of dividing human faculties into binary dichotomies, such as body and mind, matter and spirit, emotion and reason, nature and culture.[7] Early modern rationalist philosophy and the Cartesian separation between body and mind have been identified as crucial moments of this history. However, excluding sensory knowledge from the canon of objects to be taken seriously is part of a much longer history, and it includes philosophical, political and theological discourses. Concepts of "worldly matter" and "sacred spirit" had their influence on western culture, be it as polemics against a "carnal Israel", a ritualistic paganism, or set in analogy with gendered constructions of women as passive nature and men as active culture, and non-European cultures being classified according to their body-centeredness contrasted with standards of rationality.

---

7 This perspective of a History of the Study of Religion as *Problemgeschichte* (history of problems), interacting with and responding to Religious History has been offered by Hans G. Kippenberg (2002) and by Volkhard Krech (2002). This project needed to be complemented by the analysis of why the material and sensory aspects of religion/s have long been neglected, pointed out by Asad (1993), Brunotte (forthcoming), Gladigow (1988), Meyer and Verrips (2008), and Vásquez (2011).

Examining the modern history of studying religion c.1800, however, three aspects can be identified as significant in order to understand the neglect of the body and the senses in the study of religion: *text-centrism*, an *anti-ritualist* attitude and a *representationalist*, or *expressionist* understanding of aesthetic forms. In contrast to the more sociological and phenomenological French traditions[8] and the more anthropological British tradition[9] of the Academic Study of Religion, the influential Dutch, Scandinavian and German tradition entirely relied on philology, philosophy and theological history of religion. Text-centrism, as a consequence of these disciplinary roots, developed for both practical and ideological reasons. In the 19th century, religions other than the well-known traditions came from all over the colonialized world, and they came to European scholars mainly as texts. Philologist and founding father of a "science of religion", Friedrich Max Mueller, and his project of "The Sacred Books of the East" (1879–1910) stand for the effort of translating and recognising the diversity of religious traditions world-wide, yet also for the limited understanding and the adaptation of these traditions to the norms of monotheist religions relying on a Holy Scripture. The philosophical and theological tradition conceptualised the generic concept of religion according to this framework and hence regarded language, scripture and sacred books as the medium of revelation, and therefore the privileged medium in religious terms. For scholars trained as theologians, historians and philologists, exegesis and the normative content of the text were the main features of analysis, other media than texts were discredited as folk religion, or put into evolutionary patterns of expressing the ways supposedly 'uncivilised' people would express their beliefs.

Besides these practical reasons for the preference of texts for text-trained scholars, the mostly Protestant background of many of the founding figures in the Study of Religion laid grounds not only for an intellectual approach *to* religion/s, but also a preference *for* intellectual forms of religion. Using an expression from Martin Luther's reformation theology, founders of early History of Religion made clear, that "languages are the sheath in which this sword of the Spirit is contained".[10] The theology of the word, and the word only, and the critique of ritualistic "magical" practice against Catholicism had turned into a cultural-Protestant attitude that paradoxically fostered both the possibility of investigating religion in academic ways and the privilege given to rationalism, an-

---

8 Marcel Mauss (1979) and his investigation of "body techniques" is as important as Maurice Merleau-Ponty's *Phenomenology of Perception* (1962).

9 Most influential here: Mary Douglas and her understanding of the body as "natural symbol" (Douglas 1970).

10 See Gladigow (1988, 37) for quotations.

iconism, critical attitudes towards rituals and a purist understanding of religion as text and belief.

The other aspect of what has been called the Protestant bias of the Study of Religion's heritage came to be influential in the form of Schleiermacher's romantic re-definition of religion as a singular and aesthetically defined "religious experience"[11]—taken up by Rudolf Otto's influential concept of "The Holy" (1917) where he rejects any physiological, social scientific or psychological discipline as adequate to grasp the original quality of religion as an interiorized, subjective and overwhelming "experience".[12] The success of this decontextualizing approach hampered the recognition of the sensuous aspects of religion, and the development of methods with which to study them. What makes this influence even clearer is the representational model underlying the symbolic understanding of religion, regarding objects, practices and form as a "vessel" for content or carrier of 'the' meaning. Two prominent examples show that this approach did not ignore material objects and aesthetic forms, but integrated them into the superiority of the spiritual "experience". Rudolf Otto's collection of religious artefacts in the Marburg *Religionskundliche Sammlung* present the appreciation Otto had for religious matters (Bräunlein 2005)—but they were presented as expression of the generalising romantic concept of "experience" which enabled cultural difference to be considered as a variety of the essential pre-defined model of a religious experience in the singular. In addition, the impressive book on "The Holy in Art" (van der Leeuw [1957] 1963) bears witness to a fascination with sensuous and artistic expression, but it approaches the problem of how to appreciate the spiritual potential of art without putting theology under pressure, and thus presents a theology of music, dance and poetry rather than a way to study the relationship between religion and the arts.

While this conceptualisation of religion as a disembodied, undisputable "irrational" and *sui generis* mode of experience was not shared by the neighbour disciplines Anthropology or Sociology, it has often been widely underestimated just how successful this romantic concept of religion had been culturally. We would go so far to speculate that this model of religion developed as perfectly compatible with the secularism of a Western European provenience: an eminent-

---

11 For the impact of Schleiermacher's context far beyond the German context see Korsch (2011).
12 Otto's "famous page 8" where he polemicizes against an understanding of religion from the angle of "emotions of adolescence" (*Pubertäts-gefühle*), "discomforts of indigestion" (*Verdauungs-stockungen*), "or, say, social feelings" (*Sozial-gefühle*) has often been interpreted as a pledge for the phenomenological concept of religion as an experience *sui generis*; but it has rarely been mentioned that this includes a clear methodological exclusion of empirical, that is sociological, psychological or physiological explanations of religion/s (Otto [1917] 1923, 8).

ly private attitude, based on convictions or spiritual experiences which are expected to be kept invisible to the outside, the non-private world. Many of today's conflicts about mosques and veils, and much of the surprise about a rising prominence of religious forms in public, need to be understood in this context: the rejection of and the urge for religion/s being visible, tangible and demonstrating a public commitment can be seen as two sides of the same coin.

As important as it is to be critically aware of the Protestant bias in the early Study of Religion, confining this history to a narrative of repression and neglect would not tell the whole story. Its other parts are a fascination with the body, especially the naked, erotic and the painful body, which presents, on the one hand, the reversed side of the suppressed, but on the other hand the romanticised body as medium for reaching/depicting a state of lost naturalness, freedom from the repressions of culture and intellectualised life. We should also not overlook that the Cartesian divide has been developed on the backdrop of a Catholic worldview; that some of the most important theories of media and their "presence" are developed with reference to Catholic concepts;[13] and that the idealisation of the sensorium as a "natural" and "immediate" access to reality is part of movements as diverse as irrationalism, a phenomenological tradition that claims ahistorical relations with reality, and also supports notions such as the "noble savage" and the motto "back to nature" that build on Rousseau's critique of civilisation.

Facing these diverse aspects, and while there is leeway to make up for considering the body and the senses in the Study of Religion, a reflective history also should be aware of the "reasons of the body boom" (Koch 2011) in academic approaches. In a first wave, in the early 20th century, philosophers of culture such as Georg Simmel, Helmut Plessner or Henri Bergson focused on perception as a critical response to the positivistic rationalism of the natural sciences around 1900 (Riou 2014). A second wave during the 1980s was related to the "cultural turn" in the Humanities (see Bachmann-Medick 2016) and to critical work in the area of feminist philosophy, post-colonial studies and new ways of integrating sensing and imagining into history.[14] Authors such as Dietmar Kamper and Christoph Wulf still expected a desensitisation and a "dwindling of the senses" (*Das Schwinden der Sinne*, 1982) as a response to the upcoming digital media, but at the same time diagnosed a rising interest in the body especially in relation to

---

13 A prominent example is the important work of Bruno Latour. Especially in the light of his latest books (Latour 2013a, 2013b), it becomes clear that Latour's media theory cannot be understood without recognising his references to Catholic features in his philosophising.
14 The journal *Paragrana*, for instance, which can be seen as representative of the influential tradition of Historical Anthropology, features with a special issue on *Aisthesis* in 1995.

the formation of new forms of religion and spirituality (Kamper and Wulf 1981, 1987).

Today, what had been part of a subversive discourse has entered the mainstream, and scholars working on the materiality and the sensory aspects of culture are responding to a situation of extremes. Processes of mediatisation and aestheticisation in industrialised societies have intensified in a way unknown to date; working bodies are increasingly replaced by robots, and become objects of enhancement and perfectionising; the work of the senses is understood in a way that they can be technically "replaced" and stimulated by virtual worlds; and the nexus between media, body and technology has created the paradoxical situation of simultaneous desensitisation and overstimulation of the senses through computer gaming and permanent connection to online-worlds.[15] In contrast to high-tech and transhumanist visions of enhancing sensory experience, the majority of human beings are occupied with caring for the basic needs of their bodies, for food, safety and shelter. Religions are not separated from these developments, and they respond to, and shape these situations in diverse ways. Confining them to systems of belief and doctrine misses a large part of their impact and intensity.

3 Why Aesthetics? The Term's Heritage and Its Revision as a Connective Concept

Aesthetics is an ambiguous term, and it is used in a variety of ways. Mostly understood as a philosophy of aesthetic judgments or as a specific quality of art, people also call things or behaviours aesthetic that are elegant and pleasant, and distinct from practical, political or everyday life. The term, however, is derived from the Greek *aisthesis* which denotes the process of knowledge gained by sensory perception, in opposition to *noesis*, knowledge gained through intellectual capacities. In these two different understandings, we can see already a gap between a normative strand of aesthetics, on the one hand, asking about what is, or should be seen as beautiful; and on the other hand, an analytical strand of aesthetics, asking how we can understand how human beings make sense of reality through their senses.

---

15 Research suggests that teenagers' skills of "reading emotions" in other people's faces decreases considerably through the constant engagement with electronic devices (Uhls et al. 2014). For the "aestheticisation of the social" throughout commercial media, art and politics Maase (2008); Hieber and Moebius (2014) and Reckwitz et al. (2015).

3.1 Greek roots

This tension between a normative and an analytical interest can also be recognised in the historical situations upon which the modern concept of aesthetics is founded. It reaches back to the fifth and sixth centuries BCE and to the Greek investigation of human knowledge. Most prominently, it features in the work of Aristotle (384–322 BCE) who, against the Platonic distrust of appearances and aesthetic forms, developed *aisthesis* as an interface between sensation and conscious intellectual knowledge (mainly in his work on psychology, *De Anima*, in *De sensu*, and in *Metaphysics*). From this early stage, the tension between the normative and the analytical quality of aesthetics is present. While Aristotle is interested in explaining formative processes and perception through the relations between matter and form,[16] the Platonic tradition relates the sensory to the experience of beauty, and the beautiful to the sphere of morality (the Good) and metaphysics (the True). This unity has been hugely influential in European culture, for the understanding of art being tied to morality, as well as for concepts of the ugly or monstrosity as synonymous with evil. Even practices such as bodily disfigurement as punishment, e.g., marking the thief as an evildoer by mutilating the completeness of their body, can be understood to be based upon this aesthetic trinity.

3.2 Complementing Enlightenment Rationalism

The modern aesthetic project reaches back to German philosopher Alexander Gottlieb Baumgarten's work *Aesthetica* (1750–1758) and its reception through Immanuel Kant. Baumgarten defined aesthetics as a "science of sensitive cognition" (*scientia cognitionis sensitivae*, paragraph 1), and both philosophers aimed at a theory of sensuous knowledge (*sinnliche Erkenntnis*) that would complement and clarify theories of rational knowledge (*rationale Erkenntnis*). Both

---

16 Without delving into the complexities of Aristotelian philosophy, it should be noted that his model of explaining life—*hylomorphism*, that is "matter-formism"—initiated a tradition that allowed for a relational dynamic between matter and form; with this model, an alternative is offered to concepts of matter and spirit, or mind. Even if anchored in a metaphysical concept of the soul, the focus of the Aristotelian concepts lies on explaining movement and change, including the physicality of matter, the dynamics of form/formation, an agent involved and a purpose, distinct from the agent (Shields 2016, paragraph 2). This question, before Aristotelian philosophy underwent Christian interpretation, formulated the basic question of any materialist approach: how to distinguish dead and live matter.

philosophers also developed an elaborate language that enabled the discussion of qualities of perception, and the theorisation of intersubjectivity (Martin 2011).

In current critique, Kant is mostly viewed as responsible for the separation of art from political and social interests. It is sometimes forgotten, it seems, that Kant elaborated on both the normative and the analytical side of the aesthetic. Firstly, thinking art as "disinterested" also aimed to liberate art from the constraints of theology and morality, and this move towards subjectivation had simultaneously been a step towards the autonomy, and what we see today as the radical freedom, of art. Secondly, Kant's work on art as disinterested pleasure is based on his concept of a transcendental aesthetics: the acknowledgement that knowledge does not rely on the participation of an ideal world or a divine reality, but has to be conceptualised under the condition of the perceptual limits of human existence. From this perspective, Kant's theory of the sublime, for instance, still reads as extremely interesting. The affect, he states in contrast to Burke's theory of the sublime, is not dependent on the *object* causing awe and wonder. Rather, the fact that a phenomenon is too vast or too small to be grasped by the human *sensorium* causes an overwhelming confusion—which is compensated by the experience that one can cope with the vastness by applying concepts (*Begriffe*) that allow understanding and the subject to feel enthusiastic about this mastering of dimensions that eluded the human senses.

Kant even reflects on the impact of media extensions—the invention of the microscope and the telescope—and how these impact on the experience of the changed range of perceptions. We do not want to deny that the legacy of Kant's rationalism and idealism is a problem when developing a theory of the sensuous today. However, with this discussion we want to illustrate that contextualising aesthetic theories and the questions they respond too, uncovers a specific tradition of thought, concepts and questions that pertain to the overarching question we are interested in: How does sensory perception go together with religious ways of perceiving the world?

3.3 Turning *Aisthesis* into Aesthetics: The Metaphysical Project

The historical point that transformed the project of *aisthesis* into aesthetics as part of modern metaphysics has to be marked by Georg Friedrich Hegel's *Vorlesungen ueber die Aesthetik* ("Lectures on Aesthetics", 1835), in which he assigned to art a place in his teleological idealism. Also significant is the reception of Kant's theory of the sublime through romantic theorists and poets who spiritualised the "aesthetic experience" and made it the crystal point of a renewed form of religion (Vietta and Kemper 2008). We cannot elaborate on the reasons why confining *aisthesis* to art and beauty has been so successful, and why the discourse on beauty has been so critical for the 18th and 19th century of European thinking (that is another volume!). However, the emergence of aesthetics marks a turning point that has been denoted as the "aesthetic revolution" (Vietta 2008)— a reflective turn to the subject, to an objective understanding of the senses, to empiricism and the birth of "objective" knowledge. Post-romantic aesthetics, however, no longer allow for a re-enchantment of the subjective experience of the world.

3.4 Post-idealist Aesthetics: From Culture Critique to the Study of Culture

From the 1990s on, scholars such as Wolfgang Welsch (1987, 2014), Terry Eagleton (1990), and Gernot Böhme (2001) have critically revised the dominant understanding of aesthetics as art. They draw on post-modernist positions and criticise the ideological use of aesthetics to exclude the political aspects of form, and the exclusion of the sensory from the creation of democratic societies. This 1990s critique comes with strong culture-critical overtones, seeing in aesthetics a remedy of an over-mediatised and over-aestheticised capitalist society. These theorists stand in the tradition of earlier critics from the Frankfurt School and Marxist intellectuals (Walter Benjamin, Theodor Adorno, Georg Lukacs) who referred to aesthetic arguments in their analysis of fascism, and in their critique of capitalism dominating all spheres of culture. Parallel to these culture-critical, philosophical investigations of the aesthetic as a major element of modernisation processes developed, and a move in the more analytical direction took place with what has been called social aesthetics, or everyday aesthetics (for an overview, see Saito 2015).

Sociological thinkers and theorists of modernity in particular have highlighted that the aesthetic approach allows us to understand how class, group identity and power structures are linked to aesthetic practices. The key word delivered by Pierre Bourdieu is *habitus* (Distinctions [1979] 1984), and it resonates with todays' research on self-stylisation and embodied social behaviour. Jacques Rancière focussed on the "distribution of the sensible" (2010), making clear that the aesthetics with which we are surrounded organise us, corroborate or critique the sensory regimes we live by. A third strand of politico-aesthetic analysis, "social aesthetics" (Featherstone 1992; Lash 1993) and "everyday aesthetics" (Mandoki 2007), is related to theories of modernity. It is stated that aestheticisation should be taken into account as significant, because rational enlightenment ideas of modernisation processes underestimate the role of intuitive and imaginary factors, likes and distastes and the self-fashioning of reflexive modern subjects. Movies such as *The Matrix* and *The Truman Show* thematised the life in a reflexive mode, but also the vision of living in a world of 'made up' (virtual) sensations—and these are celebrated as overcoming the human condition in visions of transhumanism. Among several scholars, Michel Foucault has offered theoretical frameworks through which to investigate the ambivalence, and the dilemma of the aesthetic reflexivity of modernity: the technologies of the self are at the same time an authoritative pressure, and a matter of choice and emancipation. The structures of power are internalised in the way subjects perceive themselves and the desire to set themselves in scene/culture in order to be perceived cannot be entirely escaped.

Another far-reaching approach that binds together modern subjectivities, their socio-historical conditions, and an aesthetic perspective has been offered by Andreas Reckwitz and his team (2006). Reckwitz' work is relevant for an Aesthetics of Religion in several ways. We will focus here on the crucial question: how, after all, the aesthetic can be demarcated? On the one hand, the author joins the critique of the separation of sensory perception from rationality, and for his discipline (the sociology of culture) he clearly criticises that the ubiquity of the aesthetic has not been recognised, because Max Weber's rationalisation paradigm was understood in a way that the normativity of a rationalised society left no space for self-referential play and pleasure. Reckwitz shows in his book *The Making of Creativity* (forthcoming translation of *Die Erfindung der Kreativität*, 2012) that the implementation of rationalisation processes was dependent on aestheticisation, and that the opposition between aesthetics and rationality was a necessary part of the new social praxis. Yet, Reckwitz attempts to demarcate the aesthetic in order to provide a distinctive category. He does not oppose the aesthetic to rationality, but to a certain type of rationality that was named *Zweckrationalität* by Weber (goal – or purpose-oriented – rationality).

The aesthetic is defined as auto-referential versus instrumental; as playful and creative versus following rules and orders; and as engaging affectively versus neutrally with the environment. In contrast to the problematic category of aesthetic experience, Reckwitz' proposal allows one to touch upon a quality that has long been avoided: to address a specific experience as a desired and looked-for religious experience, without essentialising it or making it a universal. However, Reckwitz develops a contradiction with his demarcation of the aesthetic. How, we need to ask, would we describe the aesthetic quality of exactly the consequences of modern rationalisation? The metaphor Weber found for the ambivalent experience of modernity—the steel-hard shell (*stahlhartes Gehaeuse*)—could not have made clearer its aesthetic quality. This demonstrates that we need different understandings of the aesthetic, just as we have learned to distinguish different modes of knowledge as well as different types of reason (Gloy

1999). In the same way as Reckwitz refers to an aesthetics of creativity, we can speak about an aesthetics of resistance (Weiss [1975–1981] 2005), or an aesthetics of violence which are all related to social practice and their aesthetic dimensions.

3.5 Analytical Aesthetics: Embodiment, Enactivism and Aesthetics Beyond Art

Two other recent development are related to the changes in the understanding of sensory perception in psychological terms, and the opportunities provided by methods related to new scientific imagery. They are important in order to understand the dynamics fuelled by innovations in natural scientific theories of perception. The first development was that of empirical or neuro-aesthetics (e. g., Lauring 2014) which investigate the neuro-physiological and cognitive-psychological conditions of art and the features of responding to art. These approaches are related to evolutionary theories of the emergence and logics of art as a pan-human activity, but also to the patterns of aesthetic preferences—for instance in the perception of faces, its axial symmetry or its averageness—and their functions (Rusch and Voland 2013; Huston et al. 2015). While neuro-aesthetics and evolutionary theories of art provide valuable knowledge about universal features of perceptual preferences and judgements, for instance, being based on symmetry, the protagonists of the first generation of neuro-aesthetics were mostly occupied with the search for correlations with experiences of beauty (Semir Zekri, Ramachandran) making far-reaching claims based on concepts of art and beauty deeply rooted in the idealist tradition of 18th century aesthetics.[17] More recent projects have started to interrelate knowledge from both natural and the cultural studies and, for instance, investigate the status of "being moved", or the experience of disgust beyond questions of positive or negative judgements, but rather concerned with their functionality, and an intent to theorise the link between sensations and emotions in evolutionary *and* socio-cultural terms, "after Darwin" (Menninghaus 2003, 2011; Menninghaus et al 2015).

These developments have great applicability in connection with the Cognitive Science of Religion (CSR) offering such concepts[18] as minimal counter-intuitiveness, on the basis of how memorable features are (of a narrative, an image, a figure); a cognitive anthropology focuses on the concept of agency, causality and

---

17 On what can be, and should be expected from neuro-aesthetics—and what not—see Hirstein (2012) for an affirmative, and Hyman (2010) for a critical position.
18 Concise and informative one in Taves (2015).

figurative imaginations (seeing "Faces in the Cloud", Guthrie 1993); and the distinction between repetitive and innovative, creative cognitive mechanisms (McCauley and Lawson 2002). As with empirical and evolutionary aesthetics, these patterns describe aspects of the practices and activities we call religion very well and shed new light on how we look at religious efficacy and universality. Especially when related to social scientific paradigms, such as Durkheim's concept of *effervescence*, CRS perspectives provide a good basis for discussing the body-culture nexus (Schueler 2012).

The second recent development features in the psychology of perception. As psychology's main paradigms have come to be dominated by neuro-scientific concepts over the last decade, perception and cognition have also been researched from this angle. Results being partly corroborated, and partly corrected by insights into the plasticity of brain functions, and the necessity to consider brain functions as part of a brain-body unity. A first impulse to understand perception as an active organising principle rather than delivering just "raw material" for intellectual capacities came from Gestalt psychology. It provided a foundation for capturing the interrelation between visual and conceptual "figuration" of reality. Particularly the work of Rudolf Arnheim explicitly aimed at studying "visual perception as a cognitive activity—a reversal, one might say, of the historical development that led in the philosophy of the 18th century from aisthesis to aesthetics, from sensory experience in general to the arts in particular" (Arnheim 1969, v).

This topic—the relation between language, image perception and cognition —continued to produce models important in cognitive linguistics (such as *conceptual blending*; Turner and Fauconnier 2002) and for Lakoff and Johnson's (1980) conceptual metaphor theory (elaborated into a spatial theory of religion by Knott 2005). As a result of these developments—experimental knowledge about cognition and the senses and philosophical critiques—perception was no longer understood as a passive act, represented through the metaphor of mirroring an outward fixed reality (Rorty 1979), or processing a computer "input" into an intelligible "output"; rather, perception came to be seen as an active, constructive process that can be re- and deconstructed in relation to the cultural mechanism in which it is embedded.

Interestingly, the development of a "Philosophy in the Flesh" (Lakoff 1999), and of theories focusing explicitly on a somatic understanding of the aesthetic (Shusterman 1989, 2012) rediscover this potential in a moment when art has given up on aesthetics, rejecting its normative claim which anthropologist Alfred Gell has denoted aesthetics as the theology of art (Gell 1998; Elkins and Montgomery 2013). Philosopher Mark Johnson, who had earlier linked his embodiment theory to an *Aesthetics of Human Understanding* (2007), provided a clarification of the relation between the two understandings of aesthetics. The focus of traditional aesthetics, Johnson writes, such as aesthetic judgment, beauty, and art "should be seen as exemplary, intensified instances of the basic aesthetic contours and processes of human meaning-making. In other words, aesthetics is not merely a matter of aesthetic experience and art, but extends further to encompass all of the processes by which we enact meaning through perception, feeling, imagination, and bodily movement" (Johnson 2015, 24). However, it has also been shown that those developments in art that questioned meaning and representation, or rejected it in their work entirely, had much to offer for an understanding of diverse "ways of worldmaking" (Goodman 1978).

This broad spectrum of concepts and debates demonstrates that aesthetics cannot be confined to either a philosophy of art, or a theory of perception and sensory knowledge. It is the entire intellectual tradition of aesthetics, including its necessary critiques, that shed light on the affective, somatic and sensory aspects of human engagement with their environment. Especially projects such as Alfonsina Scarinzi's "Aesthetics and the Embodied Mind" (2015) that radicalise interactionist models of thinking through the senses, make clear that aesthetics provides a vibrant forum for the old question regarding how we can account for the role of the senses in human knowledge. An "enactive aesthetics" challenges the presumptions of, and offers an advantage for, the Study of Religion. It enables the analysis of sensory practices *within* religious traditions (for instance, how a religious body is created, how distinctions and norms are persuasively imagined, implemented and embodied, or experiences of "other worlds" are trained by specific engagements of the senses) and it facilitates the analysis of how perceiving and meaning-making is influenced *by* religious cultivation and judgment of the senses, independent of whether people see themselves as adherents, or not. Failing to study these aspects means missing the opportunity to understand the "efficacy" of religion/s that is rooted in layers beyond and below propositional meaning.

4 Religious Aesthetics, or an Aesthetics of Religion?

To begin with, we emphasise that we do not see religious aesthetics as essentially different from any other engagement of the senses; rather, it is seen as building upon the same evolutionary, cognitive, emotional and perceptual capacities as other cultural practices. No ahistorical *homo religiosus* is evoked by referring to moods and experiences being evoked in religious traditions, and no privileged access to other worlds is claimed. Also, the many publications on theological aesthetics ask other types of questions than those taken up by an Aesthetics of Religion approach. When speaking about *religious aesthetics*, we refer to the repertoire of practices—ways of seeing or listening, cultivating the body, implementing embodied values and imaginations—and the repertoire of products that developed in the context of religious traditions—images, architecture, texts and dances, and the institutions that teach, traditionalise and evaluate them. An Aesthetics *of* Religion, however, denotes the theoretical background, the systematic questions and the methodology which are essential for developing an academic approach. Further below, we explain in more detail in what sense we think one can speak about a distinct religious aesthetics without evoking an essentialist model of religion/s; for now it should be emphasised that such distinctions are meant as models used to describe historical transformations, for instance when religious and scientific aesthetics start to overlap, or when an aesthetics of sports is merged with religious practice.

Centring on perception and the senses in the Study of Religion/s did not develop overnight, and all scholarly work being done in this field can be seen as responding to the critical revision of the discipline's foundational concepts and its problematic legacies taking place since the 1980s and after the "cultural turn".[19] In 1990, for instance, in the journal *Visible Religion*,[20] Hans G. Kippenberg programmatically asked for an inventory of religious image practices and representational forms that would compare to the impressive achievements of text hermeneutics, allowing to take into account visual and figurative religious media with the same expertise and scrutiny as it was developed through the tradition of Biblical Studies and philology. What has been taken up by the new *Bildwissenschaft* since (visual studies, visual culture), is now being done for the other senses—smell, touch, hearing, proprioception, and the sense of time and space.

The revised concept of aesthetics has been taken up in the Study of Religion in different ways and by scholars of different backgrounds and different motivations. As a concept in ritual studies, Williams and Boyd (2006) discuss the links between the anthropology of art and aesthetics. Birgit Meyer and Jojada Verrips (2008) convincingly argue for the recognition of form when studying religion, and for considering the whole range of experiences, including the aesthetic forms considered as blasphemy and the efficacy of the an-aesthetic. In her work Meyer was confronted with a lack of methods and theories adequate to what she encountered as the bodily-engaged practice of Pentecostal Christians.

---

19 For the understanding of the "cultural turn", see Bachmann-Medick (2016)
20 For a discussion why this journal's innovative programme, which anticipated the core questions of contemporary visual and material culture applied to religious history, could not be established beyond 1982–1990, see Uehlinger (2006).

This lack, she stated, resulted from an anti-ritualist attitude especially prominent in the anthropology of Christianity. While Meyer's concepts are mainly based on a theory of religion as mediation and on the materiality of religious practice, they contributed to the applicability of aesthetic analyses of styles and "sensational forms" which create a sense of presence and modes of persuasion based on the experience of the divine (Meyer 2010, 2013). In this view, aesthetics is presented as a key term of a material approach to religion (Prohl 2015.).

S. Brent Plate (2012) introduced the suggestive metaphor of the "skin of religion" and identifies the aesthetic with the multi-functional, permeable contact zone between individual and society. The skin, it is proposed, is not only surface and outside border, as aesthetic forms are for religious traditions; it is also the inside contact holding the structures together. This view allows analysis of the interactions between objects and religious practice beyond representation. In a comparable way, David Morgan suggests technologies of embodiment as core concepts of a programme to study the material culture of religion/s (Morgan 2015, 5).

Other colleagues specifically worked out concepts of a process of aestheticisation (Svašek 2007; Johnston 2008) and theorised specific fields in the study of religion from an aesthetic point of view, such as esoteric traditions that are characterised by the reflective reference to philosophical and scientific discourses (Johnston 2008). In a recent cross-disciplinary collection, Sally Promey (2014) introduces interdisciplinary research on religion under the title *Sensational Religion*; binding together visual studies, a materiality approach and sensory perception. The volume does not draw on aesthetics or perceptual theories *per se*, perhaps because aesthetics would be identified with the arts. The articles, however, expand on aesthetic repertoire that brilliantly unfold how religion, and the impact of religion/s on the environment they are embedded in, can be explained.

A comprehensive concept of an Aesthetics of Religion has developed in the German-speaking tradition of the Academic Study of Religion. In an initial article, Hubert Cancik and Hubert Mohr offered a programmatic outline of *Religionsaesthetik* being introduced "[...] in order to describe systematically and pervade theoretically what is perceivable in religions, how religion activates, governs and restricts the body and the sensorium" (Cancik and Mohr 1988, 121). The programme draws on different sources, for instance the French École des Annales, the concept of a history of mentalities and the experiment of integrating an *imaginaire* into history writing; also Historical Anthropology underlies the emphasis on the historicity of aesthetic forms in this programme. While linking up very closely to a semiotic understanding of religion as communicative systems with assignable functions and achievements,[21] the article argued for linking meaning to sensation, perception and the materiality of sign production. Religious communication should be observed in all its media and spheres of senses: dance, music, images, architecture and landscape design, but also in under-exposed media such as fragrance, rhythm, touch, or the senses of movement and proprioception.

A strong emphasis is placed on relating body practice to cultural codes and habits, and to systemise codified, and codifying forms across history and cultures. It seems important to mention that this programmatic outline has been developed in the first handbook for a basic terminology in the Study of Religion (*Handbuch religionswissenschaftlicher Grundbegriffe*), and hence was part of embedding the Study of Religion within the larger study of culture, presenting the Aesthetics of Religion side by side with "sub-disciplines" and their history such as the Sociology of Religion, or the Psychology of Religion. The idea to specialise in approaches rather than in regions or religions stands behind the systematic construct of an Aesthetics of Religion. The concept was taken up as conference theme (Lanwerd 2003; Koch 2004), a dictionary on "everyday religion and its mediation" was conceptualised on the basis of the aesthetic approach (*Metzler Lexikon Religion*, Auffarth, Bernard, and Mohr 2000; revised and without introduction in English edition: Stuckrad 2005; more introductions can be found in articles focusing on "perception" (Mohr 2005), or on the creation of "perceptual spaces" (*Wahrnehmungsraeume*, Mohn 2010); furthermore, in publications inspired by the concept (Wilke and Moebus 2011), and in the recently published "Vocabulary for the Study of Religion" (Grieser 2015b). The concept was institutionalised in a working group in 2007, affiliated to the German association for the Study of Religion and has since regularly engaged in collaborative publications, of which this volume is one.

Although different in background and approach, these examples share the basic interest in approaching religion through sensory perception and an aim to relate physiological aspects to mechanisms of the cultivation of the senses and to "semiotic ideologies" (Keane 2006). As such they understand religious traditions as an active part of stimulating and disciplining habits of perception within a larger culture. Perception is seen as an active process of filtering and distributing attention; religions are seen as providing such "filters" and, thus, contribute to organising what is possible to perceive, feel, and think in a society.

---

21 In this concept of "religion as communication" diverse traditions converge, coming from backgrounds as different as system theory (Niklas Luhmann and Talcott Parsons), semiotics (Charles Sanders Peirce and Umberto Eco) and transcultural cybernetics (Horst Reimann).

From this point of view, an aesthetic analysis can address individual as well as collective aspects of perceptual orders. Repetitive practices and exceptional, intense experiences in relation with narratives and doctrines shape a religious *panorama of perception* that bind individual believers into a community. Across a wide variety of local forms, religious traditions can be distinguished by their *aesthetic profiles*. Without knowing much about religions, we can "sense" and identify a Buddhist or an Islamic aesthetic because religions distinguish themselves through clothes, colours, hairstyles, buildings and artefacts. These ensembles change over time and are subject to reinterpretation and adaptation (if we think, for instance, of couture Islam, the merging of orthodox and pop cultural styles of dressing or hairstyle; see Nieuwkerk et al. 2016). They reach beyond representing or symbolising religious beliefs and doctrines, because they cultivate perceptual habits that build identity within the group, and determine the mutual perception between groups and within the larger society.

The aesthetic analysis of culture also includes that normative determinations of what is beautiful and what is ugly; what is kitsch and what is worth being recorded depends on the taste of the practitioners, and not purely on normative aesthetic judgements. Aesthetic studies explicitly pay attention to the "reverse side of the expected": the use of the ugly and the monstrous, or the use of transgression, the limits of pain or disgust in liminal experiences is also addressed. This includes the non-spectacular, the an-aesthetic, the white wall of the Protestant church. Such modes are how religions "becomes effective" through aesthetic means and are named as strategies of stimulation, or deprivation of the senses by Mohr (2005). Such "work on terms", and the aim to provide analytic categories and a descriptive vocabulary marks the difference between a collection on religious aesthetics, and Aesthetics of Religion as an approach that goes beyond addressing the body and the senses in the context of religions. The research network on Aesthetics of Religion dedicated two collaborative publications to such theorisation of terms. The first special issue elaborated on *museality* from different perspectives, interlacing aspects concrete social practice of exhibiting religion, as discourse, as matrix of knowledge production and as perceptual order of relating to religion and culture (Kugele and Wilkens 2011). The second publication explored theories of imagination, and how imaginative practices are deployed in religious traditions and can be seen as the backbone of creating religious embodied realities (Traut and Wilkens 2014). In the present volume, authors expand on the terms and concepts they find useful for their cases; many of them—disfiguration, viscerality, the Hieratic—provide the basis for a list of keywords to be further elaborated.

5 Potentials of the Approach

We contend that an aesthetics of religion approach offers four innovations: (1) it takes into account new objectives and topics as well as new aspects of well-known topics (heuristic potential); (2) it offers options to describe and explain historical and political effects of religion (descriptive and explanatory potential); (3) it offers new ways of comparing religious traditions throughout history and regions (comparative potential); and (4) it allows reflexive analysis on the variety of aesthetic theories, including religious, artistic and academic ones, and their embeddedness in the religious history and the ideologies of their time, for instance that certain senses are religiously privileged or rejected, or that imagination is devalued in both religious and academic traditions (reflexive potential).

5.1 Heuristics

Taking perception as its focus and the issue of how human beings relate indirectly, metaphorically and through media to reality, new fields and sources can be explored, as has recently been done with regard to touch and odours. However, traditional fields can be approached in innovative ways. Instead of focusing on the content of texts and the hermeneutics at play, and aesthetic history of reading would include the body practice of reading (posture, aloud or silent, alone or with others, felt as a duty or as pleasure), the design and usage of texts as objects, and the way the cultural technique of reading becomes metaphors that creates new realities such as the "decoding of genes" and the reading of the code of humanity.

Developing aesthetic analysis as a repertoire of methods, a specifically trained attention is required, and results from conscious and unconscious training processes, as well as skills of collecting data and producing "thick descriptions" of sensory practices, settings and regimes. Scholars investigating the physiology and aesthetic forms of religious practice encounter two major challenges. The first is how to (re-)present the data which are not textual media. This question touches upon discussions of central concern to anthropologists for a long time. Being aware that considering music or movement is more challenging than dwelling in the seemingly same medium (text), strategies have been developed that apply innovative ways of using film and images, integrating notification techniques for dance, music or sound, finding new ways of measuring excitement, or detecting responses to the affordance of religious-aesthetic arrangements. Also, expertise requires further development, and for example, skills in notation developed (for music, for example, Laack 2008) or developing terminology and modes of analysis to appreciate performances for which one previously had no categories. Innovative forms of representation, however, do not prevent scholarly work from finding verbal ways of thinking through and reconstructing the observed and analysed; discussions from the 1980s (writing-culture debate) provide the background for rethinking the role of analytical language and qualities of academic knowledge, including the comparative difference it would make to reproduce the observed. However, the discussion sometimes tends to forget that thinking about a dance does not need to be danced, and studying religions/s does not require one to re-enact them.

In this respect, providing a descriptive language is seen as a valuable way of gaining both a closeness to religion as aesthetic practice (acknowledging the intensity and the qualities of aesthetic effects), and a position of distance, going beyond reproduction and appreciation of aesthetic forms and providing a systematic frame for comparing and analysing the single case in light of more general questions. It is an explicit goal to contribute to the "work on terms" in the study of religion that enables scholars to analytically engage with aesthetic phenomena, for example, terms such as synchronicity, extended cognition, or imagination, museality (which have been elaborated on in collaborative publications of the working group as previously noted).

The second challenge is how to interpret different modes of data if we, for instance, address physiological data and patterns of interpretation, narratives and texts as Koch and Meissner (2011) do in their pilot study, or we address extended cognition such as the "sixth sense" (Johnston 2016), or from the kinaesthetic (Mohr in this volume). As we have pointed out above, an "enactive aesthetics" as well as the discourse on bio-cultural models of religion is meant to offer a framework for this challenge. It is not the aim to find a universal solution; rather, it is seen as a great potential to make explicit the basis on which diverse modes of data are interpreted and what modes of knowledge are connected and in what ways. It is here that Vásquez' (2011) rejection of positivist naturalism and his "non-reductive materialism" needs to be extended; that Koch makes use of psycho-somatic models in order to explain spiritual healing; and that Johnston discusses adequate epistemologies that neither try to prove, nor to explain away phenomena relevant to people.

An example of how a familiar topic develops differently from the angle of an Aesthetics of Religion approach could be a sensory history of religious reading, considering that also using texts can be differentiated according to the various layers of bodily and sensorial engagement with texts. Another field develops when integrating art, again, into the aesthetic approach. If art is seen as one specific (and important) field subsumed under the heading of *aisthesis*, the relationship between religion and art turns out to be manifold:

- Art *in* religion, which is an important traditional field in aesthetic approaches to religion, and reaches beyond classical iconography (Lanwerd 2002; Belting 2011). Music, visual art, architecture, or drama within religion create multi-dimensional interrelations between the expressive, doctrinal, and perceptive spheres, and religion has fostered elaborated artistic traditions.
- Art *as* religion, a constellation which is based on art becoming an autonomous sphere during modernisation, and therewith also becoming a medium of transferring religious claims to discourses on beauty and the sublime, especially in European and American Romanticism.
- Art in *relation* to religion, either criticising religion explicitly or claiming the aestheticist position that art is not committed to morals or truth. This becomes apparent in the notion of blasphemy or in value conflicts that may result in violent responses to each other.

5.2 History and Politics

It is for two reasons that we would like to highlight the aspects of the historicity and the political character of the aesthetic. First, when we speak about perception as a somatic-sensory process, readers might be inclined to understand the "natural body" to work beyond history and relations of power. Second, when speaking about an aesthetic history of religion, we mean different aspects. A history of religion can be approached by investigating sensory practices and aesthetic forms; religious contributions to the perceptual order of a larger culture can be studied; and the ideologies about what is the aesthetic, for instance the notion of art as being separated from everyday life and the politics of power, can be analysed as being themselves dependent on the history of classes and milieus within Western societies of the modern period.

An aesthetic history of religion, and the religious-historical character of aesthetic forms make a difference in comparison to a conventional history of events (*Ereignisgeschichte*) or of concepts and ideas (*Ideengeschichte*). Taking as an example one of the most "sustainable" concepts in the history of religion, the soul; it is obvious that the focus would shift from texts and ideas to visualisations, practices such as contemplation, or healing techniques that relate touch or singing to the wellbeing of the soul. Guiding questions are what imaginative and emotional practices are performed: Which technologies of the self would be deployed? How does the soul relate to intuitive and sensory knowledge of the self and reality? Culturally different concepts can be compared on a broader basis than ideas, and the aesthetic practices and forms can be studied as a means of keeping concepts stable by adapting to new circumstances.[22]

---

22 For an aesthetic history that covers both, the history of the senses and a history through the

Works that have made this difference in approaching religious history have been presented, and we can only mention examples of the different aspects. Schneider, Wald-Fuhrmann and Watzka (2015) approach the *Aesthetics of the Spirits* by combining a historical analysis of concepts with the emerging differentiation between early modern science, religion and art. Marvin Döbler (2013) weaves together a sensory analysis of St. Bernhard's theory and practice of mysticism with its critical reflection by scholars of religion being rooted in the anti-ritual attitude of Protestant historiography. Another example of how an aesthetic concept can shed new light on, for example, the history of Christian mission in China, has been presented by Rambelli and Reinders (2012). The concepts they used, iconoclasm as practice and idolatry as ideological instrument, uncovered an unexpectedly complex—and violent—history of alliances between Protestants, Catholics, adherents of folk religion and Daoist philosophers. A final work to mention that approaches religious history through aesthetic practice concentrated on physical objects is Brent Plate's *A History of Religion in 5 ½ Objects* (2014); it demonstrates how the individual use of objects is embedded in the social and historical orders of sensing and imagining and how perception and material objects have to be understood as inevitably intertwined in their power to manage religion's dynamics of stability and change throughout history.

Mark Smith's (2007a) discussion of the problems and opportunities of a *sensory history* is interesting to us at this point. In his argument for radically historicising the senses and sensing, he outlines clearly that it cannot be the purpose to "re-enact" history on the basis of a universally shared human sensorium; nor should an immediate or privileged access to the past (or to different cultures, for that matter) be claimed through imagining how people in the past may have sensed their world. Smith makes this clear by addressing the question how to represent these imaginations if not in language and description, and using the example of the lemon sample: even if we could add to an article about the taste of lemon in early US-American history a sample of prepared

---

lens of aesthetic forms, several concepts are important and yet to be explored. Constance Classen's 6 volume project *A Cultural History of the Senses* (2014) covers time periods from 500 BCE; Robert Jütte's *History of the Senses* (2004) focuses on the interrelation between senses and media; Mark Smith (2007a, 2007b) reflects on historiographical issues. Going further back in the tradition of sensory history writing the impulse of writing a body history that undermines the paradigm of semiotics and content should certainly be included, see Duden (1990) and Feher (1989). In the same realm, the history of mentality and the exploration of the *imaginaire* in the tradition of the *Annales* School still offer the opportunity to pursue both a material history of "Things" (Meyer and Houtmann 2012) and a history of imaginaries related and relying on them (Patlagean 1978).

paper with a liquid tasting like lemon—we cannot simulate the taste of something which people were not used to at all, saw as utterly exotic, and had different experiences of, because they were not used to sweetened or strongly flavoured food at all. The other convincing argument presented is that the limits of imagining the sensed past are reached very quickly when being asked to simulate the nose of a slave-holder whose racism manifested in the conviction and perception that different skin colours have a specific odour. The specificity of whose senses are being discussed and how do they relate to class, gender, location, etc.—these are the questions that a sensory history can help to unpack and would result in the production of a more diversified history than a history of ideas and events can deliver.

It is telling, however, that Smith does not spend one word on the role of religion in his outline of a sensory history, and we may speculate that his view of religion might be confined to cognitive ideologies and beliefs being separated from the perceptual orders and the sensory regimes. Here, more conversation would make clear that an aesthetic understanding of religion needs to be included. Especially for the history of the US, religion plays a significant role on all levels of sensory history: for the definition, the use, the value and the hierarchies of the senses; sensory practices and ideals of dealing with the body; and the repertoire of aesthetic forms accompanying the conquering of the land, for instance romantic notions of wilderness, nature and freedom (Feldt 2012). *Vice versa*, the specific development of religiosity in the USA cannot be understood fully without the aesthetic history of its landscape and its new and old inhabitants. What we wanted to show here is that both an aesthetic history of religion, and a religious studies approach to sensory history have much to offer within the broader movement of extending history to aesthetic forms beyond representationalism.

In regard to the political character of the aesthetic, we have shown that especially the development in social aesthetics has made clear that there is no neutral, or unpolitical order of perception within a society. In a Foucauldian sense, practices and orders of the self are always embedded in the power structure of regulations and mechanisms of inclusion and exclusion. On this very basic level it can be said that it is the perceptual orders in the first place that determine what is possible to feel, think and believe within a society, and that what we perceive as real is politically established. In addition to the fundamentally political character of perceptual orders, extreme examples demonstrate that ideologies are not confined to conscious thought and semiotic mechanisms. As mentioned above, racist regimes manifest in a reality that is "naturalised" by a perception of differences that is anchored in sensing and feeling the otherness of the other. The slaveholder's nose creates the reality of an ideological regime, and the alleged naturalness of the smell corroborates the manifestation as real. Another extreme example can be found in the ways that totalitarian systems discipline and glorify the strong body, and succeed in creating a *Volkskoerper* (the people as one body). As outlined in Barck and Faber's (1999) volume, these ideologies do not merely express themselves in their aesthetic forms, they are rather manifesting as an emotional and perceptual reality; considering the *Aesthetic of the Political*—as their title says—also requires to consider *The Political of the Aesthetic*. At the other end of a political aesthetics, recent work on old and new forms of protest demonstrates the power of criticising and undermining dominant orders by body performance and aesthetic actions (Werbner et al. 2014).

5.3 Comparison

The notion of Comparative Religion has been under sustained critique in recent years, firstly because of the problematic concept of World Religions in which 'religions' are compared to each other as fixed units deprived of context, and secondly, because of the romantic and phenomenological heritage that neglects cultural difference by their representational model, seeing different traditions as mere expressions of the same (monotheistic) model. Comparing, however, is part and parcel of the Academic Study of Religion, and instead of giving up on the method, the point is rather to pay greater attention to what and how we compare. Against this backdrop, aesthetic analysis offers parameters of comparison—not "religions", but aesthetic schemas and forms being analysed, considering how they encounter, and how they change.

This can be done diachronically and synchronically (Schlieter 2000); for a single tradition, e.g., when migrants bring their religion and re-establish it in new forms (Svašek 2012), or when a history of the senses allows us to rethink which sense is dominating a cultural practice and their ideologies: sight (*darśan*; see Eck 2007), or sound (Wilke and Moebus 2011). Comparing different traditions, or religious encounters, can gain, for instance, from comparing the practice and the role of applying pain in rituals (Bräunlein 2010). Especially those formations which provide transitional categories, such as *subtle bodies*, allow for comparing a broad range of phenomena and cultures (Johnson and Samuel 2013).

As a third example, identifying religious aesthetic patterns helps to describe transfer processes between religious and other societal domains, such as politics, science, art, healing systems, and pop culture. For instance, what David Chidester (1986) has called "theologies of light" can be found in political staging of charismatic leaders, and in popular science as well (Grieser 2015a).

5.4 Reflexivity

Aesthetics deployed as analytical concepts are not confined to academic thinking. The senses and how to (not) use them are theorised by religious authors as well, and it is reflected upon how faculties of thought, emotion, and imagination are to be judged. Buddhism, for instance, knows elaborate normative and analytical notions about how to train and to evaluate thoughts and emotions, and the "work" of the senses. Thus, the aesthetic approach allows us to disentangle, and to be aware of the mutual influences between concepts of the soul, of *ratio* and *emotio* in academic and in religious theories of the aesthetic.

A second aspect of engaging with an aesthetic approach is that it is in itself a critical endeavour, and most scholars involved put effort in re-reading the theories we are working with in respect of how they deal with the sensuous; consider Meyer and Verrips (2008) for the Protestant foundation of the discipline; Gladigow (1998) for the phenomenological rejection of the senses; Asad (1993, 2003) for the role of the body in both formations of the religious and the secular. They look for different options when referring to "classical thinkers" that allow for a positive theory including sensory and bodily aspects of religion such as Aby Warburg or Jane Harrison (Brunotte 2013); and they critically engage with contemporary theoretical developments, for instance in a *tour de force* of assessing possible candidates for a "non-reductive materialist" theory by Vásquez (2011), aiming at establishing a "non-reductive materialism" as foundation of an "ecological-aesthetic" approach. Others delve into aesthetic traditions that oscillate between art criticism and intellectual history, making analytical use of concepts, for example, S. Brent Plate reads Walter Benjamin (2005) in a creative way.

Such reflections on the methodology and epistemology of the Study of Religion inevitably leads to the question whether there is, or will be a specific aesthetic theory of religion. An introduction is certainly not the place to propose and discuss such theory. Moreover, just as a Sociology of Religion would not be reducible to one theory or one method, an aesthetic approach provides an informed and shared analytical framework for *theorising* rather than a single theory of religions and perception. According to Stausberg (2009), a theory of religion/s should be able to respond to questions about the specificity of what we determine as religion/s; their origins, or beginnings; about assignable functions and about the structure of religion/s. These aspects provide the framework for the programmatic discussions in this volume and future theorising, including:

– Religion/s are seen as being rooted in both, universal conditions developed in evolutionary processes and in culturally contingent and changeable circumstances; for such bio-cultural understanding, diverse modes of knowledge need to be drawn together
– Religion/s are understood as modes of organising the way humans relate to reality; while humans are not seen as essentially different from other species, they face a few specific conditions, for instance that they are not only able to, but that they need to imagine beyond the situation they are situated in. Orders of perception, therefore, need to provide solutions for spheres which cannot be experienced, but can be imagined (time, being dead, wishing something that is *not*); the link between imagination, perception and bodily practice is a strong framework for theorising religion.

- The religious subject we study is conceptualised as an aesthetic subject whose decision-making is not confined to rational choice and conscious weighing of advantages and disadvantages, but rather includes preferences and styles, pleasure and boredom, satisfaction and the distribution of attention as modes that govern behaviour. If we integrate recent research on the plasticity of the brain and the perceptual system, it becomes clear that, for example, conversions cannot be studied as a change of belief systems only; rather, with a concept of aesthetic subjectivity at hand, it can be studied how not only the interpretive framework is changing, but also the perceptual orders, the intuitive reactions, and about why people might laugh or cry. The concept of an aesthetic subjectivity also challenges how we approach the relationship of ourselves as researchers and the religious agents we study. Rationalist positions that advise to suspend matters of taste, sensations, and emotions are questioned, and it is suggested that these aspects should be trained as a means of research and for academic purposes.

- Considering the religious subject as an aesthetic subject challenges the dominance of semiotics in interpreting the body and agency. The relationship between aesthetics and semiotics requires further discussion, and an enactive aesthetics might allow for acknowledging a sensory knowledge without instantly marking the body as a carrier of meaning, and without opposing sensory to abstract knowledge and meaning-making. As Margaret Wilson puts it, "the embodied cognition literature has sometimes taken a very strong stance that cognition is fundamentally and directly bound to the body in its immediate physical environment. Instead, I argue here, that the value of the embodied cognition approach is not to deny the existence of abstract and de-contextualised thought, but to explain how it grew out of previously existing sensorimotor abilities" (Wilson 2008, 375).

- Another point of discussion is the extent to which the revised understanding of aesthetics is applicable cross-culturally and how it relates to religious aesthetic theories or indigenous conceptualisation of the senses, as well as how to address them. This includes examining how scholars and practitioners negotiate between the belief in phenomena (including experience, perception, etc.) as universal or culturally specific.

- A critical conversation with theories of material agency (both old and new) is relevant, in particular the claims that an agency of things helps to de-centre the modern focus on the human subject. The point is to further discuss the status of matter and materiality in relation to perception and formative processes. Distinguishing ontological from epistemological concepts, for instance, is important when matter is discussed as the basis of a new monism.

– Especially for the Study of Religion, agency can be a helpful category; however, excluding notions of form, formation, or perception does not make sense—it is not the object that acts religiously, but the object's affordance relates to the specific sensorium of human beings. Yet, embodiment approaches and actor-network theory put human beings and their relations with the environment in perspective. Margaret Wilson's concept of "re-tooling", for instance, provides us with a model that explains the dynamics of humans being agents as well as patients of the culture they live in at the same time (Wilson 2010).

5.5 Connectivity

In the title of this volume, we qualify aesthetics as a *Connective Concept* because we think aesthetics provides connectivity on two levels: first, rather than opposing historical, sensory or interpretive approaches, it allows us to analyse the components of *aisthesis*—sensing, perceiving and sense making—in their relationality. On a second level, it connects the modes of academic knowledge we need to provide such analysis. This second aspect, though, refers to the larger problem of the fragmentation of knowledge, and to the problematic aspect of specialisation in the production and dissemination of knowledge. It also refers to a long debate about the inner organisation of the Academic Study of Religion, its status as a discipline and its place in a de-differentiating landscape of academic knowledge. Aesthetics, as an approach which thinks through the relationship between religion/s and perception, in a way is comparable to the perspective of, for example, a Sociology of Religion that thinks through the relationship between religion/s and society. As much as a Sociology of Religion is complemented by, say, an economic perspective, an Aesthetics of Religion enhances the understanding of building communities and identities by addressing the perceptual aspects of these processes. Thus, connectivity as a term may emphasise that relating diverse epistemological cultures should create a quality of knowledge which does justice to the complexity of religions as they influence and interact with possibly every other sphere of culture. Connections are enabled by allowing scholars to recognise a broader range of sources, media and data; by offering a link between perception and the history of aesthetic forms, and between individual practice and cultural ideologies; by enabling scholars to question dualist notions of body and mind, or spirit and matter; and by paving the way to critically engage diverse academic knowledge cultures—not least the polarised debate on cognition and culture. Many colleagues are in search of ways to go beyond disciplinary borders and to link different modes of knowledge to each other. Using actor-network models (Morgan 2012) or "building block approaches" (Taves 2010) to organise the academic operations of analysing and synthesising, of "assembling and disassembling" (Taves 2015, 6); proposing a "bio-cultural theory of religion" (Geertz 2010; Geertz and Jensen 2010) or laying the grounds for an epistemology of the body (Koch 2015), these are but a few examples of approaches which strive to a) produce synthetic knowledge from different academic knowledge cultures, and b) mutually advance knowledge production by developing shared questions, providing models and correct each other's assumptions.

Considering this a need for collaborative organisation of specialised knowledge, we chose the metaphor of connectivity for characterising the Aesthetics of Religion. Why this? Being at home in mathematics, computer sciences or network theories of knowledge and learning (Downes 2012), connectivity is attractive, because there are three things it does *not* suggest: it does not claim to subsume everything under one umbrella, as the word "integrative" might suggest; it does not link only two sides, as a "bridging concept" would; and it does not evoke the notion of a closed and unified whole as some "holistic theories" might. What connectivity does provide us with is a way of modelling complex processes that are not confined to a one-way causality, but are rather based on mutual responses and feedback loops, which result in learning systems. In models of brain activities, for example, connectivity is used to describe how circuits and paths are constantly re-connected in ways needed for the task to be performed—a flexible yet organised way of distributing work. The second aspect of connectivity is that it is a meta-category that does not only ask what data or knowledge we need, but also what kind of connections are important, and how we should make the connection between the different modes of knowledge and interpretation.

Connectivism, in consequence, is the name of a theory that describes how people know and learn using network processes. In this sense, the metaphor offers a concept of a non-linear learning process which allows one to be aware of possible connections, but without expecting that one contributor uses or oversees all of them. More concretely, if an Aesthetics of Religion provides us with the possibility to theorise the field of our studies through the diverse dimensions of *aisthesis*, bringing together the diverse expertise from within the Study of Religion and across the relevant disciplines is crucial. Exchanging this expertise does not make us specialists of the other disciplines—we remain experts for religious ways of approaching and creating reality; neither lumping together different ways of knowing, nor accepting a scientific naturalist causality as the only way of "explaining religion" can be the goal. Connecting expertise about religious ways of perceiving the world means to learn *from* other disciplines, but also to *add to* their expertise; it is an interdisciplinary undertaking. The question for an Aesthetics of Religion is, therefore, not only how to appropriate the fast growing knowledge about perception and cognition, simultaneously important is the question, where does the expertise of the cultural and historical Study of Religion lie? As we perceive it, in the cognitive and evolutionary study of religion/s, and also in the areas of sensory history or art studies expertise on religion/s is needed—in terms of historicising concepts of religion/s, embedding them in the cultural and comparative context and, importantly, monitoring and reflecting on the ideological and religious background of many an assumption used in natural scientific concepts in the study of "religion". Much would be gained for the study of a field as vast as religion/s if we took the time to think about how we organise, accept and exchange our expertise in order to connect specialised knowledge without being overstrained by an impossible research agenda. The structure of an aesthetic approach follows, in this respect, Max Weber's insight that "It is not the 'actual' interconnections of 'things' but the conceptual interconnections of problems which define the scope of the various sciences" (Weber 1949, 68).

6 Structure and Contributions

When looking through the table of contents, it might strike the reader that this volume is not arranged around a single period of history, a specific religion or a special region. Indeed, the chapters cover eras from Antiquity to the contemporary; disciplinary backgrounds from archaeology to ethology and literature studies; and regions from India across Europe to the Americas. This is no accidental diversity—it is exactly what we wished for the volume and the conference presentations and discussions it encapsulates. The wide-ranging topics of analysis are characteristic of an aesthetic approach in which it is the systematic questions, the methodological challenges and the epistemological reflection which provide the common foundation that links the individual chapters. According to the potential of an aesthetic approach (outlined above), we divided the contributions in four sections; it should be emphasised, however, that these divisions are not hard boundaries, and many contributions contain aspects of the other sections, as well. While focusing on one aspect, all authors show that empirical data is linked to the historicity of aesthetic forms; in many cases, their specific analysis helps to illuminate other case-studies. We also encouraged all authors to contribute to the necessary "work on terms" and to a programmatic perspective.

The chapters have been divided into four sections: *Fields and Topics*, *History and Politics*, *Comparison and Transfer*, and *Concepts and Theories*. A fifth section contains short essays by scholars who were invited to reflect—from their own point of view—on the connectivity of an Aesthetics of Religion. In this way we aim to integrate into this volume work forms employed at conferences in which colleagues were invited to act as "observers" who would provide feedback to the Working Group from their specific expertise and experience. This provided a meta-perspective and a fresh view on points that would have otherwise been overlooked. We are especially grateful to those colleagues who engaged creatively in this somewhat playful open form, most of them without having previously been part of joint events.

In the chapters of the first section, *Fields and Topics*, the reader encounters religious aesthetic forms and media that seem familiar, those usually associated with traditional approaches: texts, ritual objects, film. However, more traditional approaches mainly inquire about the content of these texts, their meaning and what we can learn about beliefs and ideas expressed therein. Through an aesthetic lens, the authors in this volume ask a different range of questions. They manage to unfold the multifaceted efficacy of text, stone and film that reaches beyond issues content and meaning (although these issues are not ignored). Investigating the ritual and social aesthetics of "petromorphic gods" in a Hindu context, Mikael Aktor demonstrates that it is not a single theoretical key but rather the interpretive combination of theories which allows one to understand how stones connect religious knowledge, performative action and the repertoire of used forms. Aktor demonstrates that neither anthropomorphic perceptions nor the agency of the stone material alone make up the ritual aesthetics in which the stones are involved. Rather, applying concepts from landscape phenomenology and cognitive theories including the role of material objects in cognitive technologies, and the structure of the human mind, Aktor unravels how the sensory and synaesthetic qualities have made these stones ritually important. In this weaving together of different aspects, Aktor illustrates the way in which an aesthetic approach forms a connective pathway within religious studies scholarship.

Another "double aspect" of aesthetics is addressed by John Hamilton and Almut-Barbara Renger, who explore German Expressionist literature between 1910 and 1925. They show that the striking combination of vitalism and scepticism, which many of the Expressionist authors inherit from Friedrich Nietzsche, complicates any naïve concept of a "re-enchanted modernity" as a regaining of un-reflected belief. These authors at the same time apply and critically thematise the undermining power of the aesthetic. Only through the mutual differentiation of art and religion as autonomous realms, a new form of de-differentiation—art deploying the purported force and efficacy of a religiously coded aesthetics—can come to the fore. It is still underestimated how important this transformation, so clearly identified by Hamilton and Renger herein, has been for understanding the varieties of modern religion.

A combination of reflective genres and their religious utilisation is presented by Adrian Herrmann who explores a "discourse of sobriety" produced by charismatic Christians. His case study addresses the 2012 documentary movie *Fathers of Light* and its audience reception ritualised in film screenings as worship in the USA and the UK. Herrmann discusses the debates within documentary studies about the nature of representation, audio-visual claims to the 'Real', and the production of visual evidence. It is an interesting twist when religious groups are using a medium that claims to represent reality in order to convincingly represent the supernatural. Drawing on an understanding of religion as a mediated practice, Herrmann examines the aesthetics of documentaries by facing the difficulties of reception research and takes a "turn to the audience". His chapter asks questions about the presentation of 'truth' and aesthetic styles that are implicitly read as 'truthful'. The aesthetics analysis provided connects changing perspectives about the production, presentation and reception of media products as shaping forms of religion in the 21st century.

Laura Feldt's chapter investigates parts of the classical religious narrative of Exodus 7–11 from the Hebrew Bible. One might think that Biblical literature has experienced enough analysis of form through the long and proficient traditions of rhetorical and exegetical analysis. However, form analysis in most cases serves a hermeneutical purpose. How can we access the *meaning* of the transmitted texts, what can we learn about concepts, ideas and theologies, and how can we bridge the historical gap of meaning making—these are the guiding questions for most historians of religion who look for information *about* religion rather than for modes of how the texts might have been used, felt or imagined. An analysis of form, theorised through the lens of cognitive narratology, leads to diverse modes of reception, and—more precisely—suggests that theological content does not exclude other reasons for the use of metaphors, suspense and other "literary-aesthetic devices". Feldt provides a pioneering shift when addressing the "efficacy" of religious texts, and how they engage their audiences by stimulating varying responses, senses and emotions: she makes evident what an aesthetic reading looks like when analysis is not subordinated to content. The important question—what do we deploy our analysis for?—offers an opportunity to bridge historical gaps by emphasising that texts and religions stimulate varying responses, senses and emotions, and are unlikely to be separated from entertainment, fascination and the sensational.

In section II, *History and Politics*, authors engage with aesthetic forms and the way they create meaning, experiences and worldviews that change throughout history. These range from the representation and cultural self-awareness of history in societies, including individual perception of biographies and fates, as well as consideration of how we as scholars are "doing history", and history of religion in particular. It is the historicity of the aesthetic as well as the aesthetic dimension of the historical which changes the way historical transformations can be described. The authors make clear that aesthetic forms do not only concern representations of ideas and theologies; rather, religious change goes along with implementing new ways of seeing, recognising and imagining. These changing perceptual habits are political in the sense that they determine what is considered true, that they include and exclude what is accepted as knowledge, represent from a certain perspective and involve the making of individual and collective identity by authenticating claims and demarcations.

Niklaus Largier opens this section by conceiving of prayer as a production of *aisthesis* and guided perception. Focusing on Theresa of Avila's *Vida*, and built on his wider investigation of medieval and early modern Christianity, Largier makes use of the rhetorical concept of *figuration—disfiguration—transfiguration* in order to show how "the invention and the rhetoric of the inner or spiritual senses allows for the creation of a space of 'experience', 'exploration' and 'amplification' of the emotional as well as of the sensory life of the soul". This investigation demonstrates a way in which the historical gap that hampers studying sensory practices can be bridged. It binds together and analyses the reading of scriptures as bodily practice; rhetorical techniques and material media. Largier argues that habitualised perceptions and experiences, created by figural networks that produce sensual and affective cognition below the level of hermeneutics, form a "material theology" which complements conceptual understanding and become an integral part of Christianity's aesthetic repertoire. The political aspect Largier highlights towards the end of his chapter consists of the impact such Catholic "aesthetic ideology" has had in the larger culture and also in academic theories, for example media theories.

Such repertoires, as it is shown in the next chapter, are not confined to religious traditions, but also find their way into the history of academic approaches and the appreciation or rejection of theories—gender politics are a topic that accompanies a sensory history of academia. Ulrike Brunotte, in her intellectual biography of classicist Jane E. Harrison, gives an excellent example of how the aesthetic perspective can be applied not only to religious historical material, but also to trace a different history of the Study of Religion and their "classical thinkers". Utilising a concept of an "aesthetics of performativity", Brunotte carves out the terms and the sources by which Harrison resisted rituals and material and bodily expressions being dominated by text, doctrines and beliefs. A pioneer of a performative approach to religion, Harrison convincingly demonstrated that simplistic dichotomies such as subject and object, spirit and matter, or form and formlessness/matter prove inadequate as methodological and theoretical concepts for a culture-historical study of religion.

Politics can be understood in different ways as demonstrated by Christoph Auffarth's close analysis of a period of massive change in Bremen, one of the Northern-German city centres of the Reformation. By looking at iconographic programmes that draw on caricature, on virtues and new symbolism, he argues that, firstly, religious change does not primarily come as ideas or doctrines in everyday life experience; rather, religious transformation develops as a change of the aesthetics in the public sphere (if we may use this term for this era). Analysing image programmes and architectural developments within the urban space, Auffarth, secondly, shows how the concept of the anti-iconic prominent in reformation theology had to negotiate ways to be visually present. "Learning a new religion", as another point made in Auffarth's approach, goes together with learning a new symbolism that is only in part explained and accounted for as theological content. Rather, the implementation of a new political and religious imaginary literally framed the perception within the city's everyday life and was not only confined to adherents and believers.

A much longer period is covered by Hubert Mohr's tracing of an aesthetic form, "the Hieratic". His chapter closely investigates one of the strategies constituting an aesthetic construction of the sacred. Based on his ground-breaking work on religion and movement, Mohr introduces "standing, not moving" as a pattern that is both grounded in basic behaviour of humans as animals, and in the cultural variations which develop as derivation from primary functions. This view—drawing from knowledge about anthropological universals, and investigating principles of cultural formations and formalisations of such behaviour—characterises Mohr's approach and stimulates the development of a descriptive vocabulary for religious aesthetics. In its programmatic dimension, a concept such as the Hieratic suggests the possibility of identifying a repertoire of religious aesthetic forms and strategies. Rooted in cognitive, kinaesthetic and behavioural studies, as well as in historical anthropology, a new type of comparison across religions and cultures is enabled by such basal forms—while fully embracing the cultural differences and the complexity which emerge from the historical layers and the political situations in which these forms exert power and implement ideologies. Mohr teaches us why hieratic standing is used in the exercise of power as well as in political protest.

Mohr's concept of a comparative repertoire of religious-aesthetic strategies makes for a fitting transition to section III, *Comparison and Transfer.* This section focuses on how observation of the usage, distribution and normative valuation of particular senses and aesthetic forms enables the comparison of religious traditions beyond doctrines and categories such as world religions. Moreover, these chapters investigate processes of differentiation and of transfer between religion and other symbolic systems, such as art, science, or politics.

The first contribution opens with an investigation of "migrating" aesthetic form, a stunningly stereotypical visualisation of the human brain. Since new image technologies have opened up possibilities to observe the "brain at work", the neurosciences have moved to the centre of attention as a new leading science (*Leitwissenschaft*) and as a provider of new technologies of the self in a Foucauldian sense. Alexandra Grieser analyses this aesthetic configuration at the interface between religious and scientific aesthetics on the backdrop of different approaches which link the perceptual qualities of the "blue brains" and "loose heads" to questions of collective imagination, as well as to concrete practices in the sphere of healing, education and entertainment. Grieser highlights the historicity of aesthetic forms, positioning the "blue brains" in a long tradition of imagining human capacities as located within and transcending the body. In this context the aestheticisation of the brain can be understood as an example of the shifting configurations of the religious and the secular within modern genres of knowledge production. Grieser introduces an *aesthetics of knowledge* as a comparative approach which assumes that all modes of knowledge are bound to aesthetic forms and considers how the formation of knowledge is organised in contemporary "knowledge societies".

A different mode of comparison is addressed by Jens Kreinath who directs his attention to inter-religious relations unfolding at Southern Turkish pilgrimage sites. In particular, he examines the concept of *mimesis* as a key term for aesthetic analysis. Reaching beyond explanatory models of representation and repetition, Kreinath discusses how perceptual qualities and the "doing together" of ritual is often more important than engaging with concepts of dialogue or contradicting theologies. It is demonstrated how rituals of saint veneration can be much more successfully conceived of as mimetic acts, and understood in the modes of becoming efficacious through aesthetic modes and solutions that balance the similarities and differences at play. It is important to note that *mimesis* here goes beyond mere simulation, or copying behaviour; rather the term bears the opportunity to interlink the evolution-based mimetic skill of human beings with the way mimetic action came to frame, design and formalise social action.

Just as Jens Kreinath bases his reflections on contemporary fieldwork data, Maruška Svašek rethinks her long-term investigation of how people—in this case, middle class families in Chennai, India—refer to "materialisations of Hindu Gods" in diverse ways. 'Comparison' here refers to an understanding that the engagement with emotionally and cognitively valuable objects is not able to be grasped by neat categories and fixations. Whether these objects are conceived of as gods, as works of art or as 'Indian heritage' is a fluid process, and can change depending upon their location and spatial arrangement. By applying the perspective of *aestheticisation*, as developed in the framework of an ethno-aesthetics (Svašek 2007), a dynamic process is conceptualised whereby artefacts and images come to be interpreted and experienced by individuals and groups of people as specifically significant, valuable and powerful objects framed by local, national, or trans-national politics.

Also commencing her study in India, Annette Wilke demonstrates that religion does not only migrate as ideas or beliefs. Her chapter "Moving Religion by Sound" builds on a detailed study of the high validity of sound in Sanskrit Hinduism through the ages (Wilke and Moebus 2011). Focusing on the concept of the "Sonic Absolute" (*Nada Brahman*), embodied in sound and modal music, Wilke traces an entangled religious-aesthetic history between India and Germany. *Nada Brahman* acquired the aura of a hoary past in India and beyond, but was in fact "invented" by the musicologist Sarngadeva in the 13th century, and re-invented in modern Europe by the Jazz historian and New Age supporter Joachim Ernst Berendt. Against any naïve idea of an "original" being transmitted to "the West", the analysis of Berendt's representation of Indian music and its impact on the rising of "spirituality" in Europe's 1980s binds together a study of religion perspective with Indology, Cultural Anthropology, sociological theories of individualisation and contemporary religion, media theory through a framework of aesthetic analysis.

The chapters of section IV, *Concepts and Theories*, comprise critical discussions about analytical concepts and tools employed to develop a theoretical and methodological framework for an aesthetic perspective. Sensory and bodily interactions cannot be fully comprehended with the methods of text hermeneutics or semiotics. Therefore, these chapters engage in discussion of concepts such as materiality, aesthetic subjectivity, the phenomenon of effervescence and a quality of the "visceral" in order to develop components for theory building and models for understanding the connectivity between the different modes of experience.

Jay Johnston's chapter, focuses on the perception and articulation of the relations between subjects and objects, inclusive of concepts of animate matter. Tracing conceptual precedents of New Materialism's 'vital matter' in western Esoteric traditions, Johnston argues that such interpretations of materiality invoke a multi-sensory aesthetics that is necessarily tied to nebulous agency, invisible dynamics and the cultivation of specific types of extra-sensory perception. This chapter plays in this realm of invisible religious aesthetics exploring their potential contribution as a connective category of experience, with specific reference to 'sacred' landscape and contemporary art created within it.

In "Aesthetics of Immersion: Collective Effervescence, Bodily Synchronisation and the Sensory Navigation of the Sacred", Sebastian Schüler introduces the concept of "aesthetics of immersion" in order to better understand some of the foundational processes involved in the emergence of collective effervescence as observed in religious rituals. This chapter both investigates a revision of Durkheim's concept of collective effervescence and considers new insights from the cognitive sciences which have given a deeper understanding to how embodied and social cognition works, especially pertaining to synchronized behaviour. Schüler presents 'immersion' as a distinct concept pertaining to an aesthetic approach to religion.

Bodies and subjectivities of a less ethereal nature are the concern of Anne Koch's chapter "The Governance of Aesthetic Subjects through Body Knowledge and Affect Economies", which draws together insights from cultural and cognitive studies to challenge normative prescriptions of the rational subject. In order to take into greater account the role of the irrational, situational and embodied agencies and factors, this chapter employs the concepts of "body knowledge" and "affect economies" in the analysis of the aesthetic dimensions of subjectivity. That is, Koch proposes that an "aesthetic subject" is created via the interplay of cognition, emotion and the social environment. Analysing the aesthetic dimension of subjects is the stepping-stone for understanding bio-political regulation. Koch analyses "spiritual dance" in public spaces to demonstrate how political and religious subjectivities are created in mutual dependence, and considers what this means in terms of ethical and political modes of expression.

In "Religion in the Flesh: Non-Reductive Materialism and the Aesthetics of Religion" Manuel A. Vásquez explores the "aesthetics of persuasion" (Meyer 2010) of transnational Brazilian Neo-Pentecostal churches—the Universal Church of the Kingdom of God and the Reborn in Christ Church. In this chapter, he develops the distinctive argument that the success of these churches is built upon a "pneumatic materialism", a dynamic and non-dualistic spirit-matter nexus, which is highly portable through global electronic media and popular cultural and highly "glocalizable": deployed in local settings where it enables embodied personal experience of the divine. The concept of *pneumatic viscerality* encompasses multi-sensorial experiences that have the power to sacralise the self in its entirety and is considered alongside eschatological monumentality understood as an aesthetic mark of Pentecostalism's efficaciousness.

For the final fifth section, *In Conversation*, we invited colleagues to reflect on, and critically discuss what we have termed the *connectivity* of aesthetics. The section includes contributions from a number of different perspectives; however, it is not designed as an instrumentalist application of the aesthetics of religion approach to other academic disciplines. Rather, the intent was more creative; it grew out of an aim to include discussions that did not automatically take-up a position of presenting a summary or overview of its contents, but rather explored the connections between the diverse fields. Therefore, responses in this section may be knowingly partial, exploratory, provide vignettes to demonstrate the advantages and limitations of this approach, focus on issues deemed 'troubling' or inspiring. We hope these essays both capture the dynamism and potential of the aesthetics of religion approach, without closing of its range of affects, and provide a wealth of directions into which its debates may range.

Fred Cummins highlights that in the cognitive sciences new approaches focused on embodiment and enactment aim to disband the all-too-familiar idea of the mind as being "located" only in the brain. That we are "seeing with our legs" is a starting point to suggest interferential points between recent cognitive studies and an aesthetics of religion approach. In his piece on "Consumer Culture and the Sensory Remodelling of Religion", Francois Gauthier investigates the links between aesthetics, sociology and an economic approach in his analysis of new forms of transnational event-religion. This demonstrates that the plausibility of religious change under the conditions of capitalism needs to be understood in terms of changing aesthetic orders rather than in terms of the production of new theologies or systems of beliefs.

Anthropologist Frank Heidemann focuses on the elusive yet important qualities which create "atmospheres", and through atmospheres create shared experiences. He discusses the classical question about the role of the researcher's own experience, and how it may help to consider the social character of the aesthetic. Heidemann argues that linking this question to proprioception—the conscious and unconscious perception of the embodied self—is seminal if one wants to understand how the power of the social is created.

Robert Yelle puts his finger on open questions about the relationship between an aesthetics and a semiotics of religion by highlighting the historicity of *aesthesis* and *semiosis* in particular. This leads him not only to compare the development of both and outline challenges that lie ahead for an aesthetics of religion; he also sees an aesthetic approach as necessary for complementing theories of humanity that emphasise the rational and exclude the aesthetic dimensions of existence. Yelle focuses on the role of Protestantism in the process of the repression of the aesthetic, and he highlights the opportunity to account for the process of repression in order to gain a better understanding of modernity.

In the final essay, S. Brent Plate takes us on a journey to a changing landscape in early 19th century USA, when the Erie Canal was built in upstate New York. He discusses this technological endeavour in terms of a *psychogeography*, and how it changes the perceptions and imaginations of American nature and culture. Plate considers this in the light of Alexander Baumgarten's distinction between natural and artificial aesthetics. It is an example of relating diverse areas of knowledge to each other as Plate is bringing Baumgarten's concepts in to conversation with contemporary theories of technology and art. This conversation allows him to unfold the multi-dimensional aesthetic history of religion, connected with technology and art.

Considering the diverse chapters of this volume collectively it is apparent that the authors view aesthetics as an opportunity to address different aspects of understanding religion that have usually not been related to each other. It might be worth enquiring about the status of an Aesthetics of Religion within the larger Academic Study of Religion, and the Study of Culture, as well. Around 1900, when Sociology was yet to be invented, founding figures such as Max Weber and Émile Durkheim were driven by the central question of what the forces were that hold a society in transition together. They were convinced that studying religion would provide them with an intense view into the laboratory of modernisation, and with a magnifying glass that helps to find answers to this question. Today, scholars across disciplines are driven by the central question of how humans perceive and construct their reality. An Aesthetics of Religion, we suggest, can help to integrate modernity's blind spot for "religion" in this crucial endeavour, and can also assist in finding new and forgotten pathways that link the two questions together.

Bibliography

Arnheim, Rudolf. 1969. *Visual Thinking*. Berkeley: University of California Press.
Asad, Talal. 1993. *Genealogies of Religion: Discipline and Reasons of Power in Christianity and Islam*. Baltimore: Johns Hopkins University Press.
— 2003. *Formations of the Secular: Christianity Islam Modernity*. Stanford: Stanford University Press.
Auffarth, Christoph, Jutta Bernard, Hubert Mohr, Agnes Imhof, and Silvia Kurre, eds. 2000. *Metzler-Lexikon Religion: Gegenwart – Alltag – Medien*. 3 Vols. Stuttgart: Metzler.

Bachmann-Medick, Doris. 2016. *Cultural Turns. New Orientations in the Study of Culture*, translated by Adam Blauhut. Boston and Berlin: de Gruyter.

Barck, Karlheinz, and Richard Faber, eds. 1999. *Ästhetik des Politischen, Politik des Ästhetischen*. Würzburg: Königshausen und Neumann.

Belting, Hans. 2011. *An Anthropology of Images: Picture, Medium, Body*. Princeton: Princeton University Press.

Böhme, Gernot. 2001. *Aisthetik: Vorlesungen über Ästhetik als allgemeine Wahrnehmungslehre*. München: Fink.

Bourdieu, Pierre. 1984. *Distinction: A Social Critique of the Judgement of Taste*. London: Routledge.

Bräunlein, Peter J. 2005. "The Marburg Museum of Religions." *Material Religion* 1/1: 177–180.

Bräunlein, Peter J. 2010. *Passyon: Rituale des Schmerzes im europäischen und philippinischen Christentum*. München: Fink.

Brunotte, Ulrike. 2013. *Dämonen des Wissens. Gender, Performativität und materielle Kultur im Werk von Jane Ellen Harrison*. Würzburg: ERGON.

—— Forthcoming. "Myth- and Ritual- Debate." In *Theory/Religion/Critique, Classic and Contemporary Approaches*, edited by Richard King. New York: Columbia University Press.

Cancik, Hubert, and Hubert Mohr. 1988. "Religionsästhetik." In *Handbuch religionswissenschaftlicher Grundbegriffe*. Vol 1, edited by Hubert Cancik, Burkhard Gladigow, and Matthias Laubscher, 121–156. Stuttgart: Kohlhammer.

Chidester, David. 1986. "The Symmetry of Word and Light: Perceptual Categories in Augustine's Confessions." *Augustinian Studies* 17: 119–134.

Classen, Constance. 1993. *Worlds of Sense: Exploring the Senses in History and Across Cultures*. London: Routledge.

—— 1998. *The Color of Angels: Cosmology, Gender, and the Aesthetic Imagination*. London: Routledge.

—— ed. 2014. *A Cultural History of the Senses*. 6 volumes, diverse volume editors. London: Bloomsbury Academics.

Classen, Constance, and David Howes. 2014. *Ways of Sensing: Understanding the Senses in Society*. London: Routledge.

Döbler, Marvin. 2013. *Die Mystik und die Sinne. Eine religionshistorische Untersuchung am Beispiel Bernhards von Clairvaux*. Göttingen: Vandenhoeck & Ruprecht.

Douglas, Mary. 1970. *Natural Symbols*. London: Barrie and Rockliff.

Downes, Stephen. 2012. "Connectivism and Connective Knowledge. Essays on Meaning and Learning Network. National Research Council Canada." Open source publication. URL: https://oerknowledgecloud.org/sites/oerknowledgecloud.org/files/Connective_Knowl edge-19May2012.pdf (last accessed 12 February 2016)

Duden, Barbara. 1999. *Body History: A Repertory (Körpergeschichte)*. Wolfenbüttel: Tandem.

Eagleton, Terry. 1990. *The Ideology of the Aesthetic*. Oxford: Blackwell.

Eck, Diana L. 2007. *Darśan: Seeing the Divine Image in India*. Delhi: Motilal Banarsidass Publications.

Elkins, James, and Harper Montgomery, eds. 2013. *Beyond the Aesthetic and the Anti-Aesthetic*, University Park, Pennsylvania: Penn State University Press.

Featherstone, Mike. 1992. "Postmodernism and the Aestheticization of Everyday Life." In *Modernity and Identity*, edited by Scott Lash and Jonathan Friedman, 265–290. Oxford: Blackwell.

Feher, Michel, ed. 1989. *Fragments for a History of the Human Body*. New York: Zone Books.

Feldt, Laura, ed. 2012. *Wilderness in Mythology and Religion—Approaching Religious Spatialities, Cosmologies and Ideas of Wild Nature*. Berlin and Boston: Walter de Gruyter.

Foucault, Michel. 1999. *Aesthetics, Method, and Epistemology: Essential Works of Foucault, 1954–1984*. 2 Vols., edited by James D. Faubion, Paul Rabinow, and Robert Hurley. Harmondsworth: Penguin.

Geertz, Armin W. 2010. "Brain, Body and Culture: A Biocultural Theory of Religion." *Method and Theory in the Study of Religion* 22: 304–321.

Geertz, Armin W., and Jeppe S. Jensen. 2010. *Religious Narrative, Cognition, and Culture: Image and Word in the Mind of Narrative*, London: Equinox Publications.

Gell, Alfred. 1998. *Art and Agency*. Oxford: Oxford University Press.

Gladigow, Burkhard. 1988–1998. "Gegenstände und wissenschaftlicher Kontext von Religionswissenschaft." *Handbuch religionswissenschaftlicher Grundbegriffe*, edited by Hubert Cancik, Burkhard Gladigow, and Matthias Laubscher, Vol. 1, 26–40. Stuttgart: Kohlhammer.

—— 1995. "Europäische Religionsgeschichte." In *Lokale Religionsgeschichte*, edited by Hans G. Kippenberg, and Brigitte Luchesi, 21–42. Marburg: diagonal Verlag. Reprinted in Burkhard Gladigow. 2005. *Religionswissenschaft als Kulturwissenschaft*, edited by Christoph Auffarth and Jörg Rüpke, 289–301. Stuttgart: Kohlhammer.

Gloy, Karen, ed. 1999. *Rationalitätstypen*. Freiburg, München: Karl Alber.

Goodman, Nelson. [1978] 1985. *Ways of Worldmaking*. Indianapolis: Hackett, 1978.

Grieser, Alexandra. 2015a. "Imaginationen des Nichtwissens: Zur Hubble Space Imagery und den Figurationen des schönen Universums zwischen Wissenschaft, Kunst und Religion." In *Religion – Imagination – Ästhetik: Vorstellungs- und Sinneswelten in Religion und Kultur*, edited by Annette Wilke and Lucia Traut. Göttingen: Vandenhoek & Ruprecht.

—— 2015b. "Aesthetics." *Vocabulary for the Study of Religion*. Vol. 1, edited by Kocku von Stuckrad and Robert Segal, 14–23. Brill: Leiden.

—— 2015c. "Rhetoric." *Vocabulary for the Study of Religion*. Vol. 3, edited by Kocku von Stuckrad and Robert Segal, 227–234. Brill: Leiden.

Guthrie, Stewart E. 1993. *Faces in the Clouds*. New York: Oxford University Press.

Hieber, Lutz, and Stephan Moebius, eds. 2014. *Ästhetisierung des Sozialen. Reklame, Kunst und Politik im Zeitalter visueller Medien*. Bielefeld: transcript.

Hirschkind, Charles. 2001. "The Ethics of Listening: Cassette-Sermon Audition in Contemporary Egypt." *American Ethnologist* 28/3: 623–649.

Hirstein, William. 2012. "Neuroaesthetics: Responding to the Critics. Ready or Not, the Neuroscience of Art Has Arrived." *Psychology Today*. Posted 18 December 2012. URL: https://www.psychologytoday.com/blog/mindmelding/201212/neuroaesthetics-re sponding-the-critics (last accessed 20 February 2016).

Howes, David, ed. 2005. *Empire of the Senses: The Sensual Culture Reader*. Oxford: Berg.

Huston, Joseph P., Marcos Nadal, Francisco Mora, Luigi F. Agnati, and Camilo J. Cela-Conde, eds. 2015. *Art, Aesthetics and the Brain*. Oxford: Oxford University Press.

Hyman, John. 2010. "Art and Neuroscience." In *Beyond Mimesis and Convention: Representation in Art and Science*, edited by Roman Frigg and Matthew Hunter, 245–262. New York: Springer.

Johnson, Mark. 2007. *The Meaning of the Body: Aesthetics of Human Understanding*. Chicago: University of Chicago Press.

—— "The Aesthetics of Embodied Life." In *Aesthetics and the Embodied Mind. Beyond Art Theory and the Cartesian Mind-Body Dichotomy*, edited by Scarinzi, Alfonsina, 23–38. Dordrecht: Springer.

Johnston, Jay. 2008. *Angels of Desire: Esoteric Bodies, Aesthetics and Ethics*. London: Equinox Publishing.

—— 2016. "Enchanted Sight/Site: An Esoteric Aesthetics of Image and Experience." In *The Relational Dynamics of Enchantment and Sacrilization: Changing the Terms of the Religion Versus Secularization Debate*, edited by Peik Ingman, Terhi Utrianen, Tuija Hovi and Mans Broo, 189–206. Sheffield: Equinox.

Jütte, Robert. 2004. *A History of the Senses: From Antiquity to Cyberspace*, translated by James Lynn. London: Polity.

Kamper, Dietmar, and Christoph Wulf, eds. 1981. *Die Wiederkehr des Körpers*, Frankfurt a. M.: Suhrkamp.

—— eds. 1982. *Das Schwinden der Sinne*. Frankfurt a.M.: Suhrkamp.

—— eds. 1987. *Das Heilige: seine Spur in der Moderne*. Frankfurt a.M.: Athenaeum.

Keane, Webb. 2006. *Christian Moderns: Freedom and Fetish in the Mission Encounter*. Berkeley: University of California Press.

Kippenberg, Hans G. 1990. "Introduction." In *Visible Religion: Annual for Religious Iconography VII*. Institute for Religious Iconography, State University Groningen (1982–1990). Leiden: Brill, vii-xix.

—— 2002. *Discovering Religious History in the Modern Age*, translated by Barbara Harshav. Princeton, New Jersey: Princeton University Press.

Knott, Kim. 2005. *The Location of Religion: A Spatial Analysis*. London: Equinox.

Koch, Anne. 2004. "Ästhetik – Kunst – Religion." *Münchener Theologische Zeitschrift* [Special Issue: *Ästhetik – Religion – Kunst*] 55/4.

—— 2011. "Reasons for the Boom of Body Discourses in the Humanities and the Social Sciences since the 1980s: A Chapter in European History of Religion." In *Menschenbilder und Körperkonzepte*, edited Angelika Berlejung, Johannes Quack, and Jan Dietrich, 3–41. Tübingen: Mohr.

—— 2015. "Körperwissen: Modewort oder Grundstein einer Religionssomatik und Religionsaesthetik." In *Die Körper der Religion – Corps en Religion*, edited by Oliver Krüger and Nadine Weibel, 15–38. Zurich: Pano.

Koch, Anne, and Karin Meissner. 2011. "Psychische und vegetative Effekte des Geistigen Heilens in ihrem rituellen und religionsgeschichtlichem Kontext: Zwei exemplarische Falldarstellungen." In *Spiritualität transdisziplinär: Wissenschaftliche Grundlagen im Zusammenhang mit Gesundheit und Krankheit*, edited by Arndt Büssing and Niko Kohls, 145–166. Heidelberg: Springer.

Korsch, Dietrich, and Amber L. Griffioen. 2011. *The Significance of Friedrich Schleiermacher's 'Reden über die Religion' for Religious Studies and Theology*. Tübingen: Mohr Siebeck.

Krech, Volkhard. 2002. *Wissenschaft und Religion. Studien zur Geschichte der Religionsforschung in Deutschland 1871 bis 1933*. Tuebingen: Mohr Siebeck.

Kugele, Jens, and Katharina Wilkens, eds. 2011. "Relocating Religion(s): Museality as a Critical Term for the Aesthetics of Religion." *Journal of Religion in Europe* [Special Issue] 4/1.

Laack, Isabel. 2008. "The Relation between Music and Religious Meaning: Theoretical Reflections." In *Religion and Music: Proceedings of the Interdisciplinary Workshop at the Institute for Scientific Studies of Religions, Freie Universität Berlin, May 2006.*, edited by Lidia Guzy, 123–153. Berlin: Weißensee-Verlag.

Lakoff, George. 1999. *Philosophy in the Flesh: The Embodied Mind and Its Challenge to Western Thought.* New York: Basic Books.

Lakoff, George, and Mark Johnson. 1980. *Metaphors We Live By.* Chicago: University of Chicago Press.

Lanwerd, Susanne. 2002. *Religionsästhetik: Studien zum Verhältnis von Symbol und Sinnlichkeit.* Würzburg: Königshausen & Neumann.

Lanwerd, Susanne, ed. 2003. *Der Kanon und die Sinne. Religionsaesthetik als akademische Disziplin.* Luxembourg: EurAssoc.

Lash, Scott. 1993. "Reflexive Modernization: The Aesthetic Dimension." *Theory, Culture & Society* 10/1: 1–23.

Latour, Bruno. 2013a. *Rejoicing: or the Torments of Religious Speech,* translated by Julie Rose. Cambridge, Polity.

—— 2013b. *An Inquiry into Modes of Existence: An Anthropology of the Moderns*, translated by Catherine Porter. Cambridge, MA: Harvard University Press.

Lauring, Jon O., ed. 2014. *An Introduction to Neuroaesthetics: The Neuroscientific Approach to Aesthetic Experience, Artistic Creativity, and Arts Appreciation.* Copenhagen: Museum Tusculanum Press.

Leroi-Gourhan, Andr. [1964] 1993. *Gesture and Speech.* Cambridge, MA, and London: MIT Press.

Maase, Kaspar. 2008. *Die Schönheiten des Populären. Ästhetische Erfahrung der Gegenwart.* Frankfurt a.M. and New York: Campus.

Mandoki, Katya. 2007. *Everyday Aesthetics: Prosaics, the Play of Cultures and Social Identities.* Aldershot: Ashgate.

Meyer, Birgit, David Morgan, and Crispin Paine, eds. *Material Religion: The Journal of Objects, Art and Belief.* London: Berg Publications.

Martin, John Levi. 2011. *The Explanation of Social Action.* Oxford: Oxford University Press.

Mauss, Marcel. 1979. *Sociology and Psychology. Essays.* London: Routledge.

McCauley, Robert N., and E. Thomas Lawson. 2002. *Bringing Ritual to Mind: Psychological Foundations of Cultural Forms.* Cambridge: Cambridge University Press.

Menninghaus, Winfried. 2003. *Disgust. Theory and History of a Strong Sensation.* Albany, New York: SUNY Press.

—— 2011. *Wozu Kunst? Ästhetik nach Darwin.* Berlin: Suhrkamp.

Menninghaus, Winifred, Valentin Wagner, Julian Hanich, Eugen Wassiliwizky, Milena Keuhnast, and Thomas Jacobsen. 2015. "Towards a Psychological Construct of Being Moved." *PLoS ONE* 10/6: e0128451. doi:10.1371/journal.pone.0128451 (last accessed 20 December 2015)

Merleau-Ponty, Maurice. 1962. *Phenomenology of Perception.* London: Routledge.

Meyer, Birgit. 2010. "Aesthetics of Persuasion: Global Christianity and Pentecostalism's Sensational Forms." *South Atlantic Quarterly* 109/4: 741–763.

—— 2013. "Material Mediations and Religious Practices of World-Making." In *Religion Across Media: From Early Antiquity to Late Modernity*, edited by Knut Lundby, 1–19. New York: Peter Lang.

Meyer, Birgit, and Dick Houtman, eds. 2012. *Things: Religion and the Question of Materiality*. New York: Fordham University Press.

Meyer, Birgit, and Jojada Verrips. 2008. "Aesthetics." In *Key Words in Religion, Media, and Culture*, edited by David Morgan, 20–30. New York: Routledge.

Michaels, Axel, and Christoph Wulf, eds. 2014. *Exploring the Senses*. London, New York, and New Delhi: Routledge.

Mohn, Jürgen. 2010. "Die Konstruktion religiöser Wahrnehmungsräume und der wissenschaftliche Blick: Religionsaisthetische Überlegungen anhand von Gartenanlagen in der europäischen Religionsgeschichte." In *Religiöse Blicke – Blicke auf das Religiöse: Visualität und Religion*, edited by Bärbel Beinauer-Köhler, Daria Pezzoli-Olgiati, and Joachim Valentin, 59–82. Zürich: Theologischer Verlag.

Mohr, Hubert. 2005. "Perception / Sensory System." In *The Brill Dictionary of Religion*. Vol. 3, edited by Kocku von Stuckrad, 1435–1448. Leiden: Brill.

Morgan David. 2012. *The Embodied Eye. Religious Visual Culture and the Social Life of Feeling*. Berkeley: University of California Press.

—— 2015. "Religion and Embodiment in the Study of Material Culture." In *Religion: Oxford Research Encyclopedias*, 1–19; DOI: 10.1093/acrefore/9780199340378.013.32 (last accessed 24 November 2016)

Nieuwkerk, Karin van, Mark Levine, and Martin Stokes, eds. 2016. *Islam and Popular Culture*. Austin: University of Texas Press.

Noyes, James. 2013. *The Politics of Iconoclasm*. London and New York: I.B. Tauris.

Otto, Rudolf. [1917] 1923. *The Idea of the Holy. On the Irrational in the Idea of the Divine and its Relation to the Rational*. London: Oxford University Press.

Patlagean, Evelyne. 1978. "L'histoire de l'imaginaire." In *La Nouvelle Histoire*, edited by Jacques Le Goff et al., 249–269. Paris: Gallimard.

Plate, S. Brent 2005. *Walter Benjamin, Religion, and Aesthetics: Rethinking Religion through the Arts*. New York: Routledge.

—— 2012. "The Skin of Religion: Aesthetic Mediations of the Sacred." *CrossCurrents* 62/2: 162–180.

—— 2014. *A History of Religion in 5 1/2 Objects: Bringing the Spiritual to Its Senses*. Boston: Beacon Press.

Prohl, Inken. 2015. "Aesthetics." In *Key Terms in Material Religion*, edited by S. Brent Plate, 9–15. London, Oxford, New York, New Delhi, Sydney: Bloomsbury Academic.

Promey, Sally M., ed. 2014. *Sensational Religion. Sensory Cultures in Material Practice*. New Haven: Yale University Press.

Rambelli, Fabio, and Eric Reinders. 2012. *Buddhism and Iconoclasm in East Asia: A History*. London: Bloomsbury.

Rancière, Jacques. 2010. *The Politics of Aesthetics: The Distribution of the Sensible*. London: Continuum.

Reckwitz, Andreas. 2006. *Das hybride Subjekt: Eine Theorie der Subjektkulturen von der bürgerlichen Moderne zur Postmoderne*. Weilerswist: Velbrück Wiss.

Reckwitz, Andreas, Sophia Prinz, and Hilmar Schäfer, eds. 2015. *Ästhetik und Gesellschaft – Grundlagentexte aus Soziologie und Kulturwissenschaften*. Berlin: Suhrkamp.

Riou, Jeanne. 2014. *Anthropology of Connection. Perception and Its Emotional Undertones in German Philosophical Discourse, 1870–1930.* Würzburg: Königshausen & Neumann.

Rorty, Richard. 1979. *Philosophy and the Mirror of Nature.* Princeton, NJ: Princeton University Press.

Rusch, Hannes, and Eckart Voland. 2013. "Evolutionary Aesthetics: An Introduction to Key Concepts and Current Issues." *Aisthesis* 6/2: 113–133.

Samuel, Geoffrey and Jay Johnston. 2013. *Religion and the Subtle Body in Asia and the West. Between Mind and Body.* London and New York: Routledge.

Saito, Yuriko. 2015. "Aesthetics of the Everyday." In *The Stanford Encyclopedia of Philosophy*, edited by Edward N. Zalta. URL: http://plato.stanford.edu/archives/win2015/entries/aesthetics-of-everyday/ (last accessed 12 February 2016).

Scarinzi, Alfonsina, ed. 2015. *Aesthetics and the Embodied Mind: Beyond Art Theory and the Cartesian Mind-Body Dichotomy.* Dordrecht: Springer.

Schlieter, Jens. 2000. "Ästhetische Handlungen: Ost und West." In *Komparative Ästhetik: Künste und ästhetische Erfahrungen zwischen Asien und Europa*, edited by Rolf Elberfeld and Günter Wohlfart, 319–333. Cologne: edition Chōra.

Schneider, Steffen, Melanie Wald-Fuhrmann, and Carlos Watzka, eds. 2015. *Aesthetics of the Spirits. Spirits in Early Modern Science, Religion, Literature and Music.* Göttingen: Vandenhoek & Ruprecht.

Schüler, Sebastian. 2012. "Synchronized Ritual Behavior: Religion, Cognition, and the Dynamics of Embodiment." In *The Body and Religion: Modern Science and the Construction of Religious Meaning*, edited by David Cave and Rebecca Sachs-Norris, 81–101. Leiden: Brill.

Shields, Christopher. 2016. "Aristotle's Psychology." In *The Stanford Encyclopedia of Philosophy*, 2016 edition, edited by Edward N. Zalta. URL: http://plato.stanford.edu/archives/spr2016/entries/aristotle-psychology/ (last accessed 20 February 2016)

Shusterman, Richard, ed. 1989. *Analytic Aesthetics.* Oxford: Blackwell.

—— 2012. *Thinking Through the Body. Essays in Somaesthetics.* Cambridge, Massachusetts: Cambridge University Press.

Smith, Mark M. 2007a. "Producing Sense, Consuming Sense, Making Sense: Perils and Prospects for Sensory History." *Journal of Social History* 40/4: 841–858.

—— 2007b. *Sensing the Past. Seeing, Hearing, Smelling, and Touching in History.* Berkeley: University of California Press.

Stausberg, Michael. 2009. "There is Life in the Old Dog Yet. An Introduction to Contemporary Theories of Religion". In *Contemporary Theories of Religion: A Critical Companion*, edited by Michael Stausberg, 1–21. London: Routledge.

Stuckrad, Kocku von, ed. *The Brill Dictionary of Religion.* Revised edition of *Metzler Lexikon Religion*. 4 Vols., edited by Christoph Auffarth. Leiden: Brill.

—— 2010. "The Code of Creation: Kabbalistic Genealogies and Modern Life Sciences." In *Myths, Martyrs, and Modernity: Studies in the History of Religions in Honour of Jan N. Bremmer.* edited by Jitse H. F. Dijkstra and Walter Ameling, 671–685. Studies in the History of Religions 127. Leiden: Brill.

Svašek, Maruška. 2007. *Anthropology, Art and Cultural Production.* London: Pluto Press.

—— 2012. "Narrating (Migrant) Belonging: Emotions and Performative Practice." In *Being Human, Being Migrant*, edited by Anne Sigfrid Grønseth, 117–136. Oxford: Berghahn.

Taves, Ann. 2010. "No Field Is an Island: Fostering Collaboration between the Academic Study of Religion and the Sciences." *Method and Theory in the Study of Religion* 22: 170–188.

—— 2015. "Reverse Engineering Complex Cultural Concepts: Identifying Building Blocks of 'Religion.'" *Journal of Cognition and Culture* 15: 191–216.

Traut, Lucia, and Annette Wilke, eds. 2015. *Religion – Imagination – Ästhetik: Vorstellungs- und Sinneswelten in Religion und Kultur.* Göttingen: Vandenhoeck & Ruprecht.

Turner, Mark, and Gilles Fauconnier. 2002. *The Way We Think. Conceptual Blending and the Mind's Hidden Complexities.* New York: Basic Books.

Uehlinger, Christoph. 2006. "Visible Religion und die Sichtbarkeit von Religion(en): Voraussetzungen, Anknüpfungsprobleme, Wiederaufnahme eines religionswissenschaftlichen Forschungsprogramms." *Berliner Theologische Zeitschrift* 23: 165–184.

Uhls, Yalda T., Minas Michikyan, Jordan Morris, Debra Garcia, Gary W. Small, Eleni Zgourou, and Patricia M. Greenfield. 2014. "Five Days at Outdoor Education Camp without Screens Improves Preteen Skills with Nonverbal Emotion Cues." *Computers in Human Behavior* 39: 387–392.

Vásquez, Manuel A. 2011. *More Than Belief: A Materialist Theory of Religion.* Oxford: Oxford University Press.

Van der Leeuw, Gerardus. [1957] 1963. *Sacred and Profane Beauty: The Holy in Art*, translated by David A. Green. New York: Holt, Rinehart and Winston.

Vietta, Silvio. 2008. "Die Ästhetikrevolution um 1800." Special Issue of *Deutsch-russische Germanistik. Ergebnisse, Perspektiven und Desiderate der Zusammenarbeit*, edited by Dirk Kemper and Iris Bäcker, 151–160.

Vietta, Silvio, and Dirk Kemper, eds. 2008. *Ästhetik – Religion – Säkularisierung I: Von der Renaissance zur Romantik. Volume II: Die klassische Moderne.* Munich: Fink.

Weber, Max. 1949. "Objectivity in Social Science and Social Policy." In *The Methodology of the Social Sciences*, translated and edited by Edward Shils and Henry Finch, 49–112. Glencoe, IL: Free Press.

Weiss, Peter. [1975–1981] 2005. *Die Ästhetik des Widerstands, A Novel*, translated by Joachim Neugroschel. Durham, NC: Duke University Press.

Welsch, Wolfgang. 1987. *Aisthesis: Grundzüge und Perspektiven der Aristotelischen Sinneslehre.* Stuttgart: Klett-Cotta.

—— 2014. *Aesthetics and Beyond.* Kaifeng (China): Henan University Press.

Werbner, Pnina, Martin Webb, and Kathryn Spellman-Poots. 2014. *The Political Aesthetics of Global Protest. The Arab Spring and Beyond.* Edinburgh: Edinburgh University Press.

Wilke, Annette, and Oliver Moebus. 2011. *Sound and Communication: An Aesthetic Cultural History of Sanskrit Hinduism.* Berlin: de Gruyter.

Williams, Ron G., and James W. Boyd. 2006. "Aesthetics." In *Theorizing Rituals: Issues, Topics, Approaches, Concepts, I*, edited by Jens Kreinath, Joannes A. M. Snoek, and Michael Stausberg, 285–306. Leiden: Brill.

Wilson, Margaret. 2008. "How Did We Get from There to Here? An Evolutionary Perspective on Embodied Cognition." In *Directions for an Embodied Cognitive Science: Towards an Integrated Approach*, edited by Paco Calvo and Toni Gomila, 375–393. Amsterdam: Elsevier.

⎯ 2010. "The Retooled Mind: How Culture Re-Engineers Cognition." *Social, Cognitive, and Affective Neuroscience* 5: 180–187.

List of Figures

https://doi.org/10.1515/9783110461015-002

PART I **Fields and Topics**

Mikael Aktor

Grasping the Formless in Stones: The Petromorphic Gods of the Hindu *Pañcāyatanapūjā*

How do people perceive their gods? What are their aesthetic properties? The answers to these questions depend not only on the specific religious tradition, but also, more generally, on the medium by which gods are perceived, imagined or conceptualised. Literary genres like myth or theology constrain by linguistic means how gods are made known to listeners or readers, and different types of ritual involve different perceptions of gods depending on both the notions of the belief system and the preferred medium of the ritual. Protestant Christians perceive their god through the audible or readable word. During church services their body language displays their attention to listening (Morgan 2012, 174–175). Quakers likewise, listen attentively to the words of their god, but through silence rather than sound (Birkel 2004, 55–58; Searl 2005, 22).[1] In Hinduism the gods can be highly audible, visible and tangible, but, still, the exact formats depend on both the ideas involved in the belief system and the ritual forms by which the gods are present for worshippers. In short, perceptions, conceptions and practices are inextricably intertwined.

1 Genres of Gods

The scholar of religion, Tord Olsson, has examined how different textual genres and different spoken-word situations in Maasai religious media constrain the perceptions of the Maasai god (*enkAi*) in different ways. In mythic narratives *enkAi* interacts socially with humans in anthropomorphic terms. In hymns, often phrased as prayers, he is sometimes addressed in cosmic terms as the sky or the earth and sometimes in more personal terms as a god who may turn his eyes upon the worshipper. In exegetic speech situations a far more agnostic style dominates where, although the focus is on *enkAi*'s almighty powers, clear identifications are avoided (Olsson 1999, 78–79). This distinction is even clearer in ancient Egyptian and Greek texts. Egyptian mythic texts present gods in anthropomorphic and theriomorphic forms, but in other texts where

---

1 I wish to thank one of my former students, Karin My Sadolin Holst, for these two references.

https://doi.org/10.1515/9783110461015-003

gods reveal themselves directly to individuals they are perceived vaguely as a "divine fragrance". Similarly, the perceptions of the gods are articulated on two different levels in the Homeric hymns: the mythic, "Olympian perspective", in which the gods appear in human shape, and the invisible perspective, in which direct encounters with the gods are expressed in direct speech in the texts as the sighting of a vaguely perceived particular type of light (Olsson 1999, 88–90). A similar division is known from Babylonian and Assyrian material (Westh 2015, 410).

This distinction resonates with reflections in Hindu theology on the nature of gods *vis à vis* the possibility of offering worship to them. Śiva, for instance, is primarily worshipped in his form as the *śivaliṅga*, an aniconic cylindrical shaft rising from a rounded pedestal (Aktor 2015, 16–17), but, secondarily, his anthropomorphic images are also worshipped; these are often placed outside or along the side walls of the sanctum containing the *liṅga*. Another type of *liṅga*, the *mukhaliṅga*, has faces emerging from the shaft that represent different aspects of Śiva. From the point of view of the theological texts, Śiva is ultimately Paramaśiva (Highest Śiva), undifferentiated (*niṣkala*), transcendent and unfathomable; but, on another level, he is accessible to his worshippers as differentiated (*sakala*) and active. It is not that one level is true and another is false. Śiva is simultaneously differentiated and undifferentiated (*sakalaniṣkala*) (Davis 1991, 113–114). This distinction is to some extent carried over to the visual "supports" of Śiva: his primary form as the aniconic *śivaliṅga* and his anthropomorphic images. These forms are distinguished according to the same divide. The aniconic *liṅga* is "undifferentiated" (*niṣkala*), corresponding to Śiva in his highest Paramaśiva aspect, the anthropomorphic image is "differentiated" (*sakala*) corresponding to Śiva as Maheśvara (Great Lord) in his various mythological aspects as yogi, dancer, teacher etc., and the *mukhaliṅga* is a mixture of the two (Davis 1991, 121–122).

It seems here that the relation between aniconic and anthropomorphic forms is thought to express the parallel relation between the undifferentiated/transcendent and differentiated/active aspects of Śiva; but the difference is carried even further. Among aniconic *śivaliṅga*s a distinction is made between manmade sculpted artefacts (*mānuṣaliṅga*) and unmanufactured stones considered to be natural, "self-manifested" forms of Śiva (*svayambhūliṅga*). Such stones are placed in the sanctums of temples and worshipped as direct manifestations of Śiva. On the level of materiality, from the anthropomorphic to the aniconic, and further from the manufactured to the unmanufactured object of worship we might see the dialectic noted by Tord Olsson on the textual level between the gods' culturally mediated well-recognized appearances and the vaguely articulated perceptions of divine transcendence which in certain religious environments are considered to be more in accordance with the essential nature of the gods.

One sub-class among the unmanufactured *svayambhūliṅgas* is that of the *bāṇaliṅgas* from Omkareshwar on the Narmada River, Madhya Pradesh. These even, oval stones originally acquired their shape as a consequence of the whirling and tumbling effect of a waterfall on the stones in an underwater cave at this point on the river, and they were therefore seen as natural *liṅgas* and thus direct manifestations of Śiva. However, since the opening of the Omkareshwar Dam in 2007 the waterfall has been submerged, and, as a consequence, the natural process that produced these stones has been terminated. Today, stones with a suitable shape from other parts of the river are processed using angle grinders, metal drums and polishing machines, and then distributed to *pūjā* shops selling items for worship and over the internet (Aktor 2015, 29 – 30). They are either placed individually on a pedestal (*pīṭha*) and worshipped singly as Śiva (see Figure 1) or clustered into a group of five to be used in the form of worship known as *pañcāyatanapūjā*.

Figure 1: An outdoor temple for Goddess Narmadā at the western point of Mandhata Island in the middle of River Narmada at Omkareshwar, Madhya Pradesh. Narmadā is both the physical river and the anthropomorphic goddess. In front, a person worshipping Śiva in the form of the *bāṇaliṅga*, which is decorated with Śiva's forehead mark, three horizontal lines (*tripuṇḍra*), and the Sanskrit ligature OM, which is *brahman* in its sonomorphic manifestation. Photo by the author, December 2012.

2 The Pañcāyatanapūjā

The *pañcāyatanapūjā* is the practice of worshipping five gods in the form of five stones. The five stones of the *pañcāyatanapūjā* are:

1. the *bāṇaliṅga*, an oval stone from the Narmada River near Omkareshwar, Madhya Pradesh, which is worshipped as a manifestation of Śiva;
2. the *śālagrāma*, an ammonite fossil from the Kali-Gandaki Gorge in the Mustang district of Nepal, which is worshipped as a manifestation of Viṣṇu;
3. the *sphaṭika*, a roundly-cut quartz crystal, traditionally sourced from near the town of Vallam, Tamil Nadu, which is worshipped as a manifestation of Sūrya (Sun);
4. the *śoṇabhadra*, a roughly rounded red jasper, traditionally sourced from the Son River at its confluence with the Ganges in Bihar, which is worshipped as a manifestation of Gaṇeśa;
5. the *suvarṇamukhi*, a pyrite (iron sulphide crystal), traditionally sourced from the Swarnamukhi River at Srikalahasti, Andhra Pradesh, which is worshipped as a manifestation of Devī, sometimes referred to as Ambikā (Mother) and sometimes by other names of the Hindu Great Goddess.

Apart from the quartz crystal and the pyrite (numbers 3 and 5 above), the exact geological identity of the stones may vary. The main criteria seem to be the visual appearance and the source locations traditionally ascribed to each of the stones. In the past, the five stones were handed down from generation to generation, but today people may have to buy them in a shop and their traditional source locations are no longer guaranteed, since not all the stones can still be found at the traditional sites (especially numbers 3–5) (Aktor 2016, 9–22).

The selection of these particular five stones is partly due to their aesthetic properties, partly due to their topographic properties. The *bāṇaliṅga* has a smooth oval shape and originates from a significant place (the Dharaji waterfall). The *śālagrāma* is marked as special due to its origin as an ammonite fossil with its circular patterns of slanting lines recognised iconographically as one of Viṣṇu's weapons, the discus (*cakra*) (see Figure 2). It may also contain cavities with smaller fossils embedded in them.

The quantity of medieval textual material about the worship of these two stones suggests that such worship has ancient roots dating back prior to any textual mention of the *pañcāyatanapūjā*, which is not much earlier than the first part of the 17th century.[2] The *pañcāyatanapūjā*, with the inclusion of the three re-

---

2 Some of the earliest references to the ritual are in Nīlakaṇṭha's *Bhagavantabhāskara* and Mi-

Figure 2: An altar with *śālagrāma*s in Śrī Muktinātha Yajñaśālā, a small building within the Muktinātha Temple precinct, Muktinath, Mustang District, Nepal. Some *śālagrāma*s are decorated with Viṣṇu's forehead mark, the U-shaped *ūrdhvapuṇḍra*. Photo by the author, September 2014.

maining stones, was therefore probably grafted on to these pre-existing practices. The *sphaṭika* is transparent and shines like a glass lens, the *śoṇabhadra* is clearly red with a smooth though sometimes uneven surface and the *suvarṇamukhi* is a cubic crystal with a metallic sheen. The source locations attributed to each add to their sacredness. Four of the stones are related to rivers, which in a Hindu context are sources of purification and spiritual transformation, and are often associated with river goddesses like Narmadā (number 1) and Gaṅgā into which both the Gandaki River (number 2) and the Son River (number 4) flow. Important pilgrimage sites are also located here. *Bāṇṇaliṅga*s originate from near Omkareshwar (number 1), which contains one of the twelve famous

tramiśra's *Pūjāprakāśa* of the *Vīramitrodaya*, both dated between 1610 and 1645. See Bühnemann (1988, 37).

*jyotirliṅga*s (*liṅga*s of light associated with Śiva's theophany in an endless column of light). *Śālagrāma*s are associated especially with Muktinath, an important *vaiṣṇava* pilgrimage site. The town of Vallam, associated with the *sphaṭika* is close to Thanjavur, whose Bṛhadīśvara Temple is one of the great pilgrimage sites of Tamil Nadu. The *śoṇabhadra* is sourced at the Gandaki-Ganges-Son River confluence (*saṃgama*), a sacred place in its own right, and Srikalahasti, the place associated with the *suvarṇamukhi*, is another important *śaiva* pilgrimage site.

Apart from these petromorphic forms, each of the five gods have other aniconic manifestations as well. The Aruṇācala hill at Tiruvannamalai in Tamil Nadu is another manifestation of Śiva. The Narmada and Ganges Rivers are both physiomorphic manifestations of the goddesses, and both are worshipped as such with *pūjā* services performed on the bathing stairs (*ghāṭs*) leading down to the river. Both Śiva and the two river goddesses have anthropomorphic forms as well. The anthropomorphic form of Narmadā, sitting on her crocodile mount, is seen behind the *bāṇaliṅga* worshipped on Figure 1. The photo is of the outdoor Narmadā Temple at the western point of the island of Mandhata located in the middle of the Narmadā River at Omkareshwar. At this site, the physiomorphic and the anthropomorphic forms of the goddess Narmadā are both present, as well as the aniconic form of Śiva in the form of the *bāṇaliṅga*.

3 Gods in the Landscape and in the Mind

The term "physiomorphic" refers to manifestations in the landscape such as mountains, hills and rivers (Gaifman 2012, 39). "Topomorphic" might be an alternative term, since what make these sites religiously and ritually relevant is not so much that they are parts of the natural world apart from fauna and flora, but that they are, or that they mark, significant places in the landscape. Rocks, as immovable parts of the landscape, belong to this category too, but stones that can be picked up and removed do not. In archaeological terminology, such stones are "manuports", that is, unmanufactured objects of nature that have been removed from their place of origin. As manuports they become markers of other landscapes and the topographical and geographical networks in which a given culture unfolds. Numbers 2, 4 and 5 in the list of *pañcāyatana* stones belong to this category. Number 1 did until *bāṇaliṅga*s produced in workshops started to replace the natural ones acquired from the Dharaji waterfall.

I think that their relation to the landscape is one explanation, among others, for the use of ritual stones like the five of the *pañcāyatanapūjā*. *Bāṇaliṅga*s and *śālagrāma*s are still specific indices of the sacred landscapes from which they are removed. Although the three remaining stones may no longer come from the areas from where they were traditionally sourced, they are still associated with these locations. Connecting these five stones from different corners of South Asia, from Nepal in the north to Tamil Nadu in the south, was also an attempt to construct a pan-Hindu geographical network of holy places transcending both political and sectarian differences.

However, the relation to the landscape may have deeper roots. The worship of stones represents an archaic element of religion, and stones themselves are special in being ancient and time-transcending. Despite the fact that large portions of the human species today live isolated from the natural landscape in modern metropolises, the human brain and mind remain evolutionarily adapted to a life of complete dependence on the landscape. Landscape knowledge has been indispensable for survival throughout human evolution, and the different types of cultural marking of the landscape, like petroglyphs and the worship of mountains and trees, have been instrumental to this knowledge. When modern humans feel compelled to collect shells at the beach or pick up beautiful or extraordinary stones or fossils they are simply being the heirs of these earlier humans. Acknowledging these archaic connections, there is today a growing body of archaeo-anthropological literature on landscape phenomenology and cultural geology (Tilley 2004; Bender, Hamilton and Tilley 2007; Cohen 2015).

Landscapes are "perceived and embodied sets of relationships between places, a structure of human feeling, emotion, dwelling, movements and practical activity within a geographic region" (Tilley 2004, 25). Living, moving and surviving in a landscape, humans engage in daily relationships with those elements that are vital for their existence. "Animism" has been analysed as certain cognitive configurations, but might as well be seen as such extended relationships with the landscape. Acknowledging the mutual agency of trees, rocks, rivers or stones has a natural basis in such human-landscape interactions. The phenomenological perspective also sharpens the attention to the synaesthetic nature of materiality (Tilley 2004, 14). The stones of the *pañcāyatanapūjā* are not only looked at like a two-dimensional image. As three-dimensional objects they are touched, moved around, washed and smeared with various anointments during the ritual; their tactile properties matter as much as their visible marks. Four of the five stones are ideally collected from rivers that have given them a smooth and shining surface.

The interaction of mind and landscape is deeply rooted in the evolution of humans. In line with the modular model of the mind prevalent in cognitive studies of the 1990s, Stephen Mithen (1996) proposes a division of such domains into realms of social intelligence, natural history intelligence and technical intelligence. At a certain point in evolution, due to the enlargement of the human brain, these divisions, Mithen suggests, became porous, resulting in a cognitive fluidity enabling the blending of cognitive content from different domains. When humans started to modify stones, bones or shells into beads and place such beads in graves, it was, according to Mithen, the result of this kind of fluidity, combining social and natural history intelligence (Mithen 1996, 76–78, 199).

Another basic cognitive categorization of the environment is the division between (a) inanimate objects, which are unable to move, grow and act on their own, (b) artefacts, which are inanimate objects that have been processed by humans, and (c) living beings. Stones are prototypical of category (a) but can also belong to category (b), and even, in some exceptional cases, share properties with entities in category (c), such as when stones are assigned some form of efficacy, or at least the ability to have an effect on human beings, for instance to protect or help them. Different aesthetic properties of a stone can trigger this ascription of efficacy, and the shape, colours or lines of a stone may be seen as anthropomorphic or theriomorphic features. It may have dots or hollows that are instantly viewed as a human face, such as the Makapangsat cobble from South Africa with its hollows resembling two eyes and a mouth, and a mark resembling a hairline (Bednarik 2002). Alternatively, it may possess aesthetic properties that are characteristic of artefacts, such as, for instance, the symmetry seen in a crystal or the colourful, shining and smooth surfaces seen in stones that have been rounded and polished by streaming water. Symmetry is also an index of living organisms, where it is usually found to a greater degree than in stones. Finally, fossils are stones that are recognized as holding imprints of various life forms.[3]

Only minds that have developed cognitive fluidity are able to combine these different characteristics into the concept that a stone can protect or help its owner by its own force (Mithen 1996, 201–202). Mithen refers to Pascal Boyer's theory that notions of the supernatural are based on intuitive distinctions, such as the three mentioned here, which have been violated by counterintuitive no-

---

3 The myths related to the *śālagrāma* fossils from the Gandaki River tell how the *cakra* marks of Viṣṇu were caused by worms with "adamantine teeth". Gaṇḍakī was originally a pious lady who lived an austere life in order to have her only wish fulfilled: that Viṣṇu and the other gods would be born from her. The gods, horrified, rejected her wish and she cursed them to become worms. They issued a counter-curse that she would become a dark river. The gods emerged as worms from the soft parts of the decaying bodies of some river monsters inside Gaṇḍakī, now transformed into the river, and started to gnaw on the stony parts of the corpses, while Viṣṇu transformed himself into his *cakra* and entered the same stony bodies. In this way, the gods as worms penetrated the stones and created the cavities in which Viṣṇu's *cakras* can be seen today (Rao 2009, Vol. 1, 29–31).

tions that assign properties from one domain to items belonging to another domain (Mithen 1996, 200 – 201). Boyer's ideas are to some extent in line with earlier theories about domain-ambiguity such as Victor Turner's "betwixt and between" (1964) and Edmund Leach's (2000) and Mary Douglas' (1984) ideas about notions of taboo and ritual efficacy emerging from these kinds of cognitive ambiguity. The five stones of the *pañcāyatanapūjā* all share some of these ambiguities.

4 Aesthetic-Conceptual Integration

How do stones from certain rivers become connected to gods? Medieval Sanskrit texts contain detailed descriptions of how to identify different specimens of *śālagrāma*s and *bāṇaliṅga*s according to the lines, patterns, dots, colours, etc. of these stones. Variations are linked to the iconographic characteristics of specific Viṣṇu and Śiva epithets and the myths related to them. Thus, a *śālagrāma* identified as Nārasiṃha (Viṣṇu's avatar as a man-lion) has a large open cavity like the wide-open jaws of a lion (Rao 2009, Vol. 1, 156; Vol. 2, 24 – 28); a *bāṇaliṅga* identified as Ardhanārīśvara (Śiva as half woman, half man) is white on one side (Śiva) and red on the other (Pārvatī) (Rao 2009, Vol. 2, 187). I have elsewhere (Aktor 2015, 29) explained these identifications in terms of the various "gazes" inherent in religious images, as suggested by David Morgan (2012, 67). Gazes are visual fields encompassing an aesthetic relationship between the viewer and the religious image in which a way of seeing is projected onto the image. Such gazes can be unilateral, like the all-seeing Buddha eyes on top of Nepalese stupas, or reciprocal, like the wide-open eyes of the images that meet the eyes of a Hindu temple visitor. Alternatively, a religious character might be identified by its gaze alone, like the all-compassionate gaze of Bodhisattva Avalokiteśvara (The Lord Looking Down) or Trilocana (The Three-Eyed Śiva). When fragments of myths and iconography are read into the *śālagrāma* and the *bāṇaliṅga* it is in the form of a "narrative gaze", a way of seeing that actively browses the mythological stock for iconic fragments that can be seen in the forms, lines and marks of these stones.

Another way of explaining this aesthetic process is by the notion of "conceptual integration", as suggested by Lambros Malafouris (2013, 99 – 102). Based on the works of Gilles Fauconnier and Mark Johnson on conceptual blends, Malafouris develops a model for how such blends integrate mental spaces and material objects. They do so by mapping some elements of the conceptual space with some of the aesthetic elements (visual, tactile or other) of the material space and projecting these and other elements of both spaces into a third space, the blend.

This is a selective process where only some conceptual elements match the material aesthetic elements, and where extra non-matching elements of both spaces can be projected into the blend. Due to these projections, the blend becomes more than the combination of the two original spaces. Some elements are augmented; some that are not present are seen as present or possibly present. Thus, from the conceptual space that is Viṣṇu, some elements, particularly his *cakra*, are mapped onto the lines of the material space that is the ammonite fossil. Both are projected into the blend which is the *śālagrāma* together with more elements from the Viṣṇu space that cannot be mapped to specific aesthetic characteristics of the ammonite, for instance his ability to offer protection and blessings. The concrete material space, the ammonite, makes it possible for the invisible qualities of Viṣṇu to be "anchored" (Malafouris 2013, 102) in the material object which is the *śālagrāma*, and, thereby, for these qualities to become present in the world.

5 Agency of Stones

A critique of the Cartesian dualism of how we understand the relation between the mind and the material environment has consequences for how we understand the role of things. Malafouris captures this consequence precisely: "We cannot bridge the Cartesian gap between persons and things without being willing to share a substantial part of our human agentive efficacy with the mediational means that made the exercise of such efficacy possible in the first place" (Malafouris 2013, 149).

Human agency acts through things and places. Not only do artefacts store knowledge that is passed on via their use through generations, but so do manuports and other aniconic objects. And not only do they store knowledge, they also shape human actions and thinking. In particular, the appropriation of things during ritual performances works to ascribe agency to them. The 'ritual efficacy' of objects of worships or of ritual implements is just another term for the agency of these objects. In their book, *Rethinking Religion*, Thomas Lawson and Robert McCauley (1990) argue that the use of such objects in larger-scale rituals should be seen as a series of embedded rituals in that each of these objects has been ritually sacralised prior to its use in the wider ritual. The choreography of rituals is such that that which is the focus of the ritual is appropriated through a behaviour that is otherwise specific to human relationships. Ritual objects are spoken to, bowed to, knelt before, kissed, honoured or otherwise brought into the sphere of human relationships. Even tools, particularly tools of high importance or those used in contexts that can be dangerous such as warfare and seafaring, are often ritualized by being offered special attention and care. Thus, the line between practical use and ritual use can be porous.

Therefore, the ritual interaction with things very often involves anthropomorphic aesthetics, that is, the bodily mediation of human relationships established through ritual. Ritual objects are often decorated with features of living creatures. It therefore seems that anthropomorphization is inherent in and a product of the ritual choreography, just as it is a product of the narrative style of mythology according to Tord Olsson and as mentioned at the start of this chapter.

This is evident in the ritual performance offered to the five stones of the *pañcāyatanapūjā*. The stones are placed on a metal plate forming a mandala with one stone in the centre, selected according to choice or the specific situation, and the other four placed around it at specific directional points (north-east, south-east, south-west and north-west; see Figure 3).

Though aniconic, the stones are offered the same sixteen services as those given to anthropomorphic images of gods. They are offered a seat and water for washing the feet, they are bathed and offered garments (a small piece of cloth wrapped around each stone) and the sacred thread (except for the Goddess), they are anointed and offered flowers, food and betel nuts, gifts and entertainment (for details, see Aktor 2016, 4–9). Two of the stones, the *bāṇaliṅga* among Śaivas and the *śālagrāma* among Vaiṣṇavas, are also worshipped separately, unlike the other three stones. In such cases they are frequently decorated with facial features, such as eyes, mouth and nose, or forehead marks (*tilaka*) typically of Śiva and Viṣṇu respectively, the former with three horizontal lines (*tripuṇḍra*) and the latter with a U-shaped mark (*ūrdhvapuṇḍra*) sometimes with a central vertical line (see Figures 1 and 2). This type of anthropomorphisation of Hindu aniconic objects is very common. It is as if pure aniconism, like pure transcendentalism, is a fragile enterprise that attracts anthropomorphic features when applied in ritual or mythological contexts.[4]

6 Grasping the Formless God in Stones

Despite the inherent anthropomorphism of the *pañcāyatana* ritual with its sixteen services, the honouring of five different gods is actually intended to stress the limitless, formless, undifferentiated and all-pervading nature of the godhead.

---

4 "Pure aniconism" is here understood in contrast to what might be labelled "symbolic aniconism", that is, the use of metonymic or metaphorical pictorial symbols like the fish for Jesus Christ or the wheel and the empty throne for the Buddha.

Figure 3: The altar and *pañcāyatana* tray and stones belonging to Mr and Mrs Atthreya, Chennai, Tamil Nadu. In this arrangement Devī is placed in the center in the form of the *śrīyantra* engraved on a silver plate. The four other deities are placed around Devī/śrīyantra in the following order: Viṣṇu in the lower right corner as the *śālagrāma* (due to the flower arrangement it has been placed a bit too high; it should have been placed at the corner of the square bronze plate like the other three); Śiva in the lower-left corner as the *bāṇaliṅga* (but here coupled with the *suvarṇamukhi* so as to form a couple: Śiva-Śakti); Gaṇeśa in the upper-left corner as the red *śoṇabhadra*; and Sūrya in the upper-right corner as the *sphaṭika*. Behind the *pañcāyatanapūjā* set with the five stones and the *śrīyantra* we see the anthropomorphic form of the goddess dressed in blue. Photo by the author, October 2014.

Pañcāyatanapūjā emerged from and is still mostly performed among certain groups of *smārta* Brahmins, primarily in southern India, who follow the *advaita-vedānta* teachings of Śaṅkara (Jackson 2013). They regard all the gods as different manifestations of the one all-pervading and formless *brahman*. Therefore they oppose the sectarian worship of *vaiṣṇavas*, *śaivas* or *śāktas*. In a sense, therefore, it does not matter what precise form is chosen for worship. The forms are only the means of focusing the mind on the transcendent, and, as such, the worship of the five petromorphic gods is merely a purification and preparation of the mind intended to gain gradually a more direct knowledge (*jñāna*) of *brahman*.[5] In fact, according to Śaṅkara's understanding, images of gods are not manifestations of these gods; rather, worshippers "superimpose" a mental idea of the god onto the object of worship (Colas 2004, 159). This is in contrast to the sectarian view of both Śaivas and Vaiṣṇavas who claim that *bāṇaliṅgas* and the *śālagrāmas* are direct manifestations of Śiva and Viṣṇu respectively.

It may seem a paradox that the abstract notion of the one formless *brahman* is projected onto something as concrete as five stones, or that Śiva in his highest undifferentiated aspect as Paramaśiva is worshipped in one of these stones, the *bāṇaliṅga*. What is the logical relationship between an undifferentiated notion of god and aniconic forms like these five stones? It seems that in this relationship two extremes from two different domains have been connected. Of the various concepts of what a god is, *brahman* and Paramaśiva are at the extreme, abstract end of the spectrum of godhead, while an unmanufactured stone collected from a river, that is a manuport, is at the extreme unmodified end of the spectrum of material culture. Returning to the ideas of Tord Olsson, we may see here the tendency to limit the perception of the abstract conception of god to the raw cosmic elements of nature—the sky, the sun or a stone. In doing so, the anthropomorphic and the cultural elements inherent in human-produced media are bracketed or set aside. As the notion of the abstract, undifferentiated god is asserted as something prior to and therefore unrelated to any human activity, so unmanufactured stones in a river are beyond human culture; or they seem to be, even when they have been picked up due to their special aesthetic and topographic properties. Such stones therefore fit the abstract notion of god by being seemingly unlimited by cultural constraints. And yet, as another paradox, we have seen that this enterprise is invaded by the anthropomorphic conduct of ritual performance. If a formless god is something that can be related to, a ritual aesthetic seems unavoidable.

Bibliography

Aktor, Mikael. 2015. "The *Śivaliṅga* Between Artifact and Nature: The Ghṛṣṇeśvaraliṅga in Varanasi and the *Bāṇaliṅgas* from the Narmada River." In *Objects of Worship in South Asian Religions: Forms, Practices and Meanings*, edited by Knut A. Jacobsen, Mikael Aktor, and Kristina Myrvold, 14–34. London: Routledge.

---

5 Interview with Mr Ramachandran Balasundara Athreya and Mrs Rajalakshmi Athreya, Chennai, on 8 October 2014.

—— 2016. "Five Stones – Four Rivers – One Town: The Hindu *Pañcāyatanapūjā*." In *Soulless Matter, Seats of Energy: Metals, Gems and Minerals in South Asian Traditions*, edited by Fabrizio M. Ferrari, and Thomas W. P. Dähnhardt, 3–27. Sheffield: Equinox.

Bednarik, Robert. 2002. "Manuports and Very Early Palaeoart." URL: http://www.ifrao.com/manuports-and-very-early-palaeoart/ (last accessed 25 April 2015)

Bender, Barbara, Sue Hamilton, and Chris Tilley. 2007. *Stone Worlds: Narrative and Reflexivity in Landscape Archeology*. Walnut Creek, CA: Left Coast Press.

Birkel, Michael L. 2004. *Silence and Witness: The Quaker Tradition*. New York: Orbis Books.

Bühnemann, Gudrun. 1988. *Pūjā: A Study in Smārta Ritual*. Leiden: Brill.

Cohen, Jeffrey Jerome. 2015. *Stone: An Ecology of the Inhuman*. Minneapolis, MN: University of Minnesota Press.

Colas, Gérard. 2004. "The Competing Hermeneutics of Image Worship in Hinduism (Fifth to Eleventh Century AD)." In *Images in Asian Religions: Texts and Contexts*, edited by Phylis Granoff, and Koichi Shinohara, 149–179. Vancouver: The University of British Columbia Press.

Davis, Richard H. 1991. *Ritual in an Oscillating Universe: Worshipping Śiva in Medieval India*. Princeton: Princeton University Press.

Douglas, Mary. [1966] 1984. *Purity and Danger: An Analysis of the Concepts of Pollution and Taboo*. London: Routledge and Kegan Paul.

Gaifman, Milette. 2012. *Aniconism in Greek Antiquity*. Oxford: Oxford University Press.

Jackson, William J. 2013. "Smārta." In *Brill's Encyclopedia of Hinduism*, edited by Knut A. Jacobsen, Helene Basu, Angelika Malinar, and Vasudha Narayanan. Leiden: Brill Online. http://referenceworks.brillonline.com/entries/brill-s-encyclopedia-ofhinduism/smarta-COM_9000000064 (last accessed 26 April 2015).

Lawson, Thomas E., and Robert N. McCauley. 1990. *Rethinking Religion*. Cambridge: Cambridge University Press.

Leach, Edmund. [1964] 2000. "Anthropological Aspects of Language: Animal Categories and Verbal Abuse." In *The Essential Edmund Leach*. Vol. 1, edited by Stephen Hugh-Jones and James Laidlaw, 322–343. New Haven: Yale University Press.

Malafouris, Lambros. 2013. *How Things Shape the Mind: A Theory of Material Engagement*. Cambridge, MA: The MIT Press.

Mithen, Steven. 1996. *The Prehistory of the Mind: A Search for the Origins of Art, Religion and Science*. London: Thames and Hudson.

Morgan, David. 2012. *The Embodied Eye: Religious Visual Culture and the Social Life of Feeling*. Berkeley, CA: University of California Press.

Olsson, Tord. 1999. "Verbal Representation of Religious Beliefs: A Dilemma in the Phenomenology of Religions." In *Comparative Studies in History of Religions: Their Aim, Scope, and Validity*, edited by Erik Reenberg Sand and Jørgen Podemann Sørensen, 75–92. Copenhagen: Museum Tusculanum Press.

Rao, S. K. Ramachandra. [1996] 2009. *Śālagrāma-Kosha*. 2 Vols. Delhi: Sri Satguru Publications.

Searl, J. Stanford, Jr. 2005. *The Meanings of Silence in Quaker Worship*. New York: The Edwin Mellen Press.

Tilley, Christopher. 2004. *The Materiality of Stone: Explorations in Landscape Phenomenology*. Oxford: Berg.

Turner, Victor W. 1964. "Betwixt and Between: The Liminal Period in Rites de Passage." In
*The Proceedings of the American Ethnological Society (1964): Symposium on New
Approaches to the Study of Religion*, 4 – 20. Seattle: University of Washington Press.
Westh, Peter. 2014. "Anthropomorphism in God Concepts: The Role of Narrative." In *Origins
of Religion, Cognition and Culture*, edited by Armin W. Geertz, 396 – 413. Oxon:
Routledge.

John T. Hamilton and Almut-Barbara Renger
Religion, Literature, and the Aesthetics of Expressionism

1 Introduction

Religious and literary texts have always been closely linked together, insofar as both are clearly grounded in human experience, desire, and reflection, which construct and mediate thought and action. For this reason alone, the generic borders that would separate religious and literary discourses are never simple to maintain. On the contrary, both bear witness to multiple and complex intersections and overlaps. To the extent that they can even be distinguished, religious impulses can often be found in literature just as literary devices may be discernible in religious texts. The Western epic tradition alone, from Homer and Vergil to Dante, Milton, and Klopstock, has long demonstrated how literary discourse can appropriate religious forms for the purpose of affirmation or critique, which allows literature to serve as a medium of religious practice beyond canonical religious doctrine. This kind of mutual effect, grossly formulated, should solicit interpretations common to both fields, both in terms of textual production and in terms of creative and critical reception. Specifically, a close consideration of these reciprocal effects and interrelated processes would call for a recalibration of *aesthetic experience*, which should here be understood as relating both to somatic-sensuous perception and to cognitive methods of interpretation.

A key example of the interrelationship between religion and literature may be found in the context of *ritual*, whereby writing, reading and listening have less to do with reflective thought and passive observation and more with immersive participation—that is, with experiences traditionally assigned to religious spheres, for example performative acts of reading in ritual recitation. A major literary consequence of reading ritualistically is the privileging of works that display vital *expression* over passive notions of *representation*, a preference for works that instigate a mode of experience that longs to move beyond mere reading or spectatorship, beyond cognitive processing and interpretive conclusions, in order to trigger the kind of profound and visceral transformation that is commonly ascribed to ritual.[1] This predilection for transformative effects is perhaps

---

[1] Along similar lines, Claude Lévi-Strauss distinguishes between *myth*, which he understands as serving a cognitive function, and *ritual*, which he grounds in a powerful lived experience that

https://doi.org/10.1515/9783110461015-004

nowhere more noticeable than in the artistic movement broadly identified as German Expressionism. After some general remarks on the connections between religion and literature, this chapter outlines the major characteristics of German Expressionist works in regard to its religious aspirations, before examining particularly Expressionist "aesthetics of redemption". In this way, a fresh, expanded understanding of aesthetics promises to shed light on the mutual indebtedness of religious and literary endeavours.

2 General Observations: Religion and Literature

The close interrelation between religion and literature is conditioned by many factors, the complexity of which defies easy generalisations or categorisations. Nonetheless, one essential trait does stand out, namely the attempt by individual writers to adapt models of religious action and thinking to current living conditions, including social and political shifts—adaptations that frequently result in transformations of original content and form. The transformative aspect of this work is bound up with the desire to convey religious themes and motifs aesthetically. The adaptable nature of religious material for literary purposes rests on the fact that religion is always already molded by languages and styles of thinking, which are deeply determined by culture, nation and epoch. Moreover, the inherited discourses are constructed in accordance with the specific subject positions of those who present themselves as religious specialists within these varied contexts: seers and prophets, priests, preachers, clergy, monks and nuns, magicians and Druids, medicine-men and shamans, and so forth. These representatives of religion are at the same time religion's intermediaries. Some work orally, others in writing, yet all claim to enjoy some special access to a realm that transcends ordinary experience as well as normal modes of perception. On this basis, they legitimise their presumed capability of conveying messages, which we could term as sacred or beyond the mundane, even if they must do so in the finite languages of humankind. For an utterance that is regarded as "holy", including the "word of God" in the monotheistic traditions, be it transmitted orally or scripturally, must be formulated in terms of human communication and therefore within the limits of certain aesthetic forms. Presumably derived from a transcendent, otherworldly source, religious discourses intervene upon and disrupt human sensibilities. As a corollary, according to the logic of

---

overrides the discontinuities implicit in intellectual reflection. See Lévi-Strauss (1981, 674–680). On the transformative capacity of ritual in this sense, see Handelman (2005).

divine inspiration, across most literary traditions, a poet may assume the sacred role of religious seer, prophet, or priest—a writer who affirms his or her power to motivate a change in *aesthetic experience.*

It is precisely in this sense that literary production and literary studies contribute to the aesthetics of religion—an area of investigation that stretches from the human body as the site of sensory perception through culturally coded semiotic systems to elaborate means of expression, like texts, artworks, and cultural institutions, rituals, and other performances related to cognitive and evidentiary modes of understanding.[2] Within this broad framework, creative and critical works further demonstrate how artistic and literary production and reception are motivated by narratives and interpretations commonly linked to religious, transformative experience. Indeed, literature in the narrow sense of the word—poetry, drama, and epic—has long served as a way for negotiating and mediating religious content. This is certainly true not only in the present day, but also particularly at the turn of the 20th century, where aestheticised religious content tends to fulfil a longing for transcendent experience, which was presumed to be unavailable through doctrinal institutions. In addition to an outpouring of religious publications—a trend only exacerbated in the wake of the First World War—there are many and diverse literary texts that engage in recognizably religious content, however transformed. Here, alongside a distinctly religious repertoire, there also stand theological assignations, which are carried over and integrated by means of creative adaptation, still discernibly religious, despite vast changes in style and content. Reaching up to present day, literature participates not only in the reception of inherited religious forms and genres, like sermons and treatises, prayers and hymns, but also in the inheritance of religious themes, plots and figures. Drawn from multiple global traditions, religious material that could impart a numinous quality of the holy consistently informs authors' fantasies.[3] This material is consequently transformed in accordance with the discursive context, a transformation that results in a recalibration of aesthetic experience, insofar as these reformulations and concomitantly new interpretations enable readers to enjoy fresh perspectives on the past by relating them to the present.

---

2 For a comprehensive account of the historical definition and theoretical breadth of the "aesthetics of religion", see Cancik and Mohr (1988). A number of studies on the aesthetics of religion have also appeared from a theological perspective. See, e. g., Viladesau (1999); and, more recently, Viladesau (2014).

3 Generally speaking, the idea of the "holy" that fascinated writers of this period corresponds to the definition and explication offered by Rudolf Otto (1917).

Literature may thus serve as an expressive medium of whatever is regarded as belonging to a venerable, transcendent reality. It comes to possess a religious value, precisely by incorporating inherited religious forms and genres, themes, plots and figures, which signal an intentional movement toward the divine, the transcendent, and the infinite.[4] This general aestheticisation of the religious, this establishment of a "sensory sacred", leads further to a sublimation or *sacralisation* of literature and art, including, on occasion, the sacralisation of the writers and artists who engage in this kind of work. Consequently, this sacralising literature proffers new alternatives for religious practices that vie with traditional modes of worship.

The sacred is here understood in the fundamental sense of *consecration*, which characterises the Latin term *sacer* as that which has been removed from everyday commerce, absolved of utilitarian purpose, and thereby dedicated to an otherworldly, "divine" sphere. With this understanding of the term, we can say that literature becomes sacred precisely by emphatically setting itself apart from the profane world, ascribing to itself a power that claims access to transcendence, to a sublime efficacy that rises above or powerfully irradiates quotidian experience. Finally, the sacralisation of literature invariably entails a *recalibration of aesthetic experience* itself on the side of both production and reception. A written text or a performance that marks itself as sacred does so by employing any number of discursive and gestural devices, which invite an appropriate adjustment of modes of interpretation and somatic dispositions that respect this sacred difference in relation to the profane.

German Expressionist writers and artists were particularly sensitive to effects of sacralisation, which they were keen to appropriate from religious traditions and implement in their work.[5] This broad and complex literary-artistic movement, which spans roughly from 1910 to 1925, stands to offer invaluable insights into the mechanisms and results that derive from the interlacing of religion, literature, and aesthetics within the European context. A consideration of this movement should illustrate some of the qualities and ramifications of the

---

4 This artistic inclination is explicitly discussed by Eckart von Sydow's 1919 essay, "The religious Consciousness of Expressionism" ("Das religiöse Bewußtsein des Expressionismus"), which demonstrates how "atavistic religious tendencies are now stirring in an entirely unambiguous manner, at least in the varying confessions of Expressionist leaders" (von Sydow 1919, 193).
5 In a number of publications from 1927, the evangelical theologian Wilhelm Knevels charted the religious potential that he discerned in Expressionist poetry: *Das Religiöse in der neuesten lyrischen Dichtung*; *Expressionismus und Religion: Gezeigt an der neuesten deutschen expressionistischen Lyrik*; and *Brücken zum Ewigen: Die religiöse Dichtung der Gegenwart*. On this theme, see the special issue of *Expressionismus: Religion* (Eichhorn and Lorenzen 2016).

terms mentioned above, namely the sacralisation of art, the turn to ritual, and the concomitant recalibration of aesthetic experience.

3 Informing Potent Discourses: Religious Aspirations and the Aesthetics of Renewal in German Expressionism

Despite a strong, Enlightenment-driven trend toward increased skepticism across German-speaking culture, Expressionist literature and works of art consistently exhibit multiple religious forms and manifestations. Alongside critical examinations of religious traditions and a general dismissal of institutional dogma, one also finds a genuine spirit of rediscovery and the revitalisation of a spectrum of religious heritages—what Wolfgang Rothe aptly defines as a "religious need" among the Expressionists (Rothe 1977, 40). Poetry, drama, and prose are saturated with metaphors and motifs drawn from religious traditions: ideas of fate, destiny, and the holy; plots of sacrifice, suffering, and redemption; allusions to the sacred and the mystical; and aspirations for messianic heroism. Words like "heart", "soul", "essence", and "god" crop up with great regularity. They function topically as a means for expressing subjective feeling and even as ciphers for humankind's relation to God and the experience of God, often in a prophetic mode.[6] At the same time, the body is addressed in highly provocative ways as the site of sensory perception, feeling and intoxication, suffering and sexuality, and placed in a tension-filled relationship to health, redemption, and transcendence. In such works, one frequently finds radicalizing alternatives to conventional modes of aesthetic experience belonging to the socio-cultural context of the bourgeoisie, where life without organised religion had become a viable possibility.

This interleaving of religious references and borrowings with aspirations of aesthetic experience is based on multiple socio-historical causes. Emerging out of a long period of industrialisation, entrepreneurship, and rationalizing bureaucratisation, which decidedly marked the German *Gründerzeit* of the late 19th century, Expressionism must be viewed within the context of the contemporary "life reform movement" (*Lebensreformbewegung*). Since the mid-19th century, especially in Germany and Switzerland, one finds common features of reform movements, which centered on a decisive critique of industrialisation, materialism, and urbanization, striving to preserve a natural state. These broad movements combined in the late 19th century with the establishment of ethnology and com-

---

6 Kurt Pinthus refers explicitly to this prophetic voice in his preface to the *Menschheitsdämmerung* collection (in Werfel 1988, 25).

parative religion, which together would come to exert a strong influence on the Expressionists. Knowledge of non-European religions significantly advanced through the decoding of writings. At the same time, however, proponents of an increasingly scholarly-industrial society on the part of modernisation demanded a renunciation of all that was handed down from the past. As a consequence, historians of religion reinforced a comparative approach to their religious-historical sources, with a focus on conceptions of humankind, nature, and society. By contrasting themes of nature-mysticism, ecstatic experience, and redemption, found in both non-European and modern European cultures, these scholars discovered views and practices which did not first and foremost contribute to posited ideals of so-called civilisation and progress.

In this way, potent discourses were informed. The subsequent reaction of the Expressionists consisted in taking up these themes against industrialisation and bureaucratisation by aesthetic means of presentation, which insisted on the spontaneity of expression and included a revolt against beauty in favour of an inner experience of the exterior world (Rothe 1977, 31–147). Important stylistic devices were put into play in the arts: the reduction and distortion of forms, the alteration of natural proportions, and the employment of distinct, clear colours and sharp contrasts. Analogously, Expressionist literature broke with the rules of conventional grammar. The writing was instead characterised by word clusters, daring neologisms, and seemingly grotesque sentence structures. In this fashion, scenes of a repulsive nature and violent excess were produced, bringing to expression masculine fantasies of creativity and claims of transcendence, and thereby inscribing the threat of material-corporeal deformation (Metzler 2003).

This turn-of-the-century rejection of the cult of beauty, which included a rejection of the theory of art's autonomy (*l'art pour l'art*—"art for art's sake") and other traditional values of the beautiful, reflected the judgment of an attitude against what it perceived as the sham values of the bourgeoisie. Moreover, it accompanied repeated gestures toward a realm beyond the perceivable earthly world with particular distinctiveness, often punctuated by scathing skepticism for the dogmas proffered by long-established religious institutions. In Expressionist literature, the arts, and theory, the search for a substitute for lost transcendence, for the "magic" of the world on the one hand and the radical affirmation of a morally nihilistic position on the other hand, stood in a tense relationship, emotionally and discursively overburdened, which built itself up successively over the decades and finally unburdened itself in protest against traditional forms of art and life. Among the central concerns of Expressionist literature we find themes like war, the metropolis, decay, anxiety, loss of self, and apocalyptic decline, in addition to over-stimulation, madness, love, intoxication, and the sheer force of nature. The presentation of corporeal, viscerally intense experiences, which elude cognitive comprehension, were especially privileged. Throughout, the bourgeois aesthetic of complacent order is flatly rejected, for example, by a notorious aesthetic of the ugly (Wolf 2004, 10). Indeed, unlike any other literary movement before, the Expressionists turned the Ugly, the Sick, and the Mad into viable subjects for artistic enterprises in order to indicate and simultaneously overcome limits of shame and disgust. This turn toward the Ugly was buttressed by apodictic statements on the Beautiful that aimed to destroy classical theories of art together with the postclassical aesthetics of the pre-modern period. Not infrequently we find an explicit denial of precisely those art theories, which postulated the aesthetic as possessing objective qualities, for example in Oskar Kanehl's programmatically Expressionist observations in *Wider die Ästhetik* ("Against Aesthetics" 1914): "Those accursed words: Aesthetics and aesthetic! Everyone feels important in using them [...]. No thing is aesthetic, no consciousness. Nothing is unaesthetic" (Kanehl 1914, 14).

Within this framework of Expressionism's aesthetically sponsored protest against the bourgeoisie and the status quo of the day, themes and motives from myth, magic, and mysticism came to play a refreshed role in portraying visions, dreams, and ecstatic experiences. This incursion into areas that entail specific cognitive and aesthetic capabilities reflects a dynamic tension between private or individual religious experience on the one hand and public religiosity or theological thought on the other—a distinction which guided the general anti-dogmatic disposition of the era and one that has repeatedly emerged across European history, for example in the Pietist movements of the 18th century. In the 20th century, the individual, non-institutionalized engagement with religion and with domains such as magic and mysticism, which presuppose augmented cognitive faculties, similarly characterises the views of many artists, writers, and thinkers, and further undermines any simplistic acceptance of conventional theories of secularisation and disenchantment.[7] This is particularly true for the era of German Expressionism. Stating that there was some fundamental loss of religious meaning would be grossly inadequate. Much to the contrary, in the first decades of the 20th century, religion and neighboring fields of belief constituted a "central", if not predominant "theme of public, cultural-political discourse and

---

7 The opposition of religious experience and the church has a long history in European history, for example in the Pietist movements of the 18th century. In the 20th century, this distinction not only characterizes the views of many artists, writers, and thinkers, but also severely undermines a simplistic acceptance of conventional theories of secularisation and disenchantment. On this point, see Pollack (2003, 132–148).

academic debates" (Graf 2004, 133–178, here 133).[8] What resulted, then, were new reformulations of the religious landscape: While the major churches were suffering a considerable loss of validity, a market of highly diverse religious offerings expanded, which gradually emerged beside traditional Christianity and ultimately entered into fierce competition with it. Particularly in German culture, a multitude of religious currents and communities evolved, whose understandings of religion were as divergent as their worldviews.[9]

What is everywhere observable are tendencies to plumb the depths of the irrational impulses against rational order. Such trends are also discernible in theological works as well, like Rudolf Otto's book *Das Heilige* ("The Idea of the Holy", 1917) or Emil Brunner's inaugural lecture *Die Grenzen der Humanität* ("The Limits of Humanity", 1922), to name only two examples. Both works reflect a then dominant discursive tendency that connects religiosity with subjective feeling and concrete individual experience. According to Otto's highly influential masterwork, a religion shorn of its rational elements cannot be comprehended conceptually or taught; it can only be experienced. In this view, the experience of the Holy involves irrational moments insofar as it conjoins feelings that elude rational, conceptual framing and can be demonstrated only by suggestive ideograms or indicative concepts. Otto characterises the irreducible moments of this experience as *mysterium tremendum* and *mysterium fascinans*. The divine is always simultaneously both a force of attraction and repulsion, something fascinating and threatening. Similarly revealing and representative for the time, even though less well-known, is Emil Brunner's lecture, the title of which directly alludes to Paul Natorp's book *Religion innerhalb der Grenzen der Humanität* ("Religion within the Bounds of Humanity", 1894). In his lecture, Brunner argues that it is correct to understand religion as a cultural factor of the highest level, and he turns against domesticated religion as a sterile, uninteresting, atrophied construct. In view of the "unleashing of Dionysian-Asiatic elements in religion", of the "great boom in mystical-romantic piety", and the "venturous religious metaphysics" of these years, the "mere humanness of all religious experience" is emphatically recalled (cited in Rothe 1969, 39).[10] There are a few other theologians who, like Brunner, extol their viewpoints as an alternative to what they consider to be an exhausted modernity. They see themselves as a theological avant-garde that motivates the overcoming of bourgeois shallowness. Similar to Otto, many of

8 On the developing emergence of religious studies in the decades before and after 1900, see Krech (2002, 9–160).
9 On this theme, see for example, Nipperdey (1988a, 1988b); Braungart, Fuchs, and Koch (1998); Habermas (2011).
10 Nietzsche's influence, which is further discussed below, is here immediately evident.

them describe fundamental experiences of the religious that are irrational, in order to distinguish their understanding of the sacred from a religion grounded in rationality.

Against this discursive background it is not surprising when, in Expressionist literature and art, religious and aesthetic experience resort to each other. Expressionist experiments frequently viewed art in religious terms and thereby redefined aesthetic experience as the surrender to some kind of spiritual, sublime energy. A deep commitment to the irrational, unpredictable, and often frightening aspects of the human or world soul drove writers and artists to shatter bourgeois expectations, complacency, and spiritual anemia. In the foreground we find concepts of the Expressionist program like "pathos", "ecstasy", and "the scream", which were especially significant not only from a religious perspective, but also in terms of poetics and style.[11] Structured around these concepts were pathos-laden outbursts, vociferous cries of ecstasy, and rhetorical proclamations of utopian visions, which functioned as complements to skeptical critiques of ideology. At the same time, the body received especial attention with its capacity for meaningful perception, for symbolic expression, and for demonstrative performance. In painting, artists like Emil Nolde, Max Beckmann, and Paul Klee created a plethora of outstanding works on religious subjects, bringing a strikingly personal, psychological content to bear on Biblical episodes. A similar approach is seen in many Expressionist films of the silent era, where manifestations of the demonic or the satanic impinge on everyday scenes. From another angle, scholars have long pointed to the employment of religious allegory in Fritz Lang's *Metropolis* (1927), which presents an intriguing mosaic of Hebrew, Christian, and pagan materials. Analogously, Mary Wigman's development of "Expressive Dance" aimed toward a reawakening of a wild spirituality, which corresponded to new directions in the study of ancient Greece and Rome that gave fresh focus to archaic forces prior to the sobriety of classical forms. Perceptual stimulations hereby functioned as signs and catalysts of an attentiveness filled with sense and meaning. In many of these cases, the influence of non-European art also played an important role. At the beginning of the 20th century, Europe's folklore museums were filled with objects from Africa and Oceania, including masks and figures, which often came from religious contexts. Their ordinarily simple and expressive forms fulfilled, among other things, the artists' longing for a new "naturalness" or "nativeness" (*Natürlichkeit*).

---

11 On this, see for example the representative excerpts of texts by Stefan Zweig, Martin Buber, Ludwig Rubiner and Rudolf Leonhard in Thomas Anz and Michael Stark (1982, 572–584).

3 Staging the Possibility of Change in Expressionist Drama: Franz Werfel

The entanglements of aesthetic and religious or spiritual aspects and moments also left their stamp on Expressionist literature and particularly on works for the modern stage, which was to be redesigned into a site where otherwise suppressed religious energies would be unleashed (Ritchie 1976). The role of Expressionist plays entailed rebelling against the drama and theatre of the day, which clearly dedicated itself to the exponential aestheticism of *Jugendstil* and Neo-Romanticism. Expressionist drama positioned itself against traditional dramaturgical and aesthetic conventions. It sought to banish "beautiful" literature from the stage, wanting instead to instigate a theatrical breakthrough that implemented poetic and dramaturgical means of liberation: exalted gestures, poses, and movement; light, colour, and image; and dialogue, at times subdued to a whisper or at other times heightened to an operatic pitch.

The early Expressionist one-act plays, written by authors like Gottfried Benn, Walter Hasenclever, and Franz Werfel—to name only a few—demonstrate this alteration in aesthetic and dramaturgical approaches and claims with especial vividness (see Denkler 1987). Gottfried Benn's one-act *Ithaka* (1914), presented in the form of a dialogue between a professor and his students, sketches out the language of rebellious youth, which longs for fantasy and intoxication. Walter Hasenclever's play *Das unendliche Gespräch* ("The Infinite Conversation", 1913) celebrates in an oratorical style the pathos of love and pain, which boldly summons the overwhelming power of the "infinite". And Franz Werfel's dialogue *Der Besuch aus dem Elysium* ("The Visit from Elysium", 1912) constitutes in hymnic-emotive language the transformation of the protagonist Markus from a state of debilitating weakness to one that exhibits the violent power of life capable of overcoming the mundane.

After 1914, we find dramas that refer in varying ways to the Great War and/or announce a coming revolution. For example, Friedrich Koffka's drama *Kain* (1917) is clearly inspired by war-related events, as is evidenced by the play's prefacing quotation from the Hebrew Bible: "And the Lord looked with favour on Abel and his offering. But on Cain and his offering He did not look" (Gen. 4:4–5). This evocation of Cain's fratricide, which is staged in a nightmarish manner, simultaneously emphasises its revolutionary force, identifying the murdered Abel as the guilty one and allowing Cain to overcome the old world embodied by his brother, yet without removing the guilt that proceeds from the murder. In contrast, *Das indische Spiel* ("Indian Play", 1920) by Alfred Brust turns to the Indo-Asian world and likewise marks the end of Expressionist drama. In an accelerated plot spanning many years, the play brings into constellation the spiritually heightened protagonist Vaddasin, the girl Sananasani and their mothers, together with a priest, who invites self-collection in the spirit of the Buddha, and a fakir, who announces that he wants to stand for twenty years on a single leg willing to pass away in body and plunge his spirit into Vaddasin's brain, in order that he might be led to great heights. Brust's piece belongs to a cycle of "plays" that succinctly create a mythical world, in which human sacrifice and priestly guides play a fundamental role—a world which is designed as a counter-image to the breakdown of civilization.

An important representative example, which grapples with the catastrophic human and civilizational consequences of the Great War, is found in Franz Werfel's play *Die Mittagsgöttin* ("The Midday Goddess", 1919), a drama of awakening to the necessity of becoming human (Werfel 1919). Here, autobiographical aspects are woven together with archaic mythic qualities and metaphors of light, which reach into mystical realms, culminating in a myth of redemption. Embedded in the play are reminiscences of Gnostic principles, which proceed from redemption through knowledge (*gnosis*) and postulate that knowledge is achieved by remembering one's own, otherworldly origin. The material world of creation appears as sorrowful, wretched, and characterised by death; the possibility of change arises by means of revealing the original, immaterial world.

This possibility, or indeed necessity, is dramatically portrayed in the staging of the play's protagonists: the vagrant Laurentin, who represents the author, and Mara, a heathen goddess who embodies the eternal feminine principle which helps Laurentin move through the painful experience toward self-realization. The figure of Mara comes from the world of Slavic sagas, reinterpreted by Werfel under the influence of his encounter with his future wife, Alma Mahler (née Schindler), for whom he wrote the play (see Grau 1966, esp. 98–108). The midday goddess of East-European mythology appears on hot days at noon, especially during the harvest, and confuses the people's understanding, paralyzes them, or kills them by lopping off their heads with her sickle. Werfel's positive reinterpretation implies a disempowerment of her mythic terror in favor of potentially productive aspects. On the level of the text, these aspects come to expression by means of apparently Gnostic references to incursions of light, which are to be understood as trace elements of the original world that Mara represents. At the same time, sensory perceptions are addressed and invoked with striking expressivity, in order to stage dramatically Laurentin's being in the world and his encounter with Mara, not only by projections of the external world of vision—for example by registering colours—but also by an intensification of the intimate, corporeal sensations like hearing and touch.

The play's broad storyline is as follows: Laurentin, unable to bear his life any longer, flees from his own mortal reality in an ardent longing for the Absolute.

This longing grows stronger in his encounter with Mara, in whom, in the noon heat, the presence of the world coalesces as the pure insistence of the maternal primal ground. As Laurentin falls asleep in the midday glow, Mara steps out from a ripe summer cornfield, adorned with garlands and surrounded by bees. For a long time she observes the sleeper, until he opens his eyes. The subsequent encounter with the goddess initiates Laurentin's transformation by means of a look, dialogue, and a repeated kiss. As he reveals to Mara, he has been in search of God:

> LAURENTIN
> *O Heidin! Viele Götter siehst du mir.*
> *Ich aber bin fremd und Landstreicher hier.*
> *Und such' den Gott allein, der streng sich schied*
> *Von seiner Welt* (180).

> LAURENTIN
> O Heathen! To me you see many gods.
> But I am a stranger here, a vagrant.
> And I seek only the god, who starkly departed
> From his world.

Mara's role is not to promise ultimate salvation to the seeker, but rather to point out the way. She informs Laurentin that he must experience "the reality of the tremendous Thou" ("Die Wirklichkeit des ungeheuren Dus" [179]) and thus exhaust his potential as man. And this is precisely what happens: United with the goddess, Laurentin is ready for renunciation and sacrifice, as Mara, at once beloved and mother, lies in painful labor, about to give birth. In this very moment Laurentin must go to the limit of his love: In order to save her, he offers a prayer to God and pledges never to touch another woman. Then, Mara, a figuration of the natural origin of the world, walks out of the cornfield with their child, instructing Laurentin, who is thankful to her for having shown the way, before she disappears:

> LAURENTIN
> *Unsterblich Sterbliche! Die höchste Gnade übtest du an mir. Du gibst mir meinen Weg.*

> MARA
> *Nun aber ruft mein Weg mich weg. Lebewohl!* (225)

> LAURENTIN
> Immortal mortal! You showed me the highest grace. You give me my way.

> MARA
> But now my way calls me off. Farewell!

The poet remains alone, carving out for himself a recluse's existence, penetrated with the thought of becoming human by becoming spirit (*Geist*). By means of a generative union with and in Mara, Laurentin has become aware of true human existence beyond material creation. Now it is necessary to follow the way out of all entanglement with the world and the ego in the sobriety of a hermit's retreat. This message is also expressed in the verbal form, which sets off with a melodically rhyming speech evoking visual, audial, and olfactory effects of summer by registering the sensuous play of yellow and gold:

LAURENTIN
Wer bist du? An deinem Gürtel hängen Ähren,
Die ganz verwirrt in goldenem Dunst sich nähren.
Die große Sonnenblume schläft in deinem Arm,
Und um dein Haar steht dicht ein Bienenschwarm (175).

LAURENTIN
Who are you? Upon your belt hang ears of grain
Which nourish confusingly in the golden haze.
The large sunflower sleeps in your arm,
And around your hair there stands close by a swarm of bees.

This sensuously rich language—further infused with vague religious allusions—unmistakably conveys an aura of mystery and longing, which stands in stark contrast to the sober prose that constitutes Laurentin's last words spoken after the disappearance of Mara:

LAURENTIN
Ich will dem gespenstischesten Gespenst begegnen: mir selbst. Denn ich bin gefeit, da das Geheimnis der kreisenden, herzklopfenden Welt durch den Kuß des höchsten Weibes mich erwählt und in mich selbst verwandelt hat.
Meine Seele erfuhr die mächtigste Wonne, erfuhr die unsagbarste Vernichtung. So müssen ihr für ewig Wonne und Schmerz ein Wahn bleiben.
Ich schaue durch euch alle wie durch farbiges Glas. Meine Lippen sind entsetzlich trocken vor Erwachtheit.
Die Welt ist ein abgestammeltes Gerücht, das dem Schöpfer aus dem Sinn gekommen ist. Ich will denken, ich will denken, bis der schwere Stein meines Ichs zur stetig weißen Flamme wird, bis meine Farben wieder vereint sind ins heilig-einfach Weiße, meine Worte gesammelt ins Schweigen, dann will ich Gott erinnern und ihm sein Rätsel zuschweigen (232).

LAURENTIN
I want to encounter the ghostly ghost: myself. For I am immune, since the secret of the rotating, palpitating world has chosen me by the kiss of the highest woman and transformed me into myself.
My soul experienced the most powerful joy, experienced the most unspeakable annihilation. Thus, joy and pain must forever remain a delusion for my soul.

> I look through you all as though through coloured glass. My lips are terribly dry from wake-
> fulness.
> The world is a stammered rumor, which came out of the Creator's mind. I want to think, I
> want to think, until the heavy stone of my ego turns to a steady white flame, until my col-
> ours recombine into the holy, simple white, my words collected into silence, then I want to
> remind God and render his riddle silent.

This passage at the end of the play stresses the protagonist's desire for spiritu-alisation (*Geistwerdung*) and is typical for the programmatic direction of many Expressionist texts and artworks that emphasise transformation. Yet these do not recapitulate the state of the world. Rather, they put themselves in the service of a "life reform, activating all transcendent and metaphysical values in cosmic relatedness" (Färber 1958, 103). Even further, they performatively seek to intro-duce change in humanity and, with it, the transmutation of the world. Aesthetic and extra-aesthetic aspects thereby penetrate each other. The cry and appeal for change are brought to expression by emotionally provocative and affective means in an effusively exaggerated gesture. Dramatic figures that represent the will to conversion and the longing for redemption convey this, as they mu-tually act upon one another.

Along these lines, Expressionist drama occasionally bears on the model of the Mystery Play, which in those years was in great demand as an attempt at the ritualisation of the theatre (for instance Sprengel 2004, 479 – 487). On the lev-els of theme and motivic content, we find this specific intention at work, for in-stance, in Werfel's one-act *Die Versuchung. Ein Gespräch des Dichters mit dem Er-zengel und Luzifer* ("Temptation: The Poet's Conversation with the Archangel and Lucifer", 1913), which explicitly alludes to the Temptation of Christ. To be sure, Werfel's meaningful allegorical deployment of mystical and mythical tensions, themes, and motifs, is not unique in Expressionist literature. Such aspects, rang-ing from the most popular to the most obscure, played a considerable role for many writers of the period. Syncretism was a common feature, audaciously blending varieties of paganism expressing pantheistic, polytheistic, or animistic beliefs together with monotheistic, particularly Catholic and Protestant themes, which often resulted in quite singular repertoires of symbolic and allegorical lan-guage. In this way, religion served as an instrument to various ends, for example, the establishment of an international, pan-religious community in Ludwig Rubiner's essay *Der Mensch in der Mitte* ("The Man in the Middle", 1917) and his anthology *Kameraden der Menschheit* ("Comrades of Humanity", 1919) or the celebration of ecstatic eroticism in the poetry of Richard Dehmel. In a phil-osophical key, one would include Ernst Bloch's *Geist der Utopie* ("Spirit of Uto-pia", 1918/1923), which offered a mystical interpretation of historical progress, as well as Franz Rosenzweig's and Walter Benjamin's heady forays in Kabbalistic prose. Finally, in addition to reoccupations of European legacies, there is ample evidence of incorporating the religions of southern and eastern Asia.[12] Figures of art and thought from Hindu, Buddhist, and Daoist traditions were engaged by writers as diverse as Alfred Döblin, Franz Werfel, Albert Ehrenstein, and Klabund. Throughout, these few examples amply demonstrate the vivacity of a religious sensibility that would instigate some of the most exhilarating and the most damning thinking of the age, from social revolutions to calls for the "New Man", from cultural innovation to insidious demagoguery, from an inspired investigation into Jewish mysticism to the detrimental consolidation of anti-Semitic stereotypes.

4 Conjuring the New Man: Nietzschean Impulses and the Aesthetics of Redemption

The discursive context of Expressionism's pronounced dealings with the body and the senses, particularly when involving issues of transcendence and salvation, sheds interesting light on the aesthetics of religion, which specifically deals with how human senses, signals, and signs are addressed, used, and engendered in and by religions. Moreover, it shows how its area of research spans all aspects of the human body, from being a site of sensory perception to serving as the means and manner of expression, for example in the mimicry, gestures, and movements, which play an important role in Expressionism and in particular in drama.

Perhaps the most important theoretical impulse for Expressionist writers and artists intent on placing corporeal experience in the foreground came from the life and work of Friedrich Nietzsche, whose enthusiastic reception in the first decades of the 20th century approximates the level of hagiography. In the famous opening sentence of Nietzsche's *Birth of Tragedy* (1871), one finds explicit reference to the possibility of readjusting aesthetic experience on the basis of Hellenic myth and ritual:

---

12 In this regard, the increased scholarship in Indology and Sinology directly motivated the development of ethnology, comparative religious studies, and comparative mythology, which toward the end of the 19th century nourished broad popular interest in esoteric lore, as evidenced for example in Helena Blavatsky's bestsellers, *Isis Unveiled* (1877) and *The Secret Doctrine* (1888). Throughout, one discerns a thoroughly creative transformation and repurposing of inherited religious traditions.

We shall have gained much for the science of aesthetics [*die aesthetische Wissenschaft*] when we have come to realize, not just through logical insight [*Einsicht*] but also with the certainty of something directly apprehended [*zur unmittelbaren Sicherheit der Anschauung*], that the continuous development of art is bound up with the duality of the Apollonian and the Dionysian in much the same way as reproduction depends on there being two sexes which co-exist in a state of perpetual conflict interrupted only occasionally by periods of reconciliation (Nietzsche 1999b, 14 [English], and 1999a, 1:25 [German]).

By evoking the mythical tension between an Apollonian principle of form and a Dionysian principle of formlessness—a tension that is emphatically compared to sexual impulses—Nietzsche prepares the ground for the expansion or recalibration of aesthetic experience that the German Expressionists, and not least Franz Werfel, would later take to heart. In Nietzsche's view, the two powerful gods, who came together in the ritualised context around the cult at Delphi, are responsible for the flourishing of Greek tragedy, which thereby attains its sacred character. Mere representation, a process ascribed to the Apollonian, must be disrupted, shattered, or even destroyed by the kind of raw vitalism associated with Dionysus. For the Expressionists who avidly read Nietzsche—as well as celebrating his heroic life, martyred in madness—art must be sacralised; aesthetic experience must become dynamic.

Nietzsche's call for the revitalization of modern culture sponsored a broad variety of movements and artistic manifestos, including above all the work of Expressionist writers. Despite the many differences among the authors and works mentioned, despite the varying references to religious materials, some common ground is nonetheless discernible: Aesthetics, which comes to serve a pioneering function within the framework of European artistic production and reception, has in Expressionism from time to time an altogether special place and value for the literary and visual exhibition of various religious forms and manifestations. The reason for this lies not least of all in the fact that at this time aesthetics, understood precisely as a mode of sense-perception (*aisthēsis*), had already for centuries enabled mankind to approach the divine by means of the divine's own human presentation. The humanization of the divine is pre-moulded in ancient paganism, for example in the anthropomorphism of the pantheon, as well as in Christianity which, with the birth, life, and passion of Christ, teaches that God has Himself become man. For the increasingly Christianized Europe of the early Middle Ages, the presupposition of the aesthetic or perceptual presentation of the divine is encountered in the so-called Byzantine iconoclasm debate of the eighth century. Crucial here is the decision that it is precisely the incarnation of the divine logos in Jesus Christ which makes possible a human presentation of God as well as Mary, the "mother of God", the prophets and the saints (see Wohlmuth 2002, 134). With this decision, the path is paved for "Christian Europe" to give an aesthetic representation of the divine, something that is precipitated in the Middle Ages in appropriations of the possibility of God's representability. Then, in the Renaissance, the aestheticisation of Christian doctrine begins, which ever since shapes the history of European literature and art. In this process, literary as well as visual arts load themselves up with religious meaning. They themselves turn into a medium of religious debate concerning the presentation of crises in religious sense as well as the search and establishment of human sense (Vietta and Uerling 2008, 10). Christian ideas of time, space, suffering, and redemption here play an essential role, albeit in a modernized—and depending on the author or artist and the social context, an aestheticised—form.

A point of reference for many Expressionists in this process of negotiation is the paradigm of the renewal of mankind. The leading postulate is galvanized in the figure of the New Man (*Der neue Mensch*), which alludes to radical changes in disposition, as well as spiritual renovation—a profound awakening that allows mankind to break free of old chains and create new capacities (Riedl 1970, 3). The concept of the New Man, as it is found paradigmatically in Werfel's dramatic encounter of Laurentin with Mara, in Laurentin's retreat for the purpose of spiritualisation, develops in the face of the gross alienation that writers and thinkers of the time linked to modernization and scientific positivism. As in the case of Neo-Kantianism, which was one of the most influential philosophical movements in the German universities of the time, Expressionism placed great emphasis on human subjectivity as the faculty that generates its objects of cognition. For the Neo-Kantians and the Expressionists alike, this creative power of the human subject should be further ascribed to ethical consciousness, which would thereby possess the potential to reshape and redirect culture, society, and even politics.[13] As Werfel famously put it in his much-quoted formula of existence—"The world begins in Man" (*Die Welt fängt im Menschen an*)—the New Man designated precisely this beginning (Werfel 1988, 291; also cited in Wright 1987, 586). The idea can be found in countless variants in the literature and art of these years, especially after the First World War, when the call for the New Man loudly resounds with especial force. The figure is embodied in Werfel's Laurentin, who awakens to his new being through intoxication and ecstasy, and is further discernible in contemporary works, with Walter Hasenclever, Georg Kaiser, Reinhard Johannes Sorge, and Ernst Stadler being particularly representative.

---

13 For a useful account, which further interrogates the masculine bias of the concept, see Wright (1987).

As mentioned above, many of these authors referred to Nietzsche, who since 1900 had become a most fashionable philosopher and, according to some actors of the time, the "great secular event of the epoch" (Max Halbe 1933, cited in Hillebrand 1978, 19). For the Expressionists as well, fundamental notions from Nietzsche's *Also Sprach Zarathustra. Ein Buch für Alle und Keinen* ("Thus Spoke Zarathustra: A Book for Everyone and No One", 1883–1885), constitute key artistic concepts, for example, the *Übermensch*, eternal return, and the will to power. These notions involve the presentation and exposition of the self-intensification and self-overcoming of a subjectivity now understood as vital and dynamic, in whose course the subject's instrumentalised role in positivist and materialist frameworks is unmasked as a paralyzing fiction. Nietzsche's repeated calls for attentiveness, for listening with "the third ear", aims at registering the breaks in normative sense and logic; life is proclaimed as an overwhelming force that fails to reach the deaf ears of bourgeois morality. Tellingly, Nietzsche frequently has recourse to religiously coded discourse. Nietzsche's general assault against moralizing Christians does not rule out an admiration for the most revolutionary aspects of the religion's divine founder. In this spirit, Expressionist-style philosophers like Ernst Bloch elaborate upon the Nietzsche's mission and persistently pit a revolutionary and even atheistic Messiah against the status quo maintained by bourgeois authority. Throughout, Nietzsche stood by as the godfather for many Expressionist works that lash out against bourgeois torpor, particularly in the "drama of awakening"—*Aufbruchsdramatik*. This strategy is paradigmatically reflected in Georg Kaiser's dramatic sketch *Die Erneuerung* ("Renewal", in Kaiser 1972 [1917/19]), which was intended as a prototype of an Expressionist drama of awakening and which is prefixed by the "Incipit tragoedia" from Nietzsche's *Die fröhliche Wissenschaft* ("The Gay Science", 1882)—a declaration that is intertextually bound not only to Nietzsche's *Zarathustra* and *Götzen-Dämmerung* ("Twilight of the Idols", 1889), but also to Bloch's *Geist der Utopie* ("Spirit of Utopia", 1917/23), whose preface modulates the Nietzschean theme in a new, Dante-inspired key: "Incipit vita nova" (Kaiser 1972, 710; Bloch 1991, 13).

The Expressionist drama of awakening is especially significant because it can be shown to offer an exemplary modern presentation of the interrelation between literature and religious sentiment. Here, the Catholic doctrine of transubstantiation proves to be particularly relevant in precisely this regard. The notion of transubstantiation, first documented in the 12th century and established as orthodox in the Fourth Lateran Council of 1215, affirmed that the consecrated Host of the Eucharist is transformed into the very body of Christ (*Hoc est corpus meum*). The participants of the mass were granted salvation by the Real Presence of Christ's body in the bread. This doctrinal belief has inspired many artists to innovate and enhance the aesthetic experiences of artistic production and reception—it transforms literature, drama, and visual art into an event replete with a real presence linked to the holy. This idea is precisely what we find in Expressionism, particularly in drama. In an often quite explicit fashion, Expressionist plays create the conditions for a kind of transubstantiation that serves as the crystalizing postulate of the artistic movement. Expressionism means an art of giving voice and making real, that is, as concretely presenting internally perceived truths and experiences in a way that empowers drama with particular force. Specifically, upon the stage, the birth of the new, *transubstantiated* man is called forth by means of abstraction and empathy, supported by music, dance, pantomime, scenery, and lighting—in a word, *presented.*

Moreover, the Expressionist play of presence, as an aestheticised ritual, results in allegorical figurations that exhibit a certain anti-mimetic drive. Allegory disrupts mimetic representation by pointing to an absence at the very core of what is being represented: an absence that can open onto a transcendent experience of the holy. Expressionist characters are thus not represented as individuals but rather as types ("Man", "Woman", "Daughter", etc.). Their portrayal is often exaggeratedly or grotesquely distorted in order to uncover psychological truths that transcend quotidian reality. Behind these gestures stands the wish of the poet, according to his self-assigned role, to assist his vision—a vision of transubstantiation into the New Man—to bring it to life not only with the given means of language but also by putting it on stage. Through a religious aesthetics the theatre is transformed into a temple—into a sacred locale of sacrifice: the ordinary bread and wine of everyday life is irradiated by the transcendent power of holy flesh and blood. Whereas bourgeois theatre consistently maintained the safe conditions of passive spectatorship and intellectual engagement, the Expressionist theatre-*cum*-temple aimed toward a more vital participation, one that, by way of ritualistic motifs and effects, should produce an internal alteration in the viewer. The implied audience of Expressionist drama is no longer protected by secure distance. On the contrary, through strategies of shock, transgression, and cognitive disturbances, the performances strive to invite rational surrender, to encourage captivation and involvement, which incite personal transformation. Stable subjective positions and the cognitive limitations that underwrite them are thereby offered up in sacrifice; the stage provides the coordinates for a true rite de passage.

In Expressionist drama, the conditions for ritualistic transformation are prepared by the hero on stage. For the hero is invariably the sacrificial victim, exposed as someone who exhibits this transubstantiation with his own body and who encompasses the program of his transformation in the word (on this theme see Denkler 1979, 136–137). Aimed at an allegorical demonstration of the realisation of ethical values, the transformation is performed for humanity conceived as the midpoint of the world, and indeed as redemption from given reality. This demonstration shares common ground with religions of redemption—not only as Judaism, Christianity, and Islam are designated, but also the Hellenistic Mysteries and Buddhism—essentially as the liberation from suffering and sickness, from prejudice and boundedness. Concepts like eternity, time, sacrifice, and sympathy equally play a crucial role. To be sure, redemption here should not be understood in the strictly religious sense as being with or in God. Expressionist dramas of transubstantiation, which are at the same time dramas of redemption—stage redemption rather in a secularized form. An isolated man appears on stage, often anonymous and masked, in order to make proclamations on universal themes that transcend the quotidian. According to this thematic intention, the interplay of the figures and their function as redeemer is hereby expressed in elevated language, accompanied by aria-like chorus parts in varying singing styles (Denkler 1979, 136 – 137). Altogether, these dramatic procedures and aesthetic means speak to a desire to transubstantiate the bodies of the actors and the audience, to effect a substantial change that adduces the holy within the communal context of the theatre.

For this reason, the body (on the one hand as the public's or the readers' means of recording, on the other hand and above all as a means of expression) plays a central role in these dramas—with its capacity for sensuous perception, signifying expression, and presentational performance by means of gestures, mimicry, and automatism. Corporeal gestures, facial expressions, the bearing and movement of the *dramatis personae* and actors on the stage are of great importance. A quick overview of Expressionist drama would illustrate these processes along various lines: As in Franz Werfel's *Mittagsgöttin,* one figure may initiate the redemption of several figures (e. g., Reinhard Goering, *Seeschlacht* ["Sea Battle"] 1917; Reinhard J. Sorge, *Odysseus,* [1911]; Walter Hasenclever, *Der Retter* ["The Savior"] 1916; and Max Brod, *Die Arche Noah* ["Noah's Ark"] 1913); several figures may seek to effectuate transubstantiation and redemption (e. g., Paul Kornfeld, *Himmel und Hölle* ["Heaven and Hell"] 1919); or the figures may seek to redeem themselves within the collective (e. g., Arnold Bronnen, *Die Geburt der Jugend* ["Birth of Youth"] 1913) (Denkler 1979, 146). As the titles alone make clear, many of these plays rely on religious borrowings and references, which attest to the roles of transubstantiation and redemption, roles that are set dramatically and expressively into the work: redemption from civil need to a more vital existence (*Die Geburt der Jugend*); redemption from war (*Seeschlacht; Der Retter*); or redemption simply from the world (*Odysseus; Die Arche Noah*). With Werfel's *Mittagsgöttin,* as is the case with Kornfeld's *Himmel und Hölle,* we are dealing with a further, frequently employed form of redemption:

redemption from spiritual, emotional, and metaphysical need and guilt. Under the evocation of numerous perceptual allurements and appeals to the senses through colour, light, movement, and tone, transformation is submitted here as the unconditional presupposition of redemption.

5. Dionysus on Stage: Reinhard Johannes Sorge

Redemption by means of transubstantiation is generally motivated by a desire to break free of quotidian reality. In German Expressionist drama the mimetic representation of social phenomena—as it was epitomized in the Realism of the previous century—comes to be disdained as restrictive obeisance, as a pusillanimous enslavement to the status quo and therefore a neglectful attitude to what *could* be, to the new and the unheard-of. Hence, Ernst Bloch's Expressionist utopianism, which explicitly promulgates Nietzsche's vitalism, illustrates a decisive turn away from representational bondage and toward a liberation fueled by expression. This allegiance to Nietzsche, to the philosopher of the Death of God, does not preclude a profound engagement with religiously transcendent motifs and themes. On the contrary, the deployment of such themes, including transubstantiation, well serves the Expressionist program of exposing the limitations of representation.

The work of Reinhard Johannes Sorge is here exemplary.[14] Whereas his major work, *Der Bettler* ("The Beggar", 1912) already bears witness to a passionate turn to Christianity—a turn reinforced in his subsequent play *Der Sieg des Christos* ("Christ's Victory", 1914)—Sorge's dramatic one act sketches of 1910 and 1911, including his "dramatic fantasy" *Odysseus* (1911), are starkly informed by an affirmative reading of Nietzsche (Sorge 1962a). In a free manner, *Odysseus* incorporates material from the Homeric epic, as the hero makes his way home to Ithaca after his long wanderings following the Trojan War. Sorge's play develops into a summarizing presentation of Books 17–22, in which Odysseus, disguised as a stranger, takes vengeance on the suitors who have invaded his home:

---

14 At first an enthusiastic follower of Nietzsche, Sorge broke free and became an opponent of Nietzsche. Following a religious awakening in February 1912, he converted to Catholicism, adopted the middle name Johannes and became a defender of the Christian faith. See Sorge's testimony in a letter to Arnold Bork from January 13, 1913, translated in Tim Cross (1989, 144): "My soul was always inherently Christian, but I was misled by Nietzsche, entangled in suns and stars. In *Der Bettler*, I invoked the Name of many a time quite unconsciously, and yet thought myself a fervent disciple of Nietzsche, who denies God's very existence."

ODYSSEUS *faßt den an einer Säule lehnenden Bogen*
Zu herbster Vollendung endlich greife ich
Den Bogen, der seit Jahren dieser Stunde harrt.
Nun soll er treffen, soll er tilgen Schändliches [...] (271).

Odysseus *grabs the bow leaning on a column*
For the bitterest accomplishment I finally seize
The bow, which for years has awaited this hour.
Now it shall hit the mark, wiping out something shameful [...]

The mass of suitors, who emerge as the chorus, begins at this point to whimper anxiously and retreat. As the stage direction reads, "*Then, everything becomes entirely silent: with a sudden jolt Odysseus tightens the bow, and as he tests the taut string, a deep droning tone floats above the stage*". Now the suitors recognize Odysseus. A "*lightning bolt streaks through the heavens*", and the hero is seen "*ready to fire, aiming the arrows at the suitors*". The suitors grasp each other's hand and "*Odysseus shoots the arrow, the bowstring springs back with a cracking sound. The shot flies through the air with a fiery streak and the suitors fall to the floor*". A ray of sunlight, "*breaking out of the heavenly depths*" repays their death; "*dawn's light is all around*". In the concluding scene, Odysseus the Redeemer stands, "*tall and proud, trembling with the joy of victory. Penelope leans upon him*" (271–273).

The final conjuration of dawn distinctly points to Nietzsche's influence, which in fact informs the entire play. Especially telling is the role of the seer, one of the central figures of the play, who clearly exhibits the traits of Nietzsche's Zarathustra. Convinced of eternal return, if not the Second Coming, he troubles the crowd of gathered suitors, by prophesying the homecoming of Odysseus with broadly open significance. Again, the emphatic conjuration of glistening gold is telling:

SEHER
Ein Glanz liegt über jener Höhe, ein goldiger, goldverräterischer, Gutes und Letztes kündend. Gutes und Letztes dieser Morgennacht, wie ich hell sie nenne, denn längst zog Mitternacht vorüber. Morgenluft spüre ich hier schon, eine tagerwartende, taglauschende, graues Morgenflattern streicht hier schon vorbei, hörbar nur für feine Ohren. Erstes Dämmer tastet, erste Morgenröte flüstert, alle lichten Dinge künden sich. Ach, Mitternacht zog längst schon vorüber! Schon rauscht Helle morgendlich ganz um mich, hoch auf letzter Höhe; ein Adler kreist über mir, dem glüht auf den Schwingen goldverräterischer Glanz goldenen Mittags. Denn er kommt, er ist nahe, der goldene Tänzer (259).

Seer
A luster lies over that peak, a golden, treacherously golden luster, announcing the Good and the Last. The Good and the Last of this night's morning, which I name bright, for midnight has long moved past. I already sense the morning air, awaiting and overhearing the

day; a gray flickering of morning already sweeps by, audible only to refined ears. The first twilight gropes, the first dawn whispers, all things of light are heralded. Ah, midnight has long moved past! Already the morning brightness rustles all around me, high up on the last peak; an eagle circles above me, the pulsing of the treacherously golden luster of golden midday glows upon him. For he comes, he is near, the golden dancer.

With Zarathustra's eagle circling above, nobly gleaming in the resplendent mid-day sky, the contrast between the fearful masses (the suitors) and the singular hero (Odysseus, who appears immediately after the seer's proclamation) is self-evident (see also Essen 2009, 112). Unlike the throng of suitors who *represent* their claims to legitimise their actions, the lone prophet *expresses*, by means of singular gestures and singular language, a religiously coded message that infuses the present with imminent futurity and novelty. To this end, Sorge's prose is replete with sensuous vividness, which intimates the imminence of transformation; hence the emphasis on the luster of morning ("the morning air", "the gray flickering of morning"), which stimulates sensuous responses ("*tasten*", "*lauschen*", "*flüstern*", "*rauschen*"—"groping", "overhearing", "whispering", "rustling", and so on). The evocation of transcendence by means of various images of lustrous, golden light efficaciously slices through conventional viewpoints, like the opinions of the suitors, who otherwise would proceed securely and comfortably with their business.

With Sorge's *Zarathustra: Eine Impression* ("Zarathustra. An Impression"), also from 1911, it is Nietzsche's book itself, which is made into an object of the drama. On stage, a vibrant mixed society of artists and the bourgeoisie, together with a criminal, engage in a heated debate with the author of *Zarathustra*, concerning the beauty and dangerousness of this writing. Whereas the artists celebrate the text, revelling in enthusiasm without restraint, the bourgeoisie, in accordance with their political and civil status, pronounce their distance or rigorous rejection of the work, while the culprit, finally, uses it to justify his murderous crime. As writer of the text in question, Nietzsche has the last word, insisting on the book's esoteric nature: "*Ich sticke an euch. Ihr könnt mich nicht kennen. Sollt mich nicht lesen. Meine Freunde können mich auch im Dunkel lesen*" ("I stitch onto you. You could not know me. You shouldn't read me. My friends can read me even in the dark") (Sorge 1962b). The statement rehearses the spirit of Nietzsche's epic, whose subtitle reads: "A Book for Everyone and for No one". The trope of unreadability, or perhaps readable unreadability, again signals a shift from the clarity of the present toward the moral inscrutability of what is to come, eternally. The affirmation of this eternal return starkly contrasts with the tremulous denial of the bourgeoisie, who would feel threatened by the powerful changes associated with a new aesthetics, with modes of sensuous experience and interpretation that undermine conventional approaches to reality.

Expressionists like Sorge adopt the position, familiar among Jewish and Christian mystics, that a failure to understand indicates a more powerful, more profound understanding. Accordingly, for his subsequent play, again explicitly inspired by the work of Nietzsche, *Antichrist. Dramatische Dichtung* ("Antichrist: A Dramatic Poem", 1911), Sorge appended a motto taken from the famous concluding lines to Nietzsche's *Ecce Homo:* "Have I been understood? Dionysus against the Crucified?" (Sorge 1962c) As the play demonstrates, Christ as master and Nietzsche-Zarathustra as his favorite disciple appear to contradict and simultaneously uphold the piece's motto, insofar as they are portrayed as brothers in spirit, transmitting the same misunderstood message, albeit in differing fashions. The master proclaims to the disciples, who pass the message on to their flock. At stake is the explicit desire for redemption:

> *Das himmlische Reich, das ich euch verhieß, ich verhieß es auch im Geiste. Es sollte euch Erlösung werden von Irrmacht dieses Lebens, Erlösung durch Begriff und Einung mit dem Geist, dessen das Reich ist. [...] Und ein Wort sagte ich euch, erlösend für alle Zeiten, stärkend, heilend, heiligend, ein Wort zur Geburt aller künftigen Geschlechter, zur Höhergeburt, zur Wiedergeburt, ein Wort aus alles Daseins tiefstem Sinn: Dieses, dieses: Das Ewige Leben.* (341–342)

> The heavenly realm that I promised you, I promised you in Spirit. It shall be your redemption from the bewilderment of this life, redemption through the notion and union with the Spirit, to whom this realm belongs. [...] And one Word I tell you, redeeming for all time, strengthening, healing, sanctifying, a Word on the birth of all future races, on a higher birth, a rebirth, from the most profound sense of all existence: This, this: *The Eternal Life.*

What Christ the Master characterises as "eternal life" is celebrated by the disciples as "the eternal return". Both parties are shown to endorse the same devotion to transcendence—a sharing of belief that bourgeois mentality would find impossible to grasp. By unifying Christ and the Antichrist Nietzsche, Sorge effectively overturns the opposition between a Christian-ascetic denial of the world and an intoxicating, Dionysian transfiguration of the world. He thus achieves a bold synopsis of life and spirit, of the God made Man and the Over-Man, of resurrection and a higher birth, of the promise of eternal life and the Dionysian affirmation of the eternal return of the same.

6 Conclusion

The ambitious agenda of the Expressionists could never be served by an aesthetics of representation, which can only understand the already understandable. Quite to the contrary, Expressionist literature offers a transformative aesthetic experience akin to ritualistic involvement, one that promises to be sensuously vital and new. Inspired by Nietzsche's formulation of the Dionysian, together with discourses proffered by theologians and religious intellectuals who were creatively co-opted for fresh statements and standpoints, the modern Expressionist stage was redesigned as a site where religious forces could find bold expression and thereby instigate the transgression of all conventional limits. Precisely through the inheritance and adaptation of religious forms and content, the aesthetics of Expressionism enhances literary and artistic production and reception; and by doing so, reveals core aspects of religious experience that otherwise have been suppressed or obfuscated by doctrinal institutions. In this regard, the Expressionist drama of awakening is especially crucial, insofar as it offers an exemplary modern interpretation of religion and literature in a manner that is also, in turn, relevant for questions concerning the aesthetics of religion. As the brief readings above should demonstrate, this effective reciprocity between religion and literature, particularly as it is found among the German Expressionists, calls for a decided redefinition of human experience as a transformative aesthetic experience, one that expands sensuous perception as well as cognitive approaches to interpretation.

Bibliography

Anz, Thomas, and Michael Stark. 1982. *Expressionismus: Manifeste und Dokumente zur deutschen Literatur 1910–1920*. Stuttgart: Metzler.

Bloch, Ernst. 1991. *Geist der Utopie*, 2nd ed. Frankfurt am Main: Suhrkamp.

Braungart, Wolfgang, Gotthard Fuchs, and Manfred Koch, eds. 1998. *Ästhetische und religiöse Erfahrungen der Jahrhundertwenden*. Vol. 2. Paderborn: Schöningh.

Brunner, Emil. 1922. *Die Grenzen der Humanität. Habilitationsvorlesung an der Universität Zürich*. Tübingen: Mohr.

Cancik, Hubert and Hubert Mohr. 1988. "Religionsästhetik". In *Handbuch religions-wissenschaftlicher Grundbegriffe*. Vol. 1, edited by Hubert Cancik, Burkhard Gladigow, and Matthias Laubscher, 121–156. Stuttgart: Kohlhammer.

Cross, Tim, ed. 1989. *The Lost Voices of World War I: An International Anthology of Writers, Poets, and Playwrights*. Ames: University of Iowa Press.

Denkler, Horst. 1979. *Drama des Expressionismus*. Munich: Wilhelm Fink.

—— ed. 1987. *Einakter und kleine Dramen des Expressionismus*. Stuttgart: Reclam.

Eichhorn, Kristin, and Johannes Lorenzen, ed. 2016. *Expressionismus: Religion*. Berlin: Neofelis.

Essen, Gesa von. 2009. "Resonanzen Nietzsches im Drama des expressionistischen Jahrzehnts." In *Friedrich Nietzsche und die Literatur der klassischen Moderne*, edited by Thorsten Valk, 101–128. Berlin: de Gruyter.

Färber, Otto Michael. 1958. *Die illusionsauflösenden Tendenzen im dramaturgischen Programm des Expressionismus*. Vienna: Diss.

Graf, Friedrich Willhelm. 2004. *Die Wiederkehr der Götter. Religion in der modernen Kultur*. Munich: Beck.

Grau, Dietrich. 1966. *Das Mittagsgespenst (daemonium meridianum): Untersuchungen über seine Herkunft, Verbreitung und seine Erforschung in der europäischen Volkskunde*. Siegburg: F. Schmitt.

Habermas, Rebekka. 2011. "Piety, Power, and Powerlessness. Religion and Religious Groups in Germany, 1870–1945." In *The Oxford Handbook of Modern German History*, edited by Helmut Walser Smith, 453–480. Oxford: Oxford University Press.

Handelman, Don. 2004. "Why Ritual in its own Right? How so?" in *Ritual in Its Own Right: Exploring the Dynamics of Transformation*, edited by Don Handelman and Galina Lindquist, 1–34. New York: Berghahn.

Hillebrand, Bruno. 1978. *Nietzsche und die deutsche Literatur*. Vol. 1, *Texte zur Nietzsche-Rezeption 1873–1963*. Munich: Deutscher Taschenbuch Verlag.

Kaiser, Georg. 1972. *Werke: Stücke 1933–1944*. Vol 6, edited by Walther Huder. Frankfurt a. M.: Propyläen Verlag.

Kanehl, Oskar. 1914. "Wider die Ästhetik." *Wiecker Bote* 1/11–12: 12–15.

Krech, Volkhard. 2002. *Wissenschaft und Religion: Studien zur Geschichte der Religionsforschung in Deutschland 1871 bis 1933*. Tübingen: Mohr.

Lévi-Strauss, Claude. 1981. *The Naked Man: Mythologiques*. Vol. 4, translated by John Weightman and Doreen Weightman. Chicago: The University of Chicago Press.

Metzler, Jan Christian. 2003. *De/Formation: Autorschaft, Körper und Materialität im expressionistischen Jahrzehnt*. Bielefeld: Aisthesis.

Nietzsche, Friedrich. 1999a. *Die Geburt der Tragödie*, edited by Giorgio Colli and Mazzino Montinari. Munich: Deutscher Taschenbuch Verlag.

⎯ 1999b. *The Birth of Tragedy*, translated by Ronald Speirs. Cambridge: Cambridge University Press.

Otto, Rudolf. 1917. *Das Heilige: Über das Irrationale in der Idee des Göttlichen und sein Verhältnis zum Rationalen*. Breslau: Trewendt & Granier, 1917.

⎯ 1958. *The Idea of the Holy: An Inquiry into the Non-Rational Factor in the Idea of the Divine and its Relation to the Rational*, translated by John W. Harvey. Oxford: Oxford University Press.

Nipperdey, Thomas. 1988a. "Religion und Gesellschaft: Deutschland um 1900." *Historische Zeitschrift* 246/3: 591–615.

⎯ 1988b. *Religion im Umbruch. Deutschland 1870–1918*. Munich: Beck.

Pollack, Detlef. 2003. *Säkularisierung – ein moderner Mythos? Studien zum religiösen Wandel in Deutschland*. Tübingen: Mohr Siebeck.

Riedl, Walter. 1970. *Der neue Mensch. Mythos und Wirklichkeit*. Bonn: Bouvier.

Ritchie, James MacPherson. 1976. "Religion and Ecstasy: Lautensack, Kornfeld, Werfel, Einstein, Jahnn, Brust, Bronnen." In *German Expressionist Drama*, 127–167. Boston: G. K. Hall/Twayne.

Rothe, Wolfgang. 1969. "Der Mensch vor Gott: Expressionismus und Theologie". In *Expressionismus als Literatur*, 37–66. Bern: Francke.

—— 1977. *Der Expressionismus: Theologische, soziologische und anthropologische Aspekte einer Literatur*. Frankfurt am Main: Klostermann.

Sorge, Reinhard Johannes. 1962a. "Odysseus: Dramatische Phantasie." In *Werke*. Vol. 1, edited by Hans Gerd Rötzer, 241–273. Nuremberg: Glock & Lutz.

—— 1962b. "Zarathustra: Eine Impression." In *Werke*. Vol. 1, edited by Hans Gerd Rötzer, 95–128. Nuremberg: Glock & Lutz.

—— 1962c. "Antichrist. Dramatische Dichtung." In *Werke*. Vol. 1, edited by Hans Gerd Rötzer, 327–350. Nuremberg: Glock & Lutz.

Sprengel, Peter. 2004. *Geschichte der deutschsprachigen Literatur 1900–1918: Von der Jahrhundert-wende bis zum Ende des ersten Weltkriegs*. Munich: Beck.

Vietta, Silvio and Herbert Uerlings. 2008. "Einleitung: Ästhetik – Religion – Säkularisierung." In *Ästhetik – Religion – Säkularisierung*. Vol. 1, *Von der Renaissance zur Romantik*, edited by Vietta and Uerlings. Munich: Fink, 7–23.

Viladesau, Richard. 1999. *Theological Aesthetics: God in Imagination, Beauty, and Art*. Oxford: Oxford University Press.

—— 2014. "Aesthetics and Religion." In *The Oxford Handbook of Religion and the Arts*, edited by Frank Burch Brown, 25–43. Oxford: Oxford University Press.

Von Sydow, Eckart. 1919. "Das religiöse Bewußtsein des Expressionismus." In *Neue Blätter für die Kunst und Dichtung*. Vol. 1, 193–199.

Werfel, Franz. 1919. *Die Mittagsgöttin. Ein Schauspiel*. Munich: K. Wolff.

—— 1988. *Menschheitsdämmerung. Ein Dokument des Expressionismus*, edited by Kurt Pinthus. Hamburg: Rowohlt.

Wohlmuth, Josef, ed. and trans. 1998. *Konzilien des ersten Jahrtausends: vom Konzil von Nizäa (325) bis zum Vierten Konzil von Konstantinopel (869/70)*. Vol. 1, 2nd ed. Paderborn: Schöningh.

Wolf, Norbert. 2004. *Expressionism*. Cologne: Taschen.

Wright, Barbara. 1987. "'New Man,' Eternal Woman: Expressionist Responses to German Feminism." *German Quarterly* 60/4: 582–599.

Adrian Hermann
Screening the *Father of Lights*: Documentary Film and the Aesthetics of the Nonfictional in Contemporary Religion

1 Introduction[1]

We arrive late for this evening's screening of the documentary "Father of Lights" at the *International Church of Las Vegas*. When we enter the auditorium the event has already started. A member of the "Wanderlust Productions" team is introducing the company and its films and projects. After he ends his presentation, the local pastor takes over. He talks about the film they will be screening tonight and what it offers to the church. The weekly offerings are collected while the lights are being dimmed and a female assistant speaks a prayer. Then the film screening starts, the intro credits roll. During the first scene, the lights in the auditorium are finally turned off completely. The film is projected onto four screens in this large hall: one central screen in the middle behind the stage, two screens left and right of the stage, and an additional projection on the rear wall. During the film the audience reacts audibly to what is shown on the screens, especially during the last third of the film. They applaud after certain scenes and shout praise to God. After the film is over, with the credits still rolling, the pastor begins to preach: "Bow your head, close your eyes". He says: "We thank you for this documentary ... how special this documentary is". He calls people to the front, those who have not yet decided to give their life to Jesus. They are asked to repeat a prayer. Then the pastor asks how many people have spoken this prayer for the first time tonight. I count about 10 hands going up. The elders of the church (about thirty men and women) are called to the front to offer prayer for people in the audience. The pastor invites anyone in need of prayer to come forward. A few follow this call, walk to the front and are prayed over by the church elders. After observing this scene for a while we leave the auditorium towards the entrance hall where merchandise is being sold.

The event described above was an evening of film screening and Christian worship held on August 8, 2012, at the *International Church of Las Vegas*

---

1 The writing of this chapter has been supported by a post-doctoral mobility fellowship of the Swiss National Science Foundation (SNSF) that allowed me to spend time as a Visiting Scholar at Utrecht University and Stanford University in 2014/2015.

https://doi.org/10.1515/9783110461015-005

(ICLV) in Las Vegas, Nevada, USA. It was part of a two-month screening tour of the documentary *Father of Lights* organised by the Chicago-based film company "Wanderlust Productions".[2] Together with a colleague I conducted ethnographic and sociological fieldwork during this tour for three weeks, in total attending eight such events. In the following, I want to draw on this research on the film *Father of Lights* and the screening tour in the summer of 2012 to reflect upon documentary media and the aesthetics of the nonfictional in contemporary religion.

In this context, the notion of "aesthetics" can serve to connect an analysis of religious (documentary) films with a focus on their performance and reception. Drawing on recent work done in the "aesthetics of religion" (Cancik and Mohr 1988; Wilke 2008, 206–232; Mohr 2010), this perspective allows us to take media in general (and films in particular) "seriously as material forms through which the senses and bodies of religious practitioners are tuned and addressed" (Meyer and Verrips 2008, 25). Contributing to the development of a systematic 'aisthetic' approach, Jürgen Mohn (2012, §43; translation mine) has argued that religious systems attempt to continuously establish "a specific perceptual space, which gives order to the world in space and time and communicates this order as a specific perceptual world-and-life-order to the human senses". In seeking to reconstruct and analyse such perceptual spaces, we can pragmatically distinguish (a) a production process, (b) a medial-material process of performance and presentation, and (c) a process of reception (see Mohn 2012, §33, §47). Each of these three aspects of religious *aisthesis* can establish and take place in its own distinctive perceptual space at a different point in time, or they might also take place simultaneously. Mohn (2012, §31) considers the analysis of such "aisthetic framings" of religious communications to be a central task for the academic study of religion.

Taking these approaches and an aesthetic perspective as a starting point therefore allows us to connect the three levels of analysing a) religious media products, b) the performative dimension of such media, and c) their audience reception. In this way, a study-of-religion perspective on certain recent documentaries, as will be presented in this chapter, could also contribute to a broader investigation of documentary film that goes beyond the paradigm of film-as-text and takes into account the analytic levels of "texts, contexts and audiences for documentary" (Austin 2007, 1).

---

2 The film is available for streaming and on DVD at http://fatheroflights.wpfilm.com/. Extended trailer: https://www.youtube.com/watch?v=bUFLWGAeaiU (last accessed 18 May 2017).

2 Screening the *Father of Lights:* A Christian Documentary and its Audience Reception

Wanderlust Productions, the company that in 2012 released the film I am concerned with in this chapter, was founded in 2006 by Darren Wilson, then Professor of Communications at Judson University, a Christian college in Chicago. Since then, the company has released four documentary films, all directed by Wilson himself: *Finger of God* (2007), *Furious Love* (2009), *Father of Lights* (2012), and recently *Holy Ghost* (2014). Wilson is now "Artist-in-Residence at Judson", which—with his support—has started offering a degree in "Film and Digital Media" where Christian filmmakers can learn to make similar films.

Wanderlust Productions "concentrates on creating feature films that are both creatively exciting and spiritually engaging", adopting the slogan "Making God Famous One Film at A Time" (www.wpfilm.com). Their films are Christian documentaries that attempt to capture 'the supernatural' on film and, over the course of the first trilogy, develop an audio-visual theology of God's fatherly love. *Finger of God*, *Furious Love*, and *Father of Lights* are composed of live-action documentary scenes as well as talking head interviews with well-known charismatic-Christian pastors and church leaders, complemented by the director's voice-over narration. While *Finger of God* follows Wilson on a journey to examine and document miracles, *Furious Love* goes on a—as stated on the DVD cover—"journey into the heart of darkness in search of love", looking for Godly love in "some of the darkest spiritual climates on the planet". In *Father of Lights*, Wilson visits various Christian activists (an Indian pastor preaching to Hindus, an American couple running an orphanage in China, a meeting between pastors and Latino gang leaders in Chicago, etc.) and interviews charismatic-Christian leaders on the topics of 'grace', the 'religious spirit', and 'misconceptions of God the father'. He travels to locations such as India, Taiwan, Israel, and various places in the USA (Los Angeles, Chicago, etc.) to record and follow a variety of charismatic Christians claiming to employ the power of the Holy Spirit to pray, prophesy, and heal, and attempts to capture the events following those prayers on film.

Father of Lights is indexed and circulated as a non-fiction film (see Carroll 1996a, 287; Carroll 1996b, 232) through the rhetoric of the film itself, but just as much in the accompanying material, the marketing, as well as the film's distribution (especially online and through social media like Facebook). At the same time, all of the films of Wanderlust Productions can be understood as 'films of inner mission', which constitute and confirm their own community and its worldview, while also offering some critique of fellow Christians, inviting them to change their opinions and views—be it on their understanding of God's love, or the possibility of the miraculous workings of God in our own time.

2.1 *Father of Lights* and the Director's On-Screen Persona: A Christian Michael Moore?

In order to understand some aspects of the appeal of the films of Wanderlust Productions, it seems useful to compare director Darren Wilson's relationship to his films and his own appearance in them to how another documentary film-maker—whose films were very successful in the last decades and whose style of production probably influenced Wilson—develops the authority of his films: Michael Moore, director of, e. g., *Roger & Me* (1989), *Bowling for Columbine* (2002), and *Fahrenheit 9/11* (2004).

In an article on Moore's filmic voice and persona, Louise Spence and Vinicius Navarro (2010, 370) have described the authority of his films as one in which the authority of an omniscient voice-of-god commentary is replaced by the authority of Moore's on-screen persona. They draw attention to the distribution of authority as one of the important if complicated ways in which a documentary represents reality (Spence and Navarro 2010, 368). In his films, Moore is not only the one telling the story and the one who assumes control over our interpretation of it through his voice-over commentary. He also, as early as in his first film *Roger & Me*, appears in the film himself, as a person on the screen who guides the viewer through the events he observes. Also referring to *Roger & Me*, Douglas Kellner (2013, 60) has highlighted Moore's contributions to what he calls "documentary films of personal witnessing". Making himself the narrative centre of his films allows Moore to take the viewers on a journey in which they are invited to share in the filmmaker's adventures and experiences. As Spence and Navarro (2010, 369) have argued, in this way, "the presence not only of the filmmaker, but the crew and recording apparatus, [...] seem to render visible what is happening. The fact that they were there, the indexical aspects of the photographic media, appears to certify [the] documentary's authenticity and authority at the same time". While there is of course a larger history behind the idea of a film's director appearing on-screen as a protagonist in a documentary (see Winston 2013, 19), Moore's style of filmmaking deploys the three documentary strategies of "personal witnessing, exploratory and confrontational quest dramas, and partisan political interventions" to create a unique take on the genre (Kellner 2013, 60). In this way "the filmmaker's screen act, the self that is performed for the camera" (Spence and Navarro 2010, 369–270) becomes a central feature of the film, its distribution of authority, and its representation of reality.

We can compare Moore's relationship to his films and the way in which he establishes his on-screen persona to the film *Father of Lights*. In this film, the director Darren Wilson similarly not only provides the voice-over commentary, but also appears on camera—even if he is not as often in the centre of our attention as Moore is in his films. He mostly guides us through his journey, leaving the bulk of the action to the other Christians he encounters around the world. Only sometimes he himself takes the centre stage, as in one scene early in the film at Venice Beach in California,[3] where Wilson confronts sign-carrying fire-and-brimstone preachers to talk with them about their reasons for their form of ministry and their understanding of God (*Father of Lights*, 0:12:02–0:16:02). In many of the other scenes we follow other Christians as Wilson follows them. Nevertheless, he is always present as the narrator in the film, lending it the credibility of his on-screen persona.

As such, he appears as our guide in a journey to "film God and understand His character" (DVD cover) culminating in Jerusalem at the end of the film. Just as Moore does (see Spence and Navarro 2010, 372), Wilson addresses the audience in the first person plural, making us his accomplices in exploring the workings of God in our time and seemingly giving us direct access to the action we see on screen. The audience is thus always implicated in the journey, and, for example, after the intro at the beginning of the film is directly addressed, when Wilson invites us to "meet Ravi" (*Father of Lights*, 0:02:12), an Indian Christian with whom he is about to visit a remote Hindu village, preaching to its inhabitants. In the very last scene, by way of the voice-over commentary, Wilson then suddenly addresses each viewer directly, telling him or her that "[t]here are seven billion people in this world, but today, right now, right at this moment, a father has found his child, and that child is you" (*Father of Lights*, 1:32:26–1:32:39).

2.2 "Documentary Gestures" and Questions of Authenticity in *Father of Lights*

Looking at the culminating scenes of the film, in which Darren Wilson and his crew seem to be lost in Jerusalem and only through a combination of curious events are able to accomplish their goal of gaining access to the Islamic shrine on the Temple Mount known as the "Dome of the Rock", we can trace the way in

---

3 See Extended trailer: https://www.youtube.com/watch?v=bUFLWGAeaiU, min. 03:04

which the reality the film claims to represent is authenticated. These scenes' authenticity is not only underscored through a variety of "documentary gestures" (Ehmann, Farocki, and Pantenburg 2012) such as the use of a hand-held camera, many out-of-focus shots with a shaking camera, awkward camera angles, technical equipment and crew members visible on screen, etc., (*Father of Lights*, 1:15:10 ff.), but also, as we have seen, through the way the director himself appears in the film and on screen as both an all-knowing voice-over and as just another regular Christian who stumbles from one adventure into the next. Drawing on Paul Arthur's reflections on Michael Moore's film *Roger & Me* and "jargons of authenticity", it can be argued that this form of documentary aesthetics exhibits a sort of "negative mastery" (Arthur 1993, 129), a post-modern form of establishing documentary authenticity. Extending this analysis, Spence and Navarro (2010, 376) describe the production of authenticity in the genre Moore has helped to establish as follows: "In other words, [such documentaries] 'technical awkwardness' and 'feigned inadequacy' becomes the sign of unvarnished truth; their combination of ineptness and sincerity makes them seem credible". All of this contributes to the feeling that had we been there, "[w]e would have seen it for ourselves" (Spence and Navarro 2010, 369; see also Nichols 1991, 27–28).

However, a documentary like *Father of Lights*, documenting a 'religious reality' and instances of 'miraculous healing' that not everyone in the audience might accept as the profilmic reality to begin with, complicates such attempts to show it 'like it was' that are implied in this form of representation. The question of 'Would we actually have seen it for ourselves?' therefore highlights the centrality of the audience's attitude towards the film and the importance of a focus on its reception. Only if the film is watched in the context of a—in the words of Marie Gillespie (1995)—"devotional viewing", in which the audience shares (or is converted to sharing) the basic premises of the profilmic reality the film is trying to represent, the authenticity produced by Wilson's aesthetics of "negative mastery" (see Arthur 1993, 129) can be substantiated. It therefore becomes important to consider the reactions of the audience to the film, to which I will turn now.

2.3 The "Father of Lights"-Tour in 2012

As described in exemplary fashion in the vignette at the beginning of this chapter, the film *Father of Lights* is not only interesting as a contemporary religious media product, but also because it was part of a series of religious events in 2012 and 2013. It was distributed, marketed, and screened in a film-screening and worship setting during the "Father of Lights"-Tour, which took place from

July to September 2012 in over 40 churches and theatres in the USA, Australia, Canada and the UK (with an additional tour in South Africa in March 2013). Through a media and event ethnography of eight of these screenings in the USA, in combination with a survey questionnaire (handed out on paper and available online), the anthropologist Lydia M. Reynolds and I have attempted to address the three levels of analysis of documentary films as religious media that I have identified above: production, performance, and reception. Drawing on recent work in film and media reception studies (Staiger 2000, 2005; Austin 2007; Barker & Mathijs 2008; Plantinga 2009a), we set out to investigate the commercial, discursive, and social contexts of the circulation and consumption of such films, as well as the audiences' expectations and responses.

By not merely screening *Father of Lights* at these churches and theatres, but also making it the central piece of a religious event which included musical performances, speeches, worship, and prayer, Wanderlust Productions created a specific 'perceptual space' (see Mohn 2012), which was supposed to invoke and facilitate religious experiences and produce a religious reception of the documentary presented on these over forty nights between July and September 2012. The structure of the film-screening events can be observed by looking at the example of a screening on August 19, 2012, at the Paramount Theatre in Aurora, Illinois. The screenings at other stops of the tour followed a similar format, with some changes depending on the location, especially whether the event took place in a church building or not. In Aurora, the structure was as follows: 1. Worship and concert by Christian singer-songwriter Jake Hamilton; 2. Darren Wilson presents Wanderlust Productions, its different products, and the film *Father of Lights*; 3. Screening of *Father of Lights*; 4. Worship and preaching (with the Vineyard pastor Robby Dawkins); 5. Prayer and prayer groups; 6. Merchandise sale (in the entrance hall of the theatre). In the following section I will discuss some results from our study of the "Father of Lights" Tour.

2.4 Audience Responses to the "Father of Lights"-Tour

In addition to attending and observing eight of the evening screenings during the "Father of Lights"-Tour 2012, we distributed surveys on paper after the end of the events. They were designed to evaluate the audience response to the film *Father of Lights* and the events organized by Wanderlust Productions. We compiled the questions with reference to the surveys used by Margaret M. Poloma and John C. Green (2010) in a study of the revitalization of American Pentecostalism and the questionnaire used by Thomas Austin (2007) in his study of the reception of recent documentary films by British cinema audiences.

While a detailed evaluation of the results of our study cannot be presented here, a short sketch of some of the results of the analysis will be highlighted below. Following the field study during the US-leg of the "Father of Lights"-Tour in 2012, Lydia M. Reynolds has continued to do fieldwork at one of the tour spots to evaluate the lasting effects and continuing use of the film in the charismatic-Christian revival culture in Urbana, Illinois. I want to highlight three aspects of our results: a) a (preliminary) typology of reactions to the truth claims of the film; b) reports of healing experiences in connection with watching the film; c) the use of the film as an evangelistic tool.

2.4.1 A Typology of Audience Trust in the Film

Asked if he trusts the film to tell the truth, one respondent to the survey wrote that "[g]iven that it was a documentary the story is not someone's imagination of what might happen or what could happen, but what actually happened to people as they connect with God" (survey results 2012). In taking a closer look at some of the answers in which respondents affirm their trust in the film, an interesting pattern emerges regarding the reasons the audience members give for their trust in the veracity of the film. These can be organized in the following typology (all answers to the question "Do you trust this film to tell the truth? Please give reasons for your answer"):

1. A resort to their *previous experiences:* e. g., "I have seen God's miracles and seen the people healed, I have witness [*sic!*] God's love and his provision... To me this film is a reflection of the reality I already walk in..." / "Yes because I've seen some of those miracles happen before in real life, I know Jesus works in those ways [...]" (survey results 2012).

2. A resort to the *authority of the filmmaker* as well as the *'celebrities' speaking with authority* in the interviews presented in the film: e. g., "Yes. Darren is very relatable and his humility shines throughout the movie. The credibility of some of the most well-known pastors around the world adds to this" (survey results 2012).

3. A resort to a *'spiritual evaluation' of the veracity of the film's claims:* e. g., "Also this might sound weird but in my spirit I could see what was happening... If it was fake I could see it... I don't know how to explain it..." (survey results 2012).

While the first two types of responses to this question probably are to be expected (resort to *experience* and to *authority*), the third type (resort to a *'spiritual evaluation'*) points to a more surprising religious reception strategy. The audience's acceptance of the film's status as a documentary and the trust in its claims to a truthful representation of reality are not only based on strategies of evaluation that could apply to any non-fictional film, e. g., in a television context, but rather, in the setting of the "Father of Lights"-Tour, a strategy of "devotional viewing" (Gillespie 1995) becomes apparent. A more detailed evaluation of our data will show whether or not this third type of answer to this question is as common as indicated by the analysis presented here.

2.4.2 Testimonies of Healing
Our study of the audience response to *Father of Lights* also includes the testimonies and reactions to the film and the film-screening tour that can be found online on the website of Wanderlust productions (www.wpfilm.com) as well as on other portals like youtube.com and social networks like facebook.com. One audience member, for example, reports the following experience on the company's website:

> My father has been suffering from a heart condition for roughly 20 years. [...] I had discovered the films 'Finger of God' and 'Furious Love' during this tough time of thought process and decision making. I found out that the newest film 'Father of Lights' was being shown in Nashville, Tn [...] and decided I had to go and see it. [...] WOW what an awesome time of worship!! I drove home and had my parents watch the film that night. These three films strengthened my faith and I knew anything was possible. My dad went to the doctor a week ago and well his heart function is normal and he needs no surgery!! (father-oflights.wpfilm.com/testimonies/)

This sort of reaction is common and can be found not only online but also in our survey data, indicating that in the charismatic-Christian culture in which most of the screenings of the "Father of Lights"-Tour took place, the documentary is thought to function as a facilitator of healing experiences. Some Christians connect an experience of healing with attending a screening of the film and testify to having such experiences in a variety of ways.

Similarly, on the social network facebook.com, the production company posted a testimony from another screening, this time reporting on a healing experience as well as a conversion connected with the film: "How's this for a testimony: someone attending the FOL tour here in Chicago was healed of scoliosis afterwards. They bought the movie, took it home, and showed it to their friend, who then accepted Jesus!" (www.facebook.com/fatheroflights, September 11, 2012). Interestingly, in the comments to this testimony we find the audience member referred to responding herself, indicating the effect the film had on her: "[Name] that was me!! I had scoliosis since I was in 6th grade and a stress fracture for a year and God healed them both!! and God totally rocked my friends heart with the video! Glory to God!! So blessed and so humbled! We are loved by a LOVING father!!" (www.facebook.com/fatheroflights, September 11, 2012)

These reported experiences and testimonies draw attention to the way in which the (mainly Christian) audience of the "Father of Lights"-Tour interacted with and responded to the screenings of the film. As is common for the evangelical and charismatic-Christian culture in which most of the screenings took place, the responses to the perceived power of the message of the film, and the experiences of watching the video are integrated into testimonies of God's miraculous working. In this way, the audience members can themselves take part in the realities represented on-screen in the film.

2.4.3 The Continuing Use of the Film as an Evangelistic Tool

Through the continuing fieldwork done by my colleague Lydia M. Reynolds among a charismatic-Christian college youth group at one of the tour stops in Urbana, Illinois, since 2012, it becomes possible to observe how *Father of Lights* is still being talked about and referred to in this community, and is regularly used as an evangelistic tool.

One testimony given during one of the college group's meetings can illustrate this continuing influence of the film. At one of the meetings Brian, a member of the youth group, told the story of how, after praying for healing for a group of teenagers at a store, the same teenagers showed up on his doorstep later in the night to ask for additional explanations. After telling them what he and the college youth group are doing in their attempt to heal people on the streets, Brian ended up talking to them most of the night and also decided to show them *Father of Lights*. When asked about why he used the film in this way, Brian responded that he and his family have been showing *Father of Lights* a lot recently, and that they are deeply identifying with the film and the people in it.

This story told in one of the college youth group's weekly meetings, as well as similar uses of the film which we have observed, hints at the way in which the documentary film discussed in this chapter is becoming an important tool of conveying a certain form of Christian experience in the charismatic-Christian communities that have come in contact with the films of Wanderlust Productions. We hope that through further analysis of the data we have collected we will be able to present a detailed case study on the importance of religious documentary films and the aesthetics of the non-fictional in the contemporary charismatic-Christian culture in the USA.

3 Religion as Mediation, the Aesthetics of the Non-Fictional, and the Production of the Religious Real

Birgit Meyer and Jojada Verrips have recently suggested "an understanding of religion as a practice of mediation [...] to which media are intrinsic" (Meyer and Verrips 2008, 25). This perspective builds on earlier reflections by Hent De Vries (2001) and Jeremy Stolow (2005) and has been further developed by Meyer in later publications (2008, 2011). Drawing on this perspective, it can be argued that in the same way that traditional religious media (e. g., books and images) became central to religious mediation practices in the past, under certain conditions specific new media like photographs or film can function as "sensational forms" (Meyer 2008) for invoking (and even 'producing') a transcendent sphere. In her work on Ghanaian video film culture, Meyer (2002, 2004, 2005) has examined how in the context of Ghanaian Pentecostal Christianity, fictional video films have become established as a "medium of revelation" (Meyer 2010, 125) that is central to establishing and transmitting "pentecostal views" (Meyer 2005). Others have also drawn attention to the importance of audio-visual media (Birman and Lehmann 1999; De Witte 2003; Asamoah-Gyadu 2005; Hirschkind 2006; Schulz 2012) and especially film (Krings 2005; Hughes and Meyer 2005; van de Port 2006) in contemporary religious mediations. Such media are therefore not antithetic to religious experience but rather can become "authorized to be suitable harbingers of immediate, authentic experiences" (Meyer 2008, 712). In this way, new media contribute to the production of the 'religious real'.

In these recent debates on religion and audio-visual media, scholars have, however, only rarely focused on documentary film (see Krüger 2012, 247–249). At the same time, a particular concern with questions of 'representation' and 'reality' has always occupied theoreticians of documentary (see, e. g., Nichols 1991; Corner 1996; Plantinga 1997; Cowie 2011), which makes an engagement with these issues interesting for the study of religion. Additionally, as we have seen above, the religious use of documentary film complicates documentary's production of and relation to the reality it seeks to represent, questions the nature of 'representation' through claims to documenting the 'supernatural', and highlights the importance of the actual response of audiences embedded in aesthetic communities, once more drawing attention to the question of 'when the documentary is' (see Eitzen 1995).

In his classic definition of "religion as a cultural system", Clifford Geertz (1973, 90) attributes to religion the creation of an "aura of facticity" around its conceptions of the order of existence. Likewise, he describes the "religious perspective" as one that—unlike art, which disengages from "the whole question of factuality"—"deepens the concern with fact and seeks to create an aura of utter actuality" (Geertz 1973, 112). This preoccupation with the creation of "the 'really real'" (Geertz 1973, 112), which the Geertzian definition of religion entails, is strikingly similar to the concerns that already for decades have been controversially debated by scholars of documentary film. Since John Grierson (1933, 8) had famously defined documentary as "the creative treatment of actuality" in the early 20th century, the 'documentary characteristics' of audio-visual media have been highly contested. Current accounts of these issues vary from perceptual realist (Currie 1996), to post-structuralist (Renov 1993), to instrumentalist (Plantinga 1996), to subjectivist (Eitzen 1995) approaches (for a recent overview see Plantinga 2009b). At stake in these debates are not only distinctions between fictional and non-fictional uses of audio-visual media, but also the question of representation as such, as well as the issue of how such media generate their 'reality effects'. Louise Spence and Vinicius Navarro, for example, in their recent book *Crafting Truth* have tried to describe "markers of authenticity" that establish an audio-visual recording as "documentary" (2011, 31). Dirk Eitzen (1995), on the other hand, already suggested twenty years ago that we should understand the documentary as a "mode of reception" rather than as a characteristic of certain audio-visual recordings, and therefore posed the question of "when" and not "what" the documentary is.

In regard to these questions, recent theoretical thinking on documentary is characterised by a 'turn to the audience'. While the question of audience reception has always been an important issue for theoreticians of documentary, Brian Winston in his introduction to the comprehensive *Documentary Film Book* has recently focused particularly on the relation between film and audience. This leads him to claim that documentary's capacity for 'representation' has always already relied on an audience's reception: "[documentary's] claim on truth cannot ever be guaranteed by the image alone; it requires audience testing of its authenticity against experience—in reality, or on the basis of other information. Never mind naivety; the claim on the real depends on the audience's prior knowledge and experience of the real" (2013, 10). Winston therefore proposes a revised description of documentary as "the narrativized recorded aspects of witnessed observation received as being a story about the world" (2013, 24), suggesting this formulation as a replacement for Grierson's "creative treatment of actuality".

For the study of religion these debates about representation provide fresh material for a rethinking of theoretical approaches to religion, particularly from an aesthetic perspective. The short investigation of the engagement of a particular audience with a religious documentary film, as presented in the case study above, has highlighted the centrality of "the audience's prior knowledge and experience of the real" (Winston 2013, 10)—in this case of a particular 'religious real'—and the importance of a "devotional viewing" for the reception of *Father of Lights* as a documentary. While a more detailed exploration of these topics cannot be presented here, it becomes apparent that a contrastive reading of theories of documentary film and theories of religion promises to be fruitful for both theoretical discourses.

4. Conclusion

This chapter has attempted to provide some insight into the use of the medium of documentary film in contemporary religion, drawing on a case study of the film *Father of Lights* and the accompanying film-screening tour organized by Wanderlust Productions in 2012. An 'aesthetic perspective' on religion makes it possible to recognize the importance of media in religion (see Meyer and Verrips 2008, 25) and to extend the range of sources studied, but it also allows us to make sure that the contemporary proliferation of religious media products is studied on all three levels of analysis: the media products themselves, their performance and presentation, and their audience reception. Such an analysis of how religious actors create 'panoramas of perception' and establish specific "perceptual spaces" (Mohn 2012) should particularly be concerned—as I have argued above—with the ways in which they draw on the discourse and aesthetics of the 'non-fictional' in their engagement with audio-visual media.

In a cultural context in which "reality television" and other TV shows which draw on the aesthetics of the "non-fictional"—no matter how staged such programmes actually are or not—have become highly successful and influential (see Biressi and Nunn 2005; Hill 2005), a Christian documentary film like *Father of Lights* is able to carve out a special niche and accomplish what the often low-budget Christian fiction films of the past have not been able to achieve in their competition with large-budget Hollywood productions. In contrast to these fiction films it is to the advantage of Christian documentaries like *Father of Lights* that their effectiveness and perceived authenticity are not diminished but rather heightened by their at times seemingly amateurish production value, and that they thus apparently succeed in becoming effective tools for evoking the religious experiences aimed at by their producers.

As a "discourse of sobriety" (Nichols 1991, 3–4), documentary films present differing "views of the world" (Nichols 1991, ix), creating perceptual spaces that can be engaged with as describing reality and telling the truth. In doing so, they rely on presenting their "relation to the real as direct, immediate, transparent" (Nichols 1991, 4). At the same time, however, the film analysed in this chapter employs the discourse of documentary in a context which is itself often concerned with establishing the reality of "the 'really real'" (Geertz 1973, 112). In their 'reality production', as Birgit Meyer (2008) and others (e.g., De Vries 2001) have claimed, religions have always relied on media. It is therefore important to evaluate how these 'reality productions' are negotiated and how religious usage affects the discourse of documentary, just as the use of documentary, as a 'discourse of sobriety', affects religion. As I have tried to establish, making use of the aesthetics of the non-fictional seems to be an especially powerful form of making religion "effective". Borrowing from Birgit Meyer (2008, 711), we could also say that in Wanderlust Productions' trilogy of films "audiovisual technologies [are] mobilized for the sake of revelation". In drawing attention to a film genre often considered to be primarily concerned with 'representations of reality', it can be shown how 'the documentary' is used as a 'medium of revelation' in contemporary religion and how filmmakers draw on this common understanding of documentary as a medium of 'the real' in attempting to present audio-visual evidence of the divine, of the miraculous workings of God.

Bibliography

Arthur, Paul. 1993. "Jargons of Authenticity (Three American Moments)." In *Theorizing Documentary*, edited by Michael Renov, 108–134. New York: Routledge.

Asamoah-Gyadu, J. Kwabena. 2005. "Anointing through the Screen: Neo-Pentecostalism and Televised Christianity in Ghana." *Studies in World Christianity* 11/1: 9–28.

Austin, Thomas. 2007. *Watching the World: Screen Documentary and Audiences*. Manchester: Manchester University Press.

Barker, Martin, and Ernest Mathijs, eds. 2008. *Watching the Lord of the Rings: Tolkien's World Audiences*. New York: Peter Lang.

Biressi, Anita, and Heather Nunn. 2005. *Reality TV: Realism and Revelation*. New York: Columbia University Press.

Birman, Patricia, and David Lehmann. 1999. "Religion and the Media in a Battle for Ideological Hegemony: the Universal Church of the Kingdom of God and TV Globo in Brazil." *Bulletin of Latin American Research* 18/2: 145–164.

Cancik, Hubert, and Hubert Mohr. 1988. "Religionsästhetik." In *Handbuch religionswissenschaftlicher Grundbegriffe*. Vol. 1, edited by Hubert Cancik, Burkhard Gladigow, and Matthias Laubscher, 121–156. Stuttgart: Kohlhammer.

Carroll, Noël. 1996a. "Nonfiction Film and Postmodernist Skepticism." In *Post-Theory: Reconstructing Film Studies*, edited by David Bordwell and Noël Carroll, 283–306. Madison: University of Wisconsin Press.

—— 1996b. *Theorizing the Moving Image*. Cambridge: Cambridge University Press.

Corner, John. 1996. *The Art of Record: A Critical Introduction to Documentary*. Manchester: Manchester University Press.

Cowie, Elizabeth. 2011. *Recording Reality, Desiring the Real*. Minneapolis: University of Minnesota Press.

Currie, Gregory. 1996. "Film, Reality, and Illusion." In *Post-Theory: Reconstructing Film Studies*, edited by David Bordwell and Noël Carroll, 325–344. Madison: University of Wisconsin Press.

De Vries, Hent. 2001. "In Media Res: Global Religion, Public Spheres, and the Task of Contemporary Comparative Religious Studies." In *Religion and Media*, edited by Samuel Weber and Hent De Vries, 3–42. Stanford: Stanford University Press.

De Witte, Marleen. 2003. "Altar Media's 'Living Word': Televised Charismatic Christianity in Ghana." *Journal of Religion in Africa* 33/2: 172–202.

Ehmann, Antje, Harun Farocki, and Volker Pantenburg. 2012. "Control and Contingency." In *Berlin Documentary Forum 2*, edited by Cordula Daus, Hila Peleg, Bert Rebhandl, and Vera Tollmann, 12–17. Berlin: Haus der Kulturen der Welt.

Eitzen, Dirk. 1995. "When Is a Documentary? Documentary as a Mode of Reception." *Cinema Journal* 35/1: 81–102.

Geertz, Clifford. 1973. "Religion as a Cultural System." In *The Interpretation of Cultures: Selected Essays*, 87–125. New York: Basic Books.

Gillespie, Marie. 1995. "Sacred Serials, Devotional Viewing, and Domestic Worship: A Case-Study in the Interpretation of Two TV Versions of the Mahabharata in a Hindu Family in West London." In *To be Continued...: Soap Operas Around the World*, edited by Robert C. Allen, 354–380. London: Routledge.

Grierson, John. 1933. "The Documentary Producer." *Cinema Quarterly* 2/1: 7–9.

Hill, Annette. 2005. *Reality TV: Audiences and Popular Factual Television*. London: Routledge.

Hirschkind, Charles. 2006. *The Ethical Soundscape: Cassette Sermons and Islamic Counterpublics*. New York: Columbia University Press.

Hughes, Stephen, and Birgit Meyer. 2005. "Introduction: Mediating Religion and Film in a Post-Secular World." *Postscripts* 1/2–3: 149–153.

Kellner, Douglas. 2013. "On Truth, Objectivity, and Partisanship: The Case of Michael Moore." In *The Documentary Film Book*, edited by Brian Winston, 59–67. Basingstoke: Palgrave Macmillan.

Krings, Matthias. 2005. "Muslim Martyrs and Pagan Vampires: Popular Video Films and the Propagation of Religion in Northern Nigeria." *Postscripts* 1/2–3: 183–205.

Krüger, Oliver. 2012. *Die mediale Religion. Probleme und Perspektiven der religionswissenschaftlichen und wissenssoziologischen Medienforschung*. Bielefeld: Transcript.

Meyer, Birgit. 2002. "Occult Forces on Screen: Representation and the Danger of Mimesis in Popular Ghanaian Films." *Etnofoor* 15/1–2: 212–221.

—— 2004. "Praise the Lord: Popular Cinema and Pentecostalite Style in Ghana's New Public Sphere." *American Ethnologist* 31/1: 92–110.

—— 2005. "Religious Remediations: Pentecostal Views in Ghanaian Video-Movies." *Postscripts* 1/2–3: 155–181.

—— 2008. "Religious Sensations. Why Media, Aesthetics and Power Matter in the Study of Contemporary Religion" In *Religion: Beyond A Concept*, edited by Hent De Vries, 704–723. New York: Fordham University Press.

—— 2010. "'There Is a Spirit in that Image': Mass-Produced Jesus Pictures and Protestant-Pentecostal Animation in Ghana." *Comparative Studies in Society and History* 52/1: 100–130.

—— 2011. "Mediation and Immediacy: Sensational Forms, Semiotic Ideologies and the Question of the Medium." *Social Anthropology* 19/1: 23–39.

—— and Jojada Verrips. 2008. "Aesthetics." In *Key Words in Religion, Media and Culture*, edited by David Morgan, 20–30. New York: Routledge.

Mohn, Jürgen. 2012. "Wahrnehmung der Religion: Aspekte der komparativen Religionswissenschaft in religionsaisthetischer Perspektive." *Erwägen Wissen Ethik* 23/2: 241–254.

Mohr, Hubert. 2010. "Material Religion/Religious Aesthetics: A Research Program." *Material Religion. The Journal of Objects, Art and Belief* 6/2: 240–242.

Nichols, Bill. 1991. *Representing Reality: Issues and Concepts in Documentary*. Bloomington: Indiana University Press.

Plantinga, Carl R. 1996. "Moving Pictures and the Rhetoric of Nonfiction: Two Approaches." In *Post-Theory: Reconstructing Film Studies*, edited by David Bordwell and Noël Carroll, 307–324. Madison: University of Wisconsin Press.

—— 1997. *Rhetoric and Representation in Nonfiction Film*. Cambridge: Cambridge University Press.

—— 2009a. *Moving Viewers*. Berkeley: University of California Press.

—— 2009b. "Documentary." In *The Routledge Companion to Philosophy and Film*, edited by Paisley Livingston and Carl R. Plantinga, 494–504. London: Routledge.

Poloma, Margaret M., and John C. Green. 2010. *The Assemblies of God: Godly Love and the Revitalization of American Pentecostalism*. New York: New York University Press.

Renov, Michael. 1993. "Introduction: The Truth About Non-Fiction." In *Theorizing Documentary*, edited by Michael Renov, 1–11. New York: Routledge.

Schulz, Dorothea E. 2012. *Muslims and New Media in West Africa: Pathways to God*. Bloomington: Indiana University Press.

Spence, Louise, and Vinicius Navarro. 2010. "Working-Class Hero: Michael Moore's Authorial Voice and Person." *The Journal of Popular Culture* 43/2: 368–380.

—— 2011. *Crafting Truth: Documentary Form and Meaning*. New Brunswick: Rutgers University Press.

Staiger, Janet. 2000. *Perverse Spectators: The Practices of Film Reception*. New York: New York University Press.

Staiger, Janet. 2005. *Media Reception Studies*. New York: New York University Press.

Stolow, Jeremy. 2005. "Religion and/as Media." *Theory, Culture & Society* 22/4: 119–145.

van de Port, Mattijs. 2006. "Visualizing the Sacred: Video Technology, 'Televisual' Style, and the Religious Imagination in Bahian Candomblé." *American Ethnologist* 33/3: 444–461.

Wilke, Anette. 2008. "Religion/en, Sinne und Medien: Forschungsfeld Religionsästhetik und das Museum of World Religions (Taipeh)." In *Im "Netz des Indra": Das Museum of World Religions, sein buddhistisches Dialogkonzept und die neue Disziplin Religionsästhetik*, edited by Anette Wilke and Esther-Maria Guggenmos, 205–295. Münster: LIT.

Winston, Brian. 2013. "Introduction: The Documentary Film." In *The Documentary Film Book*, edited by Brian Winston, 1–29. Basingstoke: Palgrave Macmillan.

Films

Finger of God. 2007. Directed by Darren Wilson. Wanderlust Productions.
Furious Love. 2010. Directed by Darren Wilson, Wanderlust Productions.
Father of Lights. 2012. Directed by Darren Wilson, Wanderlust Productions.
Holy Ghost. 2014. Directed by Darren Wilson, Wanderlust Productions.

Laura Feldt
The Literary Aesthetics of Religious Narratives: Probing Literary-Aesthetic Form, Emotion, and Sensory Effects in Exodus 7–11

1 Introduction: The Aesthetics of Religion and Literary Form

Media—understood in a broad sense—play important roles in forms of emotional and sensory practice. Understanding religion as a multi-facetted cultural phenomenon, which involves aesthetic mediations (Grieser 2015), means that religious phenomena must be analysed in their aesthetic forms and contexts, and so religious media cannot be used merely as windows to religious representations. The aesthetic form and context in which religious representations are embedded are crucial for how they are understood and used—from large rituals and processions to sermons, myths, songs, and individualized practices relating to objects or stories. In spite of these rather obvious facts, aesthetic analyses of written, religious narratives are quite rare in the general study of religion.[1] There has been surprisingly little outright theoretical reflection on the *literary-aesthetic form* of religious texts (Feldt 2011b), even if much of the traditional material is basically literary—think of Mesopotamian, Greek, Roman, Hindu, Old English, Islamic, etc., materials. This article argues that if we wish to understand how religion becomes effective in religious identity formation, analyses of how the literary-aesthetic form of written, religious narratives stimulates and affects senses, emotions, and cognition are crucial. In written religious narratives, emotional stimuli and emotion management are arguably important for understanding how religious representations are maintained as salient and significant from generation to generation, or transmitted to new members.

---

1 Of course various area-studies that belong to the study of religion, such as Hebrew Bible studies, have undertaken literary or stylistic study, but these literary studies have not to a great extent been brought back to interact with the general study of religion, nor has there been a great emphasis on emotional and sensual impact, as in an aesthetic analysis.

https://doi.org/10.1515/9783110461015-006

2 Why Literary Narratives? Emotional Practices and Religious Identity Formation

The aesthetics of religion is a perspective which can make a substantial new contribution to the study of religious texts, which can potentially free the study of religious texts from problems of theologising, i.e., the problem that may arise when scholars of religion focus on the religious representations severed from the aesthetic form, and assume that religious texts embed (more or less) consistent theologies or worldviews. This is problematic because lack of order and consistency seems to be more normal in religious narratives than consistency, and because they rarely express worldviews, which can be understood apart from genre and contexts of use. An analysis of the literary-aesthetic form of religious texts analyses the texts as media, which influence how religious representations are embedded in specific sensual, emotional, and cognitive forms and contexts, which influence their reception. The texts are thus not necessarily seen as sources for a religious system, and the analysis does not isolate context-free religious representations, but attempts to understand the aesthetic effects of written texts and assess their functions aesthetically. Often, the aesthetic form is seen as insignificant ornament from which the religious representations can be abstracted, and the sensual and emotional impact of written texts not analysed in depth.

Frequently religious texts are used in very specific ways, as windows to past religious experiences, or as sources to when and where Moses or Mohammad performed specific actions, or to their religious experiences. While religious texts of course embed religious representations, it is thus overlooked how their literary-aesthetic form stimulates emotional, sensual, and cognitive responses, and so have effects which might be important for understanding the religion in question (religious texts are rarely good historical source material), and the role of religious narrative in religion more broadly. One category that has often been used to tackle this terrain in the study of religion is that of "manifestation"; a term which has primarily been related to forms of religious experience in the phenomenology of religion, especially by Rudolf Otto (1936), Gerardus van der Leeuw ([1933] 1938²), and Mircea Eliade (1963). The perspective of the aesthetics of religion can be used to deal more appropriately with texts that tell of such "encounters" with supernatural others because the narratives about such fantastic encounters can be studied instead in terms of their literary-aesthetic mediality—how they stimulate, affect, and model experiences, emotions, and sensory responses. We cannot get to any *Erlebnisechtheit* of religious experience, for reli-

---

2 Reference quoted from Ryba (2000).

gious experience is culturally mediated experience, modelled on previous narrative expression and cultural practice. But we can analyse the aesthetic form and the aesthetic effects of different religious media; not as reflections of past religious experiences, but as flexible resources that enable multiple forms of religious engagement, as performative media modelling religious identity formation and aiding the maintenance of emotions and sensory response.

While written religious literature has been studied for information about a religion—its core ideas, tenets, practices, and its history—and the literary-aesthetic form has been left more out of sight, recent studies have made it clear that text hermeneutics is not adequate for analyses of sound, touch, or movement in religion, and some have also demonstrated the necessity of aesthetic analyses of the cultures of production and use of religious texts. Here, I argue that approaches focusing only on content and meaning are also not fully adequate for understanding the work of texts and how they engage their audiences and become effective. The aesthetics of religion offers new and vital perspectives on the literary-aesthetic form of religious narrative, which differs from classical understandings of style. Analyses of literary-aesthetic form, as part of how religious narratives stimulate varying responses, senses, and emotions, can throw new light on how religious texts become effective in the formation of religious identity. Emotional and sensual arousal and memory, which may intuitively seem to be physical, are in fact deeply socialized (Feldt 2011a). Senses and emotions play important roles in the formation of religious identity and are cultural practices situated in and composed of interdependent cognitive, somatic, and social components (Scheer 2012). Emotional and sensual arousal is always embedded in larger social frames, literary conventions, and cultural scripts.

As religious narratives are some of the primary means by which religions bridge the gap between generations and by which religious identity is negotiated and socialised, religious narrative is one of the fundamental mediating links between individual and collective religious identities (Feldt 2011a). Emotions clearly have cognitive and bodily foundations, and some degree of universality in our human patterns of emotional reaction can be reckoned with,[3] as researchers today agree that feelings are mental and bodily processes with common cognitive and somatic foundations. The basic emotions are universal and recognisable across the globe, and all emotions have a physical and bodily basis, and yet all emotions are verbalised, managed and practiced in historically and culturally

---

3 E.g., fear is one of our most basic emotions and tied to our survival instinct. In the natural sciences, research into the basic emotions is extensive. The American psychologist Paul Ekman reckons with six basic emotions: fear, disgust, anxiety, joy, surprise, and sadness, quoted by Keen (2011, 6).

variable ways. With many other scholars, we may distinguish between affect as a bodily response and emotion as the verbalised reaction.[4] As Monique Scheer and others have pointed out, emotions as bodily responses are always understood in an interplay with a verbalised or narrated form (Scheer 2012; Simecek 2015, 497–500). In and through stories and narrative framings, affects become emotions, we make sense of those emotions, and through narrative we access the emotions of others, that is, the cultural framings of experiences of others.

Ancient myths and religious texts are often complex literary works, and here, I work from the assumption that verbalised emotions can be studied historically as sources for key emotional practices in a religious culture, just as narratives can stimulate emotional responses and affects. Indeed, we might say that in any situation in which there is uncertainty and suspense—that is, in any narrative situation—emotional reactions play a part (Keen 2011, 5).[5] For these reasons, aesthetic analysis of religious narratives is vital. Aesthetic analysis of literary-religious texts involves not only the materiality of religious texts and their cultures of production, circulation, and use (e. g., Clark 2007; Stolow 2007; Hofmeyr 2008; Meyer and Verrips 2008, 28; Myrvold 2010), although these are natural arenas for aesthetic studies of religious texts. This essay argues that the form of religious texts has aesthetic effects too. Since the literary-aesthetic forms of religious texts vary greatly, it should, accordingly, not surprise us that media form impacts how religious texts become effective in differing ways. This essay will argue that literary-aesthetic form used in religious literature requires more investigation with respect to how specific senses, emotions, and reactions are stimulated in the reception process.

Aiming to discuss and to contribute to a broader aesthetic approach to religion and positing that analyses of the aesthetic form of religious narratives are ultimately crucial for understanding how they become effective, I focus on one example of literary-religious aesthetics from the Hebrew Bible, namely Exodus 7–11. I hope to bring out some of the ways in which the specific literary-aesthetic form of this influential narrative is of decisive importance for understanding how it becomes effective and to point to areas in which aesthetics may indeed be used as a connective concept between content and form-related questions and between text/mind and the body/senses. The aim of the essay is to demonstrate

---

4 Scholars disagree as to whether feelings, emotions, and affect are the same thing. Here, I use feelings and emotions as synonyms for the verbalised reaction, and affect for the bodily reaction. Suzanne Keen suggests that narratives elicit aesthetic emotions, not as discrete things bearing labels such as joy, sorrow, hope or hate, but as unifying and moving *forces* in time, pointing to the interconnectedness of emotions and narrative (Keen 2011, 1–53).
5 With reference to the American philosopher John Dewey.

the value of analyses of the literary aesthetics of religious texts for historians of religion. Not only the phenomenological content of myths and their historical source value should be of interest, but also their uses as aesthetic media with particular effects on their recipients in terms of emotional practices and religious identity formation.

3 The Aesthetic Form of Religious Narratives

We may describe religious narratives broadly perceived—i.e., myths, stories of miracles, marvels, etc., epics, legends—as texts which feature superhuman, counterintuitive, or transempirical, actors, events, actions, and spaces.[6] Religious narratives communicate about gods, demons, angels, miracles, magic, prophecies, enchanted forests, heaven, etc. (cf. Gilhus and Mikaelsson 2001, 102–120). My focus is here on religious narratives which embed—using a term from the cognitive science of religion—counterintuitive representations.[7] In order to analyse the literary-aesthetic form of religious narratives embedding counterintuitive representations, I here use terminology adapted from literary studies of the fantastic.[8] The literary genre theories of the fantastic are used to formulate a strategy of analysis for religious narratives with fantastic elements, whether they are persons/actors like deities, monsters, or saints, events or actions like miracles or magic, spaces like enchanted forests, heaven, or purgatory, or things like magical objects or relics (see Feldt 2012). Indeed, it can be used as a perspective for the analysis of the aesthetic form of all kinds of narratives which communicate about counterintuitive, superhuman, or fantastic actors, events, actions, spaces, and things, in combination with theories of emotion and cognition.

In such an analysis, it is necessary both to identify the counterintuitive elements of the texts and analyse their literary-aesthetic form in order to assess

---

6 As a minimum. For a more detailed discussion of the literary affordances of religious narratives, on which the present discussion draws, see Feldt (2016).
7 For the cognitive background, see Hirschfeld and Gelman (1994); for its use in the study of religion, see e.g., Pyysiäinen (2004).
8 Although mainly known as currently popular genres, fantasy literature and the fantastic are also sites of literary-theoretical reflections on the aesthetic form of these genres (Lachmann 2002; Jackson 1981; Todorov 1975). With some theorists of the fantastic and fantasy (Lachmann 2002; Hume 1984), I understand the fantastic as a broad literary mode of narration which presents alterity, that is, the impossible, the contra-factual and the unreal, in literature, and which uses ambiguity programmatically (Lachmann 2002, 8–25). It is a large and complex field; for more detailed discussions, see Feldt (2012).

their impact on the recipients. Such elements may be presented in varying ways —the status of the elements may be presented as clear or as contested in the text, as matter-of-fact or hallucinatory, as evoking belief, trust, or consolation, or as evoking doubt, hesitation, and ambiguity, or fear and horror. Then, an assessment of the sensual and emotional impact and functions can be made. Characteristic of the aesthetic form of the fantastic *per se* is a presentation of the counterintuitive elements which emphasizes the oscillation between categories—real and unreal, known and strange, self and other, truth and lie, good and evil (Lachmann 2002, 36–38). The aesthetic form of the fantastic emphasizes ambiguity and enigma (Lachmann 2002, 155). Not all religious texts present the superhuman elements in an aesthetically "fantastic" way. Importantly, however, this perspective throws light on how different the literary-narrative framing of counter-intuitive representations can be, and allows us to also analyse superhuman elements which are represented as factual events, or as sensorially dull or emotionally flat. The aesthetic form of the fantastic emphasizes transgressions of the boundaries of intuitive cognitive domains, ambiguity concerning the status of the fantastic elements, affects and emotional stimuli of fear, horror, disorientation, hesitation, and confusion. This aesthetic form features interesting elements because it stimulates other sensory responses than we usually attribute to *religious* literature, such as belief, trust, consolation, orientation, foundation, and meaning. Instead, a fantastic presentation of counterintuitive representations may stimulate sensory responses, which resemble those of horror-fantasy: fear, confusion, disorientation, and an atmosphere of mystery which stimulates the recipients' fascination and desire to solve the riddles ("detectivism," see Feldt 2012). Theories of the fantastic may thus assist us in analyses of the aesthetic form of religious narratives and how they create sensations by playing on emotions, anxieties, bodily reactions, and by using fascination techniques.

Often in studies of religious narrative, the focus is on the world structure or on belief in the reality of the narrated events and beings. A.K. Petersen has suggested that religious texts are unique, compared to other text types—because they posit a world divided into two domains, where the supernatural actors inhabit a sphere differing from everyday reality (Petersen 2005). To be sure, religious texts often do posit separate otherworlds inhabited by superhuman beings, which influence the human or everyday world, but as we are witnessing new forms of religion today in which the construction of an "other", transcendent sphere does not seem to be all that significant (Bruce 2011, 102–103; Taylor 2010), this aspect seems not be decisive in terms of what makes religious narratives effective. Other scholars have suggested that religious narratives are special in that they insist that their phantasms are 'real' or 'true'—what we could call a transgression of the purely verbal or literary area. Religious narratives often feature some markers of a transgression of the text-internal world, for instance in remarks which suggest that the superhuman actors or the transempirical events really exist/have existed, or are otherwise "believed" by the recipients. But while the attempt to create an overlap between text-internal world and the recipient or text-external world is indeed very often important in religious texts, it cannot be considered decisive (Feldt 2016, 2006), for religious narratives also abound which carry no such explicit markers.[9] The attempt to transgress the verbal area may indeed hold for 'religion', but it does not always hold for 'religious texts'. For some myths do not attempt to create an overlap with the text-external world by means of *deixis* or ritual prescriptions,[10] although an overlap can then be created in the community of interpretation, in ritual usage and/or institutional anchorage.

Key aspects of what makes religious narratives effective do not primarily relate to the belief in the reality of the narrated events, but rather, I suggest, to emotional and somatic involvement. The relation, in religious texts, between the narrated events or content and the authors or redactors varies from channelling, witnessing, to a visionary or imaginative relationship. Some religious texts do not even bring up the question of the relations to the text-external world; as mentioned above, fictionality is not always a problem for religions.[11] Indeed, I suggest that the aesthetic form of religious texts and the sensory and emotional stimuli provided—via its aesthetic form, as well as via its usage—are often more important than its propositional content or reality status. In the following, I analyse the aesthetic form of a text, which is *fantastic* and which attempts to transgress the verbal area and stimulate particular types of sensory and emotional responses from its recipients.

---

9 According to Petersen (2005, 17), this is one of the criteria of distinction for religious texts. However, some types of fantastic literature and fantasy present themselves as factual narrations, cf. Horace Walpole and Todorov ([1973] 1975, 27–28). According to literary scholar Renate Lachmann, part of the semantic work of fantastic literature consists precisely in an attempt to transgress the verbal area (Lachmann 2002, 137), to enter the text-external world of the recipient and make the recipient wonder whether the events of the text have actually taken place or not (Lachmann 2002). Please note here my overlapping discussion in relation to contemporary fantasy fiction in Feldt (2016).
10 One example could be the Old-Babylonian myth *Lugale* or Ninurta's Exploits.
11 See here also the argument and discussion in Feldt (2012, 242–254).

4 The Exodus Narrative as a Case Study

The Exodus narrative's importance as the narrative traditions[12] about the origins of the biblical group of "Israel", and of its religion and institutions, is undisputed in Judaism. Key strands of both biblical and Jewish tradition attest that the narrative of the Exodus is decisive for the identity and self-understanding of the collective of "Israel". Yet, the Exodus narrative's aesthetic form is peculiar and striking: we find in this text all the major fantastic, strange, and supernatural occurrences of the Hebrew Bible (Feldt 2012). In spite of this, previous literary-aesthetic analyses of the fantastic elements of the Exodus myth are surprisingly few. The 'supernatural' or fantastic elements are scarcely mentioned in previous literary or stylistic analyses, such as Gunn (1982); Fokkelman (1987); Pardes (2000)—but see Miscall (1992). The presence of these elements has been noted but treated in little detail, and they are often understood as mere ornament, entertainment, or as primitive elements.[13] The literary-aesthetic of the written form of the myth is regarded with some uneasiness, if not hostility, especially towards the 'incredible' elements, in biblical scholarship (Wyatt 2001, 4; Feldt 2012, 20 – 42). Indeed, the literary-aesthetic form of the narrative is remarkable. The interplay between an abundant use of counterintuitive representations and the literary stimulation of emotions shows, I argue, that we also need to discuss and analyse written texts aesthetically, in terms of sensual and emotional stimulation.

---

12 Historical-critical research has demonstrated that the book of Exodus consists of multiple traditions interwoven by one or more redactors; see here Propp (1997), Vervenne (1996) for extensive discussions.

13 Sometimes researchers paraphrase the superhuman elements naturalistically, as when the transformation of the Nile from water to blood by Moses and Aaron is explained by the natural appearance of red dust particles in the water, or they ascribe them to the storyteller's 'inventiveness' and 'exaggeration', and therefore see them as inconsequential ornament, and/or borrowed from the ancient Near Eastern literary tradition and accordingly inauthentic to the bible (as in van Seters 1994, 15 – 16, 33 – 34, 136 – 139). Sometimes, they are understood as expressions of (belief in) supernatural intervention into 'history,' as Yahweh's 'salvation history', and as 'demonstrating divine presence' (as in Durham 1987; Houtman 1996). Historical-critical analyses distribute the fantastic elements among the different "source" traditions (the Priestly source, the Deuteronomist, the Elohist, the Yahwist, and their hypothetical redactors, etc.) (as in Römer 2003). Contrariwise, my aim here is to show that the literary-aesthetic form of the narrative is a necessary object of analysis if we want to understand how this text becomes effective, as well as for broader discussions of how religious narratives function. A more detailed analysis of these trends in exegesis can be found in Feldt (2012).

4.1 Marvels, Magic, and Mystery in Exodus 7–11[14]

In the Exodus narrative, the counterintuitive elements are presented in an ambiguous manner and with substantial text-internal reflection on the nature, meaning, and veracity of these elements. A specific literary-aesthetic form is used which stimulates a particular sensory and emotional response in the intended recipient. The great number of fantastic elements and uncertain counterintuitive events should thus not be reduced or deemed inauthentic, for it has significant effects. I hope to show that it does not suffice to read the narrative's fantastic elements solely as materials for a cognitive analysis of counterintuitive representations, a system of beliefs, or as a celebration of the deity's great deeds, even though they have, in the latter case, previously been interpreted accordingly— as supports of the symbolic order, as it were. An aesthetic analysis shows that the literary-narrative aesthetics of the fantastic elements stimulate doubt, fear, and uncertainty. Moreover, the literary-narrative embedding of the counterintuitive representations have consequences in terms of bodily affect and emotional stimulation. A fascination with distinctions—revelation and disguise, trust and distrust, belief and doubt, fantasy and reality—dominates the narrative and elicits uncertainty and hesitation in the recipients.

The section of the Exodus narrative that I have selected for analysis here is also known as "the plagues narrative". It abounds in ambiguous and complex passages that have supported interpretations of the text as composite, and this is the view of the majority of scholars (see Feldt 2012, 20–42, for discussion of the views).[15] However, if we analyse the text's literary-aesthetic form, what is seen as compositeness from one perspective has important aesthetic effects. The interplay between repetition and variation, the complexity and ambiguity, the mounting severity, and higher degrees of excess in the plagues (Propp 1999, 315, 317–318; Fischer 1996, 165–169) stimulate sensory and emotional responses.[16] In Exod. 7:1–5, Yahweh is represented as giving a speech about the

---

14 The following analysis depends in large part on my more detailed analyses of fantastic elements in the Exodus narrative in my monograph (Feldt 2012, 77–101). While there are many overlaps, the previous analysis, however, did not focus on the aesthetics of religion as a connective concept, emotional practices, or the senses.

15 Houtman, with others, acknowledges that the narrative draws on heterogenous material, but focuses on its current unity and finds that exact analysis into literary strands is not possible (Houtman 1996, 17). Van Seters finds that it is impossible to reconstruct independent P and J documents (van Seters 1995, 579–580). More details in Feldt (2012).

16 The exact number of plagues is much discussed. The number ten appears in Jub. 48:7, and tradition (partly based on Ps. 105) considers blood the first plague and the slaying of the first-born the last, and this finds some support in Exod. 11:1, "one more plague" (this makes the death

multiplicity of his signs and wonders, i.e., about the fact that there are so many counterintuitive events. Here, it is explicitly stated that the great number is Yahweh's deliberate intention, which can certainly be read as a signal of text-internal reflection on the text's complexity.[17] The aesthetic form should not be overlooked, also because the final, composite form of the religious texts is the version to which the religious recipients relate. The deity is represented as insisting on the multiplicity of fantastic elements, and the text seems to aim for, and reflect on, the opposite of the reduction of complexity. Even the hardening of Pharaoh's heart occurs in order to multiply the wonders (Exod. 11:9).

Others have suggested that the reason for the fantastic excess is 'enhancement of the drama' (Propp 1999, 352), that is, entertainment or embellishment. However, this does not do justice to the spectacular sensory and emotional effects that distinguish this narrative from other passages of the Hebrew Bible. An aesthetic analysis supports these text-internal reflections. Taken as a whole, this narrative constitutes a catalogue of the disturbing: images of a river the size of the Nile, filled with blood and dead fish, masses of frogs, dead cattle, the firstborn. The sensory, emotional, and bodily effects of these plagues are not a far cry from those elicited by horror-fantasy. As examples I offer three readings of important passages in Exodus 7–11: the contest of magicians, the hardening of Pharaoh's heart, and the role of inconsistency.

4.2 The Contest of Magicians

Exodus 7 tells of an interesting contest of magicians. Staffs become snakes, water is turned into blood, masses of grasshoppers appear, cattle are killed, darkness prevails for days, the firstborn are killed, the sea is split, etc. These elements are not presented as matters-of-fact, but as ambiguous and difficult to understand. The text is constructed so that the distinction between knowing/understanding and not knowing/understanding the fantastic elements comes to the fore. Pharaoh and the Egyptians (and Israel, too, cf. the parallel between 7:13 and 6:9) are, according to the text, meant to understand that "I am Yahweh" (7:17; 8:6, 18; 9:14, 29; 11:7; and 15:26) by means of these signs and wonders. But the fantastic elements and their meaning and status are equivocal.

---

of the firstborn the last plague). But it is also possible to count differently; other ways of counting would be in accord with the text's talk of wonders (*môptîm*; Exod. 7:9 and 11:10).

17 With others, I would hold that the narrative does not portray pharaoh as cruel, but as stubborn or strong willed. The verb used is *qšh* in hiphil, 'to give courage', not 'to make cruel'. See Meyers (2005, 70–71).

All through the contest of magicians, the narrative insists on imitation between Israel and Egypt with respect to the performance of the wonders.[18] This is one example of how the fantastic elements are presented as ambiguous and difficult to understand.[19] There seems to be a tendency in exegesis to belittle the Egyptian magicians, even though they really, at least for a while, are represented as performing exactly the same fantastic feats as Moses and Aaron (Houtman 1996, 30; e.g., Exod. 7:11, 22; cf. Gen. 41:8). Later, when they can no longer perform the magical feats, the text still points towards imitation or comparison between them in the execution of the plagues.

However, to begin with, to let the Egyptian magicians repeat or imitate Yahweh's plagues is quite paradoxical and disturbing. For example, in the plague of turning water into blood, all of the water of the Nile has already been turned into blood by Moses and Aaron (7:21). This is in itself an episode that invokes affects and emotions relating to disgust. Therefore, it is quite strange that the narrative has the Egyptian magicians do the same in 7:22. What is the motivation for the Egyptian magicians to do something so detrimental and disgusting to Egypt, to destroy its means of subsistence? The narrative at once asserts reference for its counterintuitive elements *and* obscures it, for how can they repeat the marvel immediately afterwards? This is a literary-aesthetic feature apt to elicit uncertainty in the recipient; the water to blood transformation is a horror- and disgust-stimulating element, which jolts the audience twice, while the literary-aesthetic form elicits uncertainty.

Exodus 8 (8:3, 14–15), telling of the plagues of frogs and gnats, continues the insistence on imitation between Israelites and Egyptians, and suggests that the Egyptians can do the same as Moses and Aaron, and we also find this theme in

---

18 With respect to the sign of turning a staff into a snake, there is a difference in terms between the *nahaš* of Moses and Aaron and the *tannîn* of the Egyptian magicians. The connotations suggest that we should regard the *tannîn* as the more awesome creature (Houtman 1993, 137–138).
19 Houtman points out the similarity between the Egyptian magicians and Moses and Aaron, but still insists that there is an 'essential difference with respect to the origin of the miracle' (Houtman 1993, 535). However, Houtman unfolds the many speculations in exegesis as to how the Egyptian magicians were able to perform such impressive acts without Yahweh's support (for examples, see Houtman 1993, 534–535). These speculations, I think, confirm my argument that there is in fact a noticeable insistence on imitation. Commentators seem to feel some uneasiness with regard to the abilities of the Egyptian magicians—why does the text not simply reject them and their powers? Durham, however, insists that they are not mere magicians, but worthy opponents, and that there is no attempt in the Exodus narrative to discredit them (Durham 1987, 110).

Exodus 9 (9:11).[20] This insistence on imitation with its detrimental consequences for Egypt has been understood as an attempt to ridicule the Egyptians. Yet, this insistence on imitation is so blatant, and so strange, that it elicits uncertainty. To be sure, Israel's magicians, Moses and Aaron, are more powerful than the Egyptian ones—the abilities of the Egyptian magicians are more limited and their repertoire not as varied as Moses' and Aaron's. However, *what* they can do does not really differ: they can transform water to blood and turn a staff into a snake (a physical metamorphosis), and multiply frogs which are found in the strangest places (a hyperbolic misplacement), stimulating fascination and disgust at the same time, reiterating it.

This insistence on the imitation of Moses and Aaron by the Egyptian magicians may also point to reflections on identity and alterity: the ethnic other is not so 'other' when compared to the otherness of the deity (cf. 8:6), and the focus on imitation shows that the clear difference between Egyptians and Israelites is broken down. The deity's enigmatic election and the fantastic elements *disturb* not only Egypt but also Israel, and these form aspects also unsettle and destabilize the reception process. The strangeness of the episode seems to both assert reference for the fantastic elements *and* to render it uncertain. For how and why could so many disgusting and frightening events appear again and again? Add to this the interesting trait that the plagues can be withdrawn in an instant, the minute Pharaoh asks Moses. But who controls Pharaoh's oscillation between allowing or denying the Israelites to leave?—the deity Yahweh. Again, we see literary-aesthetic strategies which are apt to elicit uncertainty in the recipient and reflection on the nature of the deity's manifestations in the human world, and which stimulate specific emotional practices supporting a sustained fascination: horrific and enigmatic fantastic elements.

4.3 Horrors of the Mind or Paradoxes of the Heart?[21]

The hardening, or, better, strengthening,[22] of Pharaoh's heart (see Exod. 4:21) by the deity (i.e., a counterintuitive mental metamorphosis), is often seen as a dif-

---

20 According to Childs, the theme of the conflict with the magicians continues throughout several of the plagues (Exod. 7:22; 8:14; 9:11). He suggests that the theme once provided the major framework of a key plague tradition (P) (Childs 1974, 151).
21 The phrase "paradoxes of the heart" is borrowed from the title of Noël Carroll, *A Philosophy of Horror – or: Paradoxes of the Heart* (Carroll 1990).
22 The translation 'strengthen' is better here, since in English 'harden' connotes 'hard-hearted' which means 'cruel', and the meaning here is "stubborn" (Propp 1999, 217). See also Deut. 2:30;

ficult part of the Exodus narrative. In the composite text, clearly Yahweh is responsible for Pharaoh's reactions (4:21; 7:2–4; 8:15; 9:12, 34–35; 10:1, 20, 27; 11:10; 14:4, 8, 17);[23] a feature also verbalised as strange and unreasonable within the text (cf., e. g., the servants in 10:7, and Pharaoh's bargaining in 10:8). Many biblical scholars agree that the narrative is not an 'essay on the theological and philosophical issue of human freedom and divine determinism' (Meyer 1983, 77 quoted in Propp 1999, 353), and that the hardening motif should not be understood merely a way of tying together originally independent plagues (Childs 1974, 174). While both options—Pharaoh hardening his own heart and Yahweh hardening it (e. g., 8:32 vs. 9:12; Schmidt 1996, 230)—appear in the narrative, the presence of the latter option from before the plagues begin to occur, and at the beginning of the plagues narrative itself (Exod. 4:21; 7:2–4), suggests the dominance of the idea of divine causality. After 9:8–12 any ambiguity about Yahweh's responsibility for the hardened heart disappears (Gunn 1982, 77). Pharaoh's strong heart is thus literarily framed as incomprehensible, even to his servants (Exod. 10:7)—were it not for Yahweh as explaining cause. After the events of Exodus 12, the references to Yahweh's mental metamorphosis of Pharaoh in 14:4, 8 unmistakably turns Pharaoh into Yahweh's puppet (Gunn 1982, 80–81).

But, in an aesthetic analysis, how does such a narrative element become effective? If Yahweh is responsible for hardening Pharaoh's heart, is the narrative unfolding of events merely deterministic? And why must the human characters go through these horrors, if Yahweh controls all events? Why not settle for just one fantastic event to free the Hebrew slaves?[24] If we read the fantastic excess of the text and the strengthening of Pharaoh's heart in a literary-aesthetic perspective, these paradoxes and uncertainties become interesting in a different way. The literary-aesthetic form of the narrative plays on ambiguity and uncertainty to an extent that is well suited to elicit not only reflection, but also fear and horror in the recipients. If Pharaoh's stubbornness is Yahweh's doing, then this mental metamorphosis means that the horror of the story and the destructive aspects of the counterintuitive elements must be understood as commu-

---

Josh. 11:20; Ezek. 2:4; 3:7. The dominant verb used is related to being strong, then to being heavy, which is used five times, and *qšh*, to harden, which is used once (Meyers 2005, 70). The varied terminology may be literary artistry or a signal of the text's composite prehistory, but whether or not this is so, the present form can be read as literary (cf. Meyers 2005, 78).

23 See, e. g., Exod. 7:9: 'when (*kî*) pharaoh speaks...', not if. *kî* may also be translated 'if', but the 'when' option is more likely here.

24 Religious recipients have also reflected on this issue as can be seen in the Jewish Pesach song *Dayenu* ("It would have been enough for us").

nication about the deity.[25] The uncertain and ambiguous elements suggest a monstrousness, an enigma in the deity, which is apt to unsettle and scare the recipients, while the uncertainty involved also stimulates bodily responses. These elements also point to the artifice of the narrative *as narrative* because of its paradoxicality. This mental metamorphosis and the constant oscillation between Pharaoh hardening his heart himself and the deity doing it thus comes out as not just about representing and communicating divine power, but also about eliciting interruption, disturbance, and unsettling expectations in the audience. The human subjects of the story are horrified and disturbed, as is the reception process. The ambiguous communication about Yahweh, and the stimulation of emotional practices related to fear and horror, are aspects underlined in the following text segments.

In Exod. 8:15, the Egyptian magicians realise that they are dealing with a deity, and they tell Pharaoh that what happens is 'the finger of (a) god' (or 'a divine finger'). This also supports the impression that the Egyptian magicians are not simply represented as evil or stupid enemies.[26] In Exodus 9:20–21, we also find a line of division—between those who believe Yahweh's words and those who do not—which applies as much to the Egyptians as to the Israelites (see also Exod. 10:7). Repeatedly, the text states that Pharaoh comes to acknowledge and recognise Yahweh, and then, repeatedly, that Yahweh strengthens Pharaoh's resolve not to let Israel go (9:27; 10:16–17:24). The effect is that Pharaoh comes across, not as the epitome of cruelty, but as a haunted man, and this is reflected in Exodus 9:14's formulation: "…all my afflictions to you" (*kol-maggēpōtay 'el-libbᵉka*), suggesting that Pharaoh's heart suffers.[27] These and other elements suggest that a simple image of the Egyptians in Exodus as evil idolaters and simple-minded magicians, and an interpretation of the story as straightforwardly eliciting belief and trust in Yahweh, is quite difficult to maintain.[28] Pharaoh is a haunted man, a tragic character, portrayed as opaque to the recipients of the story, and to himself, stimulating uncertainty and horror in the recipients,

---

25 In line with this: Amos 3:6 and Isa. 45:6–7.
26 According to Moses' utterance in 8:20, the ethnic animosity is the wish of Pharaoh and the Egyptians. Yet this utterance seems to be meant as a trickery of Pharaoh. The ethnic distinctions are Yahweh's doing (8:19; 11:9). In Exodus 9, a speech by Yahweh makes it clear that he is the instigator of the ethnic divisions—not Egypt, and not Israel. Pharaoh and the Egyptians seemingly present an obstacle to Yahweh's plan. And in a sense, Israel is an obstacle too. I unfold this discussion more fully in Feldt (2012).
27 Ex 7:14 states that pharaoh's heart is *kābēd*, which connotes weight and mass. Defective bodily organs may also be called *kābēd* (Moses' mouth in 4:10).
28 In 11:2 it seems that the Israelites have Egyptian friends.

in combination with the disgust elicited with regard to the many different plagues.

The analysis of the literary-aesthetic form shows that the plagues narrative
does not present the story as a narrative of fair divine punishment,[29] but as one
of dangerous supernatural power, mystery, and horror. The counterintuitive elements are embedded in a literary-narrative frame, which elicits not only cognitive
disturbance, but also stimulates affect and emotional reactions.

4.4 Dead or Alive, Real or Unreal? Writing Impossibles

In the Exodus narrative, one finds several examples of 'mistakes', or contradictions. In other words, we find an explicit use of contradictory elements that challenge the mimetic-illusionist assumptions of the reader (Lachmann 2002, 108–
111; Feldt 2012, 59–62). For example, in Exod. 9:6, the Egyptian cattle die.
Strangely, in Exod. 9:19 the cattle are alive again—to be killed again in another
plague (9:25), and to be offered to Israel as sacrificial animals (10:25), even if the
Egyptians no longer possess any cattle. Some die once more in the plague of the
firstborn (11:5; 12:29), while the horses also drown in the sea (14:28; 15:1, 4, 19,
21).[30] Also, in Exod. 9:22, 25 'all the field's plants' are destroyed, and yet in
9:31 and 10:5 some vegetation is left. We may thus understand Exod. 9:31–32
as text-internal naturalistic comment, showing that it was, also in the ancient
world, quite difficult to accept that *all* the crops were indeed spoilt.

Clearly such contradictions would also be noticed by ancient recipients and
redactors, as they are quite blatant, and their effect cannot be explained merely
by reference to different background sources. From a literary-aesthetic perspective, such contradictions have their own functions and contribute to the aesthetic

---

29 E.g., Contra Propp, who understands the plagues narrative to be about how God punishes
guilty humans, animals, crops, and lands (Propp 1999, 346).

30 We could point to other contradictions, which are difficult to explain: that between Moses'
statement in Exod. 10:29 ("I'll see your face no more") and Pharaoh's address to Moses and
Aaron in 12:31–32; that of how the Egyptian magicians could duplicate the plague of blood if
there was no water. I do not agree that "the real answer" lies in 7:24 (that the Egyptians can obtain water by digging; Propp 1999, 325). In the ancient world, this paradox generated many speculations (Gregory of Nyssa, Ibn Ezra, Augustine etc.; see Houtman 1996, 30, for references). Another difficulty is how people could survive for seven days without water, something that was
also recognised as impossible in the ancient world (Houtman 1996, 29–30). Cf. 7:24 and 7:19.
21, where the issue is left unresolved by the text—stimulating reflection.

effect.[31] The extreme hypertrophy, the fantastic excess, that sometimes even disregards consistency, testifies that this narrative's aesthetic form generates ambiguity and uncertainty, it stimulates fascination, disgust, and horror. The contradictions aid the elicitation of a fantastic effect and push the events of the narrative beyond normal, everyday experience, and even further towards a withdrawal of cognitive guarantees and the transgression of standard cognitive responses. By means of the contradictions, the Exodus narrative flaunts its constructed nature and voices doubt and hesitation with respect to its counterintuitive elements.

The literary-aesthetic form of the narrative, its pervasive ambiguity, the affect and the emotions elicited, and the uncertainties that it triggers, are important to how we understand it. The summation in Exod. 11:9–10 answers the question of the fantastic excess that culminates in the slaying of the firstborn: "In order to multiply my wonders in the land of Egypt" (*lᵉmaʿan rᵉbôt môptay bᵉ'ereṣ miṣrāyim*), indicating a purpose while reiterating the futility of the signs and wonders that entail an excessive loss of human and animal life. This element places violence and the evocation of terror at the centre of the narrative, and removes the divine persona from full, verbal comprehension.[32] The mass slaughter of the Egyptian firstborn has a horrific effect, which the comments in 11:6 and 12:30 bring out clearly. This does not, as claimed by some exegetes (Meyers 2005, 93–94), entail a harsh view of the Egyptians as the evil enemy other, for the description of the cry of Egypt (Exod. 12:30) is based on empathy; it evokes terror of the deity and horror-affect. The text's aesthetic form works to make the recipients share the terror of Yahweh.

4.5 The Affect of Intimate Strangeness

The literary arrangement of the series of fantastic events in "the plagues narrative" has received some attention in biblical studies. The present composition may draw on diverse sources, but the literary arrangement of the composite text has long been recognized as such; namely as three series of signs and won-

---

31 In support of my reading strategy, please see the history of the early exegesis of the plagues narrative, which showed that the inconsistencies troubled exegesis also in ancient and medieval times (Childs 1976, 164–168).

32 Early rabbinic commentators sought to explain this horrific act; references in Sarna (1991, 52 and 244 n. 5).

ders with the same format (Meyers 2005, 77–78).[33] However, the 'materials' of the signs and wonders has not been addressed in similar detail. If this literary-aesthetic form is indeed, as I suggest, part of religious mediation, we must take into account that what is communicated is not just a message, but also a medium with aesthetic effects.

A great deal of the materials used for the hyperbolic fantastic elements relate to forms of intimate strangeness. The materials of many of the fantastic elements are taken from familiar and known natural phenomena—hail, darkness, clouds, fire—and such animals as invariably accompany human life—flies, gnats, frogs, locusts. These natural phenomena and animals are familiar elements of human, everyday life, while at the same time being conducive to a transgression of the familiar. Such phenomena and animals are normally "background", "décor" (Serres 1995, 3), but here they are made to enter the foreground to disturb and attack the familiar, making the "mute world" speak and act (Serres 1995, 3). The background moves out and forms another, shifting, alterity, beyond the anthropomorphic (cf. Connor on Serres in Connor 2005). Other fantastic elements are intimately strange because relating directly to the human body (children, boils, water, blood), and their fantastic effect proceeds from their being enlarged hyperbolically and/or from their body-related metamorphosis: where there was water, there is now the intimately strange substance of blood. The prospect of it potentially entering the body from the outside is abhorrent and disgusting; the prospect of a river of blood stimulates feelings of horror and fear.

Some fantastic elements offer disturbance because of their *multiplicity*. Flies, gnats, frogs, and locusts embody disturbance of intuitive cognitive categories simply by being an aggregation of tiny individuals, prompting a sense of wonder (Connor 2006, 91–92) and simultaneous disgust because they are misplaced. The aggregation of many small individuals in a swarm provokes reflection on the nature of multiplicity and the relationship of different scales. Such a crowd of small bodies is a form that makes multiplicity visible, and yet retains its untouchability, as suggested by Steven Connor (Connor 2006, 96–100). A swarm is at once formless, edgeless, and without an inside; it dissolves form *and* discloses it. The same might be said of the soot and the dust (Exod. 9:8–12), which are similarly amorphous and metamorphic, diffuse *and* cohesive. Such elements, appearing in culturally misplaced settings, may elicit feelings of disgust, dread, and fasci-

---

33 For the first sign in each series, Pharaoh receives a warning in the morning; for the second, a warning is mentioned, and the confrontation takes place in his palace; and the third comes without a warning or mention of site. Other features of literary arrangement have been discerned (Meyers 2005, 78).

nation. Again, we note that counter-intuitive representations are used, but embedded in a very particular aesthetic form, with particular aesthetic effects to follow.

To such disturbances of the everyday, we also find further *misplacements* of the 'material' of some of the fantastic elements. This contributes further to the fantastic-horrific effect. When the frogs (Exod. 7:28; 8:3)[34] enter houses, beds, ovens, kneading bowls, and the locusts (10:6) devour all produce and fill all houses (10:5–7, 15–16), such reversals of everyday 'background' into 'foreground', such misplacements of familiar phenomena, lead to hesitation and questioning. The message of the aesthetic form, of the fantastic "materials", is one of transformation and exchange, that mutability of given orders is possible; a mutability which can be both destructive and generative. The reiterated reversibility of the phantasms amplifies the effect: *Now you see them, now you don't.*

If we look at how the text-internal characters react to the counterintuitive elements, this analysis is corroborated, for the degree of hesitation, doubt, disbelief, and suspicion in the characters is surprisingly great, considering the great amount of fantastic events or 'miracles' they are represented as having witnessed. The personae are disoriented, confused, and bewildered, and the fantastic events are staged as emotionally and cognitively disorienting experiences (Feldt 2012, 141–145). These reactions are embedded in a narrative frame presented by the narrator's discourse; which to some extent does tell of the people's belief and trust in the deity. The cumulative effect, however, is that the Israelites are presented as finding themselves in a pendulous motion between belief and disbelief, trust and fear. The tension between the various reactions remains in the foreground of the text, naturally affecting the recipients. While the narrator predominantly speaks of belief and orientation, doubt and disorientation are not absent from the narrator's interpretations, and in combination with the disoriented and confused character reactions, the effect of disorientation and disturbance is remarkable. The literary-aesthetic form, in which the counterintuitive elements are placed, suggests disturbance and horror as appropriate reactions. In combination with the considerable confusion, hesitation, and doubt on the part of the text-internal characters, we have a narrative that elicits sensory and emotional reactions quite far removed from what we, in the study of religion, usually attribute to "myths".

---

34 Propp finds the frogs a prank and the mosquitoes humorous (1999, 349–350). Propp is right that the fantastic and the ludic certainly can go together, but here we should not overlook the uncanny effects their misplacement has; their noise and their stench.

5 Conclusions

In the narrative analysed here, the literary-aesthetic form has a sensory and emotional impact. The literary aesthetic form of this religious narrative labours to elicit a sensory, emotional, and cognitive response of hesitation, disorientation, fear, and horror, and ultimately reflection on the nature and character of divine manifestation, in its narration of the foundational events at the Exodus from Egypt. In key ways, the sensory affect of the text's aesthetic form mimics the presentation of the text-internal character experience in relation to the deity's marvels, and this also aids the stimulation of a particular response. The counterintuitive certainly does not appear in a 'pure' or abstract way, but is presented here in a particular aesthetic form, where it is mixed with literary-aesthetic forms of violation, many of which are not directly counterintuitive, but hyperbolic, or concern the culturally unusual, misplaced, or what is paradoxical in this particular literary context. Indeed, the literary-aesthetic form does make for a special treatment of key counterintuitive representations, which affects their reception and the sensual and emotional stimuli.

I think this shows that the literary-aesthetic form and the narrative contexts in which counterintuitive representations are embedded, encountered, and used by recipients, are crucial for understanding the types of interactions with superhuman agents that are prescribed and enabled for recipients, and for understanding the sensory-emotional impact of religious narratives on recipients—in short, for understanding how religious narratives become effective and how they function. Uncertainty, hesitation, disgust, horror, and a suspension between wonder and doubt may be responses to some types of religious narrative, may be cultivated by them, perhaps even be part of 'religion'. Clearly, religious narratives play on the work of the senses and form part of the emotion-management strategies of religions. Perception always occurs as a construction process, where stored social frames and cultural scripts are compared with new perceptions (Mohr 2005), and so the aesthetic forms of religious narratives also play a role in how religion becomes effective, as narratives play important roles in imaginative arousal and imitatory participation, and for religious identity formation between the collective and the individual (Feldt 2011a).[35]

---

35 As Mohr has pointed out, the ritual use of texts and material objects plays on and stimulates sensual, emotional, and cognitive arousal (Mohr 2005, 1442). I have argued here that religious narratives also play on the senses, and on emotional and cognitive arousal. Clearly, the use of the Exodus myth in the Jewish Passover ritual makes for a powerful combinatory work on the senses, emotions, and cognition.

The aesthetic perspective allows us to investigate religious stories in a way that does not over-determine which response is or should be elicited, but analyses how the narratives represent and negotiate the status of their counterintuitive or trans-empirical elements. It also allows us to fruitfully connect cognitive, somatic, and cultural studies approaches, when analysing which types of sensory, emotional, and cognitive responses are cultivated in different religions or with regard to differing forms of mediation. From the literary-aesthetic perspective presented here, religious texts are flexible media that may disorient, disturb, and unsettle, as well as orient, found, and comfort. They do not present religious explanations, truths, or models of reality, or information about deities, metamorphoses, or miracles that are separable from the media in which they are embedded. The aesthetic approach, I believe, underlines how religious texts do not necessarily alleviate incoherence or lack of meaning, and that they may also actively create and sustain incoherence, enigma, fear, ambiguity, and uncertainty. Thus, an analysis of aesthetic form may counter the too easy explanations of the work of religion and religious narratives as providing certainty and comfort.

Religious narratives are some of the primary means by which religions bridge the gap between generations and by which religious identity is socialized; narrative is one of the fundamental mediating links between individual and collective identities (Feldt 2011a), and between somatic affect and emotion management. I have suggested here that it is not only ritual performances or religious practices involving the presence of other bodies that may provide religious participants with emotional arousal and sensual stimulation. Skilfully imagined and narrated events and actions may also be intense and affective, in addition to events and actions actually performed, especially when used collectively. Ritual action is make-believe, as is narrated action (Feldt 2011a). Investigations of the varying literary-aesthetic forms of religious texts and their effects on the process of reception, on the senses, the mind, and the body, may thus bring out new, concrete perspectives on how they become effective and how they function, as parts of the many ways in which religion fundamentally relies on connections of sensual, emotional, and cognitive stimuli in order to stay in "the existential game".

Bibliography

Bruce, Steve. 2011. *Secularization. In Defence of an Unfashionable Theory*. Oxford: Oxford University Press.

Cassuto, Umberto. 1967. *A Commentary on the Book of Exodus*, translated by Israel Abrahams. Jerusalem: The Magnes Press.

Childs, Brevard S. 1974. *The Book of Exodus.* Old Testament Library. Philadelphia: The
Westminster Press.
Connor, Steven. 2005. "Michel Serres' Five Senses." In *Empire of the Senses. The
Sensual Culture Reader,* edited by David Howes, 318–334. Berg, Oxford, and New York:
Bloomsbury Academic.
—— 2006. *Fly.* London: Reaktion.
Clark, Lynn Scofield. 2007. "Identity, Belonging, and Religious Lifestyle Branding (Fashion
Bibles, Bhangra Parties and Muslim Pop)." In *Religion, Media and the Marketplace,*
edited by Lynn Schofield Clark, 1–33. New Brunswick: Rutgers University Press.
Carroll, Noël. 1990. *A Philosophy of Horror – Or: Paradoxes of the Heart.* London: Routledge.
Cusack, Carole. 2009. "Science Fiction as Scripture." In *Literature and Aesthetics* 19/2:
72–91.
Davidsen, Markus. 2010. "Fiktionsbaseret religion: Fra Star Wars til Jediisme." In
Religionsvidenskabeligt Tidsskrift 55: 3–21.
Doniger, Wendy. 1998. *The Implied Spider. Politics and Theology in Myth.* New York:
Columbia University Press.
Durham, John I. 1987. *Exodus.* Word Biblical Commentary. Waco: Word Books.
Durkheim, Emile. [1912] 1995. *The Elementary Forms of Religious Life,* translated by Karen
Fields. New York: The Free Press.
Eliade, Mircea. 1963. *Patterns in Comparative Religion,* translated by Rosemary Sheed. New
York: World Publishing Company.
Feldt, Laura. 2006. "Signs of Wonder – Traces of Doubt: The Fantastic in the Exodus
Narrative." In *Fremde Wirklichkeiten. Literarische Phantastik und antike Literatur,* edited
by N. Hömke, and M. Baumbach, 311–338. Heidelberg: Universitätsverlag Winter.
—— 2011a. "Fantastic Re-Collection: Cultural vs. Autobiographical Memory in the Exodus
Narrative." In *Religious Narrative, Cognition and Culture – Image and Word in the Mind
of Narrative,* edited by Armin W. Geertz and Jeppe S. Jensen, 191–208. London: Equinox.
—— 2011b. "Religious Narrative and the Literary Fantastic." *Religion* 41/2: 251–283.
—— 2012. *The Fantastic in Religious Narrative from Exodus to Elisha.* London: Routledge.
—— 2016. "Harry Potter and Contemporary Magic. Fantasy Literature, Popular Culture, and
the Representation of Religion." *Journal of Contemporary Religion* 18/1: 3–24.
Fields, Karen. [1995] 2005. "Religion as an Eminently Social Thing." In *The Elementary Forms
of Religious Life,* by Émile Durkheim, translated by Karen Fields, xvii–lxxiii. New York:
The Free Press.
Fischer, G. 1996. "Exodus 1–15: Eine Erzählung." In *Studies in the Book of Exodus:
Redaction–Reception–Interpretation,* edited by Marc Vervenne, 149–178. Leuven: Leuven
University Press.
Fokkelman, Jan P. 1987. "Exodus." In *The Literary Guide to the Bible,* edited by Robert Alter,
and Frank Kermode, 56–65. London: Collins.
Gilhus, Ingvild S., and Lisbeth Mikaelsson. 2001. *Nyt blikk på religion. Studiet av religion i
dag.* Oslo: Pax Forlag.
Gould, John, 2001. *Myth, Ritual, Memory and Exchange. Essays in Greek literature and
culture.* Oxford: Oxford University Press.
Greenberg, Moshe. 1969. *Understanding Exodus.* New York: Behrman House.
Grieser, Alexandra. 2015. "Aesthetics." In *Vocabulary for the Study of Religion.* Vol. 1, edited
by Kocku von Stuckrad and Robert A. Segal, 14–23. Leiden: Brill.

Gunn, David M. 1982. "The 'Hardening of Pharaoh's Heart': Plot, Character and Theology in Exodus 1–14." In *Art and Meaning: Rhetoric in Biblical Literature*, edited by David J.A. Clines, David M. Gunn, and Alan J. Hauser, 72–96. Sheffield: JSOT Press, Sheffield.

Harrison, Peter. 2006. "Miracles, Early Modern Science, and Rational Religion." *Church History* 75/3: 493–510.

Hirschfeld, Lawrence A., and Susan Gelman, eds. 1994. *Mapping the Mind: Domain Specificity in Cognition and Culture*. Cambridge: Cambridge University Press.

Hoffmann, Thomas. 2007. *The Poetic Qur'ān. Studies in Qur'ānic Poeticity*. Vol. 12, Diskurse der Arabistik. Wiesbaden: Harrasowitz.

Hoffmeyr, Isabel. 2008. "Text." In *Key Words in Religion, Media and Culture*, edited by David Morgan, 198–208. London and New York: Routledge.

Houtman, Cornelis. 1993 *Exodus. Historical Commentary on the Old Testament*. Vol. 1. Kampen: Kok Publishing House.

—— 1996. *Exodus. Historical Commentary on the Old Testament*. Vol. 2. Kampen: Kok Publishing House.

Hume, Kathryn. 1984. *Fantasy and Mimesis. Responses to Reality in Western Literature*. New York and London: Methuen.

Jackson, Rosemary. 1981. *Fantasy. The Literature of Subversion*. London: Methuen.

Johnstone, William. 1990. *Exodus*. Old Testament Guides. Sheffield: Journal for the Study of the Old Testament Press.

Keen, Suzanne. 2011. "Emotions and Narrative." *Poetics Today* 32/1: 1–53.

Lachmann, Renate. 2002. *Erzählte Phantastik. Zu Phantasiegeschichte und Semantik phantastischer Texte*. Frankfurt am Main: Suhrkamp.

Meyers, Carol. 2005. *Exodus*. The New Cambridge Bible Commentary. Cambridge: Cambridge University Press.

Miscall, Peter D. 1992. "Biblical Narrative and the Categories of the Fantastic." In *Fantasy and the Bible*. Vol. 60, Semeia, edited by G. Aichele and T. Pippin, 39–52. Atlanta: Scholars Press.

Mohr, Hubert. 2005. "Perception/Sensory System." In *The Brill Dictionary of Religion*, edited by Kocku von Stuckrad (revised edition of *Metzler Lexikon Religion*, edited by Christoph Auffarth, Jutta Bernard, and Hubert Mohr). Vol 3, 1435–1448. Leiden: Brill.

Myrvold, Kristina. 2010. *The Death of Sacred Texts*. London: Ashgate.

Otto, R. 1936. *Das Heilige. Über das Irrationale in der Idee des Göttlichen und sein Verhältnis zum Rationalen*. Munich: Ch. Beck'sche Verlagsbuchhandlung.

Paden, William E. 1994. *Religious Worlds. The Comparative Study of Religion*. Boston: Beacon.

Pardes, Ilana. 2000. *The Biography of Ancient Israel. National Narratives in the Bible*. Berkeley: University of California Press.

—— 1992. *Countertraditions in the Bible. A Feminist Approach*. Cambridge: Harvard University Press.

Petersen, Anders K. 2005. "Fra hellig til religiøs tekst." In *Litteraturen og det hellige*, edited by Ole Davidsen, Kirsten Nielsen, and Stefan Klint, 414–432. Aarhus: Aarhus University Press.

Popovic, Mladen, ed. 2010. *Authoritative Scriptures in Ancient Judaism*. Leiden: Brill.

Propp, William H.C. 1999. *Exodus 1–18. A New Translation with Introduction and Commentary*. Vol. 1, Anchor Bible Commentaries. New York: Doubleday.

—— 2006. *Exodus 19–40. A New translation with Introduction and Commentary.* Vol. 2, Anchor Bible Commentaries. New York: Doubleday.

Pyysiäinen, Ilka. 2004. *Magic, Miracles and Religious Belief.* Cognitive Science of Religion Series. Lanham: Altamira Press.

Römer, Thomas C. 2003. "Competing Magicians in Exodus 7–9: Interpreting Magic in the Priestly Theology." In *Magic in the Biblical World: From the Rod of Aaron to the Ring of Solomon*, edited by Todd Klutz, 12–22. JSOT Sup 245. London: Continuum.

Ryba, Thomas. 2000. "Manifestation." In *Guide to the Study of Religion*, edited by Willie Braun and Russell T. McCutcheon, 168–189. New York: Cassell.

Scheer, Monique. 2012. "Are Emotions a Kind of Practice (and Is That What Makes Them Have a History)? A Bourdieuian Approach to Understanding Emotion." *History and Theory* 51/2: 193–220.

Schmidt, W.H. 1996. "Die Intention der Beiden Plagenerzählungen (Exodus 7–10)" In *Studies in the Book of Exodus: Redaction-Reception-Interpretation*, edited by Marc Vervenne, 225–243. Leuven: Leuven University Press.

Segal, Robert A. 2004. *Myth. A Very Short Introduction.* Oxford: Oxford University Press.

Serres, Michel. 1995. *The Natural Contract.* Ann Arbor: University of Michigan Press.

Seters, John van. 1994. *The Life of Moses: The Yahwist as Historian in Exodus-Numbers. Contributions to Biblical Exegesis and Theology.* Kampen: Kok Pharos Publishing House.

Simecek, Karen. 2015. "Beyond Narrative: Poetry, Emotion, and the Perspectival View." *British Journal of Aesthetics* 55/4: 497–513.

Stolow, Jeremy. 2007. "Holy Pleather: Materializing Authority in Contemporary Orthodox Jewish Publishing." *Material Religion* 3/3: 314–335.

Taylor, Bron. 2010. *Dark Green Religion: Nature Spirituality and the Planetary Future.* Berkeley: University of California Press.

Todorov, Tzvetan. [1973] 1975. *The Fantastic. A Structural Approach to a Literary Genre.* Ithaca: Cornell University Press.

Vater, Ann M. 1982. "'A Plague on Both Our Houses': Form– and Rhetorical-Critical Observations on Exodus 7–11." In *Art and Meaning: Rhetoric in Biblical Literature*, edited by David J. A. Clines, David M. Gunn, and Alan J. Hauser, 62–71. JSOT Sup 19. Sheffield: JSOT Press.

van der Leeuw, Gerardus. [1933] 1938. *Religion in Essence and Manifestation: A Study in Phenomenology*, translated by J.E. Turner. Princeton: Princeton University Press.

Wisker, Gina. 2005. *Horror Fiction. An Introduction.* London: Continuum.

Wyatt, N. 2001. "The Mythic Mind." *Scandinavian Journal of the Old Testament* 15/1: 3–61.

—

PART II **History and Politics**

Niklaus Largier
Below the Horizon of Meaning: Figuration, Disfiguration, Transfiguration

1 Embodied Cognition

At a decisive moment in the story of her life Teresa of Avila notes the following:

> It happened one day, [...], that as I went to the oratory I saw an image which they had pro-
> cured for a certain festival that was observed in the house, and which they had placed
> there. It was of Christ terribly wounded and it was so moving that when I looked at it
> the very sight of Him shook me, for it clearly showed what He suffered for us. So strongly
> did I feel what a poor return I had made for those wounds, that my heart seemed to break,
> and I threw myself on the ground before Him in a great flood of tears, imploring Him to give
> me strength once and for all not to offend Him again (Teresa of Avila 1957, 67; 1997, 79–80).

Teresa goes on, confirming what the reader of this text might have been anticipating already:

> I had a very deep veneration for the glorious Magdalen, and very often thought of her con-
> version [...]"; adding a couple of lines further down: "This was my method of praying: Since
> I could not meditate intellectually, I would try to call up the picture of Christ within me, and
> I found myself the better, as I believe, for dwelling on those moments [...]. (Teresa of Avila
> 1957, 67; 1997, 80)

The experiential moments Teresa evokes in these passages about her method of
prayer are "sweat and affliction" ("sudor y aflicción"), but also "sin" ("peca-
dos"), and "many tormenting thoughts" ("tormento") (Teresa 1957, 68; 1997,
81–82). Other elements emerge in the text as moments of intense experience
that concern both the realm of affects and of sensation: joy and sadness, sweetness and bitterness, but also a wide range of sensation and affect. What Teresa
thus presents us with is a form of aesthetic experience, a specific form of the
convergence and unfolding of thought, sensation, and affect that in her understanding compensates for her inability to "meditate intellectually".

In conceiving of prayer as a production of *aisthesis* and guided perception,
Teresa follows here, as I will show further, a long tradition of contemplative
prayer and meditation where the arousal of affective and sensual experience
plays a key role. This experience is to be seen in the horizon of notions of *cognitio dei experimentalis*, an experiential cognition of the divine, or, if we want to
use a word that the church father Origen introduces, a form of *aisthesis*, i.e., a

https://doi.org/10.1515/9783110461015-007

sensual and affective experience that takes place where discursive cognition acknowledges that the divine is unknowable.

Continuing her train of thought and her teaching about her own way of prayer, Teresa emphasizes that Magdalen is the exemplary figure she imitates in this practice:

> When I made that inward picture in which I threw myself at Christ's feet, and sometimes also when I was reading, there would come to me unexpectedly such a feeling of the presence of God as made it impossible for me to doubt that He was within me, or that I was totally engulfed in Him. This was no kind of vision, I believe it is called mystical theology. The soul is then suspended that it seems entirely outside itself. The will loves; the memory is, I think, almost lost, and the mind, I believe, though it is not lost, does not reason—I mean that it does not work, but stands as if amazed at the many things it understands. For God wills it to realize that it understands nothing at all of what [he] places before it (Teresa of Avila 1957, 71; 1997, 84).

In these intricately constructed and complex passages Teresa offers not only a rich phenomenology of her religious experience, psychology, and understanding of embodied cognition, but also a reflection on the very production of this experience and—as I want to argue—a pathway into the discussion of the role of the specifically aesthetic aspects in religious practice. The very experience she recounts here is based on what we can call a practice and rhetorical technique of figuration and a phenomenology of rhetorical effects. The first, most obvious, and well-known elements, possibly also the least surprising ones in this quote are the references to late medieval practices of visual culture and 'visual piety'. Teresa's prayer is entirely rooted in the overwhelming effects of a figure, namely the image of the suffering Christ and the affective force of it. It is this image—a medium of translation that presents a biblical narrative (see McLuhan 1967, 57–58)—that acts upon her, producing a range of effects that she is then able to explore further. Thus, we can speak of *aisthesis* in simple terms of the perception effects of an image, and of the phenomenological exploration and evaluation of these effects.

In her practice, however, Teresa doesn't just contemplate the image of Christ, dwell on its effects on her soul, and frame it in terms that in our eyes make this not just an aesthetic, but a 'religious' experience. In doing so, she immediately evokes another image, namely the exemplary figure of Mary Magdalen and her position at the feet of the cross. This image of the Magdalen functions as a mediating figure, providing her with a narrative and a (quasi-)biblical anchoring point for her experience on one side, a model for her experience on the other side. Mary Magdalen is the exemplary viewer, the embodiment of a grasp of conversion that is not understood in terms of intellectual belief but of a perception

event. The Magdalen, however, is not primarily the basis for a set of hermeneutic exercises (e.g., a foil for Teresa's hermeneutics of herself, the effects of the image, and of the scriptures) but the center of a figural network and of a specifically affective and sensual form of contemplation that Teresa explores in her practice of prayer. She connects Teresa and Christ; she implies a way of seeing; she is an exemplary figure of conversion; and she is a figure of the abandonment in love, to name just a few of the figural lines that she suggests.

Prayer, we can conclude on the basis of these few elements from Teresa's *Vida*, is a rhetorical *mise-en-abîme* of mediation and translation that produces and gives shape to reason and memory, the affects and the senses. It does so in quoting images from the scriptures and in exploring the effects of this translation into a new medium. At the same time, however, prayer does not make use of that medium alone—e.g. in using the image of Christ in order to produce certain effects—but it is a highly self-conscious staging of the necessity of mediation and its impossibility itself. Thus, in focusing on the image of Christ through the image of the Magdalen, Teresa plays with the available forms of media in a strategic way, indicating that an immediate view of the divine is beyond her (and us). As she writes in the passages quoted above, conversion and the turning toward the divine take shape through figuration, through the figure of the lover Magdalen and through other figures that are deployed in a process of "aesthetic formation" (Meyer 2010).

Conversion and embodied cognition are thus defined not as acts of intellectual comprehension or hermeneutic understanding by means of illustrating images, but as acts that entail an intense absorption into affect and sensation, or, to put it in terms of the ultimate goal, an absorption in love. This very absorption is produced by the medium beyond or below all hermeneutic engagement. Not the content of the image of Christ is important to Teresa but the very effect of the image upon her soul, her perception, her affects, her memory, and her reason. In this sense we can speak of this experience—in an allusion to Marshall McLuhan and Gilles Deleuze—as a tactile event that leaves all vision behind (see Largier 2010).

The path toward this goal takes shape as a form of aesthetic experience. It is produced in prayer through means of figuration that give shape to perception. As 'aesthetic experience' it is also an experience that at its core reiterates the very fact that all sensation, affect, and cognition is mediated, and that enacts this very fact self-consciously in concrete forms of the production of sensation and affect. Playing with Deleuze's image of the Baroque (Deleuze 1988) we can say that Teresa presents us with a practice of folding: Each figure is the result of a folding, and each folding opens towards another figure. Thus, the figure of Christ, a folding of the figure of the finitude of our intellect, unfolds into the figure of the Magdalen, which in turn unfolds in the *aisthesis* and embodied cognition of the figure of Christ. The very experience Teresa is testifying to is embedded in the productivity of this very network of figuration and its formative powers. As she points out, in this embodied cognition affect, sensation, memory, and reason converge in a new and different form of knowledge.

2 Figuration, Sensation, Affect

We know from a long medieval and early modern tradition of theories of reading, prayer, and meditation that the desired absorption into the abyss of love and the experience Teresa is testifying to are not to be understood as a divine gift alone. They are also the product of an extensive training and self-fashioning that creates the very possibility for the reception of this gift and this different type of knowing. This very training starts with the reading of the scriptures, and it entails—beyond the communal rituals, the liturgy, image and colour, music and song—a dramatisation of the self and of the established perceptual and discursive order (see Foucault 1988, 48; Bataille 1988, 10 – 29).

In this dramatization we identify several constitutive moments: leaving behind the established worldly, natural, and discursive order (i.e., leaving the 'old world' and moving into the desert or the cell); configuring a new life in the imitation of an exemplary figure (i.e., following the example of an ideal follower, for example, Saint Antony or Mary Magdalen, in order to become an 'other Christ'); enacting the spiritual struggle as a translation of martyrdom (i.e., dramatizing the existential constitution in the fight between the demonic and the angelic); and transforming sensations and emotions by means of contemplative practices in order to gain a foretaste of heaven (i.e., the production of sensual sweetness and absorbing love as embodied perception events).

The very encounter with the scriptures, the revelation, and the evangelical promise turns thus into a matter not primarily of cognitive belief and knowledge but of practices of figuration and embodied aesthetic cognition. The ideal believer, we might say in a very sketchy way, is the 'convert' who follows an exemplary figure, adopting its image in a practice of mimetic refiguration; who leaves the 'old world' and the established patterns of subjectivity behind in imitating this figure; who makes this imitation a practice of figuring herself through an enactment of the constitutive moments that shape the life of the exemplary figure; and who explores the rhetorical effects of this practice in view of the dramatic distancing from the 'old world' of bitterness and sorrow and the absorption into the promised 'new world' of sweetness and bliss. In other words, the deployment of the figures that support these contemplative prayers produces a movement from figuration (the image of Christ and his followers) and disfiguration (the pain, sorrow, and the demonic face of this world) to transfiguration (the world in light of eternal sweetness). In shaping perception and thought they also produce the transition from intellectual 'belief' to an existentially new state of 'conversion', from the letter that "kills" to the embodied spirit that "makes alive" (2 Cor 3:6).

The practice of figuration, disfiguration, and transfiguration is centred primarily around the teaching that the experiential knowledge of God is not just metaphorically described in terms taken from our external sense-experience and worldly affect but that it is actually based on a phenomenology of the so-called five inner or spiritual senses. It is a teaching which is usually traced back to its origins in the hermeneutical practice and theory of the church father Origen, one of the most influential Greek theologians.[1] And it is to be called a phenomenology because it offers an alternative to the philosophical faculty psychology, which focuses on senses, sense organs, and specific media. Instead, the tradition that starts with Origen foregrounds not the faculties but the very acts of sensation that are produced in the practices of reading and remembering the scriptures. Thus, their focus lies from the beginning on the medium, the artificial production, and its formative power. Although the so-called inner or spiritual senses correspond to the five outer senses (in fact they are named in analogous ways), they are not just to be seen as analogous, metaphorical, or disembodied. In other words, they are not to be seen as a set of allegorical poetic means of expressing and representing a preceding spiritual experience. Rather, they constitute and construct a specific experiential reality, forming the basis of what I want to call a culture of arousal within the framework of memorial practices and techniques of reading. The sensations that Origen postulates form a new and previously unknown life of the soul, and they are intrinsically linked to the experience and the exploration of sensual and emotional arousal in medieval reading practices. Thus, I want to suggest, the invention and the rhetoric of the inner or spiritual senses allows for the creation of a space of 'experience', 'exploration' and 'amplification' of the emotional as well as of the sensory life of the soul—or, if we want, an exploration of the live-shaping force that inhabits the letter below its literal meaning.

I use these three terms because they refer to three aspects of this practice of prayer and its reliance on techniques of mediation: an experiential instead of a

---

1 For the theory of the 'inner and outer senses' see now: Gavrilyuk and Coakley (2012); Rudy (2002). See also: Adnès (1967); Canévet (1989); Rahner (1932, 1933); von Balthasar (1984); Fraigneau-Julien (1985); Miquel (1989).

conceptual understanding; the discovery and exploration of new and unheard-of states of emotional arousal against the 'aridity' of the soul; and finally a technique of excitement, i.e., of an amplification of the affective life by rhetorical means. This amplification is based on mnemotechnical practices, the use of scriptural quotes and visual arrangements in the theatre of memory and imagination, but also the use of artefacts in the church and liturgy. Beyond that, the amplification is based on narrative scripts, which draw from scriptural scenes, lives of martyrs, and lives of saints. These scripts—among those the life of Saint Antony and of Mary Magdalen—include the production of feelings of intense desolation, hope and hopelessness, as well as joy, but also of overwhelming sense-experience of the bitterness of hell and the sweetness of the divine, and finally of intense desire and excessive love that is mostly seen in terms of an experience of touch.

Ultimately, this theory and practice of prayer and contemplation attempts to transcend, or, to put it more precisely, inherently transcends the common and universally emphasized disjunction of 'inner' and 'outer' 'man' in medieval anthropology.[2] This is the case because the evocation of the inner senses in the practice of prayer opens up a realm of embodied emotions and sensations that compensate for the lack of the intellectual understanding and thus neutralize the common dissociation of 'inner' and 'outer' in medieval, of 'thought' and 'matter' in modern anthropology. The movement through which this is reached can be characterized as a de-naturalization of perception by artificial means— the techniques of prayer and the use of rhetorical stimuli that deploy their effect, producing a virtual reality—and a re-naturalisation, a return to the intensity of sensory and emotional experience of the world, in form of an aesthetic experience which is constructed with the help of these very rhetorical, artificial means. De-naturalisation means nothing else than dis-figuration, re-naturalisation nothing else than trans-figuration; or, more concretely: de-naturalisation makes the world appear in light of the demonic ugliness and corruption, re-naturalisation in light of divine beauty and plenitude. In many cases, the re-naturalisation follows an eschatological, often highly dramatic pattern, referring to events in the life of Christ or in the Song of Songs, anticipating ultimately a state of redemption, but emphasising at the same time the necessity of the descent into hell. However, it has to be pointed out that the logic of figuration, disfiguration, and transfiguration can never be left behind. Each moment of 'literal' understanding, each moment of understanding has to be overcome, i.e., de-na-

---

2 I am drawing here on my research presented in several earlier articles: Largier (2014a, 2015, 2008a, 2008b, 2003).

turalised and dis-figured in order to produce the transition to the 'live-giving' force that transfigures it. Otherwise all perception would be stuck in a literal 'understanding' of the world and of itself, and thus it would succumb to a stable order of discourse and idolatry.

As I pointed out, this theory of the inner or spiritual senses is a response to the desire for experience of the divine that is based on the reading of the scriptures. As I pointed out before it is in writings of early Greek theologians, especially Origen and Gregory of Nyssa, where we encounter the attempt to define the communication between man and God in terms not only of an intellectual grasp or of a stoic *apatheia* but of a grasp that must be described as 'sensory' and 'emotional'. Using the Greek term *aisthesis*, Origen indicates that he speaks about an experience that transcends the rational and discursive operations of our intellect. In fact, Origen translates the biblical verse Proverbs 2:5 (King James Version: "Then shalt thou understand the fear of the Lord, and find the knowledge of God") in a specific way, introducing the term *aisthesis* where other translations, including the Septuagint and the Vulgate, use *gnosis* or *scientia* (quoted in Rahner 1932, 116).[3] Thus Origen emphasizes that the text of the scriptures is the object of each sense of the soul, such as light for the eyes, word for the ears, bread for the taste, tactile sensation for the touch—but not metaphorically (Origenes 1991, 442).Origen points to the fact that the practice of reading the scriptures necessarily involves the practice of sensation. In his words, memorial practice and exercise (*gymnasía*) are key elements leading to the constitution of this realm of experience. Where this happens is above all in prayer. Prayer is the place, as well, where the rational, discursive, and practical level of the life of the soul is left behind in favour of the contemplative aesthetic experience of the divine.

In many cases, starting with Gregory of Nyssa and essentially based on a number of biblical verses, the emphasis of this contemplative prayer lies not on the inner vision—as one might expect from a modern perspective and from the Greek philosophical basis of a large part of Christian theology—but on inner taste and finally on inner touch as well. As we might expect, taste refers above all to the sweetness that is experienced in the perception of the divine. Honey is the expression used in many of these cases, quoting from the bible and its uses of 'milk and honey' with regard to the experience of the paradise or eternal life, but reference is also made to bitterness and other terms, evoking

---

3 Rahner (1932, 116), "Le début". Origenes: *kai aísthäsin theían heuréseis.* Septuagint: *kai epígnosin theou heuréseis*; Vulgate: *et scientiam Dei invenies.*

the exploration of a variety of experiences of taste (Gregory of Nyssa 1860, 1084c; 1960, 425 – 426).

Innumerable authors who use this terminology could be quoted here, especially those who comment on the "Song of Songs", the text which is at the basis of most elaborations on the sensory and emotional experience of the divine. Among these, William of St. Thierry plays an important role in the medieval tradition, and a Middle High German text that testifies to the importance of the theory of the inner senses is to be found in the "St. Trudperter Hohelied" (see Ohly 1998, 922 – 923).

Often the approach to this understanding of sensation chosen by the medieval authors is not systematic. It does not take shape in the form of a clearly elaborated theory of the hierarchy of the senses, but rather in the form of comments on different approaches to the divine through the scriptures and in memorial practices, which in turn find their expression in the smell, the sound, the touch, or the taste that is perceived by the soul while praying, that is, in other and more concrete words, while it is 'chewing' and 'ruminating' the words of the scriptures. In most cases, biblical verses expressing such moments of taste figure prominently in these texts—and in the case of the medieval mystic Mechthild of Magdeburg's *Flowing Light of the Godhead*, to take just one example, the memorial practice, i.e., the evocation of a specific biblical scene, always leads to the production of intense emotional and sensual experience. The texts testify to the fact that quite often, specific biblical verses and prayers are used as the stimuli, the rhetorical means that call forth specific sensations and emotions. In meditative practice the effect of memorizing and ruminating can thus, as in the case of Teresa of Ávila, result in the production of complex inner worlds of multiple layers of sensation, emotion, and thought.

Major attempts to bring this practice of prayer and contemplation into coherent shape can be found in Albert the Great and in Bonaventure. Albert relates sight, hearing, and odor to knowledge of truth, i.e., to the more cognitive intellectual realm; he relates taste and touch to the experience of the good, i.e., to the realm of love and will. Inspired by Dionysius the Pseudo-Areopagite and his negative theology, he emphasizes the passivity of this form of experience and the fact that the soul is "suffering" it and that the produced inner sensory phenomena are aspects of the reality of this suffering of the divine in the practice of reading and remembering the scriptures. Speaking of *tactus* and *sapor* with regard to the divine he accentuates the "experiential", purely "receptive", and "passive" character of this kind of perception.[4]

---

4 Albert the Great (1894, III d. 13 a. 4, 240): *Si autem objicitur contra hos duos sensus, quod sen-*

It should be pointed out that the perception of the divine in terms of an experience of taste and touch becomes most significant in Franciscan traditions, in David of Augsburg's *Septem gradus orationis*, in Bonaventure's *Itinerarium mentis ad Deum* and *Breviloquium*, but even more so in later medieval texts, e. g., in Rudolf of Biberach's *De septem itineribus aeternitatis*. Other examples where the gustatory and tactile experience is very important could be added, among those are the works of Peter of Ailly and the *Imitatio Christi* by Thomas a Kempis, one of the works that had a major influence on Ignatius of Loyola's *Spiritual Exercises*. *Delectatio* ("pleasure"), and *suavitas* ("sweetness") are the key words these authors use when they discuss the ways by which man can reach the divine in an experiential way, referring to a sensation of taste. Peter of Ailly expresses it in this way: "[...] *divinas aeternorum praemiorum delectationes jam quodammodo experimentaliter attingere, et eorum suavitatem delectabiliter sapere*" ("to reach already in this life the pleasures of the eternal rewards in an experiential way, and to taste their sweetness with delight") (Peter of Ailly 1634, 134). Rudolf of Biberach, in the treatise entitled *De septem itineribus aeternitatis*, uses the following words, largely inspired by Alcher and Bernhard of Clairvaux's, Hugh of Saint Victor's, and Saint Bonaventure's treatment of the inner senses: ... *attingens gustum interioris mentis, aperit eum ad aeternorum dulcedinem gustandam* ("reaching the inner sense of taste, it opens it up toward the tasting of eternal sweetness") (Rudolf of Biberach 1985, 467). In these texts, as for example in Richard of Saint Victor's Commentary on Psalm 28, *experientia* or *experiendo* stand for the aspect of contemplative reading and prayer that Origen has in mind when he uses *aisthesis*.

The eschatological structure of this concept of reading and remembering is often obvious, since it is in a newly produced experience[5] that sensation is sup-

---

sus est vis cognitiva: istud autem non ordinatur ad apprehendere, sed potius ad affici: dicendum, quod est cognitio per modum receptionis quasi ab extra: et est cognitio experimentalis, sicut dicit Dionysius quod Hierotheus patiendo divina, didicit divina: et haec cognitio est per gustum et tactum spirituales. ("If someone argued against these two senses that sense experience is a cognitive power, one should stress that this does not refer to active apprehension but rather to passive perception. One should reply that it is a form of cognition in the mode of an influence as if from outside. It is experiential cognition, to be understood in the way Dionysius said of Hierotheus that he knew the divine through suffering the divine. This is cognition through the spiritual senses of taste and touch".) For Albert's understanding of the inner senses, see also Albert the Great (1897, 414–415).

5 In his long treatment of the inner senses, Rudolf (n.8, 464–472) makes this experiential aspect very explicit: "*Ex quo ergo gustum illum nemo potest exprimere, sed solum per experientiam noscitur, ideo oportet viam quaerere, qualiter spiritus noster ad istam gustus experientiam possit pertingere*". (467: "This explains why nobody can express this taste. It can only be known through

posed to be rehabilitated and all perception transfigured in a way unknown since the loss of paradise. Such experiences are characterized as an anticipation of the eternal and a reconciliation with the ideal existence of man beyond the state of sin. However, it is more than that. In the Franciscan tradition this rehabilitation of the senses and of experience leads to a new affirmative mode with regard to sense experience itself and to an aesthetic justification of the world as it is to be found in Franciscan poetry and science of the late Middle Ages. Here, the practice of sense-formation in prayer translates into a liberation of sensation that produces something we might want to call a spiritual empiricism and figural materialism—or, to put it in eco-theological terms, an experience of the world in light of the promise of salvation that is enacted through the use of specific media that give redemptive shape to the ways in which we inhabit the world.

3 Figuration, Disfiguration, Transfiguration

How does this dramatic grasp of the hidden sense of the biblical text in terms of *aisthesis* and the transfiguration of sensation and affect happen? I want to sketch the process in the next couple of paragraphs, trying to explain it further based on the concept of figuration. In using this term I am referring both to the use of the notion of figure in the rhetorical tradition and to the use of '*figura*' that Erich Auerbach discusses in his essay with the title *Figura* (Auerbach 2014).In this text Auerbach points to the difference between the 'material' aspect of the notion of figure (its "plasticity" and "corporeality") and the 'hermeneutic' aspect (the possibility to read figures in terms of metaphor and allegory). This very difference underlies the practice of contemplative prayer that is at stake here. As shown above, the practice of prayer focuses on the production of experiential states in form of sensation– and affect-events that deploy an absorbing power. This is the result not of a spiritualizing and allegorizing engagement with rhetorical figures and scriptural images, in other words a hermeneutic understanding, but of a deployment of their "energetic" (Auerbach 2014, 80)[6] plastic force. This plastic effect is the form-giving aspect of rhetorical figures, i.e., *aisthesis* as affective, sensual, and cognitive formation according to the figures that are introduced and used in prayer.

---

experience, and this is why we have to look for the way in which our mind can reach the experience of this taste".)

6 Newman translates Auerbach's "*energischer Realismus*" as "emphatic realism". See Largier (2013).

As rhetorical productions, however, the new experiential states and perception-events are always problematic. They are overwhelming, forceful, and while they give a new shape to sensation, affect, and cognition they also raise suspicion. What about the nature of this experience of sweetness and joy, is thus a question Teresa asks herself repeatedly, what about the unspeakable knowledge of the divine? This is a question that all the treatises on contemplative prayer raise time and again. How can we know that the experience is divine and that it is not a simulacrum that has its origin in the activities of the devil? How can we ever be sure? This question has been raised since the early days of Christian contemplative practice, going back to the desert saints and above all to Evagrius Ponticus. The desert fathers in their prayers are all engaged in practices of figuration that evoke sensation and affect, and thus they have to address these very issues. They do so in two ways: On one side they develop techniques of evaluation, i.e., a phenomenology of the life of the soul. On the other side they conceive of the practices of figuration in terms of a *psychomachia*, a battle in the soul that engages in processes of self-transformation. Thus, they see the process of figuration, i.e., the self-formation and the shaping of perception through figures that are drawn from the scriptures and from other lives of saints, as essentially dramatic. In other words, the attempt to shape the soul in contemplative prayer will necessarily evoke the battle with demonic figures—or, to put it more concisely, it will necessarily put the surrounding world into a light that makes it look disfigured, monstrous, and utterly full of temptation. Thus, in the eyes of transformative prayer the world will look like a stage of figures of temptation, violence, and horror—before it can turn into a world of sweetness (see Largier 2014b). In the eyes of Saint Antony, the exemplary saint in this tradition of the enactment of spiritual battles, the surrounding world turns into an aesthetic experience of horror, and so an aesthetics of horror is born. Seen from the perspective of the practice of contemplative prayer, the true beauty of the world—again, an aesthetic experience—returns only when sensation and affect have been reconfigured and shaped with the help of the rhetorical figures that are drawn from the scriptural archive and deployed along the lines of a drama between an aesthetics of horror and an aesthetics of beauty.

In via, we might say, this tension and drama can never be left behind. In this production of sensation and affect and in the phenomenology of rhetorical effects nothing can be truly stable. Every prayer has to work through a drama of figuration, disfiguration, and transfiguration, leaving the literal understanding behind, producing a world of new aesthetic experience that makes the 'old world' visible as a disfigured world, and evoking the transfigured world in an embodied experience. In the goal of producing a "foretaste" of heaven (*praegustatio*) a wide range of stimulating rhetorical means is being used. This means, however, that the world itself has to emerge and to be experienced in its disfigured state time and again: as a place of horror, devastation, as something that is bare, nude, and open toward a transfiguring salvation. Contemplative prayer produces this drama with all its aspects, leading from the initial gestures of crying and abandonment to the moments of overwhelming joy in experiences of the sweetness and beauty that shines through the experience of the world itself.

Using Nietzsche's words (somewhat ironically) we might be tempted to speak of an aesthetic justification of the world that emerges on the grounds of this practice of prayer. At its centre stands the challenge not to understand conversion in terms of an intellectual and conceptual grasp but of an existential transformation that enacts the life-shaping force of the word. As we have seen in Teresa's text and in the history of prayer, this transformation relies on *aisthesis*, i.e., an active formation of perception that has to be dramatically staged and reiterated time and again. The very dynamic of figuration, disfiguration, and transfiguration cannot come to an end in this live. It does, however, open a realm of perception-events that let us understand both conversion and religious experience in terms of aesthetic experience. Its religious aspect lies not in the dynamic of figuration itself but, as Marshall McLuhan correctly saw, in the lines of analogy that are produced in these practices of figuration and figural networks of resonance. He writes in a letter—commenting on his own Catholicism in 1969—that this very rhetoric of an affirmation, dramatization, and reconfiguration of the sensual and affective worlds in prayer relies not on "concepts or ideas" but on an "analogical awareness that begins in the senses." Thus, he notes:

> Your piece on me brings to mind that I am a Thomist for whom the sensory order resonates with the divine Logos. I don't think concepts have any relevance in religion. Analogy is not concept. It is community. It is resonance. It is inclusive. It is the cognitive process itself. That is the analogy of the divine Logos. I think of Jasper [sic], Bergson, and Buber as very inferior conceptualist types, quite out of touch with the immediate analogical awareness that begins in the senses and is derailed by concepts or ideas (McLuhan 2010, 69).

The production of this "resonance" and of "analogical awareness", or of "analogical awareness" through "resonance" is indeed the very core of Teresa's practice of 'folding' and of the theory of prayer I have portrayed here.

Bibliography

Adnès, Pierre. 1967. "Goût spirituel." In *Dictionnaire de spiritualité ascétique et mystique.* Vol. 6, 626–644. Paris: Beauchesne.

Auerbach, Erich. 2014. "Figura." In *Selected Essays of Erich Auerbach: Time, History, and Literature*, edited by James I. Porter, translated by Jane O. Newman, 65–113. Princeton: Princeton University Press.

Albert the Great. 1894. *Commentarii in III Sententiarum*. Vol. 28, *Opera omnia*, edited by Stephanus Borgnet. Paris: Vivès.

— 1897. "De coelesti hierarchia." In *Opera omnia*. Vol. 14, edited by Stephanus Borgnet, 4–451. Paris: Vivès.

Balthasar, Hans Urs von. 1984. *Origen. Spirit and Fire. A Thematic Anthology of His Writings*. Washington: Catholic University of America Press.

Bataille, Georges. 1988. *Inner Experience*, translated by Leslie Ann Boldt. New York: SUNY Press.

Canévet, Mariette. 1989. "Sens spirituels." In *Dictionnaire de spiritualité ascétique et mystique*. Vol. 13, 598–617. Paris: Beauchesne.

Deleuze, Gilles. 1988. *Le pli: Leibniz et le baroque*. Paris: Minuit.

Foucault, Michel. 1988. "Technologies of the Self." In *Technologies of the Self: A Seminar with Michel Foucault*, edited by Luther H. Martin, Huck Gutman, and Patrick H. Hutton, 16–49. Amherst: University of Massachusetts Press.

Fraigneau-Julien, Bernard. 1985. *Les sens spirituels et la vision de dieu selon Syméon le Nouveau Théologien*. Paris: Beauchesne.

Gavrilyuk, Paul L., and Sarah Coakley, eds. 2012. *The Spiritual Senses: Perceiving God in Western Christianity*. Cambridge: Cambridge University Press.

Gregory of Nyssa. 1860. "In Canticum Canticorum homilia 14." In *Patrologia Graeca*. Vol. 44, edited by Jacques Paul Migne, 1061–1088. Paris: Migne.

— 1960. "In Canticum Canticorum homilia 14." In *Gregorii Nysseni Opera*. Vol. 6, *In Canticum canticorum*, edited by Hermannus Langerbeck, 425–426. Leiden: Brill.

Largier, Niklaus. 2003. "Inner Senses – Outer Senses: The Practice of Emotions in Medieval Mysticism." In *Codierung Von Emotionen Im Mittelalter / Emotions and Sensibilities in the Middle Ages*, edited by C. Stephen Jaeger and Ingrid Kasten, 3–15. Berlin and New York: de Gruyter.

— 2008a. "Praying by Numbers. An Essay on Medieval Aesthetics." *Representations* 104: 73–92.

— 2008b. "Medieval Christian Mysticism." In *The Oxford Handbook of Religion and Emotion*, edited by John Corrigan, 364–379. Oxford: Oxford University Press.

— 2010. "The Plasticity of the Soul: Mystical Darkness, Touch, and Aesthetic Experience." *Modern Language Notes* 125: 536–551.

— 2013. "Zwischen Sinnlichkeit, Rhetorik und Hermeneutik. Erich Auerbachs *Figura* und das Konzept der 'historischen Topologie'." In *Figura. Dynamiken von Zeichen und Zeiten*, edited by Katharina Mertens Fleury and Christian Kiening, 51–70. Würzburg: Königshausen & Neumann.

— 2014a. "The Art of Prayer: Conversions of Interiority and Exteriority in Medieval Contemplative Practice." In *Rethinking Emotion. Interiority and Exteriority in Premodern, Modern, and Contemporary Thought*, edited by Rüdiger Campe and Julia Weber, 58–71. Berlin and Boston: de Gruyter.

— 2014b. "Ästhetik der Disfiguration. Ein Essay zur Versuchung des Antonius durch die Dämonen." In *Das Dämonische. Schicksale einer Kategorie der Zweideutigkeit nach Goethe*, edited by Lars Friedrich, Eva Geulen and Kirk Wetters, 43–52. Paderborn: Fink.

—— 2015. "The Rhetoric of Mysticism: From Contemplative Practice to Aesthetic Experiment." In *Mysticism and Reform*, edited by Sarah Poor and Nigel Smith, 353–379. Notre Dame: University of Notre Dame Press.

Meyer, Birgit. 2010. "From Imagined Communities to Aesthetic Formations: Religious Mediations, Sensational Forms, and Styles of Binding." In *Aesthetic Formations: Media, Religion, and the Senses*, edited by Birgit Meyer, 6–11. New York: Palgrave Macmillan.

McLuhan, Marshall. 1967. *Understanding Media*. New York: McGraw-Hill.

—— 2010. *The Medium and the Light: Reflections on Religion and Media*. Eugene: Wipf and Stock.

Miquel, Pierre. 1989. *Le vocabulaire de l'expérience spirituelle dans la tradition patristique grecque du IVe au XIVe siècle*. Paris: Beauchesne.

Ohly, Friedrich, ed. 1998. *Das St. Trudperter Hohelied. Eine Lehre der Liebenden Gotteserkenntnis*. Frankfurt am Main: Deutscher Klassiker Verlag.

Origenes. 1991. *Commentarium in Canticum Canticorum. Commentaire sur le Cantique des cantiques*. Vol. 1, edited by Luc Brésard, Henri Crouzel, and Marcel Borret, 442. Paris: Cerf.

Peter of Ailly. 1634. *Compendium contemplationis* III 11. In *Opuscula spiritualia*, 67–139. Douai: Wyon.

Rahner, Karl. 1932. "Le début d'une doctrine des cinq sens spirituels chez Origène." *Revue d'ascétique et de mystique* 13: 113–145.

—— 1933. "La doctrine des 'sens spirituels' au Moyen-Age, en particulier chez Bonaventure." *Revue d'ascétique et de mystique* 14: 263–299.

Rudolf of Biberach. 1985. "De septem itineribus aeternitatis VI dist. V." In *De septem itineribus aeternitatis: Nachdruck der Ausgabe von Peltier 1866 mit einer Einleitung in die lateinische Überlieferung und Corrigenda zum Text*, edited by Margot Schmidt, 467. Stuttgart-Bad Cannstatt: Frommann-Holzboog.

Rudy, Gordon. 2002. *Mystical Language of Sensation in the Later Middle Ages*. London and New York: Routledge.

Teresa of Avila. 1957. *The Life of Saint Teresa of Ávila by Herself*, translated by John Michael. Cohen. London: Penguin.

Teresa of Avila. 1997. *Obras completas*, a cargo de Maximiliano Herráiz. Salamanca: Sigueme.

Ulrike Brunotte

The Performative Knowledge of Ecstasy: Jane E. Harrison's (1850–1928) Early Contestations of the Textual Paradigm in Religious Studies

1 Aesthetics of Performativity

In the 1990s a shift in focus occurred in cultural studies, which drew attention to cultural practices, events and acts and their power in creating and transforming meaning. Within this context, the body and body knowledge (Koch 2007; 2012, 3–42) gained significance in the cultural sciences. This shift to material culture and sensuous practices, which was partly inspired by ethnographic research, offered important new resources for the study of religion; see David Morgan (2011). Especially the new significance of ritual studies re-centred the study of religion into everyday life and cultural practices. Religious studies increasingly found its way beyond the equation of religion and belief, leaving the library and moving into "lived religion" (Hall 1997). As one of the main promoters of the so-called *performative turn* in the United States, the theatre anthropologist Richard Schechner looked back in 2003 to his own start in performance theory: "Taking a cue from Erving Goffman's 1959 breakthrough book, *The Presentation of Self in Everyday Life,* [I was] [...] learning about 'body language' and a whole range of expressive behaviour outside of spoken or written words" (Schechner [1988] 2003, ix–x). The "so-called performative turn, in the social sciences, leads toward an explicit reception of performance and theatre studies in the study of ritual" (Kreinath 2009, 235; Brunotte 2001, 85–102; 2000, 349–367; 2013a, 35–522). In the European sphere, following early works by Stanley J. Tambiah (1981), it was, and is, primarily the theatre studies scholar Erika Fischer-Lichte (2000a, 2000b, 2001, 2004, 2008), who, furthering early approaches of the theory of theatre and ritual of the *fin de siècle*, such as that of Nikolai Evreinov (1908), expanded the radius of the performative to include the moment of the theory of theatricality. At the same time she has opened up the perspective to an aesthetics of the performative that links art and religion: "Evreinov introduced the concept of theatricality as an anthropological category, which aims at the human capacity to creatively change 'the world as we perceive it' [...] and view performativity [...] as constituting reality. [...] [H]e coined the term 'theatricality', which he defined as a 'pre-aesthetic instinct' which underlies all cultural activity, i.e., reli-

https://doi.org/10.1515/9783110461015-008

gion, art, customs, law, etc." (Fischer-Lichte 2000a, 294–295; 2005, 99; Evreinov 1923).

In this context, the focus is directed away from the text and toward the transformative potential of human action to influence meaning. The term "performative" was coined by John L. Austin in his language philosophy. He introduced it in his lecture series *How to Do Things with Words* (Austin 1962). The current heterogeneous discourse on performativity links Austin and Searle's theory of *Speech Acts* and the concept of *performance* in theatre studies with the notion of *performative acts and gender constitution* introduced by Judith Butler (1990) and the theories of *social drama* and the *liminal*, as advanced by the anthropologist Victor Turner (1969, 1974). "Ceremony *indicates*, ritual *transforms*" (Turner 1982, 80) was Turner's concise and fitting distinction for a reading of ritual actions that is both somatic and aesthetic (i.e., aisthetic). Common to all of these approaches is a special link between speaking and acting, which suggests the power of the speech act to produce and transform reality. Austin developed the crucial innovations in his *Words and Deeds* lectures (1952–1954 in Oxford) and *How to Do Things with Words* (1955 in Harvard). Although Austin did not incorporate the long religious and juridical tradition of performative speech acts into his theory, it is apparent "that many of the performative utterances he examined represent the carrying out or 'part of the carrying out of a ritual,' that is, 'ritual phrases'" (Därmann 2013). This has to do with both the event *aspect* of completing a ritual and the *emergent* aspect of the physical and theatrical dimension of their perception and presentation. It is first and foremost the magical performative quality of rituals—their capacity to let something inaccessible appear—that represents an intermediary field between religion, culture, and art.

Like Mary Douglas in *Natural Symbols* (1970) and Marcel Mauss in "*techniques du corps*" (1935, 271–293) before him, Pierre Bourdieu also speaks of "performative magic" in his early analyses of North African Kabyles (Bourdieu 1991, 106; see Wulf et al. 2001, 8), that is, ritual practices that go beyond the mere *embodiment* and *enactment* of social patterns of thought and expression. For his sociology of social practice, the *habitus*, the "social made body" (Bourdieu and Wacquant 1992, 127), is not to be understood solely in the sense of a normative system of social dispositions; instead, the changing potential of an *ars vivendi* is at the same time always immanent in the *habitus*; see Krais and Gebauer (2002, 6).

All current approaches in ritual theories (see Kreinath, Snoek, and Stausberg 2006) which are part of the *performative turn* are embedded in a broader theoretical discourse and stand in tension with the two preceding turning points in the 20th-century European and Western theory of rituals, one in the late 1970s and the first around 1900. Especially in the field of theatre studies, the arts and in *comparative anthropology,* different "thrusts of performativity" (Fischer-Lichte 2001, 113) at the *fin de siècle* led to a knowledge transfer from the "colonial frontiers" (Chidester 1996, 2014)[1] to European societies. The "discovery" of a ritualistic approach to culture in Europe revolved around symbolic power *and* the corporeal, communicated practice of rituals. At the same time, under the conditions of modern pluralisation through "newly emerging needs for meaning" (Gladigow 1995, 36; 2009), the dialectic of the secularisation and constant transfer of religion to various segments of society (such as science, literature, and the arts) *and back* became meaningful—and was viewed by Burkhard Gladigow as key for the European history of religion.

In this sense, the approach of an aesthetics of ritual performances as developed especially by Jens Kreinath (Kreinath 2006, 2009) for religious studies—following Susanne K. Langer (1945, 1953), Fischer-Lichte, and Klaus Peter Köpping (Köpping and Rao 2001)—is part of the "non-traditional, dynamic concept of the European history of religion" (Kugele and Wilkens 2011, 10; see also Kippenberg, Rüpke and von Stuckrad 2009).

1.1 Affective Archives: The Ephemeral Remembered

For the new study of the aesthetics of religion the findings of *performative studies* could be fruitful, because a performative mode of observation pushes the sensual completion of the action and the effective ritualised situations, ritual performances and staged depictions into the focus of interest. As Erika Fischer-Lichte claims, an aesthetics of performativity bridges the field of the arts, theatre, everyday life and religion. Another field of research connecting performative studies and the study of the aesthetics of religion can be found in the recent debate on performativity, affect and remembrance (Plate and Smelik 2013). In these debates cultural memory is no longer seen as a static archive but as performative one: especially art objects and artistic practices are analysed as modes and media to perform the past in the present. However, the paradox of re-mediation, re-enactment, and experiences of immediacy is an intrinsic quality of religious cults and a focus of the Christian doctrine of the "real presence". In recent years this context has gained significance through the Christian material and media theory approach of religious studies analyses, such as those of David Mor-

---

1 David Chidester proposed the term "colonial frontier" as a fiercely contested zone where knowledge was produced and impacted in both directions.

gan and Birgit Meyer (Morgan 2005, 2011, 2012; Meyer 2006; 2009; 2011, 23–39; 2013b, 309–326).

The debates on the performativity, memory and the role of affect and media revolve around the question if and how the performative—which exists only in the present and in the immediate execution (performance) and then disappears—can be remembered and archived. Within the framework of the *affective approach* (Gregg and Seigworth 2010) inspired by a revival of Deleuze and Guattari's *A Thousand Plateaus* (1987), performative acts are no longer understood as "immaterial", ephemeral and thus transient, but as affective and thus "material". Ritual performances often release and transmit affective discharge that can exceed the boundaries of an enclosed time frame. They can constitute an affective archive, as affects are "material, physiological things" (Brennan 2003) that can create an *"in-between-ness, [...] the passage of forces or intensities"* (Gregg and Seigworth 2010, 1).

Recent research on the *performative* and *cultural memory* has raised the question of how a material/affective ephemeral can be remembered. Rebecca Schneider asks: "What is the evidentiary status of the trace [of past events] carried forward and backward in the form and force of affective, incorporated, 'live' actions?" (Schneider 2011, 38). In answering this question, it can be helpful to concentrate on the material-religion approach (Meyer 2006; Houtman and Meyer 2012; Keane 2008; Goa et al. 2005; Meyer et al. 2011) and the aesthetics of religion, because ritual enactments and religious feasts were not only, following Jan Assmann, the "primary forms of organizing cultural memory", they also provided the media which as "poetic form, ritual performance, and collective participation" captured the unifying knowledge in a manner that would preserve it (Assmann 2011, 41–42). It is the ritual *frame* (Jungaberle and Weinhold 2006, 7) that makes experiences of immediacy and the "presence" of the past possible in the first place. Carried forth in theatricality, "the embodied cycles of memory [...] do not delimit the remembered to the past" (Schneider 2011, 32). In religious as well as performative-artistic events, the very past-ness of the past can be challenged; re-enacted, re-felt emotions are then experienced as immediacy and absolute presence.

Cultural and especially performative studies today try to consider an "affective archive" and, as André Lepecki has put it, even a body-to-body transmission of cultural knowledge and *"embodied* actualizations" of remembrance (Lepecki 2010, 31). The "redefining action is carried out through a common articulator: the dancer's body. As we will see [...], in dance re-enactments there will be no distinctions left between archive and body. The body is archive and archive a body" (Lepecki 2010, 31). In this context it can be very insightful to refer back to researchers of ritual, affect, and images such as Jane Ellen Harrison und Aby Warburg.

Around 1900, Warburg—art historian, religious studies scholar, and founding father of iconology—already thought about a body-to-body and image-to-image-in-motion transmission of cultural memory and a gestural archive of embodied emotions. For his *energetic* concept of body-, image-, and affect-based figures and emotional forms of cultural remembrance he coined the term *pathos formula*, or "emotive formula". Warburg's pathos formulae are body-centred, comprising figures of movement and (often mythical) scenic actions—such as the rape of Persephone or the beheading of Holofernes—that, from antiquity to modernity, mediated archaic trauma. However, they were also scenes and gestures of ambivalent and highly emotional intensity: the embodied knowledge of emotions of joy, terror/horror, passion or ecstasy. He conceptualised these formulae firstly around the figure of woman-in-movement, his "Nympha" or "Ninfa Fiorentina" (Warburg [1900] 2010), but his life project focused on developing a *Mnemosyne image atlas* (Warburg 2000, 2009): "Undertaken between 1926 and 1929, the atlas of images entitled *Mnemosyne* is Aby Warburg's nearly wordless account of how and why symbolic images of great pathos persist in Western cultural memory from antiquity to the early twentieth century" (Johnson 2012, 4).

In the following I will draw on Warburg's and Harrison's pioneering work on an emotional, performative (*avant la lettre*) and transformative approach to ritual and culture, and mark ritual and theatrical (dance) as a field of study within the *aesthetics of religion*. Thereby I'll focus on the paradox of the capacity of rituals to create a virtual space of "absolute presence" and immediacy through mediation and, at the same time, to provide a symbolic gestural "form" for embodied cultural experience and memory. Not directly in line with Warburg and Harrison, but instead following Ernst Cassirer's theory of symbolic forms, Susanne K. Langer, in her 1945 book *Philosophy in a New Key: A Study in the Symbolism of Reason, Rite, and Art* (see also Langer 1952), also developed a theory of human symbol formation based on ritual and dance performances, which reinforced the role of "formed" feelings. Birgit Meyer's concept of "sensational forms", which stresses the importance of the senses as media of knowledge production without negating the role of meaning production, provides a helpful analytical tool to reflect and further elaborate on this paradox (Meyer 2006, 2011). Drawing on Webb Keane's notion of "semiotic ideology" (Keane 2007, 16) she writes:

> Sensational forms are relatively fixed modes for invoking and organizing access to the transcendental, offering structures of repetition to create and sustain links between believers in the context of particular religious regimes. [...] [A]ddressing the paradox of mediation and

immediacy requires developing a new synthesis of approaches that stress the importance of the senses and experience with those stressing the forms and codes that are at the basis of cultural and religious systems (Meyer 2011, 29–30).

2 Ritual and Theatricality: The Pre-eminence of Bodily Performance over Text

Until the late 1980s, the notion of "culture as text" dominated cultural studies and the Protestant bias governed religious studies, which privileged texts and beliefs over bodily expressions and rituals as the prime religious media. Specific cultural phenomena as well as entire cultures were conceived as structured webs of signs waiting to be deciphered. "Numerous attempts to describe and interpret culture were launched and designated as 'readings'" (Fischer-Lichte 2008, 26). But already around 1900, as ritual studies emerged in Great Britain, Jane Ellen Harrison (1850–1928), the first female Hellenist and the head of the so-called Cambridge Ritualists, revolutionised the very concept of antique Greek religion and culture: her innovation was to elevate rituals and images as means of religious expression to a status equal to that of literature. Prior to this move toward ritual around 1900, research pursued a more or less enlightened protestant understanding of religion. Jane E. Harrison herself described the eighteenth-century text paradigm of the history of religion, using as an example her research on Greek religion: "Religion, we have seen, was in the last century regarded mainly in its theoretical aspect as a doctrine. Greek religion, for example, meant to most educated persons Greek mythology" (Harrison 1915, 151–152; [1909] 2009, 506). This changed with the shift to a more ritual-centred approach around 1900; see Segal (2006, 101). Harrison described the development to a performative understanding of religion, whose point of departure was not belief and dogmas, but cultural and religious practices, again based on her research on Greek religion:

> Yet even a cursory examination shows that neither Greek nor Roman religion had any creed or dogma, any hard and fast formulation of belief. In the Greek Mysteries only we find what we should call a *Confiteor*; and this is not a confession of faith, but an avowal of rites performed. When the religion of primitive peoples came to be examined it was speedily seen that though vague beliefs necessarily abound, definite creeds are practically non-existent. Ritual is dominant and imperative. [...] In examining religion as envisaged to-day it would therefore be more correct to begin with the practice of religion, i.e. ritual, and then pass to its theory—theology or mythology (Harrison 1915, 152; 2009, 498–499).

Furthermore, not only in her book *Ancient Art and Ritual* (Harrison [1913] 1951), but already in her early studies, such as *Myth of the Odyssey in Art and Literature* (Harrison 1882) and *Introductory Studies in Greek Art* (Harrison 1885), her pioneering work on the analysis of ritual scenes on vase paintings, she "draw[s] a direct genealogical connection between ritual and theatre, emphasizing the pre-eminence of performance over text" (Fischer-Lichte 2008, 31). Like other women of her time (see Fiske 2008), Harrison thus turned around her presumed incomplete linguistic training in the Greek language, attempting a different sort of appropriation of ancient tradition, one conveyed via non-linguistic means. However, Harrison went a step further by questioning the very concept of rational, scientific objectivity that was normative in her time. This was due to her method of "sympathetic imagination"—as she put it (Harrison 1991, 164)—which very early on made her scholarship subject to criticism for its "female" qualities (Arlen 1996, 165), at the time also considered "unclear" or even "irrational". Harrison turned around this attack *ad feminan,* formulating an epistemological programme that pursued the creative role of emotion and desire in ritual and narrative processes, and in fact in the production of knowledge per se. In the aesthetics of religion today, the concept of *knowledge* and the role of sensational knowledge have got new relevance: "For the aesthetics of religion the very idea of an aesthetics of knowledge is important in order to show how knowledge is created and understood, and how different claims and different qualities of knowledge emerge" (Grieser, Hermann, and Triplett 2011, 45).

In 1913 she published her essay "Women and Knowledge", which is still relevant today, in the *New Statesman* (Harrison [1913] 1915). In the article Harrison seriously questioned an ostensibly neutral rationality: "Knowledge is never, or very rarely, divorced from emotion and action", she asserted. "M. Bergson has shown us very clearly that all science grows up out of the desire to do and to make" (Harrison 1915, 125). With respect to the role of "sex/gender" (which Harrison viewed as both biological and culturally influenced) and intellect, she continued: "To deny sex in intellect would seem to me a desperate pessimism, and would be in intent to reassert the *old obsolete dualism between body and soul.* [...] Intellect is never wholly and separately intellectual. It is a thing charged with, dependent on, arising out of, emotional desire" (Harrison 1915, 140, emphasis added).

Concerning her study of Greek tragedy, Harrison was inspired by Friedrich Nietzsche's *The Birth of Tragedy: From the Spirit of Music* (Nietzsche 1872). In her book *Themis: A Study of the Social Origin of Greek Religion* (Harrison [1912] 1977), she developed a theory of Greek theatre as originated out of social practices, mainly ritual dance and song.

2.1 The Dual Nature of the Dionysian Cult

When Harrison explored the sources of Pausanias for her edition of *Mythology and Monuments of Ancient Athens* (Harrison and Verrall 1890), she developed her initial ideas on the dual nature of the Dionysian cult while in the Dionysian theatre in Athens: "The theatre of the Greeks was originally an orchestra, or dancing-place, *that and nothing more,* yet enough for Dionysos the Dance-lover —an altar and a level place about it" (Harrison and Verrall 1890, 286). She then discovered in ritual dance the crucial connection between cult and tragedy. In the midst of the ruins "Harrison suddenly understood a Greek vase she had seen in Naples" (Peters 2008, 1). The vase had two entirely different sides. One side, she said, showed "all the ordered splendour and luxury of a regular dramatic representation—masks, tripods, costly raiment; while Bacchus and Ariadne watch the preparation of the chorus from their sumptuous couch"; and the other side depicted "the wild dance of Maenads and Satyrs—such a dance as went on by many a rustic altar" (Harrison and Verrall 1890, 288). What Harrison suddenly realised, according to Julie Peters, was "that the dancing Maenads and Satyrs, the sacrificial goat, and the primitive god were the key to the 'ordered splendour and luxury of [the] regular dramatic representation'" (Peters 2008, 1). This was because on the other side of the same vase the Maenads and Satyrs had transformed into the tragic chorus, which the goat (*tragos*) had given his name (*tragoedia*). The German archaeologist Wilhelm Dörpfeld, whom Harrison had visited on some of his excavations, had drawn her attention in Epidaurus to the fact that the circular *orchestra* was the original centre of the dramatic performances. Harrison also saw a similar, round "dancing-place" in the Athenian theatre (see Brunotte 2013a, 200). Now she was able to imagine *"the old original orchestra on which the plays of Aeschylos were performed"* (Harrison and Verrall 1890, 285–286, emphasis in original). At the same time her imagination delved yet further into the past and she saw "the early Dionysiac dance" (Harrison and Verrall 1890, 285). The ritual itself, the starting point of the tragedy, was in fact rather simple. Harrison continued, "all were worshippers, [...] none were actors, none spectators" (Harrison and Verrall 1890, 290). It is already clear from her early vision of the performative-ritual origin of theatre, in which the boundary between player and spectator is eliminated, why Harrison's work became an "essential source for the primitivist rhetoric of modern theatre" and why she "was pivotal in the transformation of theatre from the narrative and socially mimetic institution that it had been from the Renaissance into the anti-mimetic organ it became for the twentieth-century avant-garde" (Peters 2008, 3). At the same time Harrison contributed early on to resolving a key question of contemporary religious studies research on rituals by expanding her theory of ritual action to acts of everyday life, that is, combining *dromena* (things done) with religious *drama* (performance). As Guggenmos, Laack and Schüler state, in the "Ritual Dynamics" Collaborative Research Centre in Heidelberg (see Harth and Michaels 2003, 5) "similar questions have been raised regarding the context of 'rituals'; whether 'ritual' should be conceptualised as a distinctive mode of action coinciding with non-ordinary states of mind" (Guggenmos, Laack, and Schüler 2011, 116). Following Birgit Meyer, religious rituals can therefore represent "ways in which people link up with, or even feel touched by, a meta-empirical sphere that may be glossed as supernatural, sacred, divine, or transcendental" (Meyer 2006, 6). For Harrison, however, there is no "beyond", no separate area of the sacred or divine. Instead, she views rituals as a means of re-translating religious action into human collective emotions in action. Also in Harrison's later analysis of the so-called *Hymn of the Kouretes* (Harrison 1912, 1977, 7–8) she claimed a radical anti-essentialist, aesthetic, and practical approach to religion. "In some sense, for Harrison, society is always ritualised, seamlessly shifting between worldly and aesthetic praxes" (Comentale 2001, 481). In *Mythology and Monuments* not only does she already unfold the formative and theatrical potential of the Dionysian cult, she also illuminates the broad spectrum of the god (see Harrison 1991, 34), from wine-god and theatre-god to the deadly extreme of a sacrificial dance that takes place "around an altar [...] flecked with the blood of the slain goat" (Harrison and Verrall 1890, 286).

3 The Material Knowledge of Daemons: From Anthropomorphism to Hybridity

Harrison's second innovation in the study of Greek religion was her rejection of a classical approach to Greek religion with its anthropomorphism and cult of beauty. As the first female Hellenist, she devoted a monograph to the study of monsters, spirits and Greek daemons, and discovered what Eric Robertson Dodds would later define as an *irrational* antiquity of ecstasy, fear and (cultic) madness (Dodds 1951).[2]

---

2 It was not Harrison who would reap the glory of having pioneered research on Greek irrationality, but Eric Robertson Dodds, who had been inspired by her work. Dodds succeeded Gilbert Murray as the chair of Greek studies at Oxford. He supported Harrison with his interpretation of maenadic ecstasy, its "reality" and the false assumption of its Thracian origins (see also Schlesier 1994, 169n74). Dodds gained fame through his book *The Greeks and the Irrational* (1951).

But she effected yet more innovations. From 1879 to 1897 Harrison lived in London, worked at the British Museum as a lecturer and studied classical archaeology. The influence of the still young field of archaeology on Harrison was great, as was her enthusiasm for the excavations in Greece and elsewhere, which were revolutionary at the time. Harrison developed her own method of comparative image analysis. The "proof" for her thesis on the origins of the mysteries of the god Dionysus and her interpretation of his rituals, according to Mary Beard, "... are founded in visual evidence: more than one hundred and fifty 'figures' (from a modern African initiation dance to ancient coins, Minoan seal stones to Attic vase paintings) are analyzed and compared"(Beard 2000, 106). Every lecture she performed on the "stage" of the British Museum was a drama, in which she tried to demonstrate and quasi re-enacted to and before the audience the ritual embedding of the artefacts and made them "live" again: "They were also lavishly illustrated with up-to-the-minute lantern slides, laboriously handmade by Harrison's friends and pupils. These slides are the closest we can now get to the atmosphere of her lectures. Four large wooden boxes in the Newnham College Archive still contain more than a hundred of the fragile squares of glass" (Beard 2000, 55). Harrison travelled with her lectures beyond the limits of London, and she won over a large audience: "At the height of her popularity she was able to draw an audience of 1,000 in the Midland Institute in Birmingham and 1,600 in Dundee" (Evangelista 2011, 517). As a researcher in religion who was also trained in archaeology she followed a material approach to religion. For her the artefacts, especially vase paintings, figures and sculptures, which recent archaeological discoveries had brought to light, were not only important as mere illustrations of myths and rituals, "but as 'commentaries' or 'variants' of myths in their own right" (Schlesier 1994, 155).

Furthermore, in her studies on religious traditions, which were consistently connected to modern debates and questions of modernity, and which she integrated the latest approaches in psychology, cultural anthropology, sociology and philosophy, she was more concerned with the role of emotions than with that of belief, more with the sensual impulse behind ritual actions than with text-based theological systematics. Nowadays her work, which was rediscovered for German-language comparative religious studies by Walter Burkert and Renate Schlesier in the 1970s, is increasingly being re-read by literary, theatrical and religious studies scholars as well as by researchers on performativity. (Carpentier 1998; Prins 1999; Peters 2008; Evangelista 2011; Klironomos 2008; Robinson 2001; Fiske 2008; Wright 2009; Brunotte 2013a).

As previously mentioned, Harrison's performative focus was strongly connected to her shift from an approach to Greek art that was looking for "beauty" and mostly anthropomorphic works of individualised artists, to the new focus on "ugly" or "frightening" monsters. These were often hybrid animal-human figures. Her teacher, colleague and dear friend, the Greek scholar and Euripides translator Gilbert Murray, described Harrison's interest in hybrid, formless and "ugly" figures in the eulogy that he held in Newnham in October 1928, five months after Harrison's death:

> A well-written hymn to Zeus the supreme judge, the father of gods and men, left her cold. Athena the armed virgin, the seeker of wisdom, [...] was too obvious in her beauty, and slightly repelled her. But a smiling dragon with a blue beard, or a man and woman poorly carved on a stele, bearing a speechless sacrifice to a great snake, called for her understanding, for sympathetic interpretation, and always got it. She loved, and doubtless idealised, the thought or desire that could not express itself; she loved to help it out, to strip it of its mere externals and expound the aspiration that lay at its heart (Murray 1928, 8).

In her first major work in 1903, *Prolegomena to the Study of Greek Religion* (Harrison [1903] 1991), Harrison already looked beyond the anthropomorphically formed Olympian gods and the immaterial *logos* of philosophy and asked about the material knowledge of daemons and spirits. She was concerned again and again with the relationship between art and religion, or more precisely art and ritual. In *Themis* (1912) she pointedly stated that the Olympians were "*non*-religious, because really the products of art and literature" (Harrison [1912] 1977, xi).

In 1903, at the end of *Prolegomena*, Harrison summarised her ambivalence toward the popular opinion among researchers, asserting that religion develops in a linear progression that culminates in the anthropomorphism of the Olympian gods. She views the beautiful, harmonic world of Olympian mirth and well-formed (super)human divine bodies, as depicted in Germany in, for example, Schiller's poem "The Gods of Greece" ([1788] 1901), but she also sees therein a loss. She critically emphasises in particular the loss of *formlessness:*

> We are apt to regard the advance to anthropomorphism as necessarily a clear religious gain. A gain it is in so far as a certain element of barbarity is softened or extruded, but with this gain comes loss, the loss of the element of formless, monstrous mystery. The ram-headed Knum of the Egyptians is to the mystic more religious than any of the beautiful divine humanities of the Greek. Anthropomorphism provides a store of lovely motives for art, but that spirit is scarcely religious which makes Eros a boy trundling a hoop, of Apollo a youth aiming a stone at a lizard, of Nike a woman who stoops to tie her sandal. Xenophanes put his finger on the weak spot of anthropomorphism (Harrison 1991, 258).

Her pronounced fascination for monstrous classical daemons, which were always connected to the "lusts of the flesh" (Harrison 1991, 168) and hybrid in nature, implied a heightened interest in embodied, immanent or "tacit knowledge" (McCauley and Lawson 2002).

One of the resulting achievements of her ritualistic approach was to clearly show—very similar to the way Bruno Latour (1993) did this with the self-myths of modernity—that the classicism invoked by Schiller and Hegel and many others never existed in ancient Greece. Harrison did this by focussing her attention on the cultic site and the ritual embeddedness of the figures, and thus the sensuous presence and practices of the *sacred gaze* (Morgan 2005). As soon as she reconstructed the ritual enactment of the sculptures and pictures, the clear lofty serenity of the figures, which were stored separately in the museum, disappeared. David Morgan introduced the term "sacred gaze" to analyse "the manner in which a way of seeing invests an image, a viewer, or an act of viewing with spiritual significance" (Morgan 2005, 3). For him the very act of seeing is always embodied in a sensuous grounded cultural network of practices; see Morgan (2012). In the cultic context of protection, cleansing and death rituals, which she examined in *Prolegomena* in addition to the Dionysian rituals, to Harrison the figures appeared painted, draped with jewellery or animal skins, or even smeared with wine and blood. They did not contain an isolated meaning, but their meaning was performed; see Brunotte (2013a, 91–105). Harrison's distinction between Olympian and chthonic divinities is historically not unequivocal, as Renate Schlesier has emphasised (Schlesier 1994, 175). However, any reservations do nothing to change the radically new view of the ancient world of the gods that Harrison, through her concentration on a performative and "daemonic" Greek antiquity, was already able to introduce in *Prolegomena*, particularly regarding apotropaic protection and death rituals.

4 Dionysian Ecstasy: Religious and Aesthetic Impulse

The anthropomorphically fixed and individualised Olympian gods, according to Harrison, were "losing touch with life and reality"; but then "there came into Greece a new religious impulse, an impulse really religious, the mysticism that is embodied for us in the two names Dionysos and Orpheus" (Harrison 1991, 363–364). Dionysus, as representative of the group, always attended by a *thiasos*, the flock of his intoxicated admirers, and often merging with them, embodied for Harrison "what Professor Bergson calls *durée*" (Harrison [1912] 1977, xii), the "the impulse of life through all things, perennial, indivisible" (Harrison [1912] 1977, 476).

As an analyst of images and rituals she was interested, as was the somewhat younger art historian Aby Warburg, in what took place within the affective, religious and aesthetic impulses of ritual behaviour: how the violent emotional thrusts of frenzy—in other words, what the maenads, the female followers of Dionysus, experience and do (*mainomai*)—were transformed into inspirational madness (*mania*) that can create wisdom, literature and art. In this connection, she pursued a body-focused theory of art inspired by Friedrich Nietzsche which, proceeding from an impulse of movement and visionary exaltation that may be defined as Dionysian, placed the accent on the dynamics of the expressive potential inherent in the gestural patterns and inner visual forms of Dionysian ecstasy (see Brandstetter 1995).

Harrison integrated religion and art – which she viewed neither as otherworldly nor in its "autonomy"—into the plurality of social practices (see Bertram 2014). Her understanding of art and ritual is thus expanded in the direction of more general research on narrativity and performativity *avant la lettre:*

> Religious convention compelled the tragic poets to draw their plots from traditional mythology, from stories whose religious content and motive were already in Homer's days obsolete. A knowledge of, a sympathy with, the *milieu* of this primitive material is one step to the realization of its final form in tragedy. It is then in the temple of literature, if but as a hewer of wood and drawer of water, that I still hope to serve (Harrison 1903, viii).

In this linking of ritual and theatre, the written text of the tragedy, which manages to put a frightening event into word form, does not lose its emotional validity. Instead it is interpreted as a container of older ritual knowledge, and "theatre history [is shown] to be intimately linked to the broader history of human performance" (Peters 2008, 3). In a certain way, Harrison's dialectic of archaic and modern served the self-reflexive presentation of the performative affect potential of modern culture and art in the "mirror of the primitive" (see Schüttpelz 2005).[3]

4.1 Intoxication and Art: Ecstasy and Form

In Dionysian song and ritual dance Harrison localised the classical origin of intoxication *and* art (Harrison 1991, 449). The ritual pantomime dance creates a creative, powerfully symbolic space of performative events, from which aesthetic and social transformations can emerge. In her popular 1913 work *Ancient Art and Ritual*, in which she summarised her research theses for a broader audience of

---

3 English translation as "The Scene of (Media-)Technological Superiority," in Schuettpelz (without date, http://www.ny-magazine.org/issues.html).

laypeople, her goal to connect theatre and religion, and to establish her performative approach as a connective concept, is stated programmatically:

> The title of this book may strike the reader as strange and even dissonant. What have art
> and ritual to do together? The ritualist is, to the modern mind, a man concerned perhaps
> unduly with fixed forms and ceremonies, with carrying out the rigidly prescribed ordinan-
> ces of a church or sect. The artist, on the other hand, we think of as free in thought and
> untrammelled by convention in practice; his tendency is towards licence. Art and ritual,
> it is quite true, have diverged to-day; but the title of this book is chosen advisedly. Its object
> is to show that these two divergent developments have a common root, and that neither can
> be understood without the other. *It is at the outset one and the same impulse that sends a
> man to church and to the theatre* (Harrison 1951, 9, emphasis added).

Grouping together church and theatre, religion and art, in this way suggests an
ultimately *aisthetic* notion of religion, that is, one which emerges from sensuous
perception, collective emotions and the performative acts nurtured by them. This
aisthetic approach, however, does not bring the researcher to an essentialist notion of religion as an ontological value or social sphere *sui generis*; ultimately
Harrison's ritualism shields her from this. In contrast to Nietzsche, who in *The
Birth of Tragedy* attempted to establish a new cult surrounding Wagner's
music in Bayreuth (see Cancik and Cancik-Lindemaier 1999), Harrison is instead
concerned with the reconstruction of the transformation potential of concrete ancient ritual acts (see examples in Brunotte 2013a, 144–150).

All her life Harrison acted as an intermediary between the scholarly world of
Cambridge and the artistic circles of the London metropolis. In doing so, ritual
dance represented for her the decisive link between scholarship and art and between art and ritual: "We shall find in these dances", Harrison wrote in 1913,
"the meeting-point between art and ritual" (Harrison 1951, 28).

4.1.1 Emotional Communities and Aesthetic Formations

It is hardly surprising that it is the religious material of the Dionysian cult on
which Harrison based the development of, above all, her theory (theories) of ritual. For that reason too, she classified rituals as affective means of shared agitation and of producing "emotional communities" (Rosenwein 2006), since a
special mode of perception and experience is inherent in them. The concept of
"emotional communities" was introduced into historical research on emotion
by Barbara H. Rosenwein. She uses the term to refer to communities that are
larger than the nuclear family and not necessarily comprising only relatives,
but smaller than the nations and societies that Benedict Anderson referred to
as *imagined communities*. "Emotional communities" are connected to one anoth-

er through a certain emotional style and emotional patterns, and they also share values that evolved out of emotions. In religious studies research, Birgit Meyer developed the term "aesthetic formations" (Meyer 2009, esp. 6–11) with a similar intention. The new coinage "aesthetic formations" emphasises the emotional, visual, and physical-psychological elements in ritual events. Harrison's concept of an emotional or even ecstatic collectivity is derived from ritual and cultic practices, usually those of the Dionysian mysteries. In cultic acts, early forms of concrete sensual mediation occur with a claim to general validity. Here we are dealing with aisthesis, that is, with the perceptions, experiences and knowledge of seeing, smelling, tasting, touching, hearing and feeling in all of their intermediate and extreme stages. Thus, according to Aldous Huxley, "religious dances provide a religious experience that seems more satisfying and convincing than any other. ... It is with their muscles that [the faithful] most easily obtain knowledge of the divine" (Huxley 1937, 232 and 235, as cited in Dodds 1951, 271).

Harrison's early religious-psychological approach is unthinkable without Nietzsche's thesis from *The Birth of Tragedy,* according to which the Dionysian experience is at one and the same time a psychological and a collective experience and according to which individuals are transformed into a new Dionysian collective subject during their orgiastic "disintegration" in the intoxicating experience of the cult. At many points in her work, Harrison explicitly refers to Nietzsche's description of the mystical communion between man and nature in "limitless excess [...] ecstasy" (Harrison 1991, 445–446n4). Harrison first learned about Nietzsche's theory through the scholar Erwin Rohde, a friend of Nietzsche's. Rohde had placed the theory of a collective Dionysian ecstasy, albeit without mentioning Nietzsche by name, at the focus of his reflections concerning the Dionysian cult in part two of his 1894 work *Psyche: The Cult of Souls and the Belief in Immortality among the Greeks* (Rohde [1925] 2000). He also restored the central role of the maenads—one made invisible by Nietzsche—in the cultic experience of dance and intoxication. Already in an early review of the book, Harrison formulated her aisthetic approach to religion and claimed a sensuous knowledge (of the god) to be both physical and spiritual. There Harrison found enthusiastic words to describe the dance of the women intoxicated by the god: "And what a madness it must have seemed! [...] To dance till we are dizzy, to toss our heads in ecstasy" (Harrison 1894, 165). She admittedly qualifies this by raising doubts that this "may not seem to us the best means of promoting spirituality", but she "nevertheless insists that the true spirit of Dionysus is experienced through the senses. The sensuous immediacy of this experience defies the 'common sense'; ... the women who follow Dionysus have greater access to the truth, even though it is dubbed 'dangerous, disreputable, immoral, a peril to hearth and home'" (Prins 1999, 62–63, citing Harrison 1894, 165).

Harrison's remarks on the ritual and ecstatic origins of ancient tragedy stood in direct contact with the parallel reforms of modern theatre (see Fergusson 1949 and Peters 2008, 3–4). To be sure, precisely with an eye toward her reconstruction of maenadic ecstasy, Harrison at the same time influenced and commented on the movement to innovate "free dance" (see Brandstetter 1995, 33), whose break with classical ballet—just think of Isadora Duncan—proceeded via a *revival* of ancient models of movement. Her work as a whole is thus positioned in a twofold interstice—between antiquity and modernity, and between religion and art. However, she also played a great role for modern literature—from Virginia Woolf to T. S. Eliot to James Joyce, to name just a few—due in particular to the key significance she gave concrete, albeit therefore formed, emotions and desires as dynamic potentials in literature and art. The poets and artists who followed the fixed and essentially immaterial "eikonism" (Harrison 1915, 202) of classical Olympian religion "lose all touch with the confusions of actuality" (Harrison 1991, 215), which, initiated through passions, fears, and affects, were still present in earlier mythology and rites. The mysteries of Eleusis, for example, for Harrison have maintained some of that formlessness. They cultivated sensuality and desire as media of divine epiphany and revelation: "It is indeed", she said, "only in the orgiastic religions that these splendid moments of conviction could come" (Harrison 1991, 568). In *Themis* and then in *Ancient Art and Ritual*, rituals are first and foremost representations of "thing[s] desired" (Harrison 1951, 18), whose performative potential, according to Harrison, lies in its transformative quality. Like Harry C. Payne (1978), Kathy J. Phillips claims that: "Harrison could well be represented in anthologies and classes as one of the key background forces of modern literature. [...] Her linking of anthropologists with contemporary artists reveals that Harrison [...] was participating in the elaboration of Modernism in general" (Phillips 1991, 467 and 476).

4.1.2 Thiasotic Cult, Sensational Form and Remembrance

Through her search for concrete gestural forms as intermediaries between body and soul even in the ritual expressions of the deepest emotion, Harrison's work is closely allied with Aby Warburg's *Mnemosyne* project. For Warburg the *"thiasotic cult"* of Dionysus already "formed" more chaotic "confusions" of emotions, impulses, and gestures:

> The process of de-demonizing the inherited mass of impressions, created in fear, that encompasses the entire range of emotional gesture, from helpless melancholy to murderous cannibalism, also lends the mark of uncanny experience to the dynamics of human movement in the stages that lie in between these extremes of orgiastic seizure—states such as

fighting, walking, running, dancing, grasping. [...] Through its images the *Mnemosyne Atlas* intends to illustrate this process, which one could define as the attempt to absorb pre-coined expressive values by means of the representation of life in motion (Warburg 2000; 2009, 277).

Warburg focused his psycho-historical research on the models—which he referred to as "pathos formulae"—in which the "unhindered release of expressive bodily movement, especially as it occurred amongst the followers of the gods of intoxication in Asia Minor, [was performed] in all mimetic actions" (Warburg 2009, 279). For Warburg as well as for Harrison, "thiasotic" ecstasy is thus not a chaotic frenzy per se but rather an early "traceable inventory of pre-coined expressions, which demanded that the individual artist either ignore or absorb this mass of inherited impressions" (Warburg 2009, 280): It is embodied in *pathos formulae* of cultural remembrance. In the context of this gestural archive of emotional remembrance the figure of the woman-in-motion and ecstasy played a central role. Aby Warburg's *nympha project* (Warburg 2010) as well as Harrison's fascination for the female followers of Dionysus were embedded in a general "renaissance of the maenads" around 1900 (see Prins 1999; Brunotte 2013a, 190–215).

If one reviews Harrison's various interpretations of maenadic intoxication and its "daemonic" god, the entire religious polarity which she otherwise describes as the opposition between chthonic *daimones* and the "Apollonian" Olympian gods is condensed in the double face of Dionysus himself (and his cult). Thus, in Harrison's view, in addition to orgiastic dance and frenzy, there is also the relaxing, inspiring and soothing ("limb-loosening") quality of wine as an intermediary between the body and the soul. The Dionysian cult shows "how in the breaking of bread, and still more in the drinking of wine, life spiritual as well as physical is renewed, thought is re-born, [man's] equanimity, his magnanimity are restored, reason and morality rule again" (Harrison 1991, 452). All in all, according to Harrison, "the constant shift from physical to spiritual" makes up the "essence of the religion of Dionysos" (Harrison 1991, 453). Soon, however, Harrison abandons the sacramental reading of breaking bread and drinking wine—something that for her was too narrow and Christologically coded—to emphasise the aesthetic quality of Dionysian wine intoxication, which she feels goes beyond it. She enters the realm of aesthetic inspiration and erotic stimulation when in the style of the *fin de siècle* she stresses that only those who truly enjoy themselves know "what it is to be drunken with the physical beauty of a flower or a sunset, with the sensuous imagery of words, with the strong wine of a new idea, with the magic of another's personality" (Harrison 1991, 453). In such rather incidental interpretations of the ambivalence of deep Dionysian emotion, Harrison pursues only the issue of the Nietzschean dualism between Apollonian form and Dionysian formless intoxication in her earlier work; later, she instead attempts to reconstruct in the ritual ecstasy itself those elements which both create distance and provide sensational and artistic form. It was out of this immanent process of determining form, Harrison claims, that Greek tragedy developed:

> Not only did the Greeks mix their Thracian wine with water, tempering the madness of the god, but they saw in Dionysos the god of spiritual as well as physical intoxication. It cannot be forgotten that the drama was early connected with the religion of Dionysos; *his nurses are not only Maenads, they are Muses*, from him and him only comes the beauty and magic of their song: "Hail Child of Semele, only by thee. Can any singing sweet and gracious be" (Harrison 1991, 449, italics added).

Not distance-creating Apollo but rather ecstasy-producing Dionysos and his mysteries—with this I once again relate Harrison to Warburg—are the basis for the creation of *sensational forms* (Meyer 2011, 29–30) of emotional remembrance that connect ritual to arts and the performative creation of "presence" to collective embodied memory. According to Harrison maenads can transform themselves into muses and can even "dance out" their emotive knowledge of fear, joy and frenzy in highly expressive bodily movements, in songs and music. In his famous introduction to his *Mnemosyne* project, Aby Warburg, too, wrote about the liminal and creative role of the primal orgiastic experience in "thiasotic tragedy":

> Since Nietzsche's time it has no longer been necessary to adopt a revolutionary attitude in order to view the character of antiquity through the symbol of the double-headed herm of Apollo-Dionysus. On the contrary, when looking at pagan art, the superficial daily use of this theory of opposites makes it difficult to take seriously the role of sophrosyne [prudence] and ecstasy as a single, organic functional polarity that marks the limit values of the human will to expression (Warburg 2009, 279).

Roughly twenty years earlier Jane E. Harrison developed a similar interpretation of ecstatic ritual dance as a liminal or thinking space, as well as a medium of self-perception and self-reflection.

5 Mimetic Anticipation and "Thinking Space"

Since *Themis*, whose programmatic subtitle is *A Study of the Social Origins of Greek Religion* (Harrison [1912] 1977), Harrison viewed religion as a social institution, and the practices of the rituals that she studied, as primarily social practices. In her view rituals can both generate knowledge and, as creative social practices, be media of memory, desire and therefore also transformation:

> A high emotional tension is best caused and maintained by a thing felt socially. [...] If [...] [the] whole tribe dances together [...] emotion will mount to passion, to ecstasy [...]. [A *dromenon*] is a thing *re*-done or *pre*-done, a thing enacted or represented. It is sometimes *re*-done, commemorative, sometimes *pre*-done, anticipatory, and both elements seem to go to its religiousness. [...] the drama or *dromenon* here is a sort of precipitated desire, a discharge of pent-up emotion [...] [the desire] breaks out into mimetic, anticipatory action. Mimetic, not of what you see done by another, but of what you desire to do yourself". (Harrison [1912] 1977, 43, 45)

With this approach, it is beyond question that Harrison can be considered a theorist of the performative *avant la lettre*. In recent theatre studies research, such as the work of Julie Stone Peters, Harrison's writings are read precisely in this new way:

> Ritual was, then [for Harrison], in its origin, a kind of proto-drama, taking the form of mimetic dances and containing an 'element of make-believe.' This element did not, however, involve an "attempt to deceive, but a desire to *re*-live, to *re*-present" (*Themis* 43). Rather than being a mere imitative copying of life, it was a conjunction of acting, making, and doing that was essentially performative: a magic invocation of the object of desire, a creation of the event through its pre-enactment, and a collective discharge of pent-up emotion. It was *metheksis* more than *mimesis*, participation or *doing* more than imitation (126) (Peters 2008, 16).

Harrison viewed rituals as forming ecstatic states of orgiastic emotion through rhythmic movements, gestures, music and song. Thus not only is the Greek term *drama*, Harrison said, its "own cousin to the word for rite, *dromenon*" (Harrison 1913, 35), but "the beginnings of drama and of primitive magical rites are [...] intertwined at the very roots" (Harrison [1912] 1977, 31). These theatrical acts thereby open up a cultural and psychological space between the heightened collective affects and their direct realisation. This in-between space that emerges in ritual framing makes psychological and cultural creativity possible, as well as, ultimately, symbol formation: "If an impulse finds instantly its appropriate satisfaction, there is no representation," asserted Harrison. "It is out of the delay, just the space between the impulse and the reaction, that all our mental life, our images, ideas, [...] most of all our religion, arise" (Harrison [1912] 1977, 44).

Harrison's concept of the in-between space as a space of creative symbolic production not only anticipated Aby Warburg's concept of *Denkraum* ("thinking space") (Warburg [1923] 2010) and Victor Turner's theory of the transitional liminal phase in rites of passage, it is also related to Donald W. Winnicott's concept of "intermediate area" (Winnicott 1971, 1–35 and 87–114). Not least through her positive assessment of *formlessness*, a central concept of Winnicott's, who was an English child psychoanalyst and theorist on creativity, Harrison's theory on rituals approaches the psychoanalytic theory of play. Like Harrison, Winnicott analysed objects of transition and figures of the intermediary imaginative space as a production site of symbols (see Neubaur 1987). In Jane Harrison's work, rituals are generally viewed as a liminal space between *dromenon* and *drama,* and—to borrow from Meyer again, as intermediate zones and sensational forms of affect modulation, not only for the sake of cathartic purification of the emotions, as in Aristotle's theory of tragedy, but for their presentation and lasting formation. She attempted to work out a cultural space that for her lies between the perception of extreme emotions and orgiastic seizure, and the immediate realisation of these affective, sometimes murderous impulses.

6 Harrison's Topicality for the Study of the Aesthetics of Religion

In *Ancient Art and Ritual* Harrison asks at the end if her endeavour is it a purely "antiquarian enquiry" and "Why is it, apart from the mere delight of scientific enquiry, important to have seen that art arose from ritual?" (Harrison 1951, 204). She answers with a reference to the "revival of the ritual dance" (Harrison 1951, 207) in the avant-garde movements of her time, in part inspired by the *Lebensphilosophie* (philosophy of life school). This is yet further evidence of how much she participated in opening up the text-centred theatre of her time to another social field of cultural rituals (that is, cultural performances): "Some of the strenuous, exciting, self-expressive dances of to-day are the soil and some exotic, but, based as they mostly are on very primitive ritual, they stand as singular evidence of this real recurrent need. Art in these latter days goes back as it were on her steps, recrossing the ritual bridge back to life" (Harrison 1951, 207).

Harrison's work and her pursuit of the knowledge of the daemons offer a representation of the shattering of the elite, classicist Hellenism and its discursive glorification of a text-centred *logos.* The crisis of this hegemonic and male-coded order of knowledge, which to be sure was not brought about by Harrison alone, ultimately evolved into a democratisation of science and to multifarious appropriations of antiquity; see Fiske (2008). Harrison thus shed light on the performative dimensions of cultural practice that were lost in text-analytical approaches. In particular her attempts to illuminate the tension between ritual and theatre in what was then a radical new way contributed to an understanding of the specifically transformative *energeia* and the embodied knowledge of the performative *avant la lettre*. Especially in the area of English-language research on religion and in Greek studies, Harrison's openness to the knowledge of the daemons, which developed so far as to acknowledge emotion in the research process itself, led around 1900 to upheaval in the order of knowledge. Within the scope of an innovative approach to an aesthetics of religion, it would be well worth taking this up again today.

Recommended Readings:

Fischer-Lichte, Erika. 2008. *The Transformative Power of Performance: A New Aesthetics*, translated by Saskya Iris Jain. New York and Oxon: Routledge.

Fiske, Shanyn. 2008. *Heretical Hellenism: Women Writers, Ancient Greece, and the Victorian Popular Imagination*. Athens, OH: Ohio University Press.

Harrison, Jane E.. [1913] 1951. *Ancient Art and Ritual*. London: Williams & Norgate and New York: Henry Holt.

Brunotte, Ulrike. 2013. *Dämonen des Wissens. Gender Performativität und materielle Kultur im Werk von Jane Ellen Harrison*. Würzburg: Ergon Verlag.

Thies-Lehmann, Hans. 2013. *Tragödie und dramatisches Theater*. Berlin: Alexander Verlag Berlin.

Bibliography

Arlen, Shelley. 1996. "'For Love of an Idea': Jane Ellen Harrison, Heretic and Humanist." *Women's History Review* 5/2: 165–190.

Assmann, Jan. 2011. *Cultural Memory and Early Civilization: Writing, Remembrance, and Political Imagination*, translated by David Henry Wilson. Cambridge and New York: Cambridge University Press.

Austin, John L. 1962. *How to Do Things with Words*. Cambridge, MA: Harvard University Press.

Beard, Mary. 2000. *The Invention of Jane Ellen Harrison*. Cambridge, MA: Harvard University Press.

Bertram, Georg W. 2014. *Kunst als menschliche Praxis. Eine Ästhetik*. Frankfurt a.M.: Suhrkamp.

Bourdieu, Pierre. 1991. *Language as Symbolic Power*, translated by Gino Raymond and Matthew Adamson. Cambridge: Polity Press.

Bourdieu, Pierre, and Loïc Wacquant. 1992. *An Invitation to Reflexive Sociology*. Chicago: University of Chicago Press and Cambridge: Polity Press.

Brandstetter, Gabriele. 1995. *Tanz-Lektüren. Körperbilder und Raumfiguren der Avantgarde*. Frankfurt a. M.: Fischer.

Brennan, Teresa. 2003. *The Transmission of Affect*. Ithaca, NY: Cornell University Press.

Brunotte, Ulrike. 2000. "Ritual und Erlebnis. Theorien der Initiation und ihre Aktualität in der Moderne." *Zeitschrift für Religions- und Geistesgeschichte* 53/4: 349–367.

⸺ 2001. "Das Ritual als Medium 'göttlicher Gemeinschaft'. Die Entdeckung des Sozialen bei Robertson Smith und Jane Ellen Harrison." In *Theatralität 2, Wahrnehmung und*

Medialität, edited by Erika Fischer-Lichte, Christian Horn, Sandra Umathum, and Matthias Warstat, 85–102. Tübingen: Francke.

—— 2013a. *Dämonen des Wissens. Gender Performativität und materielle Kultur im Werk von Jane Ellen Harrison*. Würzburg: Ergon Verlag.

—— 2013b. "'A Body that Matters?' Jane E. Harrisons epistemologische ontdekking van de 'Grote Moeder' en de rol van de Chôra." *Tijdschrift voor Genderstudies* 16/3: 66–80.

Butler, Judith. 1990. "Performative Acts and Gender Constitution: An Essay in Phenomenology and Feminist Theory." In *Performing Feminism, Feminist Critical Theory and Theatre*, edited by Sue-Ellen Case, 270–282. Baltimore and London: Johns Hopkins University Press.

Cancik, Hubert, and Hildegard Cancik-Lindemaier. 1999. *Philolog und Kultfigur: Friedrich Nietzsche und seine Antike in Deutschland*. Stuttgart and Weimar: J.B. Metzler.

Carpentier, Martha Celeste. 1998. *Ritual, Myth, and the Modernist Text: The Influence of Jane Ellen Harrison on Joyce, Eliot, and Woolf*. Amsterdam: Gordon and Breach.

Chidester, David. 1996. *Savage Systems: Colonialism and Comparative Religion in Southern Africa*. Charlottesville and London: University of Virginia Press.

—— 2014. *Empire of Religion: Imperialism and Comparative Religion*. Chicago: Chicago University Press.

Comentale, Edward P. 2001. "Thesmophoria: Suffragettes, Sympathetic Magic, and H.D.'s Ritual Poetics." *Modernism/Modernity* 8/3: 471–492.

Därmann, Iris. 2013. *Kulturtheorien. Zur Einführung*. Dresden: Junius.

Deleuze, Gilles, and Félix Guattari. 1987. *A Thousand Plateaus*, translated by Brian Massumi. Minneapolis: University of Minnesota Press.

Dodds, Eric Robertson. 1951. *The Greeks and the Irrational*. Berkeley and Los Angeles: University of California Press.

Evangelista, Stefano. 2011. "Lessons in Greek Art: Jane Harrison and Aestheticism." *Women's Studies* (Special Issue: *Nineteenth Century Women Writers and Classical Inheritance*) 40/4: 513–536.

Evreinov, Nikolai. [1908] 1923. *Apologija teatral'nost* (Apology for Theatricality), 23–31. Berlin: Academia.

Fergusson, Francis. 1949. *The Idea of a Theater: A Study of Ten Plays – The Art of Drama in Changing Perspective*. Garden City, NY: Doubleday and Princeton, NJ: Princeton University Press.

Fischer-Lichte, Erika. 2000a. "Grenzgänge und Tauschhandel. Auf dem Weg zu einer performativen Kultur." In *Performanz*, edited by Uwe Wirth, 277–300. Frankfurt a.M.: Suhrkamp.

—— 2000b. "Theater als Modell für eine performative Kultur. Zum *performative turn* in der europäischen Kultur des 20. Jahrhunderts." *Universitätsreden* 46, Universität Saarbrücken, 4–20.

—— 2001. "Vom 'Text' zur 'Performance'. Der 'performative turn' in den Kulturwissenschaften." In *Schnittstelle. Medien und kulturelle Kommunikation*, edited by Georg Stanitzek, and Wilhelm Voßkamp, 111–115. Cologne: DuMont.

—— 2004. "Theater und Ritual." In *Die Kultur des Rituals. Inszenierungen, Praktiken, Symbole*, edited by Christoph Wulf, and Jörg Zirfas, 279–292 Munich: Fink.

—— 2005. *Theatre, Sacrifice, Ritual: Exploring Forms of Political Theatre*. Oxon and New York: Routledge.

—— 2008. *The Transformative Power of Performance: A New Aesthetics,* translated by Saskya Iris Jain. New York and Oxon: Routledge.

Fiske, Shanyn. 2008. *Heretical Hellenism: Women Writers, Ancient Greece, and the Victorian Popular Imagination.* Athens, OH: Ohio University Press.

Gladigow, Burkhard. 1995. "Europäische Religionsgeschichte." In *Lokale Religionsgeschichte,* edited by Hans G. Kippenberg and Brigitte Luchesi, 21–42. Marburg: diagonal Verlag.

—— 2009. "Europäische Religionsgeschichte der Neuzeit." In *Europäische Religionsgeschichte. Ein mehrfacher Pluralismus.* Vol.1, edited by Hans G. Kippenberg, Jörg Rüpke and Kocku von Stuckrad, 15–38. Göttingen: Vandenhoek & Ruprecht/UTB.

Gregg, Melissa, and Gregory J. Seigworth. 2010. "An Inventory of Shimmers." In *The Affect Theory Reader,* edited by Melissa Gregg and Gregory J. Seigworth, 1–25, Durham, NC: Duke University Press.

Grieser, Alexandra, Adrian Hermann, and Katja Triplett. 2011. "Museality as a Matrix of the Production, Reception, and Circulation of Knowledge Concerning Religion." *Journal of Religion in Europe* 4/1: 40–70.

Goa, David, David Morgan, Crispin Paine, and S. Brent Plate, eds. 2005. "Editorial Statement." *Material Religion: The Journal of Objects, Art and Belief* 1/1: 4–9.

Guggenmos, Esther-Maria, Isabel Laack, and Sebastian Schüler. 2011. "Agency and the Senses in the Context of Museality from the Perspective of Aesthetics of Religion." *Journal of Religion in Europe* 4/1: 102–133.

Hall, David. 1997. *Lived Religion in America: Towards a History of Practice.* Princeton, NJ: Princeton University Press.

Harrison, Jane E. 1882. *Myths of the Odyssey in Art and Literature.* London: Rivingtons.

—— 1885. *Introductory Studies in Greek Art.* London: Unwin. (repr. Cambridge University Press, 2009).

—— 1890. "Preface." In *Mythology and Monuments of Ancient Athens: Being a Translation of a Portion of the "Attica" of Pausanias,* Jane E. Harrison and Margaret de G. Verrall, i–xiv. London and New York: Macmillan.

—— 1894. "Review of Erwin Rohde's *Psyche. Seelenkult und Unsterblichkeitsglaube der Griechen.*" *Classical Review* 8: 165–166.

—— [1903] 1991. *Prolegomena to the Study of Greek Religion.* Princeton, NJ: Princeton University Press.

—— 1908. *Prolegomena to the Study of Greek Religion.* Second edition. Cambridge, UK: Cambrigde University Press.

—— [1909] 2009. "The Influence of Darwinism on the Study of Religions." In *Darwin and Modern Science Essays in Commemoration of the Centenary of the Birth of Charles Darwin,* edited by A C. Seward, 494–511. Cambridge: Cambridge University Press.

—— [1912] 1977. *Themis: A Study of the Social Origins of Greek Religion.* London: Merlin Press.

—— [1913] 1951. *Ancient Art and Ritual.* London: Williams & Norgate and New York: Henry Holt.

—— 1915. *Alpha and Omega.* London: Sidgwick & Jackson; including:

"'Homo Sum': Being a Letter to an Anti-Suffragist from an Anthropologist," 80–115.

"Scientiae sacra fames," 116–142 (published 1913 in a shorter version as "Women and Knowledge" in *New Statesman* (supplement), vi–viii).

"The Influence of Darwinism on the Study of Religions," 143–178.

"Alpha and Omega," 179–208.

Harrison, Jane, and Margaret de G. Verrall. 1890. *Mythology and Monuments of Ancient Athens: Being a Translation of a Portion of the "Attica" of Pausanias.* London and New York: MacMillan.

Harth, Dietrich, and Axel Michaels. 2003. *Grundlagen des SFB 619: Ritualdynamik – Soziokulturelle Prozesse in historischer und kulturvergleichender Perspektive.* URL: http://journals.ub.uni-heidelberg.de/index.php/ritualdynamik/article/view/361/344 (last accessed 19 November 2014).

Houtman, Dick, and Birgit Meyer, eds. 2012. *Things: Religion and the Question of Materiality.* New York: Fordham University Press.

Huxley, Aldous. 1937. *Ends and Means.* London: Chatto & Windus.

Jungaberle, Hendrik, and Jan Weinhold, eds. 2006. *Rituale in Bewegung: Rahmungs- und Reflexivitätsprozesse in Kulturen der Gegenwart.* Berlin: LIT.

Johnson, Christopher D. 2012. *Memory, Metaphor, and Aby Warburg's Atlas of Images.* Ithaca, NY: Cornell University Press.

Keane, Webb. 2007. *Christian Moderns: Freedom and Fetish in the Mission Encounter.* Berkeley: University of California Press.

—— 2008. "The Evidence of the Senses and the Materiality of Religion." *The Journal of the Royal Anthropological Institute* 14/1: 110–127.

Kippenberg, Hans G., Jörg Rüpke, and Kocku von Stuckrad, eds. 2009. *Europäische Religionsgeschichte.* Vol. 1, *Ein mehrfacher Pluralismus.* Göttingen: Vandenhoek & Ruprecht/UTB.

Klironomos, Martha. 2008. "British Women Travellers to Greece, 1880–1930." In *Women Writing Greece: Essays on Hellenism, Orientalism and Travel,* edited by Vassiliki Kolocotroni, and Efterpi Mitsi, 135–158. Amsterdam and New York: Rodopi.

Koch, Anne. 2007. *Körperwissen. Grundlegung der Religionsaisthetik.* Habilitation. Open access University of Munich: *Perspektiven der Religionswissenschaft* series. URL: http://epub.ub.uni-muenchen.de/12438/ (last accessed 28 November 2015)

—— 2012. "Reasons for the Boom of Body Discourses in Humanities and Social Sciences. A Chapter in European History of Religion." In *Menschenbilder und Körperkonzepte im Alten Israel, in Ägypten und im Alten Orient,* edited by Angelika Berlejung, Jan Dietrich, and Joachim F. Quack, 3–42. Tübingen: Mohr Siebeck.

Köpping, Peter, and Ursula Rao. 2002. *Im Rausch des Rituals. Gestaltung und Transformation der Wirklichkeit in körperlicher Performanz.* Hamburg: LIT.

Krais, Beate, and Gunter Gebauer. 2002. *Habitus. Themen der Soziologie,* Bielefeld: Transcript.

Kreinath, Jens. 2009. "Virtuality and Mimesis: Toward an Aesthetics of Ritual Performances as Embodied Forms of Religious Practice." In *Religion, Ritual, Theatre,* edited by Bent Holm, Bent Flemming Nielsen, and Karen Vedel, 229–259, Frankfurt a.M.: Peter Lang.

Kreinath, Jens, Jan Snoek, and Michael Stausberg, eds. 2006. *Theorizing Rituals: Issues, Topics, Approaches, Concepts.* Vol. 1. Leiden and Boston: Brill.

Kugele, Jens, and Katharina Wilkens, eds. 2011. "Relocating Religion(s) – Museality as a Critical Term for the Aesthetics of Religion: Introduction." *Journal of Religion in Europe* 4: 7–13.

Langer, Susanne K. 1945. *Philosophy in a New Key: A Study in the Symbolism of Reason, Rite and Art*. Cambridge, MA: Harvard University Press.

—— 1953. *Feeling and Form: A Theory of Art Developed from Philosophy in a New Key*. New York: Charles Scribner's Sons.

Latour, Bruno. 1993. *We Have Never Been Modern*, translated by Catherine Porter. Cambridge, MA: Harvard University Press.

Lepecki, André. 2010. "The Body as Archive: Will to Re-enact and the Afterlives of Dances." *Dance Research Journal* 42/2: 28–48.

McCauley, Robert N., and E. Thomas Lawson. 2002. *Bringing Ritual to Mind: Psychological Foundations of Cultural Forms*. Cambridge: Cambridge University Press.

Meyer, Birgit. 2006. "Religious Sensations: Why Media, Aesthetics, and Power Matter in the Study of Contemporary Religion." Inaugural Lecture, Free University Amsterdam: October 6. URL: https://www.vu.nl/nl/Images/Oratietekst%20Birgit%20Meyer_tcm9–44560.pdf (last accessed 28 November 2015)

—— 2009. "Introduction: From Imagined Communities to Aesthetic Formations: Religious Mediations, Sensational Forms and Styles of Binding." In *Aesthetic Formations: Media, Religion and the Senses,* edited by Birgit Meyer, 1–30. New York: Palgrave Macmillan.

—— 2011. "Mediation and Immediacy: Sensational Forms, Semiotic Ideologies and the Question of the Medium." *Social Anthropology* 19/1: 23–39.

—— 2012. *Mediation and the Genesis of Presence: Towards a Material Approach to Religion*. Inaugural lecture, University Utrecht, October 19. URL: #http://www2.hum.uu.nl/onder zoek/lezingenreeks/pdf/Meyer_Birgit_oratie.pdf

—— 2013a. "Material Mediations and Religious Practices of World-Making." In *Religion Across Media: From Early Antiquity to Late Modernity,* edited by Knut Lundby, 1–19. New York: Peter Lang.

—— 2013b. "Mediation and Immediacy: Sensational Forms, Semiotic Ideologies and the Question of the Medium." In *A Companion to the Anthropology of Religion,* edited by Janice Boddy and Michael Lambek, 309–326. Malden, MA and Oxford: Wiley-Blackwell.

Meyer, Birgit, David Morgan, Crispin Paine, and S. Brent Plate, eds. 2011. *Key Words in Material Religion* (special issue), *Material Religion* 7/1.

Morgan, David. 2005. *The Sacred Gaze: Religious Visual Culture in Theory and Practice.* Berkeley: University of California Press.

—— 2011. *Religion and Material Culture: The Matter of Belief.* London: Routledge.

—— 2012. *Embodied Eye: Religious Visual Culture and the Social Life of Feeling.* Berkeley: University of California Press.

Murray, Gilbert. 1928. *Jane Ellen Harrison.* An address delivered at Newnham College, October 27. Cambridge: Heffer.

Neubaur, Caroline. 1987. *Übergänge. Spiel und Realität in der Psychoanalyse Donald W. Winnicotts.* Frankfurt a.M.: Athenaeum.

Nietzsche, Friedrich. [1872] 1909. *The Birth of Tragedy: Out of the Spirit of Music,* translated William A. Haussmann. London: Unwin.

Payne, Harry C. 1978. "Modernizing the Ancients: The Reconstruction of Ritual Drama 1870–1920." *Proceedings of the American Philosophical Society* 122: 182–192.

Peters, Julie Stone. 2008. "Jane Harrison and the Savage Dionysus: Archaeological Voyages, Ritual Origins, Anthropology, and the Modern Theatre." *Modern Drama* 51/1: 1–41.

Phillips, Kathy J. 1991. "Jane Harrison and Modernism." *Journal of Modern Literature* 17/4: 465–476.

Plate, Liedeke, and Anneke Smelik, eds. 2013. *Performing Memory in Art and Popular Culture*. London and New York: Routledge.

Prins, Yopie. 1999. "Greek Maenads, Victorian Spinsters." In *Victorian Sexual Dissidence*, edited by Richard Dellamore, 43–81. Chicago: Chicago University Press.

Robinson, Annabel. 2002. *The Life and Work of Jane Ellen Harrison*. Oxford: Oxford University Press.

Rohde, Erwin. [1925] 2000. German original 1894. *Psyche: The Cult of Souls and the Belief in Immortality among the Greeks*, translated W.B. Hillis. Oxon: Routledge.

Rosenwein, Barbara H. 2006. *Emotional Communities in the Early Middle Ages*. Ithaca, NY: Cornell University Press.

Schechner, Richard. [1988] 2003. *Performance Theory*. London and New York: Routledge.

Schiller, Friedrich. 1901. "The Gods of Greece (1788)." In *The Poems of Schiller*, translated E. P. Arnold-Forster. 72–82. London: Heinemann.

Schlesier, Renate. 1994. *Kulte, Mythen und Gelehrte. Anthropologie der Antike seit 1800*. Frankfurt a.M.: Fischer.

Schneider, Rebecca. 2011. *Performing Remains: Art and War in Times of Theatrical Reenactment*. London and New York: Routledge.

Schüttpelz, Erhard. 2005. *Die Moderne im Spiegel des Primitiven*. Paderborn: Wilhelm Fink.

—— "The Scene of (Media-)Technological Superiority," translated by Olga von Schubert, Matt Franks and Alwin Franke. *New York Magazine of Contemporary Art and Theory* 1/5, 1–17. http://www.ny-magazine.org/issues.html last (accessed 28 November 2015).

Segal, Robert A. 2006. "Myth and Ritual." In *Theorizing Rituals: Issues, Topics, Approaches, Concepts*. Vol. 1, edited by Jens Kreinath, Jan Snoek, and Michael Stausberg, 101–121. Leiden and Boston: Brill.

Tambiah, Stanley J. 1981. "A Performative Approach to Ritual." *Proceedings of the British Academy* 65: 113–169.

Turner, Victor. 1969. *Ritual Process: Structure and Anti-Structure*. New York: Aldine P. Company.

—— 1974. *Dramas, Fields and Metaphors*. Ithaca, NY: Cornell University Press.

—— 1982. *From Ritual to Theatre: The Human Seriousness of Play*. New York: PAJ Publications.

Warburg, Aby. [1900] 2010. "Ninfa Fiorentina." In *Werke in einem Band*, edited and commentated by Martin Treml, Sigrid Weigel, and Perdita Ladewig, 187–198. Frankfurt a.M.: Suhrkamp.

—— [1923] 2010. "Bilder aus dem Gebiet der Pueblo-Indianer in Nord-Amerika. Materialien zur Psychologie primitiver Religiosität (speech given on April 21, 1923. Kreuzlingen, Heilanstalt Belle-Vue)." In *Werke in einem Band*, edited and commentated by Martin Treml, Sigrid Weigel, and Perdita Ladwid, 524–566. Frankfurt a.M.: Suhrkamp.

—— 2000. "Der Bilderatlas Mnemosyne." *Gesammelte Schriften: Studienausgabe*. Vol. II2,1, edited by Martin Warnke and Claudia Brink. Berlin: Akademie Verlag.

—— 2009. *Einleitung zum Mnemosyne-Atlas*, published in English as: "The Absorption of the Expressive Values of the Past," translated Matthew Rampley. *Art in Translation* 1/2 (Berg Journals): 273–283.

Winnicott, Donald W. 1971. *Playing and Reality*. London: Tavistock.

Wulf, Christoph, Birgit Althans, Kathrin Audem, Constanze Bausch, Michael Göhlich, Stephan Sting, Anja Tervooren, Monika Wagner-Willi, and Jörg Zirfas. 2001. *Das Soziale als Ritual. Zur performativen Bildung von Gemeinschaften*. Opladen: Leske und Budrich.

Christoph Auffarth

What Does a Reformed City Look Like? – Changes in Visible Religion During the Reformation in Bremen

The Protestant Reformation of the 16th century radically changed the visible culture in Europe. Considering a fundamental break from an iconic culture, based primarily on images and rituals, to a non-iconic culture of "the Word" and of "Belief" is a valuable typological distinction to bear in mind when describing and analyzing historical phenomena of that era. This takes into account the two conceivable arguments about the relationship between images and culture/religion which could help to assess the concrete historical situation. What was the advice and theological arguments given by the Reformators (their ideals of what should be); how did people respond; and what can be observed about how they reacted? Did the *Bildersturm* (iconoclasm) virtually remove every image? Bob Scribner's seminal article (Scribner 1981) showed that the propaganda of the Early Reformation relied to a good part on the images shown in the *Flugblätter* (pamphlets).[1] Is it the same, however, if we look at the Second Calvinist Reformation, which turned out to convey much more radical attitudes towards images? In this article, I shall first address theoretical issues, referring to the aesthetics of religion as the framework for my case study. This case is the Northern German city of Bremen, and the changes of visible religion in the city during its transformation from a medieval town—abounding in religious signs and symbols present in the public sphere—into a stronghold of Reformation:

- first by a radical reformation of a group of 104 men in 1530 – 1532, which was violently suppressed;
- followed by a Lutheran church constitution, written on behalf of and established by the City Council in 1534;
- and finally, in a third stage, into a Calvinist reformed city in the years between 1568 and 1581.

In 1612, the city's reformation process was crowned by the new façade for the Town Hall. Can we say that the visuality of religion vanished in this process—

---

1 *Flugblätter* are the single leaf prints with ingravings.

https://doi.org/10.1515/9783110461015-009

as reformers would have claimed—or did it find new realms? Is it possible to transform an iconic visual *habitus* into a non-iconic Protestant *habitus?*[2]

1. Cultural and Religious Aesthetic

In their seminal article about the aesthetics of religion as a systematic approach (Cancik and Mohr 1988), Hubert Cancik and Hubert Mohr stated that religious aesthetics form part of the aesthetic culture of a specific place and epoch with its codes of symbols, signs, and values of what is good and what is evil. The authors explain that the perception of visual, auditive, etc. impressions, on the one hand, and the cognition of the percepts as religious symbols within a larger cultural-aesthetic setting are two different activities. Although human beings share the basic structures of an anthropological nervous system, perception and cognition are encoded by cultural modes of evaluation and appreciation.

In his systematic and comprehensive description of the perception-system, and how religious traditions make use of it (see Mohr 2006, 1446–1447), Hubert Mohr differentiates between the individual act of perceiving and the percepts which—as part of a cultural symbol-system—exist independently from random or varying individual acts of ascription (*Zuschreibung*). What an individual person observes is tied to the cultural symbolic system consisting of conventions and codifications of meaning (*Festschreibung*). If a child or a foreigner at first does not identify a sign (an observation) correctly, he or she will sooner or later learn the correct (i. e., correct in the given culture) meaning of the observation as a culturally encoded sign which allows him/her to behave accordingly. Cognition, however, goes beyond de-coding signs; it is a process of perceiving, and simultaneously comparing with previous sensations. Cognition is re-cognition.

There are sharp differences between the diverse aesthetic cultures as to how religion is perceived. Annette Wilke and Oliver Moebius analysed the sounds, rattles, and rings of India, and they demonstrated how iconic cultures can be distinguished from non-iconic cultures by investigating which senses are privileged in texts and in practice (Wilke and Moebus 2011; Wilke 2012). The *aisthesis*, the relationship between stimuli and reactions, is encoded differently, which also makes it different which sounds in India or in Greece are perceived as religious,

---

2 As Jäggi and Staecker (2007) have shown for Scandinavian literature the term *habitus* is frequently used. Referring to Bourdieu's term, however, would mean there can be no break, or revolution at all.

and which are not. To support the importance of analysing the specificity of a historically and culturally bound religious *aisthesis*, it is important to note that constructivist approaches in the neurosciences do not support a direct tie between stimulus and reaction (Roth 1994, 2013). This research shows, for instance, that the nervous system does not react to a peripheral nerve stimulation if it does not match the internal program of recognition. Cognition is re-cognition.

The topic in this chapter is the revolutionary break in religious aesthetics during the Reformations, how this break was performed and how the mode of "re-cognition" has been changed as well.[3] Modelling the changes of cultural codes in the Early Modern period, it can be argued that these codes are inverted compared to the previous medieval culture – however, this inversion is only partial. Of the three confessions of the Early Modern period, Catholics would be the ones accumulating religious sensations,[4] especially in public, in the form of religious images at the corners of houses or in the centre of market places; in the form of processions clouded in the smell of incense; in the form of full orchestras accompanying masses of people moving through the cities in the Baroque era. Although the Lutherans had removed central altarpieces showing Mary and other saints, they generally resisted the iconoclastic cleansing of church interiors. New paintings were commissioned with mainly didactic themes, and even statues of "counter-saints" such as Martin Luther and Philipp Melanchthon appeared;[5] epitaphs continued to line both sides of church interiors to fill the void in the centre. In contrast, the Calvinistic or Reformed Confession treated the question of images in a more radical way. Churches were stripped of images and scents, the walls were white-washed; no sensations should interfere with the Word of God cited in the readings and the sermon: this can be described as a theoretical and practical *ritual exclusion of stimuli*, as Hubert Mohr has called it (sensory deprivation, "*ritueller Reizausschluss*"; Mohr 2003, 47–67; Mohr 2006a, 1446–1447).

The guiding questions are: On what levels can we describe the "encoding of sensations"? Does the inversion of the religious symbol-system also affect the

---

3 On the Reformation and subsequent reformations, see Lindberg (1996) and Kaufmann (2012). See also my review in: http://buchempfehlungen.blogs.rpi-virtuell.net/
4 See Meyer (2006) who developed her concept mainly for the analysis of contemporary media history.
5 Concerning a mixed Catholic and Lutheran region (Hildesheim), Renate Dürr (2006) showed that although clearly divided in terms of space, the two confessions concurred and imitated one another: Lutherans installed statues and confessionals; Catholics looked for priests who had studied at universities.

larger cultural *habitus* of perception, the system of symbols and how individual people refer to it? Do culturally defined symbols which are no longer part of the religious symbol system persist as part of the larger cultural system? As Hans Belting has shown (Belting 1993), we can speak of an era of the image as "presence"—created and received as an object of veneration—being replaced by an era when images were considered as objects of fine art, and when art was separated from religion as an autonomous subsystem. After a brief consideration of these developments, I will address the question of whether these shifts within the cultural symbol system constitute 'secularisation'. As I have noted elsewhere, in Early Modern times Calvinist engravers of maps avoided displays of religious partisanship in marginal ornaments so as not to offend their Catholic clients (Auffarth 2005, 43–68).

2 Sensual Deprivation in the Reformed City?: From Visible and Iconic to Non-Iconic Religion of the Reformation

There is ample evidence that the Reformation effected a revolutionary break in the *aisthesis* of the everyday life of the citizens: until then, religious signs were perceptible everywhere—not only inside the churches, but also outside, be it within or outside the city walls. A few examples should aptly demonstrate the omnipresence:

- Every morning the day began and ended with the ringing of the church bells; the indication of the hours. Each ring had to conform to the clock of the town hall (Dohrn-van Rossum 1992).
- St. Peter's key, opening or closing the gates to heaven, is the city of Bremen's official coat of arms.
- The giant Roland statue on the market place, symbolizing civic rights and privileges, wears a belt buckle bearing the image of an angel playing a lute.
- The blessings and the custody of the saints at every street corner within the city and at crossings outside protect everyone against the attacks of evil forces.
- The saints, the prophets, and the angels perform Divine Service to God in the churches, even at those hours when the churches are closed to the public. The images in the churches—painted on the walls or standing as statues at the columns and above the altar—perform Divine Service to the Lord perpetually. Normal laymen only join the multitude of saints and angels during Mass.
- *The Reformation changed this attitude:* the visual presence of the transcendent realm in everyday life on earth was renounced sharply. The wooden

idols, the painted panels venerated at the altars were despoiled, torn out, and burned.[6] At least, this is what the first preacher of the new religion in Bremen, the Augustinian monk Henry of Zütphen, entreats the public to do, as reported in a bill of indictment:

XIII. Item ponit et dicit, quod prefatus assertus frater Hinricus in suo sermone ad populum adhortatus fuit, sanctos colendos non esse et imagines igne cremandos fore. Quod sic fuit et est verum.

XIV. Item ponit et dicit, quod certi perversi et malivoli doctrinam dicti asserti fratris Hinrici sequentes ipsas imagines destruere et in fontem projicere fecerunt et studuerunt. Quod sic fuit et est verum.

XV. Item ponit et dicit, quod dictus assertus frater Hinricus candelas vel alia quecumque luminaria domino Deo seu eius sanctis offerre publice de ambone prohibuit, nec meritorium esse, Quod sic fuit et est verum.

XIII. It is further recorded that Brother Henry exhorted people in his sermon not to venerate the saints and to throw the images into the fire. That is the next recorded fact.

XIV. It is further recorded that certain perverse and malevolent men followed Brother Henry's instructions and destroyed the images, intending to throw them into a well. This is also recorded.

XV. Furthermore it is recorded: Brother Henry prohibited that candles and any other lights be dedicated to the Lord God or his saints. That yields no merit. That is the next recorded fact.

Though Martin Luther opposed the radical iconoclasm incited by Andreas Karlstadt in the churches of Wittenberg,[7] the Reformation in principle divested churches of their images, relics, candles, incense, altar bells, and vestments.[8]

Iconoclasm changed what might be called the sensory aspect of religion dramatically: one could no longer smell, touch, kiss, illuminate, genuflect in veneration, make an offering, and pay for the remission of sins.[9] No splendour could be seen anymore, no lavishness, no luxury transcending human potential as a sign of God's presence. Religious *aisthesis* is reduced to hearing the Word of God spoken by a man clothed in the professional robe of a professor (Kaufmann

---

6 Concerning Bremen: in the indictment against Heinrich von Zütphen Nr. 13–15: [Quellen zur Bremischen Reformationsgeschichte = Bremisches Jahrbuch II 1 (1885), Quelle 5. Staatsarchiv Stade, Reg. 5b Fach 140 Nr. 9 – *f* 27–30. See Rudloff (1987, 71–76); it follows a commentary by Ortwin Rudloff: Quod dictus asssertus frater Henricus de ambone publice praedicabat: Zu Heinrich von Zütphens Bremer Predigten im Januar und Februar 1523 (Rudloff 1987, 77–116).
7 On the rather conservative Lutheran attitude towards images, see Dürr (2006, 87–116, 181–253, 256–333).
8 For the English Reformation see Duffy (1992, 377–593).
9 On late medieval forms of piety, in general see Hamm (2009). Concerning Bremen, see Weidinger 2012, 439–498.

2012, 473–476, 479, 483). As introduced above, Hubert Mohr's concept of the cultic sensory deprivation (*kultischer Reizausschluss*, Mohr 2003) encompasses best the mechanism and effects related to remaining silent, not hearing any voice or noise, not making use of light or illumination, not allowing for drink or food, or any interesting or fascinating attraction for the eyes.

Iconoclasm demolished the images, however the Lutheran reformation did not become an entirely non-iconic culture. Images should not be venerated, therefore they were banned from the centre of the church. They could, however, help to illustrate the new creed and explain, for example, the Ten Commandments. But there were indeed radical changes to the *aisthesis* of religion that focused on beholding and venerating images.[10] The tension between the expulsion of images from sacred buildings and prohibiting their presence in religious ritual, but in a nevertheless iconic culture, brings us to the question: Did the iconic *habitus* to expect images in religion find expression in other media, other places, different motifs?

3 New Visible Symbols in the Reformed City: The First, Lutheran Reformation in the City of Bremen

To illustrate my argument, I shall present three examples of iconic change in the reformed city of Bremen.

3.1 The Epitaph of Segebade Clüver (Died 1547)

Before, during, and after reformation one iconic medium within church buildings remained in use: the epitaph. The ministers were buried outside the church in the churchyard,[11] but had the privilege of presenting themselves in form of a monument: thus, even after death they remained in the church permanently, as members of the perpetual Divine Service for God, together with the angels and the saints.[12]

---

10 Iconoclasm: the term is analyzed by Bremmer (2008). On iconoclasm in the first phase of the Reformation, see Dupeux, Jezler, and Wirth 2000.

11 Only (arch-)bishops had the privilege of being buried in the church. On the continuity of the epitaph even after see Zerbe (2007), Zerbe (2013) and my review http://buchempfehlungen.blogs. rpi-virtuell.net/2015/07/27/reformation-der-memoria/ (27 July, 2015).

12 Protestant pastors kneeling and praying in many of the examples collected by Zerbe (2007).

Figure 1: Epitaph Segebade Clüver 1547. Bremen, Dom. Photo taken by author. Before Segebade Clüver, the head of the ministers of the Cathedral in the Northern German city of Bremen, died in 1547 he ordered an epitaph. He wanted to see himself depicted as a priest praying *vis à vis* Christ, a traditional ("Catholic") motif. However, he comes out as fostering the new Protestant (*evangelische*) creed: The blood of the crucified Christ feeds the two sacramental means of salvation, both the chalice of the Eucharist and the fountain of rebirth, baptism. Salvation is needed because of the fall of the first human beings, Adam and Eve. The timber of death, the cross, has turned into the tree of life: paradise is regained. The coming eschatological New Jerusalem on the right side in the background finds its earthly equivalent in the city of Bremen on the left side. Segebade Clüver chose Protestant (*evangelische*) motifs as a commitment to the new confession.

We find one of the cathedral priests depicted after his death in his traditional vocation, praying day and night for all eternity (Trüper 2001, 40–44). On this outstanding piece, the monument of Segebade Clleba, Cathedral Provost, he is wearing the traditional liturgical vestment of a priest, not the new Protestant robe of an intellectual. But 'reading' the image on his epitaph reveals that he is an adherent of the new creed.

In the centre we see Christ Crucified. From the wounds of hands and feet rivers of blood pour forth, nourishing two vessels.

- The upper one is a Eucharist chalice, over which during Mass the priest repeats the words of Christ in 1 Corinthians 11:25: "This cup is the new testament in my blood: this do ye, as oft as ye drink it, in remembrance of me". (King James Version)
- The streaming fluid feeds a second basin in which men and women are bathing: the bath of baptism. It also resembles the Fountain of Youth, from which one emerges as a young man after diving into the waters of rejuvenation.

Reformation theology recognized only two of the previous seven sacraments: namely baptism and Eucharist. The figure at the bottom right unites both sacraments: John the Baptist. He is the man who baptises and points to the coming Saviour, the *agnus Dei*, as the banderole reads, "who takes away the sins of the world".

The Fountain of Youth here is not yet the motif of the Renaissance, but also no longer just the sacrament of baptism. A new notion emerges, albeit tentatively, and certainly not as drastically as depicted by Hieronymus Bosch as the land in which milk and honey flow, both Paradise and Cockaigne.

The cross is not just the timber of death, but it flourishes again so that it is both the cross on Golgotha and the tree of Paradise: the tree of life. The two figures to the left and to the right, Adam and Eve are led into temptation and fall; they carry the signs of death. The cross is fixed on the Calvary, i.e. the grave of Adam. But the Saviour, the "new Adam," reverses original sin into innocence.

To the left of the cross (the iconographic right side) one sees a city with its windmill. This is an indication that we are no longer in historical and biblical times, but in fact in the Lower Germany of the modern age: the church with the two different towers resembles the Bremen cathedral. On the other side, another city is depicted, with a church and a mountain in the background. As is well known, there is no mountain nearby Bremen, or even a hill. That means the epigraph is depicting not just Bremen and a parish church or the cathedral. The structure of the epitaph with its typological counterparts calls for an interpretation as a different town of religious significance. The mountain crowned by

Figure 2: Lucas Cranach the Elder (1472–1553): *The Fountain of Youth* 1546. Reproduced with permission of bpk / Gemäldegalerie, Staatliche Museen zu Berlin.
In the fountain of baptism, there are not only babies swimming, but also bearded men. Although the Lutheran Protestants insisted on the baptism of new-born children and rejected the baptism of convinced adults (as the (Ana-) Baptists required as the biblical attested rite), the motive on the epitaph combines the baptism with the bath of rejuvenation. On the contemporary picture, famous Reformation painter, Lucas Cranach, narrates how on the left side old women and men are transported to the fountain and that, while swimming in the fountain of rejuvenation, they become young and pretty again. Ascending on the other side they indulge in the desires of the youth, dancing, singing, feasting, eating and having sex.

a small round structure could be the Chapel of the Ascension on the Mount of Olives. In the valley, the round double structure of a building within a building resembles the typical architecture of the Holy Sepulcher.[13] The holy city in Lower Germany is the burial place of Segebade Clleba, who by the grace of the Saviour is now dwelling in the Heavenly Jerusalem. The typological argument, however, carries yet another meaning: Bremen is the New Jerusalem.

---

13 This is not the occasion to develop this argument in detail. I intend to do this elsewhere.

3.2 The Conversion of the Prophets on the Town Hall

My second example is found outside the church, facing the cathedral in its immediate vicinity: the Town Hall of Bremen. Four statues on the western side are easily visible to the burghers of Bremen. Contrary to an art historian,[14] who poses the question whom the statue portrays, I as an historian of religion inquire: why are they there; whom are they looking at; who sees them; who is communicating with whom?[15] On the eastern side, another group of four figures is in communication with the cathedral's façade.

Among today's residents of Bremen an often-repeated presumption is that the giant Roland statue, symbol of the city's autonomy, represents the city's liberation from the hated archbishop's regime. He is the brave man resisting ecclesiastical appetite for the citizen's wealth. But it is closer to historical reality that the Roland is not cross-eyed—he actually looks past the cathedral. He stands there rather to face Bremen's great rival, the city of Hamburg.

When the Town Hall was built 1405–1410, Bremen proudly presented itself as a Free Imperial City of the Holy Roman Empire: the eight most powerful rulers of the Empire, the seven prince-electors (*Kurfürsten*) plus the emperor himself stand above the balcony. The electors are accompanied on the right and on the left side of the building by eight figures representing the prophets of the Old Testament.

During the Reformation the figures on the western side facing the city changed identities. On the scrolls the prophets held (banderoles) that designated them as part of Christian Holy Scripture, now the names Plato,[16] Aristotle,[17] Demosthenes,[18] and Cicero[19] were inscribed. What does this conversion to representatives of pagan Antiquity mean?

---

14 Nevertheless: my interpretation relies on the fundamental work of the art historian Gramatzki (1994).

15 On the image as part of a communication process see Auffarth (2010). Horst Bredekamp (2013) now introduces a new model for the interaction between viewer and the image as two actors in what he calls the "Bildakt" (image act).

16 Plato in the Renaissance is missing in Moellendorff, Simonis, and Simonis (2013). Manuscripts, editions and translations Landfester (2007), 469–473.

17 Aristotle in the Renaissance see Fröhlich in Moellendorff, Simonis, and Simonis (2013), 95–106. Manuscripts, editions and translations Landfester (2007), 71–76; editio princeps 1495–1498.

18 Demosthenes is not part of the usual canon. In the stalls for the members of the city council in the Gothic town hall of Bremen (Gramatzki 1994, 50–61) Plato, Aristotle, Cicero, and others are represented, but Demosthenes is missing. For Demosthenes' reputation in the Renaissance see since the editio princeps 1504. Bassarion's *speech against the Turks* (1470) as a Demosthenian

The city's claim to rule over the citizens, and now even over the religious realm as well, is legitimised by a new competence: education, logical thinking, knowledge of languages, persuasion, rhetoric, in a word: *humanism*. It is a renaissance (*renatae litterae*) of the knowledge and competence of the ancient sages. The iconographic programme of the Town Hall's interior claims good government for the city council (*buon governo*).[20]

On the eastern side of the building facing the cathedral, in contrast, the other four prophets were not subjected to such a conversion; they remained in place as prophets, hinting as figures of the Old Testament at the typological prefiguration of the fulfilment in the Christian church opposite the town hall. Thus, the conversion of the prophets to ancient sages does not signify secularisation in opposition to religion, but rather a synthesis of both Christian religion and the competences in *re publica*, to be acquired from the ancient philosophers and rhetoricians.

4 A New Iconographic Program: The *New Jerusalem* after Bremen's Second Reformation to a Calvinist City

The Reformation launched a revolution within visual culture. Before that schism there was a *habitus* to admire the holy as a person, to kiss, to touch and stroke it, to smell the incense, to light a candle, to genuflect in veneration. In Calvinistic ritual all senses were deprived except hearing the Word of God (Ehrensperger 2011, esp. 213–256, 305–330). The sharp break, however, in the ritual communication at the centre of the religious service found other media, both within the church building and outside on the public town hall, to present the new program of religious and political reformation. Iconic religious motifs migrated from the centre of the church to its margins. Iconic religious motifs migrated to the centre of the public political sphere. The epitaph of Segebade Clüver continued to present the traditional motifs but with emphasis on the new Protestant program of two sacraments and Bremen as the New Jerusalem. The conversion of the prophets on the city side of the Town Hall is not meant as an act of secularisation, but

Olynthian orations. Huss in Moellendorff, Simonis, and Simonis (2013), 351–360. Düren (2012). Manuscripts, editions and translations Landfester (2007), 196–198.

19 Cicero in the Renaissance see Mueller (2013). Manuscripts, editions and translations in Landfester (2007, 148–175); orationes, ed. princ. 1470.

20 See Gramatzki (1994, 50–61). For a similar Reformation program of a city council see Koch (2008). Bremen and Lüneburg refer to a Renaissance program, the first represented by Lorenzetti's fresco *buon governo* in the town hall of Siena 1338/39.

it places the symbols of new competences in education, knowledge, and rhetoric above divine custody, authorizing the claim of political leadership (against the Archbishop's counterclaim).

Figure 3: Bremen Townhall; Allegories on the façade of 1612: caricature of the victory of the Reformed City over Papacy (in Gramatzki 2005, 51).
In the series of reliefs visible to the passing-by citizens, one of the virtues represents a bitter caricature: a young woman is mounted on a man, who lost the control over the sword she is taking away from him. She incites him by a spur in the rectum. The tiara on the head of the 'horse' makes him recognisable as the Pope. By the cruciger globe in her hand, the woman is identifiable as the (Protestant city) state who has now taken on also the spiritual sword.

To conclude our *tour d'horizon* of the visuality of religion in the reformed city, I shall take a look at the new façade of the Town Hall of 1612, a capstone, as it were, concluding the reformation century in Bremen. Religious virtues are presented as part of the civic duties within the catalogue of virtues of ancient Stoicism.[21] The iconographical program integrated religious life as part of the political body: the Calvinistic city fulfils the millenarian reign of Christ with the elect (as do the Puritans of that period in the Promised Land of America) (Brunotte 2000). Again, presenting two details helps to illustrate this point. The first is a bitter caricature of the victory of the Reformed City over Papacy. A young

---

21 In deciphering of the allegories I follow Gramatzki (1994).

woman holds the imperial regalia, in her left hand the *globus cruciger* (Imperial Orb). With her right hand she grasps the blade of the sword, of which at this moment its owner has lost command. The sword's owner is a man serving as the woman's mount. The 'horse' is wearing the triple crown of papacy. The woman rider prods the horse with a goad in form of the papal cross. A sexual connotation of the 'woman on top' ridicules the Pope as either having lost control, as being love-crazed, or as one who is unable to satisfy his lover, a reference to Aristotle and his lover Phyllis.[22] Such a polemic against the papacy could never have been exhibited in a church. We find similar drastic and polemic engravings in the leaflets of the Early Reformation. However presenting such polemic in public creates a new space for religious communication. It is enabled by the new public space that religion gained in the reformed city. Not in the dignified interior of a church, but open to the gazes of the citizens, proudly displayed on the new façade of the Town Hall. The caricature of the ridiculous leader of the opposing confession and the victorious (female) city on top fosters a process of desacralisation and decentralisation of the Holy in the public space.

Figure 4: Hans Baldung Grien: Phyllis Rides Aristotle. Woodcut 1513. Berlin, Kupferstichkabinett. Reproduced with permission of bpk / Gemäldegalerie, Staatliche Museen zu Berlin.
The caricature on the Town hall (figure 3) recalls a late medieval narrative: the model-intellectual, philosopher Aristotle, went crazy of sexual desire. His girlfriend (whore) Phyllis takes command and rides on him inciting him with the spur. The intellectual is ridiculed; the order is turned upside-down: women on top is unacceptable for confessional Early Modern Europe.

---

22 Again, a full analysis cannot be provided here. For the moment, I follow Davis (1975).

In contrast, the iconographic programme of the new façade culminates in a symbol at the very apex: the throne of God in the form of a precious stone, above the heraldic symbol of the city, St. Peter's key. God rules over the many images of the Great Adversary below, the beast of the Apocalypse named 666. Gramatzki (1994) interprets the stone as conveying two meanings: (1) the stone of the Old Testament prophet Daniel: In the dream sent by God, the history of the world is summarised by the figure of a colossus standing on clay feet. The colossus represents the four civilisations. In the Protestant interpretation, the feet of clay signify the Roman papacy (not the Roman Empire).[23] A stone rolls down the mountain from above and shatters the colossus (Dan. 2:44) (Koch 1997, 108–111, 126–130). This stone is the future eternal empire of God.

(2) In the Apocalypse, Heavenly Jerusalem is built on a foundation of twelve precious stones. Placing the emerald on the throne depersonalises God, substituting him with a symbol. This substitution allows fundamental new modes of thought: God is the Word, the Eye in the centre of a triangle (see Stoelleis 2004, 2009). It also enables dissent with the mutual legitimation of Monarchy and Monotheism. Thirteen years later, the Dutch Professor Hugo Grotius in his *De jure belli et pacis* (1625) asserted that the subject on the thrones of the city-states is the body of citizens. The stone cannot be revered, but it is a reference to an eternal rule of a Christian conduct of life, represented by the constitution of the *res publica*.

By displaying religious motifs in the public sphere in the reformed city while leaving void the church centre images were no longer objects of veneration. Religion, as conceived by the Reformation, is changed fundamentally: it is no longer a body of images, saints, sacraments, and priests to be venerated as objects. Instead, lay people are now the subject of religion. The citizens of the reformed city are called upon to actively conduct their own lives in a Christian manner. Determining the right religious path and consciously leading a religious life accordingly is posed as a daily challenge for every Christian citizen.

5 Conclusion

Considering the above discussion, what are the implications for the initial question regarding the *aisthesis* of religion and whether a revolutionary change of a visual *habitus* is even possible? For systematic considerations, re-conceptualis-

---

23 Traditionally, Daniel's four empires are interpreted as the Babylonian, the Persian, the Greek of Alexander the Great, and as the last one, the Roman Empire, which exists even after the fall of Rome as the Holy Roman Empire of the German Nation, the so-called *Translatio imperii*, see Auffarth (2002, 86–90).

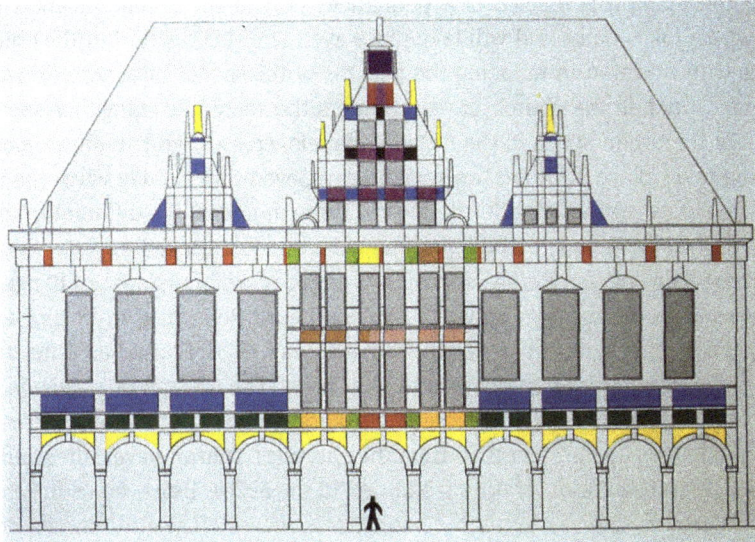

Fassadenschema mit Themenverteilung
(Rot = Christus, Gelb = Tugenden, Hellgrün = Köpfe als Zeitdarstellung)

Figure 5: Bremen Town Hall: Iconological schema by Albrecht (1993, Ausfalttafel II).
The Calvinistic programme of the second reformation pushes forward the implementation of Christian ideals in the City's politics and, thus, aims at erecting the Lutheran theological programme of the two rather autonomous reigns: the spiritual of the church and the secular of the regional princes (*Landesfürsten*). The latter will transfer into God's reign only after history and the Last Judgment. In Calvinist thought, good government has to be realised here and now by the virtues of the Christian citizens, by the redeemer and, above all, by God, who—as the *summum bonum*, the highest good—is represented by the empty throne and the precious stone.

ing urban space offers an important distinction. Up until the Reformation religious action 'takes place'[24] and dwells first and foremost in the church building. Agency is attributed to the religious specialists, and in cases of emergency, the saints may intervene on behalf of God. Through praying and offering candles and money lay people ask for, and receive, signs and actions symbolizing the sacred, such as sacraments. The church building as a space is semi-public, as lay people can enter it without asking the priest, pray and 'sacrifice' a candle, but the shareholders of the building are the priests (Dürr 2006, 87–116). The case of the epitaph follows in part the iconic (iconographic) tradition: the man for

---

24 For religious place I refer to Jonathan Z. Smith (1978, 1987). Even more systematically place is part of the conceptualising of space, as shown by Knot 2005 and 2008.

whom the epitaph is erected is a permanent part of the communication with God, which takes place and will take place even after his death. But the epitaph breaks with tradition in reducing the persons of the sacred history to Christ the redeemer. Outside the church one encounters the sacred at many, but specific, places in the urban space in the form of chapels, crosses, and statues of saints. Religion takes place in rituals, on specific days, even thrice a day when the ringing bells create regular religious moments. These moments are different from the 'every day' activities such as digging the garden, cooking, selling, etc.

Clearly, during the Reformation the concept of religious space changed in comparison to the medieval one. Yet, the Lutheran Reformation did not expel the visuality of religion in principal: rather it was re-configured as a means of a new type of veneration in the central altar piece. The epitaph of Segebade Clüver is an example of a specific genre of visual religion that Lutherans allowed to persist. Whereas images vanished from the churches' central naves, the tradition of the self-representation of priests endured in the aisles. However, as the example of Segebade Clüver's epitaph demonstrates, new Reformation motifs dominated the imagery. This means, on the one hand, that a (secondary) genre continues to impart what is, on the other hand, a new message. According to the Lutheran doctrine of the two 'reigns' the divide between the two realms—the secular of the dukes and kings opposed to the spiritual reign—would only be overcome by God in heaven (which also means: after death), but not on earth. During the Second Reformation[25] however, this was conceptualised very differently. The reign of God was meant to be realized in this life; the city itself and the every-day life of the citizens were sanctified. If we consider the concept of space again: religious space is no longer restricted to specific spots; now the city, and especially the city hall and the politics conducted from there are religious, and at the same time humanistic (scientific),[26] as the conversion of the prophets may show. Inside the church the cult became an aniconic religion – it is notable that violence against images is but one form of transition, and for the Bremen example it is not prominent. In public space the concept of religious politics, the sanctified city and citizens, can be found in a visual expression in the iconographic (but not traditional) programme of the façade of the city hall. The precious stone at the top of the Town Hall's façade conceives of God no longer as a personified figure that is arbitrarily interfering in human history. Instead, God is precious, the *summum bonum*, yet still part of a greater, magnificent order, the capstone of the

---

25 Some prefer 'Calvinist reformation', the now common term is Calvinist confessionalisation (besides the Catholic and Lutheran one).
26 The secular/sacred distinction is true only after the conception of the monopoly of the state following the French revolution.

ideal city built upon the virtues of its citizens. To fulfil God's Will in the here and now, not in some distant divine realm beyond death: in this way religion becomes Christian politics. The *aisthesis* of religion ceases to perceive religion as a material manifestation of divine power, which may be venerated by seeing, touching, tasting, smelling, and through which—by intervention of the saints and priests—one may partake in its salvific properties. Providence "calls upon man" to fulfil his divine destiny by leading an in every aspect fully Christian life: as husband, as head of a household, as citizen, in war, as senator. The precious stone is part of a divine order, which is also present in the civic order. It is a case of a revolutionary change: visual culture migrates from the semi-public interior of the church into the public space of the precious modern façade of the city hall. The iconic programme presents both the humanistic/ Renaissance revival of ancient virtues, but it integrates them as Christian in an iconographic setting dominated by a non-personified *summum bonum* that can be perceived as a symbol of God. A sharp and profiled programme of Protestant identity as opposed to the Catholic one, personified as political (military, economic) enemies paved the way for different confessional cultures that acted 'differently', and in mutual dependence on one another. The modernity of Classical humanist culture, which the Protestant to-be-pastors became acquainted with during their university studies, presented the new Protestant iconographic programs and visual culture as differing strongly from the traditional medieval sensory modes. The smell of incense made the Catholic feel the presence of the sacred; it made the Protestant visitor feeling rather sick.

Religious aesthetics as a connective concept allows one to integrate theories, methods and knowledge from different scientific approaches: iconography, history of art, *Bildwissenschaft*, ritual studies (dynamics of ritual), spatial turn, anthropology of perception, semantics, *Religionswissenschaft* (study of religion, history of religion), church history as a sub-discipline of Christian theology, philology, Renaissance studies, etc. They are connected by a systematic-analytical question (a *religionswissenschaftliche Fragestellung*), which is specific through its 'comparative view' (Auffarth 2009, 192–218), making scholars aware of the fact that for the same issue in other cultures and epochs very different solutions have been found. This way of comparing and historising a complex entanglement of perceptive and interpretive patterns comes close to Max Weber's method to construct 'ideal-types', yet with a focus on the "work of the senses." As Weber also proclaimed, an aesthetics of religion approach does not anticipate what is 'religious' or 'non-religious' *before* the material would have been analysed. Religion is but one, yet a crucial element, in a comprehensive change of visual perception, and of ways to communicate and establish new values in a wider culture. This change is not limited to religious history, and religion is not its only reason. Rather, the aesthetic approach makes clear how modes of visuality link the elements to each other.

Bibliography

Albrecht, Stephan. 1993. *Das Bremer Rathaus im Zeichen städtischer Selbstdarstellung vor dem 30-jährigen Krieg*. Marburg: Jonas.
Auffarth, Christoph. 2002. *Irdische Wege und himmlischer Lohn: Kreuzzug, Jerusalem und Fegefeuer in religionswissenschaftlicher Perspektive*. Göttingen: Vandenhoeck & Ruprecht.
— 2005. "Neue Welt und Neue Zeit: Weltkarten und Säkularisierung in der Frühen Neuzeit." In *Expansionen in der Frühen Neuzeit*, edited by Renate Dürr, Gisela Engel, and Johannes Süßmann. *Zeitschrift für Historische Forschung*, Special Issue 34: 43–68.
— 2007. "Ritual, Performanz, Theater: Die Religion der Athener in Aristophanes' Komödien." In *Literatur und Religion 1: Wege zu einer mythisch-rituellen Poetik bei den Griechen*, edited by Anton F. Bierl, Rebecca L Rebe, and Katharina Wesselmann, 387–414. Berlin and New York: de Gruyter.
— 2008. "Alle Tage Karneval? Reformation, Provokation und Grobianismus." In *Glaubensstreit und Gelächter: Reformation und Lachkultur im Mittelalter und in der Frühen Neuzeit*, edited by Christoph Auffarth, and Sonja Kerth, 79–105. Berlin et al.: LIT.
— 2009. "Mittelalterliche Modelle der Eingrenzung und Ausgrenzung religiöser Verschiedenheit." In *Europäische Religionsgeschichte: Ein mehrfacher Pluralismus*, edited by Hans G. Kippenberg, Jörg Rüpke, and Kocku von Stuckrad, 193–218. G 193–218: Vandenhoeck & Ruprecht.
— 2010. "The Materiality of God's Image: Olympian Zeus and the Ancient Christology." In *The Gods of Ancient Greece: Identities and Transformation*, edited by Jan N. Bremmer, and Andrew Erskine, 465–480. Edinburgh: Edinburgh University Press.
Auffarth, Christoph, Jutta Bernard, and Hubert Mohr, eds. *Metzler Lexikon Religion: Alltag, Medien, Gegenwart*. 4 Vols. Stuttgart and Weimar: Metzler.
Auffarth, Christoph, and Sonja Kerth, eds. 2008. "Glaubensstreit und Gelächter: Religion – Kultur – Kunst: Eine Einführung." In *Glaubensstreit und Gelächter: Reformation und Lachkultur im Mittelalter und in der Frühen Neuzeit*. Berlin et al.: LIT.
Belting, Hans. 1990. *Bild und Kult: Eine Geschichte des Bildes vor dem Zeitalter der Kunst*. Munich: Beck.
— 1993. *Likeness and Presence: A History of the Image before the Era of Art*, translated by Edmund Jephcott. University of Chicago Press (translation of Belting 1990).
Bredekamp, Horst. 2013. *Theorie des Bildakts. Frankfurter Adorno-Vorlesungen 2007*. Berlin: Suhrkamp.
Bremmer, Jan. 2008. "Iconoclast, Iconoclastic, and Iconoclasm: Notes towards a Genealogy." *Church History and Religious Culture* 88: 1–17.
Brunotte, Ulrike. 2000. *Puritanismus und Pioniergeist: Die Faszination der Wildnis im frühen Neu-England*. Berlin: de Gruyter.
Cancik, Hubert, and Hubert Mohr. 1998. "Religionsästhetik." In *Handbuch religionswissenschaftlicher Grundbegriffe*. Vol. 1, 121–156. Stuttgart: Kohlhammer.

Davis, Natalie Zemon. 1975. "Women on Top." In *Society and Culture in Early Modern France: Eight Essays*, 124–151. Stanford: Stanford University Press.

— 1987. "Die aufsässige Frau." In *Humanismus, Narrenherrschaft und die Riten der Gewalt: Gesellschaft und Kultur im frühneuzeitlichen Frankreich*, (translation of Davis 1975) 136–170. Frankfurt: Fischer TB.

Düren, Alexander. 2012 *Die Rezeption des Demosthenes von den Anfängen bis ins 17. Jh.* Diss. Bonn.

Dupeux, Cécile, Peter Jezler, and Jean Wirth, eds. 2000. *Bildersturm: Wahnsinn oder Gottes Wille?* [Exhibition catalogue Bern]. Munich: Fink.

Dohrn-van Rossum, Gerhard. 1992. *Geschichte der Stunde. Uhren und moderne Zeitordnung.* Munich: Hanser.

Duffy, Eamon. [1992] 2005. *The Stripping of the Altars: Traditional Religion in England c.1400 – c.1580.* New Haven, CT: Yale University Press.

Dürr, Renate. 2006. *Politische Kultur in der Frühen Neuzeit: Kirchenräume in Hildesheimer Stadt- und Landgemeinden 1550–1750.* Gütersloh: Gütersloher Verl.-Haus.

Ehrensperger, Alfred. 2010. *Der Gottesdienst in Stadt und Landschaft Basel im 16. und 17. Jahrhundert.* Zurich: Theologischer Verlag.

— 2011. *Der Gottesdienst in Stadt und Landschaft Bern im 16. und 17. Jahrhundert.* Zurich: Theologischer Verlag.

— 2012. *Der Gottesdienst in der Stadt St. Gallen, im Kloster und in den fürstäbtischen Gebieten vor, während und nach der Reformation.* Zurich: Theologischer Verlag.

Fröhlich, Vincent. 2013. "Aristoteles." In *Historische Gestalten der Antike: Rezeption in Literatur, Kunst und Musik. Der Neue Pauly*, Supplemente Vol.8, edited by Peter von Moellendorff, Annette Simonis, and Linda Simonis. Stuttgart: Metzler, 95–106.

Gaimster, David, and Roberta Gilchrist, eds. 2003. *The Archaeology of Reformation 1480–1580: Papers Given at the Archaeology of Reformation Conference, February 2001.* Leeds: Maney.

Gramatzki, Rolf. 1994. *Das Rathaus in Bremen: Versuch zu seiner Ikonologie.* Bremen: Hauschild.

— 2005. "Das Renaissance-Rathaus: Bürgerstolz und Glaubensbekenntnis in schwerer Zeit." In *Das Rathaus und seine Nachbarn. Macht, Pracht, Gott und die Welt am Markt zu Bremen*, edited by Gotthilf Hempel, 39–54. Bremen: Hauschild.

Hamm, Berndt. 2009. "Den Himmel kaufen: Heilskommerzielle Perspektiven des 14. bis 16. Jahrhunderts." In *Himmel auf Erden/ Heaven on Earth*, edited by Rudolf Suntrup and Jan R. Veenstra, 23–56. Frankfurt: Lang.

Huss, Bernhard. 2013. "Demosthenes." In *Historische Gestalten der Antike: Rezeption in Literatur, Kunst und Musik. Der Neue Pauly*, Supplemente Vol.8, edited by Peter von Moellendorff, Annette Simonis, and Linda Simonis, 351–360. Stuttgart: Metzler.

Jäggi, Carola, and Jörn Staecker. 2007. *Archäologie der Reformation: Studien zu den Auswirkungen des Konfessionswechsels auf die materielle Kultur.* Berlin: de Gruyter.

Kaufmann, Thomas. 2012. *Der Anfang der Reformation: Studien zur Kontextualität der Theologie, Publizistik und Inszenierung Luthers und der reformatorischen Bewegung.* Tuebingen: Mohr Siebeck.

King, Chris, and Duncan Sayer, eds. 2011. *The Archaeology of Post-Medieval Religion.* Woodbridge: Boydell.

Knott, Kim. 2005. *The Location of Religion: A Spatial Analysis.* London: Equinox.

—— 2008. "Spatial Theory and Method for the Study of Religion." *Religion Compass* 2/6: 1102–1116.

Koch, Klaus. 1997. *Europa, Rom und der Kaiser vor dem Hintergrund von zwei Jahrtausenden Rezeption des Buches Daniel.* Hamburg: Joachim-Jungius-Gesellschaft der Wissenschaften.

—— 2008. "Die Gemaelde der Grossen Ratsstube: Zur Rezeption der Daniel-Apokalyptik in der Reformationszeit. In *Jerusalem, du Schöne. Vorstellungen und Bilder einer heiligen Stadt*, edited by Bruno Reudenbach 131–166. Bern: Lang.

Koerner, Joseph Leo. 2004. *The Reformation of the Image.* London: Reaktion.

Kroesen, Justin. 2010. *Kirchen in Ostfriesland und ihre mittelalterliche Ausstattung.* Petersberg: Imhof.

Landfester, Manfred, ed. 2007. "Geschichte der antiken Texte." In *Der Neue Pauly*, Supplemente Vol. 2. Stuttgart: Metzler.

Lindberg, Carter. [1996] 2010. *The European Reformations.* Chichester: Wiley-Blackwell.

Meyer, Birgit. 2006. *Religious Sensations: Why Media, Aesthetics and Power Matter in the Study of Contemporary Religion. Inaugural Lecture, Vrije Universiteit.* Amsterdam: VU 2006. URL: http://www.fsw.vu.nl/nl/Images/Oratietekst_Birgit_Meyer_tcm249-36764.pdf (last accessed 5 December 2015)

Moellendorff, Peter von, Annette Simonis, and Linda Simonis. 2013. *Historische Gestalten der Antike: Rezeption in Literatur, Kunst und Musik. Der Neue Pauly*, Supplemente Vol. 8. Stuttgart: Metzler.

Mohr, Hubert. 2000a. "Wahrnehmung/Sinnessystem." In *Metzler Lexikon Religion.* Vol. 3, 620–633. Stuttgart: Metzler.

—— 2000b. "Vision/Audition." In *Metzler Lexikon Religion.* Vol. 3, 570–577. Stuttgart: Metzler.

—— 2003. "Kultischer Reizausschluss." In *Der Kanon und die Sinne:* Religionsästhetik als akademische Disziplin, edtied by Susanne Lanwerd, 47–67. Luxembourg: EurAssoc.

—— 2006a. "Perception/Sensory System." In *The Brill Dictionary of Religion*, edited by Kocku von Stuckrad (translation of Mohr 2000a). Vol. 4, 1435–1448. Leiden: Brill.

—— 2006b. "Vision/Auditory Experience." In *The Brill Dictionary of Religion*, edited by Kocku von Stuckrad (translation of Mohr 2000b). Brill Online, URL: http://referenceworks.bril lonline.com/entries/brill-dictionary-of-religion/visionauditory-experience-COM_00476 (last accessed 28 November 2015)

—— 2006c. "Religionsästhetik." In *Wörterbuch der Religionen*, edited by Christoph Auffarth, Hans G. Kippenberg, and Axel Michaels, 431–433. Stuttgart: Alfred Kröner.

Mohr, Hubert, and Hubert Cancik. 2001. "Kult." In *Handbuch ästhetischer Grundbegriffe.* Vol. 3, 489–510. Stuttgart: Metzler.

Müller, Gernot Michael. 2013. "Cicero." In *Historische Gestalten der Antike: Rezeption in Literatur, Kunst und Musik. Der Neue Pauly*, Supplemente Vol.8, edited by Peter von Moellendorff, Annette Simonis, and Linda Simonis. Stuttgart: Metzler, 277–296.

Roth, Gerhard. 1994. *Das Gehirn und seine Wirklichkeit. Kognitive Neurobiologie und ihre philosophischen Konsequenzen.* Frankfurt a.M.: Suhrkamp.

—— 2013. *The Long Evolution of Brains and Minds.* Berlin, New York: Springer.

Rublack, Ulinka. 2003. *Die Reformation in Europa.* Frankfurt: Fischer 2003

—— 2005. *Reformation Europe.* (translation of Rublack 2003). Cambridge: Cambridge University Press.

Rudloff, Ortwin, ed. 1987. "Häretische Sätze aus den Bremer Predigten Heinrichs von Zütphen, Januar und Februar 1523." *Hospitium Ecclesiae* 1: 71–116.

Scribner, Robert W. 1981. *For the Sake of Simple Folk: Popular Propaganda for the German Reformation.* Cambridge: Cambridge University Press.

Schlögl, Rudolf. 1998. "Öffentliche Gottesverehrung und privater Glaube in der Frühen Neuzeit : Beobachtungen zur Bedeutung von Kirchenzucht und Frömmigkeit für die Abgrenzung privater Sozialräume." In *Das Öffentliche und Private in der Vormoderne*, edited by Gert Melville, and Peter von Moos, 165–209. Cologne: Böhlau.

Smith, Jonathan Z. 1978. *Map is Not Territory: Studies in the History of Religions.* Leiden: Brill.

—— 1987. *To Take Place: Toward Theory in Ritual.* Chicago, IL: University of Chicago Press.

Stolleis, Michael. 2004. *Das Auge des Gesetzes.* Munich: Beck.

—— 2009. *The Eye of the Law: Two Essays on Legal History.* Abingdon: Birkbeck Law Press.

Tarlow, Sarah. 2003. "Reformation and Transformation: What Happened to Catholic Things in a Protestant World?" In *The Archaeology of Reformation 1480–1580: Papers Given at the Archaeology of Reformation Conference, February 2001*, edited by David Gaimster and Roberta Gilchrist, 108–121. Leeds: Maney.

Trüper, Hans G. 2001. "Segebade Clüver. *Blätter der "Maus"* 24: 40–44.

Weibezahn, Ingrid, and Detlev G. Gross, eds. 2005. *Schätze aus dem Bremer St. Petri Dom. Führer durch das Dom-Museum.*

Weidinger, Ulrich, Dieter Hägermann, and Konrad Elmshäuser. 2012. *Bremische Kirchengeschichte im Mittelalter.* Bremen: Hauschild.

Wilke, Annette. 2012. "Text, Klang und Ritual. Plädoyer fuer Religionswissenschaft als Kulturhermeneutik." In *Religionswissenschaft: Ein Studienbuch*, edited by Michael Stausberg, 407–422. Berlin and Boston: de Gruyter.

Wilke, Annette, and Oliver Moebus. 2011. *Sound and Communication. An Aesthetic Cultural History of Sanskrit Hinduism.* Berlin: de Gruyter 2011.

Zerbe, Doreen. 2013. *Reformation der Memoria: Denkmale in der Stadtkirche Wittenberg als Zeugnisse lutherischer Memorialkultur im 16. Jahrhundert.* Leipzig: Evangelische Verlagsanstalt.

—— 2007. "Memorialkunst im Wandel: Die Ausbildung eines lutherischen Typus des Grab- und Gedächtnismals im 16. Jahrhundert." In *Archäologie der Reformation. Studien zu den Auswirkungen des Konfessionswechsels auf die materielle Kultur*, edited by Carola Jäggi, and Jörn Staecker, 117–163. Berlin and Boston: de Gruyter.

Hubert Mohr

Standing, Not Walking – The Hieratic as a Key Term of an Anthropologically Based Aesthetics of Religion

*For Brigitte Luchesi,
with gratitude for the Bremen years*

1 Introduction[1]

This contribution aims at establishing the notion of *Hieratics* as a key term of religious aesthetics and, moreover, at introducing the project of an anthropologically based aesthetics of religion. The notion of an anthropological basis refers to
the general idea that we can gain a better understanding of religious aesthetic
forms and strategies by drawing on knowledge about human (and animal) behaviour, perception and cognition. It also encompasses knowledge of how
human beings orientate themselves in the environment through their sensorium
and the cultured ways of shaping and reshaping the fundamental modes of moving, sensing and perceiving. As I have shown elsewhere (Mohr 2006a), this approach engages with different perspectives about anthropological knowledge
and perceptual psychology, for example, art historical knowledge. However, it
is also inclusive of movement studies, historical anthropology and discursive understandings of history including historically changing aesthetic forms. For this
chapter, I will focus on ethology, kinaesthetics and the transition between physiologically functional body postures and their cultural and religious engagement. Human beings, it is assumed, differ gradually from other species in how
they respond to stimuli from the environment. Due to their capacity to de-couple
from instinctive responses, they perform a great variety of responses. Human beings can react differently, or not react at all to a stimulus; and most importantly,

1 An earlier stage of this chapter was presented in 2008 at the University of Bremen on the occasion of the retirement of Dr Brigitte Luchesi. Another version was presented in the Religions-
wissenschaftliches Kolloquium at the University of Basel in 2012: for the helpful discussion, I
thank Prof. Jürgen Mohn and the other participants. For the possibility to present other aspects
of the topic during the performance "absent while here – transgressive bodies" at Schwere Reiter
(Munich) in December 2009 I am very thankful to Micha Purucker. I am also grateful to Mrs Angela Baggarley (Tübingen) for improving my spoken English and discussing the topic with me.

https://doi.org/10.1515/9783110461015-010

they are able to turn the basic forms of responding into the foundation of interpretive systems and symbolic worlds (Mohr 2006a, 1441). Liturgies which engage all senses, attention attracting architecture which stands out from the landscapes and cityscapes they are embedded in, these are but a few examples of how religious systems create a significant "panorama of perception" which unmistakably distinguishes one tradition from the other – both for the adherents and a given "outside" sphere. Diverse aesthetic means and principles are at work here, many of them sharing the feature that they are "effective" by deviating from an everyday functional "neutral mode" of perceiving and acting. Religious aesthetic forms, for instance, often push behaviour to extremes by either stimulating or depriving the senses (see Mohr 2004 on the deprivation of the senses). Looking at religious practice and conceptualisations through the lens of these modes of shaping and reshaping basic bodily and perceptual functions provides an opportunity to develop a systematic and comparative overview of how religious traditions cultivate, restrict and thematise the body and the senses (for a systematic table see Mohr 2006a, 1446–1447; for a "kinaesthetic of religion", see Mohr 2003). It is in this perspective that the notion of the Hieratic is developed in this chapter. It is seen as a contribution to a terminology, a typology and a model, for a toolkit in the perspective of a larger comparative religious aesthetics, and a cultural understanding of somatic aesthetics as well.

My line of argument starts with a historical example of sacred art from nineteenth century which represents very well what I identified as the recurring form of "standing, not walking—the Hieratic" (section 1); in the paragraphs that follow the Hieratic will be explained in a systematic way. Proceeding from discourse history, the basic elements of what constitutes (or could be seen as) an *Aesthetics of the Hieratic* will be established (section 2). In a next step, the perspective will be broadened by applying ethological, anthropological and social aspects, concentrating on standing as a special form of bodily behaviour and posture both in humans and in animals (section 3). Subsequently, the Hieratic will be more specifically determined as a political, artistic, and religious "enhancement form" of everyday bodily positions and dispositions. As a basic analytical tool a typology of standing is developed (section 4). Finally, some remarks will be made on the pragmatic aspect, especially regarding the means of how Hieratic aesthetics are created, ritually and in social discourse: the *Hieratisation* (section 5). It should be noted that the consideration being presented is but a preliminary sketch which deserves more detailed arguments in a future study.

2 Hieratic Art (*Hieratische Kunst*) – The *Beuroner Kunstschule* and Father Desiderius Lenz

During the very politically agitated times of the 1860s, two young German artists developed a new religious art style adapting an hitherto unknown blend of Christian and pagan designs: Peter "Desiderius" Lenz (1832–1928) and Jakob "Gabriel" Wüger (1829–1892). Both artists were deeply impressed by the Catholicing "Nazarene movement" and, therefore, made a pilgrimage to Rome following their heroes' tracks. However, the *Bildungserlebnis* they encountered was unprecedented for the artists as well as art history. Here is an account from a letter written seven years later by Lenz to his friend Wüger:

> In the summer of 1864, when I went to the [sc. Prussian] archaeological library in Rome [...] in order to study Greek art, especially vase pictures, one day, I got around to browsing through a couple of Egyptian books. I came back again and again, and already by the second day I began noticing which pictures I was going to trace and copy myself. Inspecting these things made me both giddy and shiver inside. Never before had a form of art impressed me nearly so much, thus seized and enticed and all but soaked up my entire being, I felt just like one feels when in a quiet moment a sacred dictum of ancient wisdom enters one's consciousness and one pursues its momentum ad infinitum—on the other hand terror and awe in turn at the sight of these idols, the handiwork of hell. I wondered if I was allowed to engage with these things, if it wasn't a great sin.[2]

Lenz' Roman initiation experience induced him to create a new type of sacred art combining Christian iconography and Egyptian style. Their Christian impetus led Lenz and Wüger to join the Benedictine cloister of Beuron in the upper Danube valley. They brought together an enthusiastic group of monk artists, among them Adolf "Gabriel" Krebs (1849–1935) and Jan "Willibrord" Verkade (1868–1946). A

---

2 Letter from Peter (Desiderius) Lenz to Jakob Wüger, 5.10.1871; my own translation; the German source citation by Krins (1998, 22–23): "Als ich im Sommer 1864 die archäologische Bibliothek [sc. die der preußischen Gesandtschaft in Rom] zu besuchen anfieng, keineswegs in der Absicht, Egyptisch zu studieren, sondern nur griechisch insbes. Vasenbilder, kam ich eines Tages dazu, ein Paar Bände Egyptisch durchzusehen. Ich kam wieder und wieder und (23) schon am zweiten Tag fieng ich an zu bezeichnen, was ich mir pausen und kopieren wollte. Denn mir wurde immer warm und kalt bei Betrachtung dieser Sachen. Nie hatte auch entfernt eine Kunst so auf mich gewirkt, mein ganzes Wesen so gepackt und angezogen und gleichsam aufgesaugt, mir war zu Muthe, gleichwie einem ist, wenn in einem ruhigen Momente ein heiliger Spruch uralter Weisheit ins Bewußtsein fällt und man seine Tragweite ins Unendliche verfolgt – auf der andern Seite wieder abwechselnd Schauer und Furcht, wenn ich diese Götzengestalten sah, das Werk der Hölle. Ich fragte mich, ist es erlaubt mit diesen Dingen sich einzulassen, ist es nicht schwere Sünde [...]". – The letter is also quoted by zu Stolberg (2008, 78).

constant flow of sacred artwork—frescoes, statues, architectural sketches—demonstrates the productivity of the so called "Beuron School" until the First World War. Contemporary art critics and theologians in the first third of the twentieth century used the term *Hieratische Kunst* to describe this unfamiliar or even eccentric kind of religious art (Pöllmann 1905; Kreitmeiner 1923, 73–98). It will be necessary to go back in time by means of *Begriffsgeschichte* (*conceptual history* after Reinhardt Koselleck) in order to understand both the aesthetic of the "Beuron Boys" and their enthusiastic followers. In this study, there will be space for a short sketch (section 3.1). After which I will proceed to outline of what might be call Hieratic aesthetics or The Hieratic, a descriptive key term for religious aesthetics.

3 The Aesthetics of the Hieratic

3.1 The historical discourse – The Beuron School, *Mysterientheologie* and the *Liturgische Bewegung*

As the images (Fig. 1–2) reveal, the Beuron School and their master Desiderius Lenz had a considerable appetite for form. Their preferred figuration is geometrical, even axis-symmetrical, vertical, with the person's face turned frontally to the observant faithful. Severe, stylized, standing or sitting—such are the Beuron "Hieratics".

What does that notion mean? The first clue comes from etymology: Hieratics derives from the Greek adjective *hierós*, "holy". Accordingly, "Hieratic art" in the first instance means "sacred art". Hieratics then implies a relating quality. But that doesn't signify sacred aesthetics per se, as explained in this quotation by the Jesuit Josef Kreitmeier from 1923:

> The difference between hieratic and non-hieratic art cannot consist in the one's being 'art pour Dieu' and the other 'art pour l'homme'.
> What constitutes the difference?
> It is exactly the same one between a choral and at best the pure Palestrinian polyphony and the other kinds of church music, as between the highly solemn and majestic liturgy and the free devotion of the people.
> The former is imbued by a deeply mystical spirit, and everything is ordered by measure and rhythm; the latter is ruled by subjectivity. Hieratic art is therefore the truly liturgical art forming complete unity and harmony with the entire liturgy and melding to a homogeneous 'Gesamtkunstwerk'.[3]

---

3 "Es kann somit der Unterschied zwischen hieratischer und nicht-hieratischer Kunst nicht

Figure 1: Desiderius Lenz. Draft of an Angel (*Entwurf zu einem Engel*), 1874. Pencil and Watercolours, 22,1 x 10,1 cm. Beuron Monastery, Germany, KAB Z003/7 – 13; from Krins 1998, 63; see also Siebenmorgen, and zu Stolberg 2008, 247. © Beuroner Kunstverlag. Reproduced with permission of the Beuroner Kunstverlag.

Figure 2: Desiderius Lenz. Group of Statues of the Holy Family; Chapel of the Kolping House, Stuttgart, Germany, 1872/74. Coloured wood; 163 x 82 cm. From Krins 1998, figure 54; see also Siebenmorgen 1983, 274 and 199. © Beuroner Kunstverlag. Reproduced with permission of the Beuroner Kunstverlag.

---

darin liegen, daß die eine 'art pour Dieu' sei, die andere 'art pour l'homme'. / Worin besteht aber nun der Unterschied? / Es ist genau derselbe, der zwischen Choral und allenfalls noch der rein palestrinensischen Polyphonie und den andern Arten von Kirchenmusik, zwischen der hochfeierlichen, majestätischen Liturgie und den freien Volksandachten besteht. Dort ist alles durchdrungen von tief mystischem Geist, alles geordnet nach Maß und Rhythmus; hier waltet die Subjektivität. Hieratische Kunst ist darum die eigentlich liturgische Kunst, die mit der gesamten

Figure 3: *Group of Statues*, combining hieratic striding with hieratic standing; Pharaoh Mykerinos with Goddess Hathor (left) and the Goddess of the 6th District of Upper Egypt (right); Gizeh,
Valley Temple of the Mykerinos Pyramid, 4th Dynasty, ca. 2480 BCE. Greywacke, 95,5 x 61 x
38 cm (Inv. No.: Kairo JE 46499; in Wildung and Grimm 1978, figure 5). Photo: © Hirmer Fo-
toarchiv München 654.1024. Reproduced with permission.
Figure 4: *Saint Demetrios Between a Bishop and an Official as Donors*. Mosaic in Hagios Demetrios, Thessalonike, 6th/7th century. From *The Yorck Project: 10.000 Meisterwerke der Mal-
erei*. DVD-ROM, 2002. Distributed by DIRECTMEDIA Publishing GmbH (available on Wikimedia,
free of copyrights).

Kreitmeier's statement illustrates that we must define the Hieratic as an aesthetic
quality of cultic or ritually bound art: It denotes "priestly art", *Priesterkunst*, according to Greek *hieratikós* (from *hieréus*, "priest"), which means the representation of a—often hierarchically organized—clergy as well as a "priestly superna-
turalism"[4] derived from dogmatic or mystical belief systems (Delahunt 2011).

Liturgie die vollste Eintracht und Harmonie bildet und mit ihr zu einem völlig einheitlichen Ge-
samtkunstwerk zusammenschmilzt" (Kreitmeier 1923, 87).
4 There is another definition in Delahunt in relation to formal stylistic criteria: The Hieratic as a
style "representing the sizes of things according to their importance, rather than how they would
objectively appear in space". A different meaning of the term is applied by historians of Old

Furthermore one often finds the collocation *hieratische Strenge* ("Hieratic Severeness" or "Austerity") which indicates a special quality of this kind of aesthetics, namely its penchant for typifying reduction, for stylized formalism, for the normative, for the ideal type. As prototypical examples we can refer to the religious images of Late Antiquity and Byzantium, from the 6th century mosaic art of Ravenna (San Vitale, consecrated in 547 AD; cf. also Figure 4) to the orthodox icon writers of today—and, above all others, to ancient Egypt as a very hotbed of holy media and design—one may remember the hieroglyphic scripture style.

Though it seems obvious from these citations that the term of Hieratics was influenced by a Catholic mystical movement in Germany from the beginning of the 20th century, the so called *"Liturgische Bewegung"* (Liturgical Movement) of the Abbey Maria Laach, and, notably, by the *"Mysterientheologie"* of Odo Casel (1886–1948) (Casel 1922), the following considerations try to (re)establish the term beyond this theological tradition and its ideological burden. Instead of this, the aesthetic qualities of the Hieratic will be constructed based on its anthropological foundation in the habitus of standing.

3.2 Outline of an Aesthetic Style (and More)

Looking at the epochs and examples of religious art connected to the term of the Hieratic (Ancient Egpyt – Byzantine – The Beuron School), we firstly will try to establish a model of the characteristic qualities of hieratic aesthetics:

- *Anthropomorphism:* The image is one of a human being.
- *Standing Habit / Position:* The body posture is mostly upright, thus underlining one of the typical, differentiating features of humanity: the faculty of going upright.
- *Axiality (Axis-Symmetry)* and *Verticality:* The body is immobile, even stiff, taking up an artificial posture that gives him or her statuesque quality;
- *Frontality:* Face and body are directed to the observer (posture "face-to-face") provoking direct visual contact.
- *Constructiveness:* The body is designed according to a set of aesthetic norms implementing regularity up to geometrical construction.
- *Self-containedness* (of the Body): The body is on the one hand "closed", without, or with only a little, indication of mobility and movement. The limbs often are held tight to the body; if there are any gestures, then they are sym-

---

Egyptian script which denotes a cursive writing type originated from the Hieroglyphic script. This terminology is not connected with the aesthetic discourse here discussed.

bolically restricted. On the other hand the bodies are isolated, scarcely interacting with one another, but may be directed to a focus.

Thus stylised, the human body becomes the centre of an artistic imagination
formed into an aesthetic design with the semantic connotations of:
- *Severity* (Formula: *hieratisch streng*): The proportions of the body, its orna-
  mental design and image are in an anti-naturalistic, even abstract, way stylised and reduced. Ultimately, such as with Desiderius Lenz, the body image
  becomes a geometrical construction, a mathematical formula (see Figure 5).
- *Timelessness:* The body image connotes permanence, durability, Eternal
  Being.
- *Non-Narrativity:* The aesthetics of the Hieratic is about (mystical, liturgical,
  representative) presence, not about mythological narration; it is about a
  So-sein and *Da-sein*, not about action; it is about structure, and not about
  history and stories.
- *"High Style"*: The bodies exhibit aesthetics of (ritual) distance and of the sub-
  lime transmitting an aura of inapproachability and the superhuman.

What is this Style used for? How does it function in the context of religion? In
order to answer these questions we have to take a step back from the study of
art and look at the social, anthropological, even ethological background of the
Hieratic style. We are in search here for how bodily movements (and especially
non-movements) generate expressive forms within a ritualistic and liturgical
context. The argument will proceed from the moving to the motionless; from
the walking body to the standing and posing; and, finally, to the "super-stylized"
forms which constitute an aesthetics of "the Hieratic".

4 Standing as a Body Position – Anthropological and Ethological Foundations

4.1 Kinaesthetics

The first consideration is in regard to body postures. Body positions, body movements, bodily behaviour as such is denoted and perceived in two ways: physically and culturally. The point to consider while employing the perspective of religious aesthetics is the connection between human body habits and the aesthetic
and semiotic "overwriting" taking place in religious contexts.

Accordingly, the approach of the following considerations is an essentially
anthropological one. The aesthetic dimensions will be elaborated from this

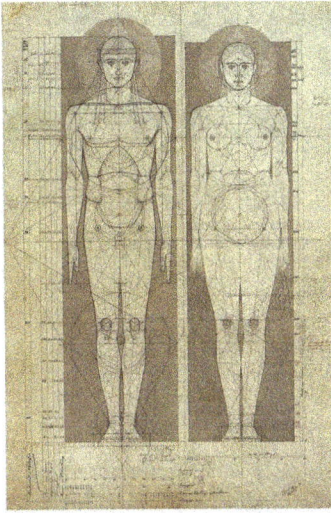

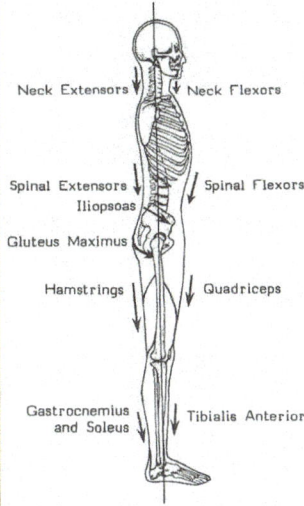

Figure 5: Desiderius Lenz. *Canonical Figures: Construction of a Masculine and a Feminine Body*, 1871. Pen and pencil, washed; 52,8 x 34,5 cm. From Krins 1998 fig. 43; see also Siebenmorgen 1983, 248. These human ideal types are constructed by triangles, rectangles, and circles—symbolizing the Christian Trinity, according to Lenz' *Versuch einer ästhetischen Geometrie* (1914). © Beuroner Kunstverlag. Reproduced with permission of the Beuroner Kunstverlag.
Figure 6: Antigravity Muscle Activity of the Erect Human Body (Schafer 1987, figure 4.1). Apart from its struggle against gravity, the upright human body has to cope with balance (i. e., orientation in space). © Frank M. Painter, D.C. Reproduced with permission of the author.

basic concept. Primarily, we look at the effects of hieratic images. Why do the images generate awe and experiences of holiness? The answer proposed here is: Because the body postures they depict are physically improbable and non-natural, artificial. Improbability and artificiality are due to the social and religious *mise-en-scène* generated by the physical efforts the body has to exert to take up and perform the postures. In sum, hieratic images are different from common physical and social behaviour. In order to learn more about this difference, applying kinaesthetics is a helpful approach (Mohr 2004, 310 – 324). It will enable us to comprehend standing as an extreme case of movement: It is movement brought to a halt; it is frozen movement, but also is the potentiality for movement. Considering the condition of the human body and its faculties of expression, movement is the foremost faculty as well as the natural one: Human bodies are continuously "on the move", by walking, by performing gestures, by moving the eyes. Therefore, if we postulate a *Homo movens*, then the posture of standing is a special case. It marks an anthropological borderline between moving and not-moving; a transient and precarious situation—a human being who stands has either just raised from sitting or lying, or has stopped running or walking. The insight we get from this stance becomes clearer when we look beyond the social performances at two other, mostly unconscious modes of the body in action: the physiological mode of the moving and standing body, and the ethological mode of basal scripts of behaviour.

Comparing walking and standing, we must not assume that the immobilized body is an idle and passive one. For standing the body requires:
- a sense of balance (the equilibrioception)
- muscle tension
- the energy to maintain this tension.

Consequently, for the body to stand is to work. Humans are standing until they fall down, due to gravitation (see Figure 6).

Furthermore, just because it is physiologically expensive and extravagant, the habitus of standing can be culturally and religiously used and laden with symbols: the upright gait, a *definiens* of the human species, is joined by the upright standing. But this polarity is not a definitive one; being a transitional state itself, it is subject to dynamic interpretations within cultural change, and it provides a pool and a playground for the creation of aesthetic forms in art, religion and politics.

4.2 Ethology

In addition to the study of human movements, ethology, the study of animal behaviour, is insightful for trying to comprehend the basal scripts underlying the visual representations of "standing, not moving". When and why does an animal straighten up? There are a couple of reasons for animal bipedalism:
- Standing Still / Keeping Still
  (a) as an attitude of observing or being at attention—one might think of the pittoresque meerkats of the Kalahari Desert in South Africa, or bears rearing up for sniffing;
  (b) as a fear reaction ("freezing")—the rabbit or tourist facing a serpent;
- Standing Still in the habit of "Facing up to"—confronting itself face to face with the unknown or an danger ("Face-off behaviour");
- Rising up / Rearing up': as a gesture of physical power and threatening (e. g. primates such as the Gorilla) (Agonal or aggressive behaviour);
- "Making Oneself Bigger": as a gesture of predominance (Display pattern).

However, it should be taken into account that sometimes the bipedalism in animals is misinterpreted by human observers who impose their fantasies, fears or imaginations upon nature. For instance, a bear who stands upright wants to observe the environment not to attack. But Western imagination makes its own images beyond reality: standing Bears are either dangerous wild beasts or cute humanized pets (Figures 7 and 8).

Figure 7: Grizzly Bear; Taxidermy, made by Pete Liewer, Burke, South Dakota (Item No. 2089) (URL: http://petestaxidermy.com/~petestaxi/mounts/animals/big-game/grizzly-bear/ (last accessed 12 December 2015). © Pete's Taxidermy, Inc. Burke, SD (Pete Liewer). Reproduced with permission of the photographer.
Figure 8: Mandy Bouriscot. *Beach Bear*; Plastic Statue; Spirit-Bears-in-the-City-Project, Vancouver 2006:[5] (URL: www.spiritbearsinthecity.com. © Mandy Bouriscot. Reproduced with permission of the artist.). *Spirit Bear* is the informal name of a rare genetic variant of Grizzly Bears, a white-coloured black bear, in Western Canada.[6]

---

5 Website *Spirit of Vancouver*; Media release" *(British Columbia Lions Society for Children with Disabilities)* 28 *April, 2006:* "Two hundred Kermode Spirit Bear sculptures will grace street corners, plazas and courtyards in communities up and down the west coast of British Columbia this summer, as part of the BC Lions Society's Kermode Spirit Bears In The City Project. [...] Each of the life-sized (seven-foot) fibreglass Kermode sculptures has been designed and decorated by well-known or up-and-coming B.C. artists, and sponsored by local businesses and individuals". URL: http://www.boardoftrade.com/sov_page.asp?pageid=1968 (received 4 December 2009)
6 "Spirit Bears" and Myth related to them: "PRINCESS ROYAL ISLAND, Canada – They're called spirit bears and fewer than 100 of these animals are alive today. They survived the Ice Age, but now could be close to extinction. Believe it or not, this white bear is really a black bear. These bears are known as white spirit bears and there are fewer than 100 of them all on Princess Royal Island off the west coast of Canada. 'A spirit bear is actually almost an oxymoron, it's a white-coloured black bear. It's not an albino, its a very rare double-recessive gene that allows this unique adaptation to occur', said Matt Reid with The Great Bear Foundation. According to Native

The Bad Bear, and the Good One: Two imaginations of a Standing Animal, an aggressive one on attack, and a friendly, tourist-proof one, "an icon of a holi-day-maker, a fun-loving, beach-bound, cool dude, with his Hawaiian shirt, surfer shorts, flip-flops, puka shell necklace, music in his pocket and boarding pass all ready for a sun and sea vacation."[7]

4.3 Social Practice

A line can be drawn from these forms of animal dominance behaviour to the aesthetics of human power, to the settings of dominance. Arguably, there is no direct dependency between animal and human behaviour but it demonstrates a comparable expressive gesture for predominance—to be bigger and thus more impressive when rearing up. It is therefore not surprising that Hieratic aesthetics is a popular medium for visualizing and performing human hierarchy. But as the ancient rites at the court of the Byzantine emperor, the Pope at the Vatican, or medieval princes demonstrate, the dominant posture could be the—more comfortable—sitting (vid. on a throne) whereas the empowering gesture of standing upright has been 'outsourced' to the entourage – as on earth so in heaven.

5 The Hieratic as an Enhancement Form

Regarding the social *mise-en-scène* we find a significant difference between commonplace and ritualistic behaviour. An overview reveals that each fundamental body posture—walking, standing, sitting, lying – has a culturally, aesthetically and ritually developed expressive form. These enhanced habits and poses are the stuff Hieratic aesthetics is made of. It should be noticed that the given examples are drawn both from art design as of the social and religious practice. It would afford another study to analyse the relationships between these two kinds of sensory representation and body cultivation.

After we have demonstrated the variety of forms of "enhanced body positions", the mode of standing will now be discussed in a more general perspective. Ex-

---

Kitasu Indians, these bears are a living reminder of a time when the world was covered with ice." November 26, 1995; From Reporter Bruce Burkhardt; http://www.cnn.com/EARTH/9511/spirit_-bears/ (last accessed 12 December 2015). The report concerns the so called Kermode Bear *(Ursus americanus kermodei)*, also called "spirit bear", a recessive genetic variation of the American Black Bear.

7 www.spiritbearsinthecity.com (last accessed 4 December 2009).

Figure 9: Table Overview 1: Aesthetic Enhancements of Body Habits; by the author.

Bodily Modes	Enhancement Form	Ritual Example
Standing	→ Standing still	Civic Ritual: Minute's Silence (vigil); *Mahnwache* (as an Act of Protest); Dominant Standing: Roman Victor during Triumph
	→ Standing in Attention	Military Guards
	→ Standing in Prayer	The Faithful and Clerics at Christian Mass
Walking	→ Striding	Christian Processions (Holy Friday; Corpus Christi); Military Ceremonies
	→ Walking Meditation	*Kinhin* rite in Zen Buddhism
Sitting	→ Being Enthroned	Pope or Bishops (Christianity); *Kumari* (Hinduism: Nepal); Kings and Queen in Europe, Asia and Africa
	→ Sitting Meditation	*Zazen* (Zen Buddhism)
Lying	→ Being Draped upon (a bed etc.)	Symposia (Ancient Greek and Rome); Deathbed displays

emplifying the argument, the guiding focus will be laid on what happens when human standing is given a cultural value; when it is enhanced by a social, political, and also an aesthetic and a religious habitus; in sum, when the transition takes place between *aisthesis* and *semiosis*, between a physiologically functional body posture and acting attitude and a culturally and religiously meaningful aesthetic form. A typological scheme can be compiled that shows, on the one hand, how standing habits are culturally framed and performed on (see overview 2 below); on the other hand a scale of enhancement can be set up which demonstrates the degree of how body positions and habits of standing are regulated and pushed to extremes, ranging from everyday standing habits to the body's "pillarization" in ascetic or artistic circumstances;

1. *'Normal' Standing:* The erect body as an everyday position resp. habit (e. g., if I am waiting for somebody).
2. *Representative Standing—Standing as a Posture and a Pose:* a decided standing which intends to express or perform a social role, a self-image (e. g., if somebody positions himself in front of a photo camera, within a photo atelier, or makes a selfie; see Figure 15 and 16).
3. *Ritual and Ceremonial Standing:* In society, politics, as well as in religious activities there are various forms of rites of immobility. These can be differ-

Figure 10: Hieratic Standing: *Votive Statue (God or King) from Abu Temple, Eshnunna* (Tell Asmar); Early Dynastic II (c. 2700 BCE); gypsum, height: 72 cm (in Eggebrecht, Walter and Pusch 1978, 62) © Roemer- und Pelizäus-Museum Hildesheim.
Figure 11: Hieratic Striding: *Monumental Statue of the Striding Buddha* by Silpa Bhirasri (aka Corrado Feroci, 1892 – 1962), casted in 1981, at Phutthamonthon Parc, Nakhon Pathom, (Thailand), displaying the gesture "Impeding the Sandalwood Statue"; height: 15,8 m. Damm, Heinrich; URL: http://upload.wikimedia.org/wikipedia/commons/3/32/Phutthamonthon03.jpg (free of copyrights; last accessed 14 December 2015).

entiated between rites of everyday life (gestures of respect, acts of courtesy; waiting rites, e. g., queuing), rites of civic ritual (wedding photo; protest and mourning acts as silent vigils or minute's silence; cf. Figure 17) and rites of civil religion (standing during a state reception, the conferring of an order, or when the national anthem is played). In regard to the religious field, standing rites occur as a main feature in liturgical practices, and, as in Christian tradition, in artwork visualizing the heavenly court. Here the ritual body is both a behavioural script expressing or reiterating internalised non-movements and a symbol fixed within a socio-religious setting and related to a belief system, an ideology, or an organization—thus a possible generator of hieratic aesthetics.

4. *STANDING, more than standing:* Standing straight can be exaggerated to extremes; forms of Intense Standing literally stand for a disciplined, expressive body. By muscular endeavours everybody can generate a great gesture, a

Figure 12: Hieratic Sitting: Daniel Chester French. *Abraham Lincoln enthroned*, 1920–22. Statue; white Marble, height with pedestal 9,1 m; Lincoln Memorial (Washington, DC), (Hirzinger, Florian. 2010. Abraham Lincoln enthroned: Lincoln Memorial (Washington). http://en. wikipedia.org/wiki/File:Lincoln_memorial.jpg (free of copyrights; last accessed 14 December 2015). The hieratic effect is amplified by architectural devices, the elevation of the throne by a pedestal as well as the sacral aesthetics of the temple design. It functions as a means to sacralise politics © Florian Hirzinger. Reproduced with permission of the author.
Figure 13: Hieratic Lying: *Reclining Buddha on his Deathbed.* Wat Suthat, Bangkok, Thailand (Damm, Heinrich. 2001. URL:http://upload.wikimedia.org/wikipedia/commons/thumb/7/77/ Buddha_recliningwsuthat.jpg/647px-Buddha_recliningwsuthat.jpg (free of copyrights; last accessed 14 December 2015).

communicative sign that transcends the daily behaviour routine culminating in a dramatic, emotional pose. However, STANDING offers not only individualistic expressive possibilities but the gesture is also an element of mass aesthetics comparable with impressive formations displaying coordinated muscular stress. There are three main types of STANDING:

a. *Standing to attention:* The gesture of "springing to attention" constitutes the military body monument. By standing flawlessly upright the soldier performs an act of self-mastery: The disciplined body, product of the "Working on Itself", thus generates prestige for being violent in the name of those who empowered it.

b. *Stretching/Erecting:* This type of enhanced standing could be a sportive exercise as well as a means for expressing emotion. In this case (and often in religious contexts), expressive STANDING generates a visual pathos formula *(Pathosformel,* Aby Warburg) as shown by the famous drawing of the German artist Fidus (i.e., Hugo Höppener, 1868–1948), *Lichtgebet* (Prayer to/in the Light; 1890 ff.) combining the body cult of the *Lebensreform movement* with neopagan nature religiosity (Frecot, Geist, and Kerbs 1997, 288–301).

Figure 14: Table Overview 2: Typology of Standing in Culture and Religion; by the author.

| Cultural Framing | The Religious Field | | | |
	Typology	Systematic Example	Religious-histori-cal Example	Visualisation
Standing as a Ritual	Ceremonial or 'Hieratic' Standing	Standing in Cultic and Liturgical Practice: 'Standing in Front of God', 'Face-to-Face'; Standing in Prayer	*wuquf* on Mount Arafat (Hadj in Mekka) *Darshan* (Hinduism)	Prayer Statues of the Ancient Near East; Art of Late Antiquity and Byzance; Beuron School
Standing as a Social Practice	Representative Standing	Standing as Role Performance (e. g. as Religious Official or Parishioner); or as visualization of an aristocratic ideal or a hero	Role Model of Priest or Pope	Memorials and Monuments of Christian Functionaries and Saints
Standing as a Body Habit	Ascetic Standing	Standing as a Religious Virtuoso or as a 'sportive' ritual practice; e. g. owing to a vow	Pillar Saints of Late Antique Syria Indian Sadhus: Vows to stand motionless	Body as Statue
Standing as Symbol and Symbolic Action	Emblematic Standing	Standing as a Message: a) Symbol for the Membership of a Religious Community b) Symbol for Personal Faith c) Standing as a Pathos Formula (Expression of an Emotion) d) Focalizing Standing	a) Standing by a Saint's Tomb b) "Here I stand. I can do no other" (Luther) c) Fidus, *Lichtgebet* (Prayer to Light) d) Position and Stance of Preachers	a) Prayer Statues b) Luther Memorials c) Baroque Sculpture; Calvary Scenes d) Statues of Gods/ Goddesses
Standing as (abbreviated) Narrative	Mythological Standing	Tableaux vivants	a) *Presepi viventi* in Italy since Frances of Assisi (Christmas Night 1223 at Greccio;	a) Statuesque Body b) Sculptural Art: "*Misteri*" in Italy and Spain (Passion Groups carried along during pro-

Figure 14: Table Overview 2: Typology of Standing in Culture and Religion; by the author. *(Continued)*

Cultural Framing	The Religious Field			
	Typology	*Systematic Example*	*Religious-histori-cal Example*	*Visualisation*
			b) *Mythological Performances (jhanki) in Hinduism* (Ramlila)	cessions; *Laocoon-Group*

c. *Provocative Standing:* Standing as a deviant posture. This type of enhanced standing is normally used in public in order to express protest or resistance to political or social authorities (e.g., by a silent vigil, see Figure 15). A famous standing performance of this kind called *duram adam* (Standing Man) was created by the Turkish artist Erdem Gündüz during the civil protests at the Taksim square on 17th June 2013.

5. *"Pillarization" (Versäulung):* The most extreme grade of standing is finally reached when the erect body in virtue of willpower multiplies its efforts to stand straight, until, getting increasingly stiffer, it will freeze into a stone-like structure or even be transformed into a pillar. In this state, every muscular exertion, every physical micro-activity has ceased and the body has undergone its metamorphosis into a cold, awesome monument. Pillarised bodies are not only stuff of fables and myths (as the Greek Pygmalion, or the biblical account of Lot's wife); they are not only crude anthropomorphic features of archaic god statues (as the Celtic God of Holzgerlingen, Germany); rather, they are also found in radical ascetic practices as there are the Pillar Saints of Late Antiquity or the *Sadhus* of Hinduism. The former ones, for instance the Syrian ascetic Simeon Stylites, merged by the eyes of the observer with their monumental underpart and thus became a hieratic icon (see Figure 21), the latter ones pillarize their bodies themselves. There is a difference between standing angels or courtiers and a *Sadhu:* in the former case, the hieratic aesthetics overpowers the audience, in the latter one, the *Sadhu* or Christian ascetic empowers oneself.

6 Pragmatics: Rites of Hieratization

Hieratic images and attitudes don't exist *per se*, but are each displayed within a setting of interaction (rites):

Figures 15 and 16: Photography: two couples, two generations in front of their houses at Gresso (Onsernone Valley, Ticino, Switzerland). Family Fiscalini, ca. 1920/30s (left), and Denise and Aschi, ca. 1986 (right); from Heyne, Maren. 1991. *Gresso, 999 m s/m. Ein Bergdorf im Wandel.* Bern: Zytglogge, 110. © Maren Heyne. Reproduced with permission of the author.
Figure 17: Standing Ritual: First *Silent Vigil* in Germany; Protest against Nuclear Weapons (Atomrüstung) at the Rathausplatz, Hamburg, 1958. Tempel, Konrad, URL: https://commons. wikimedia.org/wiki/File:Mahnwache_1958.jpg (free of copyrights; last accessed 14 December 2015).

–   *Rites of distance:* The hieratic body evokes social frames of inaccessibility and aloofness around authorities. The hieratic gaze is not communicative; it looks either straight through the observer into infinity, focusses on an authority, or upholds a statement of presence.
–   *Dominance:* Hieratic images are in the service of political and sacral modes of overpowering aesthetics: The One (emperor, pope, Christ, God) stands or sits while the other in presence (servants, followers, faithful, saints, angels) are kneeling, genuflecting, or prostrating. Or, with another hieratic setting, the bodies of the entourage standing upright around the enthroned One, both perform authority by their disciplined erectness and empower the Master, Leader, *Führer*, Pope, God by means of their standing pose. Thus, power is a constituent of the hieratic. The body is a mirror image of that power. Generally, standing rituals offer disciplined bodies, bodies formed by self-control: upright to rigid. By means of such hieratic enhancement states, the apotheosis of authority is embodied: representations of dogmatic precepts, moral virtues, role models or theological assertions. Concerning political or religious structures, one can therefore observe a close connection between hieratic aesthetics and hierarchical organizations, as in the Catholic Church. The German theologians of the Hieratic recognized that correlation. Thus Josef Kreitmaier wrote 1923 in his eulogy on the Beuron art school: "The Benedictines [...] resemble the angels of the sanctuary: dedicated to

Figure 18: The disciplined body: *Soldiers in Historical Uniforms of the Napoleonic Era, Standing in Attention.* Playmobil figures; plastic. Collection Matthias Wiedenlübbert, Overath; Spiegel online, 27.1.2008 URL: http://www.spiegel.de/fotostrecke/spielzeug-spleen-fotostrecke-108885-2.html (last accessed 14 December 2015).
The reductive design of children's toys underlines the body gesture of emphatic standing. © by permission of Matthias Wiedenlübbert.
Figure 19: Fidus (i. e., Hugo Höppener). *Spatenwacht* (Spade Watch), 1930 (in Frecot, Geist, and Kerbs, 465: 47). In the Caption it says: "All out of the soil, for the soil, and the soil for all (sc. coming) out of the soil". The standing of the masculine bodies is extremized up to frozen stiffness. The muscular men of this *völkisch* fantasy are meant to be guardians of the *Blut und Boden*. The hieratic effect is counteracted by the exaggerated design which exposes the image as a *Männerphantasie* (Klaus Theweleit) setting a straight masculine 'firewall' against the uncanny liquid, formless feminine. Mythologically, the motif is connected with the founding myth of the Greek city of Thebes: The dragon slayer Kadmos sows the dragon's teeth whereupon warriors are growing out of the furrows of the field. © Archiv Janos Frecot / Rogner & Bernhard bei 2001.

God, they incessantly stand in front of the Lamb's throne and perform the sacred service at the Christian altars. With all their praying art and their undisturbed peaceful cloister life, they are like a vision and a foreboding of the triumphant church [...]" (Kreitmeier 1923, 24).[8]

---

8 The unabridged German text is as follows: "*Am meisten zu bewundern ist die strenge, unerbittliche Notwendigkeit, mit der diese Kunst des ruhigen Versunkenseins in Gott sich dem Ordenszweck der Benediktiner einfügt. Für sie ist ja Christus "der anbetungswürdige Gott-König, dem sie dienen mit nächtlichem Psalmengebet, mit feierlich-ernstem Choral, mit einer majestätischen Liturgie, mit einer still innigen heiligen Kunst, mit einer vergeistigten Handarbeit. Und das alles fern vom Geräusch und Kampflärm der Welt, Sie sind gleich den Engeln des Heiligtums: gottgeweiht stehen sie ohne Unterlaß vor dem Throne des Lammes und vollziehen den heiligen Dienst an den christlichen Opferstätten. Sie sind mit ihrer betenden Kunst und ihrem ungestörten Klosterfrieden wie eine Vision und eine Ahnung der triumphierenden Kirche und darum erhaben über irdischen Streit und irdisches Leid.*"

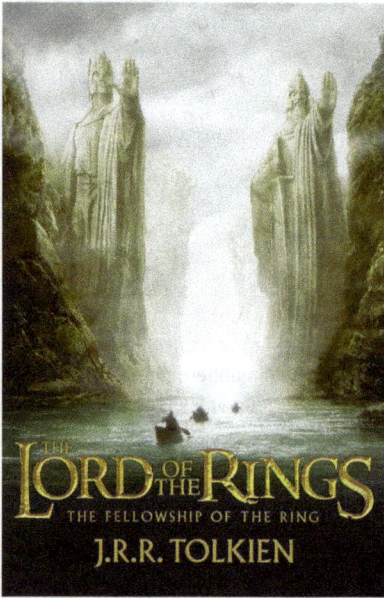

Figure 20: The Argonath. Book Cover of the film tie-in international edition of *The Lord of the Rings 1: The Fellowship of the Ring*. 2012. New York: HarperCollins (2012). The image is taken from Part I of the Film Trilogy by Peter Jackson after the novel by J.R.R. Tolkien; released 2001; URL: http://www.tolkienlibrary.com/press/images/movie-tie-in-Fellowship-of-the-Ring.jpg. © HarperCollins. Reproduced with permission of the publisher.
Figure 21: The Syrian Christian Ascetic Simeon (Stylites, 390–459). Plate, 6th century; taken from Beat Brenk. 1985. Spätantike und Frühes Christentum (= Propyläen Kunstgeschichte, Suppl.-Band), Frankfurt a.M.: Propyläen-Ullstein, Fig. 261.
Louvre, Salle de Qabr Hiram. Stohmann, André. Copyright: © Musée du Louvre. Reproduced with permission of the Musée du Louvre.

- *(A Means for) Constructing the Holy:* By the Hieratic as an aesthetic device, an aura of extraordinariness, durability, eternity and majesty is created, religious and political majesty powers get 'auratizised'; staff and scenery are put into a mode of epiphany.
- *Acclamation:* The faithful's habit is *latreutic*, fully directed to the God, "pure veneration" rather than *Erbauung*, benefits for the believer (Kreitmaier 1923, 71). The classical situation to create a hieratic impression are, therefore, the rites of *acclamatio*, of *epiclesis*, and of Triumph. Not by chance the rites originate from Greek and, especially, Roman political culture. These rites are instruments for establishing a hieratic aesthetics. In these ritual moments – and only in those moments – a dynamic element is shown. The moving fel-

lowship creates in these acts of 'hieratization' the immobility of the godly, priestly or worldly "hyper-standers".[9]
- *Overpowering:* The Hieratic is a means to create awe – and terror. Hieratic aesthetics is designed to imbue an aura of superiority by virtue and power of stylized corporeality.

7 Conclusion: Towards an Anthropologically Based Aesthetics

7.1.

The project presented here aims at developing key terms for religious aesthetic research, and moreover, for an anthropologically based aesthetics in general. It is a chance for the discipline of the Study of Religion (*Religionswissenschaft*) to develop such an approach drawing from disciplines such as cognitive science and ethology as well as from semiotics, cultural studies and the new '*Bildwissenschaft*'. A general anthropological perspective which combines physiological and culture-historical, social scientific research on the human body is proposed as the project's core.

7.2

The aesthetic design of "Hieratics", with its main features of immobility (or at least restricted mobility), frontality, axis-symmetry, verticality, was a central form of visualization of the sacred during periods of the European religious history and beyond. But is "The Hieratic" a descriptive key term of religious aesthetics as well? Yes, would be my answer, if the term can be separated from theological and romantic discourses; and, beyond it, if the hieratic design could be anthropologically understood, as an iconographic and ritual mode rooted in body habits (in both human and animal) and, even more generally, in physiological dispositions. Then we are able to describe the Hieratic as a sensory form of enhanced body postures and embodied power. It is meant to dominate and elevate the faithful visualizing overpowering structure.

---

9 On the politico-theological tradition of *acclamatio* see Agamben (2011).

7.3

However, to avoid falling back into the theological discourse as mentioned, it seems necessary to develop an aesthetic theory grounded in cultural studies and particularly in the comparative study of religion. More precisely, it seems to be necessary to build the analysis of religious phenomena as sensory phenomena on the physiological, cognitive and behavioural social practices found in the respective culture in order to understand religious arts, ritual design, or civil religious settings. Such an anthropologically based aesthetics gives us the opportunity, not only to connect different spheres of research, but to make the "breakthrough to the other side": to study religion through the human body, its interactions, its feelings and emotions, to sitting and standing.

7.4

Sto quia absurdum.

Bibliography

Agamben, Giorgio. [2007] 2011. *The Kingdom and the Glory: For a Theological Genealogy of Economy and Government*, translated by Lorenzo Chiesa and Matteo Mandarini. Stanford: Stanford University Press.

Barck, Joanna. 2008. *Hin zum Film – zurück zu den Bildern. Tableaux vivants: "Lebende Bilder" in Filmen von Antamoro, Korda, Visconti und Pasolini.* Bielefeld: transcript.

Bayertz, Kurt. 2012. *Der aufrechte Gang. Eine Geschichte des anthropologischen Denkens.* München: Beck.

Bourdieu, Pierre. [1965] 2006. *Eine illegitime Kunst. Die sozialen Gebrauchsweisen der Photographie.* Frankfurt a.M.: Europäische Verlags-Anstalt.

Carrier, David R. 2011. "The Advantage of Standing Up to Fight and the Evolution of Habitual Bipedalism in Hominins." *PLOS ONE* 6/5: e19630. (last accessed 14 December 2015)

Casel, Odo. 1922. *Die Liturgie als Mysterienfeier.* Freiburg im Breisgau: Herder.

Collins, James J., and Carlo J. De Luca. 1994. "Random Walking during Quiet Standing." *Physical Review Letters* 73: 764.

Delahunt, Michael R. 2011 (last updated). "hieratic". In *ArtLex – Art Dictionary.* URL: http://www.artlex.com/ArtLex.com (last accessed 14 December 2015)

Eggebrecht, Arne, Walter Konrad, and Edgar B. Pusch [1972] 1978. *Sumer, Assur, Babylon.* Exhibition Roemer- und Pelizaeus-Museum Hildesheim. Mainz: Zabern.

Eibl-Eibesfeldt, Irenäus. 2004. *Grundriss der vergleichenden Verhaltensforschung. Ethologie*, 8th ed. Vierkirchen-Pasenbach: Blank Media.

Frecot Janos, Johann Friedrich Geist, and Diethart Kerbs, eds. 1997. *Fidus 1868–1948. Zur ästhetischen Praxis bürgerlicher Fluchtbewegungen*. Hamburg: Rogner & Bernhard at Zweitausendeins.

Heyne, Maren. 1991. *Gresso, 999 m s/m. Ein Bergdorf im Wandel*. With texts of Giovanni Orelli und Dieter Bachmann. Bern: Zytglogge.

Kappeler, Peter M. 2012. *Verhaltensbiologie*, Berlin, Heidelberg: Springer-Verlag.

Kreitmaier, Josef, S.J. 1923. *Beuroner Kunst ; eine Ausdrucksform der christlichen Mystik*. Freiburg i. B.: Herder. Also University of Toronto, URL: http://archive.org/stream/beur onerkunstein00kreiuoft/beuronerkunstein00kreiuoft_djvu.txt (last accessed 14 December 2015)

Krins, Hubert. 1998. *Die Kunst der Beuroner Schule – "Wie ein Lichtblick vom Himmel"*. Beuron: Beuroner Kunstverlag.

Meyer, Birgit. 2009. *Aesthetic Formations: Media, Religion, and the Senses*. New York: Palgrave Macmillan.

Mohn, Jürgen. 2012. "Wahrnehmung der Religion: Aspekte der komparativen Religionswissenschaft in religionsaisthetischer Perspektive."*Erwägen – Wissen – Ethik. Forum für Erwägenskultur* 23/2: 241–254.

Mohr, Hubert. 2003. "Kultischer Reizausschluss." In *Der Kanon und die Sinne: Religionsästhetik als akademische Disziplin*, edited by Susanne Lanwerd, 47–67. Luxembourg: EurAssoc.

—— 2004. "Religion in Bewegung. Religionsästhetische Überlegungen zur Aktivierung und Nutzung menschlicher Motorik." *Münchener Theologische Zeitschrift* 55: 310–324.

—— 2006a. "Perception/Sensory System." In *The Brill Dictionary of Religion*, edited by Kocku von Stuckrad. Vol. 4, 1435–1448. Leiden: Brill.

—— 2006b. "Vision/Auditory Experience." In *The Brill Dictionary of Religion*, edited by Kocku von Stuckrad. Brill Online, URL: http://referenceworks.brillonline.com/entries/brill-dic tionary-of-religion/visionauditory-experience-COM_00476 (last accessed 28 November 2015)

—— 2006c. "Religionsästhetik." In *Wörterbuch der Religionen*, edited by Christoph Auffarth, Hans G. Kippenberg, and Axel Michaels. Stuttgart: Alfred Kröner.

Mohr, Hubert, and Hubert Cancik. 2001. "Kult." In *Handbuch ästhetischer Grundbegriffe*. Vol. 3, 489–510. Stuttgart: Metzler.

Natlacen, Christina. 2012. *Platons Ästhetik der Frontalität und der Aspekt der Maske*. URL: http://www.mediengeschichte.uni-siegen.de/files/2012/05/PDF_U%CC%88berarbeitung-1.pdf. (last accessed 14 December 2015)

Pöllmann, Ansgar. 1905. *Vom Wesen der hieratischen Kunst : ein Vorwort zur Ausstellung der Beuroner Kunstschule in der Wiener Sezession*. Beuron: Verlag der Kunstschule.

Reinle, Adolf. 1984. *Das stellvertretende Bildnis. Plastiken und Gemälde von der Antike bis ins 19. Jahrhundert*. Zürich and München: Artemis Verlag.

Schafer, R.C. 1987. *Clinical Biomechanics: Musculoskeletal Actions and Reactions*. Baltimore and London: Williams & Wilkins.

Schönhammer, Rainer. 2009. *Einführung in die Wahrnehmungspsychologie. Sinne, Körper, Bewegung, Wien*. Stuttgart: UTB.

Siebenmorgen, Harald. 1983. *Die Anfänge der "Beuroner Kunstschule". Peter Lenz und Jakob Wüger 1850–1875: ein Beitrag zur Genese der Formabstraktion in der Moderne*. Sigmaringen: J. Thorbecke.

Siebenmorgen, Harald, and Anna zu Stolberg, eds. 2008. *Ägypten, die Moderne, die "Beuroner Kunstschule": Arbeitstagung im Badischen Landesmuseum 5.–6. Oktober 2007*. Karlsruhe: G. Braun Buchverlag.

Stolberg, Anna zu. 2008. "Die Pausen des Peter Lenz." In *Ägypten, die Moderne, die "Beuroner Kunstschule": Arbeitstagung im Badischen Landesmuseum 5.–6. Oktober 2007*, edited by Harald Siebenmorgen, and Anna zu Stolberg. Karlsruhe: G. Braun Buchverlag.

Warneken, Bernd Jürgen, and Anke Blashofer-Hrusa, eds. 1990. *Der aufrechte Gang. Zur Symbolik einer Körperhaltung*. Tübingen: Tübinger Vereinigung für Volkskunde.

Warneken, Bernd-Jürgen. 1990. "'Rechtwinklig an Leib und Seele': Zur Haltungserziehung im deutschen Faschismus." In *Der aufrechte Gang. Zur Symbolik einer Körperhaltung*, edited by Bernd Juergen Warneken, 72–77. Tübingen: Tübinger Vereinigung für Volkskunde.

Wildung, Dietrich, and Günter Grimm, eds. 1978. *Götter – Pharaonen*. Mainz: Philipp von Zabern.

PART III **Comparison and Transfer**

Alexandra Grieser

Blue Brains: *Aesthetic Ideologies* and the Formation of Knowledge Between Religion and Science

1 Introduction

1.1 The Case

This chapter takes its starting point from an observation made during a long-term research project on new scientific image technologies, and how they relate to cultural ways of meaning making. Since the 1990s, it has become possible to visualise the activity of brains in living creatures. This opportunity has not only changed the methods of researching the nervous system and the brain; it has also changed the concept of what can be studied, how emotions, cognitions and thoughts of a living being can be accessed, and what can be derived from this research. Since then, arguments and practices based on neuroscientific knowledge have reached, in one way or another, all areas of life. Asking for correlations between brain activity and social behaviour has become a guiding question in the study of culture; and analysing these correlations has inspired new discussions about what constitutes a human being, how learning can be understood, whether free will is still a concept with explanatory power and how we should live our lives according to what is good for our brain, or, how it might be optimised.

This chapter aims to critically accompany the interactions between brain research and cultural imaginaries and practices. It emphasises that these interactions are not secondary aspects of recent developments, to be delegated to ethic commissions alone, but that they are determinants of how we will treat ourselves and other human and non-human creatures in the future. This chapter is not meant to devalue neuro-scientific or brain research; on the contrary, it could not have been written without the insights that force us—and allow us—to rethink our concepts of subjectivity. Science is a cultural activity, interacting with other such activities and changing not only our knowledge, but also our perception of the world. It is in this sense that neuroscientific knowledge is both a tool of research for the study of religion and culture, and a factor to be studied.

https://doi.org/10.1515/9783110461015-011

As it has been the case with the *Human Genome Project* and genetics as the leading discipline (*Leitwissenschaft*) at the end of the 20th century, researching the brain is not only a matter of scientific knowledge and of public interest, but is a major national and media issue as well. This can be seen in activities such as former U.S. president George H. W. Bush declaring a "decade of the brain" from 1990–1999; the national funding of the *BRAIN Initiative* (Brain Research through Advancing Innovative Neurotechnologies) by the Obama administration; and the launch of the European *Human Brain Project* (both 2013). These major research projects relate to national, military and academic politics, and they are embedded in structures denoted as *big science* and *Grand Challenges*, a U.S. policy term. These organisational structures of brain research responded to a joint government-industry project, that was set up initially in Japan in the 1980s (the *5th Generation*), advancing computer-scientific development of Artificial Intelligence. All of these massively funded projects grew out of an envisioned super-computer, built to understand human intelligence through the medium and possibilities of the computer. As with genetics, the links with technology, business and politics are manifold. Communication is not confined to scientific knowledge and arguments; aesthetic forms are included some of which have gained the status of icons—for example the model of the double helix—and have impacted world-wide on the social imagination of what makes a human being.

In the course of the increasing public interest in neuroscientific research, images of the brain were presented as a new form of evidence. Besides coloured versions of the computer-generated scans of the brain a vast variety of stylised transparent "human heads" emerged on the front pages of magazines, on the internet, in advertisements as well as book covers in commercial and scientific media. Diverse styles of these heads could be observed, and changing fashions as well. One of these styles has been prominent since the 1990s, and still dominates the popular aesthetics of neuroscientific knowledge. It is immediately detectable in Figure 1 below which provides a summary in images of this observation about style as presented over the last two decades. The word entered into the Avira image search was 'mind'.

The characteristic blue, with sparks and beams and glowing effects, coupled with the computer-designed head containing different versions of brains capture the basic features of this style. Such styles are mostly assessed as unimportant for the understanding of academic knowledge which is viewed as abstract and rational, produced independently from aesthetic processes and imagination. The perspective taken in this chapter claims that this style is not confined to the popularisation of science. Rather, it can be shown that any such divide between scientific and popular expressions has itself become part of the ideologies

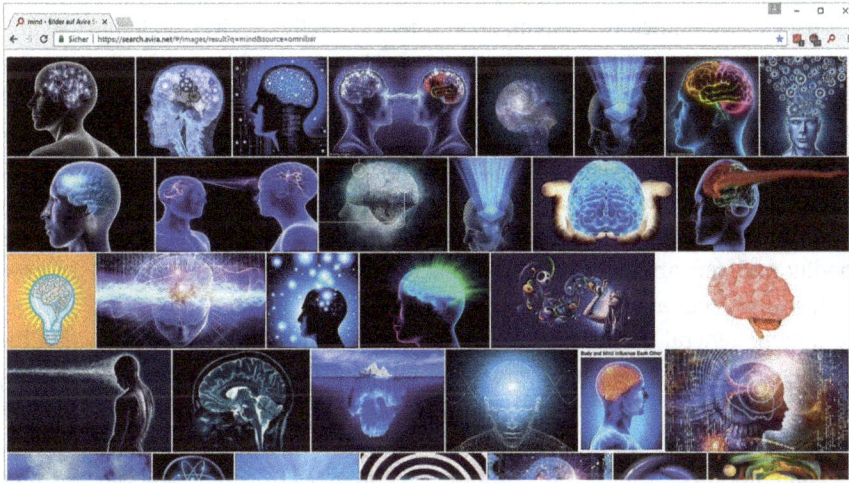

Figure 1: Result Avira Search; search word 'mind'; privatly configured computer, Ireland; 22 March 2017; reproduced with permission of Avira Operations GmbH & Co. KG.

that govern what counts as knowledge and what does not. The relationship between the two is part of science understood as a cultural practice, and the mutual influence of both needs to be considered (Kretschmann 2003; Hüppauf and Weingart 2008). In addition, in societies that define themselves as *knowledge societies* features such as the "blue brains" impact on "ways of worldmaking" (Goodman [1978] 1985) that are often not even recognised yet remain influential. Applying an aesthetics of religion view to this case shall help to unravel how religious and scientific aesthetics interact in sometimes surprising ways.

1.2 The Approach

How can we account for the sensory, bodily and affective engagement of humans in the context of religion? And how can we provide a systematic framework that coordinates and advances methods, theories and a shared debate on this challenge within the academic study of religion? These questions have fuelled the development of an *aesthetics of religion* from the early 1990s onward, and it can be seen as one of the responses to the fundamental critique of text-centrism and the predominance of belief and doctrine in conceptualising "religion" as an object of research.[1] Sharing with semiotic approaches the understanding of religion as a communicative system, an aesthetics of religion gives preference to *aisthesis*, the study of sensory perception. It is characterised by leaving behind the normative approaches to beauty and art and by providing analytical concepts for the study of culture instead. It focuses on an understanding of the interplay between intellect and sensorium, and on developing models that reach beyond such dichotomies overall.[2]

This first impulse for an aesthetics of religion resulted in a stronger focus on bodily and sensory engagement within religious contexts and opened up new fields of objects and topics for research. A second impulse, however, has led to a more general question: if we did not only study sensory practice *within* religious contexts, but rather approached religious practice *as* an aesthetic practice overall—as a specific mode of organising human perception of reality—to what extent would this give us a better position to understand the role of religion in contemporary societies?[3] In addition, this provides us with a new way to study the relations between the diverse societal sub-spheres such as religion, art and science or the sphere of healing and wellness, and how aesthetic practices and forms "migrate" between them.

Taking these preliminary questions as a framework, the goal of this chapter is threefold: first, I suggest that an *aesthetics of knowledge* can support an aesthetic approach to the Study of Religion. When investigating the interactions between religion and other societal sub-systems such as art or science it is helpful to distinguish them by different modes of how they produce and refer to knowledge. Second, the *case* I am making for an aesthetic analysis which applies the concept of knowledge to the relationship between religion and science refers to a popular aesthetic configuration observed in the context of the neurosciences, and how it reflects the cultural processing of the knowledge this academic field produces. Third, assuming that knowledge and its aesthetic forms are not confined to epistemological questions but are also involved in creating practical, political and ideological effects, the notion of an *aesthetic ideology* is discussed. Particular attention is paid to whether it allows us to complement semiotic and

---

1 It is not by accident that the programmatic outline of the aesthetic approach was published in the first ever specific handbook for key terms in the study of religion that was dedicated to integrate the discipline into a concept of culture studies (*Kulturwissenschaft*) (Cancik, and Mohr 1988).
2 For an overview of this development, see the Introduction in this volume, and Grieser (2015b).
3 These discussions were raised in different national and disciplinary contexts: Welsch (1987); Featherstone (1992); Lash (1993); Lash and Urry (1996); Rancière (2010); Reckwitz (2012).

rhetoric analyses by concentrating on the perceptual aspects of communication processes.

2 Aesthetics of Knowledge: Outline of a Comparative Concept

Recent western industrialised societies assign to themselves the label of knowledge societies as a greatly accepted self-definition.[4] This label consists of normative aspects (knowledge is a *good*; everybody *should* know), of institutions such as schools and universities and of rights and laws that regulate access to knowledge. The dominant mode of knowledge this label refers to is scientific knowledge, and with it the idea that political decision-making should be informed and directed by academic specialists. Even in those approaches that theorise the role of knowledge in public communication—for instance in the tradition of the public sphere and its structures of communication, seen in the work of Jürgen Habermas—aesthetic aspects were mostly neglected, or they were seen as mainly a matter of popular knowledge or, more recently, of the populist rejection of expert knowledge.

In contrast to these approaches, an aesthetics of knowledge starts from the assumption that the production of knowledge itself implies aesthetic forms and practices, and that *all* modes of knowledge, no matter how practical or abstract, are intrinsically related to aesthetic forms. This assumption is grounded in the view that rational thought is not seperated from, but interacts in continuity with cognition, perception, emotion and action.[5] Theories of embodiment and enactment have introduced *imagination* as a concept that links these spheres to each other. While imagination is commonly identified with fantasy and art, embodiment theories rather consider imagination a functional ability to represent sensations and perceptions independent of an actual stimulus. Fiction and fantasy, in this view, are special forms that emerged from this fundamental

---

4 This self-understanding, and the role of scientific knowledge in particular, is currently under attack through developments that have been labelled as "post-factual politics". These can be seen as the peak of the structural changes discussed in the framework of digital capitalism, networked societies and the impact of new media and the technologies of algorithms on knowledge cultures (see, for example, the analysis by Castells and Cardoso 2006). While it is still unclear how these developments will change public communication in the long term the societies in question are still largely based on their systems of education and knowledge production; it would be wrong to equal the challenge of knowledge as a value with the loss of its importance.
5 Glenberg (2015) explains the adoption of this position in the cognitive sciences in historical perspective.

capacity; memory would be another; or the ability to speak about absent persons, about past and future times, about abstract concepts or with entities such as deceased ancestors, spirits or gods.[6] It is this capacity to make present what is not present in a given moment that relates sensory and conceptual aspects to each other in any process of knowing: "Even in the absence of external stimulus, the brain can run imaginative simulations. [...] But the imaginative processes we detect in these seemingly exceptional cases are in fact always at work in even the simplest construction of meaning" (Turner and Fauconnier 2002, 6).

While embodiment theory is increasingly accepted in debates about dichotomies such as body and mind, feeling and thinking or nature and culture, and how they can be re-conceptualised or overcome, some of the positions remain astonishingly brain-centred; others seem to exclude abstract thinking from their materialist approaches entirely. Psychologist Margaret Wilson responded to these tendencies by clarifying that embodiment theory does not eliminate the differences between diverse modes of cognition and perception; rather, it makes clear that highly abstract ways of thinking and imagining are also based on bodily sensation and imagination (Wilson 2008, 375). It is this continuum, and the inseparability of bio-cultural aspects that require a *relational* approach to explain how the components work together in a specific situation, especially for phenomena that are claimed to be, or experienced as "beyond the body".[7]

For our purpose, which is to investigate interrelations between religion and science in functionally differentiated societies, these insights are important. Instead of treating both fields as ontologically separated spheres which are either essentially different, competing or in any way "reconcilable" this approach enables us to see religion and science as cultural practices that emerged from different ways of *cultivating* and *interpreting* the capacities described: perception, cognition, imagination. These forms differentiated in diverse historical processes and created different knowledge practices, institutions and claims. To a large part, but not exclusively, they developed in mutual relation to each other. Viewing imagination as being at play in both spheres provides us with a comparative concept that takes the *formation* processes of knowledge as its *tertium compara-*

---

6 For a history and application of this concept of imagination, see Grieser (2015a); see also Thomas (1999) and Kaag (2014) for explanatory models.

7 For an in-depth discussion of the role of imagination in religious practice, and how imagination can be used as an analytical concept, see the collaborative volume on "religion, imagination, aesthetics" produced by members of the German research network on Aesthetics of Religion (Traut and Wilke 2014).

tionis, and the ways of how discourses *refer* to the aesthetic forms in use. In this sense, "migrating" aesthetic forms can be observed. Only *because* religion and science separated into different discourses and practices can we now observe how the borders between them are contested and maintained, and how aesthetic forms that have emerged in one field are used in new ways in the other. For instance, when 19th century Spiritualists conducted experiments and presented photography as data *in order* to prove an afterlife, such challenges to the borders between scientific and religious practices can be observed.

Given this interest in *aesthetic knowledge practices,* however, we need a broader concept of knowledge, neither confined to scientific ways of knowing, nor conveying a normative category that ranks knowledge according to its closeness to a scientific rationality. In her pioneering work on an epistemology for somatic studies of religion, Anne Koch provides an analytical synopsis of the diverse heritage of alternative knowledge concepts, and she offers a proposal herself (Koch 2007, 2015, 2016). Koch introduces a concept of *body knowledge,* which is outlined as an interdisciplinary project in process. Distinguishing popular from academic discourse on the body, Koch does not target "knowledge *about* the body, but knowledge acquired, and practiced *through* the body (Koch 2015, 21).[8] She outlines a concept of the body as an active "organ of knowing" (*Erkenntnisorgan,* Koch 2015, 21), rather than a passively processing sensing machine lead by a steering brain.[9] The focus lies on the bodily organisation of knowledge, as all modes of knowing "are represented and repeated on the basis of receptive formation" (Koch 2015, 24). Koch uses the *ex negativo* definition of non-propositional qualities of knowledge which are, in contrast to reflexes and instincts, subject to learning processes.[10] An example would be the ability to influence the experience of pain or the heart rate through bio-feedback methods or yoga practices. With reference to the work of W. Barsalou, it is made clear that religious visions or auditions, for instance, relate to a combination of embodied knowledge from cognitive levels (convictions, texts, concepts), aesthetic

---

8 Translation of the quoted passage by Alexandra Grieser.

9 This concept is built upon reviews of embodiment philosophy, research in cognitive studies, perceptual psychology and the sociology of the body; for the use of knowledge in a broader sense than scientific knowledge, the work of Michael Polanyi ("tacit knowledge") and the re-interpretation of the sociology of knowledge by Peter Berger and Thomas Luckmann have been seminal (see Wehling 2007).

10 Arguments from the neuroscientific perspective support that somatic and somato-psychic processes are represented in older regions of the brain (e. g., amygdala) which are not monitored by the cerebrum and, thus, are not perceived consciously. They are, however, represented in the central nervous system and in this way connected to memory and to learning (Koch 2015, 30).

levels (images, haptic experiences, smells) and practices (cultivation of specific affects, movements and sensations). In order to go beyond a mere metaphorical concept of embodiment, Koch argues, we need categories and a sensibility for the "dimensions of somaticity" to describe the physical level in its importance.[11] Koch introduces three dimensions: the analysis of environmental data (a ritual setting: design of light, temperature, colours, sound); of bodily data (muscle tension, stimulation/deprivation, proprioception); and of mechanisms that regulate the interaction between the sensorium, bodily capacities and "world" (e. g., how face recognition organises emotional exchange; or how the affordance of objects regulates behaviour). Taking these dimensions—environment, body, and modes of interaction—as a model, more categories can be added in order to fine-tune observations as well as interpretations. For example, describing the qualitative interaction between humans and artefacts requires the whole range of aesthetic vocabulary such as shape, colour, contrast, composition and affectivity. In this way, the question of how to access the sensory-side of knowledge can be re-discussed and decoupled from a-historical claims about a shared experience of an assumed *sui generis* quality of religious experience in the sense of Rudolf Otto or Mircea Eliade. Rather, category building is fostered in the perspective of a developing "enactive aesthetics" (Scarinzi 2015), and the training of a specific attention needed for the analysis of aesthetic configurations. Skills, for example from the arts, can help to create an expertise in understanding the diverse religious ways of seeing or sensing, and concepts such as "detached immersion" (Johnston 2008, 187–217) enable us to reconsider the relationship between the aesthetic education of scholars and their objects of study.

An aesthetics of knowledge-perspective is further interested to integrate perception, the historicity of aesthetic forms and the social and political qualities of knowledge. This means in practice to consider the diverse aspects of knowledge formation, for example how knowing is performed in everyday life. Today, for example, in all kinds of educational situations, knowledge is transmitted by presenter slide shows. This not only impacts on perceptual habits, but also prefigures structures of knowing, for instance through the use of "smart art" which provides ready-made categories such as "list", "process" or "hierarchy". This leads to the situation that people might not first structure what they want to say, but they intuitively adapt their content to the structure the programme sug-

---

11 For healing rituals, for instance, physiological and psychological components are demonstrated in their interplay: how the change of neurotransmitters, muscular relaxation, immune markers and neuronal activity are related to expectations to be healed, processes of body learning, the direction of attention and the reduction of tension and anxieties are examples (Koch 2015, 31).

gests. A second aspect of an aesthetics of knowledge refers to creative processes, and what fosters or inhibits them. The use of mind mapping, or "sense-less" activities such as scribbling or aimlessly drawing on a piece of paper while thinking are examples of supporting intuitive synthetic processes. Thirdly, academic forms of knowing cultivate disciplined ways of perceiving. Analytical ways of looking and listening are trained, and creative interpretation is limited. Mathematic formulas are an aesthetic form, and besides their symbolic function as a tool of thinking maths they may evoke memories of school, as diverse as talent and experience.

A fourth quality is addressed when metaphors are considered that make the abstract character of knowledge concrete. Connotations of value and meaning go along with these metaphors. Knowledge is identified, for example, with *books* containing true knowledge, a concept which is fuelled by notions of sacred books. These concepts lived on in the Enlightenment ideals of the French "encyclopaedists" in the 18th century. They envisioned their project, the *Encyclopaedia, or a Systematic Dictionary of the Sciences, Arts, and Crafts*, as a *body of knowledge* that—with the progress of science—would reach comprehensiveness. This idea of a *comprehensive* knowledge, coming to an historical end, is linked to *libraries* as sites where knowledge is stored, preserved and accumulated, independent from human memory and bodies as a "carrier" of knowledge. The internet has radically changed this conceptual metaphor, not only by implementing *hypertext* and knowledge as a *network*, but also through the acceleration of changing, updating and superseding older knowledge, the logics of crowd knowledge in wiki formats and the difference between consuming and using knowledge. Evaluative notions go along with those metaphors and play a role in determining what is known in a society, and what is *not* known. Only in recent knowledge studies, attention is payed to mechanisms of forgetting, ignoring and the dynamics of non-knowledge being related to any production of new knowledge (Wehling 2007). This view challenges the predominant analogies for non-knowledge in European history, such as the narrative that scientific knowledge develops in a linear progression, minimising or wiping out non-knowledge through its growth. This notion is linked to another narrative about knowledge as an activity of exploring and conquering unknown land, bringing light to the "dark continent" and "dark periods" of non-knowledge and applying knowledge in order to tame and liberate, abolish and dry out the swamps and dangers of nature (Blackbourn 2007).

Perspectives that recognise formative processes as intrinsic to knowledge production have been deployed in science studies, and they characterise a well-researched field.[12] Yet the subject is mainly treated as a relation between science and art,[13] and it is rarely linked with religious perceptual traditions in an analytic way.[14] In the history of science, religion is often approached either in its institutional forms or as the ontological "other" of science, which includes that religions are associated with beliefs, and not with knowledge at all. In our understanding, however, the question of what can be considered *religious knowledge* does not address the classical themes of philosophy of religion: whether religious knowledge is justifiable, what knowledge we can have of god, or through god/s, or whether knowledge about an afterlife is possible. Rather, religious systems can be described with regard to the modes of knowledge they are producing or referring to. What do we need to know in order to perform a ritual correctly, for example, or what has to be done to care for the dead are typical areas of religious knowledge (we can think of the success of the *Tibetan Book of Living and Dying* in the West). Other themes include how religions regulate what is worth knowing, or how the borderline between what we can know and what we cannot know can be dealt with (Knibbe 2007). Distinguishing different forms of authorising knowledge, and how religious and scientific systems determine the scope of their knowledge are more helpful for the analysis of cultural knowledge practices than entering the debate about ontological truths. In the Weberian sense, all modes of knowledge are relevant for the understanding of culture, because they interact with and respond to each other. Even the most specific areas of religious knowledge—concerning the existence after death, eschatological and salvation knowledge (*Heilswissen*)[15]—are not confined to their relevance to believers. They are part of cultural discourse, for example, when financial ethics are re-discussed or when debates about "brain-death", or euthanasia challenge the norms of a society.

All points presented here should make clear that applying an aesthetics of knowledge approach does not necessarily corroborate the familiar borderlines between scientific and religious discourses; it might turn out that knowledge about healing overlaps with ritual and scientific approaches; that religious systems are open to argumentative critique and that scientific systems act in doctri-

---

12 See for initial concepts that have been applied and developed further by others: Rheinberger (1997, 2009); Knorr-Cetina ([1999] 2003); Krohn (2006); Bredekamp, Bruhn, and Werner (2008); Daston and Galison (2010); Epple and Zittel (2010).
13 See Jones and Galison (1998); Daston (2004); Tufte (2006).
14 See Latour and Weibel (2002); Latour and Porter (2010); Stuckrad (2010, 2014).
15 On the categories of redemption and salvation knowledge (*Erloesungswissen*, *Heilswissen*), subsumed by Kant under orientation knowledge (*Orientierungswissen*) and later theorised by Max Weber, see Meusburger (2015).

nal ways. However, this would not make religious systems scientific, or science "a" religion. The important point is that observing migrating aesthetic forms and the ends and effects of how they are deployed enables us to analyse shifts in discourse boundaries and how processes of differentiation and de-differentiation are changing.

3 Aesthetic Analysis

3.1 Brain Imagery as Cultural Practice

For cultural approaches to neuroscientific imagery, the shift in visual culture studies is seminal. Iconography—an approach that has often been confined to the study of symbolic repertoires—had been linked to the dimension of historical and cultured perceptual systems (Mitchell 1992; Meyer 2011), and to an anthropological understanding (Belting 2005) of seeing as a performative *image act* (Bredekamp 2010). Comparable with other turning points in visual history—for example, the first photograph from orbit of the earth as the 'blue planet'—the view "into the head" introduced a new imaginary repertoire. Since the 1990s, literature that investigated the changes arriving with the new scientific image technology (most significantly with functional Magnetic Resonance Imagery [fMRI]) reflected on the history of the brain as a scientific object.[16]

The first concern is to provide an understanding of the mediality of scientific images.[17] The most immediate aspects are the many steps, methods and skills that are applied to move from the generated and measured sounds[18] to storing them as digital data packages, via refined selections of what data are meaningful (among the many others recorded), to the transformation into images which translate these decisions and data into a form perceivable to the human eye. In contrast to the impression given, we are not eye witnesses[19] "watching the

---

16 This body of work provides the current development with historical and aesthetic consciousness; religion as a formative background, however, is mostly absent: Gere (2004); Borck (2005); Bredekamp, Schneider, and Duenkel (2008); Hagner (2009); Laring (2011).

17 For a technical explanation that presents images see Anonymous (1998).

18 Comparing the sensory approaches to understanding the brain, it is impressive to listen to the crackling sounds recorded, and to learn about the selection and interpolation process (and intuitive skills of "listening") at work; with gratitude to Luca Nanetti, Neuroscience Department, University of Groningen, for demonstration, explanation and patience.

19 For the epistemology of witnessing in the historical sciences, see Uehlinger (2007).

brain at work"; rather we have created a communication medium that allows us to visualise activities that we are only beginning to understand.

The second point of discussion in this literature is that the images are presented as de-coupled from the historical and cultural framework in which scientists operate. Contextualising them historically, however, it has been shown that powerful metaphors provide the imaginary tools for understanding the brain: as a machine that makes the body work; a commando bridge, resembling the military idea of central leadership; a map that can be "read" from outside in early phrenology; as a "brain in a vat", decoupled from the body; and, most influential, the brain as a computer that processes inputs into outputs, relies on bodily "hardware" and is organised by immaterial programmes. This influential metaphor—the man-made thinking machine—created an interpretive unit (see Figure 2b). Brains are understood in terms of computers, and computers are developed to imitate human thinking, to the extent that robotics, artificial intelligence and neuroscience are merged. The reconstruction of the brain in the medium of the computer turns into the construction of a computer-simulated brain.

Recent research does not share the head-centred concept of the brain as the leading body force. Rather, it focusses on a decentred understanding of the brain as interacting with the whole body's nervous system, and with other bodies in the social environment. The guiding metaphor here is the network, which allows for thinking in terms of feedback-loops and a permanent rearrangement of a complex balance between environment and all bodily functions. The insights into the plasticity of the brain are no longer compatible with the computer metaphor of the brain, and yet, the computer metaphor persists in connection with the logics, the practices and the business that developed around what has been called a "neuroculture" (Vidal and Ortega 2011). Especially in the area of neuro-enhancement (using drugs that impact on emotions, energy levels and intellectual performance for non-medical purposes), but also in everyday life situations, neuroculture is seen as the shift from the view that humans "have" brains to "the belief that human beings are essentially their brains" (Vidal and Ortega 2011, 7).

This historical and aesthetic contextualisation of scientific practice is often in turn misunderstood as dismissing scientific research, or its objectivity. Most critics, however, consider an awareness of imaginary and aesthetic forms at work not as a "contamination" of scientific work, but as a necessary support, as being part of the data. Monitoring *how* we integrate the results from the various fields of highly specialised knowledge, and with *what models* we generalise from this detailed knowledge determines how knowledge is put into practice. Critics as well as many neuroscientists agree that the interpretation of measured brain activity in relation to social behaviour is an open question (Borck 2014;

Slaby and Choudoury 2012). The "loose heads"[20] that surround us contribute to the frameworks of interpretation in diverse ways. In investigating blue brains as elements of the highly productive "neuroculture" beyond a history of ideas, three exemplary aspects will be addressed: figuration, colour and position.

3.2 Figuration: Ways of Seeing and Their Multiple Histories

In the prototypical version of the blue brains (see Figure 2a), the strong contrast between the royal blue and black, the centred position and the lack of blurring elements creates a figure-ground constellation that suggests an unambiguous recognition of "what we see": an idealised human head with a brain inside. However, we know that many preconditions are necessary to be able to decode even this seemingly simple and clear-cut pictogram.[21] This decoding is based on cultivated modes of seeing, and these modes are related to multiple "sensory histories".[22] As demonstrated in Figure 1, the variety of "loose heads" is part of a medical and scientific history and the imaginations and practices that emerged from them. Early anatomy, for example, was highly contested and went along not only with new medical techniques, but with changing ideas about the body and the soul as well (Bredekamp, Bruhn, and Werner 2008).

Comparing the image from the 14th century with the contemporary ones, the long tradition of beams and sparks linking body parts (heart, hands, head) with the divine becomes obvious. Whilst the mystic *receives* inspiration and knowledge from the heavenly *dramatis personae* (from their left hands, heart side), the modern "brain-self" provides the source of the beams itself; whilst the beams for the mystic connect the individual with the blue of the heavenly/spiritual sphere, the blue has moved *into* the neuro-heads, their corona sending out blue light into the dark space that would be enlightened by the human subject and its technologies. Examining figuration, colour and positioning in these images demonstrates a *longue durée* of a changing imaginary about the place of the subject in the world.

---

20 On the history of "disembodied heads" in the Middle Ages and early modernity, see Santing et al. (2013).
21 Research on this topic has been fuelled, for example, by the necessity to find ways of warning future generations about the dangers of nuclear waste, anticipating that over a period of 10,000 or 100,000 years media and structures of communication will change fundamentally. Since the 1980s, the field of *nuclear semiotics* brings together physicists, behavioural scientists, anthropologists and designers.
22 For a discussion of a history of the senses, and a sensory history, see Smith (2007).

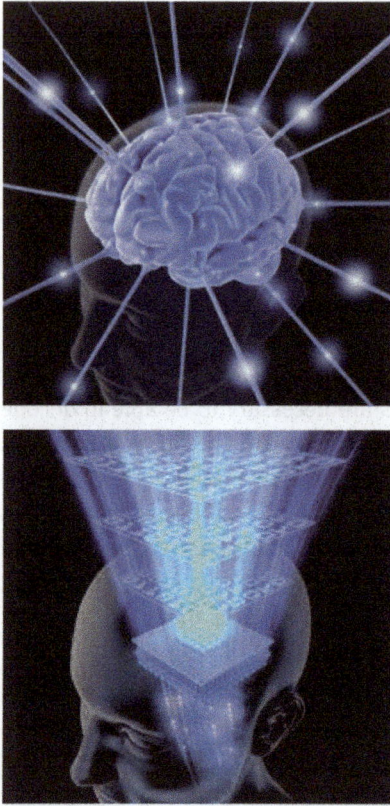

Figures 2 and 3: prototypes of the observed "blue brains" style; present since the 1990s; since then, more colourful and abstract motifs have been added. The proptotypes were produced by a graphic designer, Andrew Ostrovsky; they were traded via the agency http://de.fotolia.com, and commercial online community http://www.deviantart.com/ (a commercial online community for digital artworks; in 2010: 10 million registered users, 100 million publications; source: Wikipedia, last accessed 20 February 2016). The original is no longer traceable. Both images can be found as logos, in commercials, on book covers, power point presentation both in popular and academic media (as shown by figure 1). © Andrew Ostrovsky. Reproduced with permission of the artist.

Figure 4: Detail from St. Bridget's Eucharistic Vision, from St. Bridget of Sweden, *Revelations and Other Texts*, in Latin; Italy, Naples, late fourteenth century. Reproduced with permission of The Morgan Library & Museum, New York. MS M.498, f. 4v. Purchased by J. Pierpont Morgan (1837–1913) in 1912.

In the same way as images of the opened skull followed from anatomy, and the phrenological head followed from physiognomy, imaging the inside of the brain was linked to the new experience of X-rays and films produced in the

1980 that took the viewer on a journey through the inner body. Today, this view is extended through camera-supported minimal invasive operation methods. Conceiving of the blue brain in an unharmed transparent head moves this imagery away from the dead or injured body, and from techniques which touch and handle the brain as (dead) body tissue. As a part of media history, looking at digital scans presents a highly skilled form of analytical seeing for professionals; for an untrained viewer, however, the images do not contain specific information. They rather communicate an atmosphere and implicit assumptions that impact on unconcsious ways of how people perceive themselves—observe, for example, the gesture many people make when they talk about psychological themes or emotions, raising both hands to their head and "locating" what they are talking about in the head, rather than the heart or the chest. Such changes in the perceptual and imaginary repertoire linked to media history are a core theme of Hans Belting's work. Belting states that media technologies foster specific ways of seeing that make us see what we are led to see:

> The new technologies of vision [...] have introduced a certain abstraction in our visual experience, as we no longer are able to control the relation existing between an image and its model. We therefore entertain more confidence in usual machines than that we trust our own eyes, as a result of which their technology meets with a literal blind faith. Media appear less as a go-between than as self-referential systems, which seem to marginalise us at the receiving end (Belting 2005, 313).

Our scientific heads are a good illustration of Belting's point. While being designed for popular use by a graphic designer, Andrew Ostrovsky from Seattle, the aesthetics of the transparent heads originate in scientific computer technology. The heads serve as visual referential frameworks, for example when brain tumours need to be located and the best possibilities for operation are simulated. Individuality is not the issue in this function, and they are designed to be neutral and universal—which is precisely what they are not. Most of them carry male proportions, and if we added features of Asian or African faces we would instantly recognise how cultured, and how white, male and European these (blue) heads are. This might appear as an over-interpretation. However, the point here is neither whether these aspects lead to a correct interpretation of the meaning of the images, nor whether they were designed intentionally like this; it is rather, that these aesthetic features are effective *apart* from their intentionality, and that they are presented in other *contexts* of meaning-making. The specific features have become invisible, because they serve and corroborate the perceptual habits of the (Western) addressees. Changes in these configurations[23] reflect that more is at issue than political correctness. The functional necessity to generalise has led to a blindness towards the empirical diversity of brain features. Only in recent years it has been acknowledged that medical products are designed according to male norms, for example; it is now discussed that the neurosciences could be setting problematic universal norms around what is a healthy well-functioning, and what by implication is a "deviant" brain. Engaged scholars and self-help groups critically emphasise that it is the diverse brain that is "normal".[24]

The other prominent feature in the blue brain figuration is the beams and sparks that may denote the electro-magnetic activity of the brain (see Figure 2a). The beams visually originate in the brain, arranged as an annular rim and directed into a dark space. The sparks that would logically be located within the brain (as they are in other styles of brain depictions) transcend the human skull. For this feature, it is important to note that in sensory history as well as in the history of science, religious aesthetic traditions have been largely ignored. If we put aside whether motifs like the sparks and beams should "express" a belief or a doctrine, we can clearly see that religious modes of perception live on in different aesthetic forms and their usage. Considering religious ways of seeing does not mean that these forms, when migrating into other spheres, *create* religions elsewhere; however, ignoring religious repertoires misses an important dimension of imagining beyond the factual, especially in settings that have an interest in appearing as secular and independent from "religious heritage" entirely.

For our case, the history of locating abstract qualities in a specific part of the body is relevant, and it is well-known in all cultures and epochs. Whether it is "wisdom" situated in the liver of ancient Greeks, or "love" and "courage" being assigned to the heart, a rich iconography and metaphoric language is grounded in, and impacts on, body images and practices. Before today's dominant medicalisation of the body, these attributions to body parts were also close-

---

23 Only recently, female heads and right-directed figures appeared; features of conventionally pretty faces, comparable with styles of animated science fiction movies, change the impression of neutrality and create an aesthetic of attractive androgyny.
24 This aspect opens up a new research field, asking how natural scientific knowledge production and the practices following from them trigger social and institutional responses. As one example of many, see the lecture with the telling title "Brain Differences are not always Deficits", given by Morton Anne Gernsbacher, Professor for Psychology, University of Wisconsin-Madison, at the 25th Annual Convention of the Association for Psychological Science 2013: http://www.psychologicalscience.org/index.php/video/celebrate-brain-diversity-gernsbacher-suggests.html (last accessed 20 December 2015). Another example is provided by a field study on psychiatric patients who reject being reduced to what the scans of their brains represent and who founded self-help groups for the acceptance of brain diversity (see Cohn 2012).

ly related to comprehensive interpretive systems such as astrology or to religious hierarchies of the senses. In addition, religious communication with divine entities and spheres is related to body images and how they are linked to religious theories of the human faculties (such as the soul, reason or *imaginatio*). The eyes and the heart are body parts that often serve as the sensory interface between god/s and humans. Particularly in mysticism, the upper head and the sparks and beams as means of communication are well known (see Figure 2c).[25] The evidence of sparks as the medium for non-human, disembodied communication can be traced back to the aesthetic potential of fire. Late medieval mystic Eckhart of Hochheim ("Meister Eckhart"), for example, writes about the "little spark" (*funkelin*) as a medium between reason (*Vernunft*) and God. A new plausibility for beams and sparks as convincing perceptual and interpretive patterns later emerged from the discovery of electricity and the study of "human magnetism", including esoteric notions of an all-connecting life-force and romantic vitalism. Against this backdrop, the beams and sparks sent out by the blue brains keep open a repertoire that exceeds the notion of brains being communicative organs. They can be seen as perpetuating a "religious history of electricity" and its aesthetic forms.

Returning to Hans Belting's statement that we see what we ought to see rather than what we could see when looking a bit closer, the blue brains provide a double figuration, one that functions as an icon for scientific knowledge *about* the brain, and one that supports a universalising and de-historicising depiction *of* the brain. It is clear that these figurations are initially attributable to the practical and representational. For example, the "loose heads" are shown as separated from the body, because this is what an anatomic atlas does: showing different body parts in detail. In contrast to didactic media, however, these figures do not explain anything and they are not surrounded by other images which provide different perspectives. Through an aesthetic lens the isolation of this universal brain from other brains and from the body is amplified beyond these practical considerations, especially through the inclusion of colour and light.

3.3 Colour: The Aesthetics of Screens and the Theologies of Light

Studying the effects of colour provides a good example of the dilemma mentioned above: colour psychology often oscillates between modes of traditional popular knowledge and natural scientific research on questions so specific

---

25 See Santing et al. (2013).

that they are difficult to apply to an understanding of behaviour.[26] The main area of recent colour research is marketing and design studies. The comparative understanding of cultural colour symbolism is directed to making transnational branding predictable and successful. The utility lies in understanding effects in terms of both the conditions of evolutionary history that sets the physiological parameter *and* a cultural, social and individual history that prefigures the preferences based on taste, symbolic systems and habits of perception.[27] However, the division is not between cultural interpretation and natural sensation: both are entangled and provide a stable yet changeable way of perception-interpretation.

As summarised by Labrecque and Milne, blue as perceived by the human being is a colour rarely present in nature; however, where it presents its dimensions belong to the formative experiences of existence: the sky and atmosphere of the earth; the ocean, deep water, thick ice and snow and distant objects (e. g., mountains) appear blue to the human eye. Blue is a cold colour, not only in a metaphorical sense, but according to the wavelength measures in optics. It is the other end of the scale compared to red. In visual effects: blue "steps back" and creates distance and depth in an image; red "moves" towards the viewer; the use of red as a warning colour, or symbolising life force and activity is not mere convention (Labrecque and Milne 2012). These effects are measurable, and they are constantly used in art and advertisement, and in scientific imagery as well. Research shows that in blue or red environments the human pulse rate differs (considerably lower with blue). People working in light blue offices experience the effect as "clarity" and turn the heating slightly higher than in warmly coloured rooms (Madden, Hewett, and Roth 2000). On this basis, it is plausible that blue is an "agreeable" colour (with no bodily excitement related to it).

In religious colour codes these effects are combined with other aspects. Hell and heaven in Christian depictions clearly divide and validate the function of blue and that of the brownish-green-red-yellow (fire; "bilious green and sulphur

---

26 For a critical review of colour psychology, see Whitfield and Wiltshire (1990).
27 Differences in symbolic usage between cultures are sometimes taken as proof that these are to be understood as arbitrary entirely; other authors aim at explaining art and colour use as fully determined by evolutionary patterns (Dutton 2009). The interesting point of combining both concepts is that it allows to investigate the specific interactive dynamics at play. The differences between white and black as colour of mourning, or for weddings, for example, show cultural differences; both choices, however, make use of the "non-colours" of the spectrum and are, in this sense, not arbitrarily chosen. In addition, the use of colours (in branding or fashion styles, for example) effects back on the perception. Pink as a colour for promoting the concerns about breast cancer has been discussed in design studies as such a case.

yellow"). After all, the heavens are bright blue and the underworld is dark. However, this perceived naturalness is already part of the politics of colour and the "polemics of light" (Grieser at al. 2011) which associate the sites where the god/s are located and which set the scene for the symbolic competition between "darkness and light", be it in the encounter between Chthonic and "heavenly" religions, or the divide between "enlightened" and "dark" continents of the world. A material history of colour comes into play too in the deployment of blue: it was an extremely expensive colour to produce and to fix (based on the materials of *lapis lazuli* or *cobalt*). The assignment of blue to the garments of Mary, Jesus's mother, is a material acknowledgement of the relevance of this figure in the Christian *dramatis personae*. At the same time, she is spiritualised by the closeness of the blue to the sky/heaven and the symbolic codes of blue as cold, transparent and "distanced" colour of the spirit or the mysterious.[28]

The material and media history of royal blue is likewise embedded in the cultural habits of using it to denote "seriousness and trustworthiness", the blue of uniforms, of authority and function (business suit) and to its use in businesses that depend on association with safety and reliability such as banks, insurance and the health service.[29] Another pragmatic field of blueness is its association with cleanness. Medical institutions use blue in their environments and corporate identities; cleanness and "purity" go together in most brands of "power cleaners" ("killing all germs") as well as disinfection fluids.

The materiality and pragmatics of our royal blue is linked to media history and the technology of colour. In its glowing quality, it occurs as coloured neon gas which was instantly used by artists, in the disco culture of the 1980s and as a way to immerse stage events in effectual light, comparable to the fog machines creating a specific atmosphere. As a colour fitting the conditions of digital media, this glowing blue has become ubiquitous in TV and on websites. Game shows dye their moments of excitement in this blue light, together with tension-raising music. At the same time, contemporary spirituality makes extensive use of this colour, and where religion adapts to event culture, blue stages provide the framework for a transcendent atmosphere. For example, public performances of the passion of Christ on Easter in Dutch cities since 2013 have been im-

---

28 Observing colour codes in relation to the dichotomies spirit/mind and maleness/femaleness would make an interesting approach to gendered processes of divinisation and the theological reasoning about colour.

29 See, for instance, the collection of websites using blue for their self-presentation, presented as teaching format for design students:

http://www.onextrapixel.com/2010/01/22/anatomy-of-colors-in-web-design-blue-and-the-cool-look/ (last accessed 20 February 2016)

mersed in blue light. What we can see in this colour practice of "dyeing" a whole scene in this special blue is an overlap between religious aesthetics and the aesthetics of event culture. While religions, in fact, do not consist of the "wow" factor only, the effect of overwhelming sensations plays a seminal role in the experiential construction of religious transcendence and its maintenance through repetition and routines.[30]

Depicting brains in the same quality of light and colour places the popularisation of neuroscientific knowledge in the range of religious as well as event aesthetics. Amplified by the contrast between the royal blue and the black, the impression of an empty space is created, and the heads dwell in it. The light comes from below (an effect known from horror films), and this evokes a specific atmosphere. Based on the conditions of computer screens and digital imagery the brain is turned from a medical object—grey-fleshy coloured on white paper—into a clean and cool object that is even further detached from its mucous character than the anatomic brain. The impression of a plastic surface and the brilliance of the computer screen reinforcing the shiny hardness of the "object" sets the brain apart from the rest of the body, far beyond the pragmatics required for an anatomy atlas.

The act of seeing, as outlined above, involves and engages all senses in an "offline modus" (linking smells and sounds, emotions and memories to each other).[31] The sensory experience created, or triggered, by the blue brains viewed on the computer screen is one of a disembodied object with no sensory features such as smell or texture. In the framework of computer design, even the "hand" of the artist is missing as an individuated feature—the personal streak of an artist, or the surface of an oil painting. The skills of the designer lie in the handling of the programme which provides ready-made atmospheres such as "romantic" or "business". In a short interview about one of his images, the designer of blue brain images notes: "Additional compositional integrity was achieved with central light and a 'mystical' colour scheme."[32]

---

30 For theorising "how to capture the Wow", see Meyer (2016).

31 As Margaret Wilson puts it, an embodiment theory of imagination needs to be able to explain how—in contrast to the environment-dependent situated cognition—an "embodied cognition can go off-line" – decouple from situation-bound reactivity and use body-based resources for other purposes" (Wilson 2008, 380). For integrative theories of imagination applied to scientific imagery see also Grieser et al. (2011).

32 Andrew Ostrovsky. 5 May 2015. "Story behind the Image: Light of Ideas", fotolia image agency, https://blog.fotolia.com/us/2015/05/05/story-behind-the-image/ (last accessed 20 December 2015).

Identifying the human being with a brain that appears cool, blue and disembodied and dyed in a transcending light organises imagination and corresponds with specific practices and attitudes. David Morgan has drawn consequences from embodiment and actor-network-theory and states that certain objects are not only icons or symbols, but function as "focal objects" (Morgan 2014), binding together practices, agents, debates and discourses. The brain can well be investigated as such a focal object, and the blue brain-design is an important element of *how* this object becomes dominant and exerts its binding force.

3.4 Position: Seeing and the Placement of the Self

As pointed out for the perception of colour and surface, vision functions as an entry to a *synesthetic* experience "offline", interrelating sensations with emotions, thoughts and memory. In the same way, the act of seeing places the viewer in a position—a perspective. This interaction of seeing and being affected by the object has been examined extensively by David Morgan in his work on the heart of Jesus (Morgan 2012). With the brain as body part, we encounter an "object" that bears a more reflective potential, not externalised as the heart of the religious figure opposite the viewer, but as a mirror of "our universal self". By understanding the brain as the instance that defines who we are, when we look at the brain, it is suggested, we are looking at the brain understanding itself.

Historian of science Lorraine Daston reminds us that the investigation of the senses, and of the relationship between the knower and the knowable, took place in response to the "epistemological shock" of the Copernican turn—the insight that, for centuries, the senses had delivered the false view of reality and can, thus, not be trusted (Daston 2005). Daston explains that modern subjectivity is linked to the necessity to "re-locate" humanity, after having been pushed out of the centre of the universe, and to the differentiation between science and art as well. Securing "objective knowledge" as independent from the human self, and separating the natural *fact* from the human *imagination* "running wild", Daston states, takes place as "the polarization of the personae of artist and scientist, and the migration of imagination to the artistic pole" (Daston 2005, 17). What Daston underestimates, however, is that the differentiation between science and art is linked to religion, too.

From this viewpoint, aesthetic history and the astonishing attention paid to beauty and the sublime in 18th century philosophy can be seen in a different light. In the aesthetic discourse of romantic art, the scientific interest in the senses was reflected. It presented the shift from depicting an outward (God-made) beauty of nature to the subject that conceives of the beauty through sense perception. The scientific de-mystification *of* the senses, however, goes together with a re-mystification *through* the senses in romantic art. The famous "back figures" of romantic imagery which show the figures from the back, (see Figure 3b) invite the viewer to identify with the figure, and to see and experience what he sees. In contrast to the emergence of a scientific gaze, however, seeing and sensing is re-enchanted in romantic aesthetics. Friedrich Schleiermacher, the theologian of German romanticism, re-defined religion as "sensing and feeling" and an "intuition of the universe".[33] However, the relevance of Schleiermacher's theology for the renewal of Protestantism is not what interests us here in the first instance.[34] Rather it is that, what romanticism, in its many national and later variations, succeeds in: to provide a modern aesthetic religion that draws on feelings and individual experience rather than a personal God or doctrines. Setting the sensation of "the infinite" as an experiential ideal, romantic art strives to evoke precisely those affections which are envisioned. Art, nature and sensation become religious media by *designing* them as spiritual objects, and by cultivating practices of appreciation. The influence of this emotional and sensuous configuration is enormous. The aesthetics of overwhelming sensations in the film industry is related to it as much as new forms of spirituality and the expectations related to them.

Coming back to the "re-location" of the subject, we can see that blue brains are linked with the question of self-reflection and the position of the individual in the cosmos. This "self-placement" can be understood as an aesthetic aspect of epistemology. Literally the positioning of the body plays a role in these images of the brain and the subject-object relation in its research. Figure 3a exemplifies another recurring variant of the blue brains:[35] how the subject can gain knowledge

---

33 In the famous second of Friedrich Schleiermacher's Speeches ([1799] 1996), the central argument is based on an analysis of sensations and how they are related to perceptions and feelings; an aesthetic-argumentative reading can demonstrate how the knowledge about the senses is turned into a figure of evidence that religion is a specific form of sensation, culminating in the momentary "holy embrace" of intuitive knowledge (Schleiermacher [1799] 1996, 22–31). For the specific interest in the brain and the senses in romantic art and philosophy see Richardson (2005, 2010) and Jackson (2008).

34 The relationship between aesthetics, art and the Protestant ideal of the self-investigating subject, however, belong to the religious history of the differentiation process, as mentioned. The "invention of the inner human being" can hardly be understood without the impact of secularised religious concepts (see *Die Erfindung des inneren Menschen*, Assman and Sundermeier 1993).

35 For example, neuroscientist Andrew Newberg made use of this image as a cover for a CD he published, containing explanations and advice about religious practices which are healthy for the brain, and which ones should be avoided (Newberg 2012).

about reality without an Archimedian point outside of the world. Scientific knowledge is visualised as a given rather than as a process—represented in iconic aesthetic forms such as the double helix, computer matrices, a model of atoms, the waves of oscillography and the blue brain! The relation between brain and knowledge is depicted as identical: no reflectivity, no complication. The image positions us as looking from above on the centred subject, whose brain has turned into the colourfully arranged representations of science, being both producer and the product of scientific knowledge: subject, object and knowledge are one.

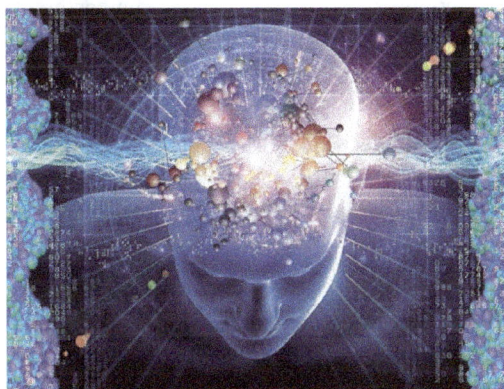

Figure 5: Andrew Ostrovsky. "Molecular Thoughts"; number 28624526 on http://de.fotolia.com/p/201652684 (last accessed 20 March 2013); re-used in many significant applications, for example, Audio CD Cover of Andrew Newberg. 2012. Spiritual Practices for a Powerful Brain. Nightingale Conant Corporation, NP. © Andrew Ostrovsky. Reproduced with permission of the artist.
Figure 6: Caspar David Friedrich. *Der Wanderer über dem Nebelmeer* (Wanderer above the Sea of Fog), around 1817/18, Hamburger Kunsthalle, Hamburg, Germany. Free of copyrights.

To conclude, we can ask what kinds of knowledge these aesthetic features transmit, and what knowledge is required to make sense of what we are seeing. These images do not impart neuroscientific knowledge; they target the level of affective attitudes rather than content and arguments. If we accept, however, that knowing includes affects, attitudes and aesthetic forms; and that engaging with images establishes multi-sensory ways of knowing through the body—body knowledge—then it is reasonable to state that the brains we are confronted with impact on how we relate to our brains, and to ourselves. The brain, we have learned, is a cool, clean, serious thing. It is detached from the rest of the body, from warmth, from flesh, blood and from the social and natural environment. Situated in an evocative dark, empty space,[36] this object covers the symbolic and perceptual configurations once occupied by notions of the spirit and the soul. At the same time, blue brain images act as a mirror, suggesting the viewer should identify with the blue brains, and sense the essence of humans in this object. Identified with scientific knowledge as well, the isolated brain is not only an *object* of investigation, but also the *target* of methods to improve and perfect it.

Ironically, the isolated, clear, clean and plastic-like brains, separated from interactions with other brains, contrast with recent findings in the neurosciences, which suggest that the brain is formed through body activities, through the way we sense, feel and act as whole bodies and with other bodies. Instead of unfolding the challenges and consequences of these findings[37] the aesthetics of disembodiment—of the brains as well as the scientific knowledge (see Figure 3a)—promote an aesthetic ideology that excludes the connectedness of both the subject and the knowledge we have about it. Putting the brain-subject in the place where once the earth was imagined to be in the geo-centric worldview, gives human cognition the highest importance. If this brain-subject, for example, is diagnosed with an Attention-Deficit Hyperactivity Disorder (ADHD), this aesthetic of disembodiment does not, in the first instance, suggest a body therapy.

There is a paradox at work in this aesthetics of disembodiment. While the computerisation of the brain fosters transhumanist dreams of replacing the susceptible human "wet-ware" by technology, bodies are at the centre of optimisation strategies through fitness sports, aesthetic surgery, enhancement drugs and in 'spiritual' ways of improving one's life.[38] This tension between dislocating and simultaneously fetishizing the body invites a discussion of disembodied brains as *objects of fascination*.

Fascination can be understood as an ambivalent state between "rejection and desire" (Kohl 1987, 2003). A history of fascination refers to aesthetic forms by which humans cope with the fear of suffering and death (Grieser 2009). Look-

---

36 How this empty space is made a coloured space-scape by adding the spectacular photos produced by the Hubble Space Telescope, see Figure 1, middle right, and Grieser (2015a).

37 These challenges concern both the complexity of *understanding* the functionality of the brain functions, and the questions how to *respond* to the findings, put on the agenda, for example, by philosopher Catherine Malabou. She targets the tension between the emancipatory potential inherent to the growing knowledge, and the neo-liberal subordination of body and brain under capitalist and exclusivist norms (Malabou [2004] 2008).

38 Research shows that in surgery, for example, the majority of people do not use these technologies for individualisation, but rather to adapt to norms that promise advantages on the job and marriage market. See Wehling (2005).

ing through this lens at the blue brain formation, they appear as part of the long history of separating the mind, the spirit and the soul from the body and also conceptualise modes of existence beyond death. To think of the brain as the organ of the highest capacities and the essence of the human self, creates a rupture with the fact that this organ is not only inseparably entangled with the mortal body, but *is* itself mortal body. The psychoanalytical category of *narcistic mortification* comes into play when understanding that the physical grey, mucous mass is aesthetically unacceptable for the cultural status that the brain has achieved. The mechanism of de-mystification—the brain as object of scientific research—and re-mystification—the brain as the seat of pure and abstract knowledge—supports the distinctive status of the human being, and the distinctive status of scientific knowledge as well. This distinctiveness is evoked, not by arguments but by the atmosphere the images are creating. It can only work on the basis of the divide pointed out by Daston: a science devoid of aesthetics, and an aesthetics devoid of body, politics and thought. Calling this an aesthetic ideology shall allow us to describe how meaning is created below the level of signification, effective yet largely unnoticed.

4 Aesthetic Ideologies

What can the notion of an a*esthetic ideology* add to the study of culture, especially in relation to rhetorical and semiotic approaches? The concept of aesthetic ideology complements rather than opposes rhetorical and semiotic approaches. It starts from the premise that ideologies not only consist of the *content* of ideas or doctrines, but also of structures: *how* we make sense. Anthropologist and semiotician Webb Keane has pursued this question, and applied C.S. Peirce's distinctions to his study on *Christian Moderns* in the colonial Dutch East Indies (Keane 2007). Keane is interested in the category of "Thirdness" (Keane 2003, 414) which allows him to include the social interaction of signs, and the materiality of artefacts. In this way he extends the scope of semiotic analysis, explicitly aiming at overcoming the separation between signs and the material world. Keane—as others in recent discussion of New Materialism[39]—turns to things, objects and their agency as the counterpart of the language paradigm. While speaking about the sensuous qualities of things (Keane 2003, 414–415), however, the *sensorium* as the interface of human interaction *with* things, is not addressed. Consequently, Keane's analysis continues to concentrate on discursive practices (Keane 2003,

---

39 For an overview of positions in New Materialism, see Hazard (2013).

422). While fully acknowledging the importance of discursive practices, an aesthetic analysis emphasises that sensation and perception are not limited to providing the "raw material" for discursive modes of meaning making. Rather, embodiment theory, enactive aesthetics and theories of imagination have shown that meaning is prefigured and organised on the level of sensation and perception as well. What can be felt, imagined and thought in a society is organised in the repertoires of signs *and* in the perceptual orders and practices that cultivate ways of imagining. If we concede with Keane that *semiotic ideologies* regulate the economy of representations, then *aesthetic ideologies* can be said to regulate the "economy of affects" (Richard and Rudnyckyj 2009). Affects, however, are not limited to emotions, but they are understood as a configuration consisting of sensations (hot, cold), perceptions (pleasant, disgusting) and affective responses (stimulating, boring, exciting, hampering or fostering movement). An exhibition in a museum, for example, can be guided by an aesthetic ideology which—on the basis of affects—creates affordances to either consume the presentations or rather to reflect or interact with them.[40] The efficacy of an aesthetic ideology is always dependent on both the aesthetic arrangement (the object or material world, endowed with agency) and the recipient's skills and habits. To develop this further, it would be helpful to draw on work that investigates the qualities of affective knowledge;[41] observations about the aesthetic quality of morality (Norton 1995; Hauskeller 1996); and approaches that think of normativity as being rooted in the process of cognition rather than in ideas, beliefs or doctrines acquired (Jensen 2013). Two arguments shall be made for recognising a specific aesthetic ideology that pre-figures what is possible to feel and perceive at all.

4.1 The Political of the Aesthetic

Aesthetic ideologies are particularly prominent in the extreme case of totalitarian political systems and how they implement, maintain and immunise their self-identity and practices (Barck and Faber 1999). This is done mainly by aesthetic means, and by influencing the perceptual orders in a way that the reality constructions appear as the natural way to perceive how reality "really is". Racist societies, for example, implement their regimes not only through racist thought or theories, but foremost on the perceptual level which establishes an order of

---

40 For *museality* as an aesthetic principle in itself, and the practices related to it see Kugele and Wilkens (2011).
41 For example, the Affect Control Theory formulates cross-cultural relations between perception an emotion; for the initial impulse, see Osgood, May, and Miron (1975).

stereotypes and evaluations. It is the "slaveholders nose" that is convinced that the black human smells differently from the white one (Smith 2007, 846). The bodily sensed uncomfortable feeling evoked when sharing a room with the racial other then needs to be overcome actively before a new way of mutual perception can be established.

Another example of aesthetic ideologies as an aspect of the political is the work of Leni Riefenstahl, the filmmaker and photographer who visually arranged the rise of the Nazis (1935, *Triumph des Willens*; "Triumph of the Will") and the Olympic Games in Nazi Germany (1938, *Olympia*). After the war, she produced photo books about the African Nuba peoples (*1973, Die Nuba, "The Last of the Nuba"*). This book has been understood as an attempt by Riefenstahl to atone for the heroic staging of the "blond beast" for the Nazi regime. However, the aesthetic strategies are not different from Riefenstahl's earlier work, and it could be argued that beauty is timeless and non-political. An analysis based on aesthetic ideologies would target the question of what makes the difference between celebrating the beauty of the human body in a way that includes, or excludes, its weakness, varieties and vulnerability. Moreover, the political quality of the aesthetic is not confined to what is visible: ideologies lie as well in what *cannot* be seen or felt, and what is made invisible through the sheer power of presence. As shown by the blue brains, it takes an effort to recognise alternative ways of imagining the brain—complexity often creates the weaker images.

4.2 The Semiotic and the Aesthetic: Can They Contradict Each Other?

Understanding the relationship between perceiving and signifying—as previously discussed—requires a research project rather than a neat solution.[42] A strong argument for adding aesthetic ideologies as a category for analysis could be founded upon demonstrating that aesthetic and semiotic ideologies can contradict each other. How can we, for example, describe the phenomenon that an organisation, which promotes a plurality of worldviews, uses a corporate design that emphasises hierarchies and centrality? Or can we learn more about radicalisation in the religious context by paying attention to the embodiment of norms, or that people change their interpretive frameworks because their affective knowledge perceives a "loss of dignity" (and what would this be in somatic terms)?

---

42 See for his discussion Yelle (2013), and in this volume.

As quoted earlier, Hans Belting states: "There is no automatism in *what* we perceive and *how* we perceive despite all attempts to prove the contrary" (Belting 2005, 310). The distinction he makes, between representation and perception, highlights what distinguishes an aesthetic ideology from the rules of signification. Perception can be trained and educated as much as ways of thinking can, and the neurosciences tell us that Belting is right: the plasticity of our body/minds is what makes us responsible for how we perceive. Belting concedes that in the politics of images, "representation is meant to rule over perception"— we see what we ought to see, otherwise, a shared reality would be hard to create. However, perception "may also lead us to resist the claims of representation". This means, perception has the capacity to generate a knowledge *differing* from representation, and therefore providing us with a position from which aesthetic ideologies can be critiqued.

Distinguishing aesthetic from semiotic aspects does not mean excluding language and text, as a last example shall demonstrate. The former leader of the prestigious European Human Brain Project, Henry Markram, gave a TED talk before being granted funding in 2009. He closed his talk by suggesting that "In summary, I think that the universe may have evolved the brain to see itself, which may be a first step in becoming aware of itself".[43] This utterance can be called a case, because Henry Markram was seen by many as a visionary scientist aiming for a paradigm shift in the neurosciences. In July 2014, however, colleagues from within the project issued an open letter to the European research commission, flagging problems with Markram's authoritarian leadership style, but also with the scientific purpose of the project. The significant point of contention is that the simulation of a brain in/as a supercomputer conflates the model with reality—as, for example, a map in relation 1:1 would likewise do. Meanwhile, more than 800 scientists have signed the letter and Markram had to step back from his position.

It is not our concern to decide about Markram's qualifications. Rather what is of concern is the phenomenon that scientists, in relation to their work and their reputation, make statements about the interpretive framing of scientific results that they would probably never accept within their scientific work. Let us not speculate whether there is a Hegelian concept of the *Weltgeist* (world spirit) coming to itself behind Markram's utterance, or esoteric patterns of a universe actively acting on us humans. The implications of conceiving of the history of the universe coming to consciousness of itself have to be left open, likewise

---

43 Henry Markram. 2009. "Henry Markram builds a Brain in a Supercomputer", https://archive. org/details/HenryMarkram_2009G (last accessed 20 December 2015).

whether it comes to itself only in the brains of those neuroscientists who will be able to build one, or in the ganglia of fruit flies, viruses, or in carrots too. This is meant less polemically than it may sound; rather it addresses the exclusivism which is related to the politics of identity between "a human" and "the universe".[44]

Comparable patterns of evoking a romantic identity between humans and "the universe" can be observed in several popular science media: slogans such as "We are all stardust" are taken up in discourses which refer to science as the formative principle of a worldview (Grieser 2015a). The point is that these patterns are not arguments, and they add nothing to the propositional knowledge about the brain. "The universe seeing itself" is an *aesthetic* suggestion which literally positions the universal human subject within the imaginary space created, and which endows "the universe" with agency and with senses. It is an *aesthetic* concept to perceive human beings as a universal unit; to imagine the universe as an agent of evolution; and "us" as being seen by this entity, and being part of a development with a *telos*. As an aesthetic ideology, however, it structures practices and discourses of knowledge, just as the blue brains do as "focal objects". If science was ever meant to provide a mode of knowledge production that limits its *semiosis* to the frames of reference they are produced in, this aesthetic ideology stands opposite to it. It hampers the exchange between different knowledge cultures, and it not only claims to replace theology and religion, but the social and cultural sciences too. In order to bring into conversation the really exciting news from the neurosciences, attention needs to be payed to aesthetic forms and the way imagination is used.

Bibliography

Anonymous. 1998. "Illustrations: The Brain." *Daedalus* 127/2: 1–16.
Assmann, Jan, ed. 1993. *Die Erfindung des inneren Menschen: Studien zur religiosen Anthropologie*. Gütersloh: Gütersloher Verlagshaus.
Barck, Karlheinz, and Richard Faber, eds. 1999. *Ästhetik des Politischen, Politik des Ästhetischen*. Würzburg: Königshausen und Neumann.
Belting, Hans. 2005. "Image, Medium, Body: A New Approach to Iconology." *Critical Inquiry* 31/2: 302–319.

---

44 Without suggesting that H. Markram subscribes to such positions, it is justifiable to hint at the compatibility of this aesthetics of identity with transhumanist concepts. Main theorist of transhumanism, Ray Kurzweil, promotes singularity (with a different meaning) as the core concept of the envisioned ideologies and practices of the future. See Kurzweil (2005), and related media such as websites, videos, talks.

Blackbourn, David. 2007. *The Conquest of Nature: Water, Landscape and the Making of Modern Germany*. London: Jonathan Cape Press.

Borck, Cornelius. 2012. "Toys Are Us: Models and Metaphors in the Neurosciences." In *Critical Neuroscience: A Handbook of the Social and Cultural Contexts of Neuroscience*, edited by Jan Slaby and Suparna Choudoury, 113–133. London: Blackwell.

—— 2005. *Hirnströme. Eine Kulturgeschichte der Elektroenzephalographie*. Göttingen: Wallstein Verlag.

Bredekamp, Horst. 2010. *Theorie des Bildakts*. Berlin: Suhrkamp.

Bredekamp, Horst, Birgit Schneider, and Vera Dünkel. 2008. *Das technische Bild. Kompendium für eine Stilgeschichte wissenschaftlicher Bilder*. Berlin: Akademie Verlag.

Bredekamp, Horst, Gabriele Werner, and Matthias Bruhn, eds. 2008. *Ikonographie des Gehirns*. Vol. 6.1, Bildwelten des Wissens. Kunsthistorisches Jahrbuch für Bildkritik. Berlin: Akademie Verlag.

Cancik, Hubert, and Hubert Mohr. 1988. "Religionsästhetik." In *Handbuch religionswissenschaftlicher Grundbegriffe*, Vol. 1, edited by Hubert Cancik, Burkhard Gladigow, and Matthias Laubscher, 121–156. Stuttgart: Kohlhammer.

Castells, Manuel, and Gustavo Cardoso, eds. 2006. *The Network Society: From Knowledge to Policy*. Washington, DC: Center for Transatlantic Relations.

Cohn, Simon. 2012. "Disrupting Images: Neuroscientific Representations in the Lives of Psychiatric Patients." In *Critical Neuroscience: A Handbook of the Social and Cultural Contexts of Neuroscience*, edited by Suparna Choudhury and Jan Slaby, 179–194. Chichester: Wiley-Blackwell.

Daston, Lorraine, ed. 2004. *Things That Talk: Object Lessons from Art and Science*. New York: Zone Books.

—— 2005. "Fear & Loathing of the Imagination in Science." *Daedalus* 134/4: 16–30.

Daston, Lorraine, and Peter Galison. 2010. *Objectivity*. New York: Zone Books.

Dutton, Denis 2009. *The Art Instinct. Beauty, Pleasure, & Human Evolution*. New York: Bloomsbury Press.

Eisenstadt, Shmuel N. 2000. "Multiple Modernities." *Daedalus* 129/1: 1–29.

Epple, Moritz, and Claus Zittel, eds. 2010. *Science as Cultural Practice*. Vol. 1, *Cultures and Politics of Research from the Early Modern Period to the Age of Extremes*. Berlin: Akademie Verlag.

Featherstone, Mike. 1992. "Postmodernism and the Aestheticization of Everyday Life." In *Modernity and Identity*, edited by Scott Lash and Jonathan Friedman, 265–290. Oxford: Blackwell Publishers Ltd.

Gere, Charlie. 2004. "Brains-in-Vats, Giant Brains and World Brains: The Brain as Metaphor in Digital Culture." *Studies in History Philosophy of Biological & Biomedical Sciences* 35: 351–366.

Glenberg, Arthur M. 2015. "Few Believe the World is Flat: How Embodiment is Changing the Scientific Understanding of Cognition." *Canadian Journal of Experimental Psychology* 69/2: 165–171.

Goodman, Nelson. [1978] 1985. *Ways of Worldmaking*. Indianapolis: Hackett, 1978.

Grieser, Alexandra. 2009. "Religion als fascinans? – Der Faszinationsbegriff in der Religionswissenschaft und die Interferenz von Faszinations- und Wissenschaftsgeschichte." In *Faszination. Historische Konjunkturen und heuristische*

Tragweite eines Begriffs, edited by Andy Hahnemann and Björn Weyand, 129–148. Frankfurt a.M. u.a.: Peter Lang.

⎯⎯ 2015a. "Imaginationen des Nichtwissens: Zur Hubble Space Imagery und den Figurationen des schönen Universums zwischen Wissenschaft, Kunst und Religion." In *Religion – Imagination – Ästhetik: Vorstellungs- und Sinneswelten in Religion und Kultur*, edited by Annette Wilke and Lucia Traut, 451–487. Göttingen: Vandenhoek & Ruprecht.

⎯⎯ 2015b. "Aesthetics." *Vocabulary for the Study of Religion*. Vol. 1, edited by Kocku von Stuckrad and Robert Segal, 14–23. Brill: Leiden.

Grieser, Alexandra, Adrian Herrmann, and Katja Triplett. 2011. "Museality as a Matrix of the Production, Reception, and Circulation of Knowledge Concerning Religion." *Journal for Religion in Europe – Special Issue Relocating Religion(s) Museality as a Critical Term for the Aesthetics of Religion* 4/1: 40–70.

Hagner, Michael. 1999. *Ecce cortex. Beiträge zur Geschichte des modernen Gehirns*. Göttingen: Wallstein.

⎯⎯ 2000. *Homo cerebralis. Der Wandel vom Seelenorgan zum Gehirn*. Frankfurt: Insel.

⎯⎯ 2009. "The Mind at Work. The Visual Representation of Visual Processes." In *The Body Within: Art, Medicine and Visualisation*, edited by Renée van de Vall and Robert Zwijnenberg, 68–90. Leiden: Brill.

Hauskeller, Michael. 1996. "Sieh hin und du weißt. Ueber die aesthetischen Grundlagen der Moral." In *Verantwortliches Handeln. Perspektiven der Kunst, Philosophie und Naturwissenschaft*, 74–89. Holzen: Hochschule Holzen.

Hazard, Sonia. 2013. "The Material Turn in the Study of Religion." *Religion and Society: Advances in Research* 4: 58–78.

Hüppauf, Bernd, and Peter Weingart, eds. 2008. *Science Images and Popular Images of the Science*. New York: Routledge.

Jackson, Noel. 2008. *Science and Sensation in Romantic Poetry*. Cambridge Studies in Romanticism 7. Cambridge: Cambridge University Press.

Jensen, Jeppe. 2013. "Normative Cognition in Culture and Religion." *Journal for the Cognitive Science of Religion* 1/1: 47–70.

Johnston, Jay. 2008. *Angels of Desire: Esoteric Bodies, Aesthetics and Ethics*. London: Equinox Publishing.

Jones, Caroline A., and Peter Galison, ed. 1998. *Picturing Science, Producing Art*. New York and London: Routledge.

Kaag, John. 2014. *Thinking Through the Imagination: Aesthetics in Human Cognition*. New York: Fordham University Press.

Keane, Webb. 2003. "Semiotics and the Social Analysis of Material Things." *Language & Communication* 23/3–4: 409–425.

⎯⎯ 2006. *Christian Moderns: Freedom and Fetish in the Mission Encounter*. Berkeley: University of California Press.

Knibbe, Kim. 2008. "The Role of Religious Certainty and Uncertainty in Moral Orientation in a Catholic Province in the Netherlands." *Social Compass* 55/1: 20–31.

Knorr-Cetina, Karin. [1999] 2003. *Epistemic Cultures: How the Sciences Make Knowledge*. Cambridge, MA: Harvard University Press.

Koch, Anne. 2007. *Körperwissen. Grundlegung einer Religionsaisthetik*. Perspectives in the Study of Religion. Habilitation Thesis, Universität München. Open access Universität

München, urn:nbn:de:bvb:19-epub-12438-7. URL: https://epub.ub.uni-muenchen.de/view/autoren/Koch=3AAnne=3A=3A.html (last accessed 20 December 2015)

—— 2015. "'Körperwissen': Modewort oder Grundstein einer Religionssomatik und Religionsaesthetik?" In *Die Koerper der Religionen – Corps en Religions*, edited by Oliver Krueger and Nadine Weibel, 21–45. Zurich: Pano.

Kohl, Karl-Heinz. 1987. *Abwehr und Verlangen. Zur Geschichte der Ethnologie.* Frankfurt am Mainand New York: Campus Verlag and Edition Qumran.

—— 2003. *Die Macht der Dinge. Geschichte und Theorie sakraler Objekte.* München: Verlag C. H. Beck.

Kretschmann Carsten. 2003. "Wissenspopularisierung – ein altes, neues Forschungsfeld". In *Wissenspopularisierung. Konzepte der Wissensverbreitung im Wandel*, edited by Carsten Kretschmann, 7–21. Berlin: Akademie 2003.

Krohn, Wolfgang. 2006. *Ästhetik in der Wissenschaft. Interdisziplinärer Diskurs über das Gestalten und Darstellen von Wissen.* Hamburg: Meiner.

Kugele, Jens, and Katharina Wilkens, eds. 2011. "Relocating Religion(s): Museality as a Critical Term for the Aesthetics of Religion." *Journal of Religion in Europe* [Special Issue] 4/1.

Kurzweil, Ray. 2005. *The Singularity is Near.* New York: Viking Books.

Labrecque, Lauren I., and George R. Milne. 2012. "Exciting Red and Competent Blue: The Importance of Color in Marketing." *Journal of the Academy of Marketing Science* 40/5: 711–727.

Laring, Wibke. 2011. *Bilder vom Gehirn: Bildwissenschaftliche Zugänge zum Gehirn als Seelenorgan.* Berlin: Akademie Verlag.

Lash, Scott. 1993. "Reflexive Modernization: The Aesthetic Dimension." *Theory, Culture & Society* 10/1: 1–23.

Lash, Scott, and John Urry. [1994] 1996. *Economies of Signs and Space.* London: SAGE and Theory, Culture & Society.

Latour, Bruno. 1999. *Pandora's Hope: Essays on the Reality of Science Studies.* Cambridge, MA: Harvard University Press.

Latour, Bruno, and Weibel, Peter, ed. 2002. *Iconoclash. Beyond the Image War in Science, Religion, and Art.* Cambridge and London: MIT Press.

Latour, Bruno, and Catherine Porter. 2010. *On the Modern Cult of the Factish Gods.* Durham, North Carolina: Duke University Press.

Lynch, Michael, and Samuel Y. Edgerton. 1988. "Aesthetics and Digital Image Processing: Representational Craft in Contemporary Astronomy." In *Picturing Power: Visual Depiction and Social Relations*, edited by Gordon Fyfe and John Law, 184–220. London: Routledge.

Madden, Thomas J., Kelly Hewett, and Martin S. Roth. 2000. "Managing Images in Different Cultures: A Cross-National Study of Color Meanings and Preferences." *Journal of International Marketing* 8/4: 90–107.

Malabou, Catherine. [2004] 2008. *What Should We Do with Our Brain?* New York: Fordham University Press.

Meyer, Birgit. 2011. "Mediating Absence. Effecting Spiritual Presence Pictures and the Christian Imagination." *Social Research* 78/4: 1029–1056.

—— 2016. "How to Capture the 'Wow': R.R. Marett's Notion of Awe and the Study of Religion". *Journal of the Royal Anthropological Institute* 22/1: 7–26.

Mitchell, William J.T. 1992. *The Reconfigured Eye: Visual Truth in the Post Photographic Era.* Cambridge and London: MIT Press.

Mohr, Hubert. 2006. "Perception/Sensory System." In *The Brill Dictionary of Religion.* Vol. 3, edited by Kocku von Stuckrad, 1435–1448. Leiden: Brill.

Morgan, David. 2012. *The Embodied Eye. Religious Visual Culture and the Social Life of Feeling.* Berkeley: University of California Press.

—— 2014. "The Ecology of Images: Seeing and the Study of Religion." *Religion and Society: Advances in Research* 5/1: 83–105

Newberg, Andrew. 2012. *Spiritual Practices for a Powerful Brain.* Nightingale Conant Corporation, NP

Norton, Robert E. 1995. *The Beautiful Soul: Aesthetic Morality in the Eighteenth Century.* Ithaca: Cornell University Press.

Osgood, Charles, W.H. May, and M.S. Miron. 1975. *Cross-Cultural Universals of Affective Meaning.* Urbana: University of Illinois Press.

Rancière, Jacques. 2006. *The Politics of Aesthetics: The Distribution of the Sensible.* London: Continuum.

Reckwitz, Andreas. 2012. *Die Erfindung der Kreativität. Zum Prozess gesellschaftlicher Ästhetisierung.* Berlin: Suhrkamp. [Forthcoming. *The Making of Creativity. How Society Has Become Art*, translated by Steven Black. Cambridge: Polity Press.]

Rheinberger, Hans-Jörg. 1997. *Toward a History of Epistemic Things: Synthesizing Proteins in the Test Tube.* Stanford: Stanford University Press.

—— 2009. "Sichtbar machen: Visualisierungen in den Naturwissenschaften." In *Bildtheorien: anthropologische und kulturelle Grundlagen des Visualistic Turn*, edited Klaus Sachs-Hombach, 127–145. Frankfurt a. M.: Suhrkamp.

Richard, Analiese, and Daromir Rudnyckyj. 2009. "Economies of Affect." *Journal of the Royal Anthropological Institute* 15/1: 57–77.

Richardson, Alan. 2005. *British Romanticism and the Science of the Mind.* Cambridge: Cambridge University Press.

—— 2010. The Neural Sublime: Cognitive Theories and Romantic Texts. Baltimore: The Johns Hopkins University Press.

Santing, Catrien, Barbara Baert, and Anita Traninger, eds. 2013. *Disembodied Heads in Medieval and Early Modern Culture.* Leiden: Brill.

Scarinzi, Alfonsina, ed. 2015. *Aesthetics and the Embodied Mind. Beyond Art Theory and the Cartesian Mind-Body Dichotomy.* Dordrecht: Springer.

Schleiermacher, F.D.E. [1799] 1996. *On Religion: Speeches to its Cultured Despisers*, edited by Richard Crouter. Cambridge: Cambridge University Press.

Slaby, Jan, and Suparna Choudoury, eds. 2012. *Critical Neuroscience: A Handbook of the Social and Cultural Contexts of Neuroscience.* London: Blackwell Publishers Ltd.

Smith, Mark M. 2007. "Producing Sense, Consuming Sense, Making Sense: Perils and Prospects for Sensory History." *Journal of Social History* 40/4: 841–858.

Stuckrad, Kocku von. 2010. *Locations of Knowledge in Medieval and Early Modern Europe: Esoteric Discourse and Western Identities.* Leiden and Boston: Brill.

—— 2014. *The Scientification of Religion: An Historical Study of Discursive Change, 1800–2000.* Berlin: De Gruyter.

Thomas, Nigel J.T. 1999. "Are Theories of Imagery Theories of Imagination? An Active Perception Approach to Conscious Mental Content." *Cognitive Science* 23: 207–245.

Traut, Lucia, and Annette Wilke, eds. 2014. *Religion – Imagination – Ästhetik: Vorstellungs- und Sinneswelten in Religion und Kultur*. Göttingen: Vandenhoeck & Ruprecht (Reihe CSRRW).

Turner, Mark, and Gilles Fauconnier. 2002. *The Way We Think. Conceptual Blending and the Mind's Hidden Complexities*. New York: Basic Books.

Uehlinger. Christoph. 2007. "Neither Eyewitnesses, nor Windows to the Past, but Valuable Testimony in Its Own Right. Remarks on Iconography, Source Criticism, and Ancient Data Processing." In *Understanding the History of Ancient Israel*, edited by Herbert G. M. Williamson, 173–228. Oxford: Oxford University Press.

Vidal, Fernando, and Francisco Ortega. 2011. "Approaching the Neurocultural Spectrum – An Introduction." In *Neurocultures: Glimpses into an Expanding Universe*, edited by Francisco Ortega and Fernando Vidal, 7–27. New York: Peter Lang.

Wehling, Peter. 2005. "Social Inequalities beyond the Modern Nature-Society-Divide? The Cases of Cosmetic Surgery and Predictive Genetic Testing." *Science, Technology & Innovation Studies* 1/1: 3–15.

—— 2007. "Wissen und Nichtwissen." In *Handbuch Wissenssoziologie und Wissensforschung*, edited by Rainer Schützeichel, 485–494. Konstanz: UVK-Verlags-Gesellschaft.

Welsch, Wolfgang. 1987. *Aisthesis: Grundzüge und Perspektiven der Aristotelischen Sinneslehre*. Stuttgart: Klett-Cotta.

Whitfield, T. W. Allan, and John Wiltshire. 1990. "Color Psychology: A Critical Review." *Genetic, Social & General Psychology Monographs* 116/4: 387–411.

Wilson, Margaret. 2008. "How Did We Get from There to Here? An Evolutionary Perspective on Embodied Cognition." In *Directions for an Embodied Cognitive Science: Towards an Integrated Approach*, edited by Paco Calvo and Toni Gomila, 375–393. Amsterdam et al.: Elsevier.

Yelle, Robert. 2013. *Semiotics of Religion*. London: Bloomsbury.

Jens Kreinath
Aesthetic Dimensions and Transformative Dynamics of Mimetic Acts: The Veneration of Habib-i Neccar Among Muslims and Christians in Antakya, Turkey[1]

1. Introduction: Mimesis as Analytical Concept for the Study of Religion

This chapter features mimesis and its contribution to the aesthetics of religion. By focusing on the aesthetic dimensions and transformative dynamics of mimetic acts, it considers aesthetics as a field of theoretical exploration and critical inquiry that emerged in close connection with the study of artworks and other forms of human creativity. Aesthetics, nowadays conceived in holistic terms, provides a conceptual framework to analyse different forms of textual representation, bodily expression, and sensual perception across cultures and religions.[2] To exemplify the methodological and theoretical potential of aesthetics as a connective concept, mimesis is taken as a key term for analysing historical and ethnographic material collected in an empirical case study. By placing mimesis at the centre of analysis, an aesthetic approach can connect different fields of research in the study of religion, which have not yet sufficiently been studied in conjunction with one another. Exemplified by a case study on the veneration of a local saint in southernmost Turkey, Habib-i Neccar, I demonstrate that mimesis not only facilitates the comparative study of textual representations and material remains along with the study of ritual practice and interreligious dynam-

1 This article was designed for the research network in Aesthetics of Religion, but there are persons and institutions I would like to acknowledge who significantly helped to shape the initial idea and the final product. It was notably Terje Stordalen who gave me the opportunity to refine my historical approach to shared sacred sites as part of his project at the Center for Advanced Studies (CAS) in Oslo. Thanks also go to Danny Praet and Jan Dumolyn who invited me to present my findings at the Centrum voor Turkse Studies (CTS) at the University of Ghent. I am grateful for the discussion of the main arguments with my former graduate research assistant William Silcott. Finally, I am thankful to Refika Sarıönder for her feedback on various versions of this article while I remain fully responsible for residual errors and ambiguities.
2 Aesthetics of religion emerged over the last twenty to thirty years as a new approach to the study of sensual perception in religious practice (Cancik and Mohr 1988; Meyer and Verrips 2008; Grieser 2016).

https://doi.org/10.1515/9783110461015-012

ics, but also helps correlate those fields of research with the forms of human sensation and perception that are central for the aesthetic formation of religious experience and cultural memory (Assmann 2006; Meyer 2009). By integrating the historical and ethnographic dimensions of religious belief and practice into a conceptual framework of analysis, I argue that mimesis facilitates an aesthetic approach to the study of religion.

Rather than delineating a precisely defined object of study, mimesis accentuates a dynamic configuration between features in human social interaction and perception that become or are made similar. In doing so, mimesis refers to acts that repeat, reiterate, represent, or imitate as well as to those that create, model, suggest, or simulate. Conceptualised as 'mimetic acts', mimesis means for someone or something to become—or be made similar—someone or something else (Benjamin 1978). On this basis, different notions of mimesis can be distinguished in different fields of research.[3] In aesthetics and related fields of study, mimesis alludes to a wide range of notions that facilitate the study of relationships established among the artist, the artwork, and its prototype, namely what a given artwork represents, or what an artist intends to imitate or simulate through a work of art (Gell 1998). Mimesis also includes the relationships that an artist establishes between the artwork and its audience and the effect that artwork has on its audience. As a relational concept, mimesis can be extended to all forms of human social practice, in which someone or something is becoming or being made similar (Gebauer and Wulf 1995). In this regard, mimesis provides a vigorous tool for analysing various configurations that unfold through mimetic acts and for determining the dynamics that emerge within the vicinity of these acts. The aesthetic dimensions of mimesis and their transformative dynamics include any kind of social human act that produces a form of similarity and differ-

---

3 In literary theory, mimesis explicates the forms of representation established in literary works and usually characterises artistic creativity as an imitation of reality and nature, and perceives literary works as the presentation of ideal situations or possible scenarios. More specifically, mimesis is often defined primarily as the representation and interpretation of reality in literary works. In theories of performing art, mimesis refers to the similarity that is created through the repetition of bodily movements, leading to the rhythms and patterns that emerge through the reiteration of gestures and motions. In other cases, mimesis is applied to the aura created through the performing arts, and the effect the theatrical and musical performances have on their audience. The concept of mimesis is further differentiated in diverse fields of research. In philosophical and psychological theories of art, mimesis implies forms of imagination and fantasy, namely when something is seen or perceived as something else in an artistic performance or an artwork; whereas in the social sciences mimesis is applied to the study of social and cultural action and means imitating a model, following an instruction, or submitting to a command.

ence that are subsequently distinguished as: *representation, imitation,* or *simulation.*

The argument proposed here is that mimesis is a concept that is applicable to the aesthetic study of religion and can be utilised on distinct but interrelated layers of analysis. Mimesis provides a conceptual framework to analyse the various aesthetic dimensions of religious beliefs and practices as in the case of the veneration of a local saint, by studying the legends of saints and the places of their veneration *as representation,* the ritual practice of saint veneration *as imitation,* and the impact of saint veneration on the devotees' perception and experience *as simulation.* By integrating these different types of mimetic acts into the holistic framework of analysis, mimesis facilitates the aesthetic study of religious beliefs and practices in saint veneration. By distinguishing the interrelated dimensions of mimetic acts, mimesis as an analytical concept goes beyond the mere imitation by integrally relating imitation to other forms of aesthetic perception and production. This focus helps engage in studying the transformative dynamics of mimetic acts through their practice of making or becoming similar. Besides, this approach facilitates empirical research and comparative analysis in the study of religion.

This chapter starts with the question what the critical theory of the Frankfurt School and the recent anthropology of art contributed to the formation of mimesis as an analytical concept, before it engages in the analysis of historical and ethnographic data. By studying the aesthetic dimensions of rituals of saint veneration along with their transformative dynamics, the objective is to integrate the different layers of mimetic acts into a holistic framework for the aesthetic study of religion.

2 Theoretical Approaches to the Aesthetic Dimensions and Transformative Dynamics of Mimesis

The concept of mimesis has a longstanding history in the study of arts and sciences since it was first coined in the philosophical work of Plato and Aristotle (Gebauer and Wulf 1995; Halliwell 2002; Potolsky 2006). As a concept for critical analysis, it gained new prominence in the mid-twentieth century, after it was reframed as a category of human social practice in the critical theory of the Frankfurt School most notably by Walter Benjamin and Theodore W. Adorno. By addressing mimesis as a conceptual lens to focus on the social dynamics, Benjamin and Adorno used mimesis as a key concept to call into question the autonomy of artworks. Their emphasis on the various relationships between artist, artwork, and its audience, as established through forms of human social intervention, stressed the efficacy of artworks within the social milieu and their role in transforming social relationships.

In his account of the mimetic faculty, Benjamin focused on reconstructing the processes by which humans discover and generate similarities between objects, persons, and events. He noticed that similarities can be found everywhere in nature, but conceived particularly the human faculty to create non-sensual similarities as uniquely human. Furthermore, he proposed a general theory of mimesis, in which he moved beyond the mere sensation of similarities. This allowed him to identify the mimetic faculty in all kinds of human social practice, stretching from profane activities, to religious practices, and magical uses, for creating similarities in occult or esoteric traditions. Benjamin defined mimesis as simulation, namely as the ability "to become and behave like something else" (Benjamin 1978, 333).

In *Aesthetic Theory*, Adorno explored mimesis as being integral to the study of art and artworks, introducing mimesis as a relational concept that ties together various types of social relationships as mediated through artworks, artists, audiences, and theorists. He accounted for the multiple relationships artworks can establish within themselves and within networks of social relationships, relating mimesis to social processes of becoming or being made similar. Mimetic processes in these terms have not only in some ways been made similar, but they also become self-similar in how they refer to themselves. Emphasising the impact artworks have on the aesthetic experience through their self-similarity, Adorno defined mimesis as being an inherently reflexive relationship, meaning that the mimetic act "does not imitate something but rather makes itself like itself" (Adorno 1997, 111). In doing so, he explicated the transformational dynamics of mimesis that becomes reflexive by way of becoming self-similar. Alongside with Benjamin, Adorno suggested that mimesis is based on the recognition of similarity and difference and refers to processes of signification and forms of representation in which the signs become similar. Both scholars theorised mimesis as a process of becoming or being made similar that relates to artworks and their surrounding social relationships. This approach insinuates that mimesis emerges in different forms of representation, imitation, and simulation.

To enhance the analytical concept of mimesis for the aesthetics of religion, it is imperative to identify the transformative dynamics of mimetic acts. The study of transformative dynamics of mimetic acts was addressed by Michael Taussig and Alfred Gell. Following the pristine insights of the Frankfurt School, both utilised mimesis as a concept to study the dynamic relationships between human social practice and aesthetic perception. Exploring the transformational dynamics of mimetic acts, both related mimesis to the organisation of social relationships in artistic production and aesthetic perception, and used mimesis to analyse the efficacy of artworks in their immediate social milieu. Developing mimesis as a concept to study the role of the senses in aesthetic perception and religious experience, Taussig combined notions of similarity and difference. In doing so, he added nuance to the notion of mimetic faculty by defining it as "the faculty to copy, imitate, make models, explore difference, yield into and become other" (Taussig 1993, xiii). Mimesis, according to him, indicates similarity on multiple levels of representation and imitation. He conceived of mimesis as initiating the process of becoming similar, as a transformative dynamic meaning that the act of imitation leads to the empowerment of the one who imitates, possibly making the image and its evocation more powerful than what it represents. The transformative dynamics of mimesis therefore consist in the type of agency attributed to the artwork as "the copy takes power from the original" (Taussig 1993, 59). Here, mimesis alludes to the form of simulation, and results in the transformation of social relations through the agency ascribed to the copy.

In *Art and Agency*, Gell (1998) refined the notion of the transformational dynamics of mimetic acts by insinuating the role of mimesis in artworks as an index that organises social relationships. He suggested that images or icons have agency and act like human agents arguing that the agency of artworks is based upon their self-similarity and complexity as created through the reiteration and repetition of formal patterns. His concept of artworks asserts that mimetic acts materialise in artworks, which become indexes of agency. They work by producing social relationships and alienating identity, in that "the primary means through which the index affects the recipient is by subverting the recipient's sense of self-possession in some way" (Gell 1998, 31). He conceptualised the transformative dynamics of artworks as indexes in terms of mimesis. Gell included the study of religious objects and interpreted them as indexes that become efficacious by transforming social relationships between the devotees, the objects, or their veneration, and prototypes these objects embody or reference. As a relational concept that accounts for the social configurations emerging through the dynamic interplay between similarity and difference, mimesis becomes a vigorous tool for identifying and analysing the different aesthetic dimensions and transformative dynamics of mimetic acts.

3 Transformational Dynamics and Aesthetic Dimensions in the Veneration of Saints

Within the parameters outlined above, mimesis can be operationalised as a key concept in the aesthetics of religion. It facilitates the study of emerging patterns of similarity and difference that occur on different scales in rituals of saint veneration. To conceptualise rituals as mimetic acts helps explicate their aesthetic qualities while emphasising their transformational dynamics. To specify the aesthetic dimensions and transformative dynamics of mimetic acts in saint veneration it is vital to analyse related rituals in terms of representation, imitation, and simulation. Studying the transformative dynamics of mimetic acts requires for each of the aesthetic dimensions a specific method of analysis as these dynamics are identified through different types of historical and ethnographic data. The objective here is to demonstrate how these data can be integrated into a holistic framework which calls for a data-driven study of the aesthetic dimensions and transformative dynamics of mimetic acts through appropriate methods of analysis.

To study acts of saint veneration in aesthetic terms places attention on the relational configurations between the visitor, the place of veneration, and the respective tradition of saint veneration. This includes exploring the dynamics of one or more of the components becoming or being made similar.[4] The ways in which the relational configuration among the saint, the site, and the devotee unfold through mimetic acts in form of oral or written traditions, ritual practices, or religious experiences and dispositions are differentiated in terms of representation, imitation, and simulation (Kreinath 2016, 160–162). The exemplary study of one case, namely the veneration of Habib-i Neccar, helps demonstrate how the analytical concept of mimesis enhances the aesthetic approach to the study of religion:

1. By *representation*, I refer to all acts of becoming or being made similar by means of different media that make past events present. These can be any kind of signs, symbols or emblems that are used to reference within a given tradition or context of interpretation. In these terms, representation refers to all kinds of oral or written accounts comprising foundational stories

---

4 Rituals are mimetic acts that have indexical and deictic features. The dynamics of similarity and difference established through rituals can be traced back to their use of repetition and reiteration. Rituals cannot exactly repeat or reproduce the same acts and thus lead to variation and change (Kreinath 2004). Mimetic acts therefore imply similarity *and* difference. Operating as mimetic acts, rituals not only refer to other actions, but also become self-referential and efficacious, resulting in transformational dynamics. Every mimetic act is similar to and different from the act that is imitated, exemplifying the indexical and deictic features through movement, gesture, or posture (Kreinath 2009). Ritual postures, gestures, and movements become indexes of agency through their repetition and reiteration and, in so doing, they create asymmetrical social relationships among the participants, even though each movement, gesture, and posture is self-referential through its indexical character. Mimesis thus has, because of its indexical and deictic character, the capacity to establish social relationships by referring to other persons' postures, gestures, and movements.

that relate to a given saint or indicate the geographic location and feature of a given pilgrimage site. The data for analysis account for oral and textual sources as well as material remains of a given site. To study the traditions and legends ascribed to a saint and the respective pilgrimage site requires methods for analysing textual accounts embracing the study of architectural records and historical remains as well.

2. By *imitation*, I refer to all observable processes of becoming or being made similar that are based on the repetition or reiteration of relevant features by following a given model or prototype. These processes consist of any kind of movement, embodiment, or rhythm performed through bodily acts. Applied to the study of saint veneration, imitation refers to ways in which a devotee follows and conforms to a given tradition by performing a prayer or ritual gestures as rituals of saint veneration that devotees perform at a given pilgrimage site. The data for analysis include acts of visiting a site or vowing at the tomb of a saint as well as those rituals that devotees perform together at a site and through which their postures, gestures, and movements become similar. To study mimetic acts through rituals of saint veneration, requires methods for analysing ethnographic data collected based on participant observation and visual documentation.

3. By *simulation*, I refer to all transformations that are achieved through mimetic acts by which something or someone is made to feel, look, act, or in any other way be or become like something or someone else. Although based on bodily acts and human social interaction, simulation unfolds in human imagination. As related to rituals of saint veneration, simulation refers to processes, in which a devotee encounters or imagines the presence of the saint at the site. This simulation can be achieved, for example, through the remembrance of the life of the saint, or through dreams or visions in which the saint is experienced as acting upon a devotee. The data for analysing simulation are based on the devotees' perception and sensation of the saint. To study the identification of the saint with the respective legends and locations, as well as the devotees' imagination of the saint, therefore requires methods for analysing personal accounts usually given in extended conversations and interviews.

Although the mimetic acts and their transformative dynamics are distinguished analytically, it should be noted that all aesthetic dimensions are, in practice, interrelated to one another. This means that each of these different mimetic acts implicates aspects of the other mimetic acts. In other words, there is no representation without imitation and simulation, just as there is no imitation and simulation without representation, or simulation without representation and imitation. Considering mimesis as a relational concept helps identify and unfold the dynamic configurations among the saint, the devotee, and the pilgrimage site through the different mimetic acts. Thus, none of the aesthetic dimensions can be sufficiently studied in isolation.

4 Mimetic Acts and the Veneration of Habib-i Neccar in Antakya

The veneration of saints is a considerably widespread phenomenon in Antakya, and in Hatay as its province. It is a tradition practiced for centuries among the different religious communities, including Muslims, Christians, and Jews. The similarities and differences in various stories and legends of the saints are found across the religious communities, even though the local interpretations of such stories and legends may differ considerably within the respective religious traditions. Besides, local interpretations are assimilated to the respective sites with which the saints are traditionally associated. Mimetic acts in rituals of saint veneration become most tangible during visits to local pilgrimage sites where their aesthetic dimensions and transformative dynamics can be observed first-hand. While ritual postures, gestures, and movements performed at these sites appear similar, the differences among the religious communities remain recognisable through visual emblems of identity embodied in postures, gestures, and movements.[5] The study of visits to local pilgrimage sites calls for the analysis of similarities and differences in rituals, which needs to be extended to the stories and legends about the respective saint. These include the social interactions among devotees of various religious communities as well as the different traditions of saint veneration devotees attach to the pilgrimage sites. The most intricate aspect of mimetic acts applies to experiences or memories devotees have with the saint as exemplified through dreams and visions, or during prayer and worship, when commemorating the life and death of the saint. This dimension of mimetic acts is the least tangible as it directly relates to the devotees' perception and sensation as in part mediated through oral or written accounts.

Despite common features, the veneration of saints differs from location to location and community to community each having its own traditions. Therefore, the relevance of the different methods of analysis varies accordingly. In some

---

5 Due to their aesthetic qualities, it can be argued that rituals are a major means of shaping and reshaping interreligious relationships (Kreinath 2016).

cases, the legends and stories related to a specific pilgrimage site can be properly identified in historical records, but the experiences of devotees become less relevant for the veneration of the saint, while in other cases the rituals of veneration and the devotees' experiences of healing are widely known and recognised, but the story of the saint and the respective site often remain unknown (Kreinath 2014, 2015). Since historical and ethnographic data available for analysis of each case differs significantly, the study of mimetic acts in the veneration of saints needs to be done on a comparative and case-by-case basis.

The saint under consideration is Habib-i Neccar, who is commonly identified with the capital city of the southernmost province of modern-day Turkey, Antakya (Gr.: Antiocheia; Lat.: Antiochia; Arab.: Antakiyyah; Turk.: Antakya). One of the mosques in the city is named after this saint and is considered a major attraction for tourists (Tekin 1998, 63–75; Türk 2012, 87–99). While the traditions attributed to Habib-i Neccar cannot be fully reconstructed, it can be stated that the veneration of this saint and the sites attributed to him played a significant role in the history of the city. Among Muslims and Christians living in Antakya, Habib-i Neccar is the most significant saint of the city and the mosque dedicated to him as the oldest and most powerful symbol for the religious coexistence in town. Among local Muslims he is believed to be the first convert, with his martyrdom giving witness for his faith in the one and only God, while among some local Christians his identity is believed to be that of John the Baptist who was beheaded due to his testimony of faith (Jacquot 1931, Vol. 2, 396; Christensen-Ernst 2013, 139). These accounts of Habib-i Neccar are based on the amalgamation of local legends originating in early Christianity, and later merged with the Qur'anic account of the Yasin Surah known as "The Companions of the City". The legendary account of the first mission of Peter and Paul in Antioch, resulting in the first conversions to Christianity was covered in the Book of Acts, reflected in early apocryphal traditions, and further developed in subsequent interpretations of the Qur'anic account. The saint also appears in different versions of this legend transmitted among Orthodox Christians in the Middle East, some of which were integrated into the corpus of Catholic legends about Christian saints.

Given that different versions of the legend about the introduction of Christianity to Antakya continue to be circulated in the Muslim and Christian community, the veneration of Habib-i Neccar not only provides a kaleidoscope for the history of interreligious relations in Antakya, but also exemplifies the aesthetic dimensions and dynamics of mimetic acts as practiced today. The aesthetic framework for this case study helps exemplify how the various legends of the saint, the sites, and rituals of veneration as well as the devotees' perceptions and experiences become or are made similar with one another. By combining and cross-referencing historical and ethnographic data, the veneration of Habib-i Neccar provides empirical evidence that devotees of different religious communities represent, imitate, and simulate each other's accounts of the saint and, in doing so, interact with one another on multiple levels. The objective is to provide evidence that each of the aesthetic dimensions of mimetic acts are related to one another and transform each other through their inherent transformative dynamics.

5 Identification of Habib-i Neccar in the Accounts of the Qur'an as Textual Representation

Although Habib-i Neccar is not mentioned in the Qur'an by name, he is associated with the protagonist of the second section of the Yasin Surah entitled "The Story of the Companions of the City" (Q.: 36:13–29 in Ali 1983, 1172–1177). The parable, or similitude, as it is called in the Qur'an, can be summarised as follows: Two messengers of God were sent, but were rejected by the people. After they were strengthened by a third, the people said that God does not send any sort of revelations and they were accused of being liars. The messengers responded that their only duty was to proclaim a clear message, but were threatened to be stoned as the people augured that an evil omen came with them. In that moment, as the messengers warned of evil omens should they be rejected, a man "came running, from the farthest part of the City" cautioning the people by saying: "O my people! Obey the Apostles" (Q.: 36:20). This, however, was of no help. He was killed and the city was wreaked with divine punishment by "no more than a single mighty Blast, and behold! they were (like ashes) quenched and silent" (Q.: 36:29).

Beginning with the earliest commentaries of the Qur'an, it is possible to reconstruct major shifts that took place in the interpretation of the Yasin Surah, most of them concerned the protagonist and location of the parable. The review of the commentaries on the Yasin Surah reveal how, compared to the accounts of the pilgrimage sites associated with Habib-i Neccar, local traditions amalgamated with the interpretation of the Yasin Surah. After the saint was identified as its main protagonist, the introduction of Christianity to Antakya became the focal point of interest in the commentaries of the Qur'an interpreting this Surah.[6]

---

6 Because the accounts of the first Christians in Antioch considerably differ within the Muslim and Christian traditions, the representations of this saint make it possible to retrace the Muslim and Christian traditions and to reconstruct the processes that lead to the amalgamation of these legends.

The earliest available commentaries of the Yasin Surah do not identify Habib-i Neccar as the protagonist of "The Companions of the City". Abdullah ibn Masud (ca. 594–650), a contemporary of the Prophet Muhammad, identified the protagonist of the Yasin Surah as 'the believer' without providing any name (Ibn Masud in Wheeler 2002, 320). Beginning in seventh century, Habib-i Neccar was identified with the Yasin Surah.[7] Abdullah ibn Abbas (619–687) specified his identity writing that, "Habib was a carpenter (Arab.: *najjar*) who had been taken suddenly by leprosy. He was very charitable but his people did not like him. When they killed him, God caused him to enter Paradise" (Ibn Abbas in Wheeler 2002, 320). Although Ibn Abbas' and Ibn Masud's interpretations of the Yasin Surah are quite similar, they only differ in their attempts to identify the protagonist. However, they do not identify the location of this event or refer to Antakya. Muhammad al-Tabari (838–923) was the first to mention Antakya in conjunction with the Yasin Surah writing that:

> [T]here was a man who lived in Antioch, whose name was Habib, and he was a silk merchant. He was sick and had become leprous. His house was near the farthest city gate. But he was a believer and gave alms. […] In the city of Antioch in which he lived was one of the Pharaohs who was called Antiochus b. Antiochus b. Antiochus. He used to worship idols and was a polytheist, so God sent messengers: Sadiq, Saduq, and Shallum. God first sent two of them to the people of the city but they rejected them, so then he reinforced them with a third. (al-Tabari in Wheeler 2002, 319)

The historian el-Mas'ūdī (896–956) provides further details about the three messengers mentioned in the Yasin Surah. He referred to Christian legends and identified the three apostles as Thomas, Paul, and Peter, "which is the Greek name of the apostle who is called Sim'an in Arabic, and Sham'un in Syriac" (el-Mas'ūdī in Sprenger 1841, 129–130). The most significant shift in el-Mas'ūdī's interpretation of the Yasin Surah is that he identified the Christian roots of the Yasin Surah and conjoined the legend of Habib-i Neccar with the introduction of Christianity to Antioch.[8]

---

7 Leaving aside the theological themes of the earliest commentaries—which included questions on the justification whether the three messengers were sent to Antioch on God's or Jesus' order, whether the martyr was entering Paradise alive, or whether the divine punishment of the earthquake was the consequence of disbelief—later interpretations focused on the identification of the protagonist and the city, or subsequently on the three disciples amalgamated with local traditions (Busse 2000, 162–163).

8 Ibn Kathir (1301–1373) gave a different account of the three messengers. Although he records the Islamic tradition identifying them as Sadiq, Masduq, and Shallum, he states that, "The

Considering that Antioch is the place where the followers of Jesus "were first called Christians" (Acts 11: 26), the implications of identifying the Yasin Surah with the introduction of Christianity to Antioch is far-reaching. Despite that the Yasin Surah is at the heart of the Qur'an and Habib-i Neccar as the greatest saint of Islam (Lassus 1934, 93), it can be argued that Habib-i Neccar is "a Muslim saint of Christian origin" (Jacquot 1931, Vol. 2, 395) or "a Christian saint of uncertain identity" who was islamised "at an unknown date" (Busse 2000, 156). Although Habib-i Neccar is recognised as the first convert to Christianity even in the Islamic tradition, he is also claimed to be "the first believer" of "the religion of Allah" (Tekin 1998, 6) or even the first convert to Islam (Busse 2000, 155, 161–162). The different accounts of the Yasin Surah indicate different historical contexts of interpretation, and it becomes obvious that they reveal very similar narrative features. The blending of these features indicates the transformative dynamics of representations as mimetic acts.

6 Identification of the Sites of Veneration Attributed to Habib-i Neccar as Local Representation

After Habib-i Neccar was identified through exemplary interpretations of the Yasin Surah, it is imperative to identify the sites of his veneration as they show how the identification of these sites shapes the ways, in which the Habib-i Neccar legend is interpreted within the local geography of Antakya. The similarities and differences of the legends are reflected in how administrators, pilgrims, and travelers identified the sites of veneration. Hence, the different versions of the legend serve to identify and justify the respective sites of saint veneration. This implies that not only the different versions of the legend shape the identification of the respective sites, but also the local geography shapes the interpretation of the Yasin Surah. The identification of the veneration sites and the interpretation of the Qur'anic accounts is yet another process of mimesis by becoming or being made similar through the mimetic acts of representation. To pursue this argument, this section traces how the sites of veneration were identified with Habib-i Neccar.

Following official accounts presented by the Office of Culture and Tourism of Antakya, the Habib-i Neccar mosque is the oldest mosque on Turkish soil built shortly after the city was conquered by Edu Ubeyde bin Cerrah (583–638), who

---

names of the first messengers were: Simeon and John, and the third was Paul. The city was Antioch" (Ibn Kathir in Wheeler 2002, 318).

instituted the Umayyad rule in Antioch in 638 (Tekin 1998, 63 – 64).[9] According to the most common version of the legend, the Habib-i Neccar mosque contains a tomb with the saint's head in its second basement, whereas the pilgrimage site is a cave of unknown age and believed to contain the tomb with the saint's body.[10] The descriptions of these sites of veneration transmitted by visitors are, despite minor differences, quite similar: however, none of the earlier accounts indicates that the tomb of Habib-i Neccar was located in a mosque.

The earliest description of the tomb of Habib-i Neccar was given by Mutah-har ibn Tahir al-Maqdisi or Muqaddasi (ca. 945 – 991), a Muslim historian who made his pilgrimage to Mecca and passed through Antakya. He noted that: "Those who visited this city [could] see a tomb in the middle of the market, whose direction is different from [that of] the Qibla of the Muslims. People claim that to be the tomb of Habib al-Najjar" (al-Maqdisi in: Busse 2000, 156). Aside from the name of the tomb, the reference about its orientation indicates that the site was venerated by Muslims but the description does not specify whether the tomb was part of a mosque or located in one. The same counts for the description given by Ali ibn Abu Bakr al-Harawī (died 1215), a Persian traveler and geographer of the late twelve and early thirteenth century who vis-ited Antakya in 1173 and described Antakya as the city where the tomb of Habib-i Neccar can be found, and in the mountain, there is "a place of worship that peo-ple come great distances to visit" (al-Harawī in: Meri 2004, 14 – 15). Al-Harawī was quite knowledgeable about the tomb's significance for Muslims by alluding to local traditions of interpreting the Yasin Surah.

After Antakya came under the rule of the Mamelukes in 1268, Ibn Battuta (1304 – 1377), one of the most widely traveled scholars of the Muslim world, vis-ited Antakya in 1355 and noted in his travelogue: "I then travelled to the town of Antakiya [Antioch], which is a great and eminent city. [...] Within it is the tomb of Habib the Carpenter (God be pleased with him), by which there is a religious house where food is supplied to all comers" (Ibn Battuta in: Gibb 1958, 103). Even though he refers to the tomb and a neighboring guest house, which could have been a Sufi lodge, he did not mention any mosque nearby. Besides,

---

9 The exact history of the mosque and the pilgrimage site remains unknown, although archaeo-logical findings seem to suggest that the mosque is of pre-Muslim origin (Lassus 1934).

10 Aside from these accounts, local Muslims and Christians often have their own views about the history of these sites and the legends attached to them. These legends deal with the first Christians in Antioch and it is not surprising that Muslims and Christians attribute these legends to the same location in the centre of the city and in the mountain slopes alike. These sites re-mained for centuries places of saint veneration and are visited by locals for purposes of vowing and healing.

the Habib-i Neccar tomb seems to be the main site of significance that Ibn Battuta found worth mentioning by name.

Another description of the tomb of Habib-i Neccar was given by the Ottoman traveler Evliyā Çelebi (1611–1682), who visited Antakya in 1648. In *Seyahatname*, the Book of Travels, he described the tomb as part of a Dervish lodge, which was visited by Muslims and Christians alike. He also identified the tomb in the pilgrimage site on the mountain slope:

> Then Habib-i Neccar was martyred by the denialists. His happy head rolled from high in the mountain to the city underneath and fell into a cave. It is buried in a lighted lodge where one goes down the stairs to enter it. Still today it is a pilgrimage site for Muslims and Christians. His sacred body is buried within the fortress on an escarpment with a park near to the sky [...] In the city below, the Habib-i Neccar lodge, filled with dervishes, is in a hole. There is another Habib-i Neccar lodge in the mountain. One can climb it within an hour, one can view the open sky from there. (Çelebi 1969, Vol. 4, 249; translated by the author)

This identification of the two sites associated with Habib-i Neccar comes closest as to how the locations could be described today. Here, the Habib-i Neccar legend is firmly tied to the description of the sites of saint veneration as lodges, both located within the confines of the city.

In these accounts, the Habib-i Neccar tomb was described as located in the centre of Antakya and part of a dervish lodge; no reference was made to a mosque in any of these accounts. The architecture of the mosque is in subsequent accounts described as being of a recent date and representative of the Ottoman architectural style.[11] Therefore, it is most likely that the Habib-i Neccar mosque did not exist before that time and this may explain its modern appearance (see Figure 1).

The earliest account of the Habib-i Neccar mosque given in a travel report dates back to the late nineteenth century. In April 1888, the Catholic priest Abbé Émile le Camus (1838–1906) visited Antakya, and gathered information from local craftsmen about the restauration of the mosque: "The workers who have recently

---

11 The earliest official records that refer to the Habib-i Neccar mosque were written by the Habib-i Neccar Foundation in the early eighteenth century. The first official record is from October 1721, in which the order is given to construct the Habib-i Neccar mosque; this record can be considered the first of its kind (Tekin 1998, 66). Subsequent records mention repairs that were made after Antakya being hit by earthquakes, one in 1828 and one in 1854 (Erel and Adatepe 2007, 244). Following these records, the minaret of the mosque was first rebuilt in January 1829 and the tomb was reconstructed in August of the same year; the tomb was thereafter again repaired in 1857 and the mosque reconstructed in 1858 subsequent to its destruction during the earthquake of 1854 (Tekin 1998, 67–69).

Figure 1: Habib-i Neccar Mosque in the Centre of Antakya. Photo by the author.
Figure 2: Tombs of Yuhanna and Pavlus at the Habib-i Neccar Mosque in Antakya. Photo by the author.

repaired the mosque argue that original building had all the characters of Greco-Roman buildings" (Le Camus 1890, Vol. 2, 259; translated by the author). Another account of the Habib-i Neccar mosque was given by the lieutenant colonel Paul Jacquot from the time when Antakya was still part of the French Mandate. He wrote, "The Habib-i Neccar mosque is the most important in Antioch. It is high above a deep crypt, which fills with water during the flooding of the Orontes. The older tower construction had the character of Greco-Roman edifices" (Jacquot 1931, Vol. 2, 393; translated by the author). An early description of the Habib-i Neccar pilgrimage site was given by Martin Hartmann (1852–1918), a German scholar of Arabic and Islamic studies, who visited Antakya in October 1892. Hartmann described the light burning during the night at this site that he saw at dusk and stated that there was always an attendant present at the pilgrimage site, which was held in high esteem among Muslims and Alawites and was even visited by Christians (Hartmann 1894, 29). In a similar way, Jacquot wrote about the Habib-i Neccar pilgrimage site that "there is a cave with a tomb called 'Saint John'. Alawites maintain lights there overnight; Muslims, Christians, Alawites are indifferently coming for pilgrimage in the summer, burn small candles, and take their meals next to the cave spending the most part of the day there" (Jacquot 1931, Vol. 2, 396; translated by the author). This practice of keeping a lamp lit was maintained until the end of the 1970s (Tekin 1998, 73). Neither the tradition of burning a light at night nor that of a servant staying at the site exists anymore.[12]

The sites of veneration as presented above as well as the legends associated with them were made similar as representations of the saint. These different representations are examples of mimetic acts that amalgamate the Qur'anic story with the geographic locations of the sites which themselves are interpreted through the different versions of the legend. Throughout the complex history of Antakya, the places of veneration and the legends associated with them remained the same in some respects, while considerably changed in others. Even though it is impossible to reconstruct the history of these changes in all detail, one aspect seems to reoccur in the examples given above, namely that the legends about the first Christians in Antakya are associated with the sites where Habib-i Neccar is venerated. However, these locations, and the legends attributed to them, are interpreted differently among Muslims and Christians.

7 Location and Design of Veneration Sites

In present-day Antakya, Habib-i Neccar is venerated at two sites, namely the Habib-i Neccar mosque (Turk.: *cami*) in the centre of the old city and the Habib-i Neccar pilgrimage site (Turk.: *ziyaret*), which is located at the outskirts east of the city in the mountain slope midway up to the Habib-i Neccar Dağı (Arab.: Jabal Habib al-Najjar; commonly Mount Silpius).

The Habib-i Neccar mosque is located right at the crossroad of the Kemal Paşa and Kurtuluş Caddesi, the oldest still existing streets of Antakya (Weulersse 1934, 47). The tomb of Habib-i Neccar is not accessible through the main prayer room of the mosque. To reach the tomb of Habib-i Neccar visitors entering the courtyard of the mosque from the main entrance on the east have to pass a side chamber east to the prayer-room with a room right beside the entrance containing a twin tomb. This room is located next to the minaret contains a large tomb, which is attributed to two Christian saints of John and Paul. Most interestingly, a plaque attached to the tomb read "Yahya ve Yunus Ziyaretleri [John and Jonah Visits]" with the name plates underneath reading "Yuhanna ve Pavlus [John and Paul]" (see Figure 2).

---

12 Until 1967, an unknown person owned the pilgrimage site which was subsequently taken over by the General Directorate of the Habib-i Neccar Foundation (Tekin 1998, 72).

Passing the minaret south to this prayer room, visitors need to enter through another side room, which connects the minaret with the mosque and serves as an antechamber, with hangers for coats and headscarves. From there a set of stairways descends to the entrance of the first crypt, which lies underneath the wall of the prayer room. This crypt again contains two tombs, one on the north side and another on the east side, the former having a name plate with Sham'un al-Safa and the latter a name plate with Habib-i Neccar (see Figure 3).

Figure 3: Tombs of Sham'un al-Safa and Habib-i Neccar in the First Crypt of the Habib-i Neccar Mosque in Antakya. Photo by the author.
Figure 4: Tomb of Habib-i Neccar in the Second Crypt of the Habib-i Neccar Mosque in Antakya. Photo by the author.

At the western end of this crypt, visitors go down another set of stairways to reach an even smaller and narrower crypt in the second basement of the mosque. This second crypt, with its low ceiling and old stonework, is a rather small and humid location and contains again two tombs attributed to the same saints; the tomb of Sham'un al-Safa is again located on the northern side of the crypt, the tomb of Habib-i Neccar facing east is integrated into the wall underneath a cellar arch with brickwork behind it (see Figure 4).

The veneration of Habib-i Neccar at the mosque is shaped by the size of the crypts and the direction of its tombs. Due to its location, visits to the tomb are rather infrequent and the place of veneration is seldom crowded. The relative quietness and intimacy of this place allows visitors to remain undisturbed in their veneration of the saint. After returning back to the mosque's courtyard, visitors can see the Habib-i Neccar pilgrimage located in the slope of mountains east of Antakya. Although the pilgrimage site is not part of the urban settlement, it is located within the confines of the massive city wall that was erected in late antiquity and includes all mountain ranges east of Antakya (Downey 1961, 612–621).

The pilgrimage site can be reached by about half an hour walk from the Habib-i Neccar mosque, located at the far end of a cul-de-sac in the middle of the mountains, providing a panoramic view of the city. The actual site is elevated and integrated into the mountain with two sets of walls that separates the pilgrimage site from the impasse. The outer wall, which stands on its own without a roof, consist of two levels with archways built on top of each other. To reach the cave visitors have to take two sets of stairs leading to a second floor from which they can enter the inner compound of the site, again covered with an archway, through two doors placed next to each other. The cave is enclosed by the inner wall and its two iron doors painted in green (see Figure 5).

Figure 5: Habib-i Neccar Pilgrimage Site in the Mountain Slope East of Antakya. Photo by the author.
Figure 6: Booklet of the Yasin Surah with Turkish Translation in the Second Crypt of the Habib-i Neccar Mosque in Antakya. Photo by the author.

The pilgrimage site has features common to cave churches with two archways carved into the ceiling. Of major interest is the pedestal next to an old iron grid at the very end in the southwest corner of the cave, which is believed the body of Habib-i Neccar. Other than that, there are no other features that could be attributed to Habib-i Neccar. Traditions shape the design and architecture of the pilgrimage site most common among Alawites, as indicated by the white and green paint used for the walls and iron work. The site also provides facilities for devotees to perform rituals of saint veneration, which include iron plates and matches for burning incense, as well as rosaries and well-worn versions of the Qur'an for the performance of prayers. The site is laid out with carpets suitable for the visitors to stay overnight during the summer months, making it suitable for dream incubation and wish making. Overall, the site is well maintained with the outer and inner walls painted in white. Even massive parts of the mountain surrounding the site and rocks stretching along the path are painted in white, so that the site can be seen from the Old Town and further.

The very location of both sites attributed to Habib-i Neccar defines which religious communities and traditions have primarily shaped those rituals that are performed and are deemed acceptable. Whereas the pilgrimage site in the mountain slope is outside of the settled area and preferred by Alawites, the tomb in the Habib-i Neccar mosque is in the centre of Antakya and primarily visited by Sunnis. Rituals performed at the Habib-i Neccar mosque clearly follow the Sunni tradition, whereas those performed in the cave at the Habib-i Neccar pilgrimage site clearly follow the Alawite tradition. The differences between the mosque and pilgrimage site also consist in the rigidity in which specific types of ritual are, or can be, officially enforced. A warning plate at the Habib-i Neccar mosque officially prohibits traditional rituals of saint veneration commonly practiced at tombs and local pilgrimage sites. It lists the prohibitions and states in twelve points those practices that are forbidden in orthodox Islam and can be translated as follows:

> Be aware during the visit at this site!
> Observe Islam devoutly
> *at this site and the tomb!*
> 1- Do not make a vow!
> 2- Do not perform a sacrifice!
> 3- Do not light a candle!
> 4- Do not knot cloth strips!
> 5- Do not rub money on the wall!
> 6- Do not enter by making a bow or kneel on the ground!
> 7- Do not throw money!
> 8- Do not leave here food offerings!
> 9- Do not touch the tomb with your hand or your face!
> 10- Do not hope to be healed at sites or tombs!
> 11- Do not circle around sites or tombs!
> 12- Do not lay down at sites!
> These and similar forms of superstition are not part of our religion and are certainly prohibited.
> *Head of the Ministry of Religious Affairs*

Barely any traces of such practices could be found at the saint's tomb in the mosque. However, during the numerous times I visited the pilgrimage site in the mountains, I could only find traces of those practices, which the Ministry of Religious Affairs explicitly prohibited and are all too common among Alawites. These include the burning of incense and lighting of candles, as well as the practice of writing down wishes or tying knots with cloth strips as visible means of sealing a vow.[13]

8 Rituals of Saint Veneration as Imitation

The veneration of saints is embodied in form of ritual postures, gestures, and movements. Rituals that devotees perform are mimetic acts as they follow a given tradition. Despite the variation in individual instances, rituals of saint veneration reveal specific patterns through their cycles of repetition and reiteration. In addition to being performed at given times and places, rituals of saint veneration are transmitted differently within the religious communities and devotees can be identified because of their ritual postures, gestures, and movements. Thus, rituals of saint veneration are mimetic in that they refer to one another and become or are made similar through their postures, gestures, and movements.[14]

The veneration of Habib-i Neccar in the mosque or the mountain cave are similar and different in unique ways. This can be explained not only because of the location and neighbourhood or the architecture and interior design of the sites, but also because of the aesthetics of the rituals performed at these sites. As common in the local Islamic tradition, primarily women visit the Habib-i Neccar tomb in the mosque for prayers and vows. Every time I visited the second crypt of the mosque I experienced a calm and subdued atmosphere with devotees only whispering their prayers. Several times, when passing the mosque on the Kurtuluş Caddesi, I witnessed a group of Muslim women sitting and praying together at the tombs of Yuhanna and Pavlus. This, however, did not happen with regard to the tomb of Habib-i Neccar, where devotees venerate the saint in solitude and quiescence.

Other than the accounts about visits to the Habib-i Neccar tomb in the mosque, I was only able to collect information from my Alawite and Orthodox Christian interlocutors about visits to the pilgrimage site. The rituals of worship at this

---

13 At one of my visits, I could even find some traces that resembled dried up blood puddles outside of the pilgrimage site close to the mountain slope that obviously indicate some form of animal sacrifice.

14 This does not only apply to the cycles of reiteration by an individual devotee or members of a specific religious community, but can also be found across members of religious communities depending on the degrees of proximity in which they interact with one another. If performed in relatively close proximity or at the same pilgrimage site, rituals of saint veneration are becoming or being made similar through processes of adaptation and assimilation (Kreinath 2016).

site are usually prayers directed to the saint, including forms of wish-making performed during the visits by the Alawite community. One of my interlocutors told me that Alawites visit the Habib-i Neccar pilgrimage site during the Feast of Sacrifice and the Kadir Hum festival, which are some of the most important festivals in this community (Türk 2001). Whereas they traditionally make visits to this site, they usually do not visit the mosque because—following a common view among Alawites—Ali was killed in a mosque. Besides, their main rituals of saint veneration are officially prohibited in the mosque.

Christians who visit these sites tend to adjust to the dominant Muslim rituals of saint veneration. One of my interlocutors told me that Christians used to visit the Habib-i Neccar tomb in the mosque's crypt to light candles or make wishes.[15] Although the Habib-i Neccar pilgrimage site is primarily visited by Alawites, I was told that Orthodox Christians still visit this site on occasion, but that this practice was more common in the past. As an elderly interlocutor told me, the whole Orthodox Christian community used to visit the Habib-i Neccar pilgrimage site on an annual basis. Following his childhood memories, it was in the early morning hours on a day early in the year that the whole community prepared to leave for a picnic at the Habib-i Neccar pilgrimage site. As he further recalled, members of the community also went into the cave to perform their prayers and made wishes; and there was an old wooden doorframe on the way up to the pilgrimage site, which was attributed to a local saint who is believed to heal headaches. Hammering nails into this frame was believed to cure them.[16]

In addition to communal visits, devotees visit the Habib-i Neccar mosque and pilgrimage site on an individual basis for purposes of praying and vowing. On these occasions the devotees informally interact with one another by performing their rituals. Despite similarities and differences in postures, gestures, and movements, these rituals can change *in situ* as devotees adapt to the given situation and site depending on who else is present. These postures, gestures, and movements may look very different at any given moment, but they are made similar depending on the context of ritual interaction among the devotees.

---

15 In the past, some Orthodox Christians visited the mosque and pilgrimage site claiming that they were both of Christian origin with the Habib-i Neccar mosque formerly being a church dedicated to John the Baptist.

16 The practice of visiting the pilgrimage site of Habib-i Neccar ended among the Orthodox Christians in Antakya. This is, according to one of my interlocutors, due to the prohibitions issued by the Turkish government in the late 1970s, which forbid climbing the mountains around Antakya due to terrorist threats common at that time. Younger members of the Orthodox Christian community in Antakya do not remember or even know about the visits of their community to the Habib-i Neccar pilgrimage site.

The performance of a prayer is an act of imitation that, depending on location and context, can lead to adaptations and assimilations of ritual postures, gestures, and movement. Due to their aesthetic qualities, rituals of saint veneration have transformative dynamics and change the interaction of the devotees. The respective ritual postures, gestures, and movements are thus comparable to those that devotees perform at this or other pilgrimage sites.

When compared, Muslim and Christian devotees in Antakya perform rituals of saint veneration in very similar ways. This becomes clear in those postures, gestures, and movements performed in the direct vicinity of the saint's tomb. To venerate the saint, devotees usually approach the tomb in a slow and ceremonial pace. They come to a stop in proximity to the tomb and while facing it they uplift their hands with the open palms facing upward and slightly raise their head as a posture of praying. After praying for a couple of minutes, they touch the tomb with their hands or kiss and touch it with their forehead. At times, devotees move with their open right hand, palm over their face. Sunnis as well as Alawites usually pray the Fatiha Surah. Less common is the reading or recitation of passages from one of the printed exemplars of the Qur'an or the Yasin Surah, which are placed in Arabic or Turkish translation on the tomb or shelves around it (see Figure 6).

When the prayer is completed, the devotee slowly moves backwards away from the tomb while still facing it. Reaching the stairways or door, devotees turn around and the prayer is completed with a hand gesture. Taking into consideration the basic sequence of bodily movements at the site, the visitors from the different religious communities cannot immediately be identified. It is still possible though that, despite sharing main features like standing in front of the tomb and praying with uplifted hands, unique differences among the members of various communities can be observed (see Figure 7).

The individual postures, gestures, and movements in rituals of saint veneration among Alawites and Sunnis differ in significant details. Alawites kiss the doorframes before entering and leaving the shrine and tend to kiss the tombs, while Sunnis place their right hand on their left chest and slightly bow their head as a sign of devotion and respect while entering the site. Another practice Alawites perform at the tomb is that they kiss the tomb and the Qur'an, often twice, in a specific sequence of movements by first kissing the tomb or Qur'an before touching them with their forehead. I observed this sequence of movements among some Sunnis and Orthodox Christians in different contexts, but Orthodox Christians usually perform these movements only once and in a much slower pace. Another ritual gesture among Alawites is that they open and close the Qur'an in front of their face. During a visit to the tomb at the Habib-i Neccar mosque with Christian and Muslim women as part of the interreligious peace prayer

Figure 7: Sunni Muslims at the Habib-i Neccar Tomb in the First Crypt of the Habib-i Neccar Mosque in Antakya. Photo by the author.
Figure 8: Catholic Christian Woman at the Habib-i Neccar Tomb in the Second Crypt of the Habib-i Neccar Mosque in Antakya. Photo by the author.

that was performed annually, I witnessed also the Christian women putting on headscarves for the occasion of visiting the site and performing a short prayer in front of the tomb as Muslim women did (see Figure 8).

In concluding their prayers, Christians made the visible sign of a cross making the forehead and chest as well as the right and left shoulder as common in the Orthodox and Catholic tradition. On one occasion, when the crypt was closed for restoration and the interreligious prayer was performed in the main prayer room of the Habib-i Neccar mosque, I witnessed an Orthodox Christian woman holding the rosary in her left hand while performing her prayers (see Figure 9).

The main difference between Muslims and Christians venerating at this site is that the Christians always include the sign of the cross at the beginning and end of their prayers and, even though they use the rosary during their prayers, the design of their rosaries obviously follows their own tradition with ten beads for the Ave Maria and a cross in the centre, not 33 or 99 beads as most of the Muslim rosaries (see Figure 10).

Despite that devotees may blend traditions in their rituals of saint veneration or avoid any form of similarity, they always establish social relationships with members of other religious communities at these sites attributed to Habib-i Neccar. These similarities and differences in the various forms of saint veneration exemplify the transformational dynamics of mimetic acts in rituals. Analysing rituals of saint veneration as mimetic acts thus helps to understand their aesthetic dimensions and transformative dynamics. With its focus on the transformational dynamics of mimetic acts, the study of interreligious rituals of saint veneration in Antakya therefore widens the breadth and depth of the aesthetics of religion by adopting mimesis as a connective concept and key term in aesthetics.

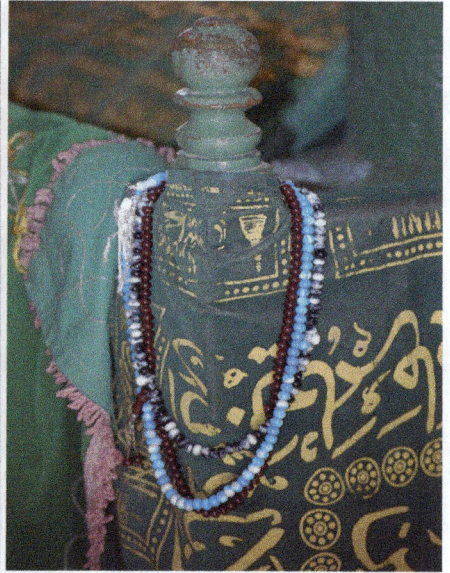

Figure 9: Orthodox Christian Woman with a Rosary in her Left Hand Praying at the Habib-i Neccar Mosque in Antakya. Photo by the author.
Figure 10: Muslim Rosaries on the Yuhanna and Pavlus Tombs at the Habib-i Neccar Mosque in Antakya. Photo by the author.

9 Imagination of the Saint's Presence as Simulation

The imagination of the saint's presence at the mosque or pilgrimage site is certainly the least tangible aspect in the aesthetics of saint veneration that devotees can evoke through rituals. The effect that the aura of the saint has on the sensation and perception of devotees exemplifies its transformative dynamics. Devotees imagine the saint's presence through the different means of simulation and imagination. In doing so, they refer to the site, and the saint who is imagined to be present at the site, through either the bodily remains or persisting spirit. Even though the ritual postures, gestures, and movements may look similar, it can be argued that the aura of the saint's presence at the site differs depending on the religious tradition a devotee follows. This applies to local traditions, namely the different meanings and legends attached to the saint as well as to the significance the site has for the respective communities. Whereas it can be argued that the sensation and perception of the saint's presence cannot be completely different, because the rituals devotees perform at the tomb of the saint share formal features. It is therefore important to demonstrate how the similarities and differences in the veneration of Habib-i Neccar can be explained and how the aesthetic formation of the saint is framed through religious discourses or simulated through ritual practices.

Compared to other saints venerated in and around Antakya, Habib-i Neccar is not known for appearances or transfigurations in dreams or visions. There are no accounts circulated in the local community that would describe Habib-i Neccar as having performed miracles or healed illnesses. Nevertheless, it is possible to reconstruct the devotees' sensation and perception of the presence at the Habib-i Neccar tombs. Habib-i Neccar is primarily of significance for local Sunnis. As my Sunni interlocutors indicated, the Yasin Surah is the centre of the Qur'an, meaning that this is the most important Surah of the Qur'an. As one of them mentioned, Habib-i Neccar serves as a role model for him and he aspires to follow him through his deeds. Another interlocutor told me that Habib-i Neccar is a true friend of God and is therefore the ideal human to imitate because he was willing to give witness for his faith in the one and only God.

By contrast, some Alawites view the figure of Habib-i Neccar with some suspicion. One of them even stated that Alawites do not venerate him at all, because he, as some legends and interpretations of the Yasin Surah seem to suggest, is believed to come from Saudi Arabia, meaning that Habib-i Neccar represents an orthodox interpretation of Sunni Islam for him. In addition, I heard that members of the Alawite community deeply admire Habib-i Neccar as their local saint. One of them considered Habib-i Neccar to be a citizen of Antioch and a friend of God who was working like Jesus as a carpenter. However, most of Alawites I talked to do not seem to have any vivid memory of a visit to one of the Habib-i Neccar tombs or even feel any strong affection toward the saint. One of my Alawite interlocutors told me when he visits the pilgrimage site he simply performs a prayer as a sign of respect for the saint and his site.

The experiences and perceptions expressed by Orthodox Christians are similar and different from those held among Alawites. One of my Orthodox Christian interlocutors admitted that he never visited either the Habib-i Neccar mosque or the pilgrimage site, stating that he feels uncomfortable going there simply because it is a mosque. He holds the view that Muslims now occupy a formerly Christian site. For him, these sites refer to John the Baptist who, because of his beheading, shared the same destiny with Habib-i Neccar. In doing so, he actually follows that aspect of the local account about the saint's death that Muslims usually attribute to Habib-i Neccar. Orthodox Christians who visited the tomb and prayed in the mosque or pilgrimage site expressed some affection toward the saint and seemed to have made their wishes while praying to the saint. At least one elder Orthodox Christian woman has vivid memories of her visits to the mosque remembering her prayers and the lighting of candles. With regret, she indicated that these are now things of the past.

As these personal accounts of devotees from the different religious communities in Antakya indicate, the veneration of Habib-i Neccar provides a shared tradition for Christians and Muslims, even if it does so in considerably different ways than the dominant discourse may seem to suggest. The respect for the saint shows that members of the Christians and Muslim communities of Antakya acknowledge the religious significance of this site. Regardless of how different the interpretations of the saint and his sites might be, all seem to share similar aesthetic formations when expressing their sense of the uniqueness of these sites. For all of them, these sites mark, despite different views, a common inheritance from the past, which is of similar importance for both the Muslim and Christian communities. The relatively close proximity and the interaction at the respective sites may explain why the devotees' sensations and perceptions become or are made similar among those who venerate Habib-i Neccar at the mosque and the pilgrimage site. The ways in which the members of the different religious communities approach the saint, and thus experience the saint's presence, one way or another suggest that there are common features of saint veneration that cut across different religious communities. Therefore, I argue that the veneration of this saint and the visits to his sites is, also for aesthetic reasons, integral to a common inheritance of the local traditions of religious coexistence in Antakya.

10 Conclusion: Transformative Dynamics of Mimetic Acts and the Aesthetics of Religion

The case study on Habib-i Neccar as a saint venerated among Christians and Muslims alike succinctly exemplified and consolidated the relevance of mimesis for the aesthetics of religion. The presentation of the empirical evidence suggested that the distinction between representation, imitation, and simulation as different aesthetic dimensions help distinguish between different layers of mimetic acts while simultaneously integrating the historical and ethnographical material into a holistic framework for analysis. As demonstrated, the concept of mimesis has the capacity to serve as an analytical tool to establish the aesthetics of religion through the tripartite feature of mimesis as a relational concept. In this configuration, mimesis allowed for determining the transformational dynamics of rituals of saint veneration as they unfold through devotees, rituals of saint veneration, and the saint as the object of veneration.

Mimesis thus facilitates the ways in which scholars of religion can study how devotees establish relationships with members of other religious communities. By following their own traditions and adjusting to traditions of other communities in their direct vicinity, the concept of mimesis unravels the transformative dynamics in the changing configuration between the performance of ritual actions, the experience of the saint's presence, and the social world outside of it. Hence, the case study exemplified the aesthetics of religion by systematically correlating the study of texts, places, and concepts as well as objects, persons, narratives, and rituals as mimetic acts. In this capacity, the concept of mimesis helps differentiate and integrate the various aesthetic dimensions of religion. By bringing the different dimensions into a fold, mimesis facilitates aesthetics as a connective concept which has proven to be vital for studying religion in a new key.

Bibliography

Adorno, Theodor W. 1997. *Aesthetic Theory*, translated by Robert Hullot-Kentor. Minneapolis: University of Minnesota Press.

Ali, A. Yusuf. 1983. *The Holy Qur'an: Text, Translation, and Commentary*. Brentwood: Amana Corporation.

Assmann, Jan. 2006. *Religion and Cultural Memory: Ten Studies*, translated by Rodney Livingstone. Stanford: Stanford University Press.

Benjamin, Walter. 1978. "On the Mimetic Faculty." In *Reflections: Essays, Aphorisms, Autobiographical Writings*, edited by Peter Demetz and translated by Edmund Jephcott, 333–336. New York and London: Harcourt Brace Jovanovich.

Busse, Heribert. 2000. "Antioch and Its Prophet Ḥabīb al-Najjār." *Jerusalem Studies in Arabic and Islam* 24: 155–179.

Cancik, Hubert, and Hubert Mohr. 1988. "Religionsästhetik." In *Handbuch religionswissenschaftlicher Grundbegriffe*, edited by Hubert Cancik, Burkhard Gladigow, and Matthias Samuel Laubscher, 121–156. Stuttgart: Kohlhammer.

Çelebi, Evliyā. 1969–1971. *Seyahatnâme* [Book of Travels]. 15 Vols. İstanbul: Zuhuri Danışman Yayınevi.

Christensen-Ernst, Jørgen. 2013. *Antioch on the Orontes*. Lanham: Hamilton Books.

Downey, Glanville. 1961. *A History of Antioch in Syria: From Seleucus to the Arab Conquest*. Princeton: Princeton University Press.

Erel, T. Levent, and Fatih Adatepe. 2007. "Traces of Historical Earthquakes in the Ancient City Life at the Mediterranean Region." *Journal of the Black Sea and Mediterranean Environment* 13/3: 241–252.

Gebauer, Gunter, and Christoph Wulf. 1995. *Mimesis: Culture, Art, Society*, translated by Don Reneau. Berkeley: University of California Press.

Gell, Alfred. 1998. *Art and Agency: An Anthropological Theory*. Oxford and New York: Clarendon Press.

Gibb, H.A.R., ed. 1958. *The Travels of ibn Battuta, A.D. 1325–1354, translated with Revisions and Notes from the Arabic Text.* Vol. 1. Cambridge: Cambridge University Press.

Grieser, Alexandra. 2016. "Aesthetics." In *Vocabulary for the Study of Religion.* Vol. 1, edited by Robert Segal and Kocku von Stuckrad, 14–23. Leiden and Boston: Brill.

Halliwell, Stephen. 2002. *The Aesthetics of Mimesis: Ancient Texts and Modern Problems.* Princeton and Oxford: Princeton University Press.

Hartmann, Martin. 1894. "Das Liwa Haleb (Aleppo) und ein Teil des Liwa Dschebel Bereket." *Zeitschrift der Deutschen Morgenlandischen Gesellschaft* 29: 142–188, 475–550.

Jacquot, Paul. 1931. *Antioche: Centre de Tourisme.* 3 Vols. Beirut: Comité de Tourisme d'Antioche.

Kreinath, Jens. 2004. "Theoretical Afterthoughts." In *The Dynamics of Changing Rituals: Religious Rituals within Their Social and Cultural Context,* edited by Jens Kreinath, Constance Hartung, and Annette Deschner, 267–282. New York: Peter Lang.

—— 2009. "Virtuality and Mimesis: Toward an Aesthetics of Ritual Performances as Embodied Forms of Religious Practice." In *Religion – Ritual – Theatre,* edited by Bent Holm, Bent Flemming Nielsen, and Karen Vedel, 219–249. Frankfurt am Main: Peter Lang.

—— 2014. "Virtual Encounters with Hızır and Other Muslim Saints: Dreaming and Healing at Local Pilgrimage Sites in Hatay, Turkey." *Anthropology of the Contemporary Middle East and Central Eurasia* 2/1: 25–66.

—— 2015. "The Seductiveness of Saints: Interreligious Pilgrimage Sites in Hatay and the Ritual Transformations of Agency." In *The Seductions of Pilgrimage: Sacred Journeys Afar and Astray in the Western Religious Tradition,* edited by Michael A. Di Giovine and David Picard, 121–143. Farnham: Ashgate.

—— 2016. "Intertextualität und Interritualität als Mimesis: Zur Ästhetik interreligiöser Beziehungen unter Juden, Christen und Muslimen in Hatay" *Zeitschrift für Religionswissenschaft:* 24/2: 1–32.

Lassus, Jean. 1934. "Sondage près de la Mosquée Habib en Najjar." In *Antioch-on-the-Orontes: I. The Excavations of 1932,* edited by George W. Elderkin, 93–100. Princeton: Princeton University Press.

Le Camus, Émile. 1890. *Notre voyage aux pays bibliques.* 3 Vols. Paris: Letouzey et Ané.

Le Strange, Guy. 1890. *Palestine under the Moslems: A Description of Syria and the Holy Land from A.D. 650 to 1500.* London: Alexander P. Watt for the Committee of the Palestine Exploration Fund.

Meri, Josef W. 2004. *A Lonely Wayfarer's Guide to Pilgrimage: 'Alī ibn Abī Bakr al-Harawī's Kitāb al-Ishārāt ilā Ma'rifat al-Ziyārāt, Studies in Late Antiquity and Early Islam.* Princeton: Darwin Press.

Meyer, Birgit. 2009. "From Imagined Communities to Aesthetic Formations: Religious Mediations, Sensational Forms, and Styles of Binding." In *Aesthetic Formations: Media, Religion and the Senses,* edited by Birgit Meyer, 1–18. New York: Palgrave Macmillan.

Meyer, Birgit, and Jojada Verrips. 2008. "Aesthetics." In *Key Words in Religion, Media, and Culture,* edited by David Morgan, 20–30. New York: Routledge.

Potolsky, Matthew. 2006. *Mimesis.* New York and London: Routledge.

Sprenger, Aloys. 1841. *El-Mas'udi's Historical Encyclopedia, Entitled "Meadows of Gold and Mines of Gems" Translated from the Arabic.* Vol. 1. London: Oriental Translation Fund of Great Britain and Ireland.

Taussig, Michael. 1993. *Mimesis and Alterity: A Particular History of the Senses.* New York and London: Routledge.

Tekin, Mehmet. 1998. *Habib-i Neccar of Antakya*, translated by Nurşin Çinçin. Antakya: Zirem Basımevi.

Türk, Hüseyin. 2001. "Hatay'da Gadir Bayramı [The Gadir Festival in Hatay]." *Folklor Edebiyat* 26: 89–96.

Türk, Muammer. 2012. *Apostles and Antioch*, translated by Isa Aydın. Iskenderun: T.C. Kültür ve Turizm Bakanlığı.

Weulersse, Jacques. 1934. "Antioche Essai de Geographie Urbaine." *Bulletin d'Études Orientales* 4: 27–79.

Wheeler, Brannon M. 2002. *Prophets in the Quran: An Introduction to the Quran and Muslim Exegesis.* London and New York: Continuum.

Maruška Svašek
Aestheticisation and the Production of (Religious) Space in Chennai

This chapter explores people-thing dynamics in the spatial settings of the homes of elite Indian families in the city of Chennai.[1] The analysis draws on the perspective of *aestheticisation*, as developed in the book *Anthropology, Art and Cultural Production* (Svašek 2007) to conceptualise a dynamic process whereby artefacts and images come to be interpreted and experienced by individuals and groups of people as specifically significant and powerful phenomena.[2] This process relies on thinking and feeling human beings, who, through their object-focussed perceptual acts, are themselves in transformation, experiencing and performing religious and other subjectivities through engagement with things in concrete social and spatio-temporal settings. The perspective of aestheticisation rejects the Kantian idea of aesthetics as realm of objective beauty (Svašek 2007), and resonates with the notion of 'aisthaesis', defined as a process of embodied perception that shapes and is shaped by multi-sensorial experiences (Verrips 2005; Morgan 2012; Bruland 2016, 254; Meyer 2008, 973). The analysis in this chapter investigates interrelated processes of the embodied perception, interpretation and framing of specific material objects in the homes of families in Chennai, examining changes in their meanings and impact as they are appropriated in different locations. I am particularly interested in the production of religious (and other) space through bodily engagement with these objects. Four interrelated questions will be answered.

---

1 In 2012, I visited ten families to ask them about the meaning and impact of artefacts displayed in their homes. The research was part of a large HERA-funded project, entitled *Creativity and innovation in a world of movement* that explored the production and appropriation of artefacts and visual imagery in an era of intensifying global interconnectedness. The overall project explored discourses, practices and experiences of creativity and cultural value in different historical and spatial contexts in four different continents. It involved twelve researchers based in the UK, Norway, the Netherland and India.

2 When writing the book *Anthropology, Art and Cultural Production*, I looked for an approach that could pull together insights provided by various strands of research. First of all, I was interested in theories of signification, in particular semiotics and poststructuralist understandings of representational practice. Secondly, I was inspired by approaches that examined commodification processes in socio-economic fields of production, marketing and consumption (Marxist and neo-Marxist analyses, Appadurai's social life of things approach). The third strand of theories explored the emotional and sensorial impact of artefacts, bringing bodily experience into focus (i.e., phenomenology, theories of agency and affect, emotions research).

https://doi.org/10.1515/9783110461015-013

1) What kind of artefacts and images are displayed in homes of the Indian elite in Chennai?
2) How are specific objects in these households aestheticized as mediators of religious experience or how are they aestheticized in alternative, possibly conflicting ways?
3) How do these dynamics shape processes of social identification and performances of (religious) selves?
4) What do the multiple processes of aestheticisation reveal about the wider politics of religion, art and heritage in the state of Tamil Nadu?

The first collection of artefacts I shall focus on was displayed in an apartment owned by a mixed Hindu-Muslim family; the second and third were exhibited in the homes of two related Muslim families. An elderly Hindu lady owned the fourth collection. Before exploring their home spaces, however, it is necessary to place them in the wider context of Chennai.

1 Chennai: Neo-Liberalism, Heritage Politics and the Glorious Hindu Past

Chennai is a city with a population of over 4.7 million (census in 2011). As Mary Hancock (2008, 9) noted, it is "one of India's mega-cities and one of the nodes through which forces of neoliberal globalization are transforming the country". While one the one hand, it is in the process of "reclaiming a regional identity" it is also becoming a "center for global software production, export processing, and back-office services", like other South Indian cities such as Bangalore (Hancock 2008, 9). In recent years, attempts have been made to brand Chennai as attractive place for investment and tourism, not only fashioning "a heritage-conscious cityscape, one with historic precincts, museums, and memorials" (Hancock 2008, 12), but also claiming to be a vibrant centre in national and global contemporary art worlds (Desai 2016, 109; Shreen 2016, 97).

The politics of heritage in Tamil Nadu reflects the religious background of the population and the impact of Dravidian politics that has promoted Tamil cultural nationalism for over a century (Hancock 2008, 12). The dominant religion is Hinduism (81.3%), followed by Islam (9.4%), Christianity (7.6%) and Jainism (1.1%), and the majority population consists of Tamils and Telugus. As tourist destination, Tamil Nadu is best known for its Hindu cultural legacy, attracting Indian and foreign tourists to its numerous ancient temples. The buildings are not just framed as centres of Hindu religious activities, but also as 'Indian heritage', resonating Hindu dominated national discourses and Hindutva ideologies. They are also promoted as 'Tamil' heritage, reflecting a Dravidian outlook. Heritages discourses are supported by regional and state-wide organisations and policies that aestheticise particular landscapes and architectural structures as materialisations of a glorious past that needs to be saved, protected, and developed. Tamil artisans and artists produce a wide variety of Hindu-themed artefacts for local and foreign markets, from expensive large bronze statues of the main deities to cheap temple souvenirs. This allows buyers to bring artefacts, perceived as 'god manifestations' and/or as signifiers of Hindu heritage into their homes.[3] The homes of the elite families focused on in this paper co-constitute the urban space of Chennai, and must be explored as part of this wider spatial context.

2 Merging Formations of Artistic and Religious Agency

The initial idea for this chapter arose when two contemporary artists, Manisha Raju and Raju Durshettiwar, took me to the homes of some buyers of their paintings.[4] The works, bought directly from the artists or through Chennai based art galleries, were most of all sensed through visual engagement, and were framed and admired as 'fine art'. As Howes (2003, 2004) and Stoller (1989) have argued, modes of sensuous perception develop through practices of learning and training that are often historically shaped and group specific. These processes of embodied knowing and 'enskilment' shape the ways in which artefacts are experienced and framed, or in other words, how they are aestheticized. Many buyers of contemporary art in Chennai have been socialised as 'art lovers' through gallery and museum visits at home and abroad, and through exposure to art collections of friends and acquaintances. The purchase of contemporary paintings and sculpture pieces, and the performance of an knowledgeable and enthusiastic 'ar-

---

3 Some churches and mosques are also mentioned in tourist guides, but the production of Christian and Muslim artefacts is limited by comparison. As Hancock (2008, 12) has noted, "[w]hile Dravidianist themes dominated urban memoryscapes during the 1970s and 1980, the 1990s saw the appearance of new narratives on the past. Tamil nationalism has remained potent, but competing notions of the past, including Dalit history, colonial nostalgia, and Hindu nationalism, have made new claims on urban space and popular loyalties. Among the sites that mediate these claims are parks, open-air museums, urban heritage districts, house museums, libraries and cultural performance spaces".

4 During the first visit to two families, I was accompanied by co-researcher Amit Desai. As part of a large collaborative research project entitled Creativity and Innovation in a World of Movement, we explored the social dynamics of the art world in Tamil Nadu. We set out to interview a number of art collectors to get a better sense of the contemporary art scene in Tamil Nadu.

tistic' gaze is one way in which well-off Chennai urbanites claim their status as member of a cultured elite.

The first family we visited was a Hindu-Muslim couple that lived with one of their daughters in an expensive apartment block. Interestingly, the walls of the L-shaped lounge were not only decorated with contemporary paintings and drawings, including works by Raju and Durshettiwar (see Figures 1 and 2); also displayed was a Tanjore piece that represented the Goddess Lakshmi (see Figure 3).

Figure 1: The lounge of the family. Photo by the author, 2012.
Figure 2: Artefacts in the lounge of the family (with the artist Manisha Raju standing in front of one of her paintings). Photo by the author, 2012.

Tanjore paintings are gilded depictions of Hindu deities, many acquired from large houses in the countryside, owned, but no longer inhabited by Chettinad people. These paintings, especially the antique pieces, were extremely popular amongst the more wealthy art buyers in Chennai as they appealed to an urban nostalgia for a glamorous Tamil or South Indian past.[5] The couple had bought

---

5 Tanjore paintings are extremely popular amongst the more wealthy art buyers in Chennai. Less expensive contemporary works are produced by contemporary artists, who are trained in techniques that are specific to the genre, and who market their products as 'traditional Indian art.' There is, however, also a relatively large market of Tanjore antiques that are much more expensive. Dealers advertise their businesses partly through the internet providing informative texts such as the following. 'Tanjore' (or Thanjavur or Thanjavoor) paintings have a very rich heritage. This style of painting has been followed widely by the people in Southern Tamil Nadu for

the work in a gallery as an exquisite example of "Indian antique" that was, like the contemporary art works in their collection, most of all valued as object of visual engagement. The performance of a knowledgeable, cultured mode of vision that could prove one's familiarity with past Indian traditions was clearly "invested with [high] social value" (Classen 1997, 401),[6] and formed an important element of middle and high class home-making practices in Chennai.

The nineteenth century Tanjore piece was an expensive and beautiful work that had once been the focus of active devotion in a wealthy Chettinad household. There were visible traces of this previous religious function, as doors were still attached to the picture frame. In the house where the piece came from, these doors would have been closed during the night, to pay respect to the Goddess who is normally treated as royalty.[7]

In its original context, the Tanjore piece had been the centre of multi-sensorial ritual engagement through *darshan* (looking into the eyes of the Goddess) and

---

the past two centuries. The art flourished in Tanjavoor, pronounced Tanjore, the capital city of the Chola dynasty, and thus got its name. Maratha princes, Nayaks of Vijaynagar dynasty, Rajus communities of Tanjore and Trichi and Naidus of Madurai patronized the art of Tanjore painting from 16 to 18th centuries. Tanjore paintings are deeply rooted in tradition and still innovative within limits. This art is sacred and dedicated. The paintings are notable for their adornment in the form of semi-precious stones, pearls, glass pieces and gold. The rich vibrant colors, dashes of gold, semi-precious stones and fine artistic work are characteristics of these paintings. They add beauty and culture to a variety of surroundings and décor. The paintings are mostly of Gods and Goddesses because this art of painting flourished at a time when fine-looking and striking temples were being constructed by rulers of several dynasties. The figures in these paintings are large and the faces are round and divine. Tracing its roots to the historical golden era of the early 18th century, Tanjore artwork is one of the many indigenous art forms for which India is noted. Originating in Tanjore about 300 kms from Chennai (Madras), which was the then capital of the Gupta empire, this form of art developed at the height of cultural evolvement achieved during that period. Crafted with meticulous care the Thanjavoor (Tanjore) pictures are unique. What sets them apart from Indian paintings in general are the embellishments made over the basic drawings with precious and semi-precious stones as well as the relief work which gives them a three dimensional effect. The pictures are of various sizes, ranging from huge works spanning whole walls to small miniatures no longer than 6-inch square. The paintings decorate the puja rooms in residences, arcades in major hotels and lobbies in Corporate Offices. They also make nice gifts for Diwali, Weddings and other special occasions? (http://tanjoreart.com/, last accessed 1 March 2011).

6 Classen argued that, when exploring the senses, scholars "must not only look at the practical uses to which the senses are put for every society will make practical use of all of the senses, but at the ways in which different sensory domains are invested with social value" (Classen 1997, 401).

7 In Hindu temples, the Priests also commonly treat the gods as highly distinguished persons, regularly feeding and bathing them, changing their clothes, and preparing them for sleep.

Figure 3 and 4: The Tanjore Piece with its doors open and closed. Photo by the author, 2012.

puja (worship involving the smell of incense and the taste of sacred food) (Eck 1998). As Christopher Pinney (2001, 158) noted, this "corpothetic" mode of perception differs from disembodied modes of absorption that show appreciation through verbal explanation. Appropriated as a collectors' item amongst other works of art in its new setting, however, the artefact was re-aestheticised as "attractive, decorative piece". As with the contemporary art works in their collection, the family's sensuous engagement was primarily visual, a mode of perception and appreciation common in globally stretching worlds of 'fine art' (Svašek 2007). Unsurprisingly, the doors of the work remained constantly open to fully expose its 'artistic' beauty (see Figure 3). When bought, the major appeal of the work had been its formal features that had made it a recognisable Tanjore work, with its characteristic subject matter, the symmetrical composition, and the shiny golden surfaces that gave it an appropriate 'lavish' look. The family also deemed it attractive because they considered it an *authentic* work; its status as real (i.e., not fake) antique implicated high commodity value, adding to the object's power to impress visitors.

Within the context of the family's domestic collection the Tanjore piece had lost its power to mediate divine agency. After a few months, however, the family began to perceive the work in radically new ways. This started when Zayna began feeling a sacred presence when looking at the work, a sense that she described as "feeling vibrations". Knowing that the artefact had originally been an object of worship, she began to treat it with respect, closing the doors at night. "Our bedroom is situated directly opposite the work", she said, "and it just felt wrong to keep the doors open". Re-sensing and re-interpreting the depiction of Lakshmi as actual divine presence, the couple could no longer admire it as "just decoration". Their new interaction with the piece turned their lounge into a religious space when Zayna began placing flowers in front of the Tanjore piece and, seated in front of it, started occasionally singing *bhajans* (Hindu devotional songs) with groups of invited female friends, most of them Hindus. All were mothers of teenage children, and were concerned with what they saw as the "moral dangers" of contemporary urban life. To counter this threat, they felt a strong need to bring "spirituality" into their home environments.

Zayna explained that, while she identified herself as a Muslim, she had "an open mind to all religions". "God is one", she said, and therefore there was no problem in adopting Hindu rituals. She did not, however, define herself as a Hindu. Unlike most of her Hindu friends, she did not visit Hindu temples to take *darshan* and her engagement with Hindu rituals was mostly through the appropriation of specific elements of Hindu ritual practice, like the occasional placing of flowers in front of the goddess. Otherwise, she continued to identify herself as Muslim, sometimes visiting Mosques and giving donations to Muslim charities. She was, she said, "an open-minded" Muslim who opposed fundamentalism in both Islam and Hinduism.

The work was displayed opposite a framed text from the Quran that she also strongly valued; her actions were to be understood as a statement about a presumed unity of the ultimate principles of Hinduism and Islam: the need to show love, respect and tolerance. During my fieldwork, I came across numerous people who expressed similar views, which was highly relevant in the wider context of local, national and global religious tensions. In India, the situation had worsened during and after the demolition of the Babri Masjid mosque in Ayodhya by Hindu extremists in 1992,[8] a political climate that had also led to the radicalisation of some groups of Tamil Muslims.[9] While Zayna did not discuss these political issues to me in detail, it was clear to me that the assemblage in her home

---

8 "The religious site where the Babri mosque was destroyed in 1992 in the northern Indian town of Ayodhya has been a flashpoint between Hindus and Muslims for years" ("Timeline" 2012).
9 In 2013, Kalanthai Peer Mohamed expressed his concern in *The Hindu* about the growing influence of Islamic reform organisations in Tamil Nadu whose members oppose syncretic Tamil Muslim practices. In his view, this is partly caused by migrant workers who spent time in the Gulf monarchies during the Gulf oil boom of the 1970s and early 1980s and were influenced by purist Wahhabi traditions in the Middle East. This process of radicalisation coincided with the rise of Hindutva politics in India and was intensified by the destruction of the Babri Mosque 1992 (Venkatachalapathy 2013).

offered a syncretic alternative to more purist Muslim and Hindu spaces in the city.

3 Sensing the Quality of Antique

The next example further discusses how objects allowed their owners to perform desired notions of self and experience religiosity in their home environments. Tamana, a Chennai based Hindu Brahmin trader of south Indian antiques, was in her late seventies when I met her in Chennai in 2012. Having musicologists as parents and a grandfather who had worked as curator in the Madras Museum, she had grown up with a strong appreciation for Indian culture, and had internalised a belief in the value of art and heritage. She had married into a strict Shaivite[10] family to a husband who, while lacking an interest in Indian arts, had not objected when she had started collecting South Indian antiques in 1975.

When I arrived at her house in May 2012, I found her on the veranda, swinging gently on a traditional wooden swing that faced the garden. Identifying herself as someone "from a family of collectors", she clearly projected herself as a person with intimate knowledge of South Indian antiques. In her view these insights had not just been built up over a lifetime, but they emerged from her biological make-up. When growing up, she said, whenever she had done an errand for her grandfather, he had given her a piece of antique. Her family background had given her the opportunity to recognise the qualities of these old pieces. "You do not acquire taste", she emphasised, "it is in your genes, it moves from generation to generation, just like musical ability". Explaining that she had been the only one of five siblings who had taken up a true interest in collecting, she conceptualised her predicament as an embodied potential.

Taking me through to the lounge, and later as we entered different rooms in the house, she talked to me about her experiences as a collector and antique dealer, speaking with passion about many artefacts on display. Her home consisted of various spaces, including a lounge, a kitchen and dinner area, several bedrooms, and a separate room adjacent to the kitchen that functioned as puja room. She used another space on the first floor as display area for her antique business.

Chatting in the living room, we were surrounded by depictions of Hindu gods and ritual attributes that she had bought from various previous owners, directly or through the help of traders. She had displayed the objects in her collection

---

10 Shaivism is one of three main forms of Hinduism and is centred on the worship

Figure 5: Artefacts in Tamana's lounge. Photo by the author, 2012.

with care, leaving empty wall space around each item. The spacious presentation gave the room a museum-feel, which was also extended to the dining room. She did not, as I had seen in other households, mix antiques with contemporary art, so the space most of all felt like a mid-twentieth century ethnographic museum. She explained that she was a "purist", preferring just antiques. On various tables she had placed antique *murtis*, statues of Hindu deities, originally produced as objects of worship. In her lounge, they were however aestheticized as museum pieces, demanding visual, appreciation, not multi-sensorial religious action. By contrast, some other Hindu families that I had visited performed daily puja for all god images displayed in their entertainment areas, adorning them with garlands of flowers and in some cases adding a *bindi* of a red powder to the gods' foreheads. These devotional practices aestheticized the pictures at least momentarily as 'active gods', protecting the household.

Tamana said she was familiar with such practices, but did not perform them herself for god-images placed *outside* her puja room. She commented that in Hinduism, devotion can be expressed in many different ways, and that the decision how to perceive and treat religious imagery, and which ones to buy and display, was personal. "There is no hard and fast rule", she said, "in many Hindu homes you find prints. I don't have them". This diversity of practice is characteristic of many strands of Hinduism, where individuals worship the Gods or Goddesses they feel personally connected to. This relative freedom rests on the belief that the different deities are all manifestations of the same divine superpower (Huyler 1999).[11]

4 Objects of Trade: Genuine Works, True Enjoyment

Tamana underplayed (but did not deny) the potential religious efficacy of the Hindu deities in her lounge. Handling them as objects of collection and trade, she most of all valued them for their beauty, uniqueness, and the craftsmanship with which they had been made. In her view, as genuine antiques, these objects were very different from contemporary copies and recently made items. She stressed that one needed skill to distinguish a genuine piece from a fake: "Even Tanjur paintings are being reproduced. You need a third eye to identify the real one. You learn by trial and error. There are no books to help out".

Her own collection provided material evidence of her 'skilled vision', a term coined by Cristina Grassini (2009, 6, emphasis in original) to draw the attention to "the ways in which vision can be shared across a community as *an enskilled sense*, to highlight the processes of apprenticeship that refine vision as a skilled *capacity*, and to focus on the institutional audiences and the contexts of labour that have historically engaged vision as a specific *form of practice*".

The sensory experience of seeing and recognising quality antique, in other words, was not only a "field of cultural elaboration" but also an "arena for structuring social roles and interactions" (Howes 2003, xi). This allowed her to claim superiority and justified her role as authenticator and high-end antique trader. During our conversation, she downplayed the fact that she profited financially from the antique trade, claiming that collecting was all about "the joy of sharing".[12] The engagement of a buyer of art with the purchased item should not be motivated by greed, she argued, but should be informed by genuine interest. "Art as investment is not good!" She complained that

> [i]n India many collectors have no passion, no taste, no knowledge. They buy Hussain, paintings worth millions, as an investment. Personally I don't like his work. There are also millions of fakes, where people copy and reproduce...copy signatures. For example Ravi Varma, [his work] is sold for fancy prices but the signature is false. Newcomers buy

---

11 Many Hindus I spoke with during my research on Hindu practices in Tamil Nadu and Northern Ireland claimed that Hinduism is "not a prescribing religion" but rather a "way of life", allowing improvisation (Svašek, 2016).

12 She did at times refer to the financial aspects of the trade. As one point she mentioned, for example, that years ago, she had bought an antique piece for "only 10 rupees". Today, she explained, "some these old pieces were worth 5 laks".

it; they don't know. Is there anyone who has knowledge to spot the fakes? Auctioneers may know, and you have to pay a nominal fee to authenticate the work.

Aestheticising the works in her home as "real antiques" and herself as "expert" who possessed the perceptual skill to identify fakes, she demanded respect for her abilities. She talked with disdain about 'ignoramuses' who wrote about antiques while lacking the required knowledge and sensitivity.

> A journalist from the *Tamil Daily* came. I told him ten times to listen carefully not to make a mistake. I showed items that women used, and he was not familiar with them. One was an antique foot scraper. In the article he wrote that it was for the face! Another time a girl came from Stella Maris (College). She wanted to write a piece for *The Hindu*. I asked her what subject she was writing about. "About antique", she said. I asked her whether she knew anything about it. "Nothing", she said. I replied that unless she had a basic idea about antiques I would not do the interview. I said, "go read, then come back". She never did. "Antiques", that's simply too vague! It is a vast subject. New graduates are ignorant. They want to write a piece, earn money and spend it in a fast food restaurant. That's why they come here. It is not easy, giving an interview to an ignoramus.

5 Objects of Religiosity in and outside the Puja Room

As noted earlier, in Tamana's lounge, the artefacts were aestheticised as unique collectables, appealing to the eye of knowledgeable collectors. While she indicated that the *potentiality* of religious engagement was always present, this was of minor importance to her. The opposite was true with the god images in her domestic shrine, and she approached them as mediators of the divine, regularly performing *puja* and *darshan*, and occasionally paying a priest to perform specific rituals (see also Svašek 2016, 220). Her embodied knowledge of Hindu rituals, passed on by her parents, did not mean that she followed strict guidelines. She explained that "Puja places are normally dark places. They suffocate you. Mine is modern, I created it in my own style. Your own character appears in your own house".

Curatorial freedom had only come, however, after the death of her mother in law. Pointing at the presence of an image of Durga amongst the deities she said:

> My mother in law was very pious. There were many laws when she was alive. No photographs in the puja room. Even she did not approve of me putting Durga in the puja room. They are strongly Shaivite. But someone gave me Durga, a good friend. If someone gives it with love and devotion, why should I not put it there? So I was pragmatic, and I put it there.

Yet even after her mother in law's death, she felt constrained. She did not allow herself to place the image that was dearest to her, a photograph of the Mother, amongst the murtis in the Puja room: "Not Mother's image though, that would hurt her. People have views on her. They say the [status of deity] was given to the wrong person. There is too much controversy [...].[13] But The Mother is my favourite. It is also pragmatism, to have it in my bedroom. When I wake up I pray, first to the Mother."[14]

Tamana recalled with much enthusiasm how the photograph has come in her possession, and the Mother had "called her" through the artefact:

> I'll tell you how I became a devotee of the Arvind Ashram in Pondicherry. Someone wanted to sell antiques, and me to appraise them [...]. I was afraid to go alone, so I took a friend, a bachelor, 65 years old and a true devotee [of the Mother]. It was a large collection, thirteen sets of silver plates, and they were all sold. I did not take any [commission] because the sellers donated all the money to the Ashram, and I thought, 'that is the least I can do for the Mother'. After some time, [my friend] visited me with three wishes from the Mother. One wish was to give her photograph to me to take it when going on a trip. I took it when I went on a business visit to Andra Pradesh, and kept it in my purse. At the first stop we had to cross a river by boat. I was the last to get on the boat, slipped and fell down in the river. I was shocked, but it wasn't deep. As I fell a flash of the Mother came in my mind. It came in my vision, I don't know. I was wet, and it made me feel all rejuvenated, I climbed 25 steps and felt really comfortable. This feeling continued four, five days during the trip. I had no injury from the fall. I felt, 'Mother is pulling me towards her'. After that experience, I go once a year to the Ashram. I go in the morning, back in the evening. There are two birthdays they celebrate. We just sit in silence and meditate; they open up the room to the public. It is a special day, and you get the Mother's blessing and a pamphlet.

"The Mother" was the first Westerner to become an India-based Guru. She has been worshipped as a reincarnation of the Divine Mother since the nineteen twenties. Born in 1878 in France as Mirra Alfassa to an Egyptian mother and a Turkish father, she studied occultism in Algeria and worked with spiritual seekers in France, before moving to India where she became the spiritual companion of Sri Aurobindo. The latter, born in Calcutta in 1872, had been educated in Britain. Returning to India, he became political activist in the Swadeshi movement and then developed a yoga-based spiritual philosophy, setting up an ashram in

---

13 A Muslim research participant told me: "My [Muslim] niece is married to a Bengali. She is a believer in the Mother. When you come into the apartment, the first thing you see is a large portrait of the Mother. Her own mother was really upset. In our community people have large portraits of Moulana Mohamed Burhanullin. Her mother was shocked that it wasn't there".

14 Sri Aurobindo Ashram Trust did not grant permission to print a photograph of The Mother in this book, but it can be found on their Website. URL: http://www.auroville.org/contents/533 (last accessed 12 May 2017).

Pondicherry. After his death in 1950, Alfassa continued his aiming for 'the manifestation of a mode of consciousness beyond mind, the 'Supramental'.[15] The ashram attracts both Indian and non-Indian seekers of spiritual truth. On the ashram's website, Sri Aurobindo is quoted claiming that "Divine Truth is greater than any religion or creed or scripture or idea or philosophy", which partly explains why many followers incorporate artefacts from different religions in their homes. The Guru also speaks to anxieties mentioned previously about the capitalist nourishment of consumer desires, especially in the context of neo-liberal economics. "The most vital issue of the age is whether the future progress of humanity is to be governed by the modern economic and materialistic mind of the West or by a nobler pragmatism guided, uplifted and enlightened by spiritual culture and knowledge".[16]

Having experienced a situation in which a photograph of the Mother had given her protection in a dangerous situation, and consequently regarding the Mother as an active manifestation of divine energy, Tamana aestheticised the picture as focal point of prayer and devotion. Defining herself as liberal Hindu, she combined practices of meditation and devotion to the Mother with religious practices in the Puja room. Interestingly, it was a cheap, mass-produced photograph that evoked the strongest sense of spiritual engagement in her.

6 Art (History) as Space of Freedom

The next example illustrates how a female academic of Muslim Shi'ite background also used the home space to negotiate a sense of individual freedom, performing a sense of self that was unconstrained by religious orthodoxy. The collection in her house included works and reproductions of contemporary Indian and European art, religious artefacts and souvenirs, and crafts bought during her extensive travels.

---

15 "The full expression of this consciousness on earth would result not only in a new species, as far beyond the human, as human race is beyond the animals, but also in a modification of the whole terrestrial creation, even more complete than the change brought about by the entrance on the world scene of the human race. Between humanity and the fully Supramental species there would have to be one or several transitional steps, represented by transitional beings, born in the human way, but able to contact and express the higher consciousness. These transitional beings would prepare the way for the advent of the Supramental Race by establishing suitable conditions" (http://www.auroville.org/contents/533, last accessed 10 January 2015).
16 See http://www.aurobindo.net/ (last accessed 10 January 2015)

Figure 6: Ashrafi's lounge. Photograph by the author, 2012.

I first met Ashrafi Bhagat (real name) in 2011 at Stella Maris College, an autonomous Catholic institution of higher education for women, affiliated with the
University of Madras. She had taught History of Art at the College since 1977
and was about to retire from her position as Head of the Department. She had
written extensively about the Madras Movement, a group of artists who had
founded Cholamandal art village in the 1960s. Having stayed in the village for
a few weeks during my fieldwork in 2011, I set out to interview her about the
Movement. When I found out that she had numerous art works displayed in
her own home, I asked her if I could photograph and interview her about her
collection.

Her house was situated in a relatively affluent part of Chennai. Sitting down
in the lounge with a cup of tea, I asked her to comment on the artefacts and pictures on display. Tellingly, projecting herself as an open-minded person, she
began talking about the range of objects "from different religions" that she
had collected over the years. "I have a variety of artefacts, things from different
religions. Christian, Hindu, Quran texts; I like them because of their aesthetic appeal". Pointing at a Korean pot on the table, she added, "I like it because of its
form; it's meant as an incense burner but I don't use it like that. I am fascinated
by the shape".

Her emphasis on form partly arose from her visual training as art historian,
having learnt to look intensely at artefacts, and describe and compare their formal features. This mode of sensorial perception influenced her value judgements

of the objects in her home. Her training at the Department of Art History and Aesthetics at the University of Baroda in Gujarat had exposed her to established artistic styles from around the world. Reproductions of conventional art history pieces, such as a Mondrian and a Vermeer, were displayed in the dining room and the kitchen areas.

In her statement about the Korean incense burner she downplayed its ritual meaning, and instead, framed it as object with an "appealing design". As became apparent when we walked through her house and she further explained why she valued other items in her collection, she projected herself as a person who admired artefacts because of their formal qualities and the skill with which they had been made. This freed her from what she saw as the burden of prescribed religious meaning. "I am not religious; I am philosophical, very spiritual", she commented several times. She explained that she did not accept strict behavioural guidelines given by any religious institution, but relied on her own judgements to decide how to shape her personal faith. Raised in a middle class Islamic Si'ite famly, also known as Bohras [17] she indicated that she had always been a rebel: "I never went to the mosque or the community hall. I have faith, but I am not religious. I don't read the Quran or pray five times a day but I believe in living a life of goodness, in helping people, in integrity".

She experienced art history as a liberating profession that had safeguarded her from having to commit to a specific religious way of sensorial engagement. "For my art history study I explored many religions. Christianity, Islam, Sikhism, Hinduism, and the principle values are all the same". She has married into a Muslim family that accepted her openness. "I am blessed with my family-in-

---

17 In 2015, when I asked her for some more information about her family background, she wrote, "I belong to a sect of Islamic shia's known as the Ismaili Mushtalian – Tayebi dawood Bohras. The word Bohra comes from the Gujarati [which is my mother tongue] word Voharas meaning traders. My grandfather and his father came from a family of agriculturalists from a place called Dhanali in Gujarat and hence the family name of Dhanaliwalla from my father's side. My paternal grandfathers name was Gulamali Abdulhusein Dhanaliwala. Before being agriculturalists his forefathers were courtiers in the court of Maratha rulers in Gujarat and Rajasthan. My grandfather came to Madras [Chennai] soon after the First World War and started his life as a office boy doing errands in a company which sold hardware goods as pipes, valves etc. Around 1925 or so he started his own business and the company he established was after his own name which still continues with my brother who is doing business on the same premises which he built in 1935. My grandfather's family are the descendents of the father of Moulana Hakim ud din whose name was Bawa Mulla Khan. Both father and son were extremely pious and had led a simple life. Hakimuddin's Rauza or mausoleum today in Burhanpur in Maharashtra State is attracting Bohra pilgrims and also from many other religions particularly the locals in the region because of his powers of performing healing miracles and many others".

law and my husband who are very open-minded", she said, "The freedom gives me space to expand and progress".

We stopped in front of three pictures displayed near to each other and she indicated that these were 'Ganesh, Jesus and verses of the Quran' (see Figure 7 and 8).

Figure 7 and 8: 'The Prophet' (by Emil Nolde), Ganesh, a Zebra and (on the wall opposite) verses of the Quran displayed in Ashrafi's house, Photo by the author, 2012.

I asked her why exactly she had decided to hang them next to each other. The unlikely combination was clearly meant to provoke a reaction. "People say, 'you're crazy, putting Ganesh next to Jesus and Qur'an verses'", she explained with a twinkle in her eye. She acknowledged that Islam forbids the portrayal of elephants and that Muslims are generally only allowed to depict flowers and certain birds. "But it is all of nature!" she exclaimed. "Many in Chennai do not understand it". Personally, she felt that she could establish a visual relationship with all elements of nature, not only directly, by being in nature, but also indirectly, through visual engagement with representations of nature in all its diversity. The pictures, aestheticized as signifiers of free curatorship, thus helped her to position herself as open-minded Muslim intellectual. I later found out that the 'Jesus' image was, in fact, a reproduction of 'The Prophet' by Emil Nolde. The fact that she had mistaken a prophet from the Hebrew Bible for Jesus was, in this context, irrelevant. What mattered was her proclaimed interest in all kinds of religious imagery. She emphasised that her interest in the image of Ganesha was informed by its form, she did not regard him as an active deity: "I do not believe in religion. I do not worship Ganesha. What matters is the form. Elephants are beautiful".[18]

---

18 Unlike Zayna, she refrained from performing Hindu-inspired rituals in front of Ganesh. Yet like Zayna, she used the term "vibration" to refer to divine manifestations of positive creative power. Commenting on the sound of her Swiss cuckoo clock, she said that, "When a bell

She contrasted the relatively strict Islamic rules concerning visual representation with what she saw as the "flexibility" of Hinduism,[19] and noted that in numerous historical periods, the boundaries between Islam and Hinduism had
been blurred by mutual stylistic influence. When I asked how her friends and relatives reacted to her appropriation of images from different religions she said,
"Some people don't accept it; they see it as a potpourri of religions. But to me
it is like a liberation, freedom. I am like a bird flying!" "To insist on specific
forms is wrong", she said, "Your faith is more important". To her faith, the
Saint Dargah-e-Hakimi more was of major importance.[20] She explained, "I
have faith in a saint in a tomb in Maharastra, in Burhanpor. For me he works
miracles. He is the saint of our community, middle class Islamic Si'ite, Bohras".
She added

> You get your values from a young age. But if religion is too much imposed it is not good. My
> mother was very religious. She taught me, it was a first step, to pray to the saint. Imbibed
> from my mother, that's how I built up the faith. It drives away problems. I offer money and
> people who travel there put it for me in a box. It is utilised for schools, poor families, it
> feeds the people. I feel more enriched because of it. You know somehow in whose shadow
> you walk. I have a one-to-one relationship with Saint Dargah-e-Hakimi. When in trouble,
> you have a hand guiding you.

Tellingly, she did not have any visual references to the Saint or his shrine (*rauza*)
in her house.

> I do not find it necessary to have such memorabilia in my home. For me he remains a spi-
> ritual guide and he gives me solutions or answers to my problems and difficulties. I am
> deeply intuitive and in my difficult moments I talk to him and there are ways and means
> [as the striking of the cuckoo clock] by which he offers answers.

Visiting her sister's house a week later, I realised the extent of Ashrafi's rebel-
lion. She had already told me that in her middle class Bhora community, people
normally displayed large portraits of their spiritual and religious head of the

---

rings, it sends vibration. I am making a connection with someone. Always when the cuckoo
clock rings something positive is confirmed. At that moment the clock says 'cuckoo'!"

19 "I love Hindu philosophy", she said, "it is a way of life, it is very flexible; it is about being
happy with yourself".

20 Saiyedi Abdul Qadir Hakimuddin (1665–1730 AD) is the holy saint who is buried in Burhanpur, India. He was a man of literature and wrote in Urdu, Sanskrit, Persian and Arabic. He translated several Sanskrit texts into Arabic in a book called Qalila Wadhima. His grave is visited by
pilgrims from all over the world. The tomb complex Dargah-e-Hakimi includes mosques, gardens, and international class accommodation facilities for visitors.

community, Moulana Mohamed Burhanuddin, on their walls.[21] In her sister's home his portrait was displayed in every room. Other decorations were sparse; they consisted of mostly oriental rugs, flower embroidered pillowcases, and a collection of glass perfume bottles. Ashrafi had only two small portraits of Burhanuddin in her house, and she admitted that this was most of all to please her mother. Otherwise, her belief in the formal quality and beauty of art and craft allowed her to freely interpret material objects, detaching them from religious meanings that she found oppressive. The collection of artefacts in her house, in other words, helped her to project the cosmopolitan mind-set of a liberal, cultured world citizen (see Figure 6).

7 Conclusion

The analysis examined how engagements with specific artefacts in different home environments in Chennai shaped their owners' performance of religious, spiritual and other subjectivities. It shed light on the ways in which the appropriated artefacts gained value, meaning and appeal in partly overlapping worlds of art, religion and politics, linking the spatial environment of the home to wider social and political fields. The study demonstrated how, for three wealthy families living in prosperous neighbourhoods in Chennai, the artefacts did not only symbolise and reinforce their socio-economic status and mediate personally felt experiences of religiosity and spirituality, but also allowed for critical reflections on various topical societal issues, including Tamil Nadu's heritage politics, the rise of Hindu and Muslim fundamentalism, and the impact of globalisation and social change on the moral outlook of the younger generation.

The ethnographic cases drew particular attention to the ways in which artefacts were drawn into, and pushed out of religious spheres of mediation, demonstrating that "religions are not objectified entities but simply dimensions of ways of life" and that "[s]yncretism, transformation and pluralism are all more likely responses" (Lambek 2008, 11). The three women expressed different views on the relationship between formal, interpretational and affective aspects of their collections. For Ashrafi, artefacts could be purely admired for their formal qualities, and this freed them from meanings and impact intended by their

---

21 She explained in January 2015 by email that "Moulana Burhanuddin is the 52nd representative of Imam Tayeb who is not visible to us but will make his appearance on the day of judgement. M. Burhanuddin is our spiritual and religious head and the entire Dawoodi Bohra community [to which I belong] follows him. Incidentally he passed away on 16th January in 2014. So we have the 53rd representative Mufaddal Saifuddin who will perform the same role".

earlier producers and users. This meant that both religious and non-religious artefacts could be aestheticized as items of art historical value, and thus appreciated as art. For her, appreciation of specific artefacts did neither evoke nor endanger religious sensibilities. She experienced faith as personal inner dialogue, a mental and affective process that was not stimulated by visually perceived forms. She claimed that artefactual form was irrelevant for her spiritual engagement, and on that basis, she strongly rejected stringent Muslim restrictions to visual representation.

Zayna also rejected such restrictions. Having married into a Hindu family, she was more directly exposed to domestic Hindu rituals than Ashrafi, and influenced by the idea that material forms of god images can become charged with divine power through ritual engagement. This explains why the Tanjore piece in her home was re-aestheticised as sacred object of affective attention, and why she began to acknowledge its spiritual potential. Its form, in other words, could not be fully uncoupled from its religious content and its ability to evoke a 'corpothetic' mode of seeing. This did not mean that the artefact demanded narrowly prescribed religious attention, but rather, that appropriate respect should be shown. Importantly, her new spiritual engagement with the Tanjore piece did not undermine her ability to also artistically appreciate it as a fine piece of Indian heritage.

Born into a devotional Hindu family, Tamana had learnt to access divine energy through sensorial interaction with god images in Hindu temples and home shrines. Through her interest in antiques, she had however also gained vast knowledge of the formal characteristics of historical pieces. As antique dealer, she was hyper-sensitised to the historicity of form, which meant that many religious artefacts were too new or fake to have any appeal to her. What also counted was availability; the less obtainable a work, the stronger its ability to impress her and her customers. By contrast, the availability of form was irrelevant to Tamana's religious life. The artefact that she valued most as object of spiritual engagement was a widely circulating and reproduced photograph of the Mother.

The perspective of aestheticisation did not only untangle the shifting significance and appeal of specific material forms, it also showed how objects became part of different performances of self, drawn into overlapping worlds of art, politics and religion. Particular instances of aestheticisation were clearly shaped by specific local, translocal and/or transnational forces through which certain worldviews and hegemonies were promoted, reinforced, or resisted.[22]

---

22 With regard to religious imagery, Meyer (2012, 29–30) has argued that this process "is not just limited to linking people with a 'beyond', but also calls forth modes of conduct and an

In all three cases, what dominated was a personally felt need to appropriate artefacts and artefact-focused behaviour in a syncretic manner, reflecting an individualistic cosmopolitan worldview. The rejection of religious orthodoxy by the three women must be understood in the light of increasing Hindu-Muslim tensions India and beyond.

Bibliography

Bruland, Stine. 2016. "'The Eye Likes It'. National Identity and the Aesthetics of Attraction Amongst Sri Lankan Tamil Catholics and Hindus." In *Creativity in Transition. Politics and Aesthetics of Cultural Production Across the Globe*, edited by Maruška Svašek and Birgit Meyer, 245–266. Oxford: Berghahn.

Classen, Constance. 1997. "Foundations for an Anthropology of the Senses." *International Social Science Journal*, 49/153: 401–412.

Desai, Amit. 2016. "Art and the Making of the Creative City of Chennai, India." In *Creativity in Transition. Politics and Aesthetics of Cultural Production Across the Globe*, edited by Maruška Svašek and Birgit Meyer, 107–130. Oxford: Berghahn.

Eck, Diana L. 1998. *Darśśan*. New York: Columbia University Press.

Grassini, Cristina. 2007. *Skilled Visions. Between Apprenticeship and Standards*. Oxford: Berghahn.

Hancock, Mary. 2008. *The Politics of Heritage from Madras to Chennai*. Bloomington: Indiana University Press.

Howes, David. 2004. *Empire of the Senses: The Sensual Culture Reader*. Oxford: Berg.

—— 2003. *Sensual Relations: Engaging the Senses in Culture and Social Theory*. Ann Arbor: University of Michigan Press.

Huyler, Stephen P. 1999. *Meeting God: Elements of Hindu Devotion*. New Haven: Yale University Press.

Lambek, Michael. 2008. *A Reader in the Anthropology of Religion*. Oxford: Blackwell.

Meyer, Birgit 2008. "Religious Sensations: Why Media, Aesthetics and Power Matter in the Study of Contemporary Religion." In *Religion: Beyond a Concept*, edited by Hent de Vries, 704–723. New York: Fordham University Press.

—— 2012. *Mediation and the Genesis of Presence. Towards a Material Approach to Religion*. Utrecht: Universiteit Utrecht.

Shreen, Kala. 2016. "The Social Life of Kottan Baskets. Craft Production, Consumption and Circulation in Tamil Nadu, India." In *Creativity in Transition. Politics and Aesthetics of Cultural Production Across the Globe*, edited by Maruška Svašek and Birgit Meyer, 86–106. Oxford: Berghahn.

Svašek, Maruška. 2007. *Anthropology, Art and Cultural Production*. London: Pluto.

—— 2012, ed. *Moving Subjects, Moving Objects: Transnationalism, Cultural Production and Emotions*. Oxford: Berghahn.

---

ethos of how to act in the world [...]. The shared partaking in religious mediation sustains collective identities [as Durkheim posits] within a particular material environment on the level of the household, religious space, the neighbourhood, the city, or even a much larger context".

—— 2016. "Undoing Absence Through Things. Creative Appropriation and Affective Engagement in an Indian Transnational Setting." In *Creativity in Transition. Politics and Aesthetics of Cultural Production Across the Globe*, edited by Maruška Svašek and Birgit Meyer, 218–244. Oxford: Berghahn.

Stoller, Paul. 1989. *The Taste of Ethnographic Things: The Senses in Anthropology.* Philadelphia: University of Pennsylvania Press.

Venkatachalapathy, A.R. 2013. "The Changing Face of Tamil Nadu's Politics." *The Hindu,* August 5.

Verrips, Jojada. 2005. "Aisthesis & An-Aesthesia." In *Off the Edge: Experiments in Cultural Analysis*, edited by Orvar Löfgren and Richard R. Wilk, 29–36. Lund: Museum of Tusculanum Press.

2012. "Timeline: Ayodhya holy site crisis." *BBC News*, December 6. URL: http://www.bbc.com/news/world-south-asia-11436552 (last accessed 1 October 2015)

Annette Wilke
Moving Religion by Sound: On the Effectiveness of the Nāda-Brahman in India and Modern Europe

This article deals with the exceptionally high valence of sound in Sanskrit Hinduism through the ages and the transference of culturally specific forms of sonic perception in India into modern European space. The prime focus is on the "Sonic Absolute" (Nāda-Brahman, lit. "Sound Brahman") which acquainted the aura of a hoary past in India and beyond, but was in fact "invented" by the musicologist Śārṅgadeva in the 13th century, and re-invented in modern Europe by the Jazz historian and New Age proponent Joachim Berendt. A major argument will be that the Nāda-Brahman or Nada Brahma of both the medieval Indian and modern Western musicians and spiritual seekers reflects the spread and conversion of religious ideas by means of a tangible holistic symbol that appeals to the senses. The metaphysical Nāda-Brahman appears embodied in audible sound—from Rāga music and devotional Bhajan song to Jazz, pop, minimal music, and even the song of dolphins in Berendt's Nada Brahma version. In the history of religion in India and modern Europe, the Nāda-Brahman was a connective concept that merged profane and sacred spaces, individual practice and cultural ideologies. Despite the different cultural coding, it crossed cultural boundaries thanks to its sensory-aesthetic properties and attributions. Berendt's representation of Indian music's impact on modern Western music and spirituality is of particular interest in this respect.

Before discussing Śārṅgadeva's Nāda-Brahman and Berendt's New Age adaption, it is important to outline the cultural context in which the Nāda-Brahman emerged: Hindu India as a strong performance culture in which religious texts are embodied in the voice, and devotion in song and music, and where sound had distinct influence on *habitus* and world-view formation (more elaborately discussed in Wilke and Moebus 2011; Wilke 2013, 2014). It makes aware of the profound difference regarding the reception of language, texts and sounds compared with Berendt's immediate European background.

1. The Nāda Brahman in Context

In Indian studies of the past decades, awareness has grown about the great plurality of traditions which "hide" behind the summary term Hinduism and about

https://doi.org/10.1515/9783110461015-014

the Orientalist construction in unifying and essentialising this plurality and transforming Hinduism into a "book religion" akin to other world-religions—particularly Christianity. If we look at the Hindus' text reception across the manifold traditions, an interesting twist of this argument emerges. We will find the importance of sound instead of scripture, starting with the preference of the spoken and sounding word even after the introduction of writing across the manifold traditions in great cultural continuity until the present day. The amazing consistency of this social practice is a unifying bond among the highly pluralistic Hindu cultures. It cuts across traditions, historical changes, and even media transformations.

Hindu India is a pronounced performance culture, in which texts are recited, memorized, sung, ritualized, preached, danced, and staged. The high value of orality, for instance memorizing systems and face-to-face communication from teacher to student, has often been noticed, but it is necessary to be aware that sonality is equally important and has its own range of meaning and impact on perception. Texts in India are performed in a semi-musical or musically pleasing way, and also composed to be heard—often the authors were very sensitive about sonic patterns and also about emotive contents and the communication of moods. Texts are sound events, embodied in the voice and also received in a sensory-emotive way. The performative approach in which text, sound and ritual form a unity, created specific *habitus* forms, based on the inherent validity of sound as a medium of communication of its own. As readings are performances and texts aesthetic events, they are not only restricted to semantic information, but speak strongly to the senses, the body, and the emotions. Sacredness is not only found in words and phrases, but also in the text as a whole and its auditive dimension. Merely hearing a religious text is believed to be auspicious and purifying. Semantic meaning can fade completely to the background or be not even there at all in a normal, lexical sense. This is particularly true for the *mantras* (sacred formulas) and devotional music. Widely spread is the belief that *mantras* have intrinsic sacrality and power without the intention of the speaker and that music can communicate devotion better than any words and tune directly into divine. Acoustic piety plays a very dominant role in daily religeous life. We are dealing with a cultural framework where a word (*śabda*) was defined by meaning *and* by sound: a word is an acoustic reality to which meaning is attached.

The importance of sound and its perception has led to rites, models of cosmic order, and abstract formulas. Sound and language were objectified in powerful religious symbols, such as the goddess Speech (Vāc) in the late Ṛgveda, the goddess Sarasvatī in classical Hinduism who is the gentle goddess of language, music and wisdom, or the great Lord God Śiva who created the world by the sounds of his hand drum. The deities of the Tantra are purely sonic, i.e., *mantra* deities, and in tantric metaphysics sonic cosmogonies were developed. The ancient Śivaitic Āgamas had seen the first expression of creation in the context of their cosmogonic *mantra* speculations in vibrant sound *(nāda)*. Sound is conceived as more basic than either mind or matter and as existing prior to them. Primeval cosmic sound pervades the universe and is a divine substance. Such ideas inspired the musicians' Nāda-Brahman, the "Sonic Absolute" pervading all existence, which is audible in music. It is a highly aesthetic symbol, intrinsically related to the senses and emotions, and blending profane and sacred world-views in the fundamental thesis that music is not only enjoyable to anybody, but also a direct way to Brahman experience, ultimate unity and bliss.

This article concentrates on the first emergence of the term, where Nāda-Brahman appears embodied in music. Indian Rāga music is by its verbal root and very definition related to "colouring" *(rakti, rañjana)* and "mood" *(rasa)*, i. e., to expressing and evoking shades of feeling, aesthetic sentiment, and emotional absorption. However, music is naturally also related to mathematics, complex rhythms, counting and summing beats. This reveals yet another typical cultural pattern. It is important to be aware that fusion and immersion, or the emotional arousal attributed to music and the magical efficacy attributed to sacred formulas were not the only effects of a life-world based on sounds. Sonic awareness was as well akin to thinking in structures and training formal thought, as obvious already in the grammarian Pāṇini (5th century BC), the trendsetter of science in India. At the core of his grammar lie certain sound codes which re-arrange the Sanskrit alphabet. A structurally similar combination of abstraction and materialization is found in the Nāda-Brahman of the musicians.

The Nāda-Brahman is the last great transformation of the Brahman concept and its "re-invention" (Wilke and Moebus 2011, 847–856). This concept has been immensely influential in Indian religious history to denote ultimate Being and a soteriology of mystical fusion. In the Nāda-Brahman the attribute-less Brahman beyond name and form becomes audible in music and colored with emotion. The Nāda-Brahman's unique blend of metaphysics and sense perception/feeling, interior and exterior space, and profane and sacred world-view answers in a most straightforward way the question: What kind of world-view is created if the basis of daily experience is sonic?

2 Śārṅgadeva's Nāda-Brahman

Śārṅgadeva (13th century), who introduced the Nāda-Brahman, came from a scholarly family in Kashmir that had immigrated into the Deccan and filled various high offices at the court of the newly established Yadava dynasty. Śārṅgadeva was the finance minister, and also an (Ayurvedic) doctor, scholar and musicologist at the court. By his encyclopaedic music handbook *Sangīta-Ratnākara*, a veritable *magnum opus* in Indian music, Śārngadeva managed to make an unforgettable name for himself. It is a thoroughly technical work on music, but contains passages on the metaphysics and soteriological relevance of music in the introductory chapters. When in this context Śārngadeva coined the term Nāda-Brahman, he was able to follow on from an idea that at his time was already widespread. The Nāda (vibrating sound) as a religious category and cosmically powerful force was well known in Śaiva-tantric milieus and already the music handbook *Bṛhaddeśī* by Matanga (ca. 7th century) had introduced it into musical discourse. But it was Śārngadeva who fused it with the Brahman and declared the Nāda-Brahman as the actual foundation of music (song, instrumental music and dance).

In later Indian history, the Nāda-Brahman became related to the contemplation of sound and resonances. It took on strongly yogic, esoteric and occult—sometimes even therapeutic—associations, and became primarily a religious category. But this is not precisely what Śārngadeva understood by it. His Nāda-Brahman was related to audible music and particularly to song. Despite of using profusely religious vocabulary, his Nāda-Brahman is first of all related to the material world: the physical body, in which song arises, and the subtle body with its psycho-physical centers (*cakras*) which Śārngadeva relates to different feelings and moods. His anthropology and world-view also includes the inner self or Ātman which the Advaita-Vedānta speaks of being one with Brahman, the hightest bliss and omnipresent source of everything. By relating the musical *nāda* ("sound") to the Brahman, Śārngadeva transforms the abstract (non-theist) Brahman into a tangible, audible substance that can be experienced by the senses—non-dual existence, consciousness, and bliss absolute can be experienced in music.

Three propositions in the introductory part of the *Sangīta-Ratnākara* are of particular interest. They develop the Nāda-Brahman concept, in which Śārngadeva makes use of nearly all discourses of this time relating to sound, language, and religion to give music a metaphysical base:

1.) Music, particularly song (*gītam*), is something divine that brings delight to everybody. As embodiment of the primordial cosmic *nāda,* music is an alloform of Śiva (SaGiRa 1.1.1). This first thesis—which could be summarized as "God is sound and Sound is god"—appears right in the initial (auspicious) verse of the work. It is indirectly communicated by the artful poetic *śleṣa* style of double coding: the verse can be read to relate to the supreme god Śiva, and also to relate to song.

2.) Listening to music is an easy and enjoyable yoga and even better, as music is audible unlike the interior soundscapes of the yogis. It appeals to feeling and is emotionally pleasing in contrast to the dry yogic contemplation, and it is able to lead directly into Brahman experience and liberation without the efforts connected with yoga (SaGiRa 1.2.164–167). This second thesis states that music is a yoga for everybody, as it easily leads to absorption and happiness. It is connected with the senses and emotion, and provides both worldly enjoyment and final liberation. The original verses use the term 'rakti', "triggering feelings", which hints to the key term 'rāga' in musicology (meaning "melody model" or melodic "mode", but also "shades of colour"). According to the classical definition a Rāga denotes a tone structure that "colours the mind", i.e., creates feelings *(rañjana)*. Deliverance in the form of music is at the same time emotionally pleasing and great fun, so that people will simply use it for its own sake, even if they do not wish to be delivered.

3.) The whole world is based on sound (SaGiRa 1.2.2)—the world is sound, as the divine source is sound (SaGiRa 1.3.1–2). This third proposition should be looked at more closely, as the term 'Nāda-Brahman' occurs here for the first time in Indian history. It is prepared by a linguistic argument: "Sound *(nāda)* manifests in the phonemes (of the alphabet), letters constitute the word, and words make a sentence. Thus, the entire business of life *(vyvahāra)* is carried on, through language. Therefore the entire world *(jagat)* is based on sound/ Nāda" (SaGiRa 1.2.2).

In the world of the musicians language becomes a subform of expressive sound in which the whole world is founded. The actual two verses on the Nāda-Brahman transpose this idea to metaphysics by compact paraphrases of several Indian language and sound discourses:

> "The consciousness *(caitanya)* of all living beings, which turns itself by itself into the world *(vivṛta)*, is the 'Sound-Brahman' *(nāda-brahman)*. In it we invoke (√upa-as) bliss, the 'One without a Second'. If we invoke sound, we also invoke without doubt [the great cosmic gods] Brahmā, Viṣṇu, and Śiva, because they are nothing other than [sound]" (SaGiRa I.3.1–2, translated by Wilke and Moebus 2011, 837).

The first verse (SaGiRa 1.3.1) alludes not only to the advaita-vedāntic Brahman—the Absolute Being who is the material and causal basis of the world and whose innate nature is pure existence-consciousness-bliss and one's own self. It alludes also to the Brahman conception of the linguist philosopher Bhartṛhari (5th century), according to whom our whole perception is based on language and ultimately founded in a universal linguistic principle or "Word-Consciousness", also called "Word-Brahman" (śabda-tattva, śabda-brahman) that forms a global form of sense and meaning going beyond single words and things. According to

Bhartṛhari, the whole world is a metamorphosis of this single language principle or Word-Brahman (Śabda-Brahman), which is the common conscious ground of all human beings. Śārṅgadeva's introduction of the Nāda-Brahman is directly imported from the Bhartṛhari school even in its terminology—the consciousness of all beings transforming itself into the world *(caitanyam sarvabhūtanāṃ viv-ṛtaṃ jagadātmanā)*, but with one decisive difference: instead of Bhartrhari's Śabda-Brahman ("Word-Brahman") there appears here the Nāda-Brahman ("Sound-Brahman"). We find a move from the mental plane of an abstract language principle and pure consciousness to a more physical substance—acoustic sound (inhering in language and music). This Sonic Absolute is more narrowly defined by the upaniṣadic-vedāntic expression "One without a Second" and "bliss". The Nāda-Brahman is non-dual world consciousness and bliss, in which God, the world and the individuals cannot be differentiated and separated.

The second verse (SaGiRa 1.3.2) follows on from the tantric interpretation of sound and paraphrases the early musicologist Mataṅga whose *Bṛhaddeśī* already postulated "the world is sound" *(nadātmakaṃ jagat)*—without, however, using the term Nāda-Brahman: "Without sound there is no song, no tones, no dance. Therefore this whole world *(jagat)* is in its nature sound.[1] [The God] Brahmā is a form of sound, Viṣṇu (here: Janārdana) is a form of sound, the transcendental power *(Parā Śakti)* is a form of sound and the great God (Maheśvara, i.e. Śiva) is a form of sound" *(Bṛhaddeśi 1.18–19, translated by Wilke and Moebus 2011, 842).

Śārṅgadeva thus immediately follows on Mataṅga. That the great gods are sound, means nothing other than that all deities have their own *mantras* and in the tantric view are actually identical to the *mantras*. Mataṅga's and Śārṅgadeva's sonic vision of the whole of reality includes both the profane and sacred sphere.

The conclusion of these statements is far-reaching: music (the epitome of sound) is a physical expression of the Brahman, and performing and hearing song and Rāga music leads directly to sensing and experiencing the soul of the world and cosmic unity. This soul is not an abstract ultimate being (as in the Vedānta or Bhartṛhari), but full of emotional colors and aesthetic moods. Despite Śārṅgadeva's otherwise very rationalistic and down-to-earth approach to music, he understood the Nāda-Brahman in quite a substantial way: as a "mythical substance" (Hübner 1985, 110, 174) that can be felt and experienced by the senses. In contrast, Śārṅgadeva's most important commentators Siṃhabhūpāla

---

[1] This proposition of extending music is prepared in *Bṛhaddeśi* 1.12.

(ca. 1330) and Kallinātha (ca. 1430) declare that the verses are not meant literally. Instead, sound is a metaphor for Brahman: contemplation of sound leads to the Brahman, but sound is not Brahman (Wilke and Moebus 2011, 844–845). However, it was more the substantial aspect that became immensely powerful in the world of musicians and in popular discourse. In keeping with Śārṅgadeva, also Tyāgarāja (1767–1847), the most famous of the carnatic musician-composers, states: "The joy of music is itself the bliss of Brahman that Vedānta speaks of" (translated by Raghavan 1994, 224).

Śārṅgadeva's introduction of the Nāda-Brahman allowed music to gain a pronouncedly cosmic dimension and be viewed as a divine service and spiritual exercise of self-cultivation. The highly individualized and modal character of Indian Rāga-music helped this aim. It is rich in overtone and based on a fundamental 'home note' and a skeleton of pitch and rhythm, the "mood" of which must be "awakened" by the musician's 'feeling' and improvising skills. Although classical Rāga music as a highly sophisticate art form was a culture of the courts until modern times, the range of music was much wider, pervading all daily activity and religious life. Music became a very powerful and central religious media in the popular *bhakti* religiosity ("loving devotion") and its manifold traditions which made their way to religious mainstream from the 9th to 13th centuries. The Nāda-Brahman concept provided both profane and courtly music a sacred (not necessarily religious) foundation and a reflexive basis for devotional music and *bhajan* singing, where it became a code-word for devotional fusion.

3 Berendt's Nada Brahma

Contemporary cultural boundaries have become so fluid that concepts can stream unimpeded from one culture to another—where it seems they sometimes even solve problems within the new host culture, at least for some of the recipients. This was definitely the idea of the jazz historian, record producer and New Age-proponent Joachim-Ernst Berendt in his postulate of a new holistic world interpretation that he popularized in his bestseller *The World Is Sound: Nada Brahma* (German 1983, Engl. [1987] 1991). He took up the Indian Nāda-Brahman concept and declared it to be a key to a "New Consciousness" (a "paradigm shift" or "New Age"), while at the same time referring to many ancient myths around the world: "Many of the world's cultures have passed down sagas and myths, legends and tales in which the world has its origin in sound" (Berendt 1991, 174).

Berendt discovered in the Nāda-Brahman a key to a new metaphysics of music, so powerful that it had the capacity to change the whole world—i.e., the supposedly spiritually impoverished Western world. In his *Nada Brahma*, which was based on his immensely popular radio discourses about "the temple of the ear", three major topics can be discerned: 1.) Berendt's cultural criticism of the Western "eye person", 2.) his New Age Nāda-Brahman, and 3.) his thesis of Indian music's impact on modern Western music history and spiritualization. Berendt himself was deeply impressed by Indian music and music making to which he ascribes an inherently spiritual attitude. His interest in India's music and the Nāda-Brahman was inspired by personal experiences and encounters with Indian musicians who came to the West. They apparently had a profound influence on his worldview, and he claimed, on the world-view of a whole generation of young musicians in the 1960s and 1970s.

3.1 Berendt's Cultural Criticism

Berendt wrote his book *Nada Brahma* especially for people in the West and associated with it a crisis diagnosis and a healing program critical of Western civilization. This cultural criticism was based on simplistic binary oppositions of East and West, ear and eye, holistic spirituality/emotional intelligence and destructive logocentrism. Berendt urged Western culture to change because it was in the process of destroying itself. He felt that only a fundamental shift in the manner of the "new consciousness" of networking prefigured in New-Age spirituality and in his generation of India-inspired musicians could avert disaster. Berendt's crisis diagnosis is that up to that time the eye was the predominant sense organ by the West, and the prevalent thought form was analytical thought.

> "The eyes are wonderful organs, but the better they are, the 'sharper' they are; 'sharpness' is a quality of knives and of cutting [...] The most admirable ideal of the 'eye-person' is to possess an 'eagle eye.' The eagle spots its prey, dives, and seizes it [...]" (Berendt 1991, 5)

Berendt thus associates the "eye person" exclusively with analytical dissection. This Aristotelian ideal, he says, has become an absolute in the age of the television and this reductionism has impoverished life in general: "Living *only* through the head has made our lives poorer" (Berendt 1991, 130). According to Berendt, this correlates directly with the shrivelling of the "most noble sense organ", the ear. People hardly "hear" anything anymore. The ear, holds Berendt, is not only a mathematical measuring instrument, but also allows sensory and emotional experience, and these two modes are dovetailed in hearing. So the ear transcends the fundamental dualism of the Western culture:

In addition to their measuring ability, there is their ability to sense. The most wonderful thing is how these two faculties are coupled together. In fact, it seems that in this coupling lies the greatest capacity of our ears: the ability to transfer, with unbelievable precision, mathematical quantities into sense perceptions, conscious into subconscious, measurable things into unmeasurable ones, abstract concepts into matters of soul—and vice versa, of course. (Berendt 1991, 136–137)

Berendt's central argument states that for precisely this reason the loss of the "capability to hear" is a grave one for the whole culture. What cannot be felt conjointly, cannot be thought of together either. Berendt's remedy is therefore to learn again to hear and listen as he had learned from Indian music and musicians: "The New Man will be a Listening Man—or will never be at all" (Berendt 1991, 7).

Berendt was inspired in this proposition by Ravi Shankar and other Indian musicians who came to the West in the 1960s and 1970s. He presents becoming acquainted with classical Indian modal music as a kind of revelation, and the practical instructions of the masters of Indian music, as an initiation into the new spiritual attitude of the "listening man", in which music and religion merge seamlessly. The Indian teachers determined the ideal attitude of a musician as follows: "*Nada Brahma*. Sound is god. Show that in your singing. Meditate on it. Cleanse your karma by it. Sing so that people will understand that, even if you haven't told them before. Sound is god, *Nada Brahma*" (Berendt 1991, 155, quoting Pandit Pran Nath).

3.2 Berendt's New Age Nada Brahma

On an optimistic note, Berendt believes that New Age change has already begun. To some extent he is trying to write it into existence with missionary zeal. Two main processes of change in the 20th century are particularly important for his argument: first, the sea-changes in modern physics brought about by Einstein, Niels Bohr and others, and second, the discovery of Eastern philosophy and Indian music. As with the pioneers of the New Age, it is no surprise that Berendt sees Eastern religion and modern sciences confirming each other: "In Hinduism, the cosmic dance of Shiva depicts the same concept of matter as found in certain aspects of the quantum and field theory in modern physics" (Berendt 1983, 169).[2]

---

2 "*[Es] wird dem Hindu durch den kosmischen Tanz des Gottes Shiva dieselbe Vorstellung von der Materie vermittelt, wie dem Physiker durch gewisse Aspekte der Quanten- und Feldtheorie.*" This statement was deleted in the English edition which, however, tellingly contains a foreword by Fritjof Capra.

Within this context the Nada Brahma concept gains importance. Berendt expresses the Hindu idea that fascinated him so much in these words: "Nada Brahman means not only: God, the Creator, is sound; but also (above all): Creation, the cosmos, the world, is sound. And: Sound is the world" (Berendt 1991, 18).

Therefore, this is not just about musicology but also about a world-view. Berendt based this world-interpretation on numerous areas of knowledge: ancient mythologies and cosmologies, modern physics, and also morphology, biology, crystallography and harmonics. No matter whether he speaks about religion, ancient music of the spheres, Indian music and *mantra* practice, quantum physics, research into the universe or protons, the behaviour of dolphins or crystals, there is always the same conclusion: the world is sound. For Berendt this was the key to a world-view that he described in terms such as "holistic", "networked", "feminine" (guided by emotional intelligence), "listening" and "spiritual".

For Berendt, music, spirituality and contemporary science were not three separate things, but intertwined with one another, and in his eyes this expressed the *kairos* of the time: "[...] something extraordinary has happened in the present generation during those same years when we became aware of the sound character of the universe, we also gained a new attitude toward music. We discovered (or re-discovered) kinds of music that correspond to the sound character of the universe in a most fascinating way" (Berendt 1991, 152).

As seen above, the sound character of the universe and the statement "the world is sound" was indeed already suggested by the Indian medieval thinker Śārṅgadeva's Nāda-Brahman. He had conceptualized music in the context of an all-pervading cosmic sound. However, the Indian Nāda-Brahman is ultimately only a formula and springboard for Berendt's intention to re-sacralise Western music and promote his New Age creed that the sound character of the universe was not Indian, but an original knowledge of humanity. His Nada Brahma metaphysics is a new "universal myth" about an age-old knowledge running through all the ancient cultures and religions and even through nature. Berendt offered "evidence" in many mythologies, from Inuit to Incas, and in the ancient Vedas, OM chanting, overtone music, the music of the spheres, singing dolphins, sounding crystals, and modern physics. No wonder that Berendt's re-invented Nada Brahma was apt to inspire all kinds of esoteric groups that centred on Nada-Yoga, Nada-therapy, etc.

3.3 Indian Music's Impact on Modern Western Music and Spirituality

Classical Indian music has little in common with classical Western music, but has some points of contact with jazz—owing to both the huge role played by improvisation and the emphasis of rhythm. However, the modal musician is by no means restricted to an absolute time system. The mode itself only determines relative time quantities. Therefore, a feeling of eternity surrounds modal music. This may have been a major reason why this music was felt to be "more peaceful and less nervous" and also to be naturally "spiritual" by people like Berendt (1991, 159) and many jazz and pop musicians who became acquainted with Indian music in the 1960s.[3] For a while it became the fashion to adapt to this style.

Berendt's argument was that modal music actually created a religious interest. The argument is interesting in terms of religious aesthetics, and cannot be rejected out of hand. From John Coltrane to John McLaughlin religion has had its standing boosted thanks to music. Indian music had at least a partial share in this. It was a different symbolic form than the familiar harmonies, and created different experience purely through aesthetic sensory aspects—which many associated with religion or spirituality (see below). Despite the great wealth of ornamentation, rhythmic and melodic diversity, and lively movement, Rāgas make an impression of something that rests within itself. Berendt saw "experiencing oneness" and "dissolution of time" as the most significant characteristics of modal music, and correlated this immediately with a nondual meditation experience:

> The music we are talking about here—classical Indian music, the music of John Coltrane and his musical heirs in jazz and rock, minimal music and the best of the new meditation music—points toward an experience that in the eastern tradition is referred to as 'becoming one'. To be sure, this music alone cannot bring about such 'at-one-ment'. No music can do that. Only years of meditation can do it. But this music paves the way [...] It is a kind of music in which time is dissolved in a manner beyond words. (Berendt 1991, 168)

This tangible, new, religion-friendly quality attributed to modal music probably explains a large part of the euphoria with which Indian music was received at that time. According to Berendt, the expressive quality of modal music is automatically tied to a different attitude in music-making and hearing, which he calls "spiritual". Modal playing of music provided the musicians with the possibility of dealing with religious feelings in a very personal form and adopting explicitly spiritual attitudes, without having to enter into institutional and dogmatic ties. For example, the tenor saxophonist Nathan Davis notes: "Playing modally has to do with spirituality. What we really mean by spirituality is religiousness.

---

3 Classical South Indian music is in fact also greatly pervaded by religious topics and the *śānta-rasa* "peaceful mood". Classical North Indian music on the other hand is often purely secular, above all in the form of love-related topics and the *rasa* of the "erotic mood".

Only we don't use that word, because we don't mean what the Christian world means by religiousness" (quoted in Berendt 1991, 160).

Berendt regarded the re-modalization of music as indicative of a new spiritual interest and religion-producing process. In his book he was in fact trying to describe the artistic self-awareness and life-feeling of a whole generation of jazz musicians, starting with John Coltrane in the 1960s (Berendt 1991, 152–172, 200 – 227). Jazz, according to Berendt, was always predestined for literally "playing off" the personal, spontaneous and individual against the dominating "brainy", mechanistic world-view. Jazz musicians play what they feel and experience, each having his 'own sound' (Berendt 1991, 97–98, 128–130, 202–203). This music just "happens" here and "NOW" (Berendt 1991, 170). According to Berendt this is precisely what made the jazz musicians especially receptive to the Indian Nāda. He believed modal music was inevitably and almost necessarily bound into a different mental attitude and, conversely, that the new spiritual thinking automatically demanded the modal style of playing.

According to Berendt, when John Coltrane (d. 1967) issued the record "Love Supreme" (1965) he was the first musician to introduce spirituality. Nowadays, Berendt states in the 1980s, this is no longer felt to be strange and inappropriate, whereas it was previously extremely unusual in jazz music (apart from gospel singing in churches). The only topics were love, passion, and longing, i.e., the standard topics of music for dancing and entertainment. Coltrane, however, wrote the following on his record cover: "Words, sounds, speech, men, memory, thoughts, fears, emotions—time—all related [...] all made from one [...] all made in one. Blessed be his name. Thought waves—heat waves—all vibrations—all paths lead to God. Thank you God".

On the same cover Coltrane documents an awakening experience in the year 1957, which he had now decided to stand by. The record was issued in the same year (1965) in which Coltrane discovered that the improvisation principle in Indian music was ideal for jazz. According to Berendt, Coltrane did most of the bridge-building between jazz and India, whereby this bridge was initially rather more based on Indian spirituality than on Indian music and, he claimed, it was also thanks to Coltrane that the aspect of spirituality spread far beyond the world of jazz (Berendt 1991, 206–207).

If Coltrane's interest in India was rather rudimentary, there were an increasing number of musicians who consciously aspired to adopt Indian spirituality— or what one imagined as Indian spirituality. India was the great role-model for making, hearing and experiencing music based on a meditative attitude. Don Cherry, for instance, studied with a master of Indian singing and became increasingly centred on India. At the end of the 1960s India was all the fashion. The Beatles became interested in TM, George Harrison learned some Indian music and even the Rolling Stones made an excursion into India by using a Sitar in "Paint it Black". This fashion passed relatively quickly, but for many musicians outside of the popular mainstream India remained a permanent force—less in relation to the musical than to the spiritual. The guitarist John McLaughlin and his group "Shakti" were real India maniacs—in fact McLaughlin himself was the only Western musician in the band. The alto saxophonist Charlie Mariano studied the local wind instrument Nadaswaram in a small village in Southern India, living without electricity and other blessings of modern civilization. Later he also played the Nadaswaram during his jazz performances. He explained the reason behind his enthusiasm for India as follows: "You know, I have observed that your jazz gets better when you have mastered Indian music. Not only in my Indian pieces, but also in others which have nothing to do with India. You simply go deeper. You say more. And what you play has more meaning" (quoted in Berendt 1991, 212).

With the opening up to India in this way, and with India as a keyword for spirituality, these ideas continued and in some cases became even stronger when the musical fashion changed (Berendt 1983, 352–371). From Woodstock to the new world music, the spiritualization and cosmopolization of music turned into a new 'creed' of perceiving music as a universal language of humanity (Berendt 1991, 212–213).

So what was still revolutionary at the time of John Coltrane in the 1960s had already become normal less than twenty years later. In 1983 Berendt took great delight in pointing out the existence of a "type of musician of which fifteen years ago there only existed a few individuals at most and of which today there are thousands" (Berendt 1983, 337). The composer Peter Michael Hamel, who was trained in classical music and at that time was strongly influenced by Indian music, noted in this epoch of the "New Consciousness":

> At present there is a broad, strong urge to open up again those clogged walls of music which alone can reveal the way to a new type of musical experience encompassing man's being in its entirety [...] Whether in avant-garde music, in jazz or in pop music, we have been witnessing a trend towards a more spiritual introverted musical language. The increasing public interest in spiritual music, both Western and non-European [...] suggests that here, too, the future role of music will not be confined to one particular dimension of human existence. (quoted in Berendt 1991, 167)

Even though New-Age-like spirituality actually became very widespread, the above prediction proved a bit too naïve—at least in relation to music. In music spirituality has not become part of the mass culture, with notable exceptions like Christian rock, or certain alternative niches, where world music inspired by India is still played and music is understood to be a "universal language" that communicates "without dogma" what all religions say (Laack 2009, 556–559). The fashion for India has largely fizzled out, but some of pop music has become more introverted, more personal, sometimes more ecstatic. Think of "trip hop" and "trance techno", which derived directly from the electronic meditation music of the 1970s and are strongly trance-inducing. These mainly instrumental music styles are completely oriented on self-sufficiency, immersion and ecstasy even if, unlike the earlier meditation music of the "New Age", they have no longer an explicitly religious character.

Central to this chapter are the transfers and the modern dissolving of religious and cultural boundaries for which Berendt's Nada Brahma is a good example. More than Ravi Shankar and other Indian musicians it was the scene of musical counter-culture, world-music and popular musicians like the Beatles whose absorption of musical elements of India and "Indian spirituality" created social effervescence. If anything, Berendt himself is the best example of the direct and indirect impact India (the real and imagined India) made on modern individualized religion, its *habitus* forms (e. g., to combine and merge many things) and its attempts to sacralize the whole of life (drawing often from Eastern cultures which remained attractive even after the Indian boom faded out).

4 Aesthetics as a Connective Concept in the Study of Religions

Whether we speak of the Indian performance culture and sounding texts, or the Nāda-Brahman in its original context and in Berendt's adoption, it is easy to detect the strength of the aesthetics of religion focus. This strength lies in bringing to light areas which often were not given enough scholarly scrutiny and in feeding in new perspectives and methods into the study of religions across different disciplines. For instance, in Indology, there was little awareness of the sounding word, even when orality was acknowledged. For many decades it was not realized (with a very few exceptions) that sacred texts were not only discursive message bearers, but also aesthetic events embodied in vocal, often musical performances and surrounded by an aura of sacredness by their mere sound, and how much this influenced individual practice and collective ideology. There was also hardly any research on the Nāda-Brahman—despite its fundamental role for the perception (of music, religion, and the world) and the Indian history of aesthetic forms beyond the musicians' circles. Its manifold imprints are still waiting to be explored.

While in academic scholarship rarely dealt with, the Nāda-Brahman entered even European space—not only esoteric practises like Nada-meditation and

Nada-healing, but also cultural temples and events of the musical establishment like the famous Salzburg festivals. In the brochure accompanying the *"ouverture spirituelle"* in 2015, devoted to Christianity and Hinduism, Walter Weidringer introduces Indian music with the suggestive words "Nada Brahma: The world is sound" referring to ancient human awareness, divine inspiration, and the Veda (Ouverture 2015a, 69). The actual program introduced the same subject with the title "Sound is god" and explained: "[...] the sacred properties of sound find expression in the Sanskrit *nada Brahma* (sound is god)" (Ouverture 2015b, 19). With a good deal of certainty, these expressions are directly imported from Berendt (without, of course, mentioning his name) rather than Sārṅgadeva. Typical for the modern reception—outside and within India—is also the hoary past attributed to the Nāda-Brahman. Its naissance in the 13th century within the musical, not religious discourse is forgotten. This reveals not only that more indological research is needed on the historical development of the term post Sārṅgadeva (and possibly also prior to him). It reveals as well the persuasive power of the term which already in Sārṅgadeva's discourse made use of potent religious symbols and certainly comprised in a nutshell already the connotations "the world is sound" and "sound is god".

The sonic world-view imbibed in the Nāda-Brahman, despite of being a strongly culture-bound symbol, has proved transcultural and transreligious efficiency. This was primarily due to its sensory-aesthetic and experiential appeal, indeed, I argue that aesthetics was the major connective concept. Or, to put it somewhat differently: for a religious aesthetics approach focussing on the sensory spaces and media of religion and everyday religiosity (and thus also on sounding religion) the Nāda-Brahman is of great interest—regarding both its emergence and developments in India and its reception outside of India.

4.1 Media, History of Mentality and Cultural Imagination

Media practices always present themselves also as techniques for absorbing certain forms of an aesthetic sense. Acoustic and written signs stimulate different senses. They connect with different patterns of perception and impart different experiential qualities. It is therefore not all one and the same, which media are given preference over others, or in which combination they appear.

India provides us with an alternative model of media history, in which orality and literacy were never separated completely. One can speak of a "third space", an in-between in view of the Western academic debates on the differences between literacy (Goody, Watt, and Gough 1986; Goody 1986, 2000) and orality (Ong 1982). In India, orality and as important sonality kept playing a vital role through the centuries. This sonic paradigm created a third space *habitus* that promoted a participative acquisition of the subject, in which the sensory, affective, performative and poeitological aspects of text-based activities were never lost from sight. Sound found its way into religious symbolizations as well as scientific symbolizations (e.g., in grammar and mathematics). We find more connectivity than in the European history not only regarding orality and literacy, and text and performance, but also regarding *mythos* and *logos*, intellect and emotion, interiority and embodiment, abstraction and materialization.

What I call "third space" regarding media history thus goes along with an intellectual history or history of mentality in which mythical embedding and abstract rationality were never set apart in equal measure as in Europe. Instead we find them (re-)united in ever new ways. The historically most influential thinkers of India invariably took holistic approaches to reality and maintained unitary visions of the world-whole, which were given a rational and analytical foundation. *Sound and Communication* (Wilke and Moebus 2011, x, 22, 50–51, 296–330) coined the term "universal myth" for this cultural pattern of holistic (often non-dualistic) world-view formation, which posits rationality within a mythical framework and explains mythical embedding in an analytical fashion. Śārṅgadeva's Nāda-Brahman or "Sound-Brahman" is a particular striking example of this pattern. Śārṅgadeva recombined several "universal myths", most prominently the Śaiva tantric cosmic Nāda (vibrating Sound) and the Advaita-Vedāntic Brahman (non-dual Absolute Being), to form a new one to arise: music's relevance to worldly happiness and religious deliverance and bliss, and to a sensory perception of unity underlying all diversity and a vision of the world whose raw material was all-pervading sound. The aesthetics of music were the connective concept which produced powerful cognitive experiential effects. The new holistic symbol amounted to the claim of somatic affective participation in the cosmos, a sensory experience of the unity of being that had been postulated by the philosophers in abstract terms, and an experience of yogic lysis without the world-denying efforts of the yogis. Śārṅgadeva's Nāda-Brahman also allowed for theistic interpretation and devotional fusion—from loving participation in the personal god to the taste of bliss flowing from the "featureless" godhead.

Berendt, the heir of a different media history, was fascinated precisely by the holism enshrined in the Nāda-Brahman and by what he perceived as "spiritual" in Indian music and music-making. His cultural criticism repeated a trope of culture critique by means of India, which had been re-appearing since the romantic period. In the age of television and deeply felt secularization, Berendt's target was the Western "eye-person". The Nāda-Brahman was the code-word for a changed world-view which was more networked, holistic, and spiritual. It became the healing principle of the logocentric, dissecting eye-oriented Western subject and the projection screen for a more intuitive and affective relation to the world. It was, in fact, a new universal myth which was not any more Indian nor purely European, but worked precisely like an Indian one: giving "evidence" for mythical embedding by rational argument, and vice versa. While Śārṅgadeva fused many earlier and contemporary theories and ideas, Berendt fused in typical New-Age manner all the world's traditions and natural science. The characteristic New-Age third space *habitus* he exposed was stern critique of a narrow dogmatic belief and a purely scientific world-view, and at the same time combining religion and science.

One may object to many things: Berendt's black and white reasoning, the romantic projection, the ahistoric approach, and some misrepresentations of the Indian concept. However, one should not skip over either the authenticity in feeling discomfort with modern Western culture and the new experiences and insights Berendt obviously gained with Indian musicians who communicated the Nāda-Brahman concept to him. Even though many things were misunderstood and misrepresented by Berendt, his general vision was not completely off the track. What he understood quite well were the holistic implications and the "substantial" aspects of the concept, and the cosmic and spiritual dimension it conferred to music. All of this existed already in Śārṅgadeva's Nāda-Brahman. Berendt's formula: "The world is sound. Sound is god" was definitely not his own invention. He apparently got the idea from native informants, and less grasped an abstract content than developing a "feeling" for the Nāda-Brahman by spending time with Indian musicians who genuinely felt their music to be the way how Śārṅgadeva had described it centuries before: the musician participates immediately in the essence of the universe and music is a kind of yoga, a spiritual discipline that generates a mood of divine peace (see, for instance, Ravi Shankar, quoted in Berendt 1991, 154).

Berendt's intercultural problem-solving "worked" on a strongly sensory symbolic level. It remains interesting that despite very divergent starting points for Berendt's complexes of imagination and those of the ancient Indians, and despite Berendt's total dehistoricisation and deculturalisation of the Nāda-Brahman, a kind of synthesis nevertheless arose that is not only the smallest common denominator but also feeds on interculturally transmittable sensory symbols. There is an equivalence between the Nāda-Brahman idea that the whole world is filled with "cosmic, primordial sound" and the monodic, extremely microtone-laden Indian modal music. In particular when overtonality is stressed, a dense, constant sound presence arises that translates the Nāda-Brahman so to speak into sensory perception and arouses a "feeling" of unity in plurality. Unity in plurality is a notion which inheres very much in the Nāda-Brahman idea. Therefore it is understandable that music was seen as a physical expression of it.

Typically, one of Berendt's key examples was the oscillation of a string (Berendt 1991, 27–30, 60–61)—discussed also by Śārṅgadeva in his more technical musicological section. The vibrating string is a truly good illustration of the "unique nature" of sound and central complexes of ideas that are associated with the Nāda-Brahman. When a string is plucked or struck, first of all a vibration arises in the whole string. However, this vibration immediately causes a second, somewhat quieter, oscillation, that of the two halves of the string. Then the three thirds of the string start to vibrate, followed by four quarters, and so on *ad infinitum*. But succeeding partial vibrations are always quieter than their predecessors and at some stage they become completely inaudible. Even though we think we are hearing one single tone, acoustic theory tells us that we are really also hearing many different tones, as each "individual tone" contains within itself all the other "individual tones" as a weak additional soundscape. Berendt was not all that wrong to lump the vibrating string and the holy syllable OṂ together and take them as physical expressions of the Nāda-Brahman. There is a continuum between the sound information from a vibrating string and the meditation on the sound of OṂ. Infinite resonances—of *mantras*—had indeed been inspiring the Indian idea of an all-pervading cosmic Nāda, and the non-dual interwovenness of notes was akin to the Brahman notion.[4]

New experiences stimulate new thoughts. Sensory symbols and new media have the power to trigger such experiences. Apparently, the discontinuities to what was known as Western classical music and religion were the ones that turned Indian music in the 20th century into a major intercultural contact zone stimulating new musical and spiritual forms of expression in Western culture, such as Berendt's New Age Nada Brahma. The jazz historian used Indian conceptions of music, because he sought a spiritualization and resacralization of life. He tried making good a cultural deficit and wanted to overcome a sense of unease with modernity. What fascinated Berendt so much about the exotic Nāda-Brahman was apparently that it was a symbol of an all-encompassing totality, whose reference in a vibrating string or overtone music could be experienced through the senses. The Nāda-Brahman provided a concept for understanding the nature of the sound as "spiritual" without necessarily being restricted to a certain culture, religious tradition or dogma. On the contrary, it

---

4 Later traditions post Śārṅgadeva (within and outside the musicians' circles) indeed developed a specific "Sound yoga" (Nāda-yoga), the contemplation of sound—irrelevant whether of music, *bhajan*, *mantra*, the name of god, or any given phonem.

could also be explained musicologically and anthropologically, i.e., by profane science. That the ear perceives sounds both in a sensory manner and mathematically, at the same time, was an important argument for Berendt. Precisely the religious charge, but also the de-differentiation of "profane" and "religious" in the Nāda-Brahman and its experience in music and all types of sound meditation made the concept attractive to the New-Age "believers". No specific religion at all now had to be associated with the Nāda-Brahman as sensory substance in the form of music. Musical lysis itself had a "spiritual quality". Overtone music and modern "world music" that mixes together all possible music styles in the world (another of Berendt's examples of Nāda-Brahman), are in the current religious culture two of many examples of re-sacralisation of life, without one having to call oneself religious. They point to the dissolution and undermining of cultural and religious boundaries, which are typical of the modern age. Many New-Age adherents regard themselves as "spiritual, but not religious"—a modern religious style whose broad popularity is well ascertained in recent research and which apparently represents an attractive alternative to traditional religion and secularism for considerable sectors of the population in modern (mostly Western) societies.

4.2 Sensory Form, Cultural Transfers and Trans-Religious Spirituality

The sensory aesthetic and cognitive qualities that made Indian music into a representation of cosmic wholeness (of Brahman itself), made it also a cross-cultural attractor. The Nāda-Brahman turned into a transreligious category in India and beyond. Here one should understand transreligiosity as transcendence of traditional religious boundaries and the conscious or unconscious fusion of different traditions. Berendt was by no means the first who adopted the Nāda-Brahman in this way and filled it with new meaning. In India, the term and its connotations became so popular that the Nāda-Brahman migrated out of classical musicians' circles and found a permanent home in different religious milieus, Hindu and non-Hindu. It infiltrated the popular Tantra and the *bhakti* literature and song, where it became a catchword for devotional fusion. It was also taken up by Veda-exegists (Mīmāṃsakas) and yogic-tantric traditions, like the Nāthyogins, where it was a springboard for intensive sound contemplation (Nāda-yoga). This "yogification" (partly also within musical practice) locates the Nāda-Brahman in resonances and inner sounds. It was incorporated into Sant, Sikh, Radhasoami and Sufi traditions, and modern Hindu movements. Each added their own ideas and practices. In this way, the Nāda-Brahman was related to all kinds of extraordinary experiences and sonic journeys to the centre of the universe, and was also associated with therapeutic power, the Pythagorean music of the spheres and popularized modern physics in India and beyond. Such ideas and corresponding esoteric practices like Nada-yoga, Nada-gnosis, Nada-healing, and Nada-music are found today in a number of esoteric groups in the West and also in India.

One may credit Berendt that Indian music had the effect of expanding religious consciousness when it became known in the West. He ascribes an inherent spiritual attitude to modal music-making and thus explains the success of Indian music in the 1960s—firstly in jazz and then in rock and pop, minimal music, meditation music and world music. He wanted not least to document this in his book *The World is Sound: Nada Brahma*. What the book certainly documents is foremost Berendt's own "discomfort in culture" and his own interest in alternative spirituality. It is a very subjective and personal source. At the same time it points to larger processes of religious change and makes the reader aware that Indian spirituality was disseminated through many channels, one of them (and not an unimportant one) being music.

Surely, Berendt's book cannot be taken at face value, and yet it is a valuable document for the shifting values and world-views, and changed religious styles initiated in the counterculture of the 1960s and the 1970s. Berendt's work *Nada Brahma* is a good document of both the India-boom of the hippies and New Age spirituality in which transreligious, "syncretistic" styles became normality. It illustrates new religious *habitus* forms that are no longer purely western or eastern, but drew a great deal of inspiration from India. Since the late 1970s they were extended to religious cultures throughout the world, which are freely drawn on and combined. Berendt's "new-aged" Nada Brahma represents a kind of prototypical structural pattern of this type of spirituality that is now widespread in Western Europe and America.

One may object with justification that New-Age spirituality has little to do with the "true India". This spirituality is certainly something quite different, something new that never previously existed in this form and extent either in India or in the West. Berendt's globalized Nada Brahma is typical of it, a hybrid with the flavour of India, a de-culturated product whose Indian original has become practically invisible. But my point is: however projected and western Berendt's "India" may be, the encounters behind it, the new experiences triggered and Berendt's desire to "hear differently with Indian ears" were real. What he "took on board" from or "heard in" his conversations with Indian musicians was "spirituality", a new attitude to making and perceiving music, and a new systematization of the world. The Nāda-Brahman/Nada Brahma was the key to a new world-view and a different spirituality than the one of the European Christian mainstream and the rationality common in Europe. It put life in the more comprehensive context of a "sacred universe" that was not tied to any particular religion. Berendt's Nāda-Brahman reception had the function of protest and of forming an alternative identity.

The intercultural exchange opened new ways of sensing the world. Not only Indian sacred literature, but also Indian music gave an impulse for new *habitus* forms by providing new ideas, aesthetic styles and attitudes. Berendt's *Nada Brahma* is of particular interest regarding aesthetics as a connective concept for the study of religions. His documentation makes clear that not only translations and teachings disseminated Indian ideas and world-views, but also aesthetic sensory forms like music. The role of Indian music for the modern history of Western music may have been overemphasized by Berendt and his "new consciousness" of a new epoch of "hearing" was more wishful thinking than reality, but for some it did indeed open new ways of sensing the world and the self and it created a space for music to take the role of an invisible religion and "universal language". Both, Indian Rāga *and* Western pop music were themselves transponders of ideas, not only their "historiographer" Berendt whose *Nada Brahma* remained a "source book" of modern esoteric thought. There was direct and indirect impact of Indian spirituality—from the India boom to New Age. Rarely, it was a complete going native or a serious study of Indian traditions. Berendt's Nada Brahma is typical for the usual de-culturalisation. Remarkably this appears in Berendt reflexively, for instance, in his (well-chosen) illustration of the Nāda-Brahman in a vibrating string whose resonances are an intersubjectively experienced and scientifically confirmed phenomenon. It is, however, just as remarkable, that Berendt *and* Śārṅgadeva (*sic!*) would see the vibrating string as a direct manifestation of the sonic nature of the universe.

Berendt himself and the scenes he describes may individually seem to be marginal minorities, but they indicate much broader and deeper processes of change in present-day religious culture than might be apparent at first glance. In fact, they are indeed good examples of a more widely spread phenomenon surpassing the sphere of music—a pluralisation and individualisation of religion, or change in subjective piety patterns, becoming apparent right at the time covered by Berendt's documentation (and by now well documented in the research literature). These new religious styles and syncretism were characterised variously as New Age, post-modern religion, late-modern religiosity, alternative spirituality, individualized religion, esotericism. Scholars struggled to capture the vast field of phenomena behind these terms in different ways and acknowledged growing popularity—from "invisible religion" (Luckmann 1967, 1991) to "popular religion" (Knoblauch 2009). Both "believing without belonging [outside the Church, but still within the Christian bracket]" (Davie 1994) and "unchurched religion [beyond the Christian bracket]" (Fuller 2001) proved to be too narrow conceptualizations. Religious styles described as "self-religion" or "subjective life spirituality" (Heelas, Woodhead 2005), "spiritual wanderer" (Gebhardt, Boching-er, Engelbrecht 2005) or even an "Easternization of the West" (Campbell 2007) are found today outside and within Christian communities. All these authors—despite their different interpretations—acknowledge a major sea-change in the late 1960s and '70s. Berendt's book documents both—the counter-culture and India-oriented hippie age of that time, and the later development of a transreli-gious spirituality which assimilates diverse cultural view-points and reinforces holism. Although by no means exclusively, Indian thought inspired and influ-enced the change of religious patterns which today are no more alternative reli-gion but part of the religious mainstream in Western Europe. Experience-based transreligious religiosity is found today not only in free floating "unchurched re-ligion", but also right within the large Christian Churches.

Berendt's book documents the shift in values and world-view that Colin Campbell (2007) called "the Easternization of the West". Campbell was one of the few sociologists who acknowledged in his theory the formative role of India or "Eastern-style outlook"—and even overemphasised it (like Berendt). Campbell's generalized "Easternization" is doubtful and some aspects that he associates with it appear far too stereotyped and sometimes erroneous. Yet, it cannot be denied, that his interesting theses, based on Max Weber, on a structur-ally necessary exchange of a "materialistic dualistic" world-view (regarded as typically western), through a "metaphysical monism" (considered as typically eastern) find support in some areas of contemporary religion. The modern reli-gious style of Berendt's New Age in the early 1980s can actually be assigned to the branch of "metaphysical monism" as described by Campbell. Campbell as-sociates with it mystical spirituality, immediate experience, sensations, feelings, and intuition, along with "an essentially spiritual approach to life" and a life philosophy of "perceiving secular activities themselves as essentially spiritual in nature" (Campbell 2007, 33–38, 46–51, 64–67, 216–249). Although this does not apply, for instance, to the high rationality of the Advaita-Vedānta and its non-dual Brahman interpretation,[5] which became "Indian philosophy" *par excellence,* it is interesting, on the other hand, that the Nāda-Brahman largely fulfils all of Campbell's claims—not only the Nada Brahma of Berendt, but also the Nāda-Brahman of Śārṅgadeva.

---

5 This was one of Śārṅgadeva's major sources and even Berendt quotes the key formula *tat tvam asi* ("that you are"). Most of all, this tradition played a very central role in forming the modern image of Hinduism, Indian philosophy, and the "mystic East".

Berendt's Nada Brahma is a useful model for analyzing how cultural concepts when transported into a new cultural field are transformed through that field. At the same time this field itself will be transformed through the addition of the new ideas. Although Berendt's Nada Brahma is no longer an Indian one, it contributed to globalizing Indian forms of thought, *habitus*, practice, and world-orientation, including the pattern of "universal myth". The Nāda-Brahman is an especially good foil exposing cultural and structural boundaries, and also their fluidity, extension and potential dissolution. It provided in medieval India and modern Europe a new definition of spirituality in which the profane and the sacred flow into each other, and which promoted highly individualized religiosity—a feature that in the Hindu traditions of course has an old history, right from the late-vedic, pre-Christian Upaniṣads. Individualized religion is not only a modern, European product.

The Nāda-Brahman was only one of the cherished exports from Sanskrit Hinduism into Western culture. But it illustrates particularly well the religious transmutations occurring in times of cultural exchange. It is instructive for the formative role of India in modern Western spirituality. Academic theories of individualization generally have too eurocentristically explained the changing religious patterns in European societies with immanent developments within these societies and too little reflected modernity as expansion of cultural horizons and trans-nationalisation of world-views. Regarding this, Joachim Berendt's Nada Brahma and his chronicle of change in music culture remain an instructive document. The example is as well of interest regarding media and aesthetic forms as producers of cultural and religious change. What becomes clear in this example is that world-views are transmitted and changed not only via ideas, but also via sensory symbols, feelings and atmospheric moods—that is, a broad range of perception and experience. The effectiveness of aesthetic media in religion and religious change—in my example moving religion by sound—proves aesthetics of religion to be a very important analytical tool and connective concept in historical and comparative studies, and in theoretical reflection.

Bibliography

Berendt, Joachim-Ernst. 1983. *Nada Brahma: Die Welt ist Klang*. Frankfurt a.M.: Insel.
—— [1987] 1991. *The World is Sound: Music and the Landscape of Consciousness*. Rochester: Destiny Books.
Campbell, Colin. 2007. *The Easternization of the West: A Thematic Account of Cultural Change in the Modern Era*. Boulder: Paradigm Publishers.

Davie, Grace. 1994. *Religion in Britain since 1945: Believing without Belonging*. Oxford: Blackwell.

Fuller, Robert C. 2001. *Spiritual, but Not Religious: Understanding Unchurched America*. New York: Oxford University Press.

Gebhardt, Winfred, Christoph Bochinger, and Martin Engelbrecht. 2005. "Die Selbstermächtigung des religiösen Subjekts. Der ‚spirituelle Wanderer' als Idealtypus spätmoderner Religiosität." *Zeitschrift für Religionswissenschaft* 05/2: 133–152.

Goody, Jack. 1986. *The Logic of Writing and the Organization of Society*. Cambridge: Cambridge University Press.

—— 2000. *The Power of the Written Tradition*. Washington: Smithsonian Institution Press.

Goody, Jack, Ian Watt, and Kathleen Gough. 1986. *Entstehung und Folgen der Schriftkultur*. Frankfurt: Suhrkamp.

Heelas, Paul, and Linda Woodhead. 2005. *The Spiritual Revolution: Why Religion is Giving Way to Spirituality*. Oxford: Blackwell.

Hübner, Kurt. 1985. *Die Wahrheit des Mythos*. Munich: Beck.

Knoblauch, Hubert. 2009. *Populäre Religion: Auf dem Weg in eine spirituelle Gesellschaft*. Frankfurt a.M.: Campus.

Laack, Isabel. 2009. *Religion und Musik in Glastonbury: Eine Fallstudie zu gegenwärtigen Formen religiöser Identitätsdiskurse*. Goettingen: Vandenhoeck & Ruprecht.

Luckmann, Thomas. 1967. *Invisible Religion*. New York: Macmillan.

—— 1991. *Die unsichtbare Religion*. Frankfurt a.M.: Suhrkamp.

Mataṅga. 1992, 1994. *Bhṛaddeśī of Śrī Mataṅga Muni*. 3 Vols., edited by Prem Lata Sharma. New Delhi: Indira Gandhi Centre for the Arts.

Ong, Walter J. 1982. *Orality and Literacy: The Technologizing of the Word*. London and New York: Methuen.

Ouverture Spirituelle. 2015a. *Christentum und Hinduismus*. Salzburger Festspiele 18 July–30 August 2015.

—— 2015b. *Hinduismus I-V: Kutiyattam, Dhrupad, Khyal, Bharatnatyam, Morgen-Ragas*. Salzburger Festspiele 18 July–30 August 2015.

Raghavan, V. 1994. *The Power of the Sacred Name. V. Raghavan's Studies in Nāma-Siddhānta and Indian Culture*, edited by William J. Jackson. Delhi: Satguru Publications.

Śārṅgadeva. 1943–1953. *Sangītaratnākara of Śārṅgadeva. With Kalānidhi of Kallināṭha and Sudhākara of Simhabhūpāla*. 4 Vols., edited by S. Subrahmanya Sastri. Madras: Adyar.

Wilke, Annette. 2013. "Sound." In *Brill's Encyclopedia of Hinduism*. Vol. 5, edited by Knut A. Jacobsen, 134–149. Leiden: Brill.

—— 2014. "Sonic Perception and Acoustic Communication in Hindu India." In *Exploring the Senses*, edited by Axel Michaels and Christoph Wulf, 120–144. London, New York, and Delhi: Routledge.

Wilke, Annette, and Oliver Moebus. 2011. *Sound and Communication. An Aesthetic Cultural History of Sanskrit Hinduism*. Berlin and New York: de Gruyter.

PART IV Concepts and Theories

Jay Johnston
Esoteric Aesthetics: The Spiritual Matter of Intersubjective Encounter

1 Introduction

The development of Material Religion and the turn to New Materialism (especially in the discipline of cultural studies) has resulted in substantive scholarly engagement with materiality, and with models that aim to replace binary concepts such as matter/mind, body/spirit or culture/nature. In the case of New Materialism the focus has been on the conceptualisation and ethical acknowledgement of 'other-than-human agency;' that is the attribution/recognition of matter (so usually cast as inert or only agential by human extension) with its own agency. However, significant questions remain regarding the conceptualisation of 'matter' upon which such studies are founded and on the *aesthetics* of these material relations. Elsewhere (Johnston 2013, 2016a, 2016b) I have noted that there are numerous precedents for the 'vital matter' that has been proposed by scholars of New Materialism which can be found in esoteric traditions, in particular concepts of 'subtle' matter. This chapter further develops this argument by turning to consider the aesthetic relations attributable to intersubjective forms of matter-consciousness and the ramifications of such aesthetic exchanges—including the ontologies upon which they are founded—for a broader aesthetics of lived experience. To exemplify this broader framework a case study examining a contemporary artwork that intersects/ works with the environment is discussed.

As elaborated in detail in its precursors (see especially Johnston 2008) the concept of subtle matter that this chapter explores wantonly traipses across, and disrupts, binary concepts of matter and consciousness (hence the use of 'matter-consciousness') and is understood as foundational to a form of radical intersubjectivity that disrupts (in creative and non-oppositional ways) other conceptual dualisms including I-Other; spirit-matter and subject-object. Therefore it equally challenges familiar methodological divides built upon such binary logic (such as 'etic' and 'emic') that have also come under sustained academic critique in the last ten years in a number of disciplines. A concept of matter, bodies, aesthetics and ethics founded on such intersubjectivity will necessarily be concerned with articulating the co-constitutional nature of phenomena and its 'messy', elusive and dynamic relations. This perspective necessarily ties a concept of aesthetics to embodied perception, its apprehension and the framework of beliefs through which these are understood. In a religious studies context, this

https://doi.org/10.1515/9783110461015-015

requires acknowledging that beliefs—especially ontological and epistemological —dictate how an individual understands not only physical and metaphysical worlds but also their lived relation. However, this is not just an issue of 'belief', such worldviews are deeply embodied, individually and collectively, and direct— consciously and unconsciously—aesthetic and ethical behaviour. As such, it is the conceptualisation and articulation of *relations* with which this chapter is concerned.

The approach taken herein is primarily a philosophical inquiry into aesthetic relations that form and emerge from intersubjective encounters between subjects and environments. The argument draws together discourses from various disciplines (religious studies, continental philosophy, art theory and cultural studies) to present concepts of matter and imagination that are ontological and explores their potential ramifications. There is no concern with truth claims, as it is considered valid enough that agential forms of matter and imagination are found within a diverse range of esoteric, indigenous and process orientated worldviews as to warrant not only respect but also careful consideration of the productive ways in which they disrupt dominant epistemological systems and their base in empirical knowledge. The argument will move from a consideration of the elemental (water, air, fire, earth) and their evocation to signal ontological forms of matter-consciousness in the work of Gaston Bachelard and Gilles Deleuze to an art installation by Roni Horn. At every turn of this pondering, the foundation is not merely matter—not an empirical matter and a consciousness localised in the brain—but an ontological matter. This understanding of materiality is sometimes considered as directly equivalent to concepts of 'subtle matter' and other times a more nebulous, less religiously orientated 'agency'. Numerous traditions link the apprehension of such matter to extrasensory forms of perception (Johnston 2008, 2016) accordingly, this chapter argues for a concomitant form of aesthetics. That is, an aesthetics that takes such unusual (and often ridiculed) forms of perception into account. As it is hoped to be demonstrated, any such aesthetics necessarily calls into account an individual's own perceptive limitations and an aesthetics of discourse mastery. There are no 'solid' subjects or 'objects' of analysis to be found within this discussion. Only glimpses of partial relations and examples of the edifices subsequently built upon them. However these glimpses are what makes the difference between judging art—or religion, for that matter— as "the other" of empirical "real life", and understanding better the quality at work in processes that influence people's lives and can be so—seemingly inexplicable—powerful.

Within this larger framework, subtle matter plays a central role when re-conceptualising subjectivity and 'vision'. The foundation upon which subjectivity and 'vision' is established herein is one of intersubjective exchange of subtle material. Vision is understood as one of many forms of perception that not only apprehend subtle material (sometimes termed spirit matter or 'energy') but is simultaneously comprised of it. An Esoteric Aesthetics is necessarily constituted by nebulous agency, invisible dynamics and the cultivation of specific types of extra-sensory perception. The discursive construction of such perception connects ontological beliefs, lived experience and aesthetic engagement. Previously (Johnston 2008, 2016a, 2016b) I have detailed the Esoteric Aesthetics' approach. I reproduce a summary of its central features here and note that these need not necessarily be concurrent:

> i) the relationship between viewer and object is radically intersubjective and co-constitutional; ii) this relationship is constitutive of other-than-human agencies which may not be perceptible to the five senses, but may be perceived by forms of extrasensory perception; iii) an esoteric aesthetics requires the utilization of a range of scopic regimes, some of which may require conscious cultivation; iv) an esoteric aesthetics is an embodied and self-reflective relationship that often requires elongated periods of time to cultivate; v) it requires continual questioning of socio-culturally defined concepts of "materiality", "subjectivity" and their interrelation; and vi) it embraces epistemological plurality in the understanding of subject-object relations (Johnston 2016b).

To commence discussion of these types of interrelationship, this chapter turns first to discuss elemental material and its perception of a more visceral nature before turning later in the chapter to consider even subtler, 'invisible' interconnections.

2 Dynamic Connections: 'Fast and Slow' Aesthetics[1]

This section presents a discussion of elemental materials and a conceptualisation of their effect/affect on the viewer via imaginative contemplation and aesthetic mediation. It will also turn to consider the 'duration' of such materials when they are purposively incorporated as central aspects of contemporary artworks. The focus is the conceptualisation and perception of the rate and rhythm of such exchanges between viewer and artwork. This approach advocates that the viewer can register and respond to such subtle exchanges if they have consciously cultivated specialised forms of perception and/or specific modes of epistemology are employed (Johnston 1999, 2008). Therefore the artworks discussed

---

1 Some material in this section was initially developed as part of a Master of Arts Honours *Subtle Exchanges: Cultivating Relations with Duration* (UWS 1999).

herein are considered as a focal point for a consideration of the horizontal and vertical extensity of matter-consciousness.

2.1 Elemental Materials

Elemental materials—water, earth, fire, air—often form the basis for the temporal works created by contemporary artists: indeed the dynamic nature of change exhibited by such materials echo the dynamic flux of the corporeal viewer. Thus the transient change and interaction of elemental materials provide for an easily observed occasion to consider temporal dynamics and also open links to the body of the observer; a point also noted by Boetzkes (2010). The viewer's own transient form is able to be understood, physically and metaphorically, to be comprised of the same elemental substances. This approach to the body establishes reciprocity of fluid and temporal substance between viewer and object. Such an intersubjective exchange can be expanded to also be inclusive of the dynamics of subtle, invisible, (even ontological) forces: a discussion taken up later in the chapter.

To commence the discussion of the aesthetic apprehension of elemental materials, I turn, no doubt predictably, to consider the work of French philosopher Gaston Bachelard (1884–1962). Working in the areas of poetry, psychology and the philosophy, particularly epistemology, of science, Bachelard is well-known to have advocated that particular 'imaginations' or modes of consciousness are required for the perception of 'matter': structuring these different types of 'material imagination' around the four elements. This is evident in *The Psychoanalysis of Fire* in which Bachelard advocated a 'material imagination' distinguished by the particularities of different elements. Writing in reflection on this text he notes:

> In *The Psychoanalysis of Fire* I have suggested classifying the different types of imagination under the heading of the *material elements* which inspired traditional philosophies and ancient cosmologies. In fact, I believe it is possible to establish in the realm of the imagination, a *law of the four elements* which classifies various kinds of material imagination by their connections with fire, air, water or earth (...). A material element must provide its own substance, its particular rules and poetics (Bachelard [1942] 1983, 3).

In Bachelard's conceptualisation, differing material elements correspond to different consciousness's—each has their own particular imagination, and arguably evolve from such a specific epistemological mode. Such an approach also stressed, as explained in the quotation below by Colette Gaudin, that images (of all types, but especially of the imagination) were 'lived' and the particular material consciousness directly participated in this 'animation'.

> "In a word, the phenomenological approach is a description of the immediate relationship of phenomena with a particular consciousness; it allows Bachelard to renew his warnings against the temptation to study images as *things*. Images are *"lived," "experienced," "re-im-agined"* in an act of consciousness which restored at once their timelessness and the new-ness" (Gaudin 1998, xli).

In order to fully grasp the implications of this approach for aesthetics as a con-nective concept Bachelard's understanding of 'imagination' also requires expli-cation. Prior to distinguishing different types of material imagination Bachelard distinguished two different modes of imagination: *formal imagination* and *mate-rial imagination*. Formal imagination pertains to forms, beauty, the surface while material imagination pertains to examining the 'hidden roots' of formal imagina-tion, the "inner recesses of substance" (1983, 1– 2). Noting that it is difficult to separate these two modes in reality, Bachelard does identify the latter—material imagination—as the defining characteristic of reverie and reverie implicitly in-volves quiet contemplation. Here then the perception of materiality is aligned both with particular modes of epistemology (material imagination) and particu-lar modes of embodied engagement (reverie).

Reverie is the mode of perception that Bachelard proposes as requisite for the practice of material imagination, the apprehension of "inner recesses of sub-stance". It is a form of contemplation, distinguished from 'day dreaming' or in-deed any form of dream-state, by its focus upon a single object, and the exten-sity, in all directions, that this contemplation emanates. In a delightful rendering of the process/ action of reverie Bachelard ([1938] 1964, 14) writes: "The reverie works in a star pattern. It returns to its centre to shoot out new beams". Indeed, Bachelard positions reverie as a practice that elicits a contemplative 'space' in which subject–object distinctions may be apprehended/experienced as ambigu-ous. It is also seen as a state of perceptive consciousness that requires a process of cultivation. As Gaudin explains: "The Bachelardian reverie, far from being a complacent drifting of the self, is a discipline acquired through long hours of reading and writing, and through a constant practice of *'surveillance de soi.'* Im-ages reveal nothing to the lazy dreamer" (Gaudin, 1998, xxviii).

Bachelard believed poetics to be the most appropriate medium through which to communicate interrelationships with material elements. This privileg-ing of language reflects his perspective that language is ontological, "the imme-diate mode of becoming" (Bachelard 1983, 188). Indeed, a form/matter dualism underlies this privileging of language. Optical vision and the creative expression reliant upon this sense faculty—including the visual arts—is affiliated with the formal imagination and a concern for surface and beauty. That is, a more traditional interpretation of aesthetics is aligned by Bachelard with his proposition of a formal imagination. In contrast, material imagination is discussed as going beyond the surface, to deeper realms of substance and is affiliated with the written word. This relation—that is a relation of connection—is demonstrated by Bachelard with a discussion of the material imagination of water:

> I will devote this conclusion almost exclusively to the most extreme of my paradoxes. It will consist of proving that the voices of water are hardly metaphoric at all; that the language of the waters is a direct poetic reality; that the streams and rivers *provide the sound* for mute country landscapes, and do it with strange fidelity; that murmuring waters teach birds and men [sic] to sing, speak, recount; and that there is, in short, a continuity between the speech of water and the speech of man [sic]. (Bachelard 1983, 15)

> Liquidity is a principle of language; language must be filled with water. (Bachelard 1983, 192).

Such a dualism between form/matter and visual art/literature is not necessary if the very nature of matter that comprises the form studied is liquefied through a Process Philosophy (or New Materialist) perspective. Further, an esoteric materiality-subjectivity enables matter-consciousness to be considered as forming a fluid ontology, in which the surfaces and depths of objects and subjects are necessarily considered porous and always in a process of interpenetration. As the delineating concept used by Bachelard, depth, would if viewed by such a perspective, not perceive different 'types' but different 'intensities' of the same (ontological) matter-consciousness. Understood thus, the material imagination would equally be at home contemplating surface as it is substance. Similarly, the cultivation of active imagination/esoteric 'vision' would render water as 'stimulus' that enables the viewer access to the perceptive realm of reverie. Therefore it is the mode of approach that is the significant factor, not necessarily the 'object' or 'form' under contemplation. In later work, more influenced by philosophical phenomenology, the relationship between the viewer and object in contemplative reverie becomes more radically intersubjective.

For Bachelard, images are lived, they enact becoming. He proposes that images exist in an ambiguous relationship to the viewer, both being an object of their consideration and their becoming. Images 'reverberate'. Bachelard adopted this term from the phenomenologist Eugène Minkowski. It is understood as a category or property of the universe, a dynamism or flow of life force understood as 'silent' but "sonorous waves" (Bachelard 1958 in Gaudin 1998, xvi–xvii) and it is the practice of reverie which opens the subject to a more conscious apprehension of such "sonorous waves"/material imagination. Here then, Bachelard's concept of substance, of 'matter' can be seen to be a corollary with esoteric forms of subtle matter and akin to ontological forms of matter proposed by New Materialists.

For Bachelard reverie enables the perception of subtle forces, of reverberations of elemental matter that inhabit the essential becoming of life. The perception of such requires an embodied aesthetic relation that commences from consideration of empirical materiality with a particular form of embodied, creative, epistemology (material imagination). Thus the perception of ontological (in some schemes 'spiritual') matter commences from a cultivated engagement with elemental material.

2.2 Invisible Elementals: Discerning the Flux and Flow

Crucial to Bachelard's proposition of reverie and the operations of material imagination—which perceives material dynamism—is a temporal aesthetics. Reverie is established via concerted, focused engagement with 'images' and/or material elements over a period of time. During which, the borders between subject and object become ambiguous and the intersubjective nature of this exchange is revealed to the viewer. This is a viewer, who as a result of body–mind cultivation techniques is able to 'see' with the material imagination as proposed by Bachelard. Such exchanges are temporal, and indeed the registering of the 'vibration' (Bachelard) or dynamics (e. g., speed) of such exchanges is requisite to the relation proposed and any understanding of this relation as an aesthetic one. The perception and exchange of 'forces' is a well-known aspect of both ontological and aesthetic relations proposed by Gilles Deleuze and Félix Guattari: "We are not in the world, we become with the world; we become by contemplating it. Everything is vision, becoming. We become universes" (Deleuze and Guattari [1991] 1994, 169).

I have argued in detail elsewhere (Johnston 2006, 2008) that the conceptualisation of ontological 'forces' developed by Deleuze and Guattari is a corollary to the way in which matter is variously conceptualised in Western Esoteric tradition—especially the subtle matter of subtle bodies—and will not repeat those argument here, except to highlight the shared concern with radical intersubjectivity and the way in which particular modes of perception are designated as having the capacity to apprehend the ontological agency of these forces (variously termed subtle, spiritual, energetic) that are understood to constitute all matter.

In the context of this chapter I'd like to specifically focus on Deleuze and Guattari's conception of sensation in *What is Philosophy* (1994). Sensations are differentiated from material by their ability to exist independently of the material. This is possible because the material has entered into the sensation (and not the other way around) and therefore can be understood to share the sensation's characteristics of exceeding the mediating subject. Bachelard's understanding of the material imagination, as enabling the extension and creation of new universes for the contemplating subject, is echoed in this material becoming (of sensation). For Deleuze and Guattari material acquired a palpable force with the potential for multiple becomings quite independent from the seemingly closed, framed surfaces of the image (they elaborate this discussion in relation to abstract painting). Without detouring into the different types of sensations distinguished by Deleuze and Guattari (1994, 168) the point of note is, thus conceptualised the viewer exists in an ontological intersubjective relation with the object of scrutiny: they and it mutually effect one another's becoming. Further, Deleuze and Guattari equate sensation (understood, as noted above, as interrelated with the material) with pure contemplation: "Sensation is pure contemplation, for it is through contemplation that one contracts, contemplating oneself to the extent that one contemplates the elements from which one originates" (Deleuze and Guattari 1994, 212).

Akin to esoteric concepts of the *mundus imaginalis*, sensation (as a practice of contemplation) is creative, it is "passive creation" (Deleuze and Guattari 1994, 212). In outlining this productive sensation–contemplation Deleuze and Guattari write further: "Plontinus defines all things as contemplations, not only as people and animals but plants, the earth, rocks. These are not Ideas that we contemplate through concepts but the elements of matter that we contemplate through sensation (Deleuze and Guattari 1994, 212). Sensation enables contemplation and contemplation enables the viewer to *enter into* sensation and to perceive its vibration or temporary form (elements of matter). These relations are possible because of a proposed shared ontological 'ground.' This contemplation requires a viewer to cultivate particular modes of perception/imagination that in turn enable the viewer to apprehend the 'forces' and flows' of elemental materials and the reciprocal intersubjective dynamics of exchange between viewer and artwork (Johnston 2008). The embodied aesthetic relation is a variable, temporal one. Central to this process is the perception of rates of material dynamism: therefore the viewer enters into fast and slow (and all gradations in between) rates of 'exchange' with various other-than-human agencies. The perception of these exchanges is an Esoteric Aesthetics.

Building on these conceptualisations of the 'material imagination' and the aesthetics of 'sensation–contemplation' developed by Deleuze and Gauttari (both of which are founded upon concepts of other-than-human agency and a 'subtle' or extensive form of embodiment) this chapter now turns to consider how this type of aesthetic relation could be understood to manifest with discussion of specific artwork examples, especially those closely aligned with the landscape, which stress the natural elements, and indeed approach the landscape as a locus of various other-than-human agencies.

3 Subtle Ecologies: The Elemental Aesthetics of Subtle Landscapes

> The artwork is the threshold at which elementals exceed the limits of perception. In simultaneously making contact with natural phenomena and withholding the drive to unify them in the viewer's field of vision, the artwork offers itself as a medium on which the earth manifests and asserts its irreducibility to human signification. In this way, the aesthetic strategies of earth art are coextensive with its ethical statement. (Boetzkes 2010, 21)

In taking up the topics of a 'subtle' and 'sacred' landscape two forms of the idea are being invoked herein. The first is the more common understanding of a landscape deemed spiritually significant for a particular group of people or broader culture. This is inclusive of landscapes noticeably altered by human activity including the addition of various structural forms (houses, churches, monuments, gardens, etc.) as well as landscapes deemed 'sacred natural sites' which evidence much lower levels of human impact and/or may be understood as inhabited by metaphysical beings. However, 'sacred landscape' also refers to 'natural' environments more broadly, from the generalist perspective that nature is "sacred, worthy of our highest respect" (Verschuuren et al. 2010, xxi).

The concept of 'nature' itself has been distinguished as highly problematic—especially when defined via reductive dualisms, e.g., nature-contra-culture. Indeed that 'nature', and what counts as 'natural' is a cultural construct is now well attested. However it is salient to note, and work with, re-definitions of nature that emerge from contemporary ecological studies. Two are of particular relevance for this context. Firstly, the concept of 'multinatural' developed by Jamie Lorimer. This term is employed to denote "the hybrid and lively character of a world animated by a vast range of human and nonhuman difference adhering to multiple and discordant spatio-temporal rhythms" (Lorimer 2015, 5). That is, environments in which the agencies of other-than-human species are taken into serious account. Lorimer's moniker 'multinatural' is used both to convey this world of diverse agencies and to critique any sense of static states induced by the term 'nature'. It is the dynamism, the processes at the heart of any environment (including those less effected by humankind) that is being invoked.

To Lorimer's 'multinatural' approach can be appended emergent concepts of spirituality found in the re-wilding movement, best illustrated by Mark Bekoff's recent discussion of re-wilding as a "mind-set" and "silent spiritual revolution" (Bekoff 2014, 30, 54). Re-wilding is an approach to conservation that receives high-profile media attention for its ambition to reintroduce now extinct apex predators, for example the lynx or wolf to Britain, as well as restoring and linking 'wild' landscapes and advocating minimal human 'management'. Of course, this is a very reductive overview with each of these aims differently emphasised by different re-wilding approaches (see, for example, www.rewilding-britain.org.uk). For Bekoff, re-wilding is attitudinal: it involves a way of viewing the world that embraces profound intersubjective relations: "When I mind animals in this way, I practice what I consider 'deep ethology.' That is, as the 'seer,' I try to become the 'seen'" (Bekoff 2014, 5). This requires a range of epistemologies, including intuition: "Historically, science dismisses and cuts off such subjective impressions, this intuitive knowledge, but this attitude has often made science 'tone deaf' to the animals they study. Too focused on proving what animals know, scientists don't hear what animals are saying: that they deserve caring, coexistence, and respect" (Bekoff 2014, 59).

Both Lorimer's *Wildlife in the Anthropocene* and Bekoff's work on re-wilding have much more to offer a consideration of the cultivation of perception (taken up elsewhere, Johnston forthcoming). They are both noted herein because of the centrality of other-than-human agencies in their work and secondly to exemplify that this issue is also of crucial concern in many academic fields outside of religious or cultural studies. Their work is employed herein to signal the inherent intersubjective and connective nature of the multispecies relations they discuss. Therefore from such a perspective 'nature' is part of a broader multispecies aesthetic ecology. Indeed, such an approach is an inherently aesthetic one: focused on cultivating and apprehending the intersubjective relations between a diverse range of agencies.

This chapter is focused less on specific multispecies agency and more on elemental agencies that collectively comprise an environment/landscape and artworks that seeks to call our attention to the other-than-human agencies of which they are formed. This is of course inclusive of the multispecies (including humans) that inhabit that landscape: a landscape of intersubjective relations.

3.1 Elemental Art: Roni Horn and the Aesthetics of Place

> What it feels like to be there is precisely not to be able to place language in a simple opposition to sensation. (Fer 2009, 24)

Vatnasafn/Library of Water, 2007, an installation by Roni Horn in Stykkishólmur, Iceland is the case study for this analysis (http://www.libraryofwater.is/landing.html). The project is comprised of a number of (overlapping) parts. Sited in a former library—also previously used as place for the collection of meteorological data—which was renovated as part of Horn's project, *Vatnasafn/Library of Water* encompasses this building and its use by the community; an installation that comprises floor-to-ceiling transparent glass columns containing glacial ice/melt-water; the floor covered in an embossed rubber inscribed with Icelandic and English words for the weather, these are adjectives that are often also used to describe an individuals' mood; and an archive of weather reports (also presented in a book) collected from local residents. The latter reflecting the history of the building as the first place in Iceland that systematic meteorological data was taken (Lingwood 2009, 15–19).

Writing in the volume that represents this Artangel project, James Lingwood (2009, 19) notes succinctly that Roni Horn has a "commitment to physical, metaphysical, political, social and moral energy". This commitment is played out in this installation that directly focuses on 'the elements': an expression commonly used to denote the weather, and in particular wild, powerful, extreme weather. Clearly, the material element water is also a central focus of the artist's exploration. Horn's installation highlights the radical reciprocity of the elements of light and water that infiltrate both subject and object; viewer and landscape. However, before turning to examine the rendering of these intersubjective relations, several distinct parts of the installation will be considered in isolation. The first of which is the landscape of Iceland itself.

As any who have ventured to Iceland know, the landscape is overwhelming. An island of contrasts: dark lava forms counterpointed by swathes of blue-mauve lupins (apparently planted to help soil regeneration); denuded scree-sided mountains dissected by waterfalls; massive glaciers bobbing about in pallid blue lakes while tourists motor out alongside them in bright orange rubber dinghies. The visual field alone is vast and can certainly lead to feeling that one's eyes are stretched in the attempt to encompass its vistas resulting in physical exhaustion due to sensory overload (and that's before you've started a hike!). It is also a literary landscape, one peppered with folk tales and saga narratives strongly bound to specific place. Metaphysical beings such as the *huldufólk* of Iceland inhabit the rocks and mounds and reverence towards these beings continues into contemporary times (Gunell 2009). It is an animate land, an enchanted landscape—whether one attributes the enchantment to otherworldly origins or not.

Roni Horn's engagement with Iceland has developed over many decades, and is a place—up until the installation at Stykkishólmur—that, as Lingwood (2009, 14) notes, from which Horn had "kept the art world at bay". Indeed, he reads the maintenance of this distance as significant to the state of the relationship: "carefully guarding the delicate ecology of her intimate relationship to the place" (Lingwood 2009, 14). Prior to *Vatnasafn/Library of Water* Horn had presented work developed and created in Iceland to audiences at a physical remove from the specific location (Lingwood 2009, 14 – 15). This is clearly evident in the book series *To Place* of which Lingwood writes that they: "convey the quiet intensity and subtle energies of a long communion between an elemental island and an enquiring mind" (Lingwood 2009, 14). *Vatnasafn/Library of Water* gives a direct invitation to the art-world, Icelanders and all other visitors to experience these "subtle energies" themselves.

This does not however, imply that Horn's invitation is a *tabula rasa*. Her installation filters the Icelandic landscape for the viewer, she plays and crafts with its elements to draw attention to their central role in the development of subjectivity, identity and relationships. That is to make evident the intersubjective relationship between human and environment. Just as she had the windows of the old library building enlarged to draw in the light and landscape to a greater degree so too she brings the more 'remote' features of landscape—remote both in terms of geography and geology—into the heart of her installation with the creation of the glacial water pillars.

The water contained in the floor-to-ceiling transparent pillars was collected from Iceland's twenty-four "major glaciers and glacial tongues" (Lingwood 2009, 14 – 17). The viewer is offered the chance to change their perspective in several ways by these glacial posts: firstly the transparent glass columns play with the light refracting in through the water, there is a mild distortion of visual perception as the translucent glass subtly breaks the viewer's field of vision, creating fissures in the smooth perception of space, or "vertical stripes, as if there are slits in it" (Fer 2009, 26). Secondly, each pillar creates a micro-world. Although the glacial ice has melted, each glass tube contains material from one particular glacier, one particular landscape, therefore the form and content of the sedimentation at the bottom of each tube is different: they form "micro-landscapes" (Lingwood 2009, 15). If a viewer peers closely into the pillars they find a miniature landscape or looking through the pillars a visual field made unstable by the curvature of the glass and the density of the water.

In a beautiful evocation of the theme of environmental concern/conservation signalled by Horn's use of glacial matter, Adrian Searle also evokes the work's bearing on the sense of hearing:

> Sound travels better through water. I imagine those melted glaciers captured inside the glass columns in the library trembling to the cries of the arriving birds, as well as registering all the other sounds, inaudible to the human ear. That fills the region of the Atlantic. Each column is itself a library: of minerals, bacteria, atomic and sub-atomic particles, of the sonorous low-frequency booms and cries of whales passing the in oceans between Iceland and Greenland (Searle 2009, 38).

The glacial waters are here presented as capturing and containing complex and invisible relationships with innumerable other-than-human agencies including the cetacean, avian, bacterial and mineral. For Searle these agencies are captured in the water's very materiality. Paying attention to this element—employing a range of different senses in such engagement—reveal complex forms of intersubjectivity. It is such intersubjective relations—between self and the environment that Horn's multi-part installation focuses upon. It aims to make evident the porous nature of the conceptual boundaries evoked in dominant culture to separate human from landscape; active from inert. The aesthetic relations evoked by Horn's elemental art are non-binary (like those proposed by Bachelard and Deleuze and Guattari). Returning to the quotation that opened this section which recounts Briony Fer's experience of *Vatnasafn/Library of Water:* "What it feels like to be there is precisely not to be able to place language in a simple opposition to sensation" (Fer 2009, 24), the binary between language and sensation is also here made porous. The elemental materials are induced to speak for themselves (within the confines of the installation) and their voice/language is sensation.

How do we listen to this other? As already recounted, Bachelard proposes a material imagination, in general an Esoteric Aesthetics would advocate an embodied engagement utilising cultivated forms of perception and alternate epistemologies. As such the 'familiar' empirical elements can be understood to speak foreign languages which the viewer needs to learn via embodied listening and exchange. The positioning of the environment as radically other is identified by Amanda Boetzkes as a feature of 'earth art' in general. Indeed, for Boetzkes it is its capacity to confound, stretch, challenge an individual's perceptive regime that gives such art its potency: "the artworks mediate contact with elemental forces that overwhelm the senses and confound the stability of one's perceptual apparatus" (Boetzkes 2010, 4).

This description comes very close to reproducing traditional concepts of 'the sublime' albeit the overawing natural world here is filtered via the contemporary artworks. Previously, with reference to the work of Kirk Pillow (2000) I have argued for the renegotiation of the beauty—sublime dualism noting how this 'other' attributed to the sublime relation has historically been easily adapted to theoaesthetic discourse (Johnston 2008). Salient to this context is the argument that a change in approach to the epistemological resources required results in different forms of aesthetic engagement and an unravelling of the beauty—sublime dualism:

> It [sublime] is a meeting with alterity that is threatening, it is a view that the inability to
> cognise is an inadequacy that undoes cohesive subjectivity. As such, an aesthetic appre-

hension is figured at the heart of relations with alterity. [...] Further, the sublime's dishar-
mony is caused by an antipathy between imagination and reason whilst there is no such
conflict between understanding and the imagination (that is, the faculties involved in
the aesthetic experience of the beautiful). Such binary frameworks are disrupted by perceptive schemes like that of *mundus imaginalis* as this Imagination is not presented as a 'lower'
or instinctive type of mental faculty but, inversely, is considered an 'advanced' faculty of
perception inclusive of ontological agency (Johnston 2008).

While not the focus of this discussion, the *mundus imaginalis* as an epistemology
found in the western esoteric tradition can be considered to have corollaries with
Bachelard's material imagination: both are *active* states of imaginative/creative
engagement between subject and object (which posit a radical form of intersubjectivity) and crucially both foreground the ontological capacity of such relations.

A similar shift is seen in Pillow's proposition of 'the Interpretative Sublime'
(Pillow 2000, 285; Johnston 2008), which highlights the partial "open-ended"
nature of the insights gleaned from sublime encounters and its ontological capacity:

> Sublime understanding helps invent our indeterminate worlds; it also violates the limits of
> current comprehension without pretending that its product is complete or that it now cap-
> tures some given reality. Aesthetic reflection's production of indeterminate webs of shared
> meaning provides constantly un-whole worlds, riven by irreducible heterogeneity, confused
> juxtapositions of incongruous interpretation, and multiple avenues for critique and trans-
> formation, but it helps articulate worlds for us nevertheless (Pillow 2000, 303).

Here then, the sublime is not purely an aesthetic response, but a mode of perceiving, interpreting and relating to the world that acknowledges its (that is
'the worlds') capacity to resist total comprehension. It is a form of relation
with alterity that does not subsume, erase or deny radical difference. As I
have highlighted previously it is an approach that calls for the *active* cultivation
of perception. Pillow presents it as requiring the "revision" of our usual "habits":
"It advocates a complicating way of seeing that pushes beyond received understanding to attempt a deeper insight. [...] Wrestling meaning from the sublime
void beyond our habits of mind, however partial and context-specific the understanding that results, leads us to constantly question our habits, to stretch out
for what has been left unthought" (Pillow 2000, 317–318).

If Boetzkes' approach to the elemental 'other' of earth art is refined with this
revised understanding of the sublime, then an account of 'nature' outside any
universal concept of 'purity' or romantic understanding of the sublime can be
proposed. As Horn's *Vatnasafn/Library of Water* exemplifies, the use of elemental
materials: "foregrounds the spectator's bodily contact with, and sensorial expe-

rience of, natural phenomena" (Boetzke 2010, 12) and part of this experience draws attention to the way in which: "The artwork is the threshold at which elementals exceed the limits of perception. In simultaneously making contact with natural phenomena and withholding the drive to unify them in the viewer's field of vision, the artwork offers itself as a medium on which the earth manifests and asserts its irreducibility to human signification" (Boetzke 2010, 21). Boetzkes presents 'earth art' as a site (both aesthetic and ethical) where the other-than-human agency of elemental material are perceivable, even if they necessarily elude any form of unified signification. To this proposal an Esoteric Aesthetics —which similarly advocates for the acknowledgment of other-than-human agency—would add an expanded understanding of what counts as perceivable (inclusive of illusive invisible 'energetic' relations), its capacity to be developed and changed via conscious cultivation and its (potential) ontological agency.

4 Conclusion: Ecologies of Esoteric Vision

ecology, *n*. **1. a.** The branch of biology that deals with the relationships between living organisms and their environment. Also: the relationships themselves, esp. those *of* a specified organism. **b.** Chiefly *Sociol.* The study of the relationships between people, social groups, and their environment; (also) the system of such relationships in an area of human settlement. [...] **c.** In extended use: the interrelationship between any system and its environment; the product of this. **2.** The study of or concern for the effect of human activity on the environment... (*OED*).

An Esoteric Aesthetics enfolds these *Oxford English Dictionary* definitions of "ecology" together. It both 'deals' with relationships between organisms and the environment, inclusive of humans as well as—exemplified by the discussion of Roni Horn's installation *Vatnasafn/Library of Water* and 'earth art' more generally—a concern for the way in which humans affect the environment. In addition, an Esoteric Aesthetics emphasises several dimensions (i) in the study of human ecologies that other-than-human agencies be taken in greater account (ii) that part of this process requires the cultivation and use of a wide variety of epistemologies, with the discussion herein focusing on Bachelard's concept of the material imagination. That is with regard to the characteristics of Esoteric Aesthetics outlined in the Introduction, any such aesthetic 'ecology' requires that perception—how these relations are apprehended—be of central concern. Once such a question is asked the ethical ramifications necessarily require a consideration of both the degree to which any alterity can be perceived and the imperative to challenge, reform, cultivate one's own perceptive literacy.

Landscapes are lived, vibrant, desolate, confusing, invigorating, perplexing, relaxing, hostile, generous, calm and endlessly changing environments. An esoteric approach to considering these material elements—in art-form or not—necessarily requires that this complexity of agencies be acknowledged even if they cannot be fully perceived or comprehended. Such relations make both the object and viewer radically permeable and unstable. This is the necessarily precarious subjective 'ground' from which an Esoteric Aesthetic unfurls.

Bibliography

Bachelard, Gaston. [1938] 1964. *The Psychoanalysis of Fire*, translated by Alan C. M. Ross. Boston: Bacon Press.
—— [1942] 1983. *Water and Dreams: An Essay on the Imagination of Matter*, translated by Edith R. Farrell. Dallas: The Pegasus Foundation, The Dallas Institute of Humanities and Culture.
Bekoff, Marc. 2014. *Rewilding Our Hearts: Building Pathways of Compassion and Coexistence*. Novato: New World Library.
Boetzkes, Amanda. 2010. *The Ethics of Earth Art*. Minneapolis: University of Minnesota Press.
Deleuze, Gilles, and Félix. Guattari. [1991] 1994. *What is Philosophy?*, translated by Graham Burchell and Hugh Tomlinson. London and New York: Verso.
Fer, Briony. 2009. "Storm of the Eye." In *Roni Horn, 'Vatnasafn/Library of Water,' Stykkishólmur, Iceland*, 146–154. London: Artangel/Steidl.
Gaudin, Colette, ed. and trans. 1998. *Gaston Bachelard on Poetic Imagination and Reverie*. Dallas: Spring Publications.
Gunnell, T. 2009. "Legends and Landscapes in the Nordic Countries." *Cultural and Social History* 6/3: 305–322.
Johnston, Jay. 2008. *Angels of Desire: Esoteric Bodies, Aesthetics and Ethics*. London: Equinox Publishing.
—— 2013. "Subtle Subjects and Ethics: The Subtle Bodies of Post-Structuralist and Feminist Philosophy." In *Religion and the Subtle Body in Asia and the West: Between Mind and Body*, edited by G. Samuel and J. Johnston, 239–248. London: Routledge.
—— 2016a. "Slippery and Saucy Discourse: Grappling with the Intersection of 'Alternate Epistemologies' and Discourse Analysis." In *Making Religion: Theory and Practice in the Discursive Study of Religion*, edited by F. Wijsen and K. von Stuckrad, 74–96. Leiden: Brill.
—— 2016b. "Enchanted Sight/Site: An Esoteric Aesthetics of Image and Experience." In *The Relational Dynamics of Enchantment and Sacralization: Changing the Terms of the Religion Versus Secularization Debate*, edited by Peik Ingman, Terhi Utriainen, Tuija Hovi and Måns Broo, 207–230. Sheffield: Equinox.
—— (forthcoming 2018/2019) *Stag and Stone: Religion, Archaeology and Esoteric Aesthetics*. Forthcoming. Sheffield: Equinox.
—— and Ruth Barcan. 2006. "Subtle Transformations: Imagining the Body in Alternative Health Practices." In *International Journal of Cultural Studies* 9/1: 25–44.

Lingwood, James. 2009. "Journey to the Library of Water." In *Roni Horn,'Vatnasafn/Library of Water,' Stykkishólmur, Iceland*, 142–145. London: Artangel/Steidl.

Lorimer, Jamie. 2015. *Wildlife in the Anthropocene: Conservation After Nature*. Minneapolis and London: University of Minnesota Press.

Oxford English Dictionary, "Ecology." URL: http://www.oed.com.ezproxy1.library.usyd.edu.au/view/Entry/59380?redirectedFrom=ecology#eid (last accessed 30 March 2016)

Pillow, Kirk. 2000. *Sublime Understanding: Aesthetic Reflection in Kant and Hegel*. Cambridge, Massachusetts: The MIT Press.

Searle, Adrian. 2009. "How Like the World Was All Over after All." In *Roni Horn, 'Vatnasafn/Library of Water,' Stykkishólmur, Iceland*, 155. London: Artangel/Steidl.

Verschuuren, Bas, Robert Wild, Jeffrey A. McNeely, and Gonzalo Oviedo. 2010. "Preface." In *Sacred Natural Sites: Conserving Nature & Culture*, edited by Bas Verschuuren, Robert Wild, Jeffrey A. McNeely and Gonzalo Oviedo, xxi-xxii. London and Washington: Earthscan.

Sebastian Schüler

Aesthetics of Immersion: Collective Effervescence, Bodily Synchronisation and the Sensory Navigation of the Sacred

[I]f collective life awakens religious thought on reaching a certain degree of intensity, it is because it brings out a state of effervescence which changes the conditions of psychic activity. Vital energies are over-extended, passions more active, sensations stronger; there are even some which are produced only at this moment. A man does not recognize himself; he feels himself transformed and consequently he transforms the environment (Durkheim [1912] 1976, 422).

1 Introduction

In this chapter I will examine the concept of aesthetics of immersion as a connective concept for the aesthetics of religion. With the term immersion I refer to typical feelings, emotions and bodily experiences of getting-drawn-into-something as they can occur in collective religious rituals or different forms of meditation. The aim of this study is to better understand the sensory side of collective ritual arousals as they were described by the famous sociologist Émile Durkheim (1976, 422) in terms of collective effervescence. Approaching the aesthetics of immersion is thus asking about the sensory perception implied when people empathetically and bodily dive, or get drawn into, a particular vibrant atmosphere. Immersion in more general terms can refer to the emotional arousal of a group, listening to music or the viewing of painted art. The aesthetics of immersion therefore asks how individuals consciously and subconsciously play with the dissolving of emotional and cognitive distances in certain situations. How does someone get drawn into a particular feeling or sensation through the special design of a room, the atmospheric use of light, the contemplation of a picture, watching a movie, playing a video game or participating in a rhythmic movement?

It is a fact that questions concerning the aesthetics of immersion have mostly been addressed in media studies and art history, focusing on immersive perception constrained and induced by space (Bieger 2007), virtual reality (Nechvatal 2009), playing video games (Jennett et al. 2008), or beholding art (Grau 2005). Sociological studies, however, have too often neglected the immersive character of collective rituals. The purpose of this article is, therefore, to broaden and sharpen the perspective of an aesthetics of immersion for the study of religions

https://doi.org/10.1515/9783110461015-016

and to develop an analytical framework for investigating collective effervescence.

I will argue that the concept of immersion is 1) a crucial aspect for understanding (the emergence of) collective effervescence, and 2) comprises a twofold dynamic that includes a feeling of *getting-drawn-into* (affect) and a feeling of *letting-go* (control). This already indicates that immersion can count as a complex mechanism in the unfolding of collective dynamics of effervescent rituals. With this aesthetics of immersion approach I hope to make a contribution to a better understanding of specific states of arousal and ecstasy as they can be found in collective effervescence and immersive forms of meditation. In order to develop this approach, I will first discuss some of the existing attempts to sharpen Durkheim's concept of collective effervescence. Secondly, I will introduce the concept of embodied synchronisation in order to corroborate the physical and sensory foundations of collective effervescence. Finally, I will elaborate on the concept and character of immersion as an aesthetical approach to collective effervescence and develop an analytical framework based on the twofold nature of immersion. This framework will be briefly applied to the phenomenon of speaking in tongues (*glossolalia*) in order to exemplify the ambivalent character and different modes of immersion.

2 Collective Effervescence: Durkheim's Concept and Beyond

Whether it be a jumping crowd in a pop concert, a singing choir, or a dancing couple, it is always sensational and agitating when people interact with each other and when this mutual interaction unfolds some kind of dynamic quality that becomes detached from the individual and, at the same time, seems to at least partly control his or her behaviour. This is what Émile Durkheim termed, about one hundred years ago, collective effervescence. Since then sociologists and psychologists have made use of Durkheim's term to explain what is commonly referred to as irrational behaviours, such as the unfolding of aggression in hooligan groups or the state of trance and ecstasy of participants in a collective ritual. The attribution of effervescent states as something irrational derives from the impression that people who enter a group dynamic do not act according to their usual standards, but somehow seem to be out of control or to have lost themselves (or their ordinary behaviours).

Durkheim's theory of collective effervescence still plays a prominent role in sociological studies of all kinds, and particularly when it comes to questions concerning the emotional and social effects of collective rituals and group dynamics. Sociologists have been mostly interested in the functional outcomes of collective arousals, such as group cohesion. What has attracted less attention, however, are the sensory and emotional foundations of collective arousals. Although the social functions of collective effervescence have been well explored in sociology, this cannot be said of the question how collective effervescence emerges in the first place. What is the material basis, what are the physiological, emotional and cognitive dispositions driving the dynamics of collective interactions that lead to collective effervescence? And how is this immersive moment of getting drawn into the social dynamic of the group perceived by the individual?

In "The Elementary Forms of Religious Life", Durkheim (1976, 215, 353) used the example of corroboree festivals among Australian aboriginal cultures to describe a prototype of social collectivisation. In his theory, during the corroboree ritual participants fall into an enthusiastic and emotional state of arousal, and at the same time this collective arousal creates a new group identity, which becomes symbolised in an icon (totem of the clan), which again becomes incorporated by the individual through the ritual dance, often demonstrated by the acting of the dancer as the totem animal. For Durkheim, in this way societies and groups create a collective identity in which the sacred becomes demarcated from the mundane, the transcendent from the everyday (Durkheim 1976, 262, 302).

Important to his theory is his observation that such forms of collectivisation, and their integrative function for a society, can be found in all cultures including modern ones, and further, that such forms of collectivisation build a starting point for transcendental (group) experiences. In his basic distinction between the profane and the sacred, Durkheim emphasised collective rituals as a core mechanism for creating a feeling for the sacred and for a communality and cohesion of the group. Although the sentiment of communality and group cohesion can be found in many different collective gatherings and group activities, it seems religious communities especially make use of this social instrument, in order to periodically restore their identity. Whether or not Durkheim's approach can sufficiently explain the social origins of religion cannot be discussed here, and this question refers to a long-standing and ongoing debate within the study of religions. For the sake of convenience, I understand forms of collective effervescence as a potential, but not inevitable, building block for the emergence or construction of things deemed sacred (Taves 2013).

The idea of effervescence—the term usually means the escape of gas in a liquid solution and the foaming effects of it—and the way Durkheim used it in his theory has inspired generations of scholars[1] in the study of religions and sociology. Some have fathomed the concept's depth by bringing it into relation with

---

1 For a comprehensive overview and discussion, see Buehler (2012). See also Pickering (1984).

other concepts such as Weber's charisma (Carlton-Ford 1992), Turner's liminality (Pickering 1984; Berger 2016) or the concept of emergence (Sawyer 2002). Others have applied it not only to religious events but also to all kinds of social collectivisations. Michel Maffesoli (1986), for example, describes all kinds of social interactions in which smaller or greater emotional arousals occur and which unfold a socially orgiastic, not-purpose-driven dynamic in terms of a collective effervescence. Yet, in the way Maffesoli uncovers collective effervescence in many different social encounters, the term is used too widely to be distinctive. In addition, Maffesoli, like Durkheim, is chiefly interested in the social function of collective arousals as social forms of integration and as mechanisms for social cohesion. This makes sense on a macro-level of analysis and for the question as to how societies work. What it fails to look at are the mechanisms on a micro-level, which lead to collective effervescence in the first place and to the individual experiences and sensations that precede and shape the emergence of collective effervescence. Durkheim's concept of effervescence starts from the assumption that the participants in a collective ritual somehow lose rational control over themselves and fall into an emotional state of uncontrolled or uncontrollable affective behaviour. He therefore points out:

> But when a corrobbori takes place, everything changes. Since the emotional and passional faculties of the primitive are only imperfectly placed under the control of his reason and will, he easily loses control of himself. Any event of some importance puts him quite outside himself. [...] There are at once transports of enthusiasm. In the contrary conditions, he is to be seen running here and there like a madman, giving himself up to all sorts of immoderate movements, crying, shrieking, rolling in the dust, throwing it in every direction, biting himself, brandishing his arms in a furious manner, etc. (Durkheim 1976, 215)

The ecstatic state of the individual seems to become decoupled from his or her cognitive control. Yet, Durkheim never saw such phenomena as pathological, as psychologists of his time did (Buehler 2012, 75). Rather, he discovered a social mechanism in collective effervescence that can be found in many social movements and group gatherings. In fact, for Durkheim emotional arousal just seems to happen as a result of people coming together. Unfortunately, he remained unclear about the concrete social arrangements, the mentalities, the sentiments, as well as collectively shared ideas, which precede the emergence of collective effervescence. What is cause, and what is effect?

A central question therefore is, what are the dispositions for collective effervescence, and how can they best be described? And how do individuals experience the moment of getting drawn into a collective dynamic—such as losing control over themselves or a high degree of apperception? There have been some efforts to look at this micro-level of collective effervescence in recent years; to follow a few examples are discussed briefly. As will be shown, all of them attempt to approach the sensuous side of collective effervescence by making use of related concepts and terminology. After this brief review, I will proceed to my own attempt to investigate this question by taking a closer look at the concept of immersion.

Not only Durkheim, and later Maffesoli, but also other scholars, such as Georg Simmel, Marcel Mauss, Max Weber, Karl Mannheim, or Randall Collins, have highlighted the energetic transference of emotional enthusiasm from one individual to another and the effects it has on individuals of losing themselves in moments of collective effervescence. Sociologist Randall Collins (2004, xii), for instance, provides the following description: "Part of the collective effervescence of a highly focused, emotionally entrained interaction is apportioned to the individuals, who come away from the situation carrying the group-aroused emotion for a time in their bodies". Yet, what Collins describes remains fuzzy for it does not explain how collective effervescence emerges from the perspective of the individual's perception or the role of the senses in that process of emergence. A more promising attempt was developed by sociologists Leistner and Schmidt-Lux (2012) who investigated the conditions and constraints that are necessary for the emergence of collective effervescence, particularly as it emerges in forms of group-aroused ecstasy, such as in fan cultures. They argue that sociology today must take emotions more seriously in order to include the affective side of social collectivisations, which can be seen as the foundation of all kinds of social phenomena. For them, ecstasy provides a good opportunity to investigate social collectivisation as it demarcates extraordinary from ordinary events (2012, 317). Thus, they define ecstasy as a collectively induced emotional state in which emotions become so intense that they seem to carry away the individual's behaviour and feelings. Leistner and Schmidt-Lux are aware of the fact that most sociologists would refer to Durkheim's concept of effervescence in order to explain the functions of group ecstasy, yet they argue that Durkheim failed to explain how effervescence emerges. They further point out that according to Durkheim effervescence seems to emerge just by the fact of people gathering. By contrast, they argue that effervescence does not occur automatically, nor does it occur very often in societies, since the dispositions that lead to the emergence of effervescence have too many prerequisites (2012, 318). Based on their own image analysis of a photograph of fans standing in a stadium watching a game of soccer, they came to the understanding that individuals stand together and watch the game as a collective event, but they seem more or less enthusiastic about it and they do not yet form a collective body of ecstasy. According to their observations, the crucial moment in collective effervescence is the point of collectively letting loose (*kollektives Fallenlassen*). In consequence, they raise three intriguing questions: 1) What are the frame conditions that lead toward and induce this moment of collectively letting loose? 2) What are the underlying dynamics that foster such a situation? and 3) When and how do people actually lose control over their bodies? Leistner and Schmidt-Lux find their answers in a combination of three instructive theories, proposed by Émile Durkheim, Randall Collins and Helmuth Plessner. I cannot unfold their complete argument here or go into the details of these three theories. But they draw our attention to the fact that a moment of collectively letting loose is conditioned by both frame conditions and situated conditions (Leistner and Schmidt-Lux 2012, 330).

Frame conditions are those that have already been described by Durkheim, such as the collective gathering of people, the spatial constraints of that gathering, and collectively performed practices such as rituals. Less attention has been given so far to what they call situated conditions. These include for instance attention or concentration on a common focus point. Gatherings of people do not necessarily lead to joint attention, even though the frame conditions might provide a dense atmosphere, for instance through the proximity of bodies in a stadium. It is the bundling of attention that boosts the likeliness of a collective effervescence. Accordingly, it could be argued that collective ecstasy is more likely in groups in which people already know each other and each other's attitudes, such as in religious rituals. As another situated condition, Leistner and Schmidt-Lux describe the internal precondition of being compassionate, which seems to be an emotional pulsation, or an alternation between observing and getting drawn into the event. For my own argument in favour of an aesthetics of immersion, this aspect is very compelling, as it demonstrates that collective effervescence oscillates between moments of control and letting go, as I will propose later in this chapter.

Another valuable approach to effervescence has been proposed by Arthur Buehler, who, in his article "The Twenty-first-century Study of Collective Effervescence", not only gives a valuable overview of recent approaches to Durkheim's concept, but also states that collective sentiments are measurable and that scholars have failed to do so; they "do not have the tools because they ignore transpersonal psychological and transpersonal anthropological methodologies when studying ritual phenomena" (Buehler 2012, 76). Buehler criticises Durkheim, and also later anthropologists, for being armchair-ethnologists who "apparently ha[ve] the superior perceptual ability to know what is really happening [during collective effervescence, S.S.] on the basis of (necessarily) flawed ethnographic data" (Buehler 2012, 78). And he continues: "Indeed, there is no evidence in Elementary Forms that collective effervescence brought about changes in the individual or in society" (Buehler 2012, 78). To give flesh to the bones of

Durkheim's theory, Buehler claims that collective effervescence is an altered state of consciousness and therefore can better be explained with insights from intense ethnographic fieldwork, including radical participation. He goes even further by contesting what he calls the scientific-materialist epistemology, what most anthropologists represent. "This so-called objectivity in doing research is intrinsic to the scientific-materialist paradigm—to the point that there is a 'taboo of subjectivity'" (Buehler 2012, 81). In order to better understand the effects of collective effervescence in terms of altered states of consciousness, Buehler claims: "To do fieldwork in a twenty-first-century context studying collective altered states of consciousness means using a methodology that produces kinds of subjective knowledge involving a change in the investigator's own state of consciousness" (Buehler 2012, 83).

Without opening up the old discussion of the insider-outsider problem here, I think on the one hand that Buehler raises an important point for the topic in question, but on the other hand I also think that we do not need to follow its radicalness. I totally agree that scholars in anthropology and in the study of religion should not be afraid of their research subjects. On the contrary, for researching contemporary religions one has to go where religion happens in real life in order to perceive for oneself how a religion is practiced in its everyday context. This is the only way to get drawn into the reality of the religious group, its rituals and sensations, and this is what participatory observation is all about. Yet, for Buehler (2012, 89) this is not enough: "The 'participant-observer' is a cognitive approach that necessarily treats the native as 'other' as it removes the anthropologist from the actual experience itself". I believe that it should be the personal decision of the scholar whether or not he/she joins religious rituals and is open for personal experiences. The crucial question is not so much that of intense participation, since this should happen anyway in the field, but the question is whether the scholar is able to take a distanced stance again after leaving the field, in order not to become an advocate of the religious tradition he or she is studying.

However, it is true that most writings on collective effervescence in recent decades were mainly theoretical, elaborating on Durkheim's idea and sociology. It is therefore necessary, first, to take more empirical examples into account in order to better understand how collective effervescence in a particular situation emerges and to describe the effects it has on the individual, and, second, to look for alternative concepts surrounding the perception and sensations involved in collective effervescence (such as altered states of consciousness) in order to enrich the sometimes ambiguous term effervescence.

These briefly discussed approaches to Durkheim's concept of collective effervescence have all highlighted the necessity of looking more closely at the micro-levels of such phenomena, and have at the same time demonstrated that the crucial question for a better understanding of the dispositions and effects of collective effervescence is that of perception and sensation. In order to develop this idea further, I will now discuss what I call the material foundations of collective effervescence, namely the synchronising effects on the body and the mind as they occur in social interactions in general and in collective effervescence in particular. From there I will proceed to the idea of "aesthetics of immersion" as a connective concept in the study of religion.

3 Bodily Synchronisation and the Material Foundation of Collective Effervescence

So far, we have taken into account new approaches to collective effervescence mainly coming from sociology. As refreshing as they are by asking new questions concerning the collective sentiments and sensations underlying the emergence of collective arousals, they seem to stop their investigations where the physical body and the senses begin. However, the body and the senses have attracted new interest recently in sociology as well as in the study of religions. Whereas the body was long taken as a mere social artefact, newer approaches have started to highlight aspects of embodiment: meaning social, as well as physical or biological foundations of the lived body. Manuel Vásquez (2011, 149–171), for instance, has underlined the importance of taking processes of embodiment more seriously in the study of religions, and at the same time he holds social constructionism in check by emphasizing the material aspects of the body rather than understanding the body only as a social artefact. In his materialist approach to religion, he does not plead for a positivist or naturalist epistemology but rather for an integrative perspective that considers sociological, neuroscientific and phenomenological approaches to understanding religion in practice. Here, I follow this materialist perspective in order to investigate the embodied dispositions at work in collective effervescence.

In recent decades, new insights from the cognitive sciences have given a deeper understanding of how embodied and social cognition works, and just lately cognitive psychologists and anthropologists have (again) become interested in the bodily and social dynamics of social interactions in general and of synchronised behaviour and collective effervescence in particular. In consequence, I will demonstrate that some of these insights into bodily and cognitive synchronisations are a more comprehensive—yet not exclusive—approach to collective effervescence (Schüler 2012). It is this multifaceted examination of effervescence, which instructs our understanding of the aesthetics of immersion as a connective concept in the study of religion.

The bodily effects of interactive behaviours and the unfolding bodily dynamics were first explored by Norman Triplett (1861–1934), one of the first scholars in social psychology, who found in 1898 that the sheer presence of other persons could enhance the physical powers of individuals (Triplett 1898; see also Davis, Huss, and Becker 2009). Triplett was able to show that cyclists became more effective and faster when they were cycling in a group-race rather than cycling alone against time. Psychological explanations usually argue that this effect results from competition. The cyclist wants to be faster than his or her competitors and, therefore, is able to release more physical power. In other words, the freed energy derives from his or her *will* to be faster. This explanation certainly contains some truth; yet, Norman Triplett added another important factor to explain his observations. In his theory, he holds "that the bodily presence of another rider is a stimulus to the racer in arousing the competitive instinct; that another can thus be the means of releasing or freeing nervous energy for him that he cannot of himself release; and, further, that the sight of movement in that other by perhaps suggesting a higher rate of speed, is also an inspiration to greater effort" (Triplett 1898, 516). Triplett points out two important factors here: 1) the bodily presence of others, and 2) the perception of movement of others. Both factors not only enhance the conscious will of the racer, but also seem to influence his behaviour on a subconscious level. The body seems to be responsive to the presence of others in such a way that this presence changes the whole autonomic nervous system. Émile Durkheim also took notice of Triplett's experiment and referred to it to support his idea of collective effervescence.

Like Triplett with his cyclists, we can argue that the term effervescence in addition to being a social phenomenon also implies cognitive, physiological and emotional dimensions of mutual perceptions. The presence of, and interaction with, another person seem to bring changes in the perception and the behaviour of an individual, resulting in a shared state of mind and a sensory connection between the two. Even Durkheim took notice of these mutual relations and the joint dynamic that occurs in groups: "When they are once come together, a sort of electricity is formed by their collecting which quickly transports them to an extraordinary degree of exaltation. Every sentiment expressed finds a place without resistance in all the minds, which are very open to outside impressions; each re-echoes the others, and is re-echoed by the others" (1976, 216–217). People connect to each other almost unconsciously as they get drawn into perception-action loops that can also be described as mutual synchronisations. In order to outline the idea of synchronisation, I will now turn to some newer insights from the social neurosciences, which throw light on the bodily and neural causes and effects in social dynamics.

Some recent experiments on bodily and cognitive synchronisation have focused on rhythmic behaviours, such as playing music or dancing, and their cognitive and social effects on the individual. One study "has discovered synchronous brain oscillations in duetting musicians, indicating a direct neural basis for interpersonally coordinated actions" (Sänger, Müller, and Lindenberger 2012). Another study demonstrates that tumultuous applause can transform itself into waves of synchronised clapping (Neda et al. 2000). This synchronised clapping is not the result of an external stimulus, such as someone clapping in front of the audience and thereby functioning as a metronome. Instead, the synchronisation appears and disappears in short waves and somehow seems to be autonomous or self-organising. In fact, the synchronised clapping results from collectively reducing the clapping speed, which leads to better physiological coordination and action-perception loops that form particular patterns of interaction. Both studies demonstrate that the emerging synchronicity of joint interactions takes place on a neural and on a bodily level.

Other experiments have shown that rhythmic and especially synchronic behaviours enhance social cooperation. In one experiment, Reddish, Fischer and Bulbulia (2013, 1) "compared a condition in which group synchrony was produced through shared intentionality to conditions in which synchrony or asynchrony were created as a by-product of hearing the same or different rhythmic beats. We found that synchrony combined with shared intentionality produced the greatest level of cooperation". In their experiment, psychologists Scott S. Wiltermuth and Chip Heath (2009, 1) even demonstrated "that positive emotions need not be generated for synchrony to foster cooperation". This shows the strong effect synchronising movements have on the perception and affective behaviours of individuals. Accordingly, these findings support Durkheim's observations that collective rituals increase group cohesion and communality.

In a broad sense, synchronisation can therefore best be understood as the way our brains and bodies effectively form *embodied interactions*. In modern cognitive sciences the term *embodiment* marks a new understanding of cognition. While cognition was understood as a solely mental operation for quite some time, recent approaches in embodied and social cognition emphasise that the emergence of cognition is always preceded by physical interaction. Highlighting this paradigmatic shift, cognitive psychologist Raymond Gibbs (2006, 13) has pointed out: "Our bodies, and our felt experiences of our bodies in action, finally take center stage in the empirical study of perception, cognition, and language and in cognitive science's theoretical accounts of human behavior".

For understanding cognition as *embodied cognition* we have to consider the body as the place where perception and action coincide. Italian neurobiologist Vittorio Gallese (2007) states that we should be wary of proposing strict dichotomies between action and perception. The elements that connect action and perception Gallese calls mirror neurons, and explains them thus: When one watches someone cry, laugh, or get punched, one can almost feel the same sadness, joy, or pain that person experiences. The reason is that by watching bodily or emotional expressions mirror-neurons are activated that trigger similar somatic and cognitive states in the brain and body of the observer. Most of the human ability for empathy is based on the function of mirror-neurons.

Raymond Gibbs (2006, 35) also emphasises a strong "connection between the mental representation of posture, the movement of one's own body, and the perception of posture and movement of other bodies". While watching others performing actions with their bodies, the same body images and body movements tend to arise in the observer, triggering similar mental representations and meanings. As the action of one person can become a stimulus for the actions of another person, this can also explain why collective rituals can enhance the emergence of action-perception loops that drive the synchronisation of bodies, emotions, and (religious) representations. In other words, the perception-action loops create a collective dynamic which on the one hand becomes an autonomous force that drives the bodily movements of the ritual participants, and on the other hand, influences the sensual perception of the participants to the extent that they cannot fully distinguish between their own actions and the actions of others. Anthropologist Maurice Bloch (Bloch 2002, 142) has described this phenomenon as follows: "One enters a ritual mode of communication by radical modifications of ordinary behavior [...] One often synchronises one's bodily and linguistic movements with those of others. This is so to the extent that one is not sure whether it is oneself or another inside oneself who is acting and using one's voice and one's body".

I therefore argue that it is the emerging dynamics of synchronising bodies that control the body (Schüler 2012). This can also help us to better understand phenomena such as glossolalia or spirit possession: the individual embodies the collective arousal in such a way that the emerging dynamics coordinate his or her body movements. Accordingly, it is the inter-subjective coordination and synchronisation of bodies in movement that constitute the basis for emerging feelings and representations of the sacred. Just as in the wordless coordination of the movements of a dancing couple, synchronicity in ritual interaction shapes the embodied experience of the ritual participants.

Finally, I would contend that the performance of collective effervescence itself produces and represents its own aesthetic of synchronisation. It *produces* an aesthetic of synchronisation by means of changing the sensual perception of the people who become part of a collective event (I have referred to this as a body-schema of collective effervescence; Schüler 2012). This way, we can also argue with Catherine Bell (2006, 538) that the ritual is a function of the body and not the other way around. Furthermore, it *represents* an aesthetic, in that bodily synchronisation shapes certain social and cultural formations, structures and images such as dancing couples or parades, which most people perceive as something 'nice to look at'.

In sum, the phenomenon of synchronisation can be found from micro-levels of neural activity to macro-levels of social and cultural formations. Synchronic behaviour seems to happen naturally wherever individuals gather in groups and start to interact through their bodies. In fact, human beings are the only living species that is able to move synchronously to rhythmic music. Sociologist Robert Bellah (2006, 161) has pointed out for instance that "This ability to 'keep together in time' is probably one of several biological developments that have evolved synchronously with the development of culture, but one of great importance for the ritual roots of society".

Taking the idea of an aesthetic of synchronisation into account, we can conclude that synchronisation works in two ways: 1) in nature and culture we can find aesthetic formations that emerge from synchronisation (school of fish, flocks of birds, collective rituals, parades); and 2) there are particular cultural achievements that enhance the effects of synchronisation and thus produce aesthetic forms such as music, dance, sports, public holidays, and of course religious rituals. In addition, these aesthetics of synchronisation mediate particular meanings and representations, and support social features such as power, cohesion or belonging. However, I have argued that for an understanding of these social functions and representations of collective effervescence, it is important to take into account the bodies in interaction and the emerging dynamics that drive this interaction. These aspects of embodied cognition and synchronised behaviour provide a sound epistemology for investigating the nature of immersion and to develop a framework for its analysis.

4 Immersion as Affect and Control: The Sensory Navigation of the Sacred (in Glossolalia)

We have now examined different sociological and anthropological attempts to go beyond Durkheim's concept of collective effervescence, and some insights developed in the cognitive sciences toward understanding the synchronising effects of embodied and social cognition. I understand both perspectives as a way of framing an aesthetics-of-immersion approach to collective effervescence. The crucial question is how immersion in collective arousals can best be described and explained in terms of the interplay of different social, physical, sensory, emotional and cognitive conditions. In this section I will argue that an aesthetic approach to immersion must connect all these perspectives to find a way of describing the ambivalent dynamics at work in moments of immersion. In this final section I will therefore, first, highlight the aspects of affect and control as the central poles of the ambivalent character of immersion, and, second, unfold these two aspects into four modes of ritual immersion in order to incorporate the intertwined conditions at work. In addition, I will tie these considerations to the empirical example of collective charismatic worship, and especially to the phenomenon of glossolalia or speaking in tongues as it can be found in the tradition of charismatic Christianity and Pentecostalism.

In media studies and art history immersion is often described as a convergence between external and internal representations, a reduction of the difference between the object observed and the perceiving subject, just as one gets drawn into a painting or loses oneself in the painting (Grabbe 2012). Even though this is a convincing description of immersion in the context of viewing art, or drawn into virtual reality, it fails to describe the manifold factors at work in immersion in the context of religious rituals, and especially in the context of collective effervescence. The divergent feelings of 'being-drawn-into-something' and 'letting-yourself-go' as they can be observed, for instance, in fan culture, already indicate that immersion as understood here always involves two sides, namely affective as well as controlling aspects, and their merging and convergence.

In more general terms affect usually refers to an occurring emotion or temper with a special quality of feeling or sensing to it, which can cause particular behaviours. To smile can therefore be an affect of having sympathy for someone. Yet, the smile can be automatic and unconscious, just like rubescence can be the affect of shame. In a ritual condition affective behaviours thus start from a certain affirmative attitude or temper someone holds towards the ritual. The feeling of 'being-drawn-into-something' can be understood as the (socially learned and expected, and therefore embodied) affect of this "emotional entrainment" (Collins 2004, xii). However, the ritual participant is not a machine that automatically falls into arousal and entrancement after entering the ritual mode. Rather he or she tunes in to the ritual atmosphere and thereby gives way for the feeling of 'being-drawn-into-something' while at the same time being able to control the moment of 'letting-yourself-go'. In order to elaborate this observation, I will briefly turn to the empirical example of glossolalia.

The phenomenon of glossolalia or speaking in tongues has always been a fascinating object of research to anthropologists, psychologists, theologians and scholars in the field of religious studies (Goodman 1972; Richardson 1973; Mills 1986; DeShane 2003; Cartledge 2006).[2] For some reason, glossolalia has attracted less attention among sociologists (Poloma 2006, 148–149), even though it involves collective effervescence. Scholars who have focused on the ritual aspect of glossolalia have highlighted the emergence of *communitas* through the moments of *liminality* in charismatic worship (Albrecht 1999). As far as I know, glossolalia has yet not been investigated as an outcome of collective effervescence and as a form of immersion.

However, with the increasing popularity of Pentecostal and charismatic Christianity around the globe, glossolalia has taken on different forms and became an identity marker of many churches and parishes. With reference to the Pentecost story in the New Testament (Acts 2:4–11), when the Holy Spirit came upon the Disciples of Christ, many charismatic Christians today believe that they receive the powers of the Holy Ghost, which causes pneumatic manifestations such as speaking in foreign or unknown languages (tongues), ecstatic bodily shaking, and even falling on the ground and trembling in the Spirit. Accordingly, glossolalia is sometimes described as a form of ecstasy or as a form of possession. It usually occurs in vivid and charismatic forms of worship, accompanied by lively or contemplative music, and under the influence of passionate preaching, praying and singing. Different techniques have been developed to support the emergence of glossolalia, such as the laying on of hands by people praying for the one who wants to receive the Spirit (sometimes professional prayer teams), or creating wind with a cloth to simulate the coming of the Holy Spirit.

In academic research, glossolalia is often described as a form of trance or possession, and depicted as solely unconscious and affective behaviour. Certainly, extreme cases of glossolalia, in which someone receives the Holy Ghost and starts shaking and rolling their eyes, easily catch the attention of researchers. Yet, not all forms of glossolalia must lead to such extreme behaviours. In fact, many long-time practitioners of glossolalia can consciously use it as a prayer technique or switch between normal prayer words and glossolalia. They may pray silently, burst out with glossolalia suddenly, and moments later fall back into their silent prayers again. Others may become deeply immersed in a state of glossolalia while remaining fully conscious. And even those who show such

---

2 It should be mentioned that much research on glossolalia is done by scholars who are also practitioners (DeShane 2003; Cartledge 2006). This provides support for the recommendation made by Buehler (2012), mentioned above, that anthropologists studying altered states of consciousness should have personal experience of the phenomenon they are studying.

extreme pneumatic reactions as rolling on the ground can have moments of conscious control. Glossolalia can thus take on different forms that are subject to the ambivalent character of immersion–oscillating between affect and control.

Taking this into account, I will now briefly sketch out four idiosyncratic modes of ritual immersion, which furthermore can be developed into correlating ideal types of the affective and controlling aspects of immersion. Describing them as ideal types already indicates that these aspects are usually merged and intertwined in ritual activities. Consequentially, this should be understood as an attempt both to differentiate between different factors at work in the perception of immersion and to illustrate their merging aspects. First of all, and in order to unfold these aspects, it is important to differentiate four basic modes or levels of ritual immersion, namely the ritual form, the ritual body, the ritual emotion, and the ritual mind. Within each mode of ritual immersion we now can develop the ideal types of affect and control: 1.) Exaltation and contemplation for the ritual form, 2.) Imagination and concentration for the ritual mind, 3.) Expansion and suspension for the ritual body, and 3.) Floating and navigating for the ritual emotions (see also Table 1).

Table 1

Modes of Ritual Immersion	Ideal Types of Immersion	
	Affect	Control
Ritual Form	Exaltation	Contemplation
Ritual Mind	Imagination	Concentration
Ritual Body	Expansion	Suspension
Ritual Emotion	Floating	Navigating

4.1 Ritual Form: Exaltation and Contemplation

Contemplation and exaltation describe two typical and widespread forms of immersion in religious rituals. Contemplation is being focused with your mind and body on sensory perception, such as listening to music or bowing down in front of an altar (or being focused on your own mind, as in meditation). Contemplation techniques can also cause a deprivation of all senses. In a contemplative state of mind one sinks into oneself, rests in oneself, and often feelings of being united with the world or of losing physical boundaries between oneself and the world are reported. In this way, contemplation (of something) and deprivation of the senses can stimulate a feeling of immersion. Exaltation, on the contrary, is to be ecstatic and enthusiastic about something, it is a rapture of sensual impressions such as music, light, or a charismatic crowd. Exaltation is often described as getting lifted up with a sense of delight. This is often the case in charismatic worship or arousing rituals. Contemplation and exaltation much depend on ritual conditions and both can cause a feeling of inebriation and therefore seem to have similar effects on the emergence of immersion. However, these ritual forms must not exclude one another but can include both aspects of immersion at once. In the case of charismatic worships phases of contemplation and exaltation often alternate, and glossolalia can occur in both states, even though with different emotional and bodily expressions.

4.2 Ritual Mind: Imagination and Concentration

For conceptual purposes, and in order to distinguish the immersive character of the ritual mind, we need to differentiate between online and offline cognition. The distinction between offline and online cognition is commonly used in cognitive sciences to describe mental processes that happen in exchange with a social environment in the here and now (online), or as more internal mental processes which imagine a what-if scenario (offline), and which can be more or less conscious in decision making (Niedenthal et al. 2005; Schilbach 2014).

Concentration is thus paying attention to a particular situation. It is being cognitively online, absorbing information such as the content and meaning of a sermon or a song. Strong concentration on cognitive information is an important step for synchronising with the ritual group. As mentioned earlier (Leistner and Schmidt-Lux 2012), in order to experience collective effervescence, the group must share a common perspective, and needs to focus its attention and act as a unit. Closely related to this kind of intellectual concentration is the act of imagination (offline cognition). Imagination is a more creative way of thinking as compared to mere concentration (Traut and Wilke 2015). With imaginations we go beyond perception of the provided content and let ourselves go with our own ideas, memories, fantasies, and associations. Both concentration and imagination can happen simultaneously or can merge in effervescent arousal (as well as in a state of deep meditation). Whereas in meditations often one goal is to let imaginaries pass the mind and not to hold on to them (in order to keep concentrated), in collective rituals one dives into the imaginary and anticipations, and dwells on the collective arousals and representations. In the case of glossolalia we can also find both aspects of the immersive mind. On the one hand ritual participants often pay attention and concentrate on the religious message and prayers of the pastor and this way become a collective unit with shared intentions and imaginaries. On the other hand, during times of worship and prayers, participants can let themselves go and this way become drawn into their imaginations (of the Holy Spirit). During glossolalia aspects of concentration (control) and imagination (affect) can both be present at the same time.

4.3 Ritual Body: Expansion and Suspension

Suspension and expansion both refer to physical rather than cognitive aspects of immersion, even though the embodied cognition approach presented above indicates that body and mind cannot be fully separated. Whereas expansion on a bodily level usually refers to collective rituals, suspension seems to be the ideal type of immersion in ritual meditation. Yet, we can also find a bodily perception of expansion in the ritual form of meditation, when the meditating person perceives his or her body expanding into space or even dissolving. In addition, we can find moments of suspension or bodily abeyance in collective rituals. Leistner and Schmidt-Lux (2012) also distinguish between suspension and expansion in their article on effervescence in fan cultures. They describe the alternating phases of a soccer game in which the fans more or less passively watch the game and then—in the next moment—passionately join in the arousing emotions when something exciting happens on the playing field. Suspension is thus being passively present in a crowd, a way to temporise one's movements, a sort of "wait and see what happens next" attitude, but always in anticipation of the next (bodily) agitation and passionate arousal. Expansion is active bodily participation, the passionate communion and the emotional arousal expressed through body movements. Like the observations made during a soccer game, in collective religious rituals such as charismatic worship, moments of physical passiveness alternate with moments of physical excitation. These bodily conditions often correlate with floating and navigating emotions, as will be described below.

4.4 Ritual Emotion: Floating and Navigating

The metaphors of floating and navigation represent an attempt to describe another relation between online and offline cognition. Floating can therefore be understood as mental absorption or immersion in a state of mind and bodily perception in which one drifts away from the actual happenings (offline cognition). A floating mind often goes along with bodily delight, a weightless feeling. Daydreaming is a good example, which demonstrates that it is more than just think-ing about something else (like what to buy for dinner) while sitting in the class-room. The emotion of floating can occur during both contemplation and exalta-tion (also often described as trance) and therefore represents a crucial moment of immersion in effervescence. In meditations a floating feeling can correlate with the perception of a dissolving body. In collective rituals floating can emerge as an affect of collective emotional arousal and intersubjectivity.

However, moments of immersion do not solely work in terms of trance or a floating feeling, but can also converge with moments of online cognition, where navigation of one's behaviour is possible. The metaphor of navigation can be un-derstood as a way of observing one's own perceptions and behaviours while being more or less able to control and direct them. In the case of trance in reli-gious rituals, for instance, there are always moments when the person in trance seems to be awake and conscious of his or her behaviours and decisions, while at the same time behaving almost out of control. Moments of offline and online cognition thus merge during immersive feelings and constitute two intriguing as-pects of immersion. As already mentioned above, for glossolalia we can often ob-serve these two ambivalent aspects, for instance, when a practitioner is deeply immersed in speaking tongues but at the same time seems to be conscious and aware of what he or she is doing.

These brief descriptions of four modes of ritual immersion are an attempt to differentiate the sensory forms and conditions at work in the phenomenon of im-mersion. They demonstrate the twofold dynamics of affect and control that con-stitute the aesthetical perception of immersion. On the one hand, affective be-haviour plays a central role in everyday practice as it coordinates our movements and thinking in an economical way. Routines can maintain affective behaviours in such a way that these behaviours more or less become subcon-scious. On the other hand, controlling our movements and thinking gives us con-fidence in what we do and it makes us rational in our decisions. Collective rituals have often been described as a loss of control and rationality. The aesthetics of immersion approach is an attempt to demonstrate that for the emergence of col-lective effervescence both affect and control play a vital role and can converge in such a way that affective and controlling behaviours seem to merge or at least unfold their own dynamics of immersion. Finally, by making use of Durkheim's concept of collective effervescence as a socially constructed (and bodily and sen-sory induced) demarcation between the profane and the sacred, we can argue that the aesthetics of immersion approach offers a contribution to describing how the collective sacred is navigated through the individual's sensory percep-tions of affect and control in moments of immersion.

5 Conclusion

In this chapter I have introduced and developed the concept of aesthetics of immersion in order to gain new insights into how collective effervescence works on the micro-level of individual perception rather than on the macro-level of a society. As has been shown, research in the social sciences has already suggested to take a closer look at the individual and interactive mechanisms involved in the emergence of collective arousals. By introducing the concept of embodied synchronisation, I have attempted to explain such interactive mechanisms using new insights from the cognitive sciences and neurosciences. In terms of epistemology, I have advocated to make a connection between social approaches and cognitive and embodied approaches to explain and describe forms of collective synchronisation and to support a material and aesthetic perspective on effervescence in order to enrich the one-sided sociological perspective that has dominated scientific discourses for so long.

With its focus on perception, the aesthetics of religion approach prepares the way for developing a basic concept of aesthetics of immersion. This concept, briefly outlined, already has the potential to describe the mechanisms at work in the emergence of collective effervescence. Finally, I have shown how the concept of immersion can be applied to the context of glossolalia. While glossolalia is often treated as a form of possession, I have argued that the immersive character of glossolalia is a twofold process of affect and control in which the ritual practitioner navigates the emergence and embodiment of sacred manifestations, as well as the dynamics of collective effervescence. Certainly this discussion of the concept of aesthetics of immersion is only a starting point for future research, and not a full-fledged theory. Nevertheless, I hope that I have been able to synchronise my thoughts with those of my readers.

Bibliography

Albrecht, Daniel E. 1999. *Rites in the Spirit. A Ritual Approach to Pentecostal/Charismatic Spirituality.* Sheffield: Sheffield Academic Press.

Bell, Catherine. 2006. "Embodiment." In *Theorizing Ritual. Issues, Topics, Approaches, Concepts*, edited by Jens Kreinath, Jan Snoek, and Michael Stausberg, 533–544. Leiden and Boston: Brill.

Bellah, Robert N. 2006. "Durkheim and Ritual." In *The Robert Bellah Reader*, edited by Robert N. Bellah, and Steven M. Tipton, 150–180. Durham and London: Duke University Press.

Berger, Peter. 2016. "Death, Ritual and Effervescence." In *Ultimate Ambiguities: Investigating Death and Liminality*, edited by Peter Berger and Justin Kroesen, 147–186. New York and Oxford: Berghahn.

Bieger, Laura. 2007. *Ästhetik der Immersion: Raum-Erleben zwischen Welt und Bild. Las Vegas, Washington und die White City*. Bielefeld: Transcript.

Bloch, Maurice. 2002. "Are Religious Beliefs Counter-Intuitive?" In *Radical Interpretation in Religion*, edited by Nancy K. Frankenberry, 129–146. Cambridge, MA: Cambridge University Press.

Buehler, Arthur. 2012. "The Twenty-First-Century Study of Collective Effervescence: Expanding the Context of Fieldwork." *Fieldwork in Religion* 7/1:70–97.

Carlton-Ford, Steven L. 1992. "Charisma, Ritual, Collective Effervescence, and Self-Esteem." *The Sociological Quarterly* 33/3: 365–387.

Cartledge, Mark J., ed. 2006. *Speaking in Tongues: Multi-Disciplinary Perspectives*. Milton Keynes, Waynesboro: Paternoster Press.

Collins, Randall. 2004. *Interaction Ritual Chains*. Princeton, Oxford: Princeton University Press.

Davis, Stephen F., Matthew T. Huss, and Angela H. Becker. 2009. "Norman Triplett: Recognizing the Importance of Competition." In *Psychology Gets in the Game: Sport, Mind, and Behavior 1880–1960*, edited by Christopher D. Green, and Ludy T. Benjamin Jr., 98–115. Lincoln: University of Nebraska Press.

DeShane, Kenneth. 2003. "A Morphology for the Pentecostal Experience of Receiving the Baptism in the Holy Spirit." *Western Folklore* 62/4: 271–291.

Durkheim, Émile. [1912] 1976. *The Elementary Forms of Religious Life*, translated by Jospeh Ward Swain and introduced by Robert Nisbet. London: George Allen & Unwin.

Gallese, Vittorio. 2007. "Embodied Simulation. From Mirror Neuron Systems to Interpersonal Relations." *Novartis Foundation Symposium* 278: 3–19.

Gibbs, Raymond W., Jr. 2006. *Embodiment and Cognitive Science*. Cambridge, et al.: Cambridge University Press.

Goodman, Felicitas D. 1972. *Speaking in Tongues: A Cross-Cultural Study of Glossolalia*. Chicago: University of Chicago Press.

Grau, Oliver. 2005. "Immersion und Emotion – Zwei Bildwissenschaftliche Schlüsselbegriffe." In *Mediale Emotionen. Zur Lenkung von Gefühlen durch Bild und Sound*, edited by Oliver Grau and Andreas Keil, 70–106. Frankfurt a.M.: Fischer.

Jennett, Charlene, Anna L. Cox, Paul Cairns, Samira Dhoparee, Andrew Epps, Tim Tijs, and Alison Walton. 2008. "Measuring and Defining the Experience of Immersion in Games." *International Journal of Human-Computer Studies* 66/9: 641–661.

Leistner, Alexander and Thomas Schmidt-Lux. 2012. "Konzentriertes Fallenlassen. Ansätze einer Soziologie kollektiver Ekstase." In *Emotionen, Sozialstruktur und Moderne*, edited by Annette Schnabel and Rainer Schützeichel, 317–333. Wiesbaden: VS-Verlag.

Maffesoli, Michel. 1986. *Der Schatten des Dionysos. Beitrag zu einer Soziologie des Orgiasmus*. Frankfurt a.M.: Syndikat.

Mills, Watson E. 1986. *Speaking in Tongues: A Guide to Research on Glossolalia*. Grand Rapids, MI: W.B. Eerdmans Publishing Co.

Nechvatal, Joseph. 2009. *Towards an Immersive Intelligence: Essays on the Work of Art in the Age of Computer Technology and Virtual Reality (1993–2006)*. New York: Edgewise Press.

Neda, Zoltan, E. Ravasz, Y. Brechet, T. Vicsek, and A.L. Barabasi. 2000. "The Sound of Many Hands Clapping." *Nature* 403: 849–850.

Niedenthal, Paula M., Lawrence W. Barsalou, Piotr Winkielman, Silvia Krauth-Gruber, and François Ric. 2005. "Embodiment in Attitudes, Social Perception, and Emotion." *Personality and Social Psychology Review* 9/3:184–211.

Pickering, W. S. F. 1984. *Durkheim's Sociology of Religion*. London: Routledge Kegan & Paul.

Poloma, Margaret M. 2006. "Glossolalia, Liminality and Empowered Kingdom Building." In *Speaking in Tongues: Multi-Disciplinary Perspectives*, edited by Mark J. Cartledge, 147–173. Milton Keynes, Waynesboro: Paternoster Press.

Reddish, Paul, Ronald Fischer, and Joseph Bulbulia. 2013. "Let's Dance Together: Synchrony, Shared Intentionality and Cooperation." *PLoS ONE* 8/8: 1–13, e71182. DOI 10.1371/journal.pone.0071182.

Richardson, James T. 1973. "Psychological Interpretations of Glossolalia: A Reexamination of Research." *Journal for the Scientific Study of Religion* 12/2: 199–207.

Sänger, Johanna, Viktor Müller, and Ulmann Lindenberger. 2012. "Intra- and Interbrain Synchronization and Network Properties when Playing Guitar in Duets." *Frontier in Human Sciences* 6: 1–19.

Sawyer, R. Keith. 2002. "Durkheim's Dilemma: Toward a Sociology of Emergence." *Sociological Theory* 20/2: 227–247.

Schilbach, Leonhard. 2014. "On the Relationship of Online and Offline Social Cognition." *Frontiers in Human Neuroscience* 8: 1–8.

Schüler, Sebastian. 2012. "Synchronized Ritual Behavior: Religion, Cognition and the Dynamics of Embodiment." In *The Body and Religion: Modern Science and the Construction of Religious Meaning*, edited by David Cave, and Rebecca Sachs Norris, 81–101. Leiden: Brill.

Taves, Ann. 2013. "Building Blocks of Sacralities." In *Handbook of Psychology of Religion and Spirituality*, 2nd ed., edited by Raymond F. Paloutzian, and Crystal Park, 138–161. New York: The Guilford Press.

Traut, Lucia, and Annette Wilke, eds. 2015. *Religion – Imagination – Ästhetik. Vorstellungs- und Sinneswelten in Religion und Kultur*. Göttingen: Vandenhoeck & Ruprecht.

Triplett, Norman D. 1898. "The Dynamogenic Factors in Pacemaking and Competition." *American Journal of Psychology* 9: 507–533.

Vásquez, Manuel A. 2011. *More than Belief: A Materialist Theory of Religion*. Oxford, New York: Oxford University Press.

Wiltermuth, Scott S., and Chip Heath. 2009. "Synchrony and Cooperation." *Psychological Science* 20/1: 1–5.

Anne Koch

The Governance of Aesthetic Subjects Through Body Knowledge and Affect Economies. A Cognitive-Aesthetic Approach

1 Introduction: Aesthetics as a Connective Approach

This chapter seeks to show that aesthetics, in the context of the study of religion, should first and foremost follow an epistemological approach rather than a neo-phenomenological, material religion or stylistic one. This is relevant for two reasons: such an approach takes into account how we, as scholars, perceive and conceptualise the object we are studying. In doing so it refers back to the epistemological process itself, and to the subjects involved in the process of knowledge generation. It is in this sense that an aesthetics of religion conceptualises its field of investigation through the lens of embodied cognition, that it offers to provide an epistemology that goes along with the core idea of transcendental philosophy which states that being aware of the conditions of knowledge production provides an understanding of the constructed nature of social and cultural reality. An important difference between this position and Kant's transcendental philosophy is that the conditions of knowledge are not referred back to "pure" and "practical" reason, but that knowledge is now understood as situated cognition by which the aesthetic subject is entangled with a related historical world. The rationale of reasoning in aesthetics of religion stems from the theory of perception (Greek *aisthesis*; see Mohr 2006) in psychology and philosophy (especially philosophy of mind, philosophy of psychology, neuro-philosophy), and it includes concepts of mediality, figuration and form.[1] Therefore, the two most

---

[1] The first programmatic article on *Religionsästhetik* is the merit of the German scholars Hubert Cancik and Hubert Mohr (1988). The authors locate the origin of their aesthetics in Alexander Gottlieb Baumgarten's eighteenth-century philosophical aesthetic that integrates sense perception into epistemology. While emphasising the role of perception, Cancik and Mohr still give most credit to the semiotic paradigm: the human body is determined being a *natural symbol* (to cite Mary Douglas's famous dictum) that has both language and expression. However, theoretical concepts that rely on the Western taxonomy of the "five senses" lack the organising somatic categories elaborated on in this chapter. In his *Philosophische Briefe des Aletheophilus* (1741), Baumgarten outlined an aesthetic theory encompassing sensory physiology, experimental physics, as well as poetology and rhetoric, focusing on the latter where he felt most competent

https://doi.org/10.1515/9783110461015-017

relevant models of knowledge for a cognitive-aesthetic approach are those of sensorial knowledge (the "*sinnliche Erkenntnis*" of A.G. Baumgarten, 1714–1763) and theories of form and performance from rhetoric, design theory, ritual and media studies (Grieser 2015).

This sketch of an aesthetics of religion pursues the double aim of clarifying the scholar's and the object's constructive principles, or rather the epistemology and the principles of cultural sensory production. Mirroring this double task, the chapter starts by sketching a philosophical anthropology of embodied agents. Grounded in our present knowledge of cognition, the category of *body knowledge* is developed and operationalised for empirical use, and other analytical categories are derived from it. In the context of a field example, the descriptive power of the partly heuristic (or still hypothetical) and partly very applicable concepts is demonstrated. The categories are applied to a very telling example of body motion in a dance practice that emerged from the New Age ideology and the spirit of the Esalen Institute in California. In a third step, the argument is further developed by distinguishing more enduring forms of subjectivity constituted by (religious) practices and regulation. It is argued that such forms of subjectivity are discursive effects. They emerge at the interface of individual biographical, socio-cultural, and political formative powers and non-discursive practices, and they are continually transformed since these powers never come to rest.

These assumptions are related to the understanding of subjectivity in the work of Michel Foucault who, in his analysis of subjectivity, focuses on institutions (clinic, prison, marketplace, gender and psychiatry) as forms of objectification of human agents. At the same time he introduced the concept of *technologies of the self* in order to grasp power, symbol systems, the production systems and the self, and in order to understand how individuals are forced into specific cognitive schemes and forms of life (Foucault [1982] 1988). In continuation of the late Foucault's special interest in a *hermeneutics of the subject* ([1981–1982] 2005), historically contingent subjectivities will be distinguished: an esoteric subjectivity, a provisional and an agnostic subjectivity. Another type would be a traumatic subjectivity (for details, see Malabou 2007; Payne and Crane-Godreau 2015) or a confessional subjectivity, which I will not elaborate on here (for details, see Foucault [1979–1980] 2014). Some of the features of these subjectivities are closely linked with religious traditions in a narrow and explicit sense; others emerge from more general features of present cultures. I will trace these aesthetically conceived subjectivities back to aesthetic politics, relat-

(Knatz and Otabe 2005, 24). By integrating the conceptual-rationalist and the perceptive subject in his aesthetic-epistemological theory he opened up the aesthetic subjectivity of modernity.

ing them to consumer behaviour, neoliberal demands, and political power. Moreover, it is asked how these framing relations do not only affect the neoliberal subjectivity, but also the other forms mentioned. My overall concern is the opportunity to re-think the epistemological foundation of the study of religion through the lens of an aesthetic approach. This should allow for a better understanding of the link between cognitive agency and forms of practice as it becomes visible in the aesthetic pattern of subjectivities. For this purpose, connective concepts for the analysis of the entanglement of politics, subjects and knowledge are essential, as these are the inseparable media of world-making.

2 The Aesthetic Subject: Body Knowledge and Synthetic Categories

What I call the aesthetic subject appears when cognitive scientific scrutiny is applied to culturally embedded situations. Recent research on embodied, distributed, enacted and situated cognition overcomes the binary of nature and culture by integrating concepts of social cognition and culturality (Wilson 2010; Davis and Markmann 2012; Lindblom 2015; Scarinzi 2015). In comparison to traditional approaches, cognitive studies increasingly take into account the historicity and cultural variability of neural processing. In this way, not only is the content of cognition addressed, but also the *how* of cognition—its mechanisms—are a subject of investigation. A good example is what Margaret Wilson called the *retooling* of the mind through the inventive practice of physical and problem-solving tools beyond an individual life span: many cognitive capacities are not genetically prescribed, but they are, rather, related to cultural inventions which affect cognitive procedures deeply. As cognitive "tools" themselves, they are then culturally transmitted as well (Wilson 2010, 180). Cognitive retooling entails a deep change in cognitive architecture. The precondition for this is sufficient plasticity of the neural system. Insights into the extent to which neural systems are flexible and adaptable have shown that the explorative-inventive ability of humans—working on the basis of habitual action and embodied cognition—can be understood as the source of innovativeness and functional inventions, even if used "off-line", without actual sensory stimuli (Wilson 2010).

In the history of emotions, cognitive studies have been combined with (Bourdieuan) praxis theory (Reddy 2001; Scheer 2012; Reckwitz 2012). In addition scholars in anthropology have applied embodiment theories in fruitful ways.[2]

---

2 Kathryn Geurts's work is a good example of how complex social categories such as moral val-

This is a development that tends to be neglected by neo-phenomenological approaches in the anthropology and sociology of the body (Gugutzer 2010) where, for example, pre-reflexive coordination of movement and communication between agents is referenced, but without addressing the question how this might happen, or how it could be explained. In the study of religion, Tanya M. Luhrmann explains the training of feelings and embodied experiences with the example of Christian prayer, especially charismatic ecstatic prayer techniques. Social learning of affective forms affects the perception in reverse. Similar to charismatic Christians who come to recognise God's presence in their bodily behavior in ecstatic prayer, participants in spiritual energy healing recognise the healing power in their body (Luhrmann 2013). Aesthetics as a connective approach bridges the explanatory gap between the rational subject, its environment and the non-rational dimensions of subjectivity. In doing so, it also binds together the classically separate disciplines of art (Scarinzi 2015), humanities and the natural sciences.

A way to provide a more specific type of cognitive epistemology for the aesthetics of religion and its potential use in cultural studies is to outline categories that help to describe and analyse implicit knowledge of agents. The following sections give an idea of how an aesthetic-cognitive analysis might be conducted by developing further a heuristic concept of *body knowledge* (somatosensory, viscerosensory, chemosensory), divided into different components. These elements are very similar to the "preparatory set" humans use to react to, avoid or adapt to environments. It is a term that was coined a hundred years ago for the rapid and sub-cortical perceptual and motor reaction time: "Preparation involves a coordination of many aspects of the organism: muscle tone, posture, breathing, autonomic functions, motivational/emotional state, attentional orientation, and expectations" (Payne and Crane-Godreau 2015, 178). This reaction is relevant for handling stress or trauma and to be able to perform new tasks. Religious traditions classically intervene here (with spiritual exercises and shared rituals), as will be demonstrated by the field example at the end of this section.

2.1 Body Scheme

The term *body scheme* denotes the self-representation of the body. It refers to how the body structures and determines self-perception. Antonio Damasio

---

ues rely on somatic categories; her case study of the African Anlo-Eve demonstrates that the names of walking styles communicate both moral and emotional states (Geurts 2002).

coined the "somatic marker hypothesis" of consciousness. By this he signals the well-proven fact that somatic and psychological self-awareness both emerge from an image of the homeostatic state of the body. This body scheme relies on interoceptions such as muscle tension, spatial position, and the symbolic meaning of body parts. It is therefore highly important for psychodynamic processes such as regression, repression, and the development of symptoms (Dornberg 2013). In fact, body schemes enable the awareness of the wholeness of the body. In recent research, body schemes are no longer understood as a class of neural representations, but rather, as a whole network of concepts (Holmes and Spence 2006). Many cultural interactions take place along the body scheme and trigger, change or manipulate it. In many rituals, body schemes become relevant when specific body parts of participants are addressed through somatic attention: for example, with rough or soft clothes, heavy masks, body paintings, the touching of body parts and their marking through singing, sensing, and bewitching. Through somatic attention, a specific body scheme is created, learned, and habituated. In this sense, Tanya M. Luhrmann uses the concept of metakinesis to describe how the self-representation of Christian-evangelicals is altered in expressive movement rituals. Evangelicals learn to identify bodily sensations, especially in trance-like prayer states, with the presence of god in their life (Luhrmann 2004, 519). For this aim, they psychologically organise what are at first bodily distinctive states, train their awareness of these states, and bind them to the semantic context of their religious group. They synthesise these sensations (Luhrmann 2004, 522) to form what one may call a specific body scheme. Luhrmann mentions "specific and dramatic mood elevations" that build up this new body scheme. This fits into recent findings on the coordination of human subjective feeling as coordination between the two hemispheres and two brain regions (the anterior insula cortex and the anterior cingulate cortex), where, as in our example here, the parasympathetic distension and connected positive emotions become relevant: "The model offers explanations for why positive emotions can reduce or block negative emotions (and vice versa), why the left (affiliative, vagal) side controls deictic pointing and verbal communication, and how increased parasympathetic activity (for example, activation of vagal afferents by gastric distension, slow breathing or electrical stimulation) can reduce negative emotions (for example, pain)" (Craig 2009, 64).

These very recent findings may be of use for closing a gap in our understanding of how interoception links to our feeling in, and with, our bodies. It indicates how afferent emotion is interrelated with the nervous system of inner organs, such as stomach, heart, lungs, muscles and skin, the endocrine system and metabolism, and directly influences our subjective well-being. These findings outline a regulatory dynamics of the body scheme: "endogenous homeostatic control mechanisms modulate the integration of afferent activity that produces the feelings from the body, which underscores the crucial dependence of subjective well-being on the physiological health of the body" (Craig 2003, 504).

As a first step, the afferent neural system represents the physiological conditions of the physical body (Herbert and Pollatos 2012). This provides a foundation for subjective feelings, self-awareness and emotions. Afferents that represent all tissues of the body project first to autonomic and homeostatic centres in the spinal cord and brainstem. As a second step, an autonomic and homeostatic interoceptive cortical image is created: "Together with afferent activity that is relayed by the nucleus of the solitary tract (NTS), it generates a direct thalamocortical representation" (Craig 2002, 655). Thirdly, "its re-representation in the anterior insular cortex of the non-dominant (right) hemisphere, possibly uniquely in humans, constitutes a basis for the subjective evaluation of one's condition, that is, 'how you feel'" (Craig 2002, 655).

What is of note is that this process can help us understand the efficacy of cultural practice: even if the neural pathway is autonomous and homeostatic, it can still be manipulated to a certain degree. This opens up the whole field of socio-cultural interaction that is always embodied, either face-to-face or by using tools of communication. Of course, for some practices or communications the manipulation of body scheme is more relevant than for others. For example, research on "breathwork", meditation and therapeutic touch have shown widely that such practices do influence self-perception and its regulation on all levels (Collins and Dunn 2005). Intensive research has been conducted on the feeling of time elapse during advanced levels of mindfulness meditation practice (Wittmann et al. 2014). *Pranayama*, for example, interferes with autonomic breathing. Some exercises double the length of exhalation; some enervate the organ systems (*uddiyana*) or reverse active inhaling and passive exhaling to an active exhale and passive inhale (*kapalabhati*) (Kuvalayananda [1931] 2010). The measurement of the heart-rate with active participants and anticipating bystanders in a fire-walking ritual reveals divergent emotional levels of anticipation: for instance, those who were carried over the live coals by relatives showed higher rates (Xygalatas et al. 2011).

Comparing the concept of the body scheme with earlier proposals of how to speak about the interplay of body, mind, and perception, G.W. Leibniz (1646–1716) comes to mind. For him, the unity of perception was an obscure representation, because the whole adds up to the entirety of imaginations he called perfection—which is conceptualised as beauty performed by the soul, not by the intellect or by perception. The body scheme as affective-embodied-cognitive representation takes on a similar role as a synthetic mode of cognition. In the implementation of a specific body scheme, rituals fulfil a range of social functions, including differentiating one group from another or from the mainstream body scheme of society; highlighting aesthetic attractiveness, producing "wellness", or cultures of touching; and implicitly criticising or privileging social body practices.

2.2 Thermoregulation

Thermoregulation is a complex and mostly autonomous regulatory circuit. Blood flow, restricted blood flow and muscle tension are only some factors that take part in this organisation. In a pilot study by Karin Meissner and myself on the efficacy of spiritual healing, it was observed how a healer fosters a feeling of warmth that symbolises the healing energy. He managed to "guide" this energy, felt as warmth, through the body of the client (Meissner and Koch 2016, 423). The perception of temperature is closely linked to emotions, ranging from comfortable to uncomfortable (Craig 2003). A sensation of warmth attracts attention on its pathway along and through the meaningful body. This attention enervates the vegetative system over time, and it may establish an established script of the path of the warmth through the body by being touched. By "moving" the warmth, the healer manipulates the body scheme. Interviews indicate that the healer may change the subjective well-being into a feeling of being "whole and healthy", of feeling "at home in one's body" and of feeling integrated and present.

2.3 Covert Imitation

According to neurological findings, imitable perceptions such as body postures, auditory noises, language sounds, and mimicry are copied and stored as isomorphic representations in brain modules. This copying, or *covert imitation*, happens routinely and automatically, and in fact the recognition of emotions is dependent on covert imitation (Wilson 2006). Experiments have shown that the connection between facial expression and body posture associated with particular emotions reveals how a particular emphasis is realised through covert imitation. Case studies have found that disrupting the covert imitation of such mimicry (for example, by chewing gum) also affects memory efficiency. In social action covert imitation is an important device for interpreting other people's actual and anticipated behaviour. From the somatological perspective such behaviour is an expression of mental states, and of the ability to synchronise mental reaction with complex behavioural reactions. In other words, the somatic category of covert imitation helps to explain how the goals and intentions of other agents are accessed by body representations.

2.4 Tattooing

The interface of the skin is often reduced to its social function of marking identity and, to its spatial function of being a border; a "skinscape" as Plate put it (2012, 165), a space for projecting identity images onto each other's bodies. Even if scholars allude to findings in neurobiology they often confine these to a metaphorical paradigm. However, the skin is an organ that is permeated with receptors, and it is the source of a huge amount of information that is received through these neural receptors, such as humidity, pain, touch, temperature, tension, etc. Since the skin is a protective shield against germs it also mirrors the state of the immune system. As any other tissue of the body, the skin memorises exposure to sun or coldness. One might talk of a skin organ sense. Sigmund Freud mentions the meaningfulness of a body zone and skin passage for one of his female patients whose father had a venous ulcer that she had to bandage. The place where his leg lay on her thigh while bandaging gained symbolic meaning for their relationship. Today, this kind of meaningfulness of body parts is no longer seen in a topological way, but rather, as a body memory of the tissue, for example in secularist or spiritual healing techniques such as osteopathy or craniosacral therapy. Instead, a functional memory of suppressed emotions or impulses might be located in a body part, for instance, in the shoulder, causing chronic pain or skin irritation. Also, mental disorders might be connected with paraesthesia when the skin or hair is touched. In this sense, *tattooing* as a category reaches beyond the "inscription" of skin; it rather relates to all sensory memories stored and actively (re-)produced through the skin which is much more than a "surface" or a screen to be written on.

2.5 Muscle Tone, Posture and Movement

Research on muscle tone, posture and movement are correlated. Work on contemplative movement practices like yoga, tai chi and contemplative dance singles out four dimensions in which self-regulation becomes operative: steering of bodily attention, meta-cognition, training of interoception and emotional regulation (van Vugt 2016). *Muscle tone* is the concept that describes the pressure at the muscle plates perceived by proprioception. Every human being has an individual tension based on connective tissue and musculature. High muscle tone lowers the risk of injury and accelerates reaction time. Sprinters, for example, stimulate their muscle tone by jumping on the spot before running, and then stretching afterwards to lower or relax their muscle tone. In meditation, the muscle tone is lowered, since breathing, like warmth, relaxes the muscles. With this in mind, body movements, breathing, and temperature fluctuations have to be taken into account in any discussion of religious rituals. Exertion, relaxation, stretching, and warming up are equally important. The physicist Edmund Jacobson's muscle relaxation therapy (which has deeply influenced Western postural Yoga) emphasises that working with muscle and body tone has strong psychological effects. Muscle tone is also important for rituals insofar as it relates body knowledge to emotionality, especially since stress and strain are localised in, or realised through, the musculature, thereby influencing posture, the power of concentration, and pain (Garde et al. 2014).

Thomas Csordas subsumes muscle tone under his concept of somatic modes of attention: "The imagined rehearsal of bodily movements by athletes is a highly elaborated somatic mode of attention, as is the heightened sensitivity to muscle tone and the appetite for motion associated with health-consciousness and habitual exercise" (Csordas 1993, 139). Mental training often addresses muscle relaxation, just as hybrid religious healing methods, for instance *reiki*, use muscle relaxation combined with activating muscle or tissue memory to recover the results from an injury or violent experiences. Hypnosis and trance often engage kinaesthetic images, and in fact the efficiency of such practices involving muscle tone—practices that can be explained by symbolic learning processes, attention focusing, and by intentional targeted muscle arousal—has been empirically proven by electromyography (EMG), a method for measuring the electricity of muscle fibres. Muscle tone is closely linked to physical and emotional *posture* aspects in a bidirectional way. Appropriate breathing may support posture. Imitation of postures and gestures has proven pivotal in psychological development. Posture influences a person's attitudes, affections and expectations. Studies have investigated this by relating expansive, involuntary or contractual postures, facial and vocal expressions with changes in endogenous substances (Payne and Crane-Godreau 2015, 7–8). Research "suggest[s] that conscious proprioceptive awareness of reflex postural preparedness may give rise to pleasant experiences of stability, readiness, and self-efficacy, or unpleasant feelings of lack of confidence and anxiety" (Payne and Crane-Godreau 2015, 7–8). Other studies have shown that "botox injections in facial muscle decreased the strength of emotional experience [...] and amygdala activity" (Ticini, Urgesi, and Calvo-Marino 2015, 107).

2.6 Prosthetic Perception

As discussed, the body scheme is highly relevant for well-being, integrative body-awareness and holistic representation. Neural plasticity lays the ground for the capacity of the body to integrate prostheses, transplanted organs, and tools or fake limbs into this representation. Part of it is the feeling of "being at home in one's body", knowing the size, expansion, and moving in a way that fits the body, for example, the doorframe, without colliding. This is the framework allowing for *prosthetic knowledge:* the sensation of a walking stick is a good example (see Polanyi 1966). We do not feel the cane in the palm of our hand, where the pressure is objectively located, but we feel the uneven, soft, or solid ground through it, as if we had a sensorium at the end of the stick. In other words, the stick is an extension, and enlargement of our sensory organ of touch. This distance perception through tool use means that tools can be integrated into the body scheme (Làdavas and Farné 2006). It does not matter if the distant object is real or imagined, if it is my limb, an imagined limb, or an artificial limb. For somatic ritual theory, this variance means that in order to explain identification (with things, movements, entities) we don't need to refer to higher cognitive processes; using the concept of prosthetic perception these effects can be explained on a sensory-action level. Also, the link between individual and collective experience in ritual action—an issue that challenges some ritual theories – need not necessarily be explained only by participation. Prosthetic enlargement and the incorporation of tools, as well as the somatic activities of other actors such as drinking or dancing, can all be displayed somatically in the embodied agent.

2.7 Peripersonal Space

Another speciality humans have developed in their way of perceiving the environment is their *peripersonal space*. This is a perceptive sector around body parts that can be detected by its specific relation to visual and tactile stimuli. The peripersonal space for hands, for example, is forty to forty-five centimetres around them, because hands are our most precious tools; it might be as narrow around the elbows, but wider around other body parts that often also have a smaller density of nociceptors. Neurological structures correspond with these specific perceptive fields. The perceptive field of the hand, again, is characterised by the cross-modal enhancement or by the extinction of visual and tactile stimuli. Another consequence of prosthetic perception is the multi-sensory coding of space, since space in relation to bodies is not metric or linear; therefore, by extension, prosthetic perception can also build on the peripersonal space. Space, at least related to the somatic dimension of agents, depends on zones of importance for protection and cross-sensory integration (Lavàdas and Farné 2006, 101). Extending the body by the use of tools, as well as reactions due to habituation and peripersonal space, show this to be the case, and violating or respecting this space makes up for a variety of ritual usages.

Prosthetic perception and peripersonal space are also closely linked to the feeling of body-ownership that is of great relevance to the cultural study of religion and is vastly neglected. Body-ownership has been studied, for instance, by fake-limb experiments, like the rubber hand experiments. Again, the protection or reaction space around the hand is tested but this time one sees at the place of one's hand a rubber hand. As a first result, the proprioceptive drift denoting the felt distance of actual and fake hand location can be measured, with the result that the rubber hand is mostly felt slightly more as one's own hand (Kerr, Agrawal, and Nayak 2016). Tai chi, which emphasises bodily attention during moving, manipulates low level sensorimotor control. It alters tactile sensation in being more aware of afferent sensory activity. In regard to all of these fine-grained experiments, further conditions have to be taken into account, like the level of mastery and the age of practitioners. Besides extending ownership, peripersonal space is intentionally manipulated in contemplative gaze training, as in yoga practice with prescribed gaze focal points (*dristi*). This strategy of looking at specific body parts (e.g. a point at the front, an imagined point in prolongation of the outstretched arm) may enhance tactile acuity and spatial attention (Schmalzl, Powers, and Blom 2016, 108).

2.8 Example: Gabrielle Roth's "5 Rhythms" Dance

To conclude this section, the fruitfulness of applying these categories can be demonstrated by the example of the contact improvisation dance called *5 Rhythms*. The preparatory set as interrelated factors of action-response is relevant insofar as this dance is widely non-reflexive. *5 Rhythms* dates back to the culturally productive time in the USA when the Esalen Institute became a centre for alternative lifestyle and humanist-psychological innovation (founded in 1962 in Big Sur, California). One of its founders, Michael Murphy, called it an "intellectual ashram" that seeks to avoid formal religious structures but nevertheless assumes a universal mystical experience (Kripal 2005, 5). Among other cultural creatives, psychologists, artists and intellectuals, Gabrielle Roth developed this dancing style from the mid-1960s; it is organised around an arc of suspense of the "wave" consisting of five phases characterised by different rhythms that stand for five energetic-affective experiences of life. The performance aims to replace a fragmented and alienated body image with an integrated, holistic image. The ultimate goal is holistic healing mediated by the dance performance and realised by the bodily expression of emotions (the unleashing of trauma) and extraordinary experiences. Gestalt therapist Fritz Perls, whom she worked at the Esalen Institute, led Roth to recognise the therapeutic potential of her dance. She further refers to an original shamanic knowledge as a source of her practical movement practice, along the lines that all human bodies "know what they need" (Roth 1997). The somatic categories sketched above may be used to explain the realisation of the holistic body experience of this dance and the healing process it promises.

Figure 1: The five rhythmic phases of the *5 Rhythms* dance by Gabrielle Roth, and how they relate to body tone; from Kunas, Markus. 2013. 'The Dancing Sangha': Die 5 Rhythmen als holistische Körpertechnik zwischen Tanz, Therapie und spätmoderner Spiritualität. Ludwig-Maximilians-University Munich. URL: http://epub.ub.uni-muenchen.de/21723/, published 13 November 2014 (last accessed 4 December 2015), 83. © Markus Kunas. Reproduced with permission of the author.

	Flowing	Staccato	Chaos	Lyrical	Stillness
Body tone	Initial state—progressively relaxing	Growing tension	Switching between easing and elevating the tension	Releasing of tension	Deeply relaxed
Bodily co-presence	Self-centred, some cautious contacts	Some two-person interactions, shared acceleration	A circle around expressive solo dancers may be formed which fortifies the loss of control in the spectator dancers	Horizontally connected	Attention to own body and exhaling

"Flowing" constitutes a preparatory phase for the wave of emotions. In this phase the feeling of sinking into the ground may occur, comparable to the practice of "earthing" in Yoga, Qi Gong and other body practices which draw attention to the soles of the feet, their sense of the temperature and texture of the ground, and their imaginative connection with the floor. Some dancers say they feel their feet are "some centimetres below floor level" (Kunas 2013, 82). This rooting is due to the prosthetic perception of an enlarged identity. The secure feeling of the ground, the walls of the building and the building itself anchored in the soil is part of imaginative training in trauma therapy, as described by Peter Levine (2005). Usually, exercises stimulating the body scheme, such as tattooing, forego the task of connecting. In tattooing, for instance, the left hand feels the right hand which lightly knocks the inner palm of the left hand, and vice versa. This knocking or sweeping of the "outer skin" of one's body can be continued with other parts of the body and can be accompanied by auto-suggestive murmuring.

The prosthetic ability to temporarily integrate tools and parts of the environment into one's own body scheme is sometimes close to experiences of disembodiment. In disembodiment the location of the body is more stable, and it is performed imaginatively, whereas prosthetic perception comes with practice. In using a tool, in moving through a space, in co-acting with other embodied agents, the tool, floor or figuration of bodies is integrated into the body. Its centre of gravity changes over the time of contact improvisation (Gugutzer 2010). In the staccato phase of *5 Rhythms* the movements intentionally come from within the body centre to address other dancers. Gestures are directed and forceful, comparable to the ones used in martial arts. Other bodies become part of prosthetically imagined motion figures. This accelerated phase leads to the next phase called "chaos" in which the activated body progresses to vibrations and uncontrolled movements or screams echoed by others. After this disintegrative phase, in the playful "lyrical" phase, the pace slows down and the centre of gravity rises to the upper body. Rotating movements become soft and light. Hands are up in the air. Within the last phase, "stillness", proprioceptive sensations are in focus. The dancers may lie on the floor, eyes closed, and direct their attention to subtle movements and sensations. The floating style of music without any song lyrics (and their semantic content) aims at supporting this susceptibility. Emotions may burst out in the form of crying.

This description gives an impression of what can be developed further as a ritual somatology. Such an approach finds support in studies based on a neuro-aesthetic hypothesis, and using Functional Magnetic Resonance Imaging (fMRI). For our case, it has been shown that people respond stronger, and more positively to movements that belong to the observer's repertoire (Ticini, Urgesi, and Calvo-Marino 2015). The same is valid for the soundscape of movements. These studies are "suggesting that the degree of covert simulation of the movements is correlated to the level of liking" (Ticini, Urgesi, and Calvo-Marino 2015, 105). The implicit aesthetic configuration corresponds to the person's own preferred postures, and this, in consequence, results in an intense non-theoretical, "simulative" understanding (Koch 2003, 187–192).

These findings are only the beginning of a more systematic way of investigating religion and ritual from a somatic point of view. Together with other parameters—for instance, kinematic properties such as speed, body parts used, directedness of motion, perceiver's ability to reproduce the movement, and vertical and horizontal displacement—can be investigated for their relevance to the implicit aesthetics of embodied agents. This approach offers a wide range of options for future research that aims at reaching beyond the limitation of non-embedded measuring and isolated interpretation of scientific imaging. As can be seen in the *5 Rhythms* example, we can describe and explain how a body-centred subjectivation process is supported. Knowledge about how to use movement for healing is performed through the bodily co-presence of the group members and through reconfiguring the body scheme during the ephemeral and non-propositional dance that constitutes a sequence of liminal phases.

3 Rethinking Subjectivity from an Aesthetic Point of View

It is a difficult task to clarify how to speak about the 'subject', the 'person', 'individual', and the 'self'—seen as some of the many historically bound inventions of human performance. As my focus is on subjectivity, I do not want to subscribe to current approaches that attribute core elements to individuals that are conceptualised within liberal social theories and their notions of freedom, singularity or referentiality. If, however, we want to talk *about* historical patterns of being ruled or being authentic in the Foucauldian sense, we will employ the concept of subjectivity, and at the same time rethink it.

What is it that makes an aesthetic approach to subjectivity special? First, from its background in cultural studies it allows for a *plurality* of modern subjectivities across sub-milieus of a society. The recent philosophical concept of subjectivity is bound to empirical findings rather than promoting singularising concepts such as a general *homo oeconomicus* or the *animal symbolicum* from which prominent cultural theories take their distance. Second, the aesthetic understanding of subjectivity relates body knowledge to political and social forms of exerting power and ruling citizens. It constructs a mid-scale layer of observing subjectivities above the individual and below the social. Subjectivities are embodied displays of behaviour, status symbols and practices (for example, which medical treatment people chose, which products they buy, what homestyle decoration they prefer, where they travel). These practices need not be coherent, they may change and intensify temporarily around cultural symbols, such as the new tablet, or Valentine's Day with its ritual of love displayed towards a chosen partner. By *subjectivity* I understand an assemblage of such clippings from social life. Subjectivity should neither be conflated with self-identity (individually felt) nor be taken as a closed unity with clear-cut borders. Subjectivity is essentially a (battle) field (if one favours war metaphors, as Bourdieu does) or a marketplace of emotional tensions, altering tastes, embodied feelings that change along with an aging personality. Some constitutive features of aesthetic subjectivity are going to be demonstrated by the following examples.

3.1 Subtle Bodies—Esoteric Ethical Subjectivity

Subtle bodies are a common concept in contemporary alternative healing and spirituality, and in practice and ideas they reach beyond the *res cogitans-res extensa* distinction of the Cartesian subject insofar as they are based on the subtle continuum ontology of the modern esoteric worldview, particularly present in the theosophical doctrine (Johnston 2012). Subtle bodies are popularly imagined as invisible energetic entities consisting of several layers or oval shapes beyond and beside the physical body characterised by energy centres and channels. They are cosmically interlinked subjectivities that are rhizomatically interwoven with the tissue of being and all humans. Jay Johnston calls them a "bridge between the individual self and the spiritual world" (Johnston 2012, 153). There is a high level of morality involved in concepts of the subtle bodies, based on their ontological "radical intersubjectivity" and indispensable subtle causalities (Johnston 2011, and in this volume). In Kandinsky's art theory, this is the rationale of why artworks can have a huge emotional effect on the beholder—it mediates materiality and form. Johnston traces the relationship of this art theory and theosophical self-conception historically and demonstrates its great impact on healing practices such as Aura Soma and most of the other forms of popular energetic healing. Modern cognitive art theory considers that displayed body movements or brushstrokes of paintings may trigger sensorimotor experiences as embodied simulations of the performed action of the painter (Ticini, Urgesi, and Calvo-Marino 2015, 104). The reason for the emotional response is also linked to materiality, even though the explanative mechanism is a neural body. The subtle subjectivity, in this view, is porous to the energetic flows of the cosmos and other human beings.

Subtle bodies can only fulfil their anthropological or spiritual task of transforming to a higher state of consciousness when they gain space in the surrounding consciousness dimensions to do so. They have to "clean up"; transforming is cleaning, and can "burn away" anger, for example. This imaginary makes Ayurveda cooking and the *agni* fire so attractive to subtle bodies, being an appropriate tool for transforming by extinguishing lower forms of consciousness. The same affect economy guides "wellbeing spirituality" for which the self is the "artwork" (Johnston 2012, 156, 162–167). Subtle body subjectivity is activist: its exposure is not a gateway for harm but for work. Jay Johnston (2011), like Binder (2011; see below), derive the formation of subtle subjectivities from (popular) esotericism, well-being spirituality, art and continental philosophy, so that we can consider it a dispositive of esoteric ethical subjectivity.

3.2 Provisional and Agnostic Subjectivities

An example of postmodern subjectivity can be found in "engaged Buddhism" groups in the tradition of Thich Nhat Hanh. I rely here on Stefan Binder's empirical work which involved participant observation and interpretation of journals kept by a Munich group of "Community of Mindful Being in Bavaria" (*Gemeinschaft für achtsames Leben Bayern e.V.*) (Binder 2011). The main practice during the weekly meetings is sitting and walking meditations, and a guided meditation with a "moderator" who reads texts authored by Thich Nhat Hanh and others in the religious tradition; the moderators also encourage further thought about and appropriation of the readings. This activity comprises prostrations towards the Buddha statue and bodhisattvas, the so-called 'earthing.' The ritual ends with dharma-sharing of experiences during meditation and of thoughts about the texts. This type of communicational exchange is called 'inter-being.' It is deeply indebted to the Buddhist doctrine of the interrelatedness of all beings. This includes the world of ancestors within the subject and causal ethical relations beyond the individual's reach (karma). The daily routine of this conditioning and being aware of emotions and sensual states is a task for lay people. A specific subjectivity is induced by the practiced techniques and by the interpretive teachings. This specific subjectivity is characterised by modality, insofar as it permanently monitors the web of meaningful relations with others and with the environment. It is also characterised by alertness in respect of an inwardly directed perception. What Binder (2011, 60–69) has formulated as a "subjectivity on hold" ("*unter Vorbehalt*") is a provisional, tentative and non-intellectual form of self-assurance. The status of being "on hold" can be seen as a technology of the self that creates the opportunity for the self to be aware of postmodern problems without resolving them. The high level of self-reflexivity contains elements of a permanent self-questioning of one's identity, and it incorporates the basic insight that all social life is constructed, contingent, related (karma-causal relations) and somehow relativistic. There is no one truth or narrative about the self, but a stream of insights and 'dazzlement' within the modal subjectivity that is 'on hold'. Instead of solving the problems, the provisional characterisation is reiterated in specific practices within the group and in individual practice. The group of the *shanga* fulfils the role of an ideal environment enforcing technologies of the self that help to intensify awareness and love towards all creatures. Awareness is the main instance for permanent self-distancing (since there is no essential self, according to Buddhist convictions) and self-observation. This absence of a fixed, or core self is counteracted by the high demand and ideal of presence through awareness, and it is this that is understood to vault the subject into the modality of being 'on hold'.

Binder also identifies this kind of subjectivity in relational psychoanalysis and sociological academic literature, as well as in forms of therapy (Binder 2011, 80 – 114). This is why he argues for a dispositive of "subjectivity on hold"; the discursive formation reaches out beyond the academic societal subfield, such as psychotherapy and spiritual practice. A similar result is to be found in attitudes towards post-mortal existence: even Christian agnostic spirituality leaves open the question of whether there is such any such existence and what it will be like (Wohlrab-Sahr, Karstein, and Schaumburg 2005).

4 Governance of Aesthetic Subjectivities

Through political forces plural subjectivities accrue in specific social milieus. The process of aestheticisation within modern societies describes a way of identity building through lifestyles which is implicit in the commodification of subjects in the context of consumer culture. In addition, recent scholarship has begun to take into account the role of matter and environment, and how they affect subjectivities. In the meantime it is well proven that the aesthetic environment of artificially featured space and healing rooms plays a significant role for optimal healing (Kohls et al. 2012). On the basis of theories of reflexive modernisa tion which presume the exchange of expert systems and processes in the empirical field (for instance Lash 1993), the question can be asked as to what extent the modern aestheticisation process and academic approach of New Materialism converge. According to Foucault, the main strategy of regulating subjects in neoliberalism is self-regulation. Subjects are "responsible" for their behaviour on the market (Turnes 2008); they engage in fitness and high performance practices such as mindfulness meditation, or cosmetic surgery. Andreas Reckwitz (2006), in his historical genealogy of "subjectivity-cultures" (bourgeois modernity, organised modernity and the instable and hybrid subject of postmodernity), has recently enquired if aesthetic subjectivities necessarily have to be creative. This leads to the question of whether we can speak about post-growth-economy subjectivities, such as a 'sustainable subjectivity', characterised by attitudes and practices that aim at extinguishing one's own CO_2 footprint, and at leaving the earth without a trace of our presence.

The critical potential of applying aesthetics to the analysis of subjectivities can also be demonstrated by looking at debates on the "dispossessed subject" and on "epidemic emotions" (Athanasiou and Butler 2013). The tired, irrational, subversive and emotional body considered as dwelling in industrial societies has been a sustained focus of attention, and the concept of body knowledge is explicitly part of this discussion in the areas of sociology of knowledge, sociology of the body, in sports and training sciences, as well as in popular discourses of health. As diverse as these approaches may be, in general they relate body knowledge to practices that promise great benefits for the capacity of memory, the inner organisation of the body and health improvement. Despite the critical concerns these discussions draw on, a new mode of suppression is developed by them: to ascribe knowledge means to ascribe an order, a hierarchy of truths, a refined system of doctrines that support or contradict other interpretations or ideologies. The moment we talk about body knowledge, we rationalise the body, and the body can be subjected to new forms of regulation. At this moment the body becomes an even more colonised landscape were governmentality is performed within a knowledge society. Introducing, and promoting the body as knowledgeable means to present the body to be the addressee for education, training and health prevention; and it also means to bring it under the rule of the political affect economy of neoliberalism. As soon as we provide a concept of body knowledge, new calculative and technocratic techniques can be applied to bodies. Neoliberalism steps into the inner body – into its intimateness of self-sovereignty. The insurance and health industries want to know what we eat, management training wants to improve our motor skills and well-being, the recreation industry offers Pilates and Co.—in order to keep people going.

Against this, dispossessed bodies may strike back. Erdem Gündüz, the Turkish dancer, choreographer and performance artist, spontaneously initiated a political performance on 16th June 2013. His intention was to protest against the construction of a new shopping mall in an urban park. He stood for eight hours in Istanbul's Gezi Park, his eyes directed towards a poster showing a portrait of Mustafa Kemal Atatürk. Through social media such as Twitter, many inhabitants of Istanbul came to know of this protest, and they copied the gesture of standing in public squares the next day, gathering together in silent protest which reached far beyond the initial shopping mall (Talbi 2013). Simply presenting the knowledgeable body, and not moving at all (see Mohr on the "hieratic" in this volume), created a new form of "movement" that differs from political demonstrations, walking, chorusing, being moved. As critical reflection shows, body knowledge can be invaded by neoliberal technocracy, being the target of rationalising manipulation; but it can also be the means of protest by repossessed bodies that were previously thought to be part of a rational choice subject that strives only to maximise gain (Athanasiou and Butler 2013). Also in *Mille Plateaux*, and much earlier than current debates, Gilles Deleuze and Félix Guattari (1980) argue for an environmentally entangled, embodied subject, and against its limitation to a bourgeois affect economy.

5 Conclusion

Speaking about an aesthetic subjectivity does not claim to provide a general philosophical theory of the subject; rather, it helps to theorise a specific form of relatedness of subjects within their socio-political historical environment. On the one hand, the concept of an aesthetic subjectivity results from the insights we gain from contemporary cognitive sciences, and the heuristic approach developed from them. On the other hand, it enables description of a contingent, yet complex, "body-world reference system": facial expression conditions feelings, and vice versa (Levenson, Ekman, and Friesen 1990; Lerner, Dahl, Hariri, and Taylor 2007); voice mirrors stress and emotions (Seifert and Kohlbrunner 2005); subjective repertoires of body posture condition the liking of how other bodies move; ways of problem-solving in the past alter the *how* of one's cognitive processing in the future. The few examples presented here demonstrate the analytical and innovative potential that lies in drawing consequences from current insights into the constitution of subjects in terms of epistemology, but also in applying these insights to the political relevance of leaving simplistic notions of the autonomous and rational subject behind—analysing the place, the agency, and the governance of the aesthetic subject should provoke a much more vigorous debate about cultural aesthetics.

The first sections of this chapter outlined how we, as scholars, conceptualise the subject we are investigating. It proposed to take as a foundation point an embodied cognition that is entangled with culture in various ways, and to use the category of body knowledge—including the outlined sub-categories – in order to describe how embodied subjectivities emerge from their interaction with societal systems. On the level of epistemology, this proposal responds to the provocative claim that a cognitive-aesthetic perspective not only focuses on other objects of research, but also changes the way we can study religion. It does this in two ways: first, it makes clear that the conceptualised agent subject we investigate is the same as the epistemological subject of the scholar: us (Koch 2003, 171, 192–212). From this follows that far more aspects than "rational" and "propositional" argumentation have to be taken into account. Further, the field under investigation in the study of religion can be developed on the assumption that it is structured by embodied agents and the historic objectification of aesthetic subjectivities.

Going back to the discussion of the relevance of how we conceptualise the subjects that we are, and that we investigate, I argue that it is important that we provide concepts such as a "project-self", and an understanding of the relatedness between the embodied subject and ethical implications. Only then we can account for, for instance, the subtle and the provisional subjectivity, as they are realised in the historically contingent religious practices and narratives that we investigate. It is here that the impact of power-knowledge from political regulation can be identified, be it intentional or unintentional. It determines how affects are evoked and then regulated, enclosed, staved off or postponed into an indeterminate future. The mastery over affect economies has a lasting effect on individuals and societies: an effect that is arduous to detect and criticise because affects are only partly connected with the linguistic realm.

On a larger scale, the concept of aesthetic subjects also changes the view of the much contested difference between the religious and the secular, and the debated (and thereby invoked) norms and forces of secularism—a not entirely new, but actual aspirant appearing on the scene, organising affects into affect economies—meaning specific discursive affect configurations, and taming them within the ties of this relatedness. I do not hold "religion" to be untranslatable to other societal systems, a *sui generis* quality, as do Jürgen Habermas or Etienne Balibar (2012). The epistemic aesthetic subject is common to all systems and, thus, religious regulation is not confined to the religious sphere. The moment the embodied agent is manipulated this transformation will also inform his and her action within other societal systems. Against this backdrop the analysis of subjectivities emerging from religious practices is highly relevant and illuminating.

Bibliography

Athanasiou, Athena, and Judith Butler. 2013. *Dispossesion: The Performative in the Political.* Cambridge: Polity Press.

Kohls, Niko, John Ives, Bonnie Sakallaris, and Wayne B. Jonas. 2012. "Towards Enhancing Healing Processes by Developing and Facilitating Technological Aspects of Optimal Healing Environments – Setting the Stage." In *Toward Optimal Healing Environments*, edited by Mathias Bachmann, John Ives, Niko Kohls, and Herbert Plischke, 18–23. Virginia: Samuel Institute Conference Proceedings.

Balibar, Étienne. 2012. *Saeculum: Culture, religion, idéologie*, Paris: Galilée.

Binder, Stefan. 2011. *Die Erzeugung von Welt in Praktiken des Selbst: Eine Dispositivanalyse von Subjektivität im zeitgenössischen Buddhismus.* Münster: LIT.

Cancik, Hubert, and Hubert Mohr. 1988. "Religionsästhetik." In *Handbuch religionswissenschaftlicher Grundbegriffe.* Vol. 1, edited by Hubert Cancik, Burkhard Gladigow, and Matthias Laubscher, 121–156. Stuttgart: Kohlhammer.

Collins Michael P., and Lucia F. Dunn. 2005. "The Effects of Meditation and Visual Imagery on an Immune System Disorder: Dermatomyositis." *Journal of Alternative & Complementary Medicine* 11: 275–284.

Craig, Arthur D. 2002. "How Do You Feel? Interoception: The Sense of the Physiological Condition of the Body." *Nature Reviews* 3: 655–666.

—— 2003. "Interoception: The Sense of the Physiological Condition of the Body." *Current Opinion in Neurobiology* 13: 500–505.

── 2009. "How Do You Feel—Now? The Anterior Insula and Human Awareness." *Nature Reviews. Neuroscience* 10: 59–70.

Csordas, Thomas. 1993. "Somatic Modes of Attention." *Cultural Anthropology* 8: 135–156.

Davis, Joshua Ian, and Arthur B. Markman. 2012. "Embodied Cognition as a Practical Paradigm: Introduction to the Topic, the Future of Embodied Cognition.'" *Topics in Cognitive Science* 4: 685–691.

Deleuze, Gilles, and Félix Guattari. 1980. *Mille Plateaux: Capitalisme et Schizophrénie.* Paris: Editions de Minuit.

Dornberg, Martin. 2013. "Dritte Körper: Leib und Bedeutungskonstitution in Psychosomatik und Phänomenologie." In *Korporale Performanz: Zur bedeutungsgenerierenden Dimension des Leibes*, edited by Arno Böhler, Christian Herzog, and Alice Pechriggl, 103–122. Bielefeld: Transcript.

Foucault, Michel. [Lecture from 1982] 1988. "Technologies of the Self." In *Technologies of the Self: A Seminar with Michel Foucault*, edited by Martin H. Luther, Huck Gutman, and Patrick H. Hutton, 16–49 ["Les techniques de soi." In *Dits et Ecrits* IV, text No. 363] London: Tavistock.

── [1981–1982] 2005. *Hermeneutics of the Subject. Lectures at the Collège de France 1981–1982* [*L'herméneutique du sujet. Cours au Collège de France 1981–82*], London: Palgrave Macmillian: UK.

── [1979–1980] 2014. *On the Government of the Living* [*Du Gouvernemet des Vivants. Cours au Collège de France* 1979–1980]. London: Palgrave Macmillian: UK.

Gard, Tim, Jessica J. Noggle, Crystal L. Park, David R. Vago, and Angela Wilson. 2014. "Potential Self-Regulatory Mechanisms of Yoga for Psychological Health." *Frontiers in Human Neurosciences* 8: 770, URL: http://journal.frontiersin.org/article/10.3389/fnhum.2014.00770/full (last accessed 1 November 2016)

Geurts, Kathryn L. 2002. *Culture and the Senses: Bodily Ways of Knowing in an African Community.* Berkeley: University of California Press.

Grieser, Alexandra. 2015. "Aesthetics." In *Vocabulary for the Study of Religion.* Vol. 1, edited by Robert S. Segal, and Kocku von Stuckrad, 14–23. Leiden, New York: Brill.

Gugutzer, Robert. 2010. "Soziologie am Leitfaden des Leibes: Zur Neophänomenologie sozialen Handelns am Beispiel der Contact Improvisation." In *Die Körperlichkeit sozialen Handelns: Soziale Ordnung jenseits von Normen und Institution*, edited by Fritz Böhle and Margit Weihrich, 165–184, Bielefeld: Transcript.

Herbert, Beate M., and Olga Pollatos. 2012. "The Body in the Mind: On the Relationship Between Interoception and Embodiment." *Topics in Cognitive Science* 4: 692–704.

Holmes, Nicholas, and Charles Spence. 2006. "Beyond the Body Schema: Visual, Prosthetic, and Technological Contributions to Bodily Perception and Awareness." In *The Human Body Perception from the Inside Out*, edited by Günther Knoblich, Ian Thornton, Marc Grosjean, and Maggie Shiffrar, 15–64. Oxford: Oxford University Press.

Johnston, Jay. 2011. "The Body in Wellbeing Spirituality: Self, Spirit and the Politics of Difference." *Religion and the Body: Scripta Instituti Donneriani Aboensis*, edited by Björn Dahla. Turku 23: 174–185.

── 2012. "Theosophical Bodies: Colour, Shape and Emotion from Modern Aesthetics to Healing Therapies." In *Handbook of New Religions and Cultural Production*, edited by Carole Cusack and Alex Norman, 153–170. Leiden and Boston: Brill.

Kerr, Catherine E., Uday Agrawal, and Sandeep Nayak. 2016. "The Effects of Tai Chi Practice on Intermuscular Beta Coherence and the Rubber Hand Illusion." In *Neural Mechanisms Underlying Movement-Based Embodied Contemplative Practices*, edited by Laura Schmalzl and Catherine E. Kerr, 188–200, Lausanne: Frontiers Media. DOI 10.3389/978-2-88919-894-8 (last accessed 11 November 2016)

Knatz, Lothar, and Tanehisa Otabe. 2005. *Ästhetische Subjektivität: Romantik & Moderne.* Würzburg: Königshausen & Neumann.

Koch, Anne. 2003. *Das Verstehen des Fremden: Eine Simulationstheorie im Anschluss an W.O. Quine.* Darmstadt: WGB.

Koch, Anne, and Karin Meissner. 2015. "Sympathetic Arousal during a Touch-Based Healing Ritual Predicts Increase in Well-Being." *eCAM. Evidence-Based Complementary and Alternative Medicine*, open access. URL: http://dx.doi.org/10.1155/2015/641704 (last accessed 11 November 2016)

—— 2016. "Holistic Medicine in Late Modernity: Some Theses on the Efficacy of Spiritual Healing." In *Religion and Illness*, edited by Annette Weissenrieder and Georg Etzelmüller, 414–435. Eugene: Wipf & Stock.

Kripal, Jeffrey. 2005. "Introducing Esalen." In *On the Edge of the Future. Esalen and the Evolution of American Culture*, edited by Jeffrey Kripal and Glenn Shuck, 1–16. Bloomington: Indiana University Press.

Kunas, Markus. 2013. *'The Dancing Sangha': Die 5 Rhythmen als holistische Körpertechnik zwischen Tanz, Therapie und spätmoderner Spiritualität.* Ludwig-Maximilians-University Munich. URL: http://epub.ub.uni-muenchen.de/21723/ (last accessed 11 November 2016).

Lash, Scott. 1993. "Reflexive Modernization: The Aesthetic Dimension." *Theory, Culture & Society* 10/1: 1–23.

Làdavas, Elisabetta, and Alessandro Farnè. 2006. "Multisensory Representation of Peripersonal Space." In *The Human Body Perception from the Inside Out*, edited by Günther Knoblich, Ian Thornton, Marc Grosjean, and Maggie Shiffrar, 98–100. Oxford: Oxford University Press.

Lerner, Jennifer S., Ronald E. Dahl, Ahmad R. Hariri, and Shelley E. Taylor. 2007. "Facial Expressions of Emotion Reveal Neuroendocrine and Cardiovascular Stress Responses." *Biological Psychiatry* 61: 253–260.

Levenson, Rober W., Paul Ekman, and Wallace V. Friesen. 2007. "Voluntary Facial Action Generates Emotions-Specific Autonomic Nervous System Activity." *Psychophysiology* 7: 363–384.

Levine, Peter. 2005. *Healing Trauma: A Pioneering Program for Restoring the Wisdom of your Body.* Boulder: Sounds True.

Lindblom, Jessica. 2015. "Meaning-Making as a Socially Distributed and Embodied Practice." In *Aesthetics and the Embodied Mind: Beyond Art Theory and the Cartesian Mind-Body Dichotomy*, edited by Alfonsina Scarinzi, 3–19. Dordrecht et al.: Springer.

Luhrmann, Tanya M. 2004. "Metakinesis: How God Becomes Intimate in Contemporary U.S. Christian Spirituality." *American Anthropologist* 106: 518–528.

—— 2013. "Building on William James. The Role of Learning in Religious Experience." In *Mental Culture. Classical Social Theory and the Cognitive Science of Religion*, edited by Dimitris Xygalatas and William W. McCorkle Jr., 145–163, Bristol, CT: Acumen.

Malabou, Catherine. 2007. *Les nouveaux blessés: De Freud à la neurologie, penser les traumatismes contemporains.* Paris: Bayard Jeunesse.

Mohr, Hubert. 2006. "Perception/Sensory System." In *Brill Dictionary of Religion*, edited by Kocku von Stuckrad, 1435–1448. Leiden and New York: Brill.

Payne, Peter, and Mardi A. Crane-Godreau. 2015. "The Preparatory Set: A Novel Approach to Understanding Stress, Trauma, and the Bodymind Therapies." *Frontiers in Human Neuroscience* 9: 178.

Plate, Brent S. 2012. "The Skin of Religion: Aesthetic Mediations of the Sacred." *Crosscurrents* 62/2: 162–180.

Polanyi, Michael. 1966. *The Tacit Dimension*. Chicago: University of Chicago Press.

Reckwitz, Andreas. 2006. *Das hybride Subjekt: Eine Theorie der Subjektkulturen von der bürgerlichen Moderne zur Postmoderne*. Weilerswist: Velbrück.

—— 2012. "Affective Spaces: A Praxeological Outlook." *Rethinking History: The Journal of Theory and Practice* 16/2: 241–258.

Reddy, William M. 2001. *The Navigation of Feeling: A Framework for the History of Emotions*. Cambridge: Cambridge University Press.

Roth, Gabriele. 1997. *Sweat Your Prayers*. New York: Tarcher.

Scarinzi, Alfonsina, ed. 2015. *Aesthetics and the Embodied Mind: Beyond Art Theory and the Cartesian Mind-Body Dichotomy*. Contributions to Phenomenology 73. Dordrecht: Springer.

Scheer, Monique. 2012. "Are Emotions a Kind of Practice (And Is That What Makes Them Have a History)? A Bourdieuian Approach to Understanding Emotion." *History and Theory* 51: 193–220.

Schmalzl, Laura, Chivon Powers, and Eva Henje Blom. 2016. "Neurophysiological and Neurocognitive Mechanisms underlying the Effects of Yoga-Based Practices: Towards a Comprehensive Theoretical Framework." In *Neural Mechanisms Underlying Movement-Based Embodied Contemplative Practices*, edited by Laura Schmalzl and Catherine E. Kerr, 96–114. Lausanne: Frontiers Media. DOI 10.3389/978-2-88919-894-8 (last accessed 11 November 2016)

Seifert, Eberhard, and Juerg Kohlbrunner. 2005. "Stress and Distress in Non-Organic Voice Disorders." *Swiss Medical Weekly* 135: 387–397.

Swami Kuvalayananda. [1931] 2010. *Pranayama*. Lonavla, India: Kaivalyadhama Institute.

Talbi, Karim. 2013. "Turkey's 'Standing Man' Protest by Erdem Gunduz Spreads Across Country." *The World Post. A Partnership of the Huffington Post and Berggruen Institute*, 6 June. URL: http://www.huffingtonpost.com/2013/06/18/turkey-standing-man-protest-erdem-gunduz_n_3458390.html (last accessed 12 December 2016)

Ticini, Luca F., Cosimo Urgesi, and Beatriz Calvo-Marino. 2015. "Embodied Aesthetics: Insight from Cognitive Neuroscience of Performing Arts." In *Aesthetics and the Embodied Mind: Beyond Art Theory and the Cartesian Mind-Body Dichotomy*, edited by Alfonsina Scarinzi, 103–116. Dordrecht: Springer.

Turnes, Corina. 2008. "Extremsport Triathlon und Michel Foucaults Konzept der Formung von Subjektivität." In *Körperliche Erkenntnis: Formen reflexiver Erfahrung*, edited by Franz Bockrath, Bernhard Boschert, and Elk Franke, 199–213. Bielefeld: Transcript.

Vugt, Marieke K. van. 2016. "Ballet as a Movement-Based Contemplative Practice? Implications for Neuroscientific Studies." In *Neural Mechanisms Underlying Movement-Based Embodied Contemplative Practices*, edited by Laura Schmalzl and

Catherine E. Kerr, 212–215. Lausanne: Frontiers Media. DOI 10.3389/978-2-88919-894-8 (last accessed 11 November 2016)

Wilson, Margaret. 2006. "Covert Imitation: How the Body Schema Acts as a Prediction Device." In *The Human Body Perception from the Inside Out*, edited by Günther Knoblich, Ian Thornton, Marc Grosjean, and Maggie Shiffrar, 111–125. Oxford: Oxford University Press.

—— 2010. "The Re-Tooled Mind: How Culture Re-Engineers Cognition." *SCAN* 5: 180–187.

Wittmann, Mark, Joachim Peter, Oksana Gutina, Simone Otten, Niko Kohls, and Karin Meissner. 2014. "Individual Differences in Self-Attributed Mindfulness Levels are Related to the Experience of Time and Cognitive Self-Control." *Personality and Individual Differences* 64: 41–45.

Wohlrab-Sahr, Monika, Uta Karstein, and Christine Schaumburg. 2005. "'Ich würd' mir das offenlassen': Agnostische Spiritualität als Annäherung an die 'große Transzendenz' eines Lebens nach dem Tode." *Zeitschrift für Religionswissenschaft* 13: 154–173.

Xygalatas, Dimitris, Ivana Konvalinka, Andreas Roepstorff, and Joseph Bulbulia. 2011. "Quantifying Collective Effervescence. Heart-Rate Dynamics at a Fire-Walking Ritual." *Communicative & Integrative Biology* 4: 735–738.

Manuel A. Vásquez

Religion in the Flesh: Non-Reductive Materialism and the Ecological Aesthetics of Religion

Over against Plato, Descartes, and other idealists, who mistrust the senses and seek to flee into the realm of abstract essences, Maurice Merleau-Ponty declared: "the world is not what I think, but what I live through". And "our body, to the extent that it moves itself about, that is to the extent that it is inseparable from a view of the world and is that view itself brought into existence, is the condition of possibility, not only of the geometrical synthesis, but of all expressive operations and all acquired views which constitute the cultural world (Merleau-Ponty 2002, 451).

In this chapter, I argue that the lived body, in particularly the senses as they summon and are summoned by the world, is central to the efficacy of religion. Borrowing from Birgit Meyer (2010), I advance this argument through an examination of the "aesthetics of persuasion" of Brazilian Neo-Pentecostalism, one of the most dynamic forces shaping the global religious field today. I will show that the appeal and power to transform of transnational Brazilian Pentecostal churches such as the *Igreja Resnacer em Cristo* (Rebirth in Christ Church) and the *Igreja Universal do Reino de Deus* (Universal Church of the Kingdom of God) emerges from compelling "sensational forms" (Meyer 2006, 2011) that enable the experience of immanent transcendence—the materialization of the supernatural—that responds to the tensions and contradictions generated by late modernity.

Epistemologically, the case of Brazilian Neo-Pentecostalism points to the limitations of traditional approaches to religion, which have tended to favour ideas, beliefs, and texts over embodiment, practices, and materiality. In order to overcome these limitations, I conclude arguing for an ecological aesthetics of religion, a relational, situated, and non-reductive materialist approach to "religion in the flesh".

* * *

The ring was set. Although it was one o'clock in the morning, the atmosphere was electric, as the crowd waited under the glare of the lights for the bouts to begin. Groups of fighters warmed up on the wings, preparing for their turn in the *vale tudo* contest. *Vale tudo*—literally "anything goes" or better yet "no holds barred"—is a very popular style of Brazilian fighting that emerged as early as the 1920s as the martial dance of *capoeira* cross-fertilized with Jiu

https://doi.org/10.1515/9783110461015-018

Jitsu, brought by Japanese immigrants. In fact, this free-style combat has become a subculture among Brazilian urban youths. On the surface, thus, there was nothing particularly unusual in this scene. It could have been taking place in any working-class or middle-class neighbourhood in Rio de Janeiro or São Paulo. Except that the ring had been installed in the middle of a church, not just any church, but the Alphaville temple of *A Igreja Renascer em Cristo* (Rebirth in Christ Church), in the greater São Paulo metropolitan region. Founded by bishops Estevam and Sônia Hernandes in the mid-1980s, Rebirth in Christ has been described by *The New York Times* as a vast "religious and business structure that includes more than 1,000 churches, a television and radio network, a recording company, real estate in Brazil and the United States, a horse-breeding ranch and a trademark on the word 'gospel' in Brazil" (Rohter 2007).

Renascer em Cristo has also the distinction of counting until recently Brazilian soccer superstar Kaká among its members. By drawing on Kaká's worldwide visibility, Rebirth in Christ introduces a definite Brazilian flavour to Neo-Pentecostalism's seamless mixture of business, media, popular culture, and religious performance. Kaká is part of what Brazilian sociologist Carmen Rial (2013) calls a new breed of Brazilian religious performer-entrepreneurs, who, taking advantage of the country's world-class prowess in soccer, travel abroad to places as diverse as Japan and Dubai not only to showcase the sport but also to spread Brazilian transnational Pentecostalism. These athletes-entrepreneurs-missionaries are performers in a global stage, in a multi-media spectacle that blends sports, entertainment, media, and pneumatic religion. As they score goals, the Christian footballers remove of their team jerseys to reveal "Jesus Saves" or "I belong to Jesus" T-shirts, or torsos tattooed with crosses. They use their bodies as billboards to deliver a holy message for millions of TV viewers. Underlining the blurring of sacred and profane genres, Kaká has declared that he plans to become a pastor after he retires from soccer.

In blending sports, entertainment, media, and pneumatic religion, Resnacer em Cristo is not alone. It competes against the "hip and happening" *Igreja Bola de Neve* (Snowball Church), which ministers specifically to Generation Xers, mixing Christian Rock, Reggae, and Rap with blogging, surfing, skateboarding, and other extreme sports. In fact, Snowball's founding and head pastor, Apostle Rina, preaches from an altar made out of his surf board. Bola de Neve has now churches in places as diverse as India, Russia (in Moscow), Canada, and the U.S. (Los Angeles and San Diego, CA, Pensacola, FL), and even Australia (Harbord, north of Sydney, where it takes advantage of the shared culture of the beautiful and buff "beach body" among Australians and Brazilians).

That Saturday evening at Renascer in Alphaville was "extreme fight night". Stepping into the middle of the ring to inaugurate the proceedings, the pastor

told the participants: "you need to practice the sport of spirituality more [...] [y]
ou need to fight for your life, for your dreams and ideals. You need to give the
Devil the old one-two punch. You need to give Him a jab to the chin" [*um soco
no queixo*]. He added that he once was a drug addict but that he had found
Jesus when he faced the direst of circumstances. He then invited the crowd to
convert. According to him, on that night "close to 60 youths gave their lives to
Christ". Our church's "first focus is God, but sports help the youth". Those
who come to us "learn the sport and abandon [*larga*] the vices".

In a clear sign of how viscerality—what Marcel Mauss (1992, 455, 461) referred to as the "biological methods of entering into communication with God,"
"actions of a mechanical, physical, or psycho-chemical order" that are nonetheless socially cultivated—has become central to affirmation of religion's authority
and authenticity in a highly competitive global religious arena, African and Af-
rican-based religions, which are often targets of Neo-Pentecostal exorcisms, have
joined the spiritual warfare. Circulating among YouTube exorcism clips is a widely popular one of a 'witch doctor' *catcheur* (wrestler) who challenges an Evangelical pastor in Kinshasa. The staged fight ends with *Luck Mistique*, the catcheur,
confronting the pastor with a smoking fétiche. As Luck Mistique blows smoke on
the face of the Pentecostal preacher, the latter falls flat on his back, shaking un-
controllably.[1] Under the catcheur's control, the pastor then proceeds to eat pages
of the Bible and to wash them, for good measure, with a large bottle of cheap
beer, as the crowd cheers on the defeat of the *faux pasteur* (fake pastor). Like
the vale tudo fights at Renascer em Cristo, this video shows that spiritual combat
is not a disembodied, purely intellectual "battle of the gods", but a visceral confrontation that has material consequences for the combats. The fake pastor is
made to eat his words literally, getting a taste of his own medicine, and thereby
affirming the materiality of the text that has been the source of his claim to transcendence.

In foregrounding viscerality, I draw from Brian Massumi (2002, 60–61) who
argues that "visceral sensibility immediately registers excitations gathered by
the five 'exteroceptive' senses even before they are fully processes by the
brain". Moreover, he rightly contends, that "the dimension of viscerality is adjacent to that of proprioception, but they do not overlap". In other words, a focus
on viscerality allows us to understand the bodily-mediated immediacy, intensity,
and generativity of religious experience in more holistic, dynamic, and non-reductive manner than traditional approaches.

---

1 See https://www.youtube.com/watch?v=Fs9 V9AjKY2Y&feature=youtu.be (last accessed 28
November 2015)

1 Ignoring the Senses and the Body: Traditional Explanations

How can we explain the efficacy of Neo-Pentecostalism? What explains the worldwide "pneumascape," to borrow from Arjun Appadurai,[2] the rapid global spread of religions that place various spirits at the core of their beliefs and practices?

A modernist attitude would regard the attribution of agency to supernatural forces and human objects as superstition, or the failure by an infantile, primitive mentality to distinguish the animate from the inanimate, as E. B. Tylor hypothesized. Or perhaps, we could say, following Max Müller, the reputed father of *Religionswissenschaft*, that it is all a "disease of language", confusing *nomina* for *numena*. But we, sociologists of religion know better than engage in these simplistic explanations, tainted by our colonial prejudices. Durkheim, for example, seems to challenge modernist prejudices about religion, reminding us that "it is an essential postulate of sociology that a human institution cannot rest upon an error or a lie, without which it could not exist" (Durkheim 1965, 14). He goes even further and states: "In reality, then, there are no religions which are false. All of them are true in their own fashion; all answer, though in different ways, to the given conditions of human existence" (Durkheim 1965, 15). Moreover, Durkheim takes the power of religion seriously—epistemologically, the sociology of religion cannot do otherwise. Religion is not some sort of dream, illusion, or hallucination. After all, "what sort of a science is it whose principal discovery is that subject of which it treats does not exist?" (Durkheim 1965, 88).

Thus, when Durkheim talks about religious efficacy he stresses religion's tangible, embodied, and material effects, drawing from the language of physics and medicine to talk about forces, energies, fields, currents, and contagion. He tells us that "to consecrate something, it is put in contact with a source of religious energy, just as to-day a body is put in contact with a sources of heat or

---

2 According to Appadurai (1996, 33–36), the cultural dimensions of contemporary globalisation can be characterised as the shifting, irregular landscapes generated by the disjunctive, perspectival relationship among at least five global flows: ethnoscapes (the movement of people, including immigrants, refuges, exiles, tourists, guest workers, and entrepreneurs, across national borders); technoscapes (the movement of technology, both mechanical and informational); financescapes (the movements of capital at blinding speeds); mediascapes (the "distribution of the electronic capabilities to produce and disseminate information […] now available to a growing number of private and public interests"); and ideoscapes (the movement of ideas, symbols, and narratives that enable people throughout the world to imagine multiple, often hybrid identities and life-worlds). Appadurai does not describe how religion enters these flows, or if religion is itself the source of flows such as "pneuma-scapes," the circulation and performance of spirits at multiple scales.

electricity to warm or electrize it; the two processes employed are not essentially different" (Durkheim 1965, 467). And when Durkheim discusses rituals, he constantly refers to heightened degrees of intensity that are produced when human bodies literally rub against each other, producing states of collective effervescence, which "change the conditions of psychic activity. Vital energies are over-excited, passions more active, sensations stronger; there are even some which are produced only at this moment. A man does not recognize himself; he feels transformed and consequently he transforms the environment which surrounds him" (Durkheim 1965, 469). So, in referring to *mana,* or other totemic principles, as forces, "we do not take the word in a metaphorical sense; they act just as veritable forces. In one sense, they are even material forces which mechanically engender physical effects. Does an individual come into contact with them without having taken proper precautions? He receives a shock which might be compared to the effect of an electric discharge. Sometimes they seem to conceive of these as a sort of fluid escaping by points" (Durkheim 1965, 218).

From the foregoing declarations, it would seem as if Durkheim really gets the generativity of religion. The power of the Holy Spirit in Neo-Pentecostalism is not an illusion or error of attribution. Or is it? Despite his critiques of E. B. Taylor and Max Müller, Durkheim ultimately fails to grasp the fullness of religious efficacy, because he sees the power of religion as a projection of the vitality and determining power of a more real reality: society. It is society that is generative, which does things. "It is society which classifies beings into superiors and inferiors, into commanding masters and obeying servants; it is society which confers upon the former the singular property which makes the command efficacious and which makes *power*" (Durkheim 1965, 409). Just as the totem is "a material expression" of society, the clan itself as "personified and represented to the imagination under the visible form of the animal or vegetable which serves as a totem," so too is religious force "only the sentiment inspired by the group in its members, but projected outside of the consciousness that experiences them, and objectified. To be objectified, they are fixed upon some object which thus becomes sacred" (Durkheim 1965, 261). So, in the end, the efficacy of a thing like the fétiche is "conferred, though purely ideal, act[ing] as if they were real [...] determin[ing] the conduct of men with the same degree of necessity as physical forces" (Durkheim 1965, 260).

In other words, Durkheim's failure to develop a more robust theory of religious efficacy is in large part due to his idealism, his representation of the "material manoeuvers" of religion as nothing more than the "external envelope under which the mental operations are hidden". In a language totally reminiscent of Hegel, Durkheim affirms that "[i]t is sometimes said that inferior religions are materialistic. Such an expression is inexact. All religions, even the crudest, are in a sense spiritualistic; for the power they put in play are before all spiritual, and also their principal object is to act upon moral life" (Durkheim 1965, 467).

Maybe what we need, then, is a Marxist approach? Could it be that Marx's historical materialism succeeds where Durkheim fails? Is the global pneuma-scape coming from the global south nothing more than the "cry of the oppressed creature", the projection of the deep longing for fullness, human dignity, and communion of vast sectors of the world's population that have been dislocated and left behind by global neoliberal capitalism? Is the ubiquity of the devil and his minions a fetishism of commodities, a displaced reflection of the contradictions and discontents of capitalist modernity? This is, in fact, what Jean and John Comaroff argue, when they observe that Neo-Pentecostalism advances a gospel of health and wealth with strong elective affinities with millennial "casino capitalism", which functions like "the cunning that made straw into gold", setting up an alchemy that "def[ies] reason in promising unnaturally large profits—to yield wealth without production, value without effort" (Comaroff and Comaroff 2001, 23) for large sectors of the world's population that have been excluded from enjoying the wealth produced by this speculative capitalism.

It would be unwise to dismiss altogether the Durkheimian and Marxist explanations. They do important critical work, allowing us to understand how religion is connected to domination and resistance, as well as to social production and reproduction. Nevertheless, Tomoko Masuzawa (2000) has demonstrated how the ambivalence toward the notion of fetishism in the early days of *Religionswissenschaft* betrays a total denigration of materiality. She notes that fetishism was associated with "absolute materiality", representing a form of consciousness even baser than idolatry and totally opposite to true spirituality. She observes: "[f]etish is materiality at its crudest and lowest; it points to no transcendent meaning beyond itself, no abstract, general, universal essence with respect to which it might be construed as a symbol" (Masuzawa 2000, 248).

It may be time to provincialize humanism, in the same way that Dipesh Chakrabarty (2000) has called us to provincialize Europe as a contingent, though binding (as a power-laden) project. In particular, it is time to challenge the thesis of human exceptionalism, which is deeply entwined with a Cartesian dualism that has proven epistemologically unsustainable and politically deleterious. Provincializing humanism means tracing genealogically the ways in which it has been implicated with a particular form of agency, a Protestant form of agency, more specifically, a Calvinist agency that is construed as rationalizing, "transcending the body, the senses, and outward religious forms" (Meyer 2010, 743). Along the same lines, philosopher Charles Taylor shows how Protestantism contributed to the "excarnation" of religious life, and life in general, that was central to the Enlightenment's project. "We have moved from an era in which religious life was more 'embodied,' where the presence of the sacred could be enacted in ritual, or seen, felt, touched, walked towards (in pilgrimage); into one which is more 'in the mind,' where the link with God passes through our endorsing contested interpretations" (Taylor 2007, 554). This movement has meant replacing Antiquity's "porous self", which was "vulnerable . . . to spirits, demons, cosmic forces" with the modern, autonomous "buffered self", which has disembedded itself from all those conditions that generated fear and dependence, "disengaging from everything outside the mind", including one's own senses and body (Taylor 2007, 38). Weber, following Nietzsche, is thus right in seeing the defining narrative of modernity as "asceticism [...] carried out of monastic cells into everyday life, and [where it] began to dominate worldly morality". In this disenchanted, bureaucratised world, the body, the senses, aesthetics, and outward religious forms (as opposed to meaning and doctrine) would be evacuated from modern societies and increasingly relegated to traditional cultures and magical religions. This is what makes sense of Weber's ambivalence toward modernity: "specialists without spirit, sensualists without heart; this nullity imagines that it has attained a level of civilization never before achieved" (Weber 1958, 181–182).

Webb Keane has documented this "dematerialization of religion" among Dutch Calvinist missionaries in Indonesia, showing that it involved a power-laden process of purification, namely the subjectivation of the convert, involving the creation of "entirely distinct ontological zones: that of human beings on the one hand; and that of nonhumans on the other" (Latour 1993, 10–11). Conversion to Protestantism meant the realization that only human beings have agency, "freedom" to receive the grace of God. Non-converts and Sumbanese Catholics were fetishists, "surrender[ing their] agency to stones, statues, and even written texts", thus diminishing their responsibility before God. This is why Calvinist missionaries sought the "entextualization of the world" of the Sumbanese, deploying a semiotic ideology that "privileged belief, associated with immaterial meaning, over practice that threatened to subordinate belief to material form" (Keane 2007, 67, 68). The missionaries "stressed the sincerity and privacy of the creed. Religious materializations such as rituals, offerings, priesthoods, sacred sites, relics, communities, holy books, and bodily disciplines persisted but usually in a position subordinate to that of statements of belief. Yet even were one to insist that belief is the very heart of religion, that insistence still depends on, and circulates by the means of, semiotic forms" (Keane 2007, 75). In other words, for all the missionaries' efforts to evoke a purified faith, the fact that they, like their potential converts, are embodied beings embedded in social and natural contexts, asserted the inescapability of the materiality that they sought to evacuate. Authentic belief can only be made present, can only be publicly recognised as sincere, through mistrusted mediators (Engelke 2007).

The dematerialisation of religion has also been the hallmark of academic study of religion. Until the recent materialist turn, the dominant approaches to religion have tended to construe it as abiding deep private belief articulated through self-conscious statements of dogma, only imperfectly represented by contingent "external" manifestations such as symbols, rituals, sacred objects and images, and institutions (Vásquez 2010). These dominant approaches, thus, fail to capture the material potency not just of the practices at Renascer em Cristo, but of the aesthetics of persuasion that gives transnational Neo-Pentecostalism its efficacy. Just as for Calvinist missionaries in Indonesia materiality is an unavoidable reality that, while making possible the implementation of their semiotic ideology, also throws into sharp relief its contradictions, so too is the global proliferation of material religion a challenge for religious studies.

2 Recovering the Senses and the Body: Neo-Pentecostal Viscerality

What would it mean to de-centre modernity's purified, overweening, and dualistic humanism, and to produce richer and more dynamic accounts of the polymorphous fecundity of matter, accounts that extend, pluralise, and render more transitive the notion of agency and that place our bodies, as flesh encountering "the flesh of the world", as an indispensable aspect of that material generativity? Could we craft robust and holistic explanations of religious phenomena such as glossolalia, divine cure, and spirit incorporation and exorcism that, while acknowledging the multiple ways in which religion is implicated in larger social processes like the deepening and widening of neo-liberal capitalism, recognise the material efficacy of the phenomena, the power to interpellate new subjects and constitute new spaces? How would an account of extreme fight nights at Renascer em Cristo look like if we focus on religion in the flesh?

Although at the theological level, within Neo-Pentecostalism's cosmology, extreme fight nights pit two forces at war with each other, ontologically, the fights point to the non-dualistic intertwining of spirit and matter, of body and soul that is at the heart of Neo-Pentecostalism's gospel of health and wealth. To carry out the Great Commission, Jesus' call to make disciples of all nations, requires a spiritual warfare that is inextricably a physical combat, since the spirits that are exorcised in the name of Jesus are embodied and territorial spirits, spirits who produce illnesses and material misfortune. How then to make sense of this fight's ontological non-dualism, of the full involvement of the body, especially of the senses, in making the salvific power of the Holy Spirit present and efficacious? We can build upon and go beyond two classical readings of agonism: Clifford Geertz's "Notes on the Balinese Cock Fight" and Roland Barthes's "On the World of Wrestling". We can reject Geertz's notion that the Balinese cock fight is primarily the enactment of an all-encompassing, self-contained cultural system, whose only function is to "say something of something", as part of an unproductive reductive textualism. However, we can say with Geertz that extreme fight nights at Renascer are "deep plays", where the "the stakes are so high" as to transcend any purely utilitarian and instrumental logic. What we have here is an on-going epic and cosmic struggle between Jesus Christ and the devil waged and displayed in and through the bodies of the fighters; it is redemptive violence territorialised in the middle of the violent city.

As in the Balinese cockfight, for followers of Renascer em Cristo attending and participating in extreme nights serves as "a kind of sentimental education" (Geertz 1973, 449). It is not an "intellectual" education about a creed, whereby the faithful engage in reflection and rational discussions of various theological aspects of Pentecostalism. Like the boxers that Loic Wacquant (2004) followed in Chicago, Neo-Pentecostals engaged in mediatised spiritual warfare develop a "pugilistic habitus" (Wacquant 2004, 16), a "rigorous management of the body [...] a meticulous maintenance of each one of its parts [...] an attention of every moment, in and out of the ring, to its proper functioning and protection" (Wacquant 2004, 127). For after all, "the pugilist's body is at once the tool of his work—an offensive weapon and a defensive shield—and the target of his opponent" (Wacquant 2004, 127).

Much has been written on the techniques of the self that accompany the production of "God's subjects", to quote Ruth Marshall (2009, 128 165). Tanya Luhrmann (2012), for example, refers to the "physical modes of discernment" through which Evangelical Christians surrounded by a culture that is deeply sceptical of the supernatural learn to experience God's presence and, eventually, establish an intimate relationship with Jesus. These modes of discernment deploy an embodied meta-kenosis, a pluri-sensorial openness to transcendence within immanence, to alterity within identity. These modes are painstakingly inculcated through a series of exercises that often involve repetition, prayers that often include particular body postures in order to heighten attention to external phenomenal as well as internal experiences. Josh Brahinsky (2012), for his part, refers to the "pedagogies of conversion and commitment" that involve "visceral modes of appraisal," (borrowing from political theorist William Connelly) or embodied conditions of felicity that enable Pentecostals to render the divine present directly and immediately. Brahinsky calls this "pneumo-poetics", an enfleshed and enfleshing religious generativity. We see here, then, how a focus on viscerality, particularly on what Félix Guattari (1995, 9) calls "preverbal intensities" enables us to recover a fuller aesthesis of religion, which includes not only conscious articulation of religious experience, but also the "gut feelings", the unreflected in-corporated habits and implicit embodied practical know-how that often exceed and ground the know-what, i.e., the narrativised accounts of religious experience.

What we have in extreme fight nights is an education of the senses, where a restless urban generation, a generation that has come of age through a steady diet of caffeine, adrenaline and virtuality, learns what Neo-Pentecostalism's embodied "ethos and [...] private sensibility looks like when spelled out externally". This is a habitus of discipline, perfect health, moral purity, optimism, and prosperity, a kind of holistic "callisthenic spirituality of corporal commitment" (Csordas 1997, 11; Coleman 2000, 134), that is part and parcel of a "muscular Christianity", one that is capable of not only protecting the body against the vices of the city but of pushing back, of purifying carving out eschatological spaces, spaces of salvation in the midst of the baffling, morally ambivalent cityscapes.[3]

In turn, the redemption of the city through vale tudo combats, exorcisms, power prayers, pilgrimages, prayer walks, and massive Christian Rock concerts is above all an exercise in place-making, the physical and spiritual labour of carving out sacred spaces against demonic strongholds.

> [T]he dirty city is also the holy city: by the conventions of the genre, it is precisely in those dark, filthy depths that God comes. The dramatic and spiritual fulfillment offered by these Christian narratives of urban conversion lies in their affirmation of the power of grace to touch absolutely the darkest, most vile, and most inhuman corners of the city's sinfulness (Orsi 1999,11).

The conquering of profane urban spaces, often marked by the construction of colossal temples or massive religious camps, together with the cleansing and healing of bodies broken by the "pathogens of poverty" (Chesnut 1997), often circulate on the Internet and church-owned media circuits, providing sensational forms that testimony to the efficacy of Neo-Pentecostalism. These forms are sensational because they both appeal to the senses, thus involving embodiment and materiality, and are spectacular (Meyer 2010, 742).

This is where Barthes comes in. Unlike wrestling, extreme fight nights at Renascer are not just simulacra in which "the function of the wrestler is not to win"

---

3 Arguably, the transnational Nigerian church Kingsway International Christian Centre offers the best short-hand characterisation of this muscular Christianity: "Raising Champions, Taking Territories".

(Barthes 1972, 16). Vale tudo at Rebirth in Christ is not simply "an immediate pantomime" in which "it no longer matters whether the passion is genuine or not"; a "human comedy in which what the public wants is the image of passion, not passion itself" (Barthes 1972, 18–19). For Barthes, "there is no more a problem of truth in wrestling than in the theater". However, Barthes's keen insight that "wrestling is not a sport, it is a spectacle" (Barthes 1972, 15) applies directly to extreme fight nights. And when he tells us "that [t]he virtue of all-in wrestling is that it is the spectacle of excess" (Barthes 1972, 15), Barthes could have also been talking of spiritual warfare. The exorcisms at the centre piece of spiritual warfare, like the bouts at extreme fight night, are ritualised displays of the power of Jesus to defeat his opponent—the Devil—and to heal. They are both enactments of morality plays that involve the "grandiloquent truth of gestures", bold moves which both the contenders and the audience apprehend as compelling through their senses: the pastor's commanding summons to the possessing demon in Jesus's name, the ushers holding tightly the convulsing body those possessed, the demon cursing back at the pastor, the shouts of the congregation at the demon "Leave now!" "Leave now!", or alternatively the smoke of the witch doctor catcheur's fétiche or the quivering vanquished body of the fake pastor.

In sharp contrast to wrestling, in spiritual warfare truth matters, and it is the sheer viscerality of the combat that is the condition for the authenticity of conversions that follow the bouts, for the affirmation of the authority of Renascer in relation to other churches which cannot go to these extremes. In a radical departure from the semiotic ideology of Calvinist missionaries in Indonesia, the body itself, restored to health and wealth, becomes the medium for vivid, immediate, and intimate experiences of the transcendent and for the assertion of the truth of the message of Neo-Pentecostalism.[4] The fight nights are not just about semiosis, the communication of meaning; they involve the "polyphonic interlacing between the individual and the social" (Guattari 1996, 267), among cognitions, emotions, affects, motions, habits, and sensations through a psycho-senso-motoric coordination apparatus.

Rebirth in Christ's success comes in large part from tapping into the rapidly expanding market of young urban generations—the Millennial and Net generations—which have emerged as Brazil enters a new stage of globalization, leapfrogging the UK as the 6th largest economy in the world. These generations

---

4 Meyer (2010, 756) highlights the centrality of the body and materiality in the generation of practices that "repeatedly persuade people of the truth and reality of their sensations". The embodied and material dynamics that are responsible for the production of truth effects, for the efficacy of religion to invoke and sustain powerful experiences of the unseen is what Meyer terms "aesthetic of persuasion".

have grown up with a steady diet of images and an increasingly short attention span. These are generations whose lives are deeply imbued with a highly "mediatized immediacy" that blurs the boundaries between virtuality and reality, producing intense enchanted simulacra, potent self-referential experiences such as being in the middle of combat (World of Warcraft), or being part of a violent heist (Grand Theft Auto) or a plot to kill an important historical figure (Assassin's Creed).

In that sense, the case of Renascer refutes Jean Baudrillard's claim that late modernity is characterised by the "omnipotence of simulacra", which act as "deterrents" to any attempts to point to the real, to have unmediated access to materiality and experience. According to Baudrillard (1994, 79), "we live in a world where there is more and more information, and less and less meaning". And this endless flow of information "dissolves meaning and dissolves the social, in a sort of nebulous state dedicated not to a surplus of innovation, but, on the contrary, to total entropy. Thus the media are producer not of socialization, but of exactly the opposite, of the implosion of the social in the masses" (Baudrillard 1994, 81). This implosion of the social, the flattening out of the life-world into the "dessert of the [hyper]real" means that "we are witnessing the end of the perspectival and panoptic space (which remains a moral hypothesis bound up with all the classical analyses on the 'objective' essence of power), and thus to the *very abolition of the spectacular*" (Baudrillard 1994, 30).

It is true that the endless waves of electronic information that wash over us at blinding speeds, particularly over young urban people, drastically exacerbate the "blasé attitude" that Georg Simmel associated with "mental life" in the metropolis.

> [T]hrough the rapidity and contradictoriness of their changes, more harmless impressions force such violent responses, tearing the nerves so brutally hither and thither that their last reserves of strength are spent; and if one remains in the same milieu they have no time to gather new strength. An incapacity thus emerges to react to new sensations with the appropriate energy. This constitutes that blasé attitude which, in fact, every metropolitan child shows when compared with children of quieter and less changeable milieus (Simmel 1950, 414).

For the blasé person in the global, digitally-connected metropolis, things appear in "an evenly flat and grey tone; no object deserves preference over any other" (Simmel 1950, 414).

However, the intensification of sensory stimulation does not just produce an exhaustion of the nerves and "a blunting of discrimination". Paradoxically, it also generates an insatiable hunger for more intensity, for more "reality", for more extreme, visceral limit-experiences as a mark of individuality, authority, creativity, and authenticity. This is the return of the repressed: the return of materiality and the flesh as a reaction to the tyranny of deterritorialised signifiers. It is in this context that we must understand the tremendous popularity of "reality TV" and "torture porn" or "gorn", which allow us to partake vicariously in the thrills of testing the body at the limits, by eating live roaches or hacking an arm off to keep on living and move to the next shocking task. Or think of the hyper-consumption of human flesh by the hordes of zombies that populate movies like *I Am a Legend, 28 Hours,* or *World War Z* and television series like *The Walking Dead,* zombies who can only be stopped by ultra-violent means.[5]

The quest for hyper-corporality is mediated and spurred by new technologies of presencing that "obliterate space through time", as David Harvey (1989) puts it, technologies that allow us to document and share globally our most intimate and banal acts by posting pictures of ourselves, our friends, and our families on Facebook and Snapchat. These technologies also play a key role in what the rise of a new transnational bio-politics, a new transnational, flexible panoptical regime that seeks to manage unruly flows that are part and parcel of the current phase of globalisation, where it be undocumented immigrants, terrorists, or drug traffickers. In particular, this regime attempts to regulate mobile populations under a rigid illegal-legal binary logic and according to a dialectic of visibility and invisibility: unauthorized immigrants must become simultaneously visible to the gaze of local, state, and federal authorities and invisible through exclusion from public and civic spaces, from schools, hospitals, and roads (Vásquez 2014).

3 Recovering Materiality: Neo-Pentecostalism's Eschatological Monumentality

I have argued elsewhere that the transportability and efficacy of Latin American and African Pentecostalisms stem from a "pneumatic materialism", a dynamic and flexible regime of discourse and practice in which the visible and the invisible, as well as the natural and supernatural, are intimately connected, such that spirit and matter are intensely involved in relations of reciprocal determination (Vásquez 2009). This pneumatic materialism operates through an *aesthetics of spectacularity* that has two main ingredients: pneumatic viscerality and eschato-

---

5 According to McAlister (2012, 462), among other things, "the zombie serves to index the excessive extremes of capitalism, the overlap of capitalism and cannibalism", of the hyper-consumption of humans by other humans.

logical monumentality. I have shown pneumatic viscerality at work in the vale tudo fights at Renascer. I would like to say a few words about eschatological monumentality before I return to the larger implications of Neo-Pentecostalism's aesthetic of persuasion. A good illustration of the aesthetics of spectacularity is the Universal Church of the Kingdom of God (UCKG), arguably the most globally visible Brazilian Neo-Pentecostal church.

The Universal unabashedly flaunts monumentality as a sign of its spiritual power, purchasing and remodelling landmark buildings, such as the Rainbow Theatre in London and Huggy Boy Theatre in East Los Angeles. The UCKG recently inaugurated a replica of Solomon's Temple in São Paulo at the cost of US$300 million. Standing 18 stories high and featuring soaring ornate columns, elaborate gardens and water fountains, and imposing gold-plated doors, the building will seat 10,000.[6] Edir Macedo, the billionaire founder of the church, spared no expense: he spent US$8 million to import stones from Israel to build the temple. When asked about why he built the Solomon's Temple, Macedo articulates a geo-spiritual pastoral project that places Brazil at the centre of a vast "globally integrated network", which, in effect, inverts the country's peripheral place in the capitalist world-system, in effect, mirroring Brazil's standing as one of the BRICS (Mafra et al. 2013).[7] Making reference to Joseph's dream in the Hebrew Bible that foretold how his brothers would eventually bow before him after having cast him out and sold him as a slave, Macedo declared that at the end of times he foresees "all religions and nations of the world bowing down [*estarão se curvando*] before Solomon's Temple".[8] Macedo has also stated that he would like Solomon's Temple to overshadow the famous Christ the Redeemer at Corcovado in Rio de Janeiro as the image that the world has of Brazil.

Spectacularity may be a common ingredient in the Neo-Pentecostal global economy of attention, as the massive events staged by the Nigerian Redeemed Christian Church of God (RCCG) in their Redemption Camp demonstrates. Drawing from Erwin Goffman, we can characterise this camp as "a total institution", a self-contained place in which the articulation of the self and the construction of everyday sociality are tightly regulated. In addition to the gigantic auditorium, the camp has its own Bible college, university, high school, guest houses,

6 Tom Phillip, "Solomon's Temple in Brazil would put Christ the Redeemer in the shade." *The Guardian*, July 21, 2010. http://www.guardian.co.uk/world/2010/jul/21/solomon-temple-brazil-christ-redeemer (last accessed 11 June 2013).
7 BRICS is an acronym for the five major emerging national economies: Brazil, Russia, India, China and South Africa. On Brazil's role in the new global religious economy, see Rocha and Vásquez (2014).
8 Here Macedo is making reference to Genesis 37:8–9.

water and electricity department, clinic, post office, bank, and supermarket. In fact, the RCCG bills Redemption Camp as "the largest city of god on earth", drawing a sharp contrast with the chaos, corruption, crime, and violence of Lagos and other Nigerian and African cities. According to the RCCG website, "[T]he Redeemed Camp is a town that works. The air is clean and fresh, the roads are free of potholes, and the general decay associated with urban living in Nigeria is almost non-existent in the Camp. Electricity supply is uninterrupted, clean water runs at the tap, environment is sanitised and decent transportation system is in place". The RCCG has purchased 800 acres of prairie land about an hour north of Dallas to build another Redemption Camp in the United States. The camp will be anchored by a temple hall with capacity for 20,000.

Whether referring to pneumatic viscerality or eschatological spectacularity, Neo-Pentecostalism's aesthetics of persuasion operates through what Meyer calls sensational forms—"relatively fixed, authorized modes of invoking, and organizing access to the transcendental, thereby creating and sustaining links between religious practitioners in the contexts of particular religious organizations" (Meyer 2006, 9). According to Meyer (2010, 751), "sensational forms are part of a specific religious aesthetics, which governs a sensory engagement of humans with the divine and each other and generates particular sensibilities. Religions operate through historically generated sensational forms that are distinctive and induce repeatable patterns of feeling and action". Furthermore, as inculcated discursive-non-discursive modes of rendering accessible the transcendental, sensational forms are paradoxical. On the one hand, in staging deep plays like extreme fight nights, these sensational forms blend media, viscerality, materiality, and transcendence so seamlessly that the media itself disappears. "The media that are involved in invoking and getting in touch with some divine power, and in binding and bonding believers, are made to 'disappear' through established and authorized religious sensational forms that mark these media as genuine to the substance they mediate" (Meyer 2011, 32). In the production of a mediated immediacy, whose immediacy is intensified, render extremely visceral, "mediation itself is sacralized".

On the other hand, Neo-Pentecostalism's pneumatic materialism makes media, particularly viscerality and materiality, "hyper-apparent". The bodies of the vale tudo fighters at Resnacer, the Universal's colossal Templo Salomão, and the RCCG's massive Redemption Camp evince the power of the Holy Spirit to break through late modernity's endless simulacra to produce converted religious subjects and to carve out highly visible heterotopias, alternative spaces of transcendence, which point to the ends of time. "[S]piritual power materializes in the medium, and is predicated to touch people in an immediate manner.

Instead of vanishing into mediation, media here become hyper-apparent" (Meyer 2011, 34).

The hyper-presence of media has important implications for the relativization of modernity's narrow understandings of agency, which attributes it only to humans, setting them against an inert and static material world that they transform through their practices. To the extent that non-human entities have agency, it is because humans have projected it into them. Here we are back to the Durkheimian and Marxist explanations that we saw could not really capture the potency of pneumascapes such the ones at Renascer. To understand religion in the flesh, to produce empirically-rich accounts of the pneumatic materialism that characterises not only Charismatic Christianities, but also a diversity of religious phenomena, ranging from the cult of the miraculous saints and their relics in traditional popular Catholicism and to Spiritism, Neo-Shamanism, and Neo-Animism, we must abandon Cartesian dualism and its accompanying somato– and geo-phobias. We must adopt a non-reductive materialism that understands matter not as fixed passive stuff, the prison of the active soul, the lifeless substance against which the sovereign subject pushes through the creative power his/her practices. Rather, we must understand that consciousness and culture are the complex, shifting-yet-relatively-stable emergent effects of the polymorphous fecundity of matter (Bennett 2010; Coole and Frost 2010). This understanding will mean that we have to relativize the sharp distinction between theology, as (fetishized and fetishistic) perspective of the religious insider, and religious studies, as the social scientific, critical approach of the outsider. A non-reductive and non-idealist aesthetic of religion will have to take seriously forms of agency and efficacy that co-operate with anthropocentric modes of perception and activity, even when these modes are fully enfleshed.

Carolyn Walker Bynum's work on Christian materiality demonstrates what I have in mind when I invoke terms such as pneumatic materialism and non-reductive materialism. She shows that for medieval Christians "matter was a dynamic substratum" (Bynum 2011, 250). "Ecclesial authorities, intellectuals, and the ordinary faithful lived in a world where blood erupted on wafers, images changed color and descended from walls, bodies broke out in stigmata". These images, objects, and bodies 'spoke' and 'acted' "their physicality in particularly intense ways that call attention to their per se 'stuffness' and 'thingness'" (Bynum 2011, 29). So that "[w]hen wood or wafer bled, matter showed itself as transcending, exactly by expressing, its own materiality. It manifested enduring life (continuity, existence) in death (discontinuity, rupture, change). Miraculous matter was simultaneously—hence paradoxically—the changeable stuff of not-God and the locus of a God revealed". Against excessively symbolicist approaches to these phenomena, matter did not merely signify something beyond itself. For medieval Christians, "[m]atter was powerful. In their insistent materiality, images thus do more than comment on, refer to, provide signs of, or gesture toward the divine. They lift matter toward God and reveal God through matter" (Bynum 2011, 35). In light of this paradox of Christian materiality—in which icons and relics call attention to materiality and how it is miraculously transformed in order to disclose that which is its opposite (God)—Bynum challenges modern theorists, including Bruno Latour and Actor-Network theorists, for thinking that matter's agency is "like that of human actors". For these theorists, "things that talk are metaphorical people", since "the power of objects increases as they approximate persons" (Bynum 2011, 282, 283).

While I share with Latour the view that networks offers a good trope to study religion in motion and embed it in various scales from the construction of the self and local everyday life to the transnational and global, I find that he still clings to the myth of human exceptionalism, to the idea that agency emerges from our interaction with non-human animals, things, and even spirits to whom we "delegate" agentic powers. But it is not just relations that matter. The materiality of the religious bodies, things, and environments we encounter matters too. It matters that an inscription is made in stone or that a text is written on parchment, for these elements afford certain sensorial possibilities and foreclose others in the manner in which we can read, touch, handle, store, transport, exchange, decorate, and amend them. For sacred landscapes, in addition to the sedimented narratives and memories that disclose them to us as singular or special, geology, topography and climate also matter. As flesh touching our flesh, the material world out of which we have emerged, upon which we depend, and in which we are inextricably embedded afford us certain embodied experiences and practices, which, in turn, transforms these affordances, opening and foreclosing new horizons of praxis.

4 Non-Reductive Materialism and an Ecological Aesthetics of Religion

I have argued that the visceral aesthetics of persuasion of Brazilian Neo-Pentecostalism make sense in the context of a generalized mediatised hunger for ever heightened intensity and life at the limits. Materiality has always been there as a constituent of our *Dasein*, our thrownness in the world. However, the present age has undermined the excarnation of the self that began with Plato but gathered considerable momentum with the Reformation and modernity, setting the stage for a return of the repressed. Rapid transformations in fields as diverse as genetics, the neurosciences, artificial intelligence, animal cognition, and computer-mediated communications have problematized what it means to be human. They have raised the issue of the uniqueness of human embodiment in relation to technologies with which our lives are increasingly entwined. If you add to this the overproduction of capitalism, which has generated more wealth that ever in history, but has also excluded large sectors of the world's population from enjoying this wealth, it is not surprising that materiality has become so salient in the humanities and social sciences. Digital media set conditions both for the generalized longing for viscerality and materiality and for the global fulfillment of this desire, by simultaneously threatening to swallow us in the "desert of the virtual" and by making possible, even at a distance, ever more vivid (hyper-real) and portable stark experiences of viscerality and materiality like the extreme fight nights at Renascer and the Universal's colossal Solomon's Temple.

The notion of viscerality not only allows us "taking into account alterity in its extreme modalities" (Guattari 1995, 107), as our discussion of fight nights and Solomon's Temple demonstrates. At deeper level, it moves us beyond traditional understandings of the essence of religion as predicational, as being only or even primarily about the profession of creed by an autonomous, disembodied, and fully transparent Cartesian self. Viscerality foregrounds the poly-sensorial-motoric and multi-modal character of religion experience—from preverbal intuitions, skin-deep affects (in Portuguese "*sentimentos à flor da pele*"), and gut feelings to habits, institutionalised regimes of sensation, and rational articulations of creed—since it departs from the embodied self in and of the world. Thus, a full-bodied aesthetics is an essential ingredient in a fully historicised and fully materialised, yet non-reductive comparative phenomenology of religion, a rigorous-yet-fallible phenomenology that eschews the limitations and contradictions of Mircea Eliade's history of religions approach.

In order to understand the efficacy of religious phenomena within our "reincarnated" present age, we must study religion "in the flesh". I borrow this expression from George Lakoff and Mark Johnson (1999), who used it to advocate for an "embodied philosophy", one that understands the mind not as some transcendental, unchanging, and pure essence standing above the contingent, fluid, and imperfect flows of history, society, and nature, but as thoroughly embodied and dynamic reality. As Varela, Thompson, and Rosch (1992, 17–173) put it, "By using the term *embodied* we mean to highlight two points: first that cognition depends upon the kinds of experience that come from having a body with various sensorimotor capacities, and second, that these individual sensorimotor capacities are themselves embedded in a more encompassing biological, psychological and cultural context". In a similar way, understanding religion in the flesh, would mean approaching it not as some fixed thing—whether the product of revelation by entity(ies) above history and nature or the inner structures of an abstract, ahistorical Cartesian-Kantian self, but rather as the contested, yet-relatively stabilised outcome of the practices of particular embodied, sensual individuals emplaced in specific socio-cultural and natural fields and networks that are themselves mediated by these practices.

I have used the notion of viscerality to point to an aesthetics of religion, a rigorous cross-disciplinary field that focuses on the production and circulation of efficacious religious experiences, practices, identities, artefacts, and institutions, as particular bodies creatively process and express biological data, emotions, and behaviours within socio-cultural and natural systems that enable and cultivate them. In that sense, aesthetics of religions is quintessentially about connectivity, about emergent phenomena that co-arise in the entanglements of culture and nature, individual and society, agency and structure, and consciousness and physio-chemistry.[9] To underline this dynamic connectivity and co-implication, I would like to propose that we develop an *ecological aesthetics of religion* that engages with but goes beyond the senses, beyond the body, to recognise the materiality that makes the senses and the body possible as part of a larger web of life. As Merleau-Ponty writes, "it is by the flesh of the world that in the last analysis one can understand the lived body (*corps proper*)". After all,

> my body is made of the same flesh as the world (it is a perceived), and moreover that this flesh of my body is shared by the world, the world reflects it, encroaches upon it and it encroaches upon the world (the felt [*senti*] at the same time the culmination of subjectivity and the culmination of materiality), they are in a relation of transgression or of overlapping (Merleau-Ponty 1968, 248, 250).

An ecological aesthetics of religion, thus, challenges the "equation of materiality with the solid substance of the earth [which] creates the impression that life goes on upon the outer surface of a world that has already congealed in its final form, rather than in the midst of a world of perpetual flux" (Ingold 2006, 16). It is an aesthetics that subscribes to "the view that things are in life rather than life in things" (Ingold 2006, 29). As such, ecological aesthetics would approach religions as the heterogeneous and hybrid products of the non-linear interplay of ecological and neuro-somatic networks, social fields, and discursive matrixes that weave the infra-structure of our life-worlds. Diverse entities co-arise, circu-

---

9 On the notion of "agential intra-activity," that "reality is composed not of things-in-themselves or things-behind-phenomena but of things-in-phenomena," actors that enact their identities and agencies within networks of intra-actions, see Barad (2007, 132–185).

late, jostle, and cross-fertilize within these networks, fields, and matrixes: wrestlers, gigantic temples, itinerant pastors, witch doctors, merchants, immigrants, tourists, pilgrims, missionaries, relics, icons, techniques of the body, sensational forms, piacular rituals, imprecatory prayers, theodicies, sacred texts, videotaped sermons, cyber-identities, and forms of constructing and managing sacred spaces, as well as gods, spirits, demons, and so forth. Our task is to elucidate with the most context-sensitive methods at hand how these entities are involved in rendering efficacious discourses, practices, institutions, and landscapes we call religious.

Bibliography

Appadurai, Arjun. 1996. *Modernity at Large: Cultural Dimensions of Globalization*. Minnesota: University of Minneapolis Press.

Barad, Karen. 2007. *Meeting the Universe Halfway: Quantum Physics and the Entanglements of Matter and Meaning*. Durham, NC: Duke University Press.

Barthes, Roland. 1972. "The World of Wrestling." In *Mythologies*, by Roland Barthes, 15–25. New York: Hill and Wang.

Baudrillard, Jean. 1994. *Simulacra and Simulation*. Ann Arbor: University of Michigan Press.

Bennett, Jane. 2010. *Vibrant Matter: A Political Ecology of Things*. Durham: Duke University Press.

Brahinsky, Josh. 2012. "Pentecostal Body Logics: Cultivating a Modern Sensorium." *Cultural Anthropology* 27/2: 215–238.

Bynum, Carolyn Walker. 2011. *Christian Materiality: An Essay on Religion in Late Medieval Europe*. New York: Zone Books.

Chakrabarty, Dipesh. 2000. *Provincializing Europe: Postcolonial Thought and Historical Difference*. Princeton: Princeton University Press.

Chesnut, R. Andrew. 1997. *Born Again in Brazil: The Pentecostal Boom and Pathogens of Poverty*. New Brunswick, NJ: Rutgers University Press.

Coleman, Simon. 2000. The Globalisation of Charismatic Christianity: Spreading the Gospel of Prosperity. Cambridge: Cambridge University Press.

Comaroff, Jean, and John Comaroff. 2001. "Millennial Capitalism: First Thoughts on a Second Coming." In *Millennial Capitalism and the Culture of Neoliberalism*, edited by John Comaroff, 1–56. Durham, NC: Duke University Press.

Coole, Diana, and Samantha Frost, eds. 2010. *New Materialisms: Ontology, Agency, and Politics*. Durham, NC: Duke University Press.

Csordas, Thomas. 1997. *Language, Charisma, and Creativity: The Ritual Life of a Religious Movement*. Berkeley: University of California Press

Durkheim, Emile. 1965. *The Elementary Forms of Religious Life*. New York: Free Press.

Engelke, Matthew. 2007. *A Problem of Presence: Beyond Scripture in an African Church*. Berkeley: University of California Press.

Freston, Paul. 2001. "The Transnationalisation of Brazilian Pentecostalism: The Universal Church of the Kingdom of God." In *Between Babel and Pentecost: Transnational*

Pentecostalism in Africa and Latin America, edited by André Corten and Ruth Marshall-Fratani, 196 – 215. Bloomington: Indiana University Press.

Geertz, Clifford. 1973. "Deep Play: Notes on the Balinese Cock Fight." *In Interpretation of Cultures*, by Clifford Geertz, 412 – 453. New York: Basic Books.

Genosko, Gary, ed. 1996. *The Guattari Reader.* London: Blackwell.

Guattari, Félix. 1995. *Chaosmosis: An Ethico-Aesthetic Paradigm.* Sydney: Power.

Harvey, David. 1989. *The Condition of Postmodernity.* London: Blackwell.

Ingold, Tim. 2011. *Being Alive: Essays on Movement, Knowledge and Description.* London: Routledge.

Keane, Webb. 2007. *Christian Moderns: Freedom and Fetish in the Mission Encounter.* Berkeley: University of California Press.

Lakoff, George, and Mark Johnson. 1999. *Philosophy in the Flesh: The Embodied Mind and Its Challenge to Western Thought.* New York: Basic Books.

Latour, Bruno. 1993. *We Have Never Been Modern.* Cambridge, MA: Harvard University Press.

Luhrmann, Tanya M. 2012. *When God Talks Back: Understanding the American Evangelical Relationship with God.* New York: Vintage.

Mafra, Clara, Camila Sampaio, and Claudia Swatowiski. 2013. "Edir Macedo's Pastoral Project: A Globally Integrated Pentecostal Network." In *The Diaspora of Brazilian Religions*, edited by Cristina Rocha and Manuel A. Vásquez, 45 – 67. Leiden: Brill.

Marshall, Ruth. 2009. *Political Spiritualities: The Pentecostal Revolution in Nigeria.* Chicago: University of Chicago Press.

Massumi, Brian. 2002. *Parables of the Virtual: Movement, Affect, Sensation.* Durham, NC: Duke University Press.

Masuzawa, Tomoko. 2000. "Troubles with Materiality: The Ghost of Fetishism in the Nineteenth Century." *Comparative Studies in Society and History*, 42/2: 242 – 267.

Mauss, Marcel. 1992 [1934]. "Techniques of the Body." In *Incorporations*, edited by Jonathan Crary and Sanford Kwinter, 455 – 477. New York: Zone.

McAlister, Elizabeth. 2012. "Slaves, Cannibals, and Infected Hyper-Whites: The Race and Religion of Zombies." *Anthropological Quarterly* 85/2: 457 – 486.

Merleau-Ponty, Maurice. 1968. *The Visible and the Invisible.* Evanston: Northwestern University Press.

—— 2002. *Phenomenology of Perception.* London and New York: Routledge.

Meyer, Birgit. 2006. "Religious Sensations: Why Media, Aesthetics and Power Matter in the Contemporary Study of Religion." Public Lecture at the Vrije Universiteit, Amsterdam.

—— 2010. "Aesthetics of Persuasion: Global Christianity and Pentecostalism's Sensational Forms." *South Atlantic Quarterly* 109/4: 741 – 763.

—— 2011. "Mediation and Immediacy: Sensational Forms, Semiotic Ideologies and the Question of the Medium." *Social Anthropology* 19/1: 23 – 39.

—— 2013. "Material Mediations and Religious Practices of World-Making." In *Religion Across Media: From Early Antiquity to Late Modernity*, edited by Knut Lundby, 1 – 19. New York: Peter Lang.

Orsi, Robert. 1999. "Introduction: Crossing the City Line." In *Gods of the City, edited by Robert Orsi, 1 – 78. Bloomington: Indiana University Press.*

Rial, Carmen. 2013. "The 'Devil's Egg': Football Players as New Missionaries of the Diaspora of Brazilian Religions." In *The Diaspora of Brazilian Religions*, edited by Cristina Rocha and Manuel A. Vásquez, 91 – 116. Leiden: Brill.

Rohter, Larry. 2007. "Brazil's Top TV Preachers Land in Hot Water in Miami." *The New York Times*, March 19. URL: http://www.nytimes.com/2007/03/19/world/americas/19brazil.html?pagewanted=all&_r=0, (last accessed 6 August 2015)

Simmel, Georg. 1950. "The Metropolis and Mental Life." In *The Sociology of Georg Simmel*, by Georg Simmel, 409–424. New York: Free Press.

Taylor, Charles. 2007. *A Secular Age*. Cambridge, MA: The Belknap Press of Harvard University Press.

Varela, Francisco, Evan Thompson, and Eleanor Rosch. 1992. *The Embodied Mind: Cognitive Science and Human Experience*. Cambridge: MIT Press.

Vásquez, Manuel. 2009. "The Global Portability of Pneumatic Christianity: Comparing African and Latin American Pentecostalism." *African Studies* 68/2: 273–286.

—— 2011. *More than Belief: A Materialist Theory of Religion*. Oxford: Oxford University Press.

—— 2014. "From Colonialism to Neo-Liberal Capitalism: Latino/a Immigrants in the U.S. and the New Biopolitics." *Journal for Cultural and Religious Theory* 13/1: 81–100.

Vásquez, Manuel and Cristina Rocha. 2013. "Introduction: Brazil in the New Global Cartography of Religion." In *The Diaspora of Brazilian Religions*, edited by Cristina Rocha and Manuel A. Vásquez, 1–42. Leiden: Brill.

Wacquant, Loic. 2004. *Body & Soul: Notebooks of an Apprentice Boxer*. New York: Oxford University Press.

Weber, Max. 1958. *The Protestant Ethic and the Spirit of Capitalism*. New York: Charles Scribner's Sons.

PART V

**In Conversation: Essays About the
Connectivity of an Aesthetics of Religion**

Fred Cummins
Subjects and Sense-Making

Preamble: the author is at home in the cognitive and language sciences and provides this contribution from some distance.

"We see with our legs", Heinz von Förster quipped (1995). He is trivially
right, of course. As we walk, we reorient ourselves with respect to the surfaces
around us, and with that, the flux on the retina changes. As the flux changes,
so we see, now this, now that. Animals are knitted into their environments
through sensory modalities and their own activity, but how that should be understood and talked about is vexed; vexed now, and vexed these last several
hundred years.

With the advent of Western modernity, the edifice of time and space, made
homogeneous and universal in the Galilean/Cartesian/Newtonian synthesis, had
no place (literally) for the soul. Descartes famously apportioned it to an entirely
distinct sphere of being, *res cogitans*. Kant made things more complex, but he
left us with a transcendental ego that was nowhere to be observed, and he considered a science of psychology to be unattainable. These moves in physics, cosmology, and the philosophy of mind all preceded the development of the modern
sciences of biology and psychology.

As the soul (ca. 1800) morphed into the mind (ca. 1900) and from there into
the cognitive system (ca. 2000), means had to be found to interrogate sensations,
perceptions, ideas, memories, and the like from a scientific standpoint. Many approaches were tried, but scientific psychology, by and large, came to view the
mind as the theatre in which the senses contributed *input* that was consumed
by *internal* processes of cogitation, assumed to be effected in the activity of
the brain. The *output* of this pipeline was the volitional activity of the autonomous individual, which we see as behaviour. The physiological distinction between peripheral and central parts of the nervous system mapped nicely onto
a distinction between input/output conduits (plumbing) and a Cartesian interiority (the mind). (Dewey 1896 provides an influential dissenting argument.)
The privileged location of the brain within the safe enclosure of the skull provided a reassuring separation of subject and the world. Theologically, this gave cre-
dence to the post-Enlightenment individual, largely Protestant in stamp, who
acted with complete autonomy, and who therefore bore full moral responsibility
for all volitional action. Socially, it accorded with the civic notion of the individual citizen, bearer of specific individualised rights and responsibilities. As noted
in the introduction, this individualisation of experience, and its positioning in an
interior realm, did duty both in theories of religious experience (e. g., James

https://doi.org/10.1515/9783110461015-019

1902), and in a secular science of psychology (e.g., Csikszentmihalyi and Larson 2014). It has become the default framing of both the subject and of experience in everyday discourse.

Two consequences of this framing of subjectivity are noteworthy. The first is a veritable hostility to movement when making any empirical observations of the subject, thereby ensuring that the many activities of daily ritualized practice, such as bead twiddling, nodding, pacing, and such are excluded from any substantive account of lived lives. The second is a blindness to the remarkable significance of joint speech (speaking identical words in synchrony), ensuring that unison speaking, which underpins many kinds of rite, ritual and prayer, but also protest and the enactment of identity in secular situations, is omitted from a scientific account of language. Both biases ensure that many of those constitutive features of everyday religious practice and everyday grounding in a familiar and shared world disappear from view, reducing accounts of religion to the enumeration of beliefs, ideologies and doctrines.

1 Hostility to Movement

A great deal of scientific work was done to shore up the view of subjective access to an exterior world through the medium of representations assembled from sensory input. Hubel and Wiesel garnered a Nobel Prize (Hubel and Wiesel 1962) for their work recording from individual neurons in the brains of cats, who, for operational reasons—the obligatory use of fine glass electrodes—had to be anaesthetized and strapped to the lab bench. When specific pattern of light and dark were projected onto the immobile retinas of the cats, intelligible activity of individual neurons was recorded. As neurons that were so monitored were selected further towards the interiority of the brain, so the apparent complexity of the relation between cat and world seemed to increase. This seminal work founded a field of computational image analysis that was construed as a model for the process of seeing (vision). The year of the Nobel Prize award, Hubel and Livingstone published a paper (Livingstone and Hubel 1981) demonstrating that pinching the tail of the cat, and thus restoring some level of conscious activity, radically changed the properties of the nerve cells, so that extrapolation from an inert inactive brain was dangerous, at best. In subsequent work, the more active the animal, the less does the brain activity admit of interpretation in this strongly representational fashion.

In the 1960s another set of experiments on cats showed something else: that self-initiated movement is essential for the development of useful vision (Held and Hein 1963). Held and Hein allowed kittens only very restricted movement opportunities. The kittens were examined in pairs. In each pair, one kitten (A = "active") got to move in a harness tethered to a central pillar (see Figure 1). The other kitten (P = "passive") was passively moved as the first walked. All walking took place inside a cylindrical chamber so that the visual stimulation received by both kittens was as nearly matched as possible. The kittens spent 3 hours a day in this chamber for some weeks. The A kittens developed normally by the measure of the tests employed (paw placement, response to a visual cliff, etc.). The P kittens, on the other hand, did not behave as normally sighted kittens. They had not learned the relation between activity and seeing.

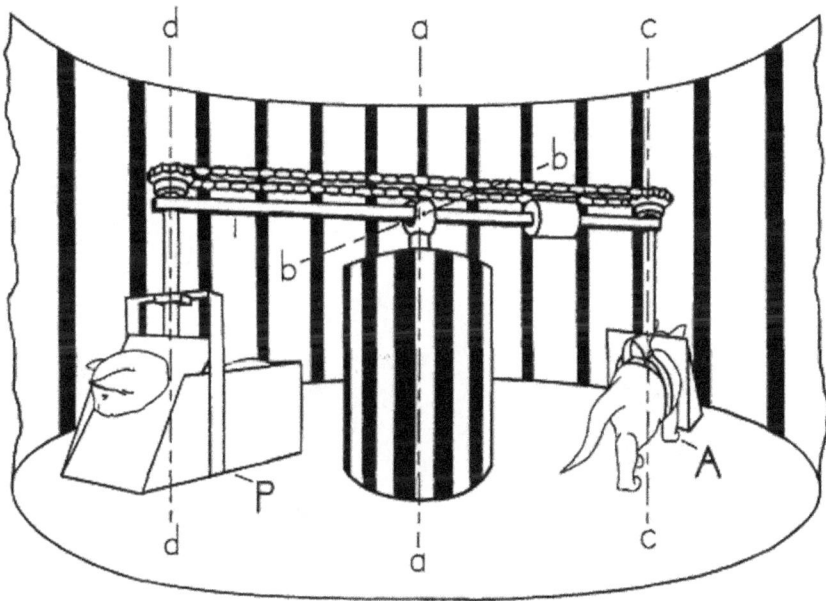

Figure 1: Apparatus for equating motion and consequent visual feedback for an active (A) and a passively moved (P) kitten. Held, Richard, and Alan Hein. 1963. "Movement-produced stimulation in the development of visually guided behavior." *Journal of Comparative and Physiological Psychology* 56/5: 872–876, figure 1. © American Psychological Association. No permission required: http://www.apa.org/about/contact/copyright/seek-permission.aspx

The importance of self-initiated action in grasping the world has likewise become apparent in the development of novel sensory modalities. Figure 2 shows an early sensory substitution device which requires the user to learn the association between user-generated motion and the corresponding pattern of stimulation on the skin (Bach-y-Rita 1972). At first, the user perceives the direct contact with the skin, but with practice, the phenomenology changes and the system becomes a means of acting in the world, locomoting, catching objects etc. In similar vein, inverting goggles that reverse the orientation of the visual field need to be mastered through activity. After about three days of continuous activity under such circumstances, one's mastery of the sensory motor contingency of visually guided action is restored. But the reported phenomenology is one of restored capacity for action, not of the inversion and subsequent righting of an image. The relation between subject and world is now clearly seen to be mediated by activity (including the legs), and the senses can be reinterpreted as a means of uncovering opportunities for goal-directed action in a meaningful world.

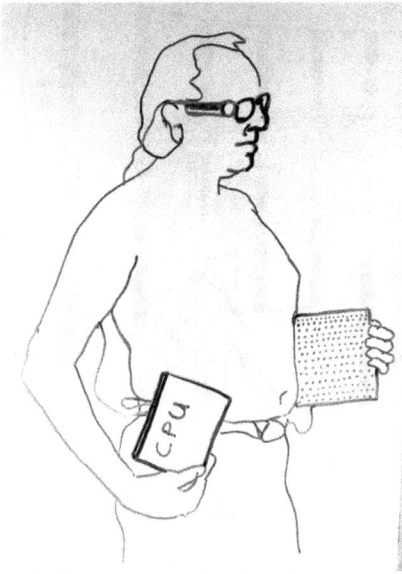

Figure 2: Early sensory substitution device. Camera attached to the eyeglasses transmits to a needle array on the belly. Graphic by the author, after Bach-y-Rita (1972). Reproduced with permission of Elsevier Publisher, UK.

But experimental psychologists still insist that their (experimental) subjects not move. Stimulus presentations are routinely preceded by a "fixation cross", to align the head (Figure 3). Most forms of neuroimaging (EEG, PET, MEG, fMRI) share this feature in common: the (experimental) subject is not allowed to move. Heads are clamped, bodies immobilized. Only under such conditions can the Cartesian subject be delineated in an imaginary interior.

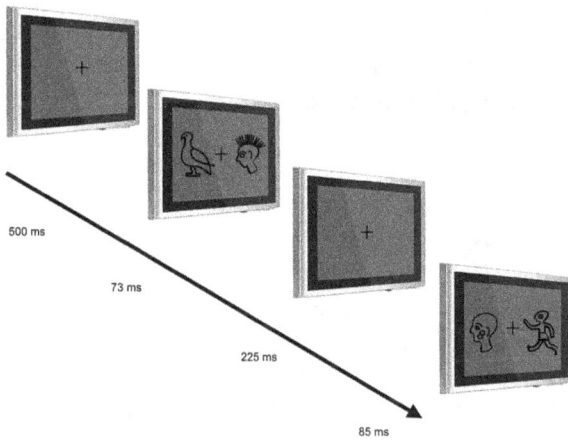

Figure 3: The ubiquitous fixation cross as used in very many cognitive psychology experiments. Graphic by the author.

A survey of standard psychology syllabi reveals that almost no attention is paid to movement as something meriting study, despite the aspirations of the discipline to be relevant to understanding behaviour, which is cast as a distal output. Yet there is a well-developed science of movement, with over a hundred years of converging empirical results that do not contribute to, or support, the interpretation of movement as a controlled output of a central executive (Cummins 2010; Latash 2008). Contemporary cognitive psychology it seems is not merely insensitive to the role of movement in grounding the relation of a person to their world, it is positively hostile to it.

2 Absence of Joint Speech

The second notable absence brought about by persistent reliance on something like the Cartesian *cogito* is evident in the scientific understanding of language. The structuralist and generative schools of linguistics that together constitute the scientific approach to language in the first and second halves of the 20th Century, respectively, both treat of human communication as the passing of encoded messages from one unobservable interiority or mind to another. This immediately serves to make human-to-human communication different in kind from all other forms of animal communication and vocalization. Both approaches rapidly abstract from the messy situated business of live interaction to the abstract systemic perspective that studies *langue* but not *parole*, or *competence* but not *performance*. This leap from the concrete and situated to the abstract and symbolic necessarily leaves much behind, including all consideration of the voice as privileged modality, and the embedding of vocal activity in many practices of daily life, from the mundane to the sacred.

Conspicuously absent from *all* scientific work on language is that form of vocal activity found when multiple people say the same thing at the same time. I have dubbed such speech *joint speech* for no term of art existed that made such speech a theme for empirical inquiry (Cummins 2009, 2013, 2014). This vocal activity necessarily evades the gaze of the Cartesian linguist, for it makes no sense as message passing. There are not necessarily distinct roles for speaker and listener, as everybody is both simultaneously. The speech is frequently characterized by a great deal of repetition, as in practices of prayer (rosary, kirtan) but also in the repeated chants of protesters and sports fans. The texts spoken are authored elsewhere. They are frequently organised as call and response, and this may find formal integration into the structures of the liturgy. Antiphonal structures, that seem to indicate collective responses that betoken generalised assent and collective uttering, are found as far back as written records stretch, to the ancient Israelites and Sumerians, and collective chanting is the manner in which the Vedas were preserved over many centuries. All human societies seem to chant in unison, yet this activity becomes invisible if we characterise language solely as the passing of encoded messages.

Attention to the many forms of joint speech found in daily life, from the solemn recitation of the *credo* to the familiar rite of singing Happy Birthday (for joint speech admits of no separation between speech and music) brings some hitherto neglected themes to the fore. In place of representation and reference, they encourage us to attend to liveness and co-presence. The commerative silence that marks public grief after tragedy may be seen as a limiting case, in which words are reduced to a minimum of zero, but the participatory collective enacts a common purpose. The words spoken are not infrequently in languages other than those used in daily life, and so it becomes important to treat of lexical content rather differently; often there is little point in asking what the words "mean", as this may not even be clear to the speakers. Rather, we learn far more by observing and understanding the *context* in which such behaviour happens. This serves to pick out a group of highly charged acts of social significance, such as the swearing of oaths of allegiance and the demands of an outraged public. It brings to the fore activities that must be participated in, and that cannot be removed to the page or to recordings. Where conversation may be understood as a dialogical negotiation of common ground, the chorusing found in overt synchronised statements of belief represent a collective and shared position with respect to the world. Joint speech, in short, does not fit the Cartesian mould, but reveals very much about the collectives who speak as one.

3 Subjects, Singular and Plural

Scientific psychology, rooted as it is in a strongly Christian world-view where the autonomy of the individual person is paramount, has never been comfortable with anything other than one mind/soul per person, and the mind/soul has been the domain of the subject. But an older, less-restrictive view that can be traced back to Aristotle, sees the subject simply as the bearer of intentional predicates. Subjects in this sense arise when we can point to a distinguishable entity to whom we can attribute beliefs, sentiments, desires, and the like. A subject, on this view, is an active entity whose activity becomes intelligible when it is viewed as teleological, or serving its own self-generated ends, survival being paramount among them. This view of what a subject is extends naturally to collective subjects, and thus to the subjects of joint speech.

The vocabulary of enaction, introduced in the 1991 volume *The Embodied Mind* (Varela at al. 1991) sought to provide a vocabulary that could address many shortcomings of the human sciences that were inherited by the Cartesian/Kantian tradition. The book self-consciously tried to introduce a Buddhist sensibility to cognitive science (though subsequent elaboration of the themes of the book have frequently played down the Buddhist lineage). Importantly, it approached the relation between subject and world not as distinct entities, but as co-defining domains that arise in activity. Space precludes any kind of comprehensive account (see Stewart et al. 2010 for a recent compilation), but two features of an enactive account are here relevant.

First, in an enactive account, the meaningful encounter *by* a subject *of* a world arises *through* activity in a specific environment. This way of treating of subjects does not allow for separation of subject and world; they are co-arising just as the surface of a bowl simultaneously gives rise to an inside and an outside. It is in the activity of the subject that a world of significance is enacted. This broad framing suggests that it might provide a profitable way to approach the (vain) repetitions found in prayer, and the associated gestures and acts that are threaded into the structures of ritual and liturgy (and sports terraces, schoolrooms, courtrooms, and beyond). It suggests that much of the activity we routinely find in the context of religious practice (as well as related contexts) might become intelligible precisely by attending to the small acts that provide a sensorimotor embedding of the individual person within a collective. It is in the aesthetics of rite, ritual, and of the grounding of everyday life that we might discover and make intelligible much of the shared world of the participants.

Secondly, the approach taken aspires to providing a vocabulary that works at many levels, from cell to society (Froese and Di Paulo 2011). Although most work in the field concerns itself with the individual multicellular organism, the basic concepts were developed in consideration of the kind of organization found in single cells, and it extends naturally beyond the individual to collective subjects, exhibiting collective intentionality through their collective practices.

And so it seems that we must appeal to a wide variety of subjects if we are to understand our own sense-making, our diversity, and our concerns. An ontological light touch seems appropriate, even necessary, if we are to avoid a premature commitment to a *subject* rooted in one religious tradition or another. This is contentious ground, for sure, but attention to the role of the senses, the embedding of action, and the manner in which meaning arises for many kinds of subjects, might just help us avoid some of the more obvious pitfalls. The aesthetics of religion then does not appear to me to be a new niche area, but a sorely necessary corrective for the negotiation of stories of our being that might garner consensus.

Bibliography

Bach-y-Rita, P. 1972. *Brain Mechanisms in Sensory Substitution*. New York: Academic Press.

Csikszentmihalyi, Mihaly, and Reed Larson. 2014. "Validity and Reliability of the Experience-Sampling Method." In *Flow and the Foundations of Positive Psychology*, by Mihaly Csikszentmihalyi, 35–54. Heidelberg, Dordrecht, London, and New York: Springer.

Cummins, Fred. 2009. "Rhythm as Entrainment: The Case of Synchronous Speech."*Journal of Phonetics*. 37/1:16–28.

—— 2010. "Coordination, not Control, Is Central to Movement." In *Towards Autonomous, Adaptive, and Context-Aware Multimodal Interfaces: Theoretical and Practical Issues*. Volume 6456, *Lecture Notes in Computer Science (LNCS)*, edited by Anna Esposito, Antonietta M. Esposito, Raffaele Martone, Vincent C. Müller, and Gaetano Scarpetta, 252–264. Heidelberg, Dordrecht, London, and New York: Springer.

—— 2013. "Towards an Enactive Account of Action: Speaking and Joint Speaking as Exemplary Domains." *Adaptive Behavior* 13/3: 178–186.

—— 2014. "The Remarkable Unremarkableness of Joint Speech." In *Proceedings of the 10th International Seminar on Speech Production*, edited by Susanne Fuchs, Martine Grice, Anne Hermes, Leonardo Lancia, and Doris Mücke, 73–77. Cologne: University of Cologne.

Dewey, John. 1896. "The Reflex Arc Concept in Psychology." *Psychological Review* 3/4: 357–370.

Froese, Tom, and Ezequiel A. Di Paolo. 2011. "The Enactive Approach: Theoretical Sketches from Cell to Society." *Pragmatics & Cognition* 19/1: 1–36.

Held, Richard, and Alan Hein. 1963. "Movement-Produced Stimulation in the Development of Visually Guided Behavior." *Journal of Comparative and Physiological Psychology* 56/5: 872–876.

Hubel, D. H., and Wiesel, T. N., 1962. "Receptive Fields, Binocular Interaction and Functional Architecture in the Cat's Visual Cortex." *The Journal of Physiology* 160/1: 106–154.

James, William. 1902. *The Varieties of Religious Experience: A Study in Human Nature.* New York: Longmans, Green & Co.

Latash, Mark L. 2008. *Synergy.* Oxford: Oxford University Press.

Livingstone, Margaret S., and D. H. Hubel. 1981. "Effects of Sleep and Arousal on the Processing of Visual Information in the Cat." *Nature* 291: 554–561.

Stewart, John, Olivier Gapenne, and Ezequiel A. Di Paolo, eds. 2010. *Enaction: Toward a New Paradigm for Cognitive Science.* Cambridge, MA: MIT Press.

Varela, Francisco J., Eleanor *Rosch, and Evan T. Thompson.* 1991. *The Embodied Mind: Cognitive Science and Human Experience.* Cambridge, MA: MIT Press.

Von Förster, Heinz 1995. "Worte." In *Interface 2: Weltbilder, Bilderwelten*, edited by K. P. Kenker and U. Hagel, 235–247. Hamburg: Im Auftrag der Kulturbehörde Hamburg.

François Gauthier
Consumer Culture and the Sensory Remodelling of Religion

How does the sociology of religion intersect with a perspective concerned with aesthetics? In my view, the very emergence of the plight voiced by this volume and its related field of research is corollary to a profound socio-cultural, historical and political shift in our societies. These have evolved towards a consumerist type of religion in which the taking into account of sensory dimensions are no longer negligible in our analyses, as was the prior case in what I call the 'national-statist' era and its corresponding secularisation epistemology. Consumer era religion appears based on the ethics of authenticity as guaranteed by experience, making sensory dimensions a requisite part of research on religion today. The Burning Man festival, held annually in the Nevada desert, as well as the global cultural movement of which it is part, provides an interesting case to observe these trends. Consumer culture is a culture of lifestyles, one in which individual choices, however menial, are ridden with symbolic meanings as they contribute in the projection of one's identity in an arena of mutual exposition so as to be recognized by significant others. Here, the sociology of religion intersects with economics as well as aesthetics, opening onto a refreshed set of questions for research.

1 The Aesthetic Concern and the Transformation of Religion

Understood as the study of the "sensory side of religion", the aesthetics approach intersects with an emergent trend within the sociology of religion. Dissatisfied with the shortcomings of instituted and institutional research methods and problematics, an increasing number of scholars is attempting to seize and understand the fluxing and complex dynamics of what is variously termed 'lived', 'vernacular' or 'everyday' religion; i.e., religion at the subjective, micro level—what I call 'religiosity' (Gauthier 2016). This trend renews with anthropological methods of enquiry and is constitutively more attentive to the sensory aspects that make up religious phenomena than classic sociological approaches. At this level, scholars aiming to distance themselves from former 'belief and belonging' perspectives must develop tools and analytics that fit the contemporary yardstick for authenticity: *lived experience*. Similarly, scholars such as Brigit Meyer have critiqued the Protestant/Christian biases of sociological concepts and methods,

https://doi.org/10.1515/9783110461015-020

showing how neglecting the sensory aspects of highly dynamic religious movements such as Pentecostalism amounted to missing out on some of its most essential aspects.

As Alexandra Grieser (2015) has argued, the neglect of the aesthetic, sensory
side of religion has been a consequence of how the nineteenth century study of
religion followed a comprehension of elite European Christianity and its valuing
of sacred texts, beliefs and pared down liturgy. From the perspective of a history
of religious studies, the interest in an aesthetic approach to religion is a product
of such a critique of the Christian biases that have underscored the discipline
and participates in a turn towards new concepts and outlooks. Yet this evolution,
which brings new legitimacy and pertinence to taking the sensory dimensions
into research accounts and theoretical discussions, is corollary to another muta-
tion—one that is socio-cultural rather than internal to the discipline. I mean by
this that religion 'itself' (i. e., those social facts that can presumably be understood as being explicitly or implicitly religious from our theoretical perspectives)
has changed in tune with wider mutations of the world we live in. Whether we
pledge allegiance to substantive or functional definitions of religion, we should
become aware of how religion is not what it used to be. In my view, religion
changed quite radically as a result of the modernisation processes of the last
couple of centuries, and yet again as a result of the globalizing forces of consumer and financial capitalism in the last three decades. To chart this evolution in a
nutshell, I would say that religion has evolved from 1) varied 'traditional' make-
ups towards 2) forms that obeyed the logics of a politically defined national-statist 'regime', and more recently still towards 3) forms that can best be understood
as being shaped (positively or negatively) by the logics of consumerism and neoliberalism—what I call the 'global-market regime'.[1]

In a nutshell, High Modern Ideals of optimal and autonomous social regulation sustained the establishment of a utopian political regulation with the state
as main actor and the nation as its preferred community of reference. What we
are used to calling 'traditional' religion is in fact not so much traditional (1)
as already modern (2): shaped into the model of the nation-state and its High-
Modern ideals. What is perhaps less acknowledged is that this process of national-statist formatting occurred not only in 'the West', but also, in variegated fashion, across the globe, namely as a result of colonialism and imperialism (cf. van
der Veer 2001). Religion was thus differentiated (in the social fabric as well as in

---

1 By regime, I mean a certain type of institutionalisation of religion, a macro-level order, a set
or array of possibilities, a socio-historically specific grammar, an episteme which shapes the varieties of religious phenomena at a given time into a structured set of manifestations.

time and space), 'freeing' other 'social spheres' (including aesthetics) to develop 'autonomously' (modern forms of art). Religion was institutionalised, bureaucratised, rationalised, scripturalised, deritualised and conscripted into nation building missions. In many cases, the state was active in the formatting of religion into this preferred frame, sometimes coercively (the case of Indonesia is ideal-typical, cf. Howell 2007).

The secularisation *paradigm* arose from this environment as an implicit frame for thinking religion as well as the other differentiated social spheres. The secularisation paradigm runs much deeper than secularisation *theories:* it precedes them both logically and historically. It is composed of a system of inter-related principles that are foundational to social sciences and modern self-comprehension: e. g., the differentiation of social spheres, individualisation, the public/private divide, de-traditionalisation, methodological nationalism, the loss of the social function of religion, the primacy of political and institutional dimensions, the opposition of modernity and religion (religion as the other of Modernity and as a phenomenon restricted to the pre–, anti– or non-modern). As such, secularisation theories appeared when the secularisation paradigm was completely naturalised, when its principles 'went without saying'.

It is not that aesthetic and sensory dimensions did not exist in this period. National-statist aesthetics of religion tended accordingly to be spiritualised, disembodied, intellectualised, against the messiness of popular culture and traditional expressions. Yet aesthetic dimensions appeared analytically negligible since the religion that was the most meaningful to observe was that which most corresponded to the framings of the national-statist regime and its correlated secularisation paradigm, i.e., Modern Christianity in the form of elite-lead, institutionalised, 'belief and belonging' concerned national churches. Such religions valued rationalised forms, while popular, sensory and ritual manifestations were dismissed as superstitious and out-dated. For some time, this type of religion could be satisfyingly enquired upon—at least for a consensual majority of scholars—by using methods that did not pay attention to such things as the body, the sensory and materiality. All of these things did not seem to matter, indeed, as long as religion was essentially a question of belief.

Contemporary sociology of religion and religious studies are still largely enmeshed in this paradigm even as they are trying to transcend it. The ambiguities of this situation are made visible by the recent popularity of the term 'post-secular', which shows an attempt to surpass secularisation and its assumptions while at the same time fatally keeping them as a starting point. It is obvious that the study of religion is undergoing a profound if not always self-conscious and self-reflexive *remise en question.* The present volume voices a novel and long overdue call for the taking into account of the aesthetic, material and sensory aspects of religion that is best understood as partaking in this shift away from the secularisation paradigm which was the 'natural' understanding of religion in the now fading national-statist regime. In other words, aesthetic and sensory concerns have become audible and mobilising *not only* because of the self-reflexive critique of the Christian, Protestant and Enlightenment assumptions in the academic study of religion, *but also* because the types of religion we are increasingly encountering present us with new types of realities in which the sensory and material are foremost as a consequence of the wider social shifts I am hinting at. Thus religion as belief and exclusive belonging is no longer a credible entry into religious phenomena. While the body, the sensory and the material could be ignored in national-statist regime religion, they can no longer as we move into the current global-market regime. These changes bring the formerly dispensable sensory dimensions to the fore. This is why the overture this volume wants to impulse with respect to aesthetics amounts to more in my view than just actualising the study of stained-glass windows in the era of Internet.

2 Religion in the Consumer Era

Many scholars seem to agree that religion today is undergoing a process of transformation whose end result is open-ended. I would argue that the characteristics of religion have been stable long enough that it is possible to define the contours and structure of the 'new' regime of religion. Cast within the political and institutional frameworks of the secularisation paradigm, the sociology of religion has been remarkably unable to seize the importance of the formidable rise of the social importance of economics as a driving force behind today's phase of globalisation (see Martikainen and Gauthier 2013; Gauthier and Martikainen 2013; Gauthier, Martikainen, and Woodhead 2013). In this new regime, the 'market'—its institutional, social and cultural reality as well as its imaginary—has replaced the state as the main actor in the utopian regulation of the social, all of this against a new global backdrop that erodes at the consistency of the nation.

Paramount in this new market regime is the rise to dominance of the consumerist ethos and its conception of the subject and citizen as a consumer. Consumerism is the culture of such a market-oriented society, in the sense that whole areas of social life are increasingly reshaped into market logics and mediated by market relations in the form of the consumption of commodities. It is a culture in which marketization, communication, branding and commoditisation are fundamental processes—all of which have heightened and specific aesthetic dimensions. Hence consumerism has developed into the dominant desirable social ethos of our time, in 'the West' and far beyond. It is "constituted as a culture both *for* consumers and *of* consumers: both a set of commodities for people to consume, and a set of representations of people as consumers" (Sassatelli 2007, 195). Consumer culture is the means of expression and actualisation of the modern project of the individualised self. It is a distinctive manner of being-in-the-world, i.e., a specific type of rapport to the self, the other, to community, to nature and the cosmos, in which symbols, material and non-material, play out an expressive function key to both identity and community construction.

Consumerism became irreversibly massified in the second half of the twentieth century in Western countries (and more recently in urban centres across the globe), accomplishing what Charles Taylor has called the 'cultural revolution of modernity'. According to Taylor, consumerism rose to such socio-cultural prominence because it provided an incredibly vast and ever-expanding array of possibilities for the expression of what he terms the 'ethics of authenticity', i.e., the conception of the self which arose in Western Romanticism according to which each individual "has his or her way of realizing one's own humanity, and that it is important to find and live out one's own" (Taylor 2002, 83) against conforming to external models and authorities, namely political or religious.

The goods and other products—including 'cultural products'—on offer in our global consumer societies provide as many symbols for the exploration and expression of this individuality. Identity becomes life-styled, as goods and products combine in aesthetic ensembles that cater to the paradox of being unique ('be yourself') while belonging to actual and/or virtual local and global 'communities'. These forms of communitization (Max Weber: *Vergemeinschaftungen*) are founded on recognizable aesthetics that include a set of worldviews, values, politics, practices and beliefs—all of which become the expression of individual 'preferences' in the terms of mainstream economics. These dynamics have profoundly changed the landscape of religiosities on the lived, micro level, while 'religion' on the meso, institutional level (see Gauthier 2016) has shifted in accordance. Seen from the perspective of the market regime, it comes as no surprise that the religious forms that are experiencing the highest levels of growth are those which correspond the most to this ethics of authenticity and expressivity: e.g., 'conservative' forms such as Pentecostal and Megachurch born-again/charismatic Christianity, or 'counter-cultural' forms such as the New Age born holistic spirituality movement (which has by now become completely mainstreamed through the personal realisation/development culture all over the world, including in places where one would not expect it). Meanwhile, those forms that most closely correspond to the framework of the former national-statist model are those experiencing the starkest decline and are transforming in tune with the new regime; hence the emergence of what scholars have called 'market Islam' (Haenni 2005; Rudnyckyj 2013) or 'market Catholicism' (Perreault 2008).

This new importance of 'objects', material and immaterial, typical of consumer culture, brings new importance to aesthetic and sensory dimensions. It should come as no surprise, from this angle, that many of the novel religious phenomena are putting emphasis on experience rather than belief and can be understood as expressions of this ethics of authenticity. One may think of the rise in importance, within Islam, of the rise of a new array of practices, from fashion veils to *niqab* fashions and other types of "Sharia-compatible" sportswear (see Gauthier and Guidi 2016). Increasingly, consumption practices (halal, vegan, etc.) and consumer goods are those means through which religion is being reconfigured. What this very brief overview leads me to suggest is that we have recently undergone a change of regime and entered a new social and cultural configuration in which the various dimensions of the social, including religion, are being modelled according to logics and dynamics of consumerism and the market.[2] If this claim is founded, it follows that aesthetics dimensions can no longer be disregarded without missing out on some of the most important dynamics of contemporary religious phenomena. This means that it suffices not that we simply 'add' these aspects to our palette of methods and approaches and continue with our otherwise normal business; rather, the shift towards a culture of authenticity places aesthetics and the sensory at the very core of the present reconfiguration of religion within the market regime. Aesthetic and sensory sensitive socio-anthropological approaches, more than perspectives focused on what I have called here 'belief and belonging', are prone to help seize and comprehend the importance and meaning of religious practices and experiences today. In my view, scholars investing the emergent field of 'aesthetics and religion' would significantly add to the relevance and impact of their contribution to the wider discipline of the study of religion by recognising the specifics of the current socio-historical environment and the heightened importance of its specific aesthetics within todays' processes of personal and community identity construction, expression and recognition.

---

2 By citing consumerism and the logics of 'the market', I am not at all calling for the use of Rational Choice Theory or any other import of neoclassical economics into social sciences ('religious capital' and what not), on the contrary. These have little or nothing to contribute to the present discussion on aesthetics and religion, and only reduce social facts to formal economic theory rather than help understand the effects of consumerism and neoliberalism on contemporary religious forms (for further discussions, see the introductory texts in Martikainen and Gauthier 2013, Gauthier and Martikainen 2013).

3 Beyond Belief: Sensory Overload at Burning Man

How can aesthetics contribute to the debate on the definition of religion? Is it possible to imagine something like an aesthetic theory of religion? How does such a perspective shape issues of method? The study of 'religion and aesthetics' should try not to focus all of its attention on the second of the two terms and take the first for granted. For a truly exciting new perspective to emerge, research crossing religion and aesthetics must avoid limiting themselves to recognised and institutionalised forms of religion, following a purely substantive, Weberian-type appreciation of what constitutes religion (Gauthier 2016). As aesthetic dimensions can be found in a theoretically indefinite array of phenomena, so does religion far exceed its institutionalisation in world religions and explicitly religious phenomena. In my view, the aesthetic focus can be particularly fecund for those phenomena that defy over-determined and conservative, substantive definitions of what is considered 'religious'. This is particularly true in the new market regime, which tends to erode traditional and modern institutions in favour of lightly instituted, networked types of associations and governance. The clear-cut boundaries between social spheres that became institutionalised during the nation-state era are increasingly blurred; this is what gives the impression that modernity has become 'liquid', as Zygmunt Baumann has put it in his many applications of the term. It is in these blurred areas of the social and cultural life that an aesthetic perspective could prove most useful.

An interesting case study and vibrant example of religious innovation outside of the institutionalised framings of the nation-state regime is the Burning Man festival (BM), an annual event that attracts a population of roughly 70,000 in the remoteness of Nevada's Black Rock Desert, in the United States. BM has emerged as one of the most important counter-cultural events of the last two decades and is at the centre of a global cultural movement aimed at disseminating its 'Ten Principles', namely: gifting, non-commodification (money-based exchanges, sponsoring and advertising are banned), community, self-expression, civic and environmental responsibility, autonomy, immediate experience, inclusion and participation. More than a festival, BM claims to be the world's largest ephemeral city, with a corresponding wide array of services catered by the participants rather than by the organisation, in accordance with the logics of gifting. While BM is neither explicitly political nor religious, its politics are rich and complex, and its religious dimensions plentiful and manifold. Rituals, processions, sweat lodges, meditation, marriages, temples, along with a smorgasbord of semi-ironic/semi-serious practices abound in this social and cultural experiment in whose centre stands a giant human figure made of wood and neon and at the edge of which rises a Temple—both of which are ritually burned at the end of the week in a highly emotional atmosphere.

Burners shun definitions of the event and are contemptuous of comparisons (the "new Woodstock", etc.). Interestingly, the only definition that seems to pass is that which coins Burning Man as a laboratory for creative and participatory arts; a self-understanding that emphasizes the importance and positive valuation of its aesthetics dimensions. The organisation does not provide any entertainment or activities and the extravaganza of artworks found on the Playa is the product of Burner initiatives, which rely heavily on collaboration. Yet 'art' here is interactive, monumental, experiential and often pyrotechnic, far from the canons of contemporary art. Playa art includes mutant art cars, monumental constructions, poetic installations, pyrotechnic machines and dragons, technically enhanced metaphysical conundrums, oneiric temples of the absurd and the complete palette of body arts. 'Art' at BM radicalises the modern critique of representation and pushes it a step further, as the works, installations and performances primarily aim to catalyse participation, community and interpersonal exchanges so to create experiences out of the ordinary. 'Art' at BM explodes the meaning of art. In a way, everything at BM is art, and art is everywhere. The boundaries of art are blurred, thrown open, just as those of religion and politics are. As a result, one cannot understand BM without paying attention to aesthetics in general, and its sensory aspects in particular. Certainly, one cannot attend to the religious (or political) dimensions of the event without considering the aesthetic and the sensory.

The fact that many of the artworks are burned at the end only emphasizes its ephemeral aspect and the importance of experience (senses, perceptions, emotions) over objects, ideas, doctrines, beliefs, ideologies and principles. Similarly, religion at BM is entirely practical and experiential, as if participants were charting the possibilities and territories of rituals without belief or dogma. Combining the harshness of the desert environment with the effervescence of the festive, the body is at the very centre of the BM experience, which oscillates between the poles of interiority (contemplation, silence, meditation, reverence) and effervescence (dance, music, sexuality, expression). BM is a sensory overload. This hyper-sensuality/sensoriality is hence intrinsically tied to the religious dimensions of the event: the sensory commands and allows for the religious, and the religious is highly sensory. All senses—touch, smell, taste, sight and audition—are assailed. As such, the body is central to the Burning Man experience, and religiosities here are more practical and experienced than represented and believed. Ritual creativity is foremost, and this creativity, as in many contemporary religiosities, draws from the symbolic potential of the body. The body and its 'parts' act as a reservoir of potential symbolic meanings anchored in shared cultural and personal histories, which rituals abundantly draw upon and mobilise. The aesthetic at BM bring the sensory to the fore. Senses, perceptions and emotions open up possibilities for the exploration of the self in its relations with itself, others, community, the world and nature. BM illustrates how the life-styling of religion and the primacy of practice over belief signifies a heightening of the sensory dimensions.

In the prior, nation-state regime, the aesthetics of a Protestant church for example—the imageless white walls, the simplified liturgy—acted in a way that focused analytical attention *away* from the sensory (or, to be more precise, oriented towards belief and its inner and outwards signs: those of reverence). Hence the study of religion could avoid paying attention to these dimensions. BM illustrates how this is no longer possible in the market regime. At the same time that its gift ethos marks a rupture with consumer society and capitalist exchanges, BM is paradoxically an ideal-typical example of the actualisation of the ethics of authenticity of consumerism understood as the culture of consumer society. This shows how mainstream and counter-culture are intertwined and form a whole that is structured within a consumerism framework.

Bibliography

Gauthier, François. 2016. "A Three-Tier, Three Level Model for the Study of Religion." In *Einheit und Differenz in der Religionswissenschaft: Standortbestimmungen mit Hilfe eines Mehr-Ebenen-Modells von Religion,* edited by Ansgar Jödicke and Karsten Lehmann 157–174. Würzburg: Ergon.

Gauthier, François, and Diletta Guidi. 2016. "Voile, Halal et Burqini. Expliquer les nouvelles formes d'expression religieuse à l'ère du consumérisme." In *Réguler le religieux,* edited by Amélie Barras, François Dermange, and Sarah Nicolet 145–169. Geneva: Labor et Fides.

Gauthier, François, and Tuomas Martikainen, eds. 2013. *Religion in Consumer Society: Brands, Consumers, Markets.* Farnham: Ashgate.

Gauthier, François, Tuomas Martikainen, and Linda Woodhead. 2013. "Acknowledging a Global Shift: A Primer for Thinking about Religion in Consumer Societies." *Implicit Religion* 16/3: 261–276.

Grieser, Alexandra. 2015. "Aesthetics." In *Vocabulary for the Study of Religion.* Vol. 1, edited by Robert A. Segal, and Kocku von Stuckrad, 14–23. Leiden: Brill.

Haenni, Patrick. 2005. *L'islam de marché: L'autre révolution conservatrice.* Paris: Seuil.

Howell, Julia Day. 2007. "Modernity and Islamic Spirituality in Indonesia's New Sufi Network." In *Sufism and the 'Modern' Islam,* edited by Martin Van Bruinessen and Julia Day Howell, 217–241. London: IB Tauris.

Martikainen, Tuomas and François Gauthier, eds. 2013. *Religion in the Neoliberal Age: Political Economy and Modes of Governance.* Farnham: Ashgate.

Perreault, Jean-Philippe. 2008. "Les jeunes et le catholicisme québécois: Dynamiques et 'vitalité paradoxale.'" In *Jeunes et religion au Québec*, edited by François Gauthier and Jean-Philippe Perreault, 123–140. Sainte-Foy: Presses de l'Université Laval.

Rudnyckyj, Daromir. 2013. "Engineering Entrepreneurial Ethics: Islam after Development in Indonesia." *Moussons* 21/1: 37–49.

Sassatelli, Roberta. 2007. *Consumer Culture: History, Theory and Politics*. London: Sage.

Taylor, Charles. 2002. *Varieties of Religion Today: William James Revisited*. London: Harvard University Press.

van der Veer, Peter. 2001. *Imperial Encounters: Religion and Modernity in India and Britain*. Princeton: Princeton University Press.

Frank Heidemann
Social Aesthetics, Atmosphere and Proprioception

Fieldwork in aesthetics of religion is often described as a special experience. The researcher and their contemporaries are in a particular mood and state of mind. They co-produce an intense atmosphere but consider it as an external force or fact. I shall discuss this process with an emphasis on social aesthetics as an implicit theory of everyday perception and on the resulting proprioception as a subjective feeling of belonging. Atmosphere, aesthetics and proprioception constitute a sensuous trinity: the first includes an unaccountable number of factors, the second is perceived as a totality, and the third is an idiosyncratic positioning. The dialectical relationship of god and devotee and of devotee and co-believer is based on aesthetic principles, it appears in emotionally charged contexts, and it accompanies the process of belonging. Whole bodies perform, all senses are addressed.

Most writers on social aesthetics refer to aisthesis as cognition through sensory perception; an approach proposed by Alexander Gottlieb Baumgarten in contradistinction to the concept of aesthetics as beauty or sublime put forward by his contemporary, Immanuel Kant (see Berleant 2005; Grant 2013; Griffero 2015; MacDougall 2006, 95–99; Miyahara 2014. See also the special issue of *Aesthetics* vol. 23 [2013]). There is a long history of related studies in philosophy, art history and comparative religion (Grieser 2015). Social aesthetics involves all senses including proprioception—an awareness of one's own body, motion, and spatial positioning (MacDougall 2015), and concepts of proximity and movement (Heidemann 2013). These studies consider social aesthetics as structured and structuring, constituting powerful affective dimensions in each society. Social aesthetics are, therefore, the principles of everyday perception: they place objects into contexts, connect people to artefacts, and create meaning and totalities. Especially in culturally demarcated spaces, such as in the boarding schools studied by David MacDougall or in temple compounds, the results of these principles can be perceived and may even seem obvious. "By the creation of a social aesthetic", MacDougall explains, "I do not mean a system of signs and meanings [...] but rather a creation of an aesthetic space or sensory structure" (2006, 105).

One way of investigating such complex totalities as schools, ships, or monasteries is to focus on their specific atmospheres, because they—unlike the aesthetic principles—are unstable, fluid and may change within seconds. Further, I would argue that the study of atmospheres reflects on the principles of percep-

https://doi.org/10.1515/9783110461015-021

tion. Gernot Böhme (2013) has pointed out that the person who senses an atmosphere is also its co-creator. Atmosphere emerges, then, in the co-presence, and co-experience, of person and environment. The emotional state of the perceiving actor influences the space they experience. To experience a complex and emotionally loaded space we have to simultaneously encounter the space—bodily, emotionally, spiritually—and know about that space. We have to taste atmosphere like a meal. We experience the whole, but our capacity to disassemble it into its component parts is limited. Like a meal, an atmosphere tangibly and intangibly enters our body: we breathe, feel the temperature, are exposed to sunlight or humidity, and are affected by emotional states. Some of the effects of an atmosphere create lingering bodily-felt experiences that are remembered long afterward. The sound of a dentist's drill triggers fear; the smell of a particular perfume, pleasure. In both cases, sound and smell are part of greater contexts, which are remembered, revived, and relived when we perceive similar sensory sensations.

The Japanese verb *ajiwau* combines better than any English word the components I aim to bring together. It means to taste, to go through or experience, and to appreciate. This verb is not intrinsically value-positive, but can be used in the case of bad food or a negative experience and has the implication "to know". To experience sadness—*ajiwau* sadness—for example, is more than an affective reaction; it also connotes having learned about sadness. The sociologist Kojiro Miyahara adopted the "methodological act of *ajiwau*" from the literary critic Hideo Koabyashi. He then employed the approach in his study of shopping areas near Kobe using interviews and explicitly auto-ethnographic description (Miyahara 2014, 66–67). In this study, what is at stake is the link between multi-sensual experience and knowing through a close investigation of *ajiwau* in his subjects. In our own discipline, extreme examples exist in the corpus of ethnographic classics: Renato Rosaldo (1984) understood the rage of the head hunter after his wife's fatal accident, and Paul Stoller (1989) was overwhelmed when he—an apprentice—realised that his magic worked. In both cases, the researcher's experience in an ethnographic context helped them to reflect on the experience of others. Though not conceptualised as such, Rosaldo and Stoller's self-reflective practice approximated the methodological act and approach of *ajiwau*. I propose that *ajiwau* offers a privileged point of departure from which to investigate in the sensuous trinity described above.

Proprioception is one of the neglected senses, but the feeling of having a body and being within a space is nonetheless powerful and ingrained (MacDougall 2015). We perceive a room in a building as a complex embodied multisensory experience: light, shadow, colour, silence, noise, echo, odours, temperature, humidity, air movement, the texture of the floor, the feel of the seats, and the ex-

perience of our body in the space. All these sensations are linked to and modified by our connection of them to a broader contextualisation of the room as part
of the building, the building as part of our personal geographies, and by the social and religious factors we carry with us or encounter there. If a person is in a
prison cell it makes a difference whether they are an inmate or a visitor to a jail-
turned-museum, like the Cellular Jail in Port Blair. But in both cases the sensory,
situational, and sapient totality—the particular proprioception—is stored in our
mind, and, experience becomes knowledge.

Beyond the feeling and sensory encounter of being in a manageable space
such as a room, there is also a similar experience of greater entities, like
ships, campuses, villages or towns or even larger geo-political assemblages
like nation states. I contend that this socio-political proprioception is present
and distinct in religious processions and, specifically, in pilgrimages in India.
To move to a distinct destination involves a statement about a spatial order.
To join a procession results in comprehensive and enduring experience, and
modifies the feeling for space, boundaries, and belonging. To see a place from
a great distance and to be in that place makes a difference as perception is transformed from a long-range vision to "tactile space" (MacDougall 2015, 5). Experiences oscillate in scale and in time-frame.

A major methodological problem is how to translate sensual perception and
experience into words, texts, and ethnographic description. There is no ready-
made answer to the question: how can we know about the feelings of others?
The understanding that we never reach certainty should not prevent asking
this question. What we know is what we see (beyond our bodies) and what we
feel (in our bodies). The ethnographer can observe, participate and include his
and her introspection in their account. To illustrate this process I shall recall
my participation in an annual event in South India, when people move from
their villages in the Nilgiri Hills to the northern foothills.

Thousands of people walk from the plateau, located about 1,800–2,200 m
above sea level to temples devoted to the "Seven Sisters" or "Seven Mariamman"
in the Moyar Ditch. In the 1990s and again in first decade of the twentieth century I had the chance to follow the steps of these pilgrims, most belonging to the
Badaga farming community. I walked from Ebbanadu to Anekatti with men re-
nowned and revered for fire-walking, and joined families from Kookal to Siriyur.
We travelled by Jeep to other festivals in Bokkapuram and Sokkanalli. Later, we
remembered our shared journey and spoke of the nights around the camp fire,
sleeping in the open air, fresh morning baths in the river, chanting devotional
songs, the sound of the birds, spotting fresh elephant dung on our path, heat,
thirst, cold water from a spring, muscle pain and sore feet, minor wounds, reaching the jungle temple, collecting firewood, the sleepless night before the fire-

walking, the sacrifice and cooking of chicken and goats after the main ritual, the release of tension and fresh energy in exhausted bodies, a feeling that the Goddess was there and in each of the pilgrim's bodies. In the experiences and the telling, we shared similar moments of the richness of *ajiwau*.

Before I joined my Badaga friends on their pilgrimages to the temples of Seven Mariamman I had the plan fixed in my mind: we would leave Badaga territory, descend to the plains and enter a national park where Jenu-Kurumbas, Kasuvas, and Sholegas live. The territory once belonged to these ethnic groups exclusively but it was included in a national wildlife sanctuary, giving rise to conflicts between the original inhabitants and the state with which Badagas are not involved. When we left, I felt that we were going to "visit" temples; the priests were Sholegas and Jenu-Kurumbas, the temples on their lands, therefore we would be guests. But on the way, my friends told me repeatedly that Badaga literally means "Northerner" because they came from the region north of the Nilgiri. Their forefathers used to graze their cattle there and they have inalienable rights on this land. As such, the Badagas pay Jenu-Kurumbas and Sholegas for acting as priests in Badaga temples. Now they go to visit their land. The dispute about the wildlife sanctuary is a recent, modern, topic. The Badagas are not worried about it. For one week I enjoyed the company of my friends and experienced their peaceful and god-fearing mood. They did not express any claim to the territory, but they had no doubt that it was theirs.

We reached a temple far from any settlement. It was covered by young vegetation, and we cleared the ground and spent the nights chanting devotional songs and dancing. We experienced the presence of the God when elderly persons fell into trance. I had the feeling that the place welcomed us. We collected firewood, cooked next to the temple, worked for three days to prepare for the festival, and slept soundly each night. On the last day thousands of people came and Mariamman was worshipped. On our return journey, we stopped at the same rest places as we did a week before. I remember vividly one vista at the rim of the plateau. I stopped and looked down toward the temple and I saw a familiar place. Mentally I included this region, the Moyar Ditch, as a part of my research on Badagas. I cannot tell how, but somehow it *was* Badaga land. Perhaps the palpability of the land reorganised the ownership. Not Jenu-Kurumba, Kasuva, or Sholega, not a national park, ... it was *Badaga land*. For me, the Badaga spatial order was—in that moment—an undisputed fact.

Michael Jackson discusses the emotional and affective involvement of the ethnographer in their field and advocates a "radical empirical method", the inclusion of the researcher's lived experience as part of ethnographic praxis. In Jackson's words: "we make ourselves experimental subjects and treat our experiences as primary data. Experience, in this sense, becomes a mode of experimentation, of testing and exploring the ways in which our experiences conjoin or connect us with others, rather than the ways the set us apart" (Jackson 1989, 4). A short answer to the question of how I was convinced about the inclusion of the Moyar Ditch in Badaga territory despite my pre-existing knowledge to the contrary, would be: a certain homology of positive and affirmative experiences included the spatial order within a greater worldview, which became "true" in the process of the pilgrimage. I stayed with dedicated believers and enjoyed their hospitality and friendship. I lived, "felt", and experienced being *in*, if not *of*, their world. In that experience, the realities of their lives became "true" for me.

According to Birgit Meyer, who studies Pentecostalism in Ghana, an "aesthetic of persuasion is intrinsic to sensational form [... and] responsible for the 'truth effect' of religion" (2010, 756). She was "struck by the specific way in which the spiritual and the physical are related" and developed her concept of sensational forms as "part of a specific religious aesthetics, which governs a sensory engagement of humans with the divine and each other and generates particular sensibilities" (Meyer 2010, 751). The study of symbols and ritual (Kertzer 1988, 11) shows how the coexistence of sensual moments and ample, condensed evidence in ambiguous form contribute to a process of persuasion. Multiple sensations and plural meanings do not just add to, but stabilize each other. Badagas feel a totality that is more than the sum of—and also precedes—its "elements". Walking barefoot, listening to devotional songs, dancing and sleeping outside constitute a total social fact, a performed constitution with a half-life of one year (Heidemann 1997, 68). The entire experience is a structured totality, but the multiple sensations are not organized like other known systems of order.

If anarchy is understood as a structured condition absent in the exercise of power by a central institution, without the imposition of physical force, but still regulating on-going affairs by convincing participants to act in a coordinated and organised way, then anarchy has something in common with atmosphere. The felt qualities of the surrounding space have an impact on those who are present; the atmosphere affects their emotions and structures performances (see Böhme 2013; Griffero 2015; and Stewart 2011). As in an anarchic situation, all participants contribute to the atmosphere around them. An atmosphere "is not an effect of other forces but a lived affect—a capacity to affect and to be affected" (Stewart 2011, 452). Perception itself has no fixed hierarchy of the senses but vision, sound, smell and texture become objects of synesthetic totality. To study atmosphere aesthetically seems appropriate, since "aesthetic phenomena are neither incidental nor epiphenomenal to social structure" (de la Fuenete 2007, 93). But the object of its investigation appears to be vague, elusive, or even chaotic. Therefore, I was not surprised to read, that "probably the first book ever published with a title including social aesthetic" was authored by Sanshiro Ishikawa, "a social thinker and anarchist activist in Japan in the first half of the 20th century" (Miyahara 2014, 76). Ishikawa's *Anarchism as Social Aesthetics* centred on the proposal to study society aesthetically (Miyahara 2014).[1] This is a radical and captivating proposition, not the least because it harnesses anarchism and aesthetics to the otherwise elusive study of the organising and experience of work and life.

It would be wrong to describe the worship of the Seven Mariamman as anarchic. Badaga headman call for meetings, mediate decisions and organise the pilgrimage. There is an underlying and functioning order for the temporal and spatial arrangements of the festival, separating and unifying tribes from the plains and peasants from the hills. On the festival day the police and personnel from the Forest Department are present, oversee the rituals, and keep the crowd at some distance from the firewalkers. While structures and institutions of law and order play an important role other forces impact on the situation as well. It was not a decision of the Badaga council, the rhetoric of Badaga headman, or a state institution that made me believe for a while that the Moyar Ditch is Badaga land. I am still puzzled at what caused my change of mind. The impressive fire-walk did not convert me into a believer of Mariamma, and I did not share the hierarchical values assigned to the different ethnic groups involved in the pilgrimage and celebration. My religious orientation and belief in ethnic equality were not destabilised. But I modified my perception of the spatial order toward the Badaga view. The connectivity of the spiritual and the physical ("truth effect"; Meyer 2010) and of experience and knowing (*ajiwau*; Miyahara 2014), and the principles of atmosphere (you participate in what you perceive; Böhme 2013) support the radical empiricism (Jackson 1989), which connects the ethnographer with their host community.

The process, which I described autobiographically, does not differ much from what Badagas told me about their pilgrimages to other locations. They experienced new places and new forms of worship and modified their religious orientation: their narrative and interpretation approach; what can be called atmosphere. At various temples they visited in Southern India they encountered an atmosphere. But in Moyar the pilgrims created the atmosphere around them. There is an anarchic element involved, because atmosphere does not follow strict rules, and has no central authority. Each pilgrim had the power to modify the atmosphere within the group. From this point of view a doubtless democratic

---

1 Ishikawa's focus was on the social beauty that is distinct from natural beauty and artistic beauty. In 1896, Georg Simmel published the essay "Sociological Aesthetics" (see de la Fuente 2007, 96), but he wanted to study aesthetics sociologically, while Ishikara "proposed an aesthetics of the social" (Miyahara 2014, 76).

quality governs the process. But atmosphere in a small place, at gathering of vol-
unteers, pilgrims or peers, is different from atmospheres in coercive contexts. In
hierarchical spaces authorities monitor much of the available sensual perception. In prisons, guards control lines of sight, light, smell, sound, texture,
daily rhythms, food quality and supply, and the presence and timing of darkness. They police mobility, interaction with others, and limit the flow of air.
The systematic and coercive control of sensual perception is a means of power
in totalitarian settings. However, this did not apply to the pilgrimages I had
the chance to witness in South India. Here, atmospheres are structured not by
a central institution, but by an anarchic force.

Still, there is a political dimension to sensational forms. As products of history with a remarkable stability, they "are authorized modes for invoking and organizing access to the transcendental that shape both religious content [...] and
norms" (Meyer 2010, 751). The cult of Seven Mariamman produces pleasant atmospheres with anarchic strategies among the pilgrims, but they constitute a
spatial regime that favours the dominant group. The need for a positive atmosphere offers agency to all participants, including those at the lowest end of
the status hierarchy. Humphrey and Laidlaw (1994, 88) are right when they
point out that the ritual commitment is a precondition for the working of ritual
itself. Passive resistance of subaltern groups may alter the auspicious atmosphere that is needed to welcome the Goddess. The weeks before interethnic festivals offer better bargaining positions for tribal groups, because Badagas know
about the anarchic character of atmosphere.

Reviewing my own experience in Moyar, I consider my commitment as part
of the effects of experience and atmosphere, which changed my felt geography.
Years later I stayed in a Jenu-Kurumba homestead at the Nilgiri foothills near the
Mariamman temples and wondered why I had felt that the Moyar region belonged to the Badagas. Any answer must remain partial, in both senses of the
word, but part of the aesthetics of persuasion was my firm conviction that ritual
processions connect places belonging to each other, and that—at least in local
understanding—a metaphysical force confirmed the Badaga view. My hosts,
the Jenu-Kurumbas, consider Badagas as visitors who paid for permission to
camp at the temple. Suddenly, Moyar became into tribal land, a national park
inhabited by Kurumbas, Sholegas and Kasuvas. The persuasive force of rituals
has a half-life and the agency of atmospheres is like atmosphere itself: vague,
unbound, and temporal. The social aesthetics of religious acts proves to be a
structured and structuring actant that suggests a comprehensive societal order.
It is expressed and experienced in social and religious contexts as a multi-sensual totality.

Bibliography

Berleant, Arnold. 2005. "Ideas for a Social Aesthetic." In *The Aesthetics of Everyday Life*, edited by Andrew Light and Jonathan M. Smith, 23–38. New York: Columbia University Press.

Böhme, Gernot. 2013. *Atmosphäre: Essays zur Neuen Ästhetik.* Frankfurt a.M.: Suhrkamp.

de la Fuente, Eduardo. 2007. "On the Promise of a Sociological Aesthetics: From Georg Simmel to Michel Maffesoli." *Distinktion* 15: 93–112.

Grant, Stuart. 2013. "Performing an Aesthetics of Atmosphere." *Journal of Literature and Aesthetics* 23/1: 12–32.

Grieser, Alexandra. 2015. "Aesthetics." In *Vocabulary for the Study of Religion*. Vol. 1, edited by Robert A. Segal and Kocku von Stuckrad, 14–23. Leiden: Brill.

Griffero, Tonino. 2015. *Atmospheres: Aesthetics of Emotional Spaces.* Farnham: Ashgate.

Heidemann, Frank. 2014. "Objectification and Social Aesthetics: Memoranda and the Celebration of 'Badaga Day.'" *Asian Ethnology* 3/1–2: 91–109.

—— 2013. "Social Aesthetics of Proximity: The Cultural Dimension of Movement and Space in South India." *Literature and Aesthetics* 23/1: 49–67.

—— 1997. "Der Kult der Sieben Mariamman am Nordrand der Nilgiri Südindiens: Ritual als Konstitution von Gesellschaft." *Mitteilungen der Berliner Gesellschaft für Anthropologie, Ethnologie und Urgeschichte* 18: 57–68.

Humphrey, Caroline, and James Laidlaw. 1994. *The Archetypical Actions of Ritual: A Theory of Ritual Illustrated by the Jain Rite of Worship.* Oxford: Clarendon.

Jackson, Michael. 1989. *Paths Towards a Clearing: Radical Empiricism and Ethnographic Inquiry.* Bloomington: Indiana University Press.

Kertzer, David I. 1988. *Ritual, Politics, and Power.* New Haven and London: Yale University Press.

Larsen, L.B. 1999. "Social Aesthetics." In *Participation: Documents of Contemporary Art*, edited by Claire Bishop, 172–173. London: Whitechapel Art Gallery.

MacDougall, David. 2015. "Social Aesthetics and Embodied Cinema." *Working Papers in Social and Cultural Anthropology* 18. Ludwig Maximilian University of Munich. URL: http://www.ethnologie.uni-muenchen.de/aktuelles/news/macdougall_band_18/index.html (last accessed 2 December 2015)

MacDougall, David. 2006. *The Corporeal Image: Film, Ethnography, and the Senses.* Princeton: Princeton University Press.

Meyer, Birgit. 2010. "Aesthetics of Persuasion: Global Christianity and Pentecostalism's Sensational Forms." *South Atlantic Quarterly* 109/4: 741–763.

Miyahara, Kojiro. 2014. "Exploring Social Aesthetics: Aesthetic Appreciation as a Method for Qualitative Sociology and Social Research." *International Journal of Japanese Sociology* 23/1: 63–79.

Rosaldo, Renato. 1984. "Grief and a Headhunter's Rage." In *Text, Play, and Story: The Construction and Reconstruction of Self and Society*, edited by Edward M. Bruner, 178–195. Prospect Hights, IL: Waveland Press.

Stewart, Kathleen. 2011. "Atmospheric Attunements." *Environment and Planning D: Society and Space* 29/3: 445–453.

Stoller, Paul. 1989. *The Taste of Ethnographic Things.* Philadelphia: University of Pennsylvania Press.

Robert Yelle

Semiotics and Aesthetics: Historical and Structural Connections

Aesthetics of religion is a relatively new approach, especially outside of the German-speaking academy. Nevertheless, it bears some striking affinities with older movements. The word "Ästhetik" itself resonates with German Enlightenment, Classicism, and Romanticism: with Alexander Baumgarten's definition of the term in his *Aesthetica* (1750); with Gotthold Ephraim Lessing's *Laokoon* (1766), which compared literary and pictorial modes of expression; and with Immanuel Kant's *Kritik der Urteilskraft* (1790), including its discussion of the "sublime".[1] The focus on perception and sensation recalls idealism; the practice of lingering on the meaning of particular symbols or images, perhaps some of the later Romantic mythologists, such as Friedrich Creuzer (1771–1858) or Johann Jakob Bachofen (1815–1887).

While much of this background appears specifically Germanic, there are resonances also with other movements that do not share this background. While preparing recently to lecture to my students in religious studies on the topic of aesthetics, I turned first to the classic programmatic statement by Hubert Cancik and Hubert Mohr, the article on "Religionsästhetik" in the *Handbuch für Grundbegriffe der Religionswissenschaft* (Cancik and Mohr 1988), and was a bit surprised to see that much of what is referred to there as falling within the domain of the aesthetics of religion was immediately recognizable to me from my background as a semiotician. First and most obviously is the concern with signs (*Zeichen*), as well as with particular types of signs, such as divination, miracles (*Wundertaten:* in the Greek New Testament, *semeion*, or signs), and gestures, all of which have been addressed also under the rubric of semiotics. Cancik and Mohr present a typology of signs, albeit one that deviates from the now-standard Peircean triad of icon, index, and symbol (Cancik and Mohr 1988, 142–147). Structuralist and symbolic anthropology, or leading figures of these movements, are also cited as precedents, as is Charles Sanders Peirce.[2]

What, then, is different about an aesthetics—as opposed to a semiotics—of religion? Cancik and Mohr answer this question thusly: "Eine Ästhetik der Religion, wie sie im ersten Teil umschrieben wurde, beginnt nicht – wie eine Semi-

---

1 For Baumgarten as a precedent, see Jens Kugele and Katharina Wilkens (2011, 7–8).
2 These symbolic and structuralist anthropologists include, e.g., Clifford Geertz, Victor Turner, and Mary Douglas.

https://doi.org/10.1515/9783110461015-022

otik – mit dem (religiösen) Zeichen, dessen Arten und Kombinationen, sondern mit dem ‚Sinnenbewußtsein' des wahrnehmenden Menschen, dessen Körper Zeichen aufnimmt und produziert" (Cancik and Mohr 1988, 132). An aesthetics of religion is focused, not (or not only) on the formal system of signs, but rather (or in addition) on the sensory perception or consciousness of the embodied human being who is the receiver and producer of signs. Aesthetics thus places emphasis on how signs are perceived, and on the *Sitz im Leben* of semiosis, which is always a corporeal but also potentially a subjective experience.

In addition, as made quite clear already in the same, seminal essay, the aesthetics of religion is by no means limited in its focus to language and texts, but aims to cover the entirety of corporeal experience, through all of the senses. As Alexandra Grieser puts it in her introduction to this volume, "the aesthetic approach... striv[es] to overcome biased categories that confined religion... to texts and abstract beliefs". While this does not mean that aesthetics excludes texts, it does suggest that the special contribution of aesthetics, even when considering texts as objects, will be to take into consideration, not only what they mean, but also how they are perceived and used, in a way that exceeds the strictly semantic function of the language that they contain. Thus, a book can be an object of reverence or visual pleasure, also to the illiterate, in addition to something to be read aloud or silently. Sacred texts can be buried behind walls or incorporated into other physical objects, such as statues, in a way that destroys their functionality as objects for reading. Prayer wheels may include tiny texts of prayers that are automatically "recited" as the wheels turn mechanically. In none of these cases is any actual reading going on, but they remain interesting in terms of ritual practice and material religion.

The focus in aesthetics on modes of semiosis other than the linguistic represents a significant step forward from traditional, text- and language-centred semiotic approaches. Semiotics has endeavoured on occasion to extend its domain beyond language. There do exist subfields such as visual semiotics, the semiotics of music, of gesture (the latter sometimes called kinesics), of practically anything you can imagine. Yet the core of semiotics has been and arguably remains language. One of the two major founding schools of semiotics originated in the structural linguistics and semiology of Ferdinand de Saussure—the semiotic of Peirce was never so tightly bound to language—and the most successful applications of semiotics to date have all been to linguistic phenomena, from Russian formalism, Roman Jakobson's poetics, and Claude Lévi-Strauss's structuralist mythology to the broader fields of literary criticism and linguistic anthropology. So we should welcome this effort by aesthetics to move beyond language

—an effort that is not without precedent[3]—as a necessary complement to a language-centred semiotics.

At the same time, we should recognise that this effort involves significant challenges. There are reasons why semiotics has remained bound to language: why it has continued to focus on texts and discourse; why its theories, even when applied beyond language, have been derived from linguistics; why other modes of semiosis, such as gesture, have often been interpreted as languages. Linguistics has developed into a refined science, capable of minutely parsing language, its phonological, morphological, syntactic, and semantic structure. Once we move beyond language, there is scarcely any mode of expression that is susceptible of such refined description, at least given the limitations of our current scholarly practice. Two partial exceptions are music, for which European culture has long possessed an accurate system of notation; and dance, for which Labanotation has been invented more recently. Moving beyond simple descriptive notation, our language dependence intrudes into the understanding of extra-linguistic phenomena in a different way. The end product of scholarship, in the aesthetics of religion as in ethnography and other related disciplines, is a writing that translates aesthetic or other observed phenomena into words. That often requires providing not only an accurate description, but also the "sense" or "meaning" of a phenomenon, despite the fact that, arguably, non-linguistic phenomena do not and cannot "mean" in the same way that language does.[4] In this case, the old saying, "*Traduttore, traditore*" applies: the translator betrays her subject in the very act of translation, in this case by converting non-speech into speech, thus giving it a meaning that it may not otherwise have. Putting things in a more positive light, I would argue that, even if the ambition of the aesthetics of religion is to go beyond language to focus on non-linguistic phenomena, it still is necessary to grapple with the problems of analysis that are entailed in this move, problems that are signalled by the limits of semiotic approaches. Moreover, as semiotics has made its greatest progress in the understanding of language, why not begin by reviewing what has already been achieved in that field? Some of that work might also turn out to be relevant for those who are interested in the sensory, material, and embodied dimensions of religion.

---

3 Cancik and Mohr (1988), as noted above, acknowledge symbolic anthropology as a precedent. Contemporary with Cancik's and Mohr's essay are two essays by Lawrence E. Sullivan that seek to go beyond the text to address other senses (Sullivan 1986, 1990).

4 For an extended argument on this point concerning the semiotics of gesture, see Robert Yelle (2006).

Given the affinities between semiotics and aesthetics, it may be relevant also for the latter field to note developments in the former. The semiotics of religion appears to be experiencing something of a revival, after a relative quiescence of a few decades. This revival has not taken the form of a simple rebirth of classical structuralism, however. The aspirations of structuralism to a universal set of explanatory principles grounded in the nature of language or the human mind, while partly realized, are now widely acknowledged, except by the most doctrinaire practitioners perhaps, as having limits. In particular, recent work on semiotics has focused on detailing the cultural and historical differences among different traditions with respect to the "semiotic (or linguistic) ideologies" that they endorse. Apart from whatever universal features they might share, different traditions vary in their manner of signifying; and such variations also reflect, to some extent, normative regimes that govern, not only what is expressed, but how it gets expressed, or indeed whether it can be expressed at all. Thus, to take a well-known example from the history of religions, certain traditions, especially the "Abrahamic" religions that stem historically from ancient Israelite monotheism, share the prohibition against representing the Godhead (or indeed any of its creations) in pictorial or plastic images. Despite the differences, not only among Judaism, Christianity, and Islam, but also internal to each of these traditions,[5] with respect to the interpretation and enforcement of this prohibition, the ban on idolatry and accompanying drive to iconoclasm has played an important cultural role in each tradition, one that also relates, in complex ways, to the role of sacred texts in each. Such differences in semiotic ideology reflect and articulate with, e.g., differences in conceptions of human and divine agency, and their interaction.[6]

By shifting to focus on such ideological differences, semiotics has lost some of its pretensions to elaborate a universal science of communication, while gaining in relevance for the historical sciences. I would argue that a parallel move should be made by aesthetics: rather than only seeking the cross-culturally

---

5 E.g., the differences between the biblical ideal of non-representation of creatures and the actual images at Dura Europus analysed by Erwin Goodenough; the 8th-century controversy among Orthodox Christians over the use of icons; the Protestant Reformation's attack on Roman Catholic imagery; the greater freedom of imagery in earlier Persianate Islam; etc.
6 I have in mind here Webb Keane's important emphasis on the manner in which Protestant affirmations of the need for sincerity in speaking, at the expense of formalism and ritualism, coordinated with a new idea of subjectivity, one that emphasized the independence of the human subject with respect to his or her own speech, which merely conveyed, as a transparent medium, the authentic sentiments of the speaker. As Keane has persuasively argued, such ideas, which may have originated in the domain of liturgy, nevertheless have been more broadly influential in shaping the contours of the modern, Western subject. See Webb Keane (2002).

valid principles of aesthetics, conceived as a science, we should recognise also the role played by different "aesthetic ideologies", governing regimes that structure sensation, perception, and expression. This obviously requires accepting the same principle that, at the birth of structuralism, Saussure recognised as essential to the understanding of the functioning of signs: signs are arbitrary. They have no value in themselves, but only in relation to the system of which they constitute a part. There can be no way back to the belief that particular signs "naturally" (or iconically) express particular meanings. Aesthetics must also embrace this limiting principle, in order to advance. Thus, there is no way to know the "meaning" or "correct interpretation" of a particular sensory phenomenon, just from observing it. Aesthetic phenomena are always ipso facto cultural phenomena. While it may be possible to apply mass spectrometry to the smells of incense, or to precisely measure the wavelength of the colours of a painting, none of this matters to the cultural study of aesthetic phenomena, any more than the recording of the wavelengths of sound matters to the interpretation of the spoken word.

It may appear to some that this proposed shift of focus would unduly limit the prospects for an aesthetics of religion, understood as a scientific endeavour. While that may be true, in a certain sense, the focus on aesthetic ideologies also, I believe, represents a powerful argument in favour of the need for such a discipline. For it is arguably precisely a shift in aesthetic ideology that, by repressing the sensory, material, and embodied dimensions of religious experience and expression, has necessitated the work of the present discipline of the aesthetics of religion, as an act of recuperation of those aspects of human experience that have been, as it were, sanitised or whitewashed, and so made to appear invisible. Cancik and Mohr allude to this on more than one occasion in their seminal article. What they refer to as the "deodorisation" (*Desodorierung*) of religion— what Hubert Mohr referred to elsewhere as the "exclusion of sensory stimuli" in ritual[7]—is this process of repressing the sensory dimensions of religion (Cancik and Mohr 1988, 136). They also note as precedent for the aesthetics of religion the liturgical movement, the reaction within Roman Catholicism against some of the modernizing reforms in the liturgy made pursuant to Vatican II that had resulted in a more austere, less engaging experience of worship for some (Cancik and Mohr 1988, 125). A number of these reforms resemble changes in liturgy made earlier by Protestants during and after the Reformation.[8]

---

7 See Christoph Auffarth's essay in this volume.

8 See Robert Yelle (forthcoming) for an account of the semiotic ideology of the major document concerning the reform of the liturgy produced by Vatican II, and how it encodes certain theological positions, the history of which relates to older post-Reformation debates.

An extreme example of "deodorisation" is the Puritan Richard Baxter's (1615–1691) diatribe against Catholic practices and their perpetuation in the insufficiently reformed Church of England:

> To worship as the Papists do, with Images, *Agnus Dei*'s, Crucifixes, Crossings, Spittle, Oyl, Candles, Holy Water, kissing the Pax, dropping Beads, praying to the Virgin *Mary*, and to other Saints, repeating over the Name of *Jesus* nine times in a breath, and saying such and such sentences so oft, praying to God in an unknown Tongue, and saying to him they know not what, adoring the consecrated Bread as no Bread, but the very flesh of Christ himself, choosing the tutelar Saint whose name they will invocate, fasting by feasting upon Fish instead of Flesh, saying so many Masses a day, and offering Sacrifice for the quick and the dead, praying for souls in Purgatory, purchasing Indulgences for their deliverance out of Purgatory from the Pope, carrying the pretended bones or other Relicts of their Saints, the Popes canonizing now and then one for a Saint, pretending miracles to delude the people, going on Pilgrimages to Images, Shrines or Relicks, offering before the Images, with a multitude more of such parcells of Devotion do most heinously dishonour God, and as the Apostle truly saith do make *unbelievers* say, *They are mad*, 1 Cor. 14.23. and that they are *children in understanding*, and not *men: v.* 20. (Baxter 1673, 179)

Baxter excludes, one by one, every form of ritual mediation used to intercede or communicate with the deity: not only images, but also repeated prayers, pilgrimage, relics, shrines, fasting and feasting. Speech or prayer is left, but must be strictly regulated: one of Baxter's points is to condemn the "vain repetitions" used by Catholics in their accustomed forms of prayer, such as the Rosary (see Yelle 2013, 103–135). It so happens that, by removing (almost) all of the sensory, embodied, and material dimensions of religion, Baxter is helping to reinforce the stereotypically Puritan idea that God is distant, cannot be influenced by ritual means, and must be addressed by an individual worshiper with correct intent, without hope of such influence: as Keane says, "sincerely". One monad addresses another. Religion is about belief, or doctrine, and is in any case mainly interior.[9] Paring down the ornament, the formalities, the externalities of ritual is key to enforcing this view. Incidentally, Baxter was one of the theological authorities cited by Max Weber in his famous account of the Protestant ethic (Weber 2009, 141–146). Now we should perhaps speak of a "Protestant aesthetic": while recognizing the great diversity among different reformed groups, Baxter's form of Puritanism represents an "ideal type" expressed also in the austerity of early Presbyterian churches, with due allowance for Christoph Auffarth's reserva-

---

9 See Alexandra Grieser's comment about "confin[ing] religion… to texts or abstract beliefs, or to an indisputable *sui generis* mode of experience" (Grieser 2015, 14).

tions regarding the homogeneity of the Protestant position, as conveyed in his essay in the present volume.

Such an aesthetic ideology does not only attempt to eliminate, as far as possible, the aesthetic dimensions of its own practice. It also systematically denigrates the role of the material, bodily, and sensory aspects of religion, and excludes these as valid objects of theorising. The aesthetics of religion is necessary as a countermovement against such an ideology, in order to recuperate for theory the marginalized or neglected domains of religious experience and expression. It is necessary precisely as a form of what Friedrich Nietzsche called "genealogy": as a recovery of the repressed, which is necessary for a comprehensive theory of humanity; and as an account of the process of its repression, which is necessary for a specific historical understanding of modernity.

Bibliography

Baxter, Richard. 1673. *A Christian Directory*. London.

Cancik, Hubert, and Hubert Mohr. 1988. "Religionsästhetik." In *Handbuch religionswissenschaftlicher Grundbegriffe*, edited by Hubert Cancik, Burkhard Gladigow, and Matthias Laubscher, 121–156. Stuttgart: Kohlhammer.

Grieser, Alexandra. 2015. "Aesthetics." In *Vocabulary for the Study of Religion*. Vol. 1, edited by Kocku von Stuckrad and Robert A. Segal, 14–23. Leiden: Brill.

Keane, Webb. 2002. "Sincerity, Modernity, and the Protestants." *Cultural Anthropology* 17: 65–92.

Kugele, Jens, and Katharina Wilkens. 2011. "Relocating Religion(s): Museality as a Critical Term for the Aesthetics of Religion." *Journal of Religion in Europe* 4: 7–3.

Sullivan, Lawrence E. 1986. "Sound and Senses: Toward a Hermeneutics of Performance." *History of Religions* 26: 1–33.

—— 1990. "'Seeking an End to the Primary Text' or 'Putting an End to the Text as Primary.'" In *Beyond the Classics: Essays in Religious Studies and Liberal Education*, edited by Frank E. Reynolds and Cheryl Burkhalter, 41–59. Atlanta: Scholars Press.

Weber, Max. 2009. *The Protestant Ethic and the Spirit of Capitalism,* with Other Writings on the Rise of the West, 4th ed., edited by Stephen Kalberg. New York: Oxford University Press.

Yelle, Robert. 2006. "The Rhetoric of Gesture in Cross-Cultural Perspective." *Gesture* 6: 223–240.

—— 2013. *The Language of Disenchantment: Protestant Literalism and Colonial Discourse in British India*. New York: Oxford University Press.

—— Forthcoming. "Reflections on the Semiotic Theory of the Sacrosanctum Concilium." In *Commentaire à Sacrosanctum Concilium: État de la Question*, edited by Ângelo Cardita (in French translation). Montréal: Novalis.

S. Brent Plate
The Artificiality of Aesthetics: Making Connections on the Erie Canal

Construction began on the Erie Canal in upstate New York on 4 July, 1817. When the technological marvel was completed eight years later it cut through 363 miles of nature with eighty-three locks that raised and lowered passenger and freight barges. Though it was no more than 40 feet (12 meters) wide, its influence well overflowed its edges: the waterway became the heart of the "Empire State" (i.e., New York), launching notions of manifest destiny as the canal opened up a passageway from the eastern seaboard into the bosom of the continent, connecting inland farming land with coastal industry and creating a network that stood at the heart of the rising American Empire.

The historian Paul Johnson suggested the canal is "the outstanding example of a human artifact creating wealth rapidly in the whole of history" (Johnson 1997, 368). It made New York City the great seaport and urban environment it continues to be today, just as the canal made the world smaller and more easily accessible with grains, timber, and other raw materials traveling across the North American continent, connecting ultimately to the European and African continents. And along its banks grew some of the most vibrant new religious movements of its age: Mormonism, Adventism, Spiritualism, utopian communities, a revived millennialism, and faith-based social causes such as abolition of slavery and women's rights. The beginning of modern American evangelicalism was largely shaped here as Charles Finney and the Second Great Awakening moved through this "burned over district", deeply indebted to the transportation and communication revolution that the canal created. To rephrase Johnson's historical-economic quip above, the canal is "the outstanding example of a human artefact creating *religions* rapidly in the whole of history".

I begin with this geo-historical scenario, and will soon return to it, because it opens up a dialogue on an old idea of aesthetics and how it may be used to approach religious history. Aesthetics, as I and most other contributors to this volume are thinking about the field, begins its modern designation with Alexander Baumgarten, not long before the Canal was being dreamed up. Baumgarten revived the ancient Greek notion of *aesthesis*, and differentiated between "natural aesthetics" (the realm of sense perception) and "artificial aesthetics" (the realm of human-made beauty and art), with aesthetics being defined as the "science of sensible cognition" (Baumgarten 1750 §1; cited in Shusterman 2000, 263–267;

https://doi.org/10.1515/9783110461015-023

Nanay 2014, 112–113).[1] Baumgarten saw humans possessing a natural "disposition" toward beauty, and was interested in what the senses could reveal for epistemological concerns, but only as that natural ability was refined and enculturated by a particular form of logical thinking. Beauty impacts the senses, which in turn impacts human understanding. The senses were thus useful, though remained under the domain of the rational mind. Whether Baumgarten may or may not be rightfully regarded as the progenitor of modern aesthetics is beside my point here. His distinction between the natural and artificial is of interest to me as a way to reframe a network of dualistic modes of aesthetic understanding (see Plate 2005; Meyer and Verrips 2008).

The subjugation of aesthetics to logic—of body to mind—notwithstanding, Baumgarten's rethinking of the sensual dimensions of existence at this point in philosophical history was crucial. In recounting this history, literary critic Terry Eagleton exclaimed:

> It is as though philosophy suddenly wakes up to the fact that there is a dense, swarming territory beyond its own mental enclave which threatens to fall utterly outside its sway. That territory is nothing less than the whole of our sensate life together—the business of affections and aversions, of how the world strikes the body on its sensory surfaces, of that which takes root in the gaze and the guts and all that arises from our most banal, biological insertion into the world. (Eagleton 1990, 13)

Eagleton's telling gloss on Baumgarten's re-discovery extends our understanding of the operations of the senses and how they open up a "territory", as our biological, bodily surfaces are inserted into the world, a connection I've elsewhere noted as a "skinscape" (Plate 2012). Eagleton is using the term "territory" somewhat metaphorically, but I want to ground this metaphor in actual territory: the physical, natural land of upstate New York.

What I am attempting to demonstrate here is that the study of religious history can be rethought through aesthetic means, that religious life itself is a product of syntheses and clashes between natural aesthetics and artificial aesthetics, as for example when a "human artefact" like the Erie Canal creates wealth as well as religious movements. Which is another way to say that the physical world affects us humans in ways far precedent to that of doctrines, texts, symbol systems, or institutions. By paying attention to the aesthetics of material practices—including bodies inserted into waters that move across vast wild spaces, the spread of media through new transportation devices, as well as the impact of hy-

---

1 Baumgarten first mentioned the new field of aesthetics in his 1735 thesis on poetry, and then developed it further with the first and second volumes of *Aesthetica* (1750, 1758).

draulic technologies rearranging the lines between natural and artificial territories—we find new ways of understanding the roots of past religious lives.

1. Natural and Artificial, Art and Technology

One way to establish a connection between the natural and artificial is to move internally, to the mind and its abilities to make sense of the world around. In general, this was Baumgarten's move, modernist that he was, seeing the thinking individual as the source of knowledge. There are a number of interesting contemporary studies in cognitive science examining the ways sense perception is indeed cultivated, though in ways that would have surprised Baumgarten. All would agree that sense perception begins with a set of raw biological materials (neurons, an olfactory bulb, a visual cortex, etc.) that are shaped by the stimuli humans are exposed to, thus allowing social and cultural institutions to, in part, form the very understandings of what we call reality. These newer studies extend Baumgarten's aesthetics and its relations to the arts, while refuting the underlying universalism of them (see Zeki 1999; Seeley 2006; Nanay 2014). Some of these studies on visual perception could be fruitfully linked with cognitive theories of religion (e.g., Geertz and Jensen 2014; Barrett forthcoming), but so far have not.

But there is another connection between the natural and artificial that I'd like to think about here briefly, and that is to go outside, to the natural world, and think about how "art" and "artefacts" affect nature. Coupled with Baumgarten's two-part aesthetics, there is a well-known, longstanding philosophical tradition that contrasts the natural (*physis*) and the artificial (*techne*), perhaps most famously taken up in the modern age by Heidegger (1977). I am not concerned to apply Heidegger's ideas in a rigorous fashion here, but suffice it to say that his view of *techne* is somewhere in the background of the following, as is a useful definition of technology given by Alfred Gell, "Technology, in the widest sense, is those forms of social relationships which make it socially necessary to produce, distribute and consume goods and services using 'technical' processes" (Gell 1988, 6). To talk critically about technology is not merely to discuss tool use and invention, it is also to discuss the social processes that make use of the tools, to enquire about their purposes, and to think about how these tools and the things they create, in turn, shape that social world.

Moreover, what we call technology today was, in earlier times, what was thought about in terms of "art" (which isn't to say that the word "art" was necessarily the one used). This confusion is key here, in part because it illuminates other ways of thinking about these connections. In so doing I want to suggest we do not leave art, or technology, behind in an investigation of aesthetics as sense perception. To think about aesthetics as a connective concept for religious history, and to flesh out the natural-artificial relation, I bring art and technology together, noting some of their overlapping, intertwined histories in the Erie Canal.

With that in the background, I turn from the abstract philosophical questions to think briefly about connections between natural and artificial aesthetics, between the physical world and the technological world, rooting these connections in the connective technology of the Erie Canal. For in the social, economic, cultural, religious, political, and artistic realms of the canalway (which includes all the cities it gave rise to—Utica, Syracuse, Rochester, Buffalo—and a vast network of trade, media production, and social life) we catch a glimpse onto the lived, material reality where natural and artificial aesthetics, nature and technology, meet.

2. The Artificial River

For New Yorkers, a common moniker for the Erie Canal was the "artificial river". Rivers exist with or without human intervention. They are, in a term, *natural*. To create an artificial body of water connecting disparate geographic regions is, at first glance, just short of madness to the unbelieving critics. To the believers it is symbolic of human potential. One way or other, building a 363-mile canal through nature's forests, swamps, and hills is an artificial intrusion into the natural world. With the canal, as with art, the artificial transforms the natural. There is no going back.

When art and technology meet nature in upstate New York nature is altered in artificial ways, but in this altercation the socio-religious life of humans is also rearranged. Spaces, whether "god-given" natural forests, or human-made cities, impacts human life, as human geographers have long noted. In his "Introduction to a Critique of Urban Geography", avant-garde theorist Guy Debord coined the term "psychogeography", defining it as "the study of the precise laws and specific effects of the geographical environment, consciously organized or not, on the emotions and behavior of individuals" (Debord [1955] 2006, 8). While Debord was interested in alternative, aesthetically based urban practices, the assumptions made about the impact of geographic environments on human behaviour are crucial to maintain. Aesthetic theories, of the sensate and artistic, natural and artificial, kinds can be utilized in a variety of ways that are not limited to the temple or museum, or even within a single tradition. Vast geographies like upstate New York become spaces where, to use Tom Tweed's phrase, "crossings and dwellings" occur (Tweed 2006). As they do we find new arrangements of religious life and experience. Technology and art meet in the creation and use of the Erie Canal, a work of the technical arts that offered connection, and in so doing transformed perceptions of individual and social religious orders.

By building and using the canal, New Yorkers were participating in a grand artwork. According to historian Paul E. Johnson, one of the key nineteenth-century understandings of "art" was that it was an "identity-defining skill. There was the shoemaker's art, the carpenter's art, the multiform arts of husbandry —the whole range of combined mental and manual performances through which trained men provided the wants and needs of their communities" (Johnson 1988, 440). But with the canal, and related innovations in transportation technologies, the view of art began to change from an individual's skills to those "works of technology and entrepreneurial vision that were transforming nature and the social order in their generation. Art was the Erie Canal, a man-made river that turned a wilderness into new farms and towns. It was the whole range of projects by which civilization was conquering nature and putting it to human use" (Johnson 1988, 442). This renewed understanding of art calls to mind the social-based definition of technology given by Alfred Gell above.

The theological and social implications here are immense. Most prominently is that conceptions of time and space were altered. What once took three weeks of travel could now be achieved in a week. Which meant that grains from the western parts of the fledgling United States could quickly and cheaply be shipped to hungry port cities like New York, Boston, and Philadelphia. This in turn sparked economic and social innovations both inland and on the coast. On a personal level too, as more and more people migrated from England and New England alike and moved to the boomtowns that grew along the canal, they could feel connected to life "back home". A letter written in 1840 by a woman who had moved from Connecticut to Western New York attests to this, "I am nearly six hundred miles from all my friends, and it is indeed a great distance but then the mail accommodation and our facilities for traveling at the present day are such as it is indeed consolation" (quoted in Sheriff 1997, 68). News in general also travelled quicker along the canalway, allowing a strong sense of bonding: "imagined communities" developed in terms of family, national pride, and religious sentiment as bodies were inserted in these new territories.

Through similar media channels, revivalists and charismatic leaders such as the preacher/revivalist Charles Finney, Oneida Community founder John Humphrey Noyes, and the initial instigators of the global movement called Spiritualism, the Fox sisters, had their messages quickly passed from town to town through print media and word of mouth, creating a rapid spread of new religious beliefs and practices. Mormonism began in the canal town of Palmyra, Joseph Smith's hometown, while the printing press he used to print the first 5000 copies of the Book of Mormon was shipped to Palmyra by the Erie Canal. When Smith and his first followers were forced out of town, they packed their belongings in a canal boat and headed west. And pastors of churches, along with other activists, created one leg of the Underground Railroad along the Erie Canal, while outspoken advocates of slavery's abolition, such as Frederick Douglass, lived, worked, and printed their newspapers in canal towns. Ongoing connections from town to town helped solidify new waves of spiritual work, as leaders were more mobile, and discussion of current religious events travelled readily. Religious movements were not confined to one place and time, but quickly gained momentum across great distances.

The artistic technology of the Erie Canal laid the ground for these new religious experiments. And just as the canal opened paths for free market economics, it also opened up a free market spirituality. Possibility and progress enabled a questing form of religious life in which multiple options were available. The result of which is seen two hundred years later in sociologist Wade Clark Roof's designation of the baby-boomers as a "generation of seekers" (Roof 1993).[2]

Even though the people of the time were participating in grand alterations of time and space, there were seldom any arrogant gestures that humans were somehow replacing divinity. At least at first. Instead, progress meant they "were taking an active role in realizing a divinely sanctioned movement toward the perfectibility of the natural and human worlds" (Sheriff 1997, 5). Indeed, from George Washington on, people believed that the site where the canal was eventually dug was a place designed by Providence: the site of the canal was the only gap in the Appalachian mountain range that stretched from Georgia to Maine. In other words, the entire East Coast of the young United States was essentially cut off from anything to the west because of the mountains, but here was one valley that went through, and that by the hand of God. Humans were simply completing what God started. Progress was God's sanction.

Experiences with the arts of progress linked, as Johnson puts it, "developmentalism and romanticism, material progress and spiritual improvement, prosperity and uplift" (Johnson 1988, 443). There was no bifurcation of these forces, though one of the key outcomes was that this new sense of progress linked with the predominant Christian worldview of the time, and connected to a belief that this was the "New Jerusalem", and Jesus would return soon. Rather than the Second Coming being an event that is out of one's control, the people believed they

---

2 There is no space to develop this further, but part of my broader argument that I'll be making elsewhere is that the Erie Canal was in large part responsible for the currents that gave rise to a "seeker" generation, and the "spiritual but not religious" designation.

had to work for it and bring it on. Women's Rights, the abolition of slavery, and utopian communal living, among other actions, were undertaken because they were aiming to usher in the Kingdom of God. The end of the world was coming, so people believed they better get things right. Physical work leads to spiritual liberation.

On the other hand, we have to remember, for all the progress that the canal enabled, it still ran through the "wilderness" for most of its 363 miles. For the visiting and migrating Europeans and New Englanders alike, this was a chance to see nature in all its sublime glory. As passengers rode the canalboats, they could look out at the vast stretches of still untamed nature, thus sampling the wilderness from the relatively safe perspective of engineered boats. And, at first anyway, this exposure to the wild provided an encounter with the natural wonders of God's world and God's power. Here, it was the sublime affect of both canal *and* nature that moved people. A choice between the artificiality of human progress and the natural realm of God's creation were not at odds. For a great many of the tourists who rode the boats, there was a harmony between the two. In its reorientations of space, it also reconceived time. The canal was a "middle landscape between nature (the past) and civilization (the future)" (Sheriff 1997, 26).

The sublime could be seen in nature, the untamed wilderness, but also in the technology, the engineered arts. The merchant Ira Blossom was an early rider of the canalboats, and as he ascended and descended through a series of locks, he noted that the experience was "somewhat calculated to bewilder the senses. [...] Unmoved as I usually am by surrounding objects, I am willing to confess that I was more astonished than I ever was by anything I had before witnessed" (Sheriff 1997, 31). His is not an uncommon expression of first experiences on the canal.

Nature was sublime, and the engineering arts were sublime, facts that drew visual artists and writers to the area in the second quarter of the nineteenth century. European writers such as Frances Trollope and Alexis de Tocqueville travelled the canalways during their visits, as did American authors Nathaniel Hawthorne and Herman Melville. At one point Tocqueville ventured just a few miles from the canalway where he found "one of those deep forest of the New World whose somber savage majesty strikes at the imagination and fills the soul with a sort of religious terror" (quoted in Bernstein 2005, 203).

Such sombre savage majesty became the focus as well of the so-called "Hudson River School" painters, including the European-born Albert Bierstadt and Thomas Cole, and the American-born Asher Durand. In art historical terms, the Hudson River movement is dated to begin in 1825, the year the Erie Canal opened. These artists were in awe of the natural worlds, and their paintings display this, even as nature is exaggerated through their artificial representations of it. And, crucial to note, these artists painted the rugged landscapes of upstate New York, even as they travelled by steamboat and canalboat. Their visions were part of an emerging American religious aesthetic that would extend through the continent in manifest destiny, creating a national identity of rugged individualism, the sole person turning away from the past (the east) and standing up to the nature of the west.

In sum, the Erie Canal created a series of affects that profoundly changed social and religious life in the young United States, and whose impact was felt across the emerging, westering nation. Those who dug, trenched, and gouged their way through the natural landscape of upstate New York unwittingly changed conceptions and perceptions of what seemed natural. The hard work of engineering and digging was followed by settlers, merchants, revivalists, and artists, who took advantage of the artificial intrusions on nature to create a new world. The oxymoronic tag, "the artificial river", attests to the ways the natural and artificial came together and created something new. The artificial river was an artistic river: It connected people, places, and things, and in so doing recreated ideas, practices, and behaviours along the way. The canal was a medium, a connective aesthetic.

3. Conclusion

As many have noted in recent years, and as the editors to this volume reiterate, aesthetics is currently undergoing a kind of "rescue mission", finding in the old Greek term the roots of a body-based, sensual reconception that helps us moderns analyse not only our world, but the worlds of religious people in many times and places. These are the initial broader leanings of aesthetics that I find useful in looking back two hundred years in the past to reimagine the place of natural territory, and the artificial manipulation thereof, for how religious experience begins.

The religious experiences that the Erie Canal engendered cannot be surveyed in intellectual historical terms alone. In other words, Charles Finney was not a central figure in the Second Great Awakening because he came up with some new theology that people intellectually sat and listened to and cognitively consented to. Instead, the revivalist movement, and Finney himself, was pushed along the waters of the canal corridor. There was no free will theology of Finney without the artificial river and the new social life it engendered. Likewise, the intellectual conceptions of manifest destiny, the coming end of the world, or nature as God's world, to say nothing of freedom itself, are reliant on the aesthetic experiences with the Erie Canal, and the technological arts that made it all possible.

My attention, however brief, to the Erie Canal intends to expand our horizons of how we think about aesthetics in relation to religious history. The canal is an artistic medium, as are railroads, airplanes, and airports, all of which operate within particular geographical spaces. Broadening the category of aesthetics beyond "theories of art" or "beauty" is crucial, while the subject matter of aesthetics can still go beyond the senses, sacred things, and art in general. Greater attention to modes of transportation, and to natural landscapes will also deepen the study of aesthetics, which will in turn deepen our understanding of religion.

What these forays into *psychogeography*, these crossings of nature and technology show, is that aesthetics can move the study of religion into newer grounds. If we begin with the natural-artificial aesthetic correlation, connecting "art" with the human body, then academic studies of new religious movements, of "individual" historical persons (be it Charles Finney or Immanuel Kant), and of historical time periods begin to take on new nuances. Knowledge of art—with all its consistencies and inconsistencies—connects with aesthetic theories of bodily sense perception, which then supplies a mode for doing historical religious studies, literally from the ground up.

Bibliography

Barrett, Nathaniel F. Forthcoming. "Cognitive Science, Embodiment, and Materiality." In *The Wiley-Blackwell Companion to Religious Materiality*, edited by Manuel Vásquez and Vasudha Narayanan. Malden: Wiley-Blackwell.

Baumgarten, Alexander Gottlieb. 1750. *Aesthetica*. Frankfurt: Ioannis Christiani Kleyb.

⸺ 1758. *Aestheticorum Parsaltera*. Frankfurt: Ioannis Christiani Kleyb.

Bernstein, Peter L. 2005. *Wedding of the Waters: The Erie Canal and the Making of a Great Nation*. New York: Norton.

Debord, Guy. [1955] 2006. "Introduction to a Critique of Urban Geography." In *Situationist International Anthology*, edited by Ken Knabb. 8–11. Berkeley, CA: Bureau of Public Secrets.

Eagleton, Terry. 1990. *The Ideology of the Aesthetic*. Malden, MA: Blackwell.

Gell, Alfred. 1988. "Technology and Magic." *Anthropology Today* 4/2: 6–9.

Geertz, Armin W., and Jeppe Sinding Jensen, eds. 2014. *Religious Narrative, Cognition and Culture: Image and Word in the Mind of Narrative*. London: Routledge.

Heidegger, Martin. 1977. "The Question Concerning Technology." In *The Question Concerning Technology and Other Essays*, translated by William Lovitt, 3–35. New York: Harper and Row.

Johnson, Paul. 1997. *A History of the American People*. New York: HarperCollins.

Johnson, Paul E. 1988 "'Art' and the Language of Progress in Early Industrial Paterson: Sam Patch at Clinton Bridge." *American Quarterly* 40/4: 433–449.

Livingstone, Margaret. 2014. *Vision and Art: The Biology of Seeing*. New York: Harry Abrams.

Meyer, Birgit, and Jojada Verrips. 2008. "Aesthetics." In *Key Words in Religion, Media and Culture*, edited by David Morgan, 20–30. New York and London: Routledge.

Nanay, Bence. 2014. "Philosophy of Perception as a Guide to Aesthetics." In *Aesthetics and the Sciences of Mind*, edited by Gregory Currie, Matthew Kieran, Aaron Meskin, and Jon Robson, 101–120. Oxford: Oxford University Press.

Plate, S. Brent. 2005. *Walter Benjamin, Religion, and Aesthetics: Rethinking Religion Through the Arts*. New York: Routledge.

—— 2012. "The Skin of Religion: Aesthetic Mediations of the Sacred." *CrossCurrents* 62/2: 162–180.

Roof, Wade Clark. 1993. *A Generation of Seekers*. San Francisco: HarperSanFrancisco.

Seeley, William P. 2006. "Naturalizing Aesthetics: Art and the Cognitive Neuroscience of Vision." *Journal of Visual Art Practice* 5/3: 195–213.

Sheriff, Carol. 1997. *The Artificial River: The Erie Canal and the Paradox of Progress, 1817–1862*. Paris: Farrar, Straus and Giroux. Kindle Edition.

Shusterman, Richard. 2000. *Pragmatist Aesthetics: Living Beauty, Rethinking Art*. Second Edition. Lanham, UK: Rowman & Littlefield.

Tweed, Thomas A. 2006. *Crossing and Dwelling: A Theory of Religion*. Cambridge, MA: Harvard University Press.

Zeki, Semir. 1999. *Inner Vision: An Exploration of Art and the Brain*. New York: Oxford University Press.

Authors Biographies

Mikael Aktor is Associate Professor, Department of History, Study of Religions, University of Southern Denmark, Odense, Denmark. His research has been focused on two particular subjects. One is the study of Hindu Law Books (*dharmaśāstra*) with a special focus on rules of Untouchability, and the other is Material Religion in general and aniconic objects of worship in the Hindu tradition in particular. His publications include *Objects of Worship in South Asian Religions* (Routledge 2015; edited with Knut A. Jacobsen and Kristina Myrvold); "Negotiating Karma: Penance in the Classical Indian Law Books", in *Negotiating Rites*, edited by Ute Hüsken and Frank Neubert (Oxford University Press 2012); *Ritualisation and Segregation: The Untouchability Complex in Indian Dharma Literature with Special Reference to Parāśarasmṛti and Parāśaramādhavīya* (CESMEO 2008); "Rules of Untouchability in Ancient and Medieval Law Books: Householders, Competence and Inauspiciousness", in *International Journal of Hindu Studies* 6/3: 243–274 (2002).

Christoph Auffarth is a Full Professor of Christian History and Theology at the University of Bremen's Department of Comparative Religion since 2001. Christoph Auffarth is chief editor of the journal *Zeitschrift für Religionswissenschaft* and co-editor of the academic series *Religionen in der pluralen Welt* (LIT Verlag). His major research focuses are ancient Greek and Roman religions, the history of medieval European religions, the religious history of the "Third Reich", and the history of science and religion in the 20th century. The central theme of his works are the plurality and interactional dynamics of different religions or intra-religious factions. He contributed essentially to the project of *Aesthetics of Religion*, and he is the co-editor of the first Dictionary on religion which focuses on its mediality and its aesthetic character: *Metzler Lexikon Religion*, 4 Vols. (1999–2002; revised English Edition by Kocku von Stuckrad, Brill 2006). Further Information: http://www.religion.uni-bremen.de/personen/personal-religion/auffarth/christoph-auffarth.html.

Ulrike Brunotte is Associate Professor at the Faculty of Arts and Social Sciences, Maastricht University. From 2001 to 2006, she was Associate Professor at the Institute for Cultural Studies at Humboldt-University Berlin. Cooperation in the DFG-priority-programme "Theatralität. Theater als kulturelles Modell in den Kulturwissenschaften" (1999–2002). Since 2013, Brunotte has been chair of the international research network Rengoo: "Gender in Orientalism, Occidentalism and Antisemitism" www.rengoo.net (promoted by NWO). She is also co-editor of the book-series "Diskurs Religion" (ERGON-Verlag). With her monograph *Das Wissen der Dämonen. Gender, Performativität und materielle Kultur im Werk Jane E. Harrisons* (Ergon 2013), she analysed a pioneer of *Aesthetics of Religion*. Fields of Research: history of religious studies, ritual theory and performativity, history of fascination, Orientalism, gender and postcolonial studies, studies in North American Puritanism, literature and religion; history of masculinity. Selected publications: *Das Wissen der Dämonen. Gender, Performativität und materielle Kultur im Werk Jane E. Harrisons* (Ergon 2013); *Helden des Todes. Studien zur Religion, Ästhetik und Politik moderner Männlichkeit* (Ergon 2015); *Orientalism, Gender, and the Jews. Literary and Artistic Transformations of European National Discourses* (de Gruyter 2015; edited with Anne D. Ludewig and Axel Stähler); *Puritanismus und Pioniergeist. Zur Faszination der Wildnis im frühen Neu-England*, RGVV (de Gruyter 2000).

Fred Cummins is Associate Professor and Co-director of the Cognitive Science Programme at University College Dublin, Ireland. He obtained a BA in Computer Science, Linguistics and German at Trinity College Dublin, an MA in Linguistics and a PhD with joint majors in Cognitive Science and Linguistics in 1997 from Indiana University. His work has focussed on coordination in speech both within an individual, in speech production, and among individuals, in unison speaking found in prayer and protest. His interest in the intentional characteristics of collective behaviour in chant and ritual has led him to look for ways of doing science that are not beholden to a single view on mind.

Laura Feldt is Associate Professor in the History of Religions, University of Southern Denmark, head of the cross-disciplinary research programme *Authority, Materiality and Media* at the University of Southern Denmark, and from 2017 co-managing editor of NVMEN, with Gregory Alles. Her publications include *The Fantastic in Religious Narrative from Exodus to Elisha* (Routledge 2012) and the edited volume *Wilderness in Mythology and Religion* (de Gruyter 2012), articles on myth, the fantastic and monstrous in ancient Mesopotamia, The Hebrew Bible and ancient Christianity, as well as on religion and contemporary popular culture. Her current research project is about wilderness mythologies, and space and religious identity formation in ancient religions.

François Gauthier (PhD) is Professor of Sociology of Religion in the Religious Studies programme of the Department of Social Sciences, Université de Fribourg, Switzerland. He completed his MA and PhD in Religious Studies at the Université du Québec à Montréal (UQAM) and two post-doctoral fellowships at Paris-Ouest Nanterre and Rennes-2 universities in France. His training is multi-disciplinary and aims towards a general social scientific outlook on contemporary religious dynamics with a growing global concern. His publications include *Religion in Consumer Society. Brands, Consumers, Markets* and *Religion in the Neoliberal Age. Political Economy and Modes of Governance* (Ashgate 2013; edited with Tuomas Martikainen), *Jeunes et religion au Québec* (PUL 2008; edited with Jean-Philippe Perreault), as well as upcoming and published special issues of the *Revue du MAUSS semestrielle*, *Archives des sciences sociales des religions*, *Social Compass* and *Entropia*. He is presently working on editing the *Routledge Handbook of Religion in Global Society* (with Linda Woodhead, Tuomas Martikainen and Jayeel Serrano Cornelio) and is a member of the Groupe Religions, Sociétés, Laïcités (EPHE-CNRS, Paris). He is active in the France-based interdisciplinary Mouvement anti-utilitariste en sciences sociales (MAUSS) founded by Prof Alain Caillé and is part of the editorial board of the *Revue du MAUSS semestrielle*.

Alexandra Grieser is Assistant Professor for the Theory of Religion at Trinity College, Dublin. She is trained in the Academic Study of Religion, German Literature and General Rhetoric (University of Tuebingen). She held positions at the University of Bremen, at the LMU Munich and at the University of Groningen (the Netherlands). Her research focuses on Method and Theory in the Study of Religion; European Pluralism; the History and Theory of Knowledge; Religion and Rhetoric; and Aesthetics of Religion. She is a founding member of the working group for the Aesthetics of Religion (German Association for the Study of Religion, DVRW) and a member of AESToR NET, funded by the German Research Foundation. She has published on changing plausibility patterns in modern religion (*Transformations of Immortality*, Peter Lang 2008), articles and book chapters on fascination as an aesthetic strategy (Peter Lang 2009); on "Museality as a Matrix of the Production, Reception, and Circulation of Knowledge"

(Journal for Religion in Europe 4/1, 2011), and on the popular aesthetics of Hubble Space photography (Vandenhoek & Ruprecht 2015). She is the editor of *Aesthetics of Religion: A Connective Concept*, de Gruyter 2017; with Jay Johnston). A special focus of her recent work lies on developing the Aesthetics of Religion as a systematic approach to the Study of Religion in an international and interdisciplinary context (for example: "Aesthetics" in *The Vocabulary for the Study of Religion* [Brill 2015]).

John Hamilton is the William R. Kenan Professor of German and Comparative Literature at Harvard University, Cambridge, USA. Together with Almut Renger, he co-organises the International Study Group *Religion and Literature* (*HolyLit*), which features members from institutions across the globe. Previous publications include *Soliciting Darkness: Pindar, Obscurity, and the Classical Tradition* (Harvard University Press 2004); *Music, Madness, and the Unworking of Language* (Columbia University Press 2008); and *Security: Politics, Humanity, and the Philology of Care* (Princeton University Press 2013).

Frank Heidemann is Professor of Social and Cultural Anthropology at the Ludwig-Maximilians-University of Munich. Besides his work on visual anthropology, he works on the broad spectrum of religion and politics, migration, labour recruitment and social movements. Recently his interest moved to social aesthetics and to social atmosphere. The regional focus of his research is South Asia, where he conducted fieldwork in Tamil Nadu, in the Nilgiri Hills, and also on the Andaman Islands and in Sri Lanka. His publications include *Akka Bakka. Religion, Politik und duale Souveränität der Badaga* (LIT 2006), *Ethnologie. Eine Einführung* (Vandenhoek 2011), *The Modern Anthropology of India* (Routledge 2013; edited with Peter Berger), *The Bison and the Horn. Indigeneity, Performance, and the State of India* (*Asian Ethnology*, special issue 2014; edited with Richard Wolf) and *Manifestations of History. Time, Space, and Community in the Andaman Islands* (Delhi, Primus Books 2016; edited with Philipp Zehmisch).

Adrian Hermann is Professor of Religion and Society at the Forum Internationale Wissenschaft, University of Bonn, Germany. From 2015 to 2017 he was Assistant Professor of Religious Studies and World Christianity at the University of Hamburg. In 2011 he graduated with a PhD in the Study of Religion from the University of Basel, Switzerland. He studied Comparative Religion, Theatre Studies and North American Literature as well as Sociology in Munich, Bielefeld, and Basel. His work focuses on method and theory in the study of religion, non-Western Christianity (with a focus on Southeast Asia), as well as on the religious history of the globalised world. From September 2014 to March 2015 he was a Visiting Scholar at the Department of Philosophy and Religious Studies at Utrecht University and the Department of Anthropology at Stanford University. His first book *Unterscheidungen der Religion: Analysen zum globalen Religionsdiskurs und dem Problem der Differenzierung von 'Religion' in buddhistischen Kontexten des 19. und frühen 20. Jahrhunderts* was published in June 2015 by Vandenhoeck & Ruprecht. He is the co-editor of two of books discussing a polycentric approach to the history of Christianity and has also published on Buddhist modernism in the nineteenth and early twentieth century.

Jay Johnston is Associate Professor in the Department of Studies in Religion, University of Sydney. Her current research examines concepts of materiality, embodiment, environment and image agency in religious and archaeological discourse and practice. She led the international collaborative project: "The Function of Images in Magical Papyri and Artefacts of Ritual Power from Late Antiquity", funded by the Australian Research Council (2012–2015). Publications include *Angels of Desire: Esoteric Bodies, Aesthetics and Ethics* (Routledge 2008); *Religion and the Subtle Body in Asia and the West: Between Mind and Body* (Routledge 2013; co-edited with Geoffrey Samuel) and forthcoming *Stage and Stone: Religion, Archaeology and Esoteric Aesthetics* (Equinox forthcoming 2018/2019).

Anne Koch is Full Professor of Religious Studies at the Paris Lodron University, Salzburg. Her main interests are contemporary normative orders across societal domains and across global institutional fields. In her most recent work she combines aesthetic and economic theories to describe religious change, for example the commodification of belonging and affects, the pricing of social capital and beauty or the supply side of embodied psycho-techniques that stem from religious traditions. Her publications include *Religionsökonomie* (Kohlhammer 2014), *Körperwissen* (open access 2007), a special issue on the *Aesthetics of Civil Religion* (*Journal of Religion in Europe* 10/1–2, 2017), and several articles on body knowledge/embodied cognition, museality, alternative healing and its efficacy, global yoga and secularism. She is a founding member of the working group for the *Aesthetics of Religion* (affiliated to German Association for the Study of Religion); she was a member of the ThinkLab at the Institute of Medical Psychology at Munich University and is part of AESToR NET, a German-European research network on aesthetics of religion (German Research Foundation 2015–2018). At the American Academy of Religion she is a member of the Religion in Europe-group.

Jens Kreinath is Associate Professor in Social and Cultural Anthropology at Wichita State University, USA. He received academic training in philosophy, religious studies, theology, and social and cultural anthropology at University of Heidelberg. Kreinath conducted fieldwork in Istanbul and Hatay on rituals among religious minorities, including Jews, Christians, and Muslims. His research interests focus on theoretical and methodological issues in the anthropological study of religion and ritual within the fields of semiotics and aesthetics. Aside from editing or co-editing volumes such as *The Anthropology of Islam Reader* (Routledge 2012), *Theorizing Rituals* (Brill 2006–2007), and *The Dynamics of Changing Rituals* (Peter Lang 2004), he is contributor to *The Vocabulary for the Study of Religion* (Brill 2015), *Religion in Past and Present* (Brill 2013–2014), *International Encyclopaedia of Anthropology* (2018) and published articles in *Journal of Ritual Studies* (2012), *Visual Anthropology* (2012); *Anthropology of the Contemporary Middle East and Central Eurasia* (2014) and *Zeitschrift für Religionswissenschaft* (2016).

Niklaus Largier holds the Sidney and Margaret Ancker Chair in the Humanities as a Professor of German and Comparative Literature at the University of California, Berkeley. He has published extensively on medieval mysticism, the history of ascetic practices, prayer, and aesthetic experience. His books include *In Praise of the Whip: A Cultural History of Arousal* (Zone Books 2007) and *Die Kunst des Begehrens: Dekadenz, Askese und Sinnlichkeit* (C. H. Beck 2007). In a number of recent essays he discusses medieval practices of contemplation, the stimulation of sensation and affect, and the emergence of aesthetic experience. He is currently working on a book on figuration, tentatively entitled *Figures of Possibility*.

Hubert Mohr is trained in Classics (Latin) and History at the University of Tübingen. From 2002 to 2008 he was a research assistant at the University of Bremen and built up a project on religion and the media; since 2008 he teaches at the University of Basel, Switzerland. He participated in publishing the *Handbuch religionswissenschaftlicher Grundbegriffe* (Kohlhammer 1988–2002; edited by Hubert Cancik, Burkhard Gladigow, and Karl-Heinz Kohl) and the *Metzler Lexikon Religion* (Metzler 1999–2002; edited with Christoph Auffarth and Jutta Bernard) which both were ground-breaking for an aesthetic approach to religion. His main research topics are: Aesthetics of Religion, (Neo-)Paganism, Religion and the Media.

S. Brent Rodriguez Plate is visiting associate professor of religious studies at Hamilton College, USA, and co-founder and managing editor of *Material Religion: The Journal of Objects, Art, and Belief.* He has authored/edited twelve books at the nexus of media, religion, and culture, most recently *A History of Religion in 5½ Objects* (Beacon Press 2014) and the edited *Key Terms in Material Religion* (Bloomsbury Academic 2015). His essays have appeared in the *Los Angeles Review of Books, Huffington Post, Chronicle of Higher Education, Religion Dispatches,* and elsewhere. Rodríguez-Plate also serves on several international advisory boards.

Almut-Barbara Renger is Professor of Ancient Religion, Culture and their Reception History at the Institute for the Scientific Study of Religion at the Freie Universität Berlin, and Associate Fellow in the Department of Comparative Literature at Harvard University. Her research and teaching focus on the reception of Greco-Roman antiquity, diverse aspects of cultural and religious theory, dynamics in the history of religions between Asia, Europe and America, and the relationship of religion and literature. She is editor of the journal *Zeitschrift für Religions- und Geistesgeschichte (Journal of Religious and Cultural Studies)* and of the series *Metaforms. Studies in the Reception of Classical Antiquity.* Together with John Hamilton she co-organises the International Study Group *Religion and Literature* (HolyLit), which features members from institutions across the globe. Most recently, she published *Körperwissen. Transfer und Innovation* (= *Paragrana* 25/1, De Gruyter 2016; with Christoph Wulf); *Meister und Schüler. Master and Disciple: Tradition, Transfer, Transformation* (VDG 2016; with Jeong-hee Lee-Kalisch); *Pythagorean Knowledge from the Ancient to the Modern World* (Harrassowitz 2016; with Alessandro Stavru); and *Erleuchtung. Kultur-und Religionsgeschichte eines Begriffs* (Herder 2016).

Sebastian Schüler is Assistant Professor for the Study of Religions at Leipzig University. Trained in the Study of Religions and Cultural Anthropology at Goethe-University Frankfurt, he completed his PhD at the University of Münster in 2010 with a dissertation on the Cognitive Science of Religion. He then held a post-doctoral research position at the "Cluster of Excellence for Religion and Politics" in Münster, focusing on the Anthropology of Christianity in general and on postmodern transformations within Evangelical Christianity in particular. His working areas include cognitive and evolutionary theories of religion, theories of embodiment, methods in the Study of Religion, evangelical and charismatic Christianity, and alternative spirituality. Publications include "Establishing a 'Culture of Prayer': Holistic Spirituality and the Social Transformation of Contemporary Evangelicalism", *Annual Review of the Sociology of Religion* 4 (2013). "Synchronized Ritual Behavior: Religion, Cognition and the Dynamics of Embodiment", in *The Body and Religion: Modern Science and the Construction of Religious Meaning* (Brill 2012; edited by David Cave and Rebecca Sachs Norris). "Agency and the Senses in the Context of Museality from the Perspective of Aesthetics of Religion", *Journal of Religion in Europe* 4/1 (2011).

Maruška Svašek is Reader in Anthropology at Queen's University Belfast. She studied Painting and Graphics at Art Academy Minerva in Groningen (1985) and completed doctoral research in Anthropology at the University of Amsterdam (1996). Svašek's main research interests include art, artefacts, migration and emotions. In her most recent work she seeks to bring these strands together, exploring mobility and agency of humans, objects and images in an era of intensifying globalisation and transnational connectivity. Major publications include *Creativity in Transition. Politics and Aesthetics of Cultural Production across the Globe* (Berghahn 2016; with Birgit Meyer); *Moving Subjects, Moving Objects: Transnationalism, Cultural Production and Emotions* (Berghahn 2012); *Emotions and Human Mobility. Ethnographies of Movement* (Routledge 2012); *Postsocialism: Politics and Emotions in Central and Eastern Europe* (Berghahn 2006); *Mixed Emotions. Anthropological Studies of Feeling* (Berg 2005; with Kay Milton). Svašek led the Interdisciplinary Research Project Creativity and Innovation in a World of Movement from 2010 to 2012, and co-edits the Book Series Material Mediations with Birgit Meyer (Berghahn).

Manuel A. Vásquez is an independent scholar and the author of *More than Belief: A Materialist Theory of Religion* (Oxford 2011) and *The Brazilian Popular Church and the Crisis of Modernity* (Cambridge 1998). He also co-authored *Living 'Illegal': The Human Face of Unauthorized Immigration* (New Press 2011) and *Globalizing the Sacred: Religion across the Americas* (Rutgers 2003). Moreover, he has published a number of co-edited volumes, including *A Place to Be: Brazilian, Guatemalan, and Mexican Immigrants in Florida's New Destinations* (Rutgers 2009), *Latin American Religions: Histories and Documents in Context* (NYU 2008), and *Immigrant Faiths: Transforming Religious Life in America* (AltaMira 2005).

Annette Wilke is professor for the Study of Religion and head of the department at the Westfalian Wilhelms University of Muenster, Germany. She received academic training in the Study of Religion, Philosophy, Theology, and Indology in Switzerland, India and the US, and her PhD (Dr. phil.) in the History of Religions at the University of Berne (1994) with a dissertation on comparative mysticism. Major fields of research are textual studies and fieldwork in Hindu traditions past and present (sound in Hinduism, goddesses, Advaita Vedanta, Tantra, reform and diaspora Hinduism); cultural theory, aesthetics of religion, mysticism, ritual studies, religious transfers, and contemporary religion. She is member of the Cluster of Excellence *Religion and Politics* at Muenster University and also member of the DVRW (German Association for the Study of Religion) working group for the Aesthetics of Religion and of AESToR NET. She has published widely in the field of Aesthetics of Religion, in particular on the sonic character of Hindu traditions. Selected Publications: *Sound and Communication. An Aesthetic Cultural History of Sanskrit Hinduism* (de Gruyter 2011; with Oliver Moebus); "Sound" in *Brill's Encyclopedia of Hinduism* Vol. 5 (2013, 134–149); *Imagination – Religion – Ästhetik* (Vandenhoeck 2015; edited with Lucia Traut).

Robert Yelle is Professor for the Theory and Method of Religious Studies and Chair of the Interfaculty Program in Religious Studies at Ludwig-Maximilians-University, Munich. He studied at Harvard University, the University of California at Berkeley, and the University of Chicago, where he received a Ph.D. in the History of Religions (2002). Prior to arriving in Munich, Yelle was Associate Professor at the University of Memphis. He has received fellowships from the University of Toronto, the University of Illinois at Urbana-Champaign, New York University School of Law, and the John Simon Guggenheim Memorial Foundation. Yelle is presently editor of the American Academy of Religion/Oxford University Press book series *Religion, Culture, and History* and co-editor of the de Gruyter series *Semiotics of Religion*. He was previously Executive Secretary of the North American Association for the Study of Religion (2007 – 2011). In addition to numerous essays and a volume, *After Secular Law* (Stanford University Press 2011), co-edited with Winnifred Sullivan and Mateo Taussig-Rubbo, Yelle has published three monographs: *Explaining Mantras* (Routledge 2003), *The Language of Disenchantment* (Oxford University Press 2013), and *Semiotics of Religion* (Bloomsbury 2013). His next monograph, *Sovereignty and the Sacred*, will be published by the University of Chicago Press.

Index

https://doi.org/10.1515/9783110461015-024

9 783110 686333